REPAIR MANUAL

MUSTANG CAPRI MERKUR 1979-88

**All U.S. and Canadian models of FORD Mustang ●
MERCURY Capri ● MERKUR**

President GARY R. INGERSOLL
Senior Vice President, Book Publishing and Research RONALD A. HOXTER
Publisher KERRY A. FREEMAN, S.A.E.
Editor-In-Chief DEAN F. MORGANTINI, S.A.E.
Senior Editor RICHARD J. RIVELE, S.A.E.
Senior Editor W. CALVIN SETTLE, JR., S.A.E.
Editor WAYNE EIFFES

CHILTON BOOK COMPANY
Radnor, Pennsylvania
19089

CONTENTS

SAFETY NOTICE

Proper service and repair procedures are vital to the safe, reliable operation of all motor vehicles, as well as the personal safety of those performing repairs. This book outlines procedures for servicing and repairing vehicles using safe, effective methods. The procedures contain many NOTES, CAUTIONS and WARNINGS which should be followed along with standard safety procedures to eliminate the possibility of personal injury or improper service which could damage the vehicle or compromise its safety.

It is important to note that repair procedures and techniques, tools and parts for servicing motor vehicles, as well as the skill and experience of the individual performing the work vary widely. It is not possible to anticipate all of the conceivable ways or conditions under which vehicles may be serviced, or to provide cautions as to all of the possible hazards that may result. Standard and accepted safety precautions and equipment should be used during cutting, grinding, chiseling, prying, or any other process that can cause material removal or projectiles.

Some procedures require the use of tools specially designed for a specific purpose. Before substituting another tool or procedure, you must be completely satisfied that neither your personal safety, nor the performance of the vehicle will be endangered.

Although the information in this guide is based on industry sources and is as complete as possible at the time of publication, the possibility exists that the manufacturer made later changes which could not be included here. While striving for total accuracy, Chilton Book Company cannot assume responsibility for any errors, changes, or omissions that may occur in the compilation of this data.

PART NUMBERS

Part numbers listed in this reference are not recommendations by Chilton for any product by brand name. They are references that can be used with interchange manuals and aftermarket supplier catalogs to locate each brand supplier's discrete part number.

SPECIAL TOOLS

Special tools are recommended by the vehicle manufacturer to perform their specific job. Use has been kept to a minimum, but where absolutely necessary, they are referred to in the text by the part number of the tool manufacturer. These tools can be purchased, under the appropriate part number, from Owatonna Tool Company, Owatonna, MN 55060 or an equivalent tool can be purchased locally from a tool supplier or parts outlet. Before substituting any tool for the one recommended, read the SAFETY NOTICE at the top of this page.

ACKNOWLEDGMENTS

The Chilton Book Company expresses its appreciation to the Ford Motor Company, Dearborn, Michigan for their generous assistance.

Copyright © 1989 by Chilton Book Company
All Rights Reserved
Published in Radnor, Pennsylvania 19089, by Chilton Book Company

Manufactured in the United States of America
    4567890   876543210

Chilton's Repair Manual: Mustang/Capri/Merkur 1979–88
ISBN 0-8019-7825-4 pbk.
Library of Congress Catalog Card No. 87-47944

General Information and Maintenance

HOW TO USE THIS BOOK

Chilton's Repair & Tune-Up Guide for the Mustang, Capri and Merkur is intended to teach you about the inner workings of your car and save you money on its upkeep.

The first two chapters will be the most used, since they contain maintenance and tune-up information and procedures. Studies have shown that a properly tuned and maintained car can get at least 10% better gas mileage (which translates into lower operating costs) and periodic maintenance will catch minor problems before they turn into major repair bills. The other chapters deal with the more complex systems of your car. Operating systems from engine through brakes are covered to the extent that the average do-it-yourselfer becomes mechanically involved. This book will not explain such things as rebuilding the differential for the simple reason that the expertise required and the investment in special tools make this task impractical and uneconomical. It will give you the detailed instructions to help you change your own brake pads and shoes, tune-up the engine, replace spark plugs and filters, and do many more jobs that will save you money, give you personal satisfaction and help you avoid expensive problems.

A secondary purpose of this book is a reference guide for owners who want to understand their car and/or their mechanics better. In this case, no tools at all are required. Knowing just what a particular repair job requires in parts and labor time will allow you to evaluate whether or not you're getting a fair price quote and help decipher itemized bills from a repair shop.

Before attempting any repairs or service on your car, read through the entire procedure outlined in the appropriate chapter. This will give you the overall view of what tools and supplies will be required. There is nothing more frustrating than having to walk to the bus stop on Monday morning because you were short one gasket on Sunday afternoon. So read ahead and plan ahead. Each operation should be approached logically and all procedures thoroughly understood before attempting any work. Some special tools that may be required can often be rented from local automotive jobbers or places specializing in renting tools and equipment. Check the yellow pages of your phone book.

All chapters contain adjustments, maintenance, removal and installation procedures, and overhaul procedures. When overhaul is not considered practical, we tell you how to remove the failed part and then how to install the new or rebuilt replacement. In this way, you at least save the labor costs. Backyard overhaul of some components (such as the alternator or water pump) is just not practical, but the removal and installation procedure is often simple and well within the capabilities of the average car owner.

Two basic mechanic's rules should be mentioned here. First, whenever the LEFT side of the car or engine is referred to, it is meant to specify the DRIVER'S side of the car. Conversely, the RIGHT side of the car means the PASSENGER'S side. Second, all screws and bolts are removed by turning counterclockwise, and tightened by turning clockwise.

Safety is always the most important rule. Constantly be aware of the dangers involved in working on or around an automobile and take proper precautions to avoid the risk of personal injury or damage to the vehicle. See the section in this chapter, Servicing Your Vehicle Safely, and the SAFETY NOTICE on the acknowledgment page before attempting any service procedures and pay attention to the instructions provided. There are 3 common mistakes in mechanical work:

1. Incorrect order of assembly, disassembly or adjustment. When taking something apart or putting it together, doing things in the wrong

order usually just costs you extra time; however it CAN break something. Read the entire procedure before beginning disassembly. Do everything in the order in which the instructions say you should do it, even if you can't immediately see a reason for it. When you're taking apart something that is very intricate (for example a carburetor), you might want to draw a picture of how it looks when assembled at one point in order to make sure you get everything back in its proper position. We will supply exploded views whenever possible, but sometimes the job requires more attention to detail than an illustration provides. When making adjustments (especially tune-up adjustments), do them in order. One adjustment often affects another and you cannot expect satisfactory results unless each adjustment is made only when it cannot be changed by any other.

2. Overtorquing (or undertorquing) nuts and bolts. While it is more common for overtorquing to cause damage, undertorquing can cause a fastener to vibrate loose and cause serious damage, especially when dealing with aluminum parts. Pay attention to torque specifications and utilize a torque wrench in assembly. If a torque figure is not available remember that, if you are using the right tool to do the job, you will probably not have to strain yourself to get a fastener tight enough. The pitch of most threads is so slight that the tension you put on the wrench will be multiplied many times in actual force on what you are tightening. A good example of how critical torque is can be seen in the case of spark plug installation, especially where you are putting the plug into an aluminum cylinder head. Too little torque can fail to crush the gasket, causing leakage of combustion gases and consequent overheating of the plug and engine parts. Too much torque can damage the threads or distort the plug, which changes the spark gap at the electrode. Since more and more manufacturers are using aluminum in their engine and chassis parts to save weight, a torque wrench should be in any serious do-it-yourselfer's tool box.
There are many commercial chemical products available for ensuring that fasteners won't come loose, even if they are not torqued just right (a very common brand is Loctite®). If you're worried about getting something together tight enough to hold, but loose enough to avoid mechanical damage during assembly, one of these products might offer substantial insurance. Read the label on the package and make sure the product is compatible with the materials, fluids, etc. involved before choosing one.

3. Crossthreading. This occurs when a part such as a bolt is screwed into a nut or casting at the wrong angle and forced, causing the threads to become damaged. Crossthreading is more likely to occur if access is difficult. It helps to clean and lubricate fasteners, and to start threading with the part to be installed going straight in, using your fingers. If you encounter resistance, unscrew the part and start over again at a different angle until it can be inserted and turned several times without much effort. Keep in mind that many parts, especially spark plugs, use tapered threads so that gentle turning will automatically bring the part you're threading to the proper angle if you don't force it or resist a change in angle. Don't put a wrench on the part until it's been turned in a couple of times by hand. If you suddenly encounter resistance and the part has not seated fully, don't force it. Pull it back out and make sure it's clean and threading properly.
Always take your time and be patient; once you have some experience, working on your car will become an enjoyable hobby.

TOOLS AND EQUIPMENT

Naturally, without the proper tools and equipment it is impossible to properly service your vehicle. It would be impossible to catalog each tool that you would need to perform each or every operation in this book. It would also be unwise for the amateur to rush out and buy an expensive set of tools an the theory that he may need one or more of them at sometime.

The best approach is to proceed slowly, gathering together a good quality set of those tools that are used most frequently. Don't be misled by the low cost of bargain tools. It is far better to spend a little more for better quality. Forged wrenches, 6 or 12 point sockets and fine tooth ratchets are by far preferable to their less expensive counterparts. As any good mechanic can tell you, there are few worse experiences than trying to work on a car with bad tools. Your monetary savings will be far outweighed by frustration and mangled knuckles.

Certain tools, plus a basic ability to handle tools, are required to get started. A basic mechanics tool set, a torque wrench, and a Torx® bits set. Torx® bits are hexlobular drivers which fit both inside and outside on special Torx® head fasteners used in various places on some cars.

Begin accumulating those tools that are used most frequently; those associated with routine maintenance and tune-up.

In addition to the normal assortment of screwdrivers and pliers you should have the following tools for routine maintenance jobs (your car, depending on the model year, uses both SAE and metric fasteners):

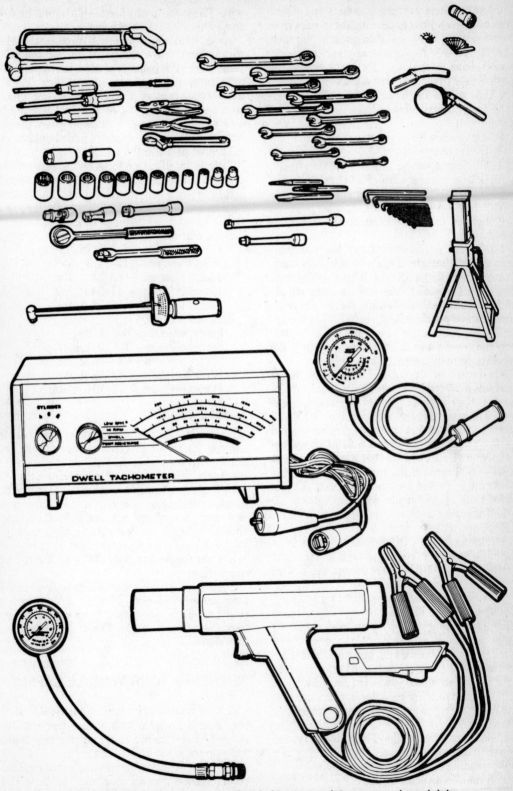

You need this basic assortment of tools for most maintenance and repair jobs

1. SAE/Metric wrenches, sockets and combination open end/box end wrenches in sizes from 1/8″ (3mm) to 3/4″ (19mm), and a spark plug socket ($^{13}/_{16}$″ or 5/8″). If possible, buy various length socket drive extensions. One break in this department is that the metric sockets available in the U.S. will all fit the ratchet handles and extensions you may already have (1/4, 3/8, and 1/2″ drive).

2. Jackstands for support.

3. Oil filter wrench.

4. Oil filler spout or funnel.

5. Grease gun for chassis lubrication.

6. Hydrometer for checking the battery.

7. A low flat pan for draining oil.

8. Lots of rags for wiping up the inevitable mess.

In addition to the above items there are several others that are not absolutely necessary, but handy to have around. These include oil-dry, a transmission funnel and the usual supply of lubricants, antifreeze and fluids, although these can be purchased as needed. This is a basic list for routine maintenance, but only your personal needs and desires can accurately determine your list of necessary tools.

The second list of tools is for tune-ups. While the tools involved here are slightly more sophisticated, they need not be outrageously expensive. There are several inexpensive tach/dwell meters on the market that are every bit as good for the average mechanic as a $100.00 professional model. Just be sure that it goes to at least 1,200–1,500 rpm on the tach scale and that it works on 4-, 6- and 8-cylinder engines. A basic list of tune-up equipment could include:

1. Tach-dwell meter

2. Spark plug wrench

3. Timing light (a DC light that works from the car's battery is best, although an AC light that plugs into 110V house current will suffice at some sacrifice in brightness)

4. Wire spark plug gauge/adjusting tools

5. Set of feeler blades.

Here again, be guided by your own needs. A feeler blade will set the point gap as easily as dwell meter will read dwell, but slightly less accurately. And since you will need a tachometer anyway ... well, make your own decision.

In addition to these basic tools, there are several other tools and gauges you may find useful. These include:

1. A compression gauge. The screw-in type is slower to use, but eliminates the possibility of a faulty reading due to escaping pressure

2. A manifold vacuum gauge

3. A test light

4. An induction meter. This is used for determining whether or not there is current in a wire. These are handy for use if a wire is broken somewhere in a wiring harness.

As a final note, you will probably find a torque wrench necessary for all but the most basic work. The beam type models are perfectly adequate, although the newer click (breakaway) type are more precise, and you don't have to crane your neck to see a torque reading in awkward situations. The breakaway torque wrenches are more expensive and should be recalibrated periodically.

Torque specification for each fastener will be given in the procedure in any case that a specific torque value is required. If no torque specifications are given, use the following values as a guide, based upon fastener size:

Bolts marked 6T

    6mm bolt/nut — 5–7 ft. lbs.
    8mm bolt/nut — 12–17 ft. lbs.
    10mm bolt/nut — 23–34 ft. lbs.
    12mm bolt/nut — 41–59 ft. lbs.
    14mm bolt/nut — 56–76 ft. lbs.

Bolts marked 8T

    6mm bolt/nut — 6–9 ft. lbs.
    8mm bolt/nut — 13–20 ft. lbs.
    10mm bolt/nut — 27–40 ft. lbs.
    12mm bolt/nut — 46–69 ft. lbs.
    14mm bolt/nut — 75–101 ft. lbs.

Special Tools

Normally, the use of special factory tools is avoided for repair procedures, since these are not readily available for the do-it-yourselfer mechanic. When it is possible to perform the job with more commonly available tools, it will be pointed out, but occasionally, a special tool was designed to perform a specific function and should be used. Before substituting another tool, you should be convinced that neither your safety nor the performance of the vehicle will be compromised.

Some special tools are available commercially from major tool manufacturers. Others for your car can be purchased from you dealer or from Owatonna Tool Co., Owatonna, Minnesota 55060.

SERVICING YOUR VEHICLE SAFELY

It is virtually impossible to anticipate all of the hazards involved with automotive maintenance and service but care and common sense will prevent most accidents.

The rules of safety for mechanics range from "don't smoke around gasoline," to "use the proper tool for the job." The trick to avoiding injuries is to develop safe work habits and take every possible precaution.

Do's

• Do keep a fire extinguisher and first aid kit within easy reach.

• Do wear safety glasses or goggles when cutting, drilling, grinding or prying. If you wear glasses for the sake of vision, then they should be made of hardened glass that can serve also as safety glasses, or wear safety goggles over your regular glasses.

• Do shield your eyes whenever you work around the battery. Batteries contain sulfuric acid. In case of contact with the eyes or skin, flush the area with water or a mixture of water and baking soda and get medical attention immediately.

• Do use safety stands for any under-car service. Jacks are for raising vehicles; safety stands are for making sure the vehicle stays raised until you want it to come down. Whenever the vehicle is raised, block the wheels remaining on the ground and set the parking brake.

• Do use adequate ventilation when working with any chemicals. Asbestos dust resulting from brake lining wear cause cancer.

• Do disconnect the negative battery cable when working on the electrical system.

• Do follow manufacturer's directions whenever working with potentially hazardous materials. Both brake fluid and antifreeze are poisonous if taken internally.

• Do properly maintain your tools. Loose hammerheads, mushroomed punches and chisels, frayed or poorly grounded electrical cords, excessively worn screwdrivers, spread wrenches (open end), cracked sockets, slipping ratchets, or faulty droplight sockets can cause accidents.

• Do use the proper size and type of tool for the job being done.

• Do when possible, pull on a wrench handle rather than push on it, and adjust you stance to prevent a fall.

• Do be sure that adjustable wrenches are tightly adjusted on the nut or bolt and pulled so that the face is on the side of the fixed jaw.

• Do select a wrench or socket that fits the nut or bolt. The wrench or socket should sit straight, not cocked.

• Do strike squarely with a hammer. avoid glancing blows.

• Do set the parking brake and block the wheels if the work requires that the engine be running.

Don't's

• Don't run an engine in a garage or anywhere else without proper ventilation—EVER!

Carbon monoxide is poisonous. It is absorbed by the body 400 times faster than oxygen. It takes a long time to leave the human body and you can build up a deadly supply of it in your system by simply breathing in a little every day. You may not realize you are slowly poisoning yourself. Always use power vents, windows, fans or open the garage doors.

• Don't work around moving parts while wearing a necktie or other loose clothing. Short sleeves are much safer than long, loose sleeves. Hard-toed shoes with neoprene soles protect your toes and give a better grip on slippery surfaces. Jewelry such as watches, fancy belt buckles, beads, or body adornment of any kind is not safe while working around a car. Long hair should be hidden under a hat or cap.

• Don't use pockets for toolboxes. A fall or bump can drive a screwdriver deep into you body. Even a wiping cloth hanging from the back pocket can wrap around a spinning shaft or fan.

• Don't smoke when working around gasoline, cleaning solvent or other flammable material.

• Don't smoke when working around the battery. When the battery is being charged, it gives off explosive hydrogen gas.

• Don't use gasoline to wash your hands. There are excellent soaps available. Gasoline may contain lead, and lead can enter the body through a cut, accumulating in the body until you are very ill. Gasoline also removes all the natural oils from the skin so that bone dry hands will suck up oil and grease.

• Don't service the air conditioning system unless you are equipped with the necessary tools and training. The refrigerant, R-12, is extremely cold and when exposed to the air, will instantly freeze any surface it comes in contact with, including your eyes. Although the refrigerant is normally non-toxic, R-12 becomes a deadly poisonous gas in the presence of an open flame. One good whiff of the vapors from burning refrigerant can be fatal.

SERIAL NUMBER IDENTIFICATION

Vehicle Identification Number
1979-80

The official vehicle identification number for title and registration purposes is stamped on a metal tag, which is fastened to the top of the instrument panel. The tag is located on the driver's side, visible through the windshield. The first digit in the vehicle identification number is the model year of the car (9 = 1979, 0 = 1980, etc.). The second digit is the assembly plant code for the plant in which the vehicle was built. The third and fourth digits are the body serial code designations (2-dr sedan, 4-dr sedan). The fifth digit is the engine code which identifies the type of engine originally installed in the vehicle (see the Engine Codes chart). The last six digits are the consecutive unit numbers

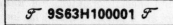

Vehicle identification number through 1980

1FABP34D9CB100001

Vehicle Identification Number, 1981–82

MFD. BY FORD MOTOR CO. OF CANADA LTD.

NOTE:

CANADIAN LABEL
PARALLELS U.S.A.
LABEL EXCEPT
FOR WORDING
"MFD. BY FORD
MOTOR CO. OF
CANADA LTD.

VEH. IDENT. NO.			TYPE				
COLOR	DSO	BODY	TRIM	SCH. DATE	AXLE	TRANS.	A/C

Vehicle certification label (Canada)

MFD. BY FORD MOTOR CO. IN U.S.A.

DATE: 08 78
GAWR: FRONT 3222

GVWR 6538
REAR 3375

THIS VEHICLE CONFORMS TO ALL APPLICABLE FEDERAL MOTOR VEHICLE SAFETY STANDARDS IN EFFECT ON THE DATE OF MANUFACTURE SHOWN ABOVE.

F0012 R0165

9S63H100001   PASSENGER

VEH. IDENT. NO.			TYPE				
COLOR	DSO	BODY	TRIM	SCH. DATE	AXLE	TRANS.	A/C
ICYA	4R	53H	DD	08H	6	X	A

① Consecutive unit no.
② Body serial code
③ Model year code
④ Assembly plant code
⑤ Engine code
⑥ Body color code
⑦ Vinyl roof type/color
⑧ District—special equipment
⑨ Body type code
⑩ Trim code (First letter = Type of trim; Second letter = color of trim)
⑪ Scheduled build date
⑫ Rear axle code
⑬ Transmission code
⑭ Air conditioning
⑮ Vehicle type
⑯ Accessory reserve load

Vehicle certification label (United States)

Engine Codes

Year	Model	Code	Number of Cylinders	Litres	Cu. in.	Carb. Barrels
1979	Mustang, Capri	Y	4	2.3	140	2
		W	4	2.3	140	2-Turbo
		Z	6	2.8	170	2
		F	8	5.0	302	2
1980	Mustang, Capri	A	4	2.3	140	2
		T	4	2.3	140	2-Turbo
		B	6	3.3	200	1
		D	8	4.2	255	2
1981	Mustang, Capri	A	4	2.3	140	2
		T	4	2.3	140	2-Turbo
		B	6	3.3	200	1
		D	8	4.2	255	2
1982	Mustang, Capri	A	4	2.3	140	2
		T	4	2.3	140	2-Turbo ①
		B	6	3.3	200	1
		D	8	4.2	255	2
		F	8	5.0	302	2
1983–88	Mustang, Capri Merkur	A	4	2.3	140	2
		W	4	2.3	140	Turbo
		B	6	3.3	200	1
		3	V6	3.8	232	CFI
		F	V8	5.0	302	CFI
		M	V8	5.0	302HO	②

① Canada Only
② 4 bbl or CFI
CFI—Fuel Injection

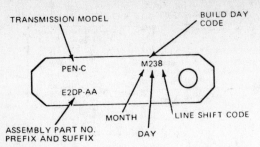

Identification tag—C-5 automatic. Under lower intermediate servo cover

which start at 100,001 for the first car of a model year built in each assembly plant.

From 1981

Beginning in 1981, the serial number contains seventeen or more digits or letters. The first three give the world manufacturer code. The fourth is the type of restraint system. The fifth will remain the letter **P**. The sixth and seventh are the car line, series and body type. The eighth is the engine type. The ninth is a check digit. The tenth is the model year. The eleventh is the assembly plant. The remaining numbers are the production sequence.

Transmission Codes

1.	Three speed
2.	Five speed overdrive
4.	Four speed overdrive (SROD)
5.	Five speed
5.	Five speed overdrive (RAP)
6.	Four speed (Borg Warner)
7.	Four speed overdrive (RUG)
7.	Four speed (ET) (Hummer)
C.	C5 automatic
S.	JATCO automatic
T.	AOD (automatic overdrive)
U.	C6 automatic
V.	C3 automatic
W.	C4 automatic
X.	FMX automatic
Y.	Borg Warner automatic
Z.	C6 police automatic

Refer to the vehicle certification plate on the driver's door frame for transmission identification code.

ROUTINE MAINTENANCE

Air Cleaner Element

All engines are equipped with a dry type, replaceable air filter element. The element should be replaced the the recommended intervals shown on the Maintenance Chart in this Chapter. If your vehicle is operated under severely dusty conditions or severe operating conditions, more frequent changes are necessary. Inspect the element at least twice a year. Early spring and at the beginning of fall are good times for the inspection. Remove the element and check for holes in the filter. Check the cleaner housing for signs of dirt or dust that has leaked through the filter element. Place a light on the inside of the element and look through the filter at the light. If no glow of light can be seen through the element material, replace the fil-

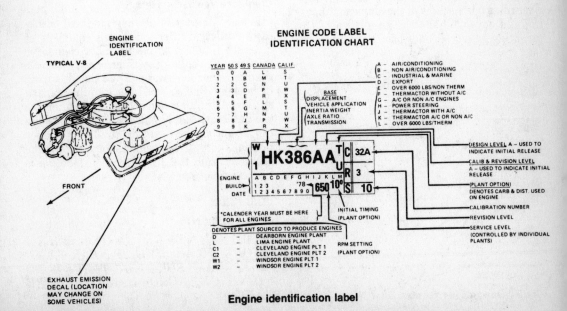

Engine identification label

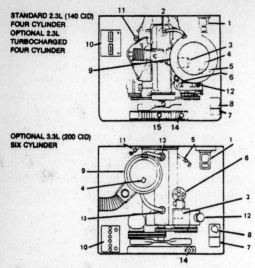

STANDARD 2.3L (140 CID) FOUR CYLINDER OPTIONAL 2.3L TURBOCHARGED FOUR CYLINDER

OPTIONAL 3.3L (200 CID) SIX CYLINDER

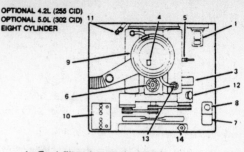

OPTIONAL 4.2L (255 CID) OPTIONAL 5.0L (302 CID) EIGHT CYLINDER

1. Brake master cylinder
2. Engine oil filler cap & PCV filter (2.3L)
3. Engine oil filter

4. Fuel filter (on carburetor)
5. Engine oil dipstick
6. Distributor
7. Coolant expansion bottle
8. Windshield washer reservoir
9. Air cleaner assembly
10. Battery
11. Automatic transmission dipstick
12. Power steering reservoir dipstick
13. PCV valve & grommet &
    oil filler cap (3.3L & 4.2L)
14. Radiator cap (all except 2.3L non-A/C)
15. Radiator cap (2.3L non-A/C)

Vehicle service points

ter. If holes in the filter are apparent or signs of dirt leakage through the filter are noticed, replace the filter.

REMOVAL AND INSTALLATION

Air Cleaner Assembly

1. Disconnect all hoses, ducts and vacuum tubes from the air cleaner assembly.

2. Remove the top cover wing nut and grommet (if equipped). Remove any side bracket mount retaining bolts (if equipped). Remove the air cleaner assembly from the top of the carburetor or intake assembly.

3. Remove the cover and the element, wipe clean all inside surfaces of the air cleaner housing and cover. Check the condition of the mounting gasket (cleaner base to carburetor).

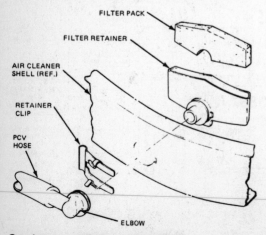

Crankcase ventilation system filter

Replace the mounting gasket if it is worn or broken.

4. Reposition the cleaner assembly, element and cover on the carburetor or intake assembly.

5. Reconnect all hoses, duct and vacuum hoses removed. Tighten the wing nut finger tight.

Element

The element can, in most cases, be replaced by removing the wing nut and cleaner assembly cover. If the inside of the housing is dirty, however, remove the assembly for cleaning to prevent dirt from entering the carburetor.

Crankcase Ventilation Filter

Replace or inspect cleaner mounted crankcase ventilation filter (on models equipped) at the same time the air cleaner filter element is serviced. To replace the filter, simply remove the air cleaner top cover and pull the filter from its housing. Push a new filter into the housing and install the air cleaner cover. If the filter and plastic holder need replacement, remove the clip mounting the feed tube to the air cleaner housing (hose already removed) and remove the assembly from the air cleaner. Installation is the reverse of removal.

Fuel Filter

REPLACEMENT

CAUTION: *NEVER SMOKE WHEN WORKING AROUND OR NEAR GASOLINE! MAKE SURE THAT THERE IS NO IGNITION SOURCE NEAR YOU WORK AREA!*

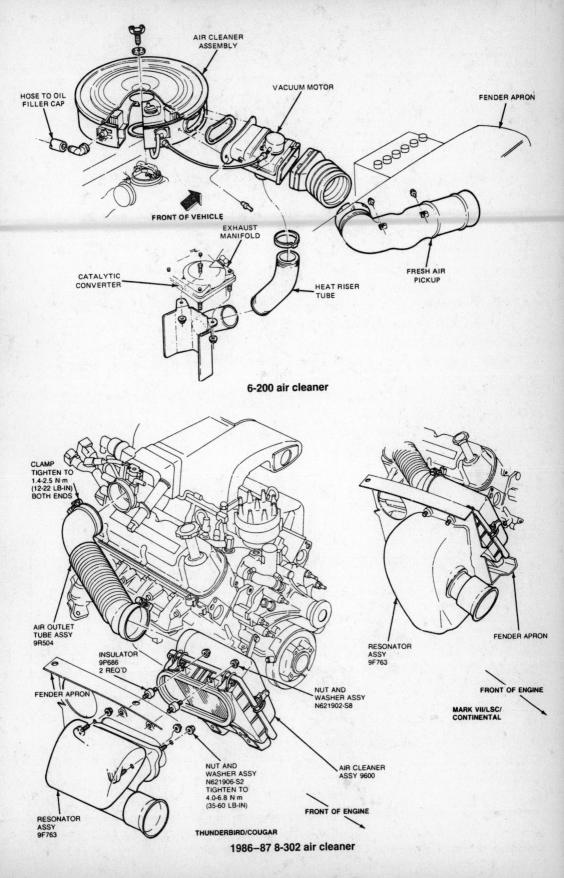

AIR CLEANER ASSEMBLY

VACUUM MOTOR

FENDER APRON

HOSE TO OIL FILLER CAP

FRONT OF VEHICLE

EXHAUST MANIFOLD

CATALYTIC CONVERTER

HEAT RISER TUBE

FRESH AIR PICKUP

6-200 air cleaner

CLAMP TIGHTEN TO 1.4-2.5 N·m (12-22 LB-IN) BOTH ENDS

AIR OUTLET TUBE ASSY 9R504

INSULATOR 9P686 2 REQ'D

FENDER APRON

NUT AND WASHER ASSY N621902-S8

RESONATOR ASSY 9F763

FENDER APRON

FRONT OF ENGINE

MARK VII/LSC/ CONTINENTAL

NUT AND WASHER ASSY N621906-S2 TIGHTEN TO 4.0-6.8 N·m (35-60 LB-IN)

AIR CLEANER ASSY 9600

RESONATOR ASSY 9F763

FRONT OF ENGINE

THUNDERBIRD/COUGAR

1986–87 8-302 air cleaner

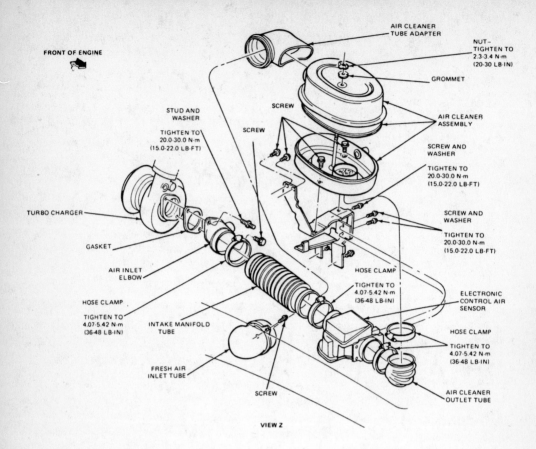

FRONT OF ENGINE

AIR CLEANER
TUBE ADAPTER

NUT—
TIGHTEN TO
2.3-3.4 N·m
(20-30 LB·IN)

GROMMET

SCREW

SCREW

AIR CLEANER
ASSEMBLY

STUD AND
WASHER

TIGHTEN TO
20.0-30.0 N·m
(15.0-22.0 LB·FT)

SCREW AND
WASHER

TIGHTEN TO
20.0-30.0 N·m
(15.0-22.0 LB·FT)

TURBO CHARGER

SCREW AND
WASHER

TIGHTEN TO
20.0-30.0 N·m
(15.0-22.0 LB·FT)

GASKET

AIR INLET
ELBOW

HOSE CLAMP

HOSE CLAMP

TIGHTEN TO
4.07-5.42 N·m
(36-48 LB·IN)

ELECTRONIC
CONTROL AIR
SENSOR

TIGHTEN TO
4.07-5.42 N·m
(36-48 LB·IN)

INTAKE MANIFOLD
TUBE

HOSE CLAMP

TIGHTEN TO
4.07-5.42 N·m
(36-48 LB·IN)

FRESH AIR
INLET TUBE

AIR CLEANER
OUTLET TUBE

SCREW

VIEW Z

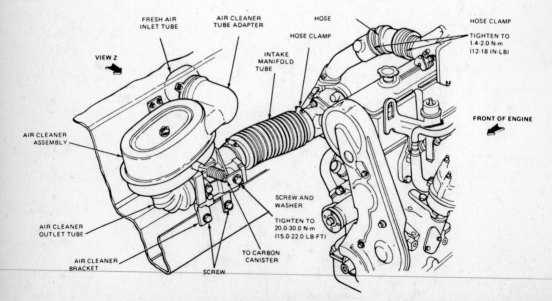

FRESH AIR
INLET TUBE

AIR CLEANER
TUBE ADAPTER

HOSE

HOSE CLAMP

HOSE CLAMP

TIGHTEN TO
1.4-2.0 N·m
(12-18 IN·LB)

VIEW Z

INTAKE
MANIFOLD
TUBE

HOSE CLAMP

FRONT OF ENGINE

AIR CLEANER
ASSEMBLY

SCREW AND
WASHER

TIGHTEN TO
20.0-30.0 N·m
(15.0-22.0 LB·FT)

AIR CLEANER
OUTLET TUBE

AIR CLEANER
BRACKET

TO CARBON
CANISTER

SCREW

1984—86 4-140 Turbo air cleaner

Carbureted Engines

6-200
6-232
8-255
8-302 w/Motorcraft 2150

A carburetor mounted gas filter is used. These filters screw into the float chamber. To replace one of these filters:

1. Wait until the engine is cold.
2. Remove the air cleaner assembly.
3. Place some absorbant rags under the filter.
4. Remove the hose clamp and slide the rubber hose from the filter.

CAUTION: *It is possible for gasoline to spray in all directions when removing the hose!*

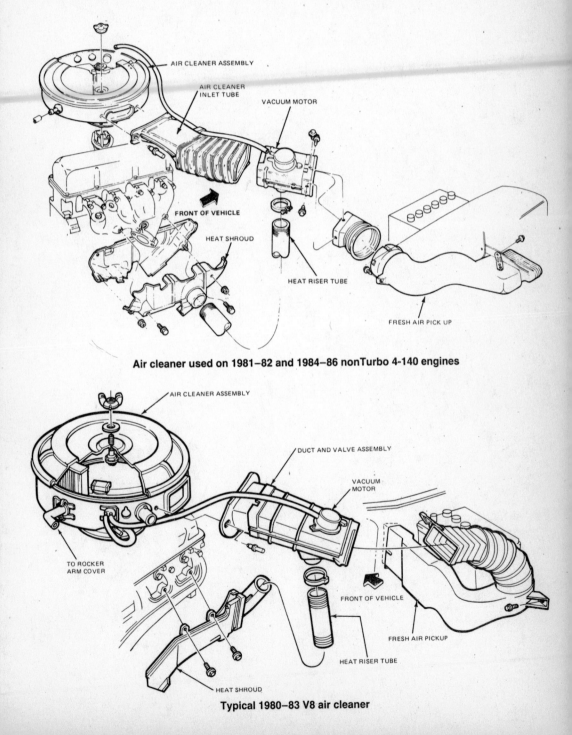

Air cleaner used on 1981–82 and 1984–86 nonTurbo 4-140 engines

Typical 1980–83 V8 air cleaner

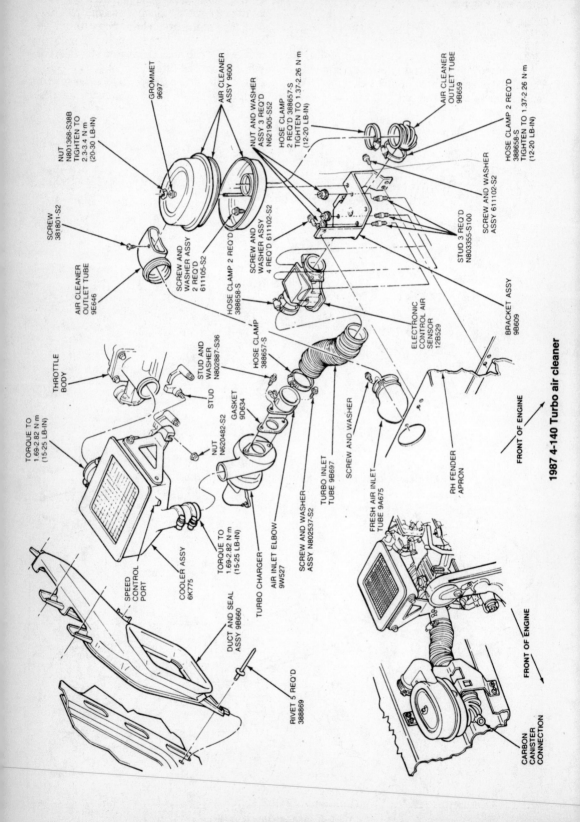

1987 4-140 Turbo air cleaner

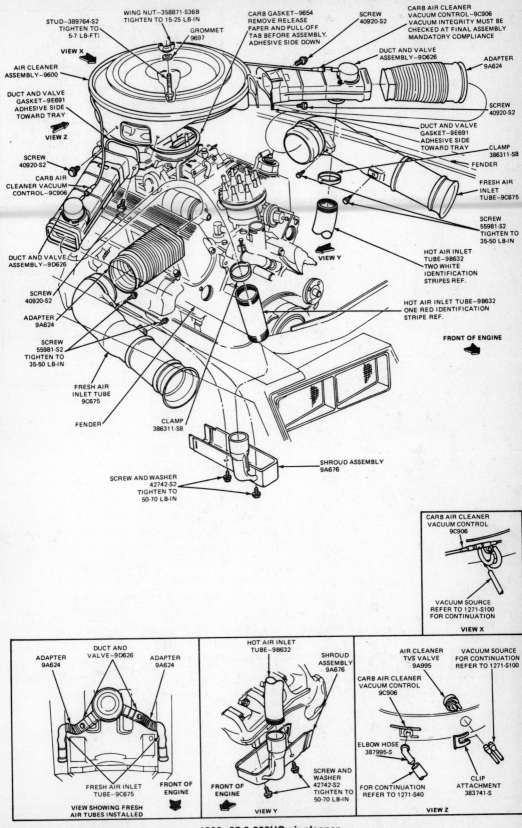

STUD–389764-S2 TIGHTEN TO 5-7 LB-FT)

WING NUT–358871-S36B TIGHTEN TO 15-25 LB-IN

GROMMET 9697

CARB GASKET–9654 REMOVE RELEASE PAPER AND PULL-OFF TAB BEFORE ASSEMBLY. ADHESIVE SIDE DOWN

SCREW 40920-S2

CARB AIR CLEANER VACUUM CONTROL–9C906 VACUUM INTEGRITY MUST BE CHECKED AT FINAL ASSEMBLY MANDATORY COMPLIANCE

VIEW X

AIR CLEANER ASSEMBLY–9600

DUCT AND VALVE GASKET–9E691 ADHESIVE SIDE TOWARD TRAY

VIEW Z

SCREW 40920-S2

CARB AIR CLEANER VACUUM CONTROL–9C906

DUCT AND VALVE ASSEMBLY–9D626

SCREW 40920-S2

ADAPTER 9A624

SCREW 55981-S2 TIGHTEN TO 35-50 LB-IN

FRESH AIR INLET TUBE 9C675

FENDER

CLAMP 386311-S8

SCREW AND WASHER 42742-S2 TIGHTEN TO 50-70 LB-IN

DUCT AND VALVE ASSEMBLY–9D626

ADAPTER 9A624

SCREW 40920-S2

DUCT AND VALVE GASKET–9E691 ADHESIVE SIDE TOWARD TRAY

CLAMP 386311-S8

FENDER

FRESH AIR INLET TUBE–9C675

SCREW 55981-S2 TIGHTEN TO 35-50 LB-IN

VIEW Y

HOT AIR INLET TUBE–9B632 TWO WHITE IDENTIFICATION STRIPES REF.

HOT AIR INLET TUBE–9B632 ONE RED IDENTIFICATION STRIPE REF.

FRONT OF ENGINE

SHROUD ASSEMBLY 9A676

CARB AIR CLEANER VACUUM CONTROL 9C906

VACUUM SOURCE REFER TO 1271-S100 FOR CONTINUATION

VIEW X

ADAPTER 9A624

DUCT AND VALVE–9D626

ADAPTER 9A624

FRESH AIR INLET TUBE–9C675

FRONT OF ENGINE

VIEW SHOWING FRESH AIR TUBES INSTALLED

HOT AIR INLET TUBE–9B632

SHROUD ASSEMBLY 9A676

FRONT OF ENGINE

SCREW AND WASHER 42742-S2 TIGHTEN TO 50-70 LB-IN

VIEW Y

AIR CLEANER TVS VALVE 9A995

VACUUM SOURCE FOR CONTINUATION REFER TO 1271-S100

CARB AIR CLEANER VACUUM CONTROL 9C906

ELBOW HOSE 387995-S

FOR CONTINUATION REFER TO 1271-S40

CLIP ATTACHMENT 383741-S

VIEW Z

1983–85 8-302HO air cleaner

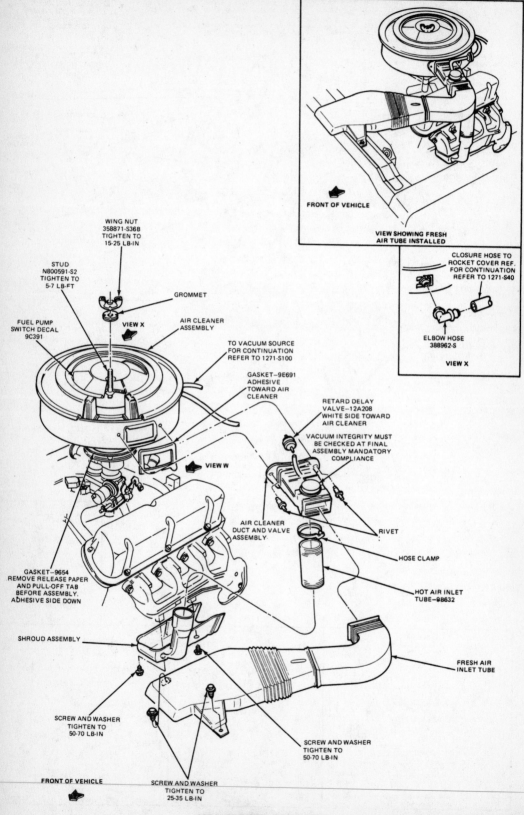

FRONT OF VEHICLE

VIEW SHOWING FRESH
AIR TUBE INSTALLED

CLOSURE HOSE TO
ROCKET COVER REF.
FOR CONTINUATION
REFER TO 1271-S40

ELBOW HOSE
388962-S

VIEW X

WING NUT
358871-S36B
TIGHTEN TO
15-25 LB-IN

STUD
N800591-S2
TIGHTEN TO
5-7 LB-FT

GROMMET

VIEW X

FUEL PUMP
SWITCH DECAL
9C391

AIR CLEANER
ASSEMBLY

TO VACUUM SOURCE
FOR CONTINUATION
REFER TO 1271-S100

GASKET—9E691
ADHESIVE
TOWARD AIR
CLEANER

RETARD DELAY
VALVE—12A208
WHITE SIDE TOWARD
AIR CLEANER

VACUUM INTEGRITY MUST
BE CHECKED AT FINAL
ASSEMBLY MANDATORY
COMPLIANCE

VIEW W

AIR CLEANER
DUCT AND VALVE
ASSEMBLY

RIVET

HOSE CLAMP

GASKET—9654
REMOVE RELEASE PAPER
AND PULL-OFF TAB
BEFORE ASSEMBLY.
ADHESIVE SIDE DOWN

HOT AIR INLET
TUBE—9B632

SHROUD ASSEMBLY

FRESH AIR
INLET TUBE

SCREW AND WASHER
TIGHTEN TO
50-70 LB-IN

SCREW AND WASHER
TIGHTEN TO
50-70 LB-IN

FRONT OF VEHICLE

SCREW AND WASHER
TIGHTEN TO
25-35 LB-IN

1984–85 8-302 air cleaner

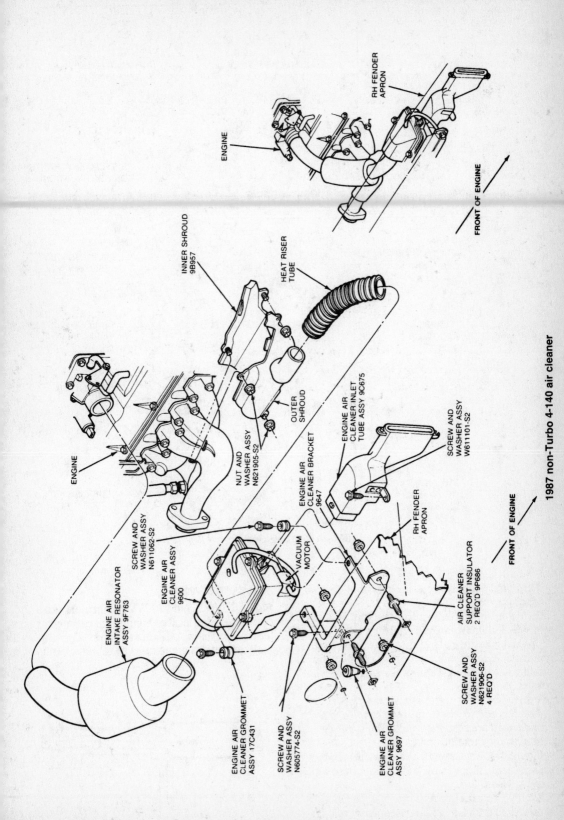

1987 non-Turbo 4-140 air cleaner

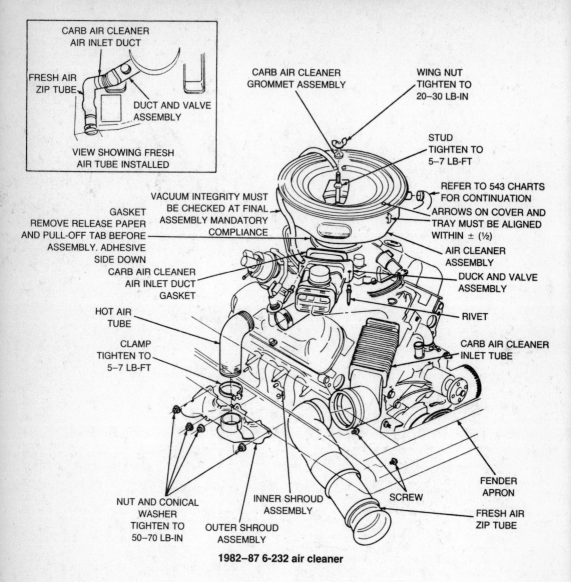

CARB AIR CLEANER
AIR INLET DUCT

FRESH AIR
ZIP TUBE

DUCT AND VALVE
ASSEMBLY

VIEW SHOWING FRESH
AIR TUBE INSTALLED

CARB AIR CLEANER
GROMMET ASSEMBLY

WING NUT
TIGHTEN TO
20–30 LB-IN

STUD
TIGHTEN TO
5–7 LB-FT

REFER TO 543 CHARTS
FOR CONTINUATION

ARROWS ON COVER AND
TRAY MUST BE ALIGNED
WITHIN ± (½)

VACUUM INTEGRITY MUST
BE CHECKED AT FINAL
ASSEMBLY MANDATORY
COMPLIANCE

GASKET
REMOVE RELEASE PAPER
AND PULL-OFF TAB BEFORE
ASSEMBLY. ADHESIVE
SIDE DOWN
CARB AIR CLEANER
AIR INLET DUCT
GASKET

AIR CLEANER
ASSEMBLY

DUCK AND VALVE
ASSEMBLY

RIVET

HOT AIR
TUBE

CLAMP
TIGHTEN TO
5–7 LB-FT

CARB AIR CLEANER
INLET TUBE

FENDER
APRON

SCREW

FRESH AIR
ZIP TUBE

NUT AND CONICAL
WASHER
TIGHTEN TO
50–70 LB-IN

OUTER SHROUD
ASSEMBLY

INNER SHROUD
ASSEMBLY

1982–87 6-232 air cleaner

This rarely happens, but it is possible, so protect your eyes!

5. Move the fuel line out of the way and unscrew the filter from the carburetor.

6. Coat the threads of the new filter with non-hardening, gasoline-proof sealer and screw it into place by hand. Tighten it snugly with the wrench.

WARNING: *Do not overtighten the filter! The threads in the carburetor bowl are soft metal and are easily stripped! You don't want to damage these threads!!*

7. Connect the hose to the new filter. Most replacement filters come with a new hose and clamps. Use them.

8. Remove the fuel-soaked rags, wipe up any spilled fuel and start the engine. Check the filter connections for leaks.

8-302 w/2700VV or 7200VV

Model 2700VV and 7200VV carburetors use a replaceable filter located behind the carburetor inlet fitting. To replace these filters:

1. Wait until the engine is cold.

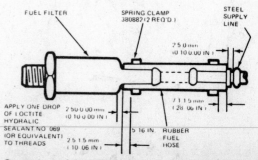

Screw-in type fuel filter with hose connection

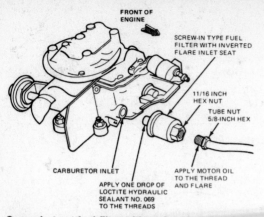

Screw-in type fuel filter with an inverted flare inlet seat

2. Remove the air cleaner assembly.

3. Place some absorbant rags under the inlet fitting.

4. Using a back-up wrench on the inlet fitting, unscrew the fuel line from the inlet fitting.

CAUTION: *It is possible for gasoline to spray in all directions when unscrewing the line! This rarely happens, but it is possible, so protect your eyes!*

5. Move the fuel line out of the way and unscrew the inlet fiting from the carburetor.

6. Pull out the filter. The spring behind the filter may come with it.

7. Install the new filter. Some new filters come with a new spring. Use it.

8. Coat the threads of the inlet fitting with non-hardening, gasoline-proof sealer and screw it into place by hand. Tighten it snugly with the wrench.

WARNING: *Do not overtighten the inlet fitting! The threads in the carburetor bowl are soft metal and are easily stripped! You don't want to damage these threads!!*

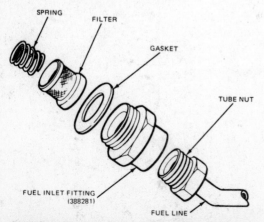

In-carburetor type filter used on the 2700VV and 7200VV

9. Using the back-up wrench on the inlet fitting, screw the fuel line into the fitting and tighten it snugly. Do not overtighten the fuel line!

10. Remove the fuel-soaked rags, wipe up any spilled fuel and start the engine. Check the connections for leaks.

4-140

1. Wait until the engine is cold.

2. Remove the air cleaner assembly.

3. Place some absorbant rags under the filter.

4. Using a back-up wrench on the filter, unscrew the fuel line from the filter.

CAUTION: *It is possible for gasoline to spray in all directions when unscrewing the line! This rarely happens, but it is possible, so protect your eyes!*

5. Move the fuel line out of the way and unscrew the filter from the carburetor.

6. Coat the threads of the new filter with non-hardening, gasoline-proof sealer and screw it into place by hand. Tighten it snugly with the wrench.

WARNING: *Do not overtighten the filter! The threads in the carburetor bowl are soft metal and are easily stripped! You don't want to damage these threads!!*

7. Using the back-up wrench on the filter, screw the fuel line into the filter and tighten it snugly. Do not overtighten the fuel line!

8. Remove the fuel-soaked rags, wipe up any spilled fuel and start the engine. Check the connections for leaks.

Fuel Injected Gasoline Engines

The inline filter is mounted on the same bracket as the fuel supply pump on the frame rail under the car, back by the fuel tank. To replace the filter:

1. Raise and support the rear end on jackstands.

2. With the engine off, depressurize the fuel system. See Chapter 5.

3. Remove the quick-disconnect fittings at both ends of the filter. See Chapter 5.

4. Remove the filter and retainer from the bracket.

5. Remove the rubber insulator ring from the filter.

6. Remove the filter from the retainer.

7. Install the new filter into the retainer, noting the direction of the flow arrow.

8. Install a new rubber insulator ring.

9. Install the retainer and filter on the bracket and tighten the screws to 60 in. lbs.

10. Install the fuel lines using new retainer clips.

11. Start the engine and check for leaks.

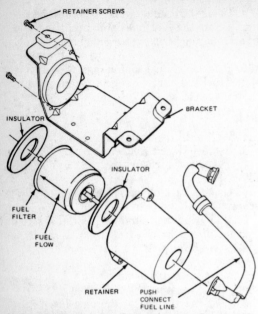

In-line fuel filter used on Thunderbird and Cougar with fuel injection

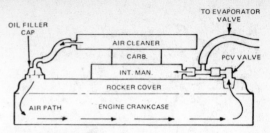

Typical PCV system

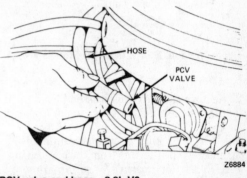

PCV valve and hose—2.8L V6

PCV Valve

All models use a closed ventilation system with a sealed breather cap connected to the air cleaner by a rubber hose. The PCV valve is usually mounted in the valve cover and connected to the intake manifold by a rubber hose. Its task is to regulate the amount of crankcase (blow-by) gases which are recycled.

Since the PCV valve works under severe load it is very important that it be replaced at the interval specified in the maintenance chart. Replacement involves removing the valve from the grommet in the rocker arm cover disconnecting the hose(s) and installing a new valve. Do not attempt to clean a used valve.

Heat Riser

Some models are equipped with exhaust control (heat riser) valves located near the head

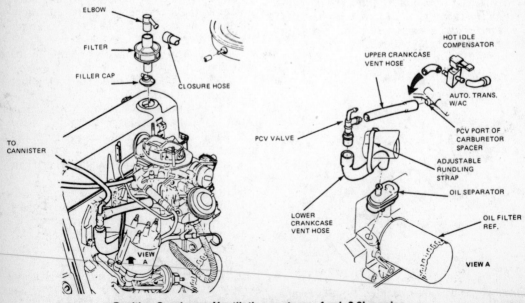

Positive Crankcase Ventilation system—4 cyl. 2.3L engine

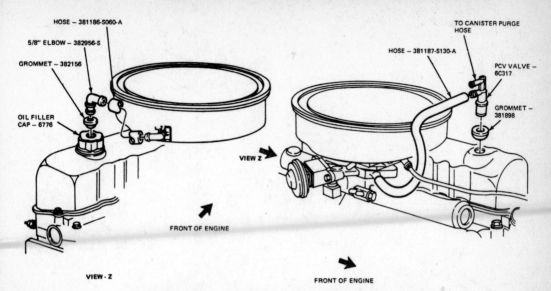

Positive Crankcase Ventilation system—6 cyl. 3.3L engine

pipe connection in the exhaust manifold. These valves aid initial warm-up in cold weather by restricting exhaust gas flow slightly. The heat generated by this restriction is transferred to the intake manifold where it results in improved fuel vaporization.

The operation of the exhaust control valve should be checked every 6 months or 6,000 miles. Make sure that the thermostatic spring is hooked on the stop pin and that the tension holds the valve shut. Rotate the counterweight by hand and make sure that it moves freely through about 90° of rotation. A valve which is operating properly will open when light finger

pressure is applied (cold engine). Lubricate the shaft bushings with a mixture of penetrating oil and graphite. Operate the valve manually a few times to work in the lubricant.

Evaporative Emissions Canister

The canister functions to cycle the fuel vapor from the fuel tank and carburetor float chamber into the intake manifold and eventually into the cylinders for combustion. The activated charcoal element within the canister acts as a storage device for the fuel vapor at times when the engine operating condition will not permit fuel vapor to burn efficiently.

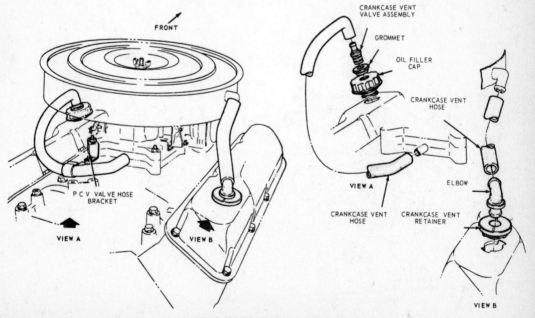

PCV valve installation—302 V8

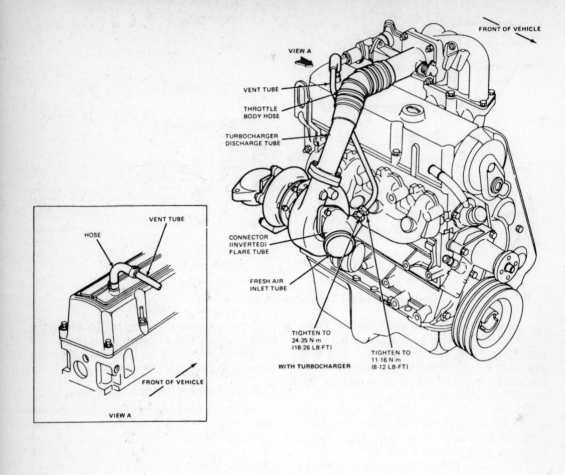

FRONT OF VEHICLE

VIEW A

VENT TUBE

THROTTLE
BODY HOSE

TURBOCHARGER
DISCHARGE TUBE

CONNECTOR
(INVERTED)
FLARE TUBE

FRESH AIR
INLET TUBE

HOSE

VENT TUBE

FRONT OF VEHICLE

VIEW A

TIGHTEN TO
24-35 N·m
(18-26 LB-FT)

WITH TURBOCHARGER

TIGHTEN TO
11-16 N·m
(8-12 LB-FT)

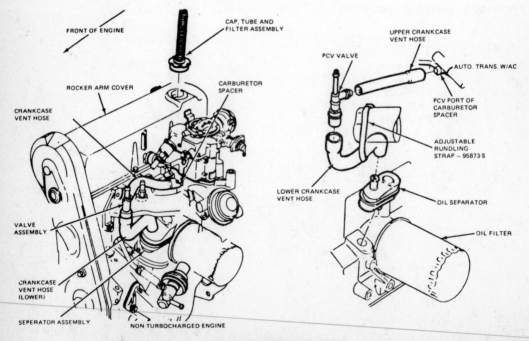

FRONT OF ENGINE

CAP, TUBE AND
FILTER ASSEMBLY

ROCKER ARM COVER

CARBURETOR
SPACER

CRANKCASE
VENT HOSE

VALVE
ASSEMBLY

CRANKCASE
VENT HOSE
(LOWER)

SEPERATOR ASSEMBLY

NON TURBOCHARGED ENGINE

UPPER CRANKCASE
VENT HOSE

PCV VALVE

AUTO. TRANS. W/AC

PCV PORT OF
CARBURETOR
SPACER

ADJUSTABLE
RUNDLING
STRAP – 95873-S

LOWER CRANKCASE
VENT HOSE

OIL SEPARATOR

OIL FILTER

4-140 late model PCV system

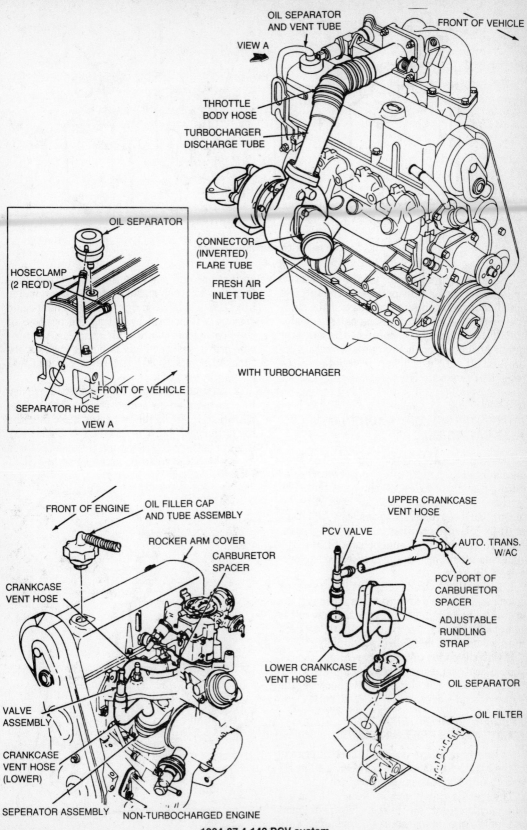

OIL SEPARATOR AND VENT TUBE

FRONT OF VEHICLE

VIEW A

THROTTLE BODY HOSE

TURBOCHARGER DISCHARGE TUBE

CONNECTOR (INVERTED) FLARE TUBE

FRESH AIR INLET TUBE

OIL SEPARATOR

HOSECLAMP (2 REQ'D)

FRONT OF VEHICLE

SEPARATOR HOSE

VIEW A

WITH TURBOCHARGER

FRONT OF ENGINE

OIL FILLER CAP AND TUBE ASSEMBLY

ROCKER ARM COVER

CARBURETOR SPACER

CRANKCASE VENT HOSE

VALVE ASSEMBLY

CRANKCASE VENT HOSE (LOWER)

SEPERATOR ASSEMBLY

NON-TURBOCHARGED ENGINE

UPPER CRANKCASE VENT HOSE

PCV VALVE

AUTO. TRANS. W/AC

PCV PORT OF CARBURETOR SPACER

ADJUSTABLE RUNDLING STRAP

LOWER CRANKCASE VENT HOSE

OIL SEPARATOR

OIL FILTER

1984-87 4-140 PCV system

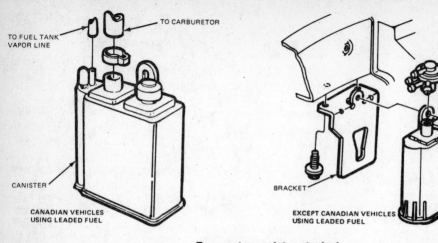

Evaporator canister—typical

The only required service for the evaporative emissions canister is inspection at the interval specified in the maintenance chart. If the charcoal element is gummed up the entire canister should be replaced. Disconnect the canister purge hose(s), loosen the canister retaining bracket, lift out the canister. Installation is the reverse of removal.

Battery

FLUID LEVEL (EXCEPT MAINTENANCE FREE BATTERIES)

Check the battery electrolyte level at least once a month, or more often in hot weather or during periods of extended car operation. The level can be checked through the case on translucent polypropylene batteries; the cell caps must be removed on other models. The electrolyte level in each cell should be kept filled to the split ring inside, or the line marked on the outside of the case.

If the level is low, add only distilled water, or colorless, odorless drinking water, through the opening until the level is correct. Each cell is completely separate from the others, so each must be checked and filled individually.

If water is added in freezing weather, the car should be driven several miles to allow the water to mix with the electrolyte. Otherwise, the battery could freeze.

SPECIFIC GRAVITY (EXCEPT MAINTENANCE FREE BATTERIES)

At least once a year, check the specific gravity of the battery. It should be between 1.20 in.Hg and 1.26 in.Hg at room temperature.

The specific gravity can be check with the use of an hydrometer, an inexpensive instrument available from many sources, including auto parts stores. The hydrometer has a squeeze bulb at one end and a nozzle at the other. Battery electrolyte is sucked into the hydrometer until the float is lifted from its seat. The specific gravity is then read by noting the position of the float. Generally, if after charging, the specific gravity between any two cells varies more than 50 points (0.50), the battery is bad and should be replaced.

It is not possible to check the specific gravity in this manner on sealed (maintenance free) batteries. Instead, the indicator built into the top of the case must be relied on to display any signs of battery deterioration. If the indicator is dark, the battery can be assumed to be OK. If

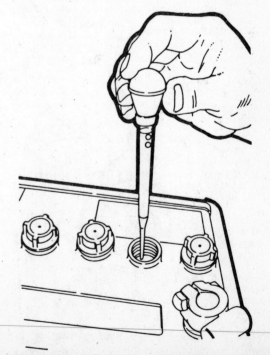

Checking the battery with a hydrometer

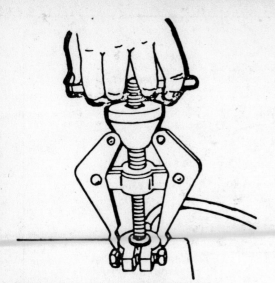

Use a puller to remove the battery cable

the indicator is light, the specific gravity is low, and the battery should be charged or replaced.

CABLES AND CLAMPS

Once a year, the battery terminals and the cable clamps should be cleaned. Loosen the clamps and remove the cables, negative cable first. On batteries with posts on top, the use of a puller specially made for the purpose is recommended. These are inexpensive, and available

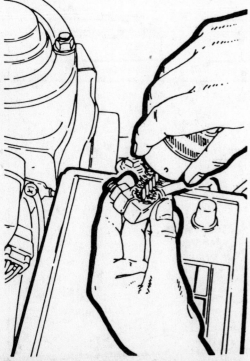

Clean the battery cable clamps with a wire brush

in auto parts stores. Side terminal battery cables are secured with a bolt.

Clean the cable lamps and the battery terminal with a wire brush, until all corrosion, grease, etc., is removed and the metal is shiny. It is especially important to clean the inside of the clamp thoroughly, since a small deposit of foreign material or oxidation there will prevent a sound electrical connection and inhibit either starting or charging. Special tools are available for cleaning these parts, one type for conventional batteries and another type for side terminal batteries.

Before installing the cables, loosen the battery holddown clamp or strap, remove the battery and check the battery tray. Clear it of any debris, and check it for soundness. Rust should be wire brushed away, and the metal given a coat of anti-rust paint. Replace the battery and tighten the holddown clamp or strap securely, but be careful not to overtighten, which will crack the battery case.

After the clamps and terminals are clean, reinstall the cables, negative cable last; do not hammer on the clamps to install. Tighten the clamps securely, but do not distort them. Give the clamps and terminals a thin external coat of grease after installation, to retard corrosion.

Check the cables at the same time that the terminals are cleaned. If the cable insulation is cracked or broken, or if the ends are frayed, the cable should be replaced with a new cable of the same length and gauge.

CAUTION: *Keep flame or sparks away from the battery; it gives off explosive hydrogen gas. Battery electrolyte contains sulphuric acid. If you should splash any on your skin or in your eyes, flush the affected area with plenty of clear water. If it lands in your eyes, get medical help immediately.*

Windshield Wipers

For maximum effectiveness and longest element lift, the windshield and wiper blades should be kept clean. Dirt, tree sap, road tar and so on will cause streaking, smearing and blade deterioration if left on the glass. It is advisable to wash the windshield carefully with a commercial glass cleaner at least once a month. Wipe off the rubber blades with the wet rag afterwards. Do not attempt to move the wipers by hand; damage to the motor and drive mechanism will result.

If the blades are found to be cracked, broken or torn, they should be replaced immediately. Replacement intervals will vary with usage, although ozone deterioration usually limits blade lift to about one year. If the wiper pattern is smeared or streaked, or if the blade chatters

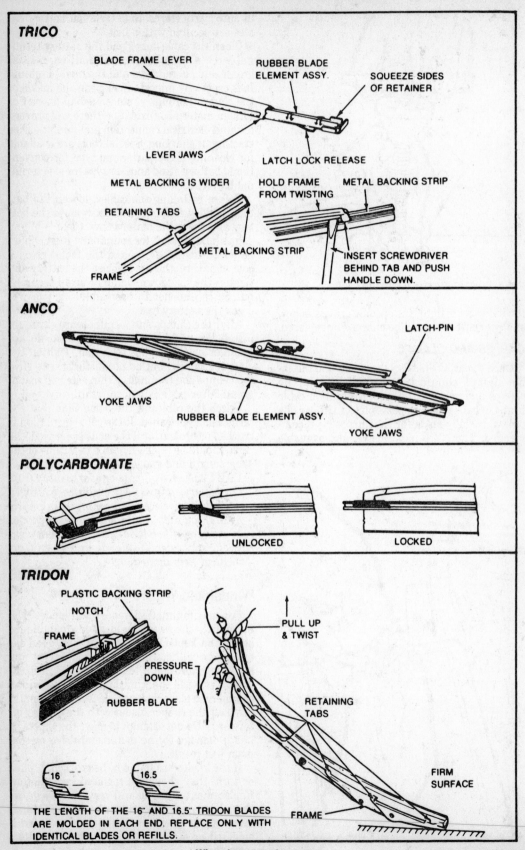

TRICO

BLADE FRAME LEVER

RUBBER BLADE ELEMENT ASSY.

SQUEEZE SIDES OF RETAINER

LEVER JAWS

LATCH LOCK RELEASE

METAL BACKING IS WIDER

HOLD FRAME FROM TWISTING

METAL BACKING STRIP

RETAINING TABS

METAL BACKING STRIP

FRAME

INSERT SCREWDRIVER BEHIND TAB AND PUSH HANDLE DOWN.

ANCO

LATCH-PIN

YOKE JAWS

RUBBER BLADE ELEMENT ASSY.

YOKE JAWS

POLYCARBONATE

UNLOCKED

LOCKED

TRIDON

PLASTIC BACKING STRIP

NOTCH

FRAME

PULL UP & TWIST

PRESSURE DOWN

RUBBER BLADE

RETAINING TABS

16   16.5

FIRM SURFACE

THE LENGTH OF THE 16" AND 16.5" TRIDON BLADES ARE MOLDED IN EACH END. REPLACE ONLY WITH IDENTICAL BLADES OR REFILLS.

FRAME

Wiper insert replacement

across the glass, the elements should be replaced. It is easiest and most sensible to replace the elements in pairs.

There are basically three different types of refills, which differ in their method of replacement. One type has two release buttons, approximately ⅓ of the way up from the ends of the blade frame. Pushing the buttons down releases a lock and allows the rubber filler to be removed from the frame. The new filler slides back into the frame and locks in place.

The second type of refill has two metal tabs which are unlocked by squeezing them together. The rubber filler can then be withdrawn from the frame jaws. A new refill is installed by inserting the refill into the front frame jaws and sliding it rear ward to engage the remaining frame jaws. There are usually four jaws. Be certain when installing that the refill is engaged in all of them. At the end of its travel, the tabs will lock into place on the front jaws of the wiper blade frame.

The third type is a refill made from polycarbonate. The refill has a simple locking device at one end which flexes downward out of the groove into which the jaws of the holder fit, allowing easy release. By sliding the new refill through all the jaws and pushing through the slight resistance when it reaches the end of its travel, the refill will lock into position.

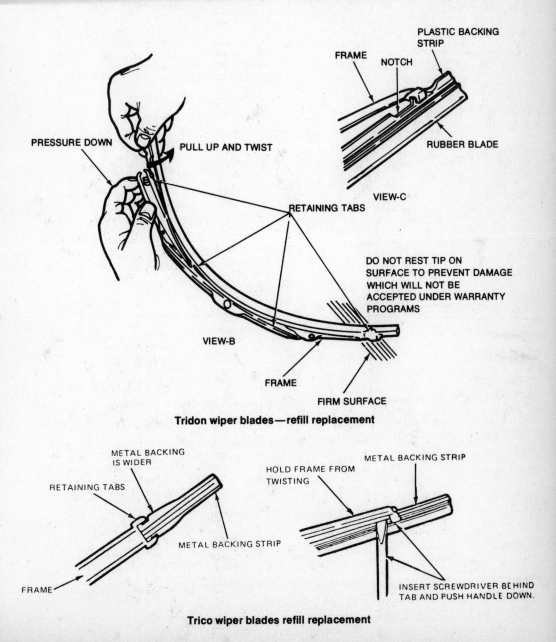

PLASTIC BACKING STRIP

FRAME   NOTCH

RUBBER BLADE

VIEW-C

PRESSURE DOWN

PULL UP AND TWIST

RETAINING TABS

DO NOT REST TIP ON SURFACE TO PREVENT DAMAGE WHICH WILL NOT BE ACCEPTED UNDER WARRANTY PROGRAMS

VIEW-B

FRAME

FIRM SURFACE

Tridon wiper blades—refill replacement

METAL BACKING IS WIDER

RETAINING TABS

METAL BACKING STRIP

HOLD FRAME FROM TWISTING

METAL BACKING STRIP

METAL BACKING STRIP

FRAME

INSERT SCREWDRIVER BEHIND TAB AND PUSH HANDLE DOWN.

Trico wiper blades refill replacement

Regardless of the type of refill used, make sure that all of the frame jaws are engaged as the refill is pushed into place and locked. The metal blade holder and frame will scratch the glass if allowed to touch it.

ARM AND BLADE REPLACEMENT

A detailed description and procedures for replacing the wiper arm and blade is found in Chapter 6.

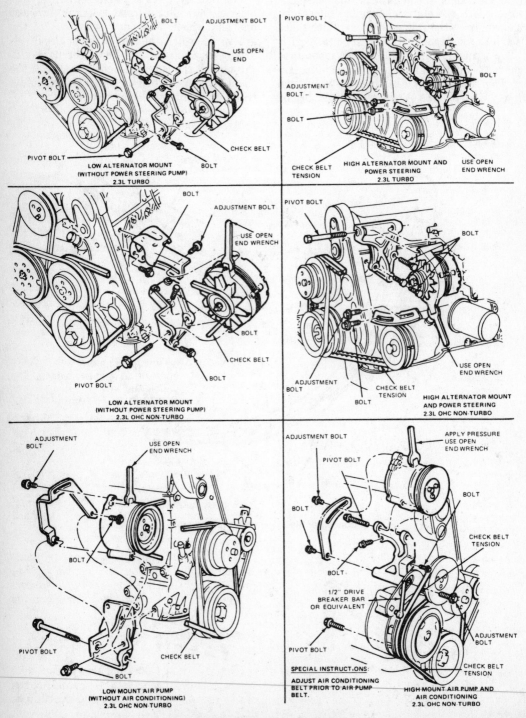

Belt tension adjustment 2.3L engines

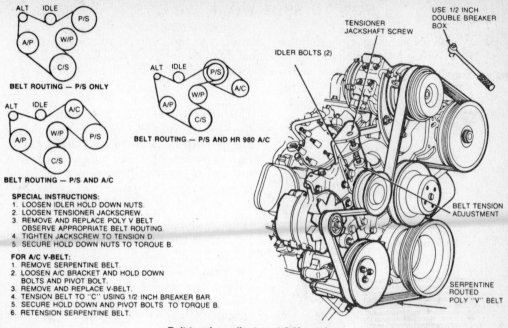

BELT ROUTING — P/S ONLY

BELT ROUTING — P/S AND HR 980 A/C

BELT ROUTING — P/S AND A/C

SPECIAL INSTRUCTIONS:
1. LOOSEN IDLER HOLD DOWN NUTS.
2. LOOSEN TENSIONER JACKSCREW.
3. REMOVE AND REPLACE POLY V BELT OBSERVE APPROPRIATE BELT ROUTING.
4. TIGHTEN JACKSCREW TO TENSION D.
5. SECURE HOLD DOWN NUTS TO TORQUE B.

FOR A/C V-BELT:
1. REMOVE SERPENTINE BELT.
2. LOOSEN A/C BRACKET AND HOLD DOWN BOLTS AND PIVOT BOLT.
3. REMOVE AND REPLACE V-BELT.
4. TENSION BELT TO "C" USING 1/2 INCH BREAKER BAR.
5. SECURE HOLD DOWN AND PIVOT BOLTS TO TORQUE B.
6. RETENSION SERPENTINE BELT.

Belt tension adjustment 3.8L engine

Belts

Once a year or at 12,000 mile intervals, the tension (and condition) of the alternator, power steering (if so equipped), air conditioning (if so equipped), and Thermactor air pump drive belts should be checked, and, if necessary, adjusted. Loose accessory drive belts can lead to poor engine cooling and diminish alternator, power steering pump, air conditioning compressor or Thermactor air pump output. A belt that is too tight places a severe strain on the water pump, alternator, power steering pump, compressor or air pump bearings.

Replace any belt that is so glazed, worn or stretched that it cannot be tightened sufficiently.

NOTE: *The material used in late model drive belts is such that the belts do not show wear. Replace belts at least every three years.*

On vehicles with matched belts, replace both belts. New ½", ⅜" and $^{15}/_{32}$" wide belts are to be adjusted to a tension of 140 lbs.; ¼" wide belts are adjusted to 80 lbs., measured on a belt tension gauge. Any belt that has been operating for a minimum of 10 minutes is considered a used belt. In the first 10 minutes, the belt should stretch to its maximum extent. After 10 minutes, stop the engine and recheck the belt tension. Belt tension for a used belt should be maintained at 110 lbs. (all except ¼" wide belts) or 60 lbs. (¼" wide belts). If a belt tension gauge is not available, the following procedures may be used.

ADJUSTMENTS FOR ALL EXCEPT THE SERPENTINE (SINGLE) BELT

CAUTION: *On models equipped with an electric cooling fan, disconnect the negative battery cable or fan motor wiring harness connector before replacing or adjusting drive belts. The fan may come on, under certain circumstances, even though the ignition is off.*

Alternator (Fan Drive) Belt

1. Position the ruler perpendicular to the drive belt at its longest straight run. Test the tightness of the belt by pressing it firmly with your thumb. The deflection should not exceed ¼".
2. If the deflection exceeds ¼", loosen the alternator mounting and adjusting arm bolts.
3. Place a 1" open-end or adjustable wrench on the adjusting ridge cast on the body, and pull on the wrench until the proper tension is achieved.
4. Holding the alternator in place to maintain tension, tighten the adjusting arm bolt. Recheck the belt tension. When the belt is properly tensioned, tighten the alternator mounting bolt.

Power Steering Drive Belt

4-140, 6-200

1. Hold a ruler perpendicular to the drive belt at its longest run, test the tightness of the belt by pressing it firmly with your thumb. The deflection should not exceed ¼".

HOW TO SPOT WORN V-BELTS

V-Belts are vital to efficient engine operation—they drive the fan, water pump and other accessories. They require little maintenance (occasional tightening) but they will not last forever. Slipping or failure of the V-belt will lead to overheating. If your V-belt looks like any of these, it should be replaced.

Cracking or weathering

This belt has deep cracks, which cause it to flex. Too much flexing leads to heat build-up and premature failure. These cracks can be caused by using the belt on a pulley that is too small. Notched belts are available for small diameter pulleys.

Softening (grease and oil)

Oil and grease on a belt can cause the belt's rubber compounds to soften and separate from the reinforcing cords that hold the belt together. The belt will first slip, then finally fail altogether.

Glazing

Glazing is caused by a belt that is slipping. A slipping belt can cause a run-down battery, erratic power steering, overheating or poor accessory performance. The more the belt slips, the more glazing will be built up on the surface of the belt. The more the belt is glazed, the more it will slip. If the glazing is light, tighten the belt.

Worn cover

The cover of this belt is worn off and is peeling away. The reinforcing cords will begin to wear and the belt will shortly break. When the belt cover wears in spots or has a rough jagged appearance, check the pulley grooves for roughness.

Separation

This belt is on the verge of breaking and leaving you stranded. The layers of the belt are separating and the reinforcing cords are exposed. It's just a matter of time before it breaks completely.

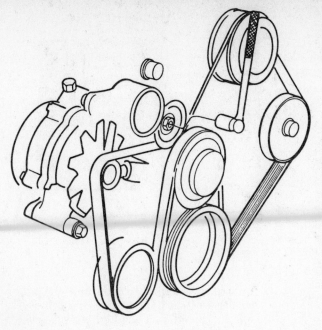

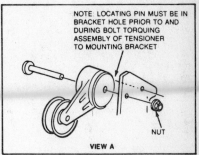

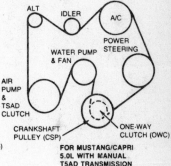

NOTE:
THE SINGLE BELT, SERPENTINE DRIVE ARRANGEMENT OF THE 5.0L ENGINE USES AN
AUTOMATIC BELT TENSIONER. NO BELT TENSION ADJUSTMENT IS REQUIRED.

SPECIAL INSTRUCTIONS:
1. LIFT AUTO TENSIONER PULLEY BY APPLYING
   TORQUE TO IDLER PULLEY PIVOT BOLT
   WITH WRENCH & SOCKET
2. INSTALL DRIVE BELT OVER PULLEYS
   PER APPROPRIATE BELT ROUTING
3. CHECK BELT TENSION. REFERENCE TENSION CODE E (MUST/CAPRI, MARK/CONTI, LTD/MARQUIS)
   OR F (LTD POLICE)
4. IF TENSION IS NOT WITHIN SPECIFICATION
   INSTALL A NEW AUTOMATIC TENSIONER.
   LOCATE TANG AS SHOWN IN VIEW A.

Belt tension adjustment 5.0L engine

REPLACEMENT INSTRUCTIONS FOR THE SERPENTINE DRIVE BELT
ARE COMMON WITH THE OTHER 5.0L SERPENTINE BELTS.
BECAUSE OF THE ROUTING IT IS POSSIBLE TO REMOVE AND
REPLACE THE REARWARD SHEAVE SERPENTINE BELT WITHOUT
DISTURBING THE FOREWARD SHEAVE JACKSHAFT BELT.

TO INSTALL A NEW JACKSHAFT BELT LOOSEN THE THREE
CLUTCH HOLD DOWN BOLTS. THEN LOOSEN THE JACKSCREW NUT
TO PERMIT BELT REMOVAL AND REPLACEMENT. ADJUST JACKSCREW
NUT   SECURE HOLD DOWN BOLTS

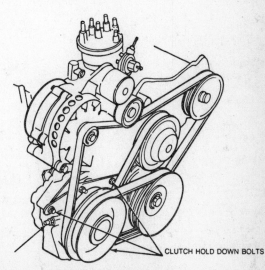

JACKSCREW TENSION ADJUSTMENT NUT   CLUTCH HOLD DOWN BOLTS

Belt tension adjustment 5.0L engine with two speed accessory drive

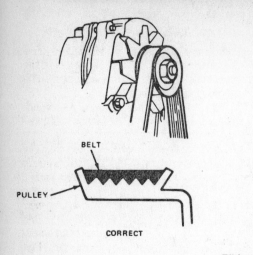

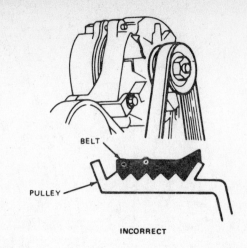

BELT

PULLEY

CORRECT

BELT

PULLEY

INCORRECT

Ribbed belt alignment

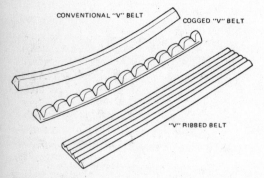

CONVENTIONAL "V" BELT

COGGED "V" BELT

"V" RIBBED BELT

Drive belt types

2. To adjust the belt tension, loosen the adjusting and mounting bolts on the front face of the steering pump cover plate (hub side).

3. Using a pry bar or broom handle on the pump hub, move the power steering pump to-

ward or away from the engine until the proper tension is reached. Do not pry against the reservoir as it is relatively soft and easily deformed.

4. Holding the pump in place, tighten the adjusting arm bolt and then recheck the belt tension. When the belt is properly tensioned tighten the mounting bolts.

V6 and V8 MODELS

1. Position a ruler perpendicular to the drive belt at its longest run. Test the tightness of the belt by pressing it firmly with your thumb. The deflection should be about ¼".

2. To adjust the belt tension, loosen the three bolts in the three elongated adjusting slots at the power steering pump attaching bracket.

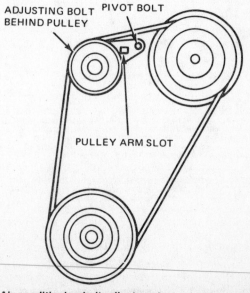

ADJUSTING BOLT BEHIND PULLEY

PIVOT BOLT

PULLEY ARM SLOT

PIVOT BOLT

PULLEYS

ADJUSTING BOLT

DRIVE BELT

Alternator belt adjustment

Air conditioning belt adjustment

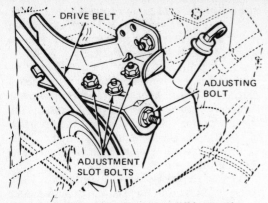

Power steering belt adjustment (slider type)

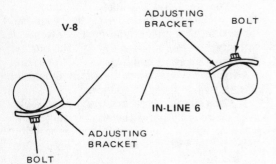

Air pump adjustment points

3. Turn the steering pump drive belt adjusting nut as required until the proper deflection is obtained. Turning the adjusting nut clockwise will increase tension and decrease deflection; counterclockwise will decrease tension and increase deflection.

4. Without disturbing the pump, tighten the three attaching bolts.

Air Conditioning Compressor Drive Belt

1. Position a ruler perpendicular to the drive belt at its longest run. Test the tightness of the belt by pressing it firmly with your thumb. The deflection should not exceed ¼".

2. If the engine is equipped with an idler pulley, loosen the idler pulley adjusting bolt, insert a pry bar between the pulley and the engine (or in the idler pulley adjusting slot), and adjust the tension accordingly. If the engine is not equipped with an idler pulley, the alternator must be moved to accomplish this adjustment, as outlined under Alternator (Fan Drive) Belt.

3. When the proper tension is reached, tighten the idler pulley adjusting bolt (if so equipped) or the alternator adjusting and mounting bolts.

Thermactor Air Pump Drive Belt

1. Position a ruler perpendicular to the drive belt at its longest run. Test the tightness of the belt by pressing it firmly with your thumb. The deflection should be about ¼".

2. To adjust the belt tension, loosen the adjusting arm bolt slightly. If necessary, also loosen the mounting belt slightly.

3. Using a pry bar or broom handle, pry against the pump rear cover to move the pump toward or away from the engine as necessary. CAUTION: *Do not pry against the pump housing itself, as damage to the housing may result.*

4. Holding the pump in place, tighten the adjusting arm bolt and recheck the tension. When the belt is properly tensioned, tighten the mounting bolt.

SERPENTINE (SINGLE) DRIVE BELT MODELS

Most late models (starting in 1979) feature a single, wide, ribbed V-belt that drives the water pump, alternator, and (on some models) the air conditioner compressor. To install a new belt, loosen the bracket lock bolt, retract the belt tensioner with a pry bar and slide the old belt off of the pulleys. Slip on a new belt and release the tensioner and tighten the lock bolt. The spring powered tensioner eliminates the need for periodic adjustments.

WARNING: *Check to make sure that the V-ribbed belt is located properly in all drive pulleys before applying tensioner pressure.*

Hoses

CAUTION: *On models equipped with an electric cooling fan, disconnect the negative battery cable, or fan motor wiring harness connector before replacing any radiator/heater hose. The fan may come on, under certain circumstances, even though the ignition is Off.*

REPLACEMENT

Inspect the condition of the radiator and heater hoses periodically. Early spring and at the beginning of the fall or winter, when you are performing other maintenance, are good times. Make sure the engine and cooling system are cold. Visually inspect for cracking, rotting or collapsed hoses, replace as necessary. Run your hand along the length of the hose. If a weak or swollen spot is noted when squeezing the hose wall, replace the hose.

1. Drain the cooling system into a suitable container (if the coolant is to be reused).

CAUTION: *When draining the coolant, keep in mind that cats and dogs are attracted by*

*the ethylene glycol antifreeze, and are quite
likely to drink any that is left in an uncovered
container or in puddles on the ground. This
will prove fatal in sufficient quantity. Always
drain the coolant into a sealable container.
Coolant should be reused unless it is contaminated or several years old.*

2. Loosen the hose clamps at each end of the
hose that requires replacement.

3. Twist, pull and slide the hose off the radiator, water pump, thermostat or heater
connection.

4. Clean the hose mounting connections. Position the hose clamps on the new hose.

5. Coat the connection surfaces with a water
resistant sealer and slide the hose into position.
Make sure the hose clamps are located beyond
the raised bead of the connector (if equipped)
and centered in the clamping area of the
connection.

6. Tighten the clamps to 20-30 in. lbs. Do not
overtighten.

7. Fill the cooling system.

8. Start the engine and allow it to reach normal operating temperature. Check for leaks.

Air Conditioning
GENERAL SERVICING PROCEDURES

The most important aspect of air conditioning service is the maintenance of pure and adequate charge of refrigerant in the system. A refrigeration system cannot function properly if a
significant percentage of the charge is lost.
Leaks are common because the severe vibration
encountered in an automobile can easily cause a
sufficient cracking or loosening of the air conditioning fittings. As a result, the extreme operating pressures of the system force refrigerant
out.

The problem can be understood by considering what happens to the system as it is operated
with a continuous leak. Because the expansion
valve regulates the flow of refrigerant to the
evaporator, the level of refrigerant there is fairly constant. The receiver-drier stores any excess of refrigerant, and so a loss will first appear
there as a reduction in the level of liquid. As
this level nears the bottom of the vessel, some
refrigerant vapor bubbles will begin to appear
in the stream of liquid supplied to the expansion valve. This vapor decreases the capacity of
the expansion valve very little as the valve
opens to compensate for its presence. As the
quantity of liquid in the condenser decreases,
the operating pressure will drop there and
throughout the high side of the system. As the
R-12 continues to be expelled, the pressure
available to force the liquid through the expan-

sion valve will continue to decrease, and, eventually, the valve's orifice will prove to be too
much of a restriction for adequate flow even
with the needle fully withdrawn.

At this point, low side pressure will start to
drop, and severe reduction in cooling capacity,
marked by freeze-up of the evaporator coil, will
result. Eventually, the operating pressure of
the evaporator will be lower than the pressure
of the atmosphere surrounding it, and air will
be drawn into the system wherever there are
leaks in the low side.

Because all atmospheric air contains at least
some moisture, water will enter the system and
mix with the R-12 and the oil. Trace amounts of
moisture will cause sludging of the oil, and corrosion of the system. Saturation and clogging of
the filter-drier, and freezing of the expansion
valve orifice will eventually result. As air fills
the system to a greater and greater extend, it
will interfere more and more with the normal
flows of refrigerant and heat.

A list of general precautions that should be
observed while doing this follows:

1. Keep all tools as clean and dry as possible.

2. Thoroughly purge the service gauges and
hoses of air and moisture before connecting
them to the system. Keep them capped when
not in use.

3. Thoroughly clean any refrigerant fitting
before disconnecting it, in order to minimize
the entrance of dirt into the system.

4. Plan any operation that requires opening
the system beforehand in order to minimize the
length of time it will be exposed to open air. Cap
or seal the open ends to minimize the entrance
of foreign material.

5. When adding oil, pour it through an extremely clean and dry tube or funnel. Keep the
oil capped whenever possible. Do not use oil
that has not been kept tightly sealed.

6. Use only refrigerant 12. Purchase refrigerant intended for use in only automotive air
conditioning system. Avoid the use of refrigerant 12 that may be packaged for another use,
such as cleaning, or powering a horn, as it is
impure.

7. Completely evacuate any system that has
been opened to replace a component, other than
when isolating the compressor, or that has
leaked sufficiently to draw in moisture and air.
This requires evacuating air and moisture with
a good vacuum pump for at least one hour.

If a system has been open for a considerable
length of time it may be advisable to evacuate
the system for up to 12 hours (overnight).

8. Use a wrench on both halves of a fitting
that is to be disconnected, so as to avoid placing
torque on any of the refrigerant lines.

HOW TO SPOT BAD HOSES

Both the upper and lower radiator hoses are called upon to perform difficult jobs in an inhospitable environment. They are subject to nearly 18 psi at under hood temperatures often over 280°F., and must circulate nearly 7500 gallons of coolant an hour—3 good reasons to have good hoses.

A good test for any hose is to feel it for soft or spongy spots. Frequently these will appear as swollen areas of the hose. The most likely cause is oil soaking. This hose could burst at any time, when hot or under pressure.

Swollen hose

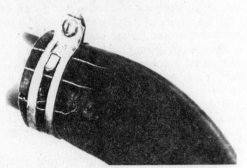

Cracked hoses can usually be seen but feel the hoses to be sure they have not hardened; a prime cause of cracking. This hose has cracked down to the reinforcing cords and could split at any of the cracks.

Cracked hose

Weakened clamps frequently are the cause of hose and cooling system failure. The connection between the pipe and hose has deteriorated enough to allow coolant to escape when the engine is hot.

Frayed hose end (due to weak clamp)

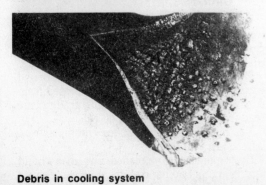

Debris, rust and scale in the cooling system can cause the inside of a hose to weaken. This can usually be felt on the outside of the hose as soft or thinner areas.

Debris in cooling system

ADDITIONAL PREVENTIVE MAINTENANCE CHECKS

Antifreeze

In order to prevent heater core freeze-up during A/C operation, it is necessary to maintain permanent type antifreeze protection of +15°F (–9°C) or lower. A reading of –15°F (–26°C) is ideal since this protection also supplies sufficient corrosion inhibitors for the protection of the engine cooling system.

WARNING: *Do not use antifreeze longer than specified by the manufacturer.*

Radiator Cap

For efficient operation of an air conditioned car's cooling system, the radiator cap should have a holding pressure which meets manufacturer's specifications. A cap which fails to hold these pressure should be replaced.

Condenser

Any obstruction of or damage to the condenser configuration will restrict the air flow which is essential to its efficient operation. It is therefore, a good rule to keep this unit clean and in proper physical shape.

NOTE: *Bug screens are regarded as obstructions.*

Condensation Drain Tube

This single molded drain tube expels the condensation, which accumulates on the bottom of the evaporator housing, into the engine compartment.

If this tube is obstructed, the air conditioning performance can be restricted and condensation buildup can spill over onto the vehicle's floor.

SAFETY PRECAUTIONS

Because of the importance of the necessary safety precautions that must be exercised when working with air conditioning systems and R-12 refrigerant, a recap of the safety precautions are outlined.

1. Avoid contact with a charged refrigeration system, even when working on another part of the air conditioning system or vehicle. If a heavy tool comes into contact with a section of copper tubing or a heat exchanger, it can easily cause the relatively soft material to rupture.

2. When it is necessary to apply force to a fitting which contains refrigerant, as when checking that all system couplings are securely tightened, use a wrench on both parts of the fitting involved, if possible. This will avoid putting torque on the refrigerant tubing. (It is advisable, when possible, to use tube or line wrenches when tightening these flare nut fittings.)

3. Do not attempt to discharge the system by merely loosening a fitting, or removing the service valve caps and cracking these valves. Precise control is possibly only when using the service gauges. Place a rag under the open end of the center charging hose while discharging the system to catch any drops of liquid that might escape. Wear protective gloves when connecting or disconnecting service gauge hoses.

4. Discharge the system only in a well ventilated area, as high concentrations of the gas can exclude oxygen and act as an anesthetic. When leak testing or soldering this is particularly important, as toxic gas is formed when R-12 contacts any flame.

5. Never start a system without first verifying that both service valves are backseated, if equipped, and that all fittings are throughout the system are snugly connected.

6. Avoid applying heat to any refrigerant line or storage vessel. Charging may be aided by using water heated to less than 125°F (52°C) to warm the refrigerant container. Never allow a refrigerant storage container to sit out in the sun, or near any other source of heat, such as a radiator.

7. Always wear goggles when working on a system to protect the eyes. If refrigerant contacts the eye, it is advisable in all cases to see a physician as soon as possible.

8. Frostbite from liquid refrigerant should be treated by first gradually warming the area with cool water, and then gently applying petroleum jelly. A physician should be consulted.

9. Always keep refrigerant can fittings capped when not in use. Avoid sudden shock to the can which might occur from dropping it, or from banging a heavy tool against it. Never carry a refrigerant can in the passenger compartment of a car.

10. Always completely discharge the system before painting the vehicle (if the paint is to be baked on), or before welding anywhere near the refrigerant lines.

TEST GAUGES

Most of the service work performed in air conditioning requires the use of a set of two gauges, one for the high (head) pressure side of the system, the other for the low (suction) side.

The low side gauge records both pressure and vacuum. Vacuum readings are calibrated from 0 to 30 inches Hg and the pressure graduations read from 0 to no less than 60 psi.

The high side gauge measures pressure from 0 to at last 600 psi.

Both gauges are threaded into a manifold that contains two hand shut-off valves. Proper manipulation of these valves and the use of the

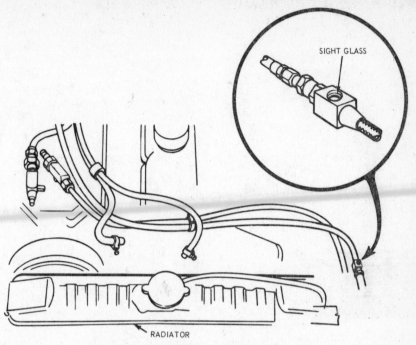

SIGHT GLASS

RADIATOR

Typical air conditioning sight glass location

attached test hoses allow the user to perform the following services:

1. Test high and low side pressures.
2. Remove air, moisture, and contaminated refrigerant.
3. Purge the system (of refrigerant).
4. Charge the system (with refrigerant).

The manifold valves are designed so that they have no direct effect on gauge readings, but serve only to provide for, or cut off, flow of refrigerant through the manifold. During all testing and hook-up operations, the valves are kept in a close position to avoid disturbing the refrigeration system. The valves are opened only to purge the system or refrigerant or to charge it.

INSPECTION

CAUTION: *The compressed refrigerant used in the air conditioning system expands into the atmosphere at a temperature of –21.7°F (–30°C) or lower. This will freeze any surface, including your eyes, that it contacts. In addition, the refrigerant decomposes into a poisonous gas in the presence of a flame. Do not open or disconnect any part of the air conditioning system.*

Sight Glass Check

You can safely make a few simple checks to determine if your air conditioning system needs service. The tests work best if the temperature is warm (about 70°F [21.1°C]).

NOTE: *If your vehicle is equipped with an*

aftermarket air conditioner, the following system check may not apply. You should contact the manufacturer of the unit for instructions on systems checks.

1. Place the automatic transmission in Park or the manual transmission in Neutral. Set the parking brake.
2. Run the engine at a fast idle (about 1,500 rpm) either with the help of a friend or by temporarily readjusting the idle speed screw.
3. Set the controls for maximum cold with the blower on High.
4. Locate the sight glass in one of the system lines. Usually it is on the left alongside the top of the radiator.
5. If you see bubbles, the system must be recharged. Very likely there is a leak at some point.
6. If there are no bubbles, there is either no refrigerant at all or the system is fully charged. Feel the two hoses going to the belt-driven compressor. If they are both at the same temperature, the system is empty and must be recharged.
7. If one hose (high pressure) is warm and the other (low pressure) is cold, the system may be all right. However, you are probably making these tests because you think there is something wrong, so proceed to the next step.
8. Have an assistant in the car turn the fan control on and off to operate the compressor clutch. Watch the sight glass.
9. If bubbles appear when the clutch is disen-

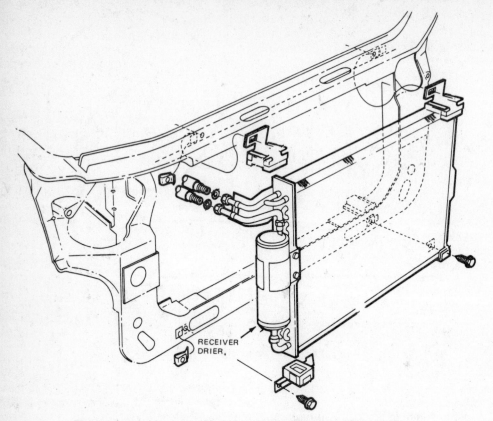

RECEIVER
DRIER.

The receiver—drier assembly is mounted to the side of the condenser

gaged and disappear when it is engaged, the system is properly charged.

10. If the refrigerant takes more than 45 seconds to bubble when the clutch is disengaged, the system is overcharged. This usually causes poor cooling at low speeds.

CAUTION: *If it is determined that the system has a leak, it should be corrected as soon as possible. Leaks may allow moisture to enter and cause a very expensive rust problem.*
NOTE: *Exercise the air conditioner for a few minutes, every two weeks or so, during the cold months. This avoids the possibility of the compressor seals drying out from lack of lubrication.*

TESTING THE SYSTEM

1. Connect a gauge set.
2. Close (clockwise) both gauge set valves.
4. Park the car in the shade, at least 5 feet from any walls. Start the engine, set the parking brake, place the transmission in NEUTRAL and establish an idle of 1,100-1,300 rpm.
5. Run the air conditioning system for full cooling, in the MAX or COLD mode.
6. The low pressure gauge should read 5-20 psi; the high pressure gauge should indicate 120-180 psi.

WARNING: *These pressures are the norm for an ambient temperature of 70-80°F (21-27°F). Higher air temperatures along with high humidity will cause higher syustem pressures. At idle speed and an ambient temperature of 110°F (43°F), the high pressure reading can exceed 300 psi.*

Under these extreme conditions, you can keep the pressures down by directing a large electric floor fan through the condenser.

DISCHARGING THE SYSTEM

1. Remove the caps from the high and low pressure charging valves in the high and low pressure lines.
2. Turn both manifold gauge set hand valves to the fully closed (clockwise) position.
3. Connect the manifold gauge set.
4. If the gauge set hoses do not have the gauge port actuating pins, install fitting adapters T71P-19703-S and R on the manifold gauge set hoses. If the car does not have a service access gauge port valve, connect the gauge set low pressure hose to the evaporator service access gauge port valve. A special adapter, T77L-19703-A, is required to attach the manifold gauge set to the high pressure service access gauge port valve.

5. Place the end of the center hose away from you and the car.

6. Open the low pressure gauge valve slightly and allow the system pressure to bleed off.

7. Whe the system is just about empty, open the high pressure valve very slowly to avoid losing an excessive amount of refrigerant oil. Allow any remaining refrigerant to escape.

EVACUATING THE SYSTEM

NOTE: *This procedure requires the use of a vacuum pump.*

1. Connect the manifold gauge set.

2. Discharge the system.

3. On 1983 and later models, make sure that the low pressure gauge set hose is connected to the low pressure service gauge port on the top center of the accumulator/drier assembly and the high pressure hose connected to the high pressure service gauge port on the compressor discharge line.

4. Connect the center service hose to the inlet fitting of the vacuum pump.

5. Turn both gauge set valves to the wide open position.

6. Start the pump and note the low side gauge reading.

7. Operate the pump until the low pressure gauge reads 25-30 in.Hg. Continue running the vacuum pump for 10 minutes more. If you've replaced some component in the system, run the pump for an additional 20-30 minutes.

8. Leak test the system. Close both gauge set valves. Turn off the pump. The needle should remain stationary at the point at which the pump was turned off. If the needle drops to zero rapidly, there is a leak in the system which must be repaired.

LEAK TESTING

Some leak tests can be performed with a soapy water solution. There must be at least a ½ lb. charge in the system for a leak to be detected. The most extensive leak tests are performed with either a Halide flame type leak tester or the more preferable electronic leak tester.

In either case, the equipment is expensive, and, the use of a Halide detector can be **extremely** hazardous!

CHARGING THE SYSTEM

CAUTION: *NEVER OPEN THE HIGH PRESSURE SIDE WITH A CAN OF REFRIGERANT CONNECTED TO THE SYSTEM! OPENING THE HIGH PRESSURE SIDE WILL OVERPRESSURIZE THE CAN, CAUSING IT TO EXPLODE!*

1979-82

1. Connect the gauge set.

2. Close (clockwise) both gauge set valves.

3. Connect the center hose to the refrigerant can opener valve.

CAUTION: *KEEP THE CAN IN AN UPRIGHT POSITION!*

4. Make sure the can opener valve is closed, that is, the needle is raised, and connect the valve to the can. Open the valve, puncturing the can with the needle.

5. Loosen the center hose fitting at the pressure gauge, allowing refrigerant to purge the hose of air.

6. Open the low side gauge set valve and the can valve.

7. Start the engine and turn the air conditioner to the maximum cooling mode. Run the engine at about 1,500 rpm. The compressor will operate and pull refrigerant gas into the system.

NOTE: *To help speed the process, the can may be placed, upright, in a pan of warm water, not exceeding 125°F (52°C).*

8. If more than one can of refrigerant is needed, close the can valve and gauge set low side valve when the can is empty and connect a new can to the opener. Repeat the charging process until the sight glass indicates a full charge. The frost line on the outside of the can will indicate what portion of the can has been used.

CAUTION: *NEVER ALLOW THE HIGH PRESSURE SIDE READING TO EXCEED 240 psi.*

9. When the charging process has been completed, close the gauge set valve and can valve. Run the system for at least five minutes to allow it to normalize. Low pressure side reading should be 4-25 psi; high pressure reading should be 120-210 psi at an ambient temperature of 70-90°F (21-32°C).

10. Loosen both service hoses at the gauges to allow any refrigerant to escape. Remove the gauge set and install the dust caps on the service valves.

NOTE: *Multi-can dispensers are available which allow a simultaneous hook-up of up to four 1 lb. cans of R-12.*

CAUTION: *Never exceed the recommended maximum charge for the system.*

The maximum charge for systems is:

1979: 4¼ lbs.

1980-81: 3½ lbs.

1982: 2½ lbs.

1983-88

1. Connect the gauge set.

2. Close (clockwise) both gauge set valves.

3. Connect the center hose to the refrigerant can opener valve.

4. Make sure the can opener valve is closed, that is, the needle is raised, and connect the valve to the can. Open the valve, puncturing the can with the needle.

5. Loosen the center hose fitting at the pressure gauge, allowing refrigerant to purge the hose of air. When the air is bled, tighten the fitting.

CAUTION: *IF THE LOW PRESSURE GAUGE SET HOSE IS NOT CONNECTED TO THE ACCUMULATOR/DRIER, KEEP THE CAN IN AN UPRIGHT POSITION!*

6. Disconnect the wire harness snap-lock connector from the clutch cycling pressure switch and install a jumper wire across the two terminals of the connector.

7. Open the low side gauge set valve and the can valve.

8. Allow refrigerant to be drawn into the system.

9. When no more refrigerant is drawn into the system, start the engine and run it at about 1,500 rpm. Turn on the system and operate it at the full high position. The compressor will operate and pull refrigerant gas into the system.

NOTE: *To help speed the process, the can may be placed, upright, in a pan of warm water, not exceeding 125°F (52°C).*

10. If more than one can of refrigerant is needed, close the can valve and gauge set low side valve when the can is empty and connect a new can to the opener. Repeat the charging process until the sight glass indicates a full charge. The frost line on the outside of the can will indicate what portion of the can has been used.

CAUTION: *NEVER ALLOW THE HIGH PRESSURE SIDE READING TO EXCEED 240 psi.*

11. When the charging process has been completed, close the gauge set valve and can valve. Remove the jumper wire and reconnect the cycling clutch wire. Run the system for at least five minutes to allow it to normalize. Low pressure side reading should be 4-25 psi; high pressure reading should be 120-210 psi at an ambient temperature of 70-90°F (21-32°C).

12. Loosen both service hoses at the gauges to allow any refrigerant to escape. Remove the gauge set and install the dust caps on the service valves.

NOTE: *Multi-can dispensers are available which allow a simultaneous hook-up of up to four 1 lb. cans of R-12.*

CAUTION: *Never exceed the recommended maximum charge for the system.*

The maximum charge for systems is 2½ lb.

Front Wheel Bearings

ADJUSTMENT

The front wheels each rotate on a set of opposed, tapered roller bearings as shown in the accompanying illustration. The grease retainer at the inside of the hub prevents lubricant from leaking into the brake drum.

1. Raise and support the front end on jackstands.

2. Remove the grease cap and remove excess grease from the end of the spindle.

3. Remove the cotter pin and nut lock shown in the illustration.

4. Rotate the wheel, hub and drum assembly while tightening the adjusting nut to 17-25 ft. lbs. in order to seat the bearings.

5. Back off the adjusting nut ½, then retighten the adjusting nut to 10-15 in. lbs.

6. Locate the nut lock on the adjusting nut so that the castellations on the lock are lined up with the cotter pin hole in the spindle.

7. Install the new cotter pin, bending the ends of the cotter pin around the castellated flange of the nut lock.

8. Check the wheel for proper rotation, then install the grease cap. If the wheel still does not rotate properly, inspect and clean or replace the wheel bearings and cups.

REMOVAL, REPACKING, AND INSTALLATION

Before handling the bearings, there are a few things that you should remember to do and not to do.

Remember to DO the following:

• Remove all outside dirt from the housing before exposing the bearing.

• Treat a used bearing as gently as you would a new one.

• Work with clean tools in clean surroundings.

• Use clean, dry canvas gloves, or at least clean, dry hands.

• Clean solvents and flushing fluids are a must.

• Use clean paper when laying out the bearings to dry.

• Protect disassembled bearings from rust and dirt. Cover them up.

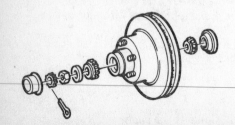

Front wheel bearings

WITH WHEEL ROTATING,
TORQUE ADJUSTING NUT,
TO 17-25 FT. LBS.

BACK ADJUSTING
NUT OFF 1/2 TURN

TIGHTEN ADJUSTING
NUT TO 10-15 IN.-LBS.

INSTALL THE LOCK
AND A NEW COTTER PIN

Front wheel bearing adjusting sequence

- Use clean rags to wipe bearings.
- Keep the bearings in oil-proof paper when they are to be stored or are not in use.
- Clean the inside of the housing before replacing the bearing.

Do NOT do the following:
- Don't work in dirty surroundings.
- Don't use dirty, chipped or damaged tools.
- Try not to work on wooden work benches or use wooden mallets.
- Don't handle bearings with dirty or moist hands.
- Do not use gasoline for cleaning; use a safe solvent.
- Do not spin-dry bearings with compressed air. They will be damaged.

- Do not spin dirty bearings.
- Avoid using cotton waste or dirty cloths to wipe bearings.
- Try not to scratch or nick bearing surfaces.
- Do not allow the bearing to come in contact with dirt or rust at any time.

1. Raise and support the front end on jackstands.

2. Remove the wheel cover. Remove the wheel.

3. Remove the caliper from the disc and wire it to the underbody to prevent damage to the brake hose. For floating caliper brakes, follow Steps 3, 4, 5, and 6 under Caliper Assembly Service.

4. Remove the grease cap from the hub.

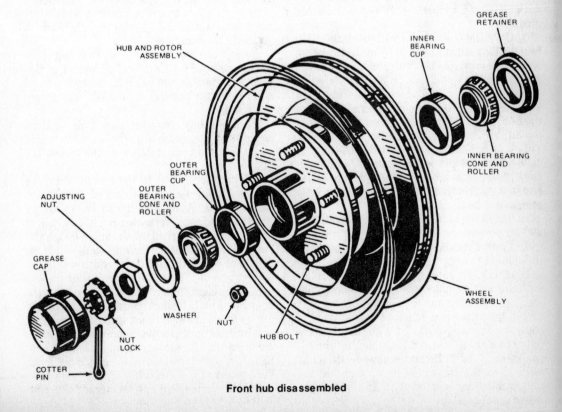

Front hub disassembled

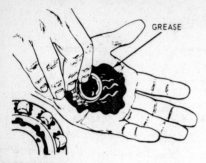

GREASE

Packing bearings

Then, remove the cotter pin, nut lock, adjusting nut and flat washer from the spindle. Remove the outer bearing assembly from the hub.

5. Pull the hub and disc assembly off the wheel spindle.

6. Remove and discard the old grease retainer. Remove the inner bearing cone and roller assembly from the hub.

7. Clean all grease from the inner and outer bearing cups with solvent. Inspect the cups for pits, scratches, or excessive wear. If the cups are damaged, remove them with a drift.

8. Clean the inner and outer cone and roller assemblies with solvent and shake them dry. If the cone and roller assemblies show excessive wear or damage, replace them with the bearing cups as a unit.

9. Clean the spindle and the inside of the hub with solvent to thoroughly remove all old grease.

10. Covering the spindle with a clean cloth, brush all loose dirt and dust from the brake assembly. Remove the cloth carefully so as to not get dirt on the spindle.

11. If the inner and/or outer bearing cups were removed, install the replacement cups on the hub. Be sure that the cups seat properly in the hub.

12. It is imperative that all old grease be removed from the bearings and surrounding surfaces before repacking. The new lithium-based grease is not compatible with the sodium base grease used in the past.

13. Install the hub and disc on the wheel spindle. To prevent damage to the grease retainer and spindle threads, keep the hub centered on the spindle.

14. Install the outer bearing cone and roller assembly and the flat washer on the spindle. Install the adjusting nut.

15. Adjust the wheel bearings by torquing the adjusting nut to 17-25 ft. lbs. with the wheel rotating to seat the bearing. Then back off the adjusting nut ½ turn. Retighten the adjusting nut to 10-15 in. lbs. Install the locknut so that the castellations are aligned with the cotter pin

hole. Install the cotter pin. Bend the ends of the cotter pin around the castellations of the locknut to prevent interference with the radio static collector in the grease cap. Install the grease cap.

WARNING: *New bolts must be used when servicing floating caliper units. The upper bolt must be tightened first. For floating caliper units, follow Steps 19, 20, and 21 under Caliper Assembly Service in Chapter 8. For sliding caliper units, follow Steps 12-19 under Shoe and Lining Replacement in Chapter 8.*

16. Install the wheels.

17. Install the wheel cover.

Tires and Wheels

Inspect the tires regularly for wear and damage. Remove stones or other foreign particles which may be lodged in the tread. If tread wear is excessive or irregular it could be a sign of front end problems, or simply improper inflation.

The inflation should be checked at least once per month and adjusted if necessary. The tires must be cold (driven less than one mile) or an inaccurate reading will result. Do not forget to check the spare.

The correct inflation pressure for your vehicle can be found on a decal mounted to the car. Depending upon model and year, the decal can be located at the driver's door, the passenger's door or the glove box. If you cannot find the decal a local automobile tire dealer can furnish you with information.

Inspect tires for uneven wear that might indicate the need for front end alignment or tire rotation. Tires should be replaced when a tread wear indicator appears as a solid band across the tread.

When you buy new tires, give some thought to these points, especially if you are switching to larger tires or to another profile series (50, 60, 70, 78):

1. The wheels must be the correct width for the tire. Tire dealers have charts of tire and rim compatibility. A mismatch can cause sloppy handling and rapid tread wear. The old rule of thumb is that the tread width should match the rim width (inside bead to inside bead) within an inch. For radial tires, the rim width should be 80% or less of the tire (not tread) width.

2. The height (mounted diameter) of the new tires can greatly change speedometer accuracy, engine speed at a given road speed, fuel mileage, acceleration, and ground clearance. Tire makers furnish full measurement specifications. Speedometer drive gears are available from Ford dealers for correction.

NOTE: *Dimensions of tires marked the same*

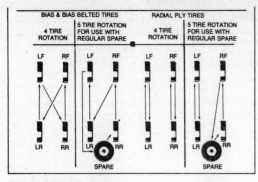

Tire rotation diagram

size may vary significantly, even among tires from the same maker.

3. The spare tire should be usable, at least for low speed operation, with the new tires.

4. There shouldn't be any body interference when loaded, on bumps, or in turning.

The only sure way to avoid problems with these points is to stick to tire and wheel sizes available as factory options.

TIRE ROTATION

Tires should be rotated periodically to get the maximum tread lift available. A good time to do this is when changing over from regular tires to snow tires, or about once per year. If front end problems are suspected have them corrected before rotating the tires. Torque the lug nuts to 70-115 ft. lbs.

NOTE: *Mark the wheel position or direction of rotation on radial, or studded snow tires before removing them.*

CAUTION: *Avoid overtightening the lug nuts to prevent damage to the brake disc or drum. Alloy wheels can also be cracked by overtightening. Use of a torque wrench is highly recommended. Tighten the lug nuts in a criss-cross sequence shown to 85 ft. lbs.*

FLUIDS AND LUBRICANTS

Fuel Recommendations
GASOLINE ENGINES

It is important to use fuel of the proper octane rating in your car. Octane rating is based on the quantity of anti-knock compounds added to the fuel and it determines the speed at which the gas will burn. The lower the octane rating, the faster it burns. The higher the octane, the slower the fuel will burn and a greater percentage of compounds in the fuel prevent spark ping (knock), detonation and preignition (dieseling).

As the temperature of the engine increases, the air/fuel mixture exhibits a tendency to ig-

nite before the spark plug is fired. If fuel of an octane rating too low for the engine is used, this will allow combustion to occur before the piston has completed its compression stroke, thereby creating a very high pressure very rapidly.

Fuel of the proper octane rating, for the compression ratio and ignition timing of your car, will slow the combustion process sufficiently to allow the spark plug enough time to ignite the mixture completely and smoothly. Many non-catalyst models are designed to run on regular fuel. The use of some super-premium fuel is no substitution for a properly tuned and maintained engine. Chances are that if your engine exhibits any signs of spark ping, detonation or pre-ignition when using regular fuel, the ignition timing should be checked against specifications or the cylinder head should be removed for decarbonizing.

Vehicles equipped with catalytic converters must use UNLEADED GASOLINE ONLY. Use of unleaded fuel shortened the life of spark plugs, exhaust systems and EGR valves and can damage the catalytic converter. Most converter equipped models are designed to operate using unleaded gasoline with a minimum rating of 87 octane. Use of unleaded gas with octane ratings lower than 87 can cause persistent spark knock which could lead to engine damage.

Light spark knock may be noticed when accelerating or driving up hills. The slight knocking may be considered normal (with 87 octane) because the maximum fuel economy is obtained under condition of occasional light spark knock. Gasoline with an octane rating higher than 87 may be used, but it is not necessary (in most cases) for proper operation.

If spark knock is constant, when using 87 octane, at cruising speeds on level ground, ignition timing adjustment may be required.

Engine
OIL RECOMMENDATION

When adding the oil to the crankcase or changing the oil or filter, it is important that oil of an equal quality to original be used in your car. The use of inferior oils may void your warranty. Generally speaking, oil that has been rated **SF** by the American Petroleum Institute will prove satisfactory.

Oil of the SF variety performs a multitude of functions in addition to its basic job of reducing friction of the engine's moving parts. Through a balanced formula of polymeric dispersants and metallic detergents, the oil prevents high temperature and low temperature deposits and also keeps sludge and dirt particles in suspension. Acids, particularly sulphuric acid, as well

Capacities

Year	Engine No. Cyl. Displacement (Cu. In.)	Engine Crankcase Add 1 Qt For New Filter	Transmission Pts to Refill After Draining			Drive Axle (pts)	Gasoline Tank (gals)	Cooling System (qts)	
			Manual		Automatic (Total Capacity) ⑮			With Heater	With A/C
			3-Speed	⅘-Speed					
'79–'82 Mustang, Capri	4-140	4	—	2.8	②③	①	11.5⑤	8.6⑦	10⑨
	4-140T	4.5	—	3.5	②③	①	11.5⑤	8.6⑧	10.2⑧
	6-170	4.5	—	4.5	②③	①	12.5	9.2	9.2
	6-200	4	—	4.5	12②④	①	16⑤⑥	9⑩	9⑩
	8-255	4	—	4.5	19④	①	12.5⑥	13.4⑪	13.7⑫
	8-302	4	—	4.5	19	①	12.5⑥	13.9	14.2
'83–'88 Mustant/Capri	4-140	4⑬	—	2.8⑭	16	①	15.4	8.6	9.4
	6-232	4	—	—	22	①	15.4	8.4	8.4
	8-302	4	—	4.5	—	①	15.4	13.1	13.4
'85–'88 Merkur	4-140T	4	—	2.64	16	3.2	15	10.5	10.5

① 6.75 in.—2.5 pts
　7.50 in.—3.5 pts
　Traction-Lok—3.55 pts
② C3—16 pts; C4—14 pts
③ '81—C4—13.25 pts; 19 pts w/V8
④ '82—C5—22 pts
⑤ '82—15.4 gal
⑥ '80–'81—12.5 gal
⑦ '82—10.2 qts
⑧ '80–'81—9.2 qts
⑨ '80–'81—9.0 qts; '82—10.2 qts
⑩ '80–'82—8.1 qts
⑪ '82—14.7 qts
⑫ '82—15 qts
⑬ 4.5 Turbo/add .5 w/filter
⑭ 5 speed—4.75 pts
⑮ Capacity when totally dry. When changing pan contents, add 2 qts, run engine and check with dipstick. Add fluid as necessary to correct level.

as other products of combustion of sulphur fuels, are neutralized by the oil. These acids, if permitted to concentrate, may cause corrosion and rapid wear of the internal parts of the engine.

It is important to choose an oil of the proper viscosity for climatic and operational conditions. Viscosity in an index of the oil's thickness at different temperatures. A thicker oil (higher numerical rating) is needed for high tempera-

Oil Viscosity—Temperature Chart

When Outside Temperature is Consistently	Use SAE Viscosity Number
SINGLE GRADE OILS	
− 10°F to 32°F	10W
10°F to 60°F	20W-20
32°F to 90°F	30
Above 60°F	40
MULTIGRADE OILS	
Below 32°F	5W-30*
− 10°F to 90°F	10W-30
Above—10°F	10W-40
Above 10°F	20W-40
Above 20°F	20W-50

*When sustained high-speed operation is anticipated, use the next higher grade.

ture operation, whereas thinner oil (lower numerical rating) is required for cold weather operation. Due to the need for an oil that embodies both these characteristics in parts of the country where there is wide temperature variation within a small period of time, multigrade oils have been developed. Basically a multigrade oil is thinner at low temperatures and thicker at high temperatures. For example, a 10W-40 oil exhibits the characteristics of a 10 weight oil when the car is first started and the oil is cold. Its lighter weight allows it to travel to the lubricating surfaces quicker and offer less resistance to starter motor cranking then, let's say, a straight 30 weight oil. But after the engine reaches operating temperature, the 10W-40 oil begins acting like a straight 40 weight oil, its heavier weight providing greater lubricating protection and less susceptibility to foaming than a straight 30 weight oil. Whatever your driving needs, the oil viscosity/temperature chart should prove useful in selecting the proper grade. The SAE viscosity rating is printed or stamped on the top of every oil container.

OIL LEVEL CHECK

The engine oil level should be checked frequently. For instance, at each refueling stop. Be

ADD 2 I ADD → SAFE ←   WARRANTY

ADD →SAFE ←   WARRANTY

ADD ← SAFE→ ←MAX. OVERFILL

(Note lubricant level should be within the safe range) typical engine oil dipstick

sure that the vehicle is parked on a level surface with the engine off. Also, allow a few minutes after turning off the engine for the oil to drain into the pan or an inaccurate reading will result.

1. Open the hood and remove the engine oil dipstick.

2. Wipe the dipstick with a clean, lint-free rag and reinsert it. Be sure to insert it all the way.

3. Pull out the dipstick and note the oil level. It should be between the SAFE (MAX) mark and the ADD (MIN) mark.

4. If the level is below the lower mark, replace the dipstick and add fresh oil to bring the level within the proper range. Do not overfill.

5. Recheck the oil level and close the hood.

NOTE: *Use a multi-grade oil with API classification SF.*

OIL CHANGE

NOTE: *The engine oil and oil filter should be changed at the same time, at the recommended intervals on the maintenance schedule chart.*

1. Run the engine to normal operating temperature.

2. After the engine has reached operating temperature, shut it off, firmly apply the parking brake, and block the wheels.

3. Raise and support the front end on jackstands.

4. Place a drip pan beneath the oil pan and remove the drain plug.

CAUTION: *The oil could be very hot! Protect yourself by using rubber gloves if necessary.*

5. Allow the engine to drain thoroughly.

WARNING: *On some V8 engines a dual sump oil pan was used. When changing the oil, both drain plugs (front and side) must be removed. Failure to remove both plugs can lead to an incorrect oil level reading.*

6. While the oil is draining, replace the filter as described below.

7. When the oil has completely drained, clean the threads of the plug and coat them with non-

hardening sealer or Teflon® tape and install the plug. Tighten it snugly.

WARNING: *The threads in the oil pan are easily stripped! Don not overtighten the plug!*

8. Fill the crankcase with the proper amount of oil shown in the Capacities Chart in this chapter.

9. Start the engine and check for leaks.

REPLACING THE OIL FILTER

1. Place the drip pan beneath the oil filter.

2. Using an oil filter wrench, turn the filter counterclockwise to remove it.

CAUTION: *The oil could be very hot! Protect yourself by using rubber gloves if necessary.*

3. Wipe the contact surface of the new filter clean and coat the rubber gasket with clean engine oil.

4. Clean the mating surface of the adapter on the block.

5. Screw the new filter into position on the block using hand pressure only. Do not use a strap wrench to install the filter! Then hand-turn the filter ½-¾ additional turn.

NOTE: *Certain operating conditions may warrant more frequent oil changes. If the vehicle is used for short trips, where the engine does not have a chance to fully warm up before it is shut off, water condensation and low temperature deposits may make it necessary to change to oil sooner. If the vehicle is used mostly in stop-and-go traffic, corrosive acids and high temperature deposits may necessitate shorter oil changing intervals. The shorter intervals also apply to industrial or rural areas where high concentrations of dust and other airborne particulate matter contaminate the oil. Finally, if the car is used for towing trailers, a severe load is placed on the engine causing the oil to thin out sooner, making necessary the shorter oil changing intervals.*

Transmission

FLUID RECOMMENDATIONS

Manual Transmissions:
- ET 4-sp – SAE 85W/90
- RAD 4-sp – SAE 85W/90
- T5 OD 5-sp – Dexron®II ATF
- Merkur 5-sp – Dexron®II ATF

85W/90 gear oil may be used in the T5 OD transmission in very warm climates or if gear/bearing noise is excessive. Conversely, Dexron®II may be used in the ET 4-sp in very cold climates, or if hard shifting is a continuing problem.

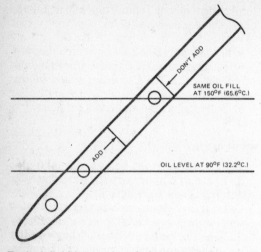

Typical fluid expansion during automatic transmission warm-up

Automatic Transmissions:
- 1979-80 C3 — Type F
- 1981-86 C3 — Dexron®II
- 1979 C4 — Type F
- 1980-81 C4 — Dexron®II
- 1982-88 C5 — Type H
- 1980-88 AOD — Dexron®II

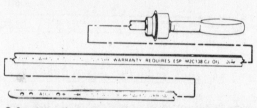

Typical automatic transmission dipstick

C-6 automatic transmission dipstick (note the special fluid designation)

LEVEL CHECK

Automatic Transmissions

It is very important to maintain the proper fluid level in an automatic transmission. If the level is either too high or too low, poor shifting operation and internal damage are likely to occur. For this reason a regular check of the fluid level is essential.

1. Drive the vehicle for 15-20 minutes to allow the transmission to reach operating temperature.

2. Park the car on a level surface, apply the parking brake and leave the engine idling. Shift

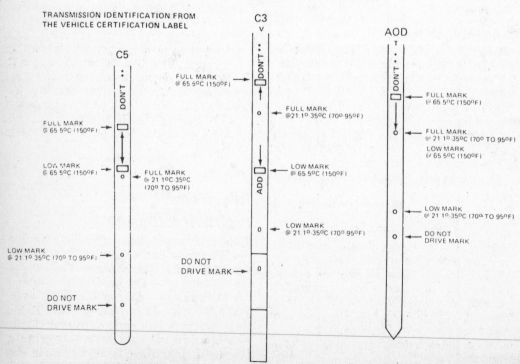

Automatic transmission dipstick markings for late models

the transmission and engage each gear, then place the gear selector in P (PARK).

3. Wipe away any dirt in the areas of the transmission dipstick to prevent it from falling into the filler tube. Withdraw the dipstick, wipe it with a clean, lint-free rag and reinsert it until it seats.

4. Withdraw the dipstick and note the fluid level. It should be between the upper (FULL) mark and the lower (ADD) mark.

5. If the level is below the lower mark, use a funnel and add fluid in small quantities through the dipstick filler neck. Keep the engine running while adding fluid and check the level after each small amount. Do not overfill.

Mustang and Capri Manual Transmission

The fluid level should be checked every 6 months/6,000 miles, whichever comes first.

1. Park the car on a level surface, turn off the engine, apply the parking brake and block the wheels.

2. Remove the filler plug from the side of the transmission case with a proper size wrench. The fluid level should be even with the bottom of the filler hole.

3. If additional fluid is necessary, add it through the filler hole using a siphon pump or squeeze bottle.

4. Replace the filler plug; do not overtighten.

Merkur Manual Transmission

Check the oil level on early production models with the aid of a fabricated dipstick. The oil level will not be in line with the oil filler hole. The oil level will be approximately 1 in. (24mm) below the filler hole. These transmissions can be identified by a yellow paint square on the side of the extension housing. The fill plug location on later production models are lowered to make the bottom of the fill hole even with the lubrication level.

DRAIN AND REFILL

Automatic Transmission

C3, C4, C5

1. Raise the vehicle, so that the transmission oil pan is readily accessible. Safely support on jackstands.

2. Disconnect the fluid filler tube from the pan and allow the fluid to drain into an appropriate container.

3. Remove the transmission oil pan attaching bolts, pan and gasket.

To install the transmission oil pan:

4. Clean the transmission oil pan and transmission mating surfaces.

5. Install the transmission oil pan in the reverse order of removal, torquing the attaching bolts to 10-16 ft. lbs. and using a new gasket. Fill the transmission with 3 qts. of the correct type fluid.

6. Lower the vehicle. Start the engine and move the gear selector through shift pattern. Allow the engine to reach normal operating temperature.

7. Check the transmission fluid. Add fluid, if necessary, to maintain correct level.

AOD

1. Raise the car and support on jackstands.

2. Place a drain pan under the transmission.

3. Loosen the pan attaching bolts and drain the fluid from the transmission.

4. When the fluid has drained to the level of the pan flange, remove the remaining pan bolts working from the rear and both sides of the pan to allow it to drop and drain slowly.

5. When all of the fluid has drained, remove the pan and clean it thoroughly. Discard the pan gasket.

6. Place a new gasket on the pan, and install the pan on the transmission. Tighten the attaching bolts to 12-16 ft. lbs.

7. Add three 3 quarts of fluid to the transmission through the filler tube.

8. Lower the vehicle. Start the engine and move the gear selector through shift pattern. Allow the engine to reach normal operating temperature.

9. Check the transmission fluid. Add fluid, if necessary, to maintain correct level.

Manual Transmission

1. Place a suitable drain pan under the transmission.

2. Remove the drain plug and allow the gear lube to drain out.

3. Replace the drain plug, remove the filler plug and fill the transmission to the proper level with the required fluid.

4. Reinstall the filler plug.

Rear Axle (Differential)

FLUID LEVEL CHECK

Like the manual transmission, the rear axle fluid should be checked every six months/6,000 miles. A filler plug is provided near the center of the rear cover or on the upper (driveshaft) side of the gear case. Remove the plug and check to ensure that the fluid level is even with the bottom of the filler hole. Add SAE 85W/90/95 gear lube as required. If the vehicle is equipped with a limited slip rear axle, add the required special fluid. Install the filler plug but do not overtighten.

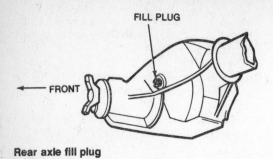

Rear axle fill plug

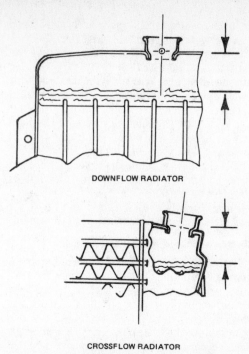

DOWNFLOW RADIATOR

CROSSFLOW RADIATOR

Fill level—crossflow and downflow radiator

DRAIN AND REFILL

Normal maintenance does not require changing the rear axle fluid. However, to do so, remove the rear drain plug (models equipped), the lower two cover bolts, or the cover. Catch the drained fluid in a suitable container. If the rear cover was removed, clean the mounting surfaces of the cover and rear housing. Install a new gasket (early models) or (on late models) apply a continuous bead of Silicone Rubber Sealant (D6AZ-19562-A/B or the equivalent) around the rear housing face inside the circle of bolt holes. Install the cover and tighten the bolts. Parts must be assembled within a half hour after the sealant is applied. If the fluid was drained by removing the two lower cover bolts, apply sealant to the bolts before reinstallation. Fill the rear axle through the filler hole with the proper lube. Add friction modifier to limited slip models if required.

Coolant

FLUID RECOMMENDATIONS

When additional coolant is required to maintain the proper level, always add a 50/50 mixture of antifreeze/coolant and water.

LEVEL CHECK

CAUTION: *Exercise extreme care when removing the cap from a hot radiator. Wait a few minutes until the engine has time to cool somewhat, then wrap a thick towel around the radiator cap and slowly turn it counterclockwise to the first stop. Step back and allow the pressure to release from the cooling system. Then, when the steam has stopped venting, press down on the cap, turn it one more stop counterclockwise and remove the cap.*

The coolant level in the radiator should be checked on a monthly basis, preferably when the engine is cold. On a cold engine, the coolant level should be maintained at one inch below the filler neck on vertical flow radiators, and 2½" below the filler neck at the **COLD FILL** mark on crossflow radiators. On cars equipped

with the Coolant Recovery System, the level is maintained at the **COLD LEVEL** mark in the translucent plastic expansion bottle. Top up as necessary with a mixture of 50% water and 50% ethylene glycol antifreeze, to ensure proper rust, freezing and boiling protection. If you have to add coolant more often than once a month or if you have to add more than one quart at a time, check the cooling system for leaks. Also check for water in the crankcase oil, indicating a blown cylinder head gasket.

DRAIN AND REFILL

CAUTION: *When draining the coolant, keep in mind that cats and dogs are attracted by the ethylene glycol antifreeze, and are quite likely to drink any that is left in an uncovered container or in puddles on the ground. This will prove fatal in sufficient quantity. Always drain the coolant into a sealable container. Coolant should be reused unless it is contaminated or several years old.*

Completely draining and refilling the cooling system every two years at least will remove accumulated rust, scale and other deposits.

NOTE: *Use a good quality antifreeze with water pump lubricants, rust inhibitors and other corrosion inhibitors along with acid neutralizers. Use a permanent type coolant that meets specification ESE-M97B44A or the equivalent.*

1. Drain the existing antifreeze and coolant.

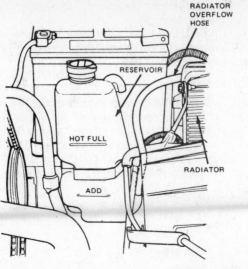

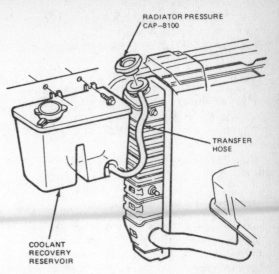

Coolant recovery system variations

Open the radiator and engine drain petcocks (models equipped), or disconnect the bottom radiator hose, at the radiator outlet. Set the heater temperature controls to the full HOT position.

NOTE: *Before opening the radiator petcock, spray it with some penetrating lubricant.*

2. Close the petcock or reconnect the lower hose and fill the system with water.

3. Add a can of quality radiator flush. If equipped with a V6 engine, be sure the flush is safe to use in engines having aluminum components.

4. Idle the engine until the upper radiator hose gets hot.

5. Drain the system again.

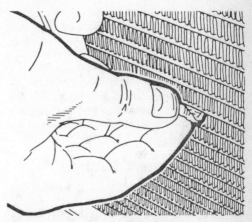

Clean debris from the radiator fins

6. Repeat this process until the drained water is clear and free of scale.

7. Close all petcocks and connect all the hoses.

8. If equipped with a coolant recovery system, flush the reservoir with water and leave empty.

9. Determine the capacity of your cooling system (see capacities specifications). Add a 50/50 mix of quality antifreeze (ethylene glycol) and water to provide the desired protection.

SYSTEM INSPECTION

Most permanent antifreeze/coolant have a colored dye added which makes the solution an excellent leak detector. When servicing the cooling system, check for leakage at:

• All hoses and hose connections

• Radiator seams, radiator core, and radiator draincock

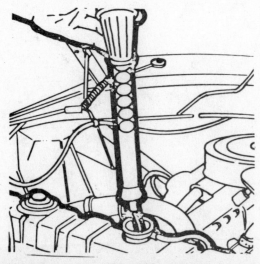

Testing coolant condition with a tester

● All engine block and cylinder head freeze (core) plugs, and drain plugs
● Edges of all cooling system gaskets (head gaskets, thermostat gasket)
● Transmission fluid cooler
● Heating system components, water pump
● Check the engine oil dipstick for signs of coolant in the engine oil
● Check the coolant in the radiator for signs of oil in the coolant

Investigate and correct any indication of coolant leakage.

Check the Radiator Cap

While you are checking the coolant level, check the radiator cap for a worn or cracked gasket. If the cap doesn't seal properly, fluid will be lost and the engine will overheat.

A worn cap should be replaced with a new one.

Clean Radiator of Debris

Periodically clean any debris such as leaves, paper, insects, etc., from the radiator fins. Pick the large pieces off by hand. The smaller pieces can be washed away with water pressure from a hose.

Carefully straighten any bent radiator fins with a pair of needle nose pliers. Be careful, the fins are very soft. Don't wiggle the fins back and forth too much. Straighten them once and try not to move them again.

CHECKING SYSTEM PROTECTION

A 50/50 mix of coolant concentrate and water will usually provide protection to −35°F (−37°C). Freeze protection may be checked by using a cooling system hydrometer. Inexpensive hydrometers (floating ball types) may be obtained from a local department store (automotive section) or an auto supply store. Follow the directions packaged with the coolant hydrometer when checking protection.

Master Cylinder
LEVEL CHECK

The brake fluid in the master cylinder should be checked every 6 months/6,000 miles.

Cast Iron Reservoir

1. Park the vehicle on a level surface and open the hood.
2. Pry the retaining spring bar holding the cover onto the master cylinder to one side.
3. Clean any dirt from the sides and top of the cover before removal. Remove the master cylinder cover and gasket.
4. Add fluid, if necessary, to within ⅜" of the top of the reservoir, or to the full level indicator (on models equipped).
5. Push the gasket bellows back into the cover. Reinstall the gasket and cover and position the retainer spring bar.

Plastic Reservoir

Check the fluid level on the side of the reservoir. If fluid is required, remove the screw on the and remove the filler cap and gasket from the master cylinder. Fill the reservoir to the full line in the reservoir. Install the filler cap, making sure the gasket is properly seated in the cap.

FLUID RECOMMENDATION

Use only Heavy Duty Brake Fluid meeting DOT3 specifications.

Power Steering
LEVEL CHECK

Check the power steering fluid level every 6 months/6,000 miles.

1. Park the vehicle on a level surface. Run the engine until normal operating temperature is reached.
2. Turn the steering all the way to the left and then all the way to the right several times. Center the steering wheel and shut off the engine.
3. Open the hood and check the power steering reservoir fluid level.
4. Remove the filler cap and wipe the dipstick attached clean.
5. Re-insert the dipstick and tighten the cap. Remove the dipstick and note the fluid level indicated on the dipstick.
6. The level should be at any point below the Full mark, but not below the Add mark.
7. Add fluid as necessary. Do not overfill.

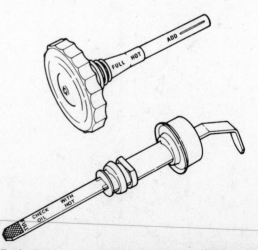

Typical power steering pump reservoir dipsticks

FLUID RECOMMENDATION

Add power steering fluid; do not overfill the reservoir.

Chassis Greasing

NOTE: *Depending on the year and model, vehicles may have plugs or grease fittings in all steering/suspension linkage or pivot points. Follow the instructions under Ball Joints if equipped with these plugs. Newer models have sealed points and lubrication is not necessary.*

BALL JOINTS

1. Park the vehicle on a level surface, set the parking brake, block the rear wheels, raise the front end and support it with jackstands.
2. Wipe away any dirt from the ball joint lubrication plugs.
3. Pull out the plugs and install grease fittings.
4. Using a hand-operated grease gun containing multi-purpose grease, force lubricant into the joint until the joint boot swells.
5. Remove the grease fitting and push in the lubrication plug.
6. Lower the vehicle.

STEERING ARM STOPS

The steering arm stops are attached to the lower control arm. They are located between

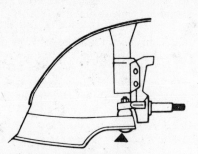

Lower ball joint lubrication points

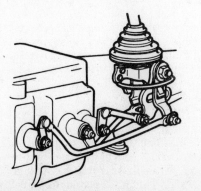

Typical manual transmission linkage lube points

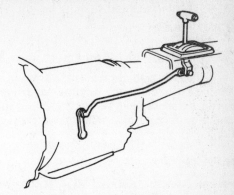

Automatic transmission linkage lube points

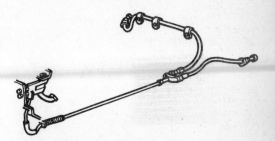

Typical parking brake lube points

each steering arm and the upturned end of the front suspension strut.

1. Park the vehicle on a level surface, set the parking brake, block the rear wheels, raise the front end and support it with jackstands.
2. Clean the friction points and apply multi-purpose grease.
3. Lower the vehicle.

MANUAL TRANSMISSION AND CLUTCH LINKAGE

On models so equipped, apply a small amount of chassis grease to the pivot points of the transmission and clutch linkage as per the chassis lubrication diagram.

AUTOMATIC TRANSMISSION LINKAGE

On models so equipped, apply a small amount of 10W engine oil to the kickdown and shift linkage at the pivot points.

PARKING BRAKE LINKAGE

At yearly intervals or whenever binding is noticeable in the parking brake linkage, lubricate the cable guides, levers and linkage with a suitable chassis grease.

OUTSIDE VEHICLE MAINTENANCE

Lock Cylinders

Apply graphite lubricant sparingly through the key slot. Insert the key and operate the lock several times to be sure that the lubricant is worked into the lock cylinder.

Door Hinges and Hinge Checks

Spray a silicone lubricant on the hinge pivot points to eliminate any binding conditions. Open and close the door several times to be sure that the lubricant is evenly and thoroughly distributed.

Trunk Lid

Spray a silicone lubricant on all of the pivot and friction surfaces to eliminate any squeaks or binds. Work the trunk lid to distribute the lubricant

Body Drain Holes

Be sure that the drain holes in the doors and rocker panels are cleared of obstruction. A small screwdriver can be used to clear them of any debris.

PUSHING AND TOWING

WARNING: *Push-starting is not recommended for cars equipped with a catalytic converter. Raw gas collecting in the converter may cause damage. Jump starting is recommended.*

To push-start your manual transmission equipped car (automatic transmission models cannot be push started), make sure of bumper alignment. If the bumper of the car pushing does not match with your car's bumper, it would be wise to tie an old tire either on the back of your car, or on the front of the pushing car. Switch the ignition to **ON** and depress the clutch pedal. Shift the transmission to third gear and hold the accelerator pedal about halfway down. signal the push car to proceed, when the car speed reaches about 10 mph, gradually release the clutch pedal. The car engine should start, if not have the car towed.

If the transmission and rear axle are in proper working order, the car can be towed with the rear wheels on the ground for distances under 15 miles at speeds no greater then 30 mph. If the transmission or rear is known to be damaged or if the car has to be towed over 15 miles or over 30 mph the car must be dollied or towed with the rear wheels raised and the steering wheel secured so that the front wheels remain in the straight-ahead position. The steering wheel must be clamped with a special clamping device designed for towing service. If the key controlled lock is used damage to the lock and steering column may occur.

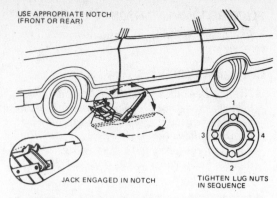

USE APPROPRIATE NOTCH (FRONT OR REAR)

JACK ENGAGED IN NOTCH

TIGHTEN LUG NUTS IN SEQUENCE

Positioning of scissors jack

JACKING

Your car is equipped with either a scissors type jack, or a bumper jack. The scissor-type jack is placed under the side of the car so that it fits into the notch in the vertical rocker panel flange nearest the wheel to be changed. These jacking notches are located approximately 8 inches from the wheel opening on the rocker panel flanges. Bumper jack slots or flats are provided on the front and rear bumper. Be sure the jack is inserted firmly and is straight before raising the vehicle.

When raising the car with a scissors or bumper jack follow these precautions: Park the car on level spot, put the selector in P (PARK) with an automatic transmission or in reverse if your car has a manual transmission, apply the parking brake and block the front and the back of the wheel that is diagonally opposite the wheel being changed. These jacks are fine for changing a tire, but never crawl under the car when it is supported only by the scissors or bumper jack.

CAUTION: *If you're going to work beneath the vehicle, always support it on jackstands.*

TRAILER TOWING

Factory trailer towing packages are available on most cars. However, if you are installing a trailer hitch and wiring on your car, there are a few thing that you ought to know.

Trailer Weight

Trailer weight is the first, and most important, factor in determining whether or not your vehicle is suitable for towing the trailer you have in mind. The horsepower-to-weight ratio should be calculated. The basic standard is a ratio of 35:1. That is, 35 pounds of GVW for every horsepower.

JUMP STARTING A DEAD BATTERY

The chemical reaction in a battery produces explosive hydrogen gas. This is the safe way to jump start a dead battery, reducing the chances of an accidental spark that could cause an explosion.

Jump Starting Precautions

1. Be sure both batteries are of the same voltage.
2. Be sure both batteries are of the same polarity (have the same grounded terminal).
3. Be sure the vehicles are not touching.
4. Be sure the vent cap holes are not obstructed.
5. Do not smoke or allow sparks around the battery.
6. In cold weather, check for frozen electrolyte in the battery. Do not jump start a frozen battery.
7. Do not allow electrolyte on your skin or clothing.
8. Be sure the electrolyte is not frozen.

CAUTION: *Make certain that the ignition key, in the vehicle with the dead battery, is in the OFF position. Connecting cables to vehicles with on-board computers will result in computer destruction if the key is not in the OFF position.*

Jump Starting Procedure

1. Determine voltages of the two batteries; they must be the same.
2. Bring the starting vehicle close (they must not touch) so that the batteries can be reached easily.
3. Turn off all accessories and both engines. Put both cars in Neutral or Park and set the handbrake.
4. Cover the cell caps with a rag—do not cover terminals.
5. If the terminals on the run-down battery are heavily corroded, clean them.
6. Identify the positive and negative posts on both batteries and connect the cables in the order shown.
7. Start the engine of the starting vehicle and run it at fast idle. Try to start the car with the dead battery. Crank it for no more than 10 seconds at a time and let it cool off for 20 seconds in between tries.
8. If it doesn't start in 3 tries, there is something else wrong.
9. Disconnect the cables in the reverse order.
10. Replace the cell covers and dispose of the rags.

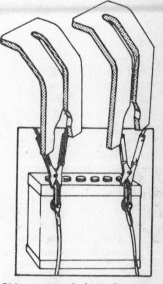

Side terminal batteries occasionally pose a problem when connecting jumper cables. There frequently isn't enough room to clamp the cables without touching sheet metal. Side terminal adaptors are available to alleviate this problem and should be removed after use.

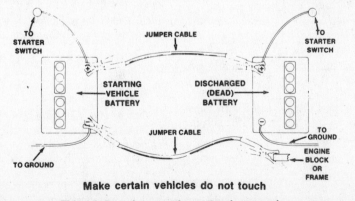

TO STARTER SWITCH

JUMPER CABLE

TO STARTER SWITCH

STARTING VEHICLE BATTERY

DISCHARGED (DEAD) BATTERY

JUMPER CABLE

TO GROUND

TO GROUND

ENGINE BLOCK OR FRAME

Make certain vehicles do not touch

This hook-up for negative ground cars only

To calculate this ratio, multiply you engine's rated horsepower by 35, then subtract the weight of the vehicle, including passengers and luggage. The resulting figure is the ideal maximum trailer weight that you can tow. One point to consider: a numerically higher axle ratio can offset what appears to be a low trailer weight. If the weight of the trailer that you have in mind is somewhat higher than the weight you just calculated, you might consider changing your rear axle ratio to compensate.

Hitch Weight

There are three kinds of hitches: bumper mounted, frame mounted, and load equalizing.

Bumper mounted hitches are those which attach solely to the vehicle's bumper. Many states prohibit towing with this type of hitch, when it attaches to the vehicle's stock bumper, since it subjects the bumper to stresses for which it was not designed. Aftermarket rear step bumpers, designed for trailer towing, are acceptable for use with bumper mounted hitches.

Frame mounted hitches can be of the type which bolts to two or more points on the frame, plus the bumper, or just to several points on the frame. Frame mounted hitches can also be of the tongue type, for Class I towing, or, of the receiver type, for classes II and III.

Load equalizing hitches are usually used for large trailers. Most equalizing hitches are welded in place and use equalizing bars and chains to level the vehicle after the trailer is hooked up.

The bolt-on hitches are the most common, since they are relatively easy to install.

Check the gross weight rating of your trailer. Tongue weight is usually figured as 10% of gross trailer weight. Therefore, a trailer with a maximum gross weight of 2,000 lb. will have a maximum tongue weight of 200 lb. Class I tarilers fall into this category. Class II trailers are those with a gross weight rating of 2,000-3,500 lb., while Class III trailers fall into the 3,500-6,000 lb. category. Class IV trailers are those over 6,000 lb. and are for use with fifth wheel trucks, only.

When you've determined the hitch that you'll need, follow the manufacturer's installation instructions, exactly, especially when it comes to fastener torques. The hitch will subjected to a lot of stress and good hitches come with hardened bolts. Never substitute an inferior bolt for a hardened bolt.

Wiring

Wiring the car for towing is fairly easy. There are a number of good wiring kits available and these should be used, rather than trying to design your own. All trailers will need brake lights and turn signals as well as tail lights and side marker lights. Most states require extra marker lights for overly wide trailers. Also, most states have recently required back-up lights for trailers, and most trailer manufacturers have been building trailers with back-up lights for several years.

Additionally, some Class I, most Class II and just about all Class III trailers will have electric brakes.

Add to this number an accessories wire, to operate trailer internal equipment or to charge the trailer's battery, and you can have as many as seven wires in the harness.

Determine the equipment on your trailer and buy the wiring kit necessary. The kit will contain all the wires needed, plus a plug adapter set which included the female plug, mounted on the bumper or hitch, and the male plug, wired into, or plugged into the trailer harness.

When installing the kit, follow the manufacturer's instructions. The color coding of the wires is standard throughout the industry.

One point to note, some domestic vehicles, and most imported vehicles, have separate turn signals. On most domestic vehicles, the brake lights and rear turn signals operate with the same bulb. For those vehicles with separate turn signals, you can purchase an isolation unit so that the brake lights won't blink whenever the turn signals are operated, or, you can go to your local electronics supply house and buy four diodes to wire in series with the brake and turn signal bulbs. Diodes will isolate the brake and turn signals. The choice is yours. The isolation units are simple and quick to install, but far more expensive than the diodes. The diodes, however, require more work to install properly, since they require the cutting of each bulb's wire and soldering in place of the diode.

One final point, the best kits are those with a spring loaded cover on the vehicle mounted socket. This cover prevents dirt and moisture from corroding the terminals. Never let the vehicle socket hang loosely. Always mount it securely to the bumper or hitch.

Cooling
ENGINE

One of the most common, if not THE most common, problem associated with trailer towing is engine overheating.

With factory installed trailer towing packages, a heavy duty cooling system is usually included. Heavy duty cooling systems are available as optional equipment on most cars, with or without a trailer package. If you have one of

Maintenance Interval Chart
(Intervals in months or miles in thousands whichever occurs first)

Operation	Miles/Months	See Chapter
ENGINE		
Air cleaner element replacement	24	1
Carburetor Idle speed and mixture	22.5	1
Cooling system check	12	1
Coolant replacement; system draining and flushing	24	1
Crankcase breather filter replacement (in air cleaner)	24	1
Drive belts check and adjust	10	1
Evaporator control system check; inspect carbon canister	30	1
Exhaust gas recirculation system (EGR) check	15	4
Fuel filter replacement	12	1
Ignition timing adjustment	①	2
Oil change	7.5 ②	1
Oil filter replacement	②,③	1
PCV valve replacement	20	1
Spark plug replacement	20	2
CHASSIS		
Automatic transmission band adjustment	④	6
Automatic transmission fluid level check	20	1
Brake system inspection, lining replacement	30	9
Brake master cylinder reservoir fluid level check	30	1
Clutch pedal free play adjustment	10	6
Front suspension ball joints and steering linkage lubrication	30	1
Front wheel bearings cleaning, adjusting and repacking	30	9
Manual transmission fluid level check	⑤	1
Power steering pump fluid level check	15	1
Rear axle fluid level check	15	1
Steering arm stop lubrication; steering linkage inspection	15	1

① Periodic adjustment unnecessary
② All 4 cyl. turbocharged vehicles require an oil and oil filter change at 3,000 mile intervals
③ Every oil change
④ Normal service—12,000 miles, Severe (fleet) service—6,000/18,000/30,000 miles
⑤ Periodic fluid level check is unnecessary

these extra-capacity systems, you shouldn't have any overheating problems.

If you have a standard cooling system, without an expansion tank, you'll definitely need to get an aftermarket expansion tank kit, preferably one with at least a 2 quart capacity. These kits are easily installed on the radiator's overflow hose, and come with a pressure cap designed for expansion tanks.

Another helpful accessory is a Flex Fan. These fan are large diameter units are designed to provide more airflow at low speeds, with blades that have deeply cupped surfaces. The blades then flex, or flatten out, at high speed, when less cooling air is needed. These fans are far lighter in weight than stock fans, requiring less horsepower to drive them. Also, they are far quieter than stock fans.

If you do decide to replace your stock fan with a flex fan, note that if your car has a fan clutch, a spacer between the flex fan and water pump hub will be needed.

Aftermarket engine oil coolers are helpful for prolonging engine oil life and reducing overall engine temperatures. Both of these factors increase engine life.

While not absolutely necessary in towing Class I and some Class II trailers, they are recommended for heavier Class II and all Class III towing.

Engine oil cooler systems consist of an adapter, screwed on in place of the oil filter, a remote filter mounting and a multi-tube, finned heat exchanger, which is mounted in front of the radiator or air conditioning condenser.

TRANSMISSION

An automatic transmission is usually recommended for trailer towing. Modern automatics have proven reliable and, of course, easy to operate, in trailer towing.

The increased load of a trailer, however, causes an increase in the temperature of the automatic transmission fluid. Heat is the worst enemy of an automatic transmission. As the temperature of the fluid increases, the life of the fluid decreases.

It is essential, therefore, that you install an automatic transmission cooler.

The cooler, which consists of a multi-tube, finned heat exchanger, is usually installed in front of the radiator or air conditioning compressor, and hooked inline with the transmission cooler tank inlet line. Follow the cooler manufacturer's installation instructions.

Select a cooler of at least adequate capacity, based upon the combined gross weights of the car and trailer.

Cooler manufacturers recommend that you use an aftermarket cooler in addition to, and not instead of, the present cooling tank in your car radiator. If you do want to use it in place of the radiator cooling tank, get a cooler at least two sizes larger than normally necessary.

NOTE: *A transmission cooler can, sometimes, cause slow or harsh shifting in the transmission during cold weather, until the fluid has a chance to come up to normal operating temperature. Some coolers can be purchased with or retrofitted with a temperature bypass valve which will allow fluid flow through the cooler only when the fluid has reached operating temperature, or above.*

JACKING AND HOISTING

Scissors jacks or hydraulic jacks are recommended for all cars. To change a tire, place the jack beneath the spring plate, below the axle, near the wheel to be changed.

Make sure that you are on level ground, that the transmission is in Reverse or with automatic transmissions, Park; the parking brake is set, and the tire diagonally opposite to the one to be changed is blocked so that it will not roll. Loosen the lug nuts before you jack the wheel to be changed completely free of the ground.

If you use a hoist, make sure that the pads of the hoist are located in such a way as to lift on the car frame and not on a shock absorber mount, floor boards, oil pan, or any other part that cannot support the full weight of the vehicle.

Engine Performance and Tune-Up

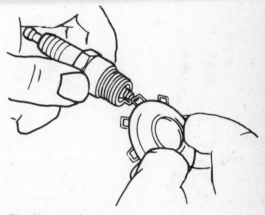

2

TUNE-UP PROCEDURES

In order to extract the full measure of performance and economy from your engine it is essential that it be properly tuned at regular intervals. A regular tune-up will keep your vehicle's engine running smoothly and will prevent the annoying minor breakdowns and poor performance associated with an untuned engine.

A complete tune-up should be performed every 12,000 miles or twelve months, whichever comes first. This interval should be halved if the vehicle is operated under severe conditions, such as trailer towing, prolonged idling, continual stop and start driving, or if starting or running problems are noticed. It is assumed that the routine maintenance described in Chapter 1 has been kept up, as this will have a decided effect on the results of a tune-up. All of the applicable steps of a tune-up should be followed in order, as the result is a cumulative one.

If the specifications on the tune-up sticker in the engine compartment disagree with the Tune-Up Specifications chart in this chapter, the figures on the sticker must be used. The sticker often reflects changes made during the production run.

Spark Plugs

A typical spark plug consists of a metal shell surrounding a ceramic insulator. A metal electrode extends downward through the center of the insulator and protrudes a small distance. Located at the end of the plug and attached to the side of the outer metal shell is the side electrode. The side electrode bends in at a 90° angle so that its tip is even with, and parallel to, the tip of the center electrode. The distance between these two electrodes (measured in thousandths of an inch) is called the spark plug gap. The spark plug in no way produces a spark but merely provides a gap across which the current can arc. The coil produces anywhere from

Checking spark plug gap

20,000 to 40,000 volts or more, which travels to the distributor where it is distributed through the spark plug wires to the spark plugs. The current passes along the center electrode and jumps the gap to the side electrode, and, in so doing, ignites the air/fuel mixture in the combustion chamber.

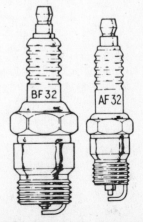

Typical spark plugs—left is $^{13}/_{16}$ in. (18 mm); right is $^{5}/_{8}$ in. (14 mm)

Troubleshooting Engine Performance

Problem	Cause	Solution
Hard starting (engine cranks normally)	• Binding linkage, choke valve or choke piston	• Repair as necessary
	• Restricted choke vacuum diaphragm	• Clean passages
	• Improper fuel level	• Adjust float level
	• Dirty, worn or faulty needle valve and seat	• Repair as necessary
	• Float sticking	• Repair as necessary
	• Faulty fuel pump	• Replace fuel pump
	• Incorrect choke cover adjustment	• Adjust choke cover
	• Inadequate choke unloader adjustment	• Adjust choke unloader
	• Faulty ignition coil	• Test and replace as necessary
	• Improper spark plug gap	• Adjust gap
	• Incorrect ignition timing	• Adjust timing
	• Incorrect valve timing	• Check valve timing; repair as necessary
Rough idle or stalling	• Incorrect curb or fast idle speed	• Adjust curb or fast idle speed
	• Incorrect ignition timing	• Adjust timing to specification
	• Improper feedback system operation	• Refer to Chapter 4
	• Improper fast idle cam adjustment	• Adjust fast idle cam
	• Faulty EGR valve operation	• Test EGR system and replace as necessary
	• Faulty PCV valve air flow	• Test PCV valve and replace as necessary
	• Choke binding	• Locate and eliminate binding condition
	• Faulty TAC vacuum motor or valve	• Repair as necessary
	• Air leak into manifold vacuum	• Inspect manifold vacuum connections and repair as necessary
	• Improper fuel level	• Adjust fuel level
	• Faulty distributor rotor or cap	• Replace rotor or cap
	• Improperly seated valves	• Test cylinder compression, repair as necessary
	• Incorrect ignition wiring	• Inspect wiring and correct as necessary
	• Faulty ignition coil	• Test coil and replace as necessary
	• Restricted air vent or idle passages	• Clean passages
	• Restricted air cleaner	• Clean or replace air cleaner filler element
	• Faulty choke vacuum diaphragm	• Repair as necessary
Faulty low-speed operation	• Restricted idle transfer slots	• Clean transfer slots
	• Restricted idle air vents and passages	• Clean air vents and passages
	• Restricted air cleaner	• Clean or replace air cleaner filter element
	• Improper fuel level	• Adjust fuel level
	• Faulty spark plugs	• Clean or replace spark plugs
	• Dirty, corroded, or loose ignition secondary circuit wire connections	• Clean or tighten secondary circuit wire connections
	• Improper feedback system operation	• Refer to Chapter 4
	• Faulty ignition coil high voltage wire	• Replace ignition coil high voltage wire
	• Faulty distributor cap	• Replace cap
Faulty acceleration	• Improper accelerator pump stroke	• Adjust accelerator pump stroke
	• Incorrect ignition timing	• Adjust timing
	• Inoperative pump discharge check ball or needle	• Clean or replace as necessary
	• Worn or damaged pump diaphragm or piston	• Replace diaphragm or piston

Troubleshooting Engine Performance (cont.)

Problem	Cause	Solution
Faulty acceleration (cont.)	• Leaking carburetor main body cover gasket	• Replace gasket
	• Engine cold and choke set too lean	• Adjust choke cover
	• Improper metering rod adjustment (BBD Model carburetor)	• Adjust metering rod
	• Faulty spark plug(s)	• Clean or replace spark plug(s)
	• Improperly seated valves	• Test cylinder compression, repair as necessary
	• Faulty ignition coil	• Test coil and replace as necessary
	• Improper feedback system operation	• Refer to Chapter 4
Faulty high speed operation	• Incorrect ignition timing	• Adjust timing
	• Faulty distributor centrifugal advance mechanism	• Check centrifugal advance mechanism and repair as necessary
	• Faulty distributor vacuum advance mechanism	• Check vacuum advance mechanism and repair as necessary
	• Low fuel pump volume	• Replace fuel pump
	• Wrong spark plug air gap or wrong plug	• Adjust air gap or install correct plug
	• Faulty choke operation	• Adjust choke cover
	• Partially restricted exhaust manifold, exhaust pipe, catalytic converter, muffler, or tailpipe	• Eliminate restriction
	• Restricted vacuum passages	• Clean passages
	• Improper size or restricted main jet	• Clean or replace as necessary
	• Restricted air cleaner	• Clean or replace filter element as necessary
	• Faulty distributor rotor or cap	• Replace rotor or cap
	• Faulty ignition coil	• Test coil and replace as necessary
	• Improperly seated valve(s)	• Test cylinder compression, repair as necessary
	• Faulty valve spring(s)	• Inspect and test valve spring tension, replace as necessary
	• Incorrect valve timing	• Check valve timing and repair as necessary
	• Intake manifold restricted	• Remove restriction or replace manifold
	• Worn distributor shaft	• Replace shaft
	• Improper feedback system operation	• Refer to Chapter 4
Misfire at all speeds	• Faulty spark plug(s)	• Clean or replace spark plug(s)
	• Faulty spark plug wire(s)	• Replace as necessary
	• Faulty distributor cap or rotor	• Replace cap or rotor
	• Faulty ignition coil	• Test coil and replace as necessary
	• Primary ignition circuit shorted or open intermittently	• Troubleshoot primary circuit and repair as necessary
	• Improperly seated valve(s)	• Test cylinder compression, repair as necessary
	• Faulty hydraulic tappet(s)	• Clean or replace tappet(s)
	• Improper feedback system operation	• Refer to Chapter 4
	• Faulty valve spring(s)	• Inspect and test valve spring tension, repair as necessary
	• Worn camshaft lobes	• Replace camshaft
	• Air leak into manifold	• Check manifold vacuum and repair as necessary
	• Improper carburetor adjustment	• Adjust carburetor
	• Fuel pump volume or pressure low	• Replace fuel pump
	• Blown cylinder head gasket	• Replace gasket
	• Intake or exhaust manifold passage(s) restricted	• Pass chain through passage(s) and repair as necessary
	• Incorrect trigger wheel installed in distributor	• Install correct trigger wheel

Troubleshooting Engine Performance (cont.)

Problem	Cause	Solution
Power not up to normal	• Incorrect ignition timing • Faulty distributor rotor • Trigger wheel loose on shaft • Incorrect spark plug gap • Faulty fuel pump • Incorrect valve timing • Faulty ignition coil • Faulty ignition wires • Improperly seated valves • Blown cylinder head gasket • Leaking piston rings • Worn distributor shaft • Improper feedback system operation	• Adjust timing • Replace rotor • Reposition or replace trigger wheel • Adjust gap • Replace fuel pump • Check valve timing and repair as necessary • Test coil and replace as necessary • Test wires and replace as necessary • Test cylinder compression and repair as necessary • Replace gasket • Test compression and repair as necessary • Replace shaft • Refer to Chapter 4
Intake backfire	• Improper ignition timing • Faulty accelerator pump discharge • Defective EGR CTO valve • Defective TAC vacuum motor or valve • Lean air/fuel mixture	• Adjust timing • Repair as necessary • Replace EGR CTO valve • Repair as necessary • Check float level or manifold vacuum for air leak. Remove sediment from bowl
Exhaust backfire	• Air leak into manifold vacuum • Faulty air injection diverter valve • Exhaust leak	• Check manifold vacuum and repair as necessary • Test diverter valve and replace as necessary • Locate and eliminate leak
Ping or spark knock	• Incorrect ignition timing • Distributor centrifugal or vacuum advance malfunction • Excessive combustion chamber deposits • Air leak into manifold vacuum • Excessively high compression • Fuel octane rating excessively low • Sharp edges in combustion chamber • EGR valve not functioning properly	• Adjust timing • Inspect advance mechanism and repair as necessary • Remove with combustion chamber cleaner • Check manifold vacuum and repair as necessary • Test compression and repair as necessary • Try alternate fuel source • Grind smooth • Test EGR system and replace as necessary
Surging (at cruising to top speeds)	• Low carburetor fuel level • Low fuel pump pressure or volume • Metering rod(s) not adjusted properly (BBD Model Carburetor) • Improper PCV valve air flow • Air leak into manifold vacuum • Incorrect spark advance • Restricted main jet(s) • Undersize main jet(s) • Restricted air vents • Restricted fuel filter • Restricted air cleaner • EGR valve not functioning properly • Improper feedback system operation	• Adjust fuel level • Replace fuel pump • Adjust metering rod • Test PCV valve and replace as necessary • Check manifold vacuum and repair as necessary • Test and replace as necessary • Clean main jet(s) • Replace main jet(s) • Clean air vents • Replace fuel filter • Clean or replace air cleaner filter element • Test EGR system and replace as necessary • Refer to Chapter 4

Tune-Up Specifications

Year	Engine No. Cyl Displacement (cu. in.)	Spark Plugs Orig Type	Gap (in.)	Distributor	Ignition Timing (deg) ▲ Man	Auto	Intake Valve Opens (deg)	Fuel Pump Pressure (psi)	Idle Speed (rpm) ▲ Man	Auto
1979	4-140	AWSF-42	.034	Electronic	6B	20B	22	5.5–6.5	850	850(750)
	4-140 (Turbo)	AWSF-32	.034	Electronic	2B	—	22	6.5–7.5	900	—
	6-170	AWSF-42	.034	Electronic	—	9(6)B	28	3.5–5.8	—	650(600)
	8-302	ASF-52	.050	Electronic	12B	6B	16	5.5–6.5	800	600
	8-302 (Calif.)	ASF-52-6	.060	Electronic	12B	6B	16	5.5–6.5	800	600
1980	4-140	AWSF-42	.035	Electronic	6B	20(12)B	22	5.5–6.5	850	750
	4-140 (Turbo)	AWSF-32	.050	Electronic	6(2)B	8(2)B	22	6.5–7.5	900	800
	6-200	BSF-82	.050	Electronic	10B	10B	20	5.5–6.5	700①	550(600)②
	8-255	ASF-42	.050	Electronic	8B	8B	16	4.0–6.0	500	550(500)
1981	4-140	AWSF-42	.034	Electronic	6B	20(12)B	22	5.5–6.5	850	750
	4-140 (Turbo)	AWSF-42	.034	Electronic	6(2)B	—	22	6.5–6.5	900	800(600)
	6-200	BSF-92	.050	Electronic	10B	10B	20	5.5–6.5	700①	550④
	8-255	ASF-52	.050	Electronic	8B	8B	16	5.5–6.5	—	550
1982	4-140	AWSF-42	.034	Electronic	6B	20(12)B	22	5.5–6.5	850	750
	4-140 (Turbo) ③	AWSF-42	.034	Electronic	6B	—	22	6.5–7.5	900	—
	6-200	BSF-92	.050	Electronic	10B	10B	20	6.0–8.0	—	700
	8-255	ASF-52	.050	Electronic	—	10B	16	6.0–8.0	—	500
	8-302	ASF-42	.044	Electronic	12B	—	15	6.5–8.0	800	—
1983–88	4-140	AWSF-44	.044	Electronic	⑤	⑤	22	5½–6½	850	800
	4-140 (Turbo)	AWSF-32C	.034	Electronic	⑤	⑤	—	—	⑤	⑤
	6-200	BSF-92	.050	Electronic	⑤	⑤	20	6–8	—	550
	6-232	AWSF-52	.044	Electronic	⑤	⑤	13	6–8⑦	—	700
	8-302	ASF-42 ⑥	.044	Electronic	⑤	⑤	16	6–8⑧	700	550

NOTE: The underhood specifications sticker often reflects tune-up specification changes made in production. Sticker figures must be used if they disagree with those in the chart.
① 900 with air conditioning
② 700 with air conditioning
③ Canada only
④ 49 states; 700 w/A/C, 600 Calif. and 700 Calif. w/A/C
⑤ Refers to emission sticker
⑥ 1985—ASF52/HO-ASF42
⑦ In tank pump—40–45
⑧ CFI—39 psi
▲ Figures in parentheses are for California; automatic figures taken w/transmission in "Drive"

SPARK PLUG HEAT RANGE

Spark plug heat range is the ability of the plug to dissipate heat. The longer the insulator (or the farther it extends into the engine), the hotter the plug will operate; the shorter the insulator the cooler it will operate. A plug that absorbs little heat and remains too cool will quickly accumulate deposits of oil and carbon since it is not hot enough to burn them off. This leads to plug fouling and consequently to misfiring. A plug that absorbs too much heat will have to de-posits, but, due to the excessive heat, the electrodes will burn away quickly and in some instances, pre-ignition may result. Pre-ignition takes place when plug tips get so hot that they glow sufficiently to ignite the fuel/air mixture before the actual spark occurs. This early ignition will usually cause a pinging during low speeds and heavy loads.

The general rule of thumb for choosing the correct heat range when picking a spark plug is: if most of your driving is long distance, high speed travel, use a colder plug; if most of your driving is stop and go, use a hotter plug. Original equipment plugs are compromise plugs, but most people never have occasion to change their plugs from the factory recommended heat range.

REPLACING SPARK PLUGS

A set of spark plugs usually requires replacement after about 10,000 miles on cars with conventional ignition systems and after about 20,000 to 30,000 miles on cars with electronic ignition, depending on your style of driving. In normal operation, plug gap increases about 0.001" (0.0254mm) for every 1,000-2,500 miles. As the gap increases, the plug's voltage requirement also increases. It requires a greater voltage to jump the wider gap and about two to three times as much voltage to fire a plug at high speeds than at idle.

When you're removing spark plugs, you should work on one at a time. Don't start by removing the plug wires all at once, because unless you number them, they may become mixed up. Take a minute before you begin and number the wires with tape. The best location for numbering is near where the wires come out of the cap.

NOTE: *On models equipped with electronic ignition, apply a small amount of silicone dielectric compound (D7AZ-19A331-A or the equivalent) to the inside of the terminal boots whenever an ignition wire is disconnected from the plug, or coil/distributor cap connection.*

1. Twist the spark plug boot and remove the boot and wire from the plug. Do not pull on the wire itself as this will ruin the wire.

2. If possible, use a brush or rag to clean the area around the spark plug. Make sure that all the dirt is removed so that none will enter the cylinder after the plug is removed.

3. Remove the spark plug using the proper size socket. Either a ⅝" or ¹³⁄₁₆" size socket depending on the engine. Turn the socket counterclockwise to remove the plug. Be sure to hold the socket straight on the plug to avoid breaking the plug, or rounding off the hex on the plug.

4. Once the plug is out, check it against the plugs shown in the Color section in this book to determine engine condition. This is crucial since plug readings are vital signs of engine condition.

5. Use a round wire feeler gauge to check the plug gap. The correct size gauge should pass through the electrode gap with a slight drag. If you're in doubt, try one size smaller and one larger. The smaller gauge should go through easily while the larger one shouldn't go through at all. If the gap is incorrect, use the electrode

bending tool on the end of the gauge to adjust the gap. When adjusting the gap, always bend the side electrode. The center electrode is non-adjustable.

6. Squirt a drop of penetrating oil on the threads of the new plug and install it. Don't oil the threads too heavily. Turn the plug in clockwise by hand until it is snug.

7. When the plug is finger tight, tighten it with a wrench. Take care not to overtighten. Torque to 15 ft.lb.

8. Install the plug boot firmly over the plug. Proceed to the next plug.

CHECKING AND REPLACING SPARK PLUG CABLES

Visually inspect the spark plug cables for burns, cuts, or breaks in the insulation. Check the spark plug boots and the nipples on the distributor cap and coil. Replace any damaged wiring. If no physical damage is obvious, the wires can be checked with an ohmmeter for excessive resistance. (See the tune-up and troubleshooting section).

NOTE: *On models equipped with electronic ignition, apply a small amount of silicone dielectric compound (D7AZ-19A331-A or the equivalent) to the inside of the terminal boots whenever an ignition wire is disconnected from the plug. or coil/distributor cap connection.*

When installing a new set of spark plug cables, replace the cables one at a time so there will be no mixup. Start by replacing the longest cable first. Install the boot firmly over the spark plug. Route the wire exactly the same as the original. Insert the nipple firmly into the tower on the distributor cap. Repeat the process for each cable.

ELECTRONIC IGNITION SYSTEMS

DuraSpark Ignition

Basically, four electronic ignition systems have been used in Ford Motor Company vehicles from 1977-88:

1. DuraSpark I
2. DuraSpark II
3. DuraSpark III
4. Universal Distributor-TFI (EEC-IV)

In 1977, the DuraSpark systems, were introduced. DuraSpark I and DuraSpark II systems are nearly identical in operation, and virtually identical in appearance. The DuraSpark I uses a special control module which senses current flow through the ignition coil and adjust the dwell, or coil on-time for maximum spark intensity. If the DuraSpark I module senses that the ignition is ON, but the distributor shaft is not

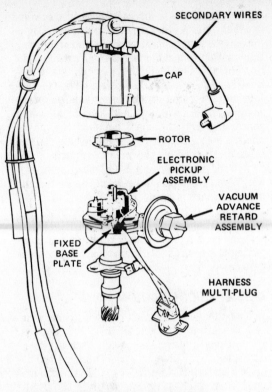

Dura Spark II distributor, disassembled

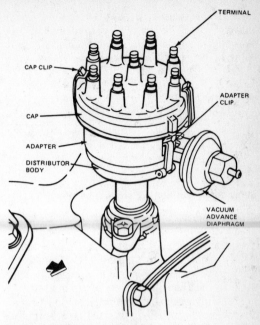

Typical distributor assembly

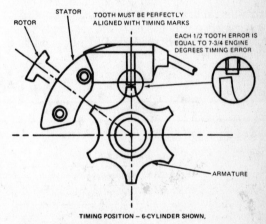

Static timing position, six cylinder shown, four cylinder very similar

turning, the current to the coil is turned OFF by the module. The DuraSpark II system does not have this feature. The coil is energized for the full amount of time that the ignition switch is ON. Keep this in mind when servicing the DuraSpark II system, as the ignition system could inadvertently fire while performing ignition system services (such as distributor cap removal) while the ignition is ON. All DuraSpark II systems are easily identified by having a two-piece, flat topped distributor cap.

In 1980, the new DuraSpark III system was introduced. This version is based on the previous systems, but the input signal is controlled by the EEC system, rather than as function of engine timing and distributor armature position. The distributor, rotor, cap, and control module are unique to this system; the spark plugs and plug wires are the same as those used with the DuraSpark II system. Although the DuraSpark II and III control modules are similar in appearance, they cannot be interchanged between systems.

Some 1978 and later engines use a special DuraSpark Dual Mode ignition control module. The module is equipped with an altitude sensor, an economy modulator, or pressure switches (turbocharged engines only). This module, when combined with the additional switches and sensor, varies the base engine timing ac-

cording to altitude and engine load conditions. DuraSpark Dual Mode ignition control modules have three wiring harness from the module.

1981 49-state and 1982 Canadian 4-140 engines with automatic transmissions have Dual Mode Crank Retard ignition module, which has the same function as the DuraSpark II module plug an ignition timing retard function which is operational during engine cranking. The spark timing retard feature eases engine starting, but allows normal timing advance as soon as the engine is running. This module can be identified by the presence of a white connector shell on the four-pin connector at the module.

Some 1981 and later DuraSpark II systems

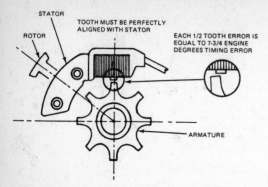

Static timing position, V8 engine; V6 similar

used with some 8-255 and 8-302 cu. in. engines are quipped with a Universal Ignition Module (UIM) which includes a run-retard function. The operation of the module is basically the same as the DuraSpark Dual Mode module.

The Universal Distributor (EEC-IV) has a diecast base which incorporates an externally mounted TFI-IV ignition module, and contains a Hall Effect vane switch stator assembly and provision for fixed octane adjustment. No distributor calibration is required and initial timing adjustment is normally not required. The primary function of the EEC-IV Universal Distributor system is to direct high secondary voltage to the spark plugs. In addition, the distributor supplies crankshaft position and frequency information to a computer using a profile Ignition Pickup. The Hall Effect switch in the distributor consists of a Hall Effect device on one side and a magnet on the other side. A rotary cup which has windows and tabs rotates and passes through the space between the device and the magnet. When a window is between the sides of the switch the magnetic path is not completed and the switch is Off, sending no signal. When a tab passes between the switch the magnetic path is completed and the Hall Effect Device is turned On and a signal is sent. The voltage pulse (signal) is used by is EEC-IV system for sensing crankshaft position and computing the desired spark advance based on engine demand and calibration.

DURASPARK OPERATION

With the ignition switch **ON**, the primary circuit is on and the ignition coil is energized. When the armature spokes approach the magnetic pickup coil assembly, they induce the voltage which tells the amplifier to turn the coil primary current off. A timing circuit in the amplifier module will turn the current on again after

Test Sequence

	Test Voltage Between	Should Be	If Not, Conduct
1980–82			
Key On	Socket #4 and Engine Ground	Battery Voltage ±0.1 Volt	Module Bias Test
	Socket #1 and Engine Ground	Battery Voltage ±0.1 Volt	Battery Source Test
Cranking	Socket #5 and Engine Ground	8 to 12 volts	Cranking Test
	Jumper #1 to #8—Read Coil "Bat" Term & Engine Ground	more than 6 volts	Starting Circuit Test
	Sockets #7 and #3	½ volt minimum wiggle	Distributor Hardware Test
Key Off	Sockets #7 and #3 Socket #8 and Engine Ground Socket #7 and Engine Ground Socket #3 and Engine Ground	400 to 800 ohms 0 ohms more than 70,000 ohms more than 70,000 ohms	Magnetic Pick-up (Stator) Test
	Socket #4 and Coil Tower	7000 to 13,000 ohms	Coil Test
	Socket #1 and Coil "Bat" Term	1.0 to 2.0 ohms Breakerless & Dura Spark II	
		0.5 to 1.5 ohms Dura-Spark I	
	Socket #1 and Engine Ground	more than 4.0 ohms	Short Test
	Socket #4 and Coil "Bat" Term (Except Dura-Spark I)	1.0 to 2.0 ohms Breakerless	Resistance Wire Test
		0.7 to 1.7 ohms Dura Spark II	

IGNITION SYSTEM
II. Primary (Low Voltage) Portion—A. Dura Spark II

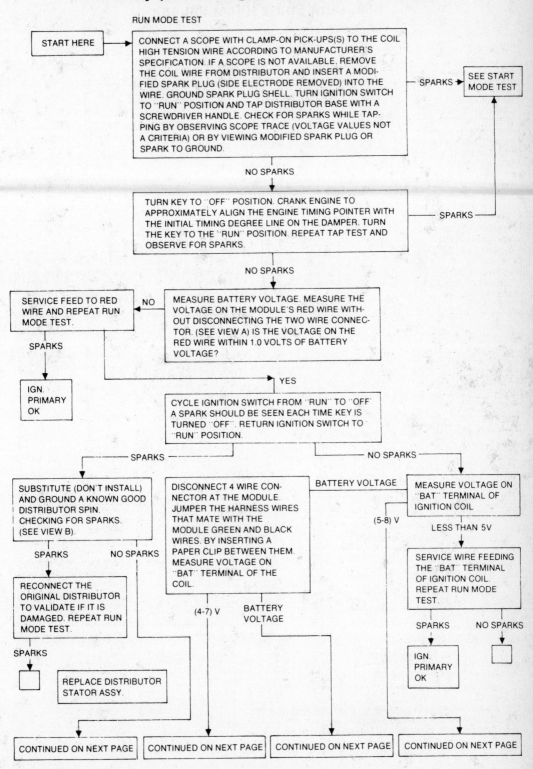

IGNITION SYSTEM (CONTINUED)
II. Primary (Low Voltage) Portion (continued)
A. Dura Spark II (continued)

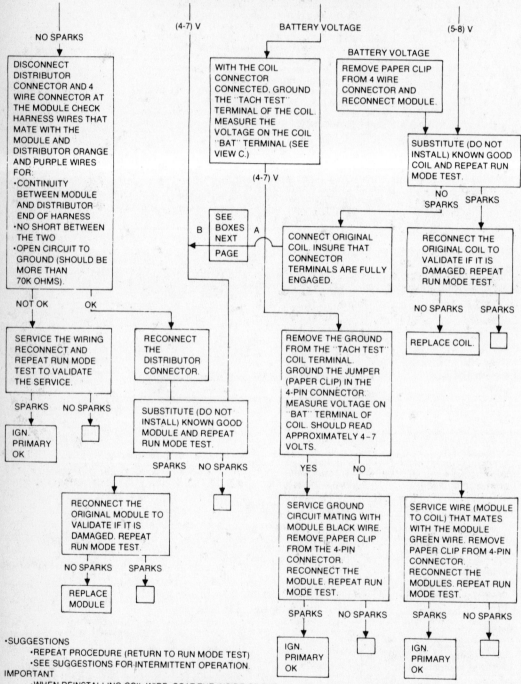

NO SPARKS

DISCONNECT DISTRIBUTOR CONNECTOR AND 4 WIRE CONNECTOR AT THE MODULE CHECK HARNESS WIRES THAT MATE WITH THE MODULE AND DISTRIBUTOR ORANGE AND PURPLE WIRES FOR:
•CONTINUITY BETWEEN MODULE AND DISTRIBUTOR END OF HARNESS
•NO SHORT BETWEEN THE TWO
•OPEN CIRCUIT TO GROUND (SHOULD BE MORE THAN 70K OHMS).

(4-7) V

BATTERY VOLTAGE

WITH THE COIL CONNECTOR CONNECTED, GROUND THE "TACH TEST" TERMINAL OF THE COIL. MEASURE THE VOLTAGE ON THE COIL "BAT" TERMINAL (SEE VIEW C.)

BATTERY VOLTAGE

(5-8) V

REMOVE PAPER CLIP FROM 4 WIRE CONNECTOR AND RECONNECT MODULE.

SUBSTITUTE (DO NOT INSTALL) KNOWN GOOD COIL AND REPEAT RUN MODE TEST.

(4-7) V

SEE BOXES NEXT PAGE

B   A

CONNECT ORIGINAL COIL. INSURE THAT CONNECTOR TERMINALS ARE FULLY ENGAGED.

NO SPARKS   SPARKS

RECONNECT THE ORIGINAL COIL TO VALIDATE IF IT IS DAMAGED. REPEAT RUN MODE TEST.

NOT OK   OK

NO SPARKS   SPARKS

SERVICE THE WIRING RECONNECT AND REPEAT RUN MODE TEST TO VALIDATE THE SERVICE.

RECONNECT THE DISTRIBUTOR CONNECTOR.

REMOVE THE GROUND FROM THE "TACH TEST" COIL TERMINAL. GROUND THE JUMPER (PAPER CLIP) IN THE 4-PIN CONNECTOR. MEASURE VOLTAGE ON "BAT" TERMINAL OF COIL. SHOULD READ APPROXIMATELY 4–7 VOLTS.

REPLACE COIL.

SPARKS   NO SPARKS

IGN. PRIMARY OK

SUBSTITUTE (DO NOT INSTALL) KNOWN GOOD MODULE AND REPEAT RUN MODE TEST.

SPARKS   NO SPARKS

YES   NO

RECONNECT THE ORIGINAL MODULE TO VALIDATE IF IT IS DAMAGED. REPEAT RUN MODE TEST.

SERVICE GROUND CIRCUIT MATING WITH MODULE BLACK WIRE. REMOVE PAPER CLIP FROM THE 4-PIN CONNECTOR. RECONNECT THE MODULE. REPEAT RUN MODE TEST.

SERVICE WIRE (MODULE TO COIL) THAT MATES WITH THE MODULE GREEN WIRE. REMOVE PAPER CLIP FROM 4-PIN CONNECTOR. RECONNECT THE MODULES. REPEAT RUN MODE TEST.

NO SPARKS   SPARKS

REPLACE MODULE

SPARKS   NO SPARKS

IGN. PRIMARY OK

SPARKS   NO SPARKS

IGN. PRIMARY OK

•SUGGESTIONS
    •REPEAT PROCEDURE (RETURN TO RUN MODE TEST)
    •SEE SUGGESTIONS FOR INTERMITTENT OPERATION.
IMPORTANT
    •WHEN REINSTALLING COIL WIRE. COAT THE INSIDE OF THE BOOT WITH SILICONE GREASE (D7AZ-19A331-A OR EQUIVALENT) USING SMALL. CLEAN SCREWDRIVER BLADE.

IGNITION SYSTEM (CONTINUED)
II. Primary (Low Voltage) Portion (Continued)
A. Dura Spark II (continued)

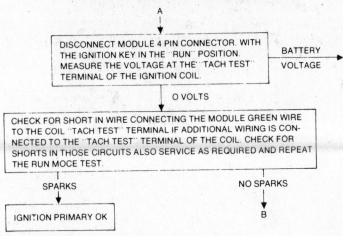

the coil field has collapsed. When the current is on, it flows from the battery through the ignition switch, the primary windings of the ignition coil, and through the amplifier module circuits to ground. When the current is off, the magnetic field built up in the ignition coil is allowed to collapse, inducing a high voltage into the secondary windings of the coil. High voltage is produced each time the field is thus built up and collapsed. When DuraSpark is used in conjunction with the EEC, the EEC computer tells the DuraSpark module when to turn the coil primary current off or on. In this case, the armature position is only a reference signal of engine timing, used by the EEC computer in combination with other reference signals to determine optimum ignition spark timing.

The high voltage flows through the coil high tension lead to the distributor cap where the rotor distributes it to one of the spark plug terminals in the distributor cap. This process is repeated for every power stroke of the engine.

Ignition system troubles are caused by a failure in the primary and/or the secondary circuit; incorrect ignition timing; or incorrect distributor advance. Circuit failures may be caused by shorts, corroded or dirty terminals, loose connections, defective wire insulation, cracked distributor cap or rotor, defective pick-up coil assembly or amplifier module, defective distributor points or fouled spark plugs.

If an engine starting or operating trouble is attributed to the ignition system, start the engine and verify the complaint. On engines that will not start, be sure that there is gasoline in the fuel tank and the fuel is reaching the carbu-

retor. Then locate the ignition system problem using the following procedures.

TROUBLESHOOTING DURASPARK I

The following DuraSpark II troubleshooting procedures may be used on DuraSpark I systems with a few variations. The DuraSpark I module has internal connections which shut off the primary circuit in the run mode when the engine stalls. To perform the above troubleshooting procedures, it is necessary to by-pass these connections. However, with these connections by-passed, the current flow in the primary becomes so great that it will damage both the ignition coil and module unless a ballast resistor is installed in series with the primary circuit at the BAT terminal of the ignition coil. Such a resistor is available from Ford (Motorcraft part number DY-36). A 1.3Ω, 100 watt wire-wound power resistor can also be used.

To install the resistor, proceed as follows.
WARNING: *The resistor will become very hot during testing.*

1. Release the BAT terminal lead from the coil by inserting a paper cup through the hole in the rear of the horseshoe coil connector and manipulating it against the locking tab in the connector until the lead comes free.

2. Insert a paper clip in the BAT terminal of the connector of the coil. Using jumper leads, connect the ballast resistor as shown.

3. Using a straight pin, pierce both the red and white leads of the module to short these two together. This will by-pass the internal connections of the module which turn off the ignition circuit when the engine is not running.

IGNITION SYSTEM (CONTINUED)
II. Primary (Low Voltage) Portion (continued)
A. Dura Spark II (continued)

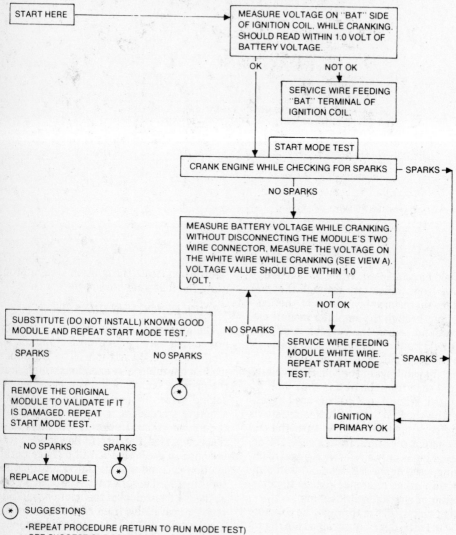

START HERE → MEASURE VOLTAGE ON "BAT" SIDE OF IGNITION COIL, WHILE CRANKING. SHOULD READ WITHIN 1.0 VOLT OF BATTERY VOLTAGE.

OK / NOT OK

NOT OK → SERVICE WIRE FEEDING "BAT" TERMINAL OF IGNITION COIL.

START MODE TEST
CRANK ENGINE WHILE CHECKING FOR SPARKS — SPARKS →

NO SPARKS

MEASURE BATTERY VOLTAGE WHILE CRANKING. WITHOUT DISCONNECTING THE MODULE'S TWO WIRE CONNECTOR, MEASURE THE VOLTAGE ON THE WHITE WIRE WHILE CRANKING (SEE VIEW A). VOLTAGE VALUE SHOULD BE WITHIN 1.0 VOLT.

NOT OK

NOT OK → SERVICE WIRE FEEDING MODULE WHITE WIRE. REPEAT START MODE TEST. — SPARKS →

NO SPARKS

SUBSTITUTE (DO NOT INSTALL) KNOWN GOOD MODULE AND REPEAT START MODE TEST.

SPARKS / NO SPARKS

REMOVE THE ORIGINAL MODULE TO VALIDATE IF IT IS DAMAGED. REPEAT START MODE TEST.

NO SPARKS / SPARKS

REPLACE MODULE.

IGNITION PRIMARY OK

(*) SUGGESTIONS
•REPEAT PROCEDURE (RETURN TO RUN MODE TEST)
•SEE SUGGESTIONS FOR INTERMITTENT OPERATION.

IMPORTANT
•WHEN REINSTALLING COIL WIRE, COAT THE INSIDE OF THE BOOT WITH SILICONE GREASE (D7AZ-19A331-A OR EQUIVALENT DOW 111 OR GE-G627) USING A SMALL, CLEAN SCREWDRIVER BLADE.

CAUTION: *Pierce the wires only AFTER the ballast resistor is in place or you could damage the ignition coil and module.*

4. With the ballast resistor and by-pass in place, proceed with the DuraSpark II troubleshooting procedures.

TROUBLESHOOTING DURASPARK II

The following procedures can be used to determine whether the ignition system is working or not. If these procedures fail to correct the problem, a full troubleshooting procedure should be performed.

Preliminary Checks

1. Check the battery's state of charge and connections.

2. Inspect all wires and connections for breaks, cuts, abrasions, or burn spots. Repair as necessary.

3. Unplug all connectors one at a time and inspect for corroded or burned contacts. Repair

RUN MODE TEST

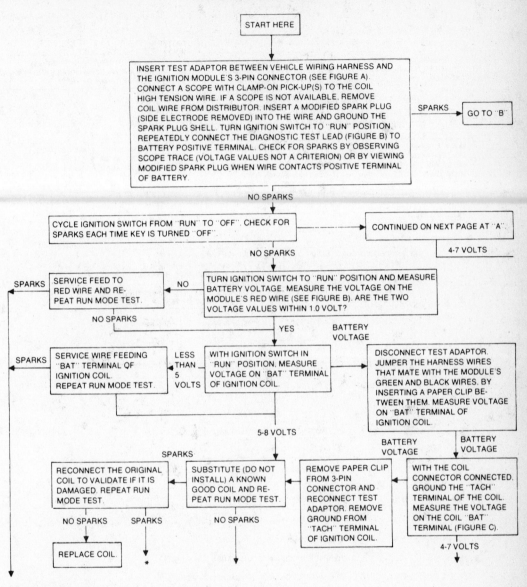

START HERE

INSERT TEST ADAPTOR BETWEEN VEHICLE WIRING HARNESS AND THE IGNITION MODULE'S 3-PIN CONNECTOR (SEE FIGURE A). CONNECT A SCOPE WITH CLAMP-ON PICK-UP(S) TO THE COIL HIGH TENSION WIRE. IF A SCOPE IS NOT AVAILABLE, REMOVE COIL WIRE FROM DISTRIBUTOR. INSERT A MODIFIED SPARK PLUG (SIDE ELECTRODE REMOVED) INTO THE WIRE AND GROUND THE SPARK PLUG SHELL. TURN IGNITION SWITCH TO "RUN" POSITION. REPEATEDLY CONNECT THE DIAGNOSTIC TEST LEAD (FIGURE B) TO BATTERY POSITIVE TERMINAL. CHECK FOR SPARKS BY OBSERVING SCOPE TRACE (VOLTAGE VALUES NOT A CRITERION) OR BY VIEWING MODIFIED SPARK PLUG WHEN WIRE CONTACTS POSITIVE TERMINAL OF BATTERY.

SPARKS → GO TO "B"

NO SPARKS

CYCLE IGNITION SWITCH FROM "RUN" TO "OFF". CHECK FOR SPARKS EACH TIME KEY IS TURNED "OFF".

CONTINUED ON NEXT PAGE AT "A".

4-7 VOLTS

NO SPARKS

SPARKS ← SERVICE FEED TO RED WIRE AND RE-PEAT RUN MODE TEST. ← NO ← TURN IGNITION SWITCH TO "RUN" POSITION AND MEASURE BATTERY VOLTAGE. MEASURE THE VOLTAGE ON THE MODULE'S RED WIRE (SEE FIGURE B). ARE THE TWO VOLTAGE VALUES WITHIN 1.0 VOLT?

NO SPARKS

YES

BATTERY VOLTAGE

SPARKS ← SERVICE WIRE FEEDING "BAT" TERMINAL OF IGNITION COIL. REPEAT RUN MODE TEST. ← LESS THAN 5 VOLTS ← WITH IGNITION SWITCH IN "RUN" POSITION, MEASURE VOLTAGE ON "BAT" TERMINAL OF IGNITION COIL.

DISCONNECT TEST ADAPTOR. JUMPER THE HARNESS WIRES THAT MATE WITH THE MODULE'S GREEN AND BLACK WIRES. BY INSERTING A PAPER CLIP BE-TWEEN THEM. MEASURE VOLTAGE ON "BAT" TERMINAL OF IGNITION COIL.

5-8 VOLTS

BATTERY VOLTAGE

BATTERY VOLTAGE

SPARKS

RECONNECT THE ORIGINAL COIL TO VALIDATE IF IT IS DAMAGED. REPEAT RUN MODE TEST. ← SUBSTITUTE (DO NOT INSTALL) A KNOWN GOOD COIL AND RE-PEAT RUN MODE TEST. ← REMOVE PAPER CLIP FROM 3-PIN CONNECTOR AND RECONNECT TEST ADAPTOR. REMOVE GROUND FROM "TACH" TERMINAL OF IGNITION COIL. ← WITH THE COIL CONNECTOR CONNECTED, GROUND THE "TACH" TERMINAL OF THE COIL. MEASURE THE VOLTAGE ON THE COIL "BAT" TERMINAL (FIGURE C).

NO SPARKS   SPARKS   NO SPARKS

4-7 VOLTS

REPLACE COIL.

*

*SUGGESTIONS:

•REPEAT PROCEDURE (START AT RUN MODE TEST)

•SEE SUGGESTIONS FOR INTERMITTENT OPERATION

and plug connectors back together. DO NOT re-move the dielectric compound in the connectors.

4. Check for loose or damaged spark plug or coil wires. A wire resistance check is given at the end of this section. If the boots or nipples are removed on 8mm ignition wires, reline the inside of each with new silicone dielectric com-pound (Motorcraft WA-10).

Special Tools

To perform the following tests, two special tools are needed; the ignition test jumper shown in the illustration and a modified spark plug. Use the illustration to assembly the igni-tion test jumper. The test jumper must be used when performing the following tests. The modi-fied spark plug is basically a spark plug with the

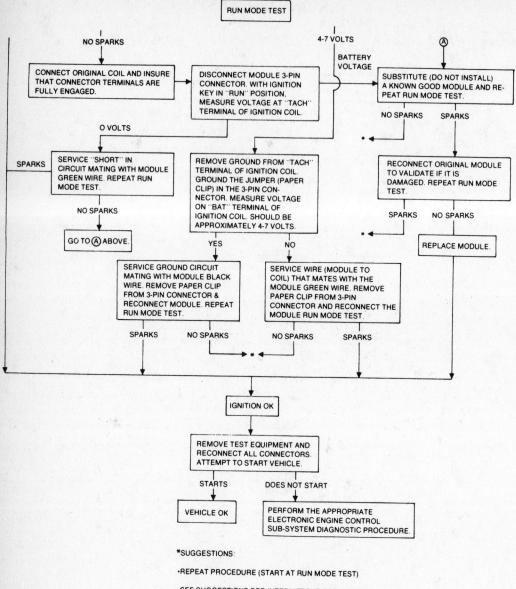

RUN MODE TEST

NO SPARKS

CONNECT ORIGINAL COIL AND INSURE THAT CONNECTOR TERMINALS ARE FULLY ENGAGED.

DISCONNECT MODULE 3-PIN CONNECTOR. WITH IGNITION KEY IN "RUN" POSITION, MEASURE VOLTAGE AT "TACH" TERMINAL OF IGNITION COIL.

4-7 VOLTS

BATTERY VOLTAGE

Ⓐ

SUBSTITUTE (DO NOT INSTALL) A KNOWN GOOD MODULE AND RE-PEAT RUN MODE TEST.

NO SPARKS   SPARKS

O VOLTS

SPARKS

SERVICE "SHORT" IN CIRCUIT MATING WITH MODULE GREEN WIRE. REPEAT RUN MODE TEST.

REMOVE GROUND FROM "TACH" TERMINAL OF IGNITION COIL. GROUND THE JUMPER (PAPER CLIP) IN THE 3-PIN CON-NECTOR. MEASURE VOLTAGE ON "BAT" TERMINAL OF IGNITION COIL. SHOULD BE APPROXIMATELY 4-7 VOLTS.

RECONNECT ORIGINAL MODULE TO VALIDATE IF IT IS DAMAGED. REPEAT RUN MODE TEST.

NO SPARKS

GO TO Ⓐ ABOVE.

YES   NO

SPARKS   NO SPARKS

REPLACE MODULE.

SERVICE GROUND CIRCUIT MATING WITH MODULE BLACK WIRE. REMOVE PAPER CLIP FROM 3-PIN CONNECTOR & RECONNECT MODULE. REPEAT RUN MODE TEST.

SERVICE WIRE (MODULE TO COIL) THAT MATES WITH THE MODULE GREEN WIRE. REMOVE PAPER CLIP FROM 3-PIN CONNECTOR AND RECONNECT THE MODULE RUN MODE TEST.

SPARKS   NO SPARKS   NO SPARKS   SPARKS

IGNITION OK

REMOVE TEST EQUIPMENT AND RECONNECT ALL CONNECTORS. ATTEMPT TO START VEHICLE.

STARTS   DOES NOT START

VEHICLE OK

PERFORM THE APPROPRIATE ELECTRONIC ENGINE CONTROL SUB-SYSTEM DIAGNOSTIC PROCEDURE.

*SUGGESTIONS:

•REPEAT PROCEDURE (START AT RUN MODE TEST)

•SEE SUGGESTIONS FOR INTERMITTENT OPERATION

side electrode removed. Ford makes a special tool called a Spark Tester for this purpose, which besides not having a side electrode is equipped with a spring clip so that it can be grounded to engine metal. It is recommended that the Spark Tester be used as there is less change of being shocked.

Run Mode Spark Test

NOTE: *The wire colors given here are the main colors of the wires, not the dots or hashmarks.*

STEP 1

1. Remove the distributor cap and rotor from the distributor.

2. With the ignition off, turn the engine over by hand until one of the teeth on the distributor armature aligns with the magnet in the pickup coil.

3. Remove the coil wire from the distributor cap. On 1978 and later models, install the modified spark plug (see Special Tools, above) in the coil wire terminal and using heavy gloves and insulated pliers, hold the spark plug shell against the engine block.

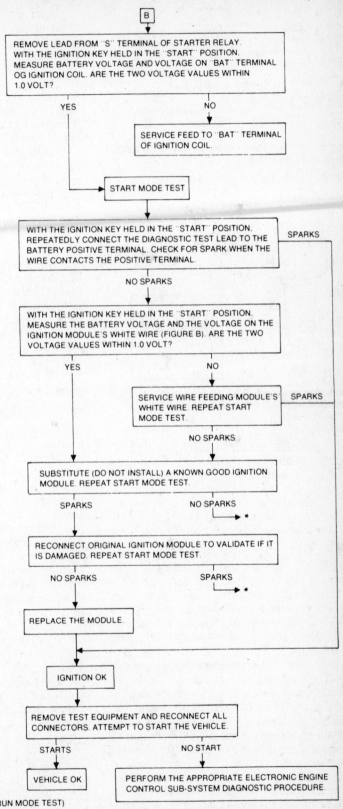

B

REMOVE LEAD FROM "S" TERMINAL OF STARTER RELAY. WITH THE IGNITION KEY HELD IN THE "START" POSITION. MEASURE BATTERY VOLTAGE AND VOLTAGE ON "BAT" TERMINAL OG IGNITION COIL. ARE THE TWO VOLTAGE VALUES WITHIN 1.0 VOLT?

YES

NO

SERVICE FEED TO "BAT" TERMINAL OF IGNITION COIL.

START MODE TEST

WITH THE IGNITION KEY HELD IN THE "START" POSITION, REPEATEDLY CONNECT THE DIAGNOSTIC TEST LEAD TO THE BATTERY POSITIVE TERMINAL. CHECK FOR SPARK WHEN THE WIRE CONTACTS THE POSITIVE TERMINAL.

SPARKS

NO SPARKS

WITH THE IGNITION KEY HELD IN THE "START" POSITION, MEASURE THE BATTERY VOLTAGE AND THE VOLTAGE ON THE IGNITION MODULE'S WHITE WIRE (FIGURE B). ARE THE TWO VOLTAGE VALUES WITHIN 1.0 VOLT?

YES

NO

SERVICE WIRE FEEDING MODULE'S WHITE WIRE. REPEAT START MODE TEST.

SPARKS

NO SPARKS

SUBSTITUTE (DO NOT INSTALL) A KNOWN GOOD IGNITION MODULE. REPEAT START MODE TEST.

SPARKS

NO SPARKS
*

RECONNECT ORIGINAL IGNITION MODULE TO VALIDATE IF IT IS DAMAGED. REPEAT START MODE TEST.

NO SPARKS

SPARKS
*

REPLACE THE MODULE.

IGNITION OK

REMOVE TEST EQUIPMENT AND RECONNECT ALL CONNECTORS. ATTEMPT TO START THE VEHICLE.

STARTS

NO START

VEHICLE OK

PERFORM THE APPROPRIATE ELECTRONIC ENGINE CONTROL SUB-SYSTEM DIAGNOSTIC PROCEDURE.

*SUGGESTIONS:

•REPEAT PROCEDURE (START AT RUN MODE TEST)

•SEE SUGGESTIONS FOR INTERMITTENT OPERATION

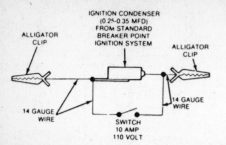

Test jumper wire switch used for testing Dura Spark ignition systems

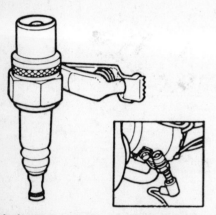

Spark plug tester; actually a modified spark plug (side electrode removed) with a spring for ground

4. Turn the ignition to RUN (not START) and tap the distributor body with a screwdriver handle. There should be a spark at the modified spark plug or at the coil wire terminal.

5. If a good spark is evident, the primary circuit is OK: perform the Start Mode Spark Test. If there is no spark, proceed to STEP 2.

STEP 2

1. Unplug the module connector(s) which contain(s) the green and black module leads.

2. In the harness side of the connector(s), connect the special test jumper (see Special Tools, above) between the leads which connect to the green and black leads of the module pig tails. Use paper clips on connector socket holes to make contact. Do not allow clips to ground.

3. Turn the ignition switch to RUN (not START) and close the test jumper switch. Leave closed for about 1 second, then open. Repeat several times. There should be a spark each time the switch is opened. On DuraSpark I systems, close the test switch for 10 seconds is adequate.

4. If there is no spark, the problem is probably in the primary circuit through the ignition switch, the coil, the green lead or the black lead, or the ground connection in the distributor; Perform STEP 3. If there is a spark, the prima-

ry circuit wiring and coil are probably OK. The problem is probably in the distributor pick-up, the module red wire, or the module: perform STEP 6.

STEP 3

1. Disconnect the test jumper lead from the black lead and connect it to a good ground. Turn the test jumper switch on and off several times as in STEP 2.

2. If there is no spark, the problem is probably in the green lead, the coil, or the coil feed circuit: perform STEP 5.

3. If there is spark, the problem is probably in the black lead or the distributor ground connection: perform STEP 4.

STEP 4

1. Connect an ohmmeter between the black lead and ground. With the meter on its lowest scale, there should be no measurable resistance in the circuit. If there is resistance, check the distributor ground connection and the black lead from the module. Repair as necessary, remove the ohmmeter, plug in all connections and repeat STEP 1.

2. If there is no resistance, the primary ground wiring is OK: perform STEP 6.

STEP 5

1. Disconnect the test jumper from the green lead and ground and connect it between the TACH-TEST terminal of the coil and a good ground to the engine.

2. With the ignition switch in the RUN position, turn the jumper switch on. Hold it on for about 1 second then turn it off as in Step 2. Repeat several times. There should be a spark each time the switch in turned off. If there is no spark, the problem is probably in the primary circuit running through the ignition switch to the coil BAT terminal, or in the coil itself. Check coil resistance (test given later in this section), and check the coil for internal shorts or opens. Check the coil feed circuit for opens, shorts, or high resistance. Repair as necessary, reconnect all connectors and repeat STEP 1. If there is spark, the coil and its feed circuit are OK. The problem could be in the green lead between the coil and the module. Check for an open or short, repair as necessary, reconnect all connectors and repeat STEP 1.

STEP 6

To perform this step, a voltmeter which is not combined with a dwell meter is needed. The slight needle oscillations (½v) you'll be looking for may not be detectable on the combined voltmeter/dwell meter unit.

1. Connect a voltmeter between the orange

and purple leads on the harness side of the module connectors.

CAUTION: *On catalytic converter equipped cars, disconnect the air supply line between the Thermactor by-pass valve and the manifold before cranking the engine with the ignition off. This will prevent damage to the catalytic converter. After testing, run the engine* *for at least 3 minutes before reconnecting the by-pass valve, to clear excess fuel from the exhaust system.*

2. Set the voltmeter on its lowest scale and crank the engine. The meter needle should oscillate slightly (about ½v). If the meter does not oscillate, check the circuit through the magnetic pick-up in the distributor for open, shorts,

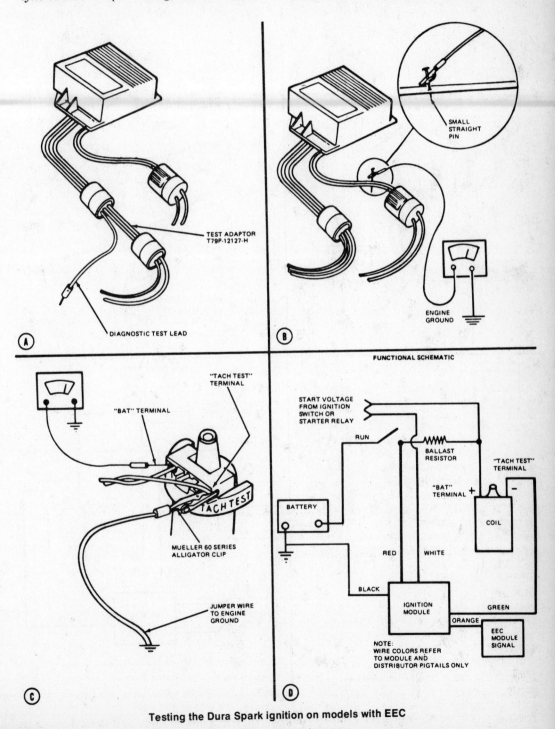

Testing the Dura Spark ignition on models with EEC

shorts to ground and resistance. Resistance between the orange and purple leads should be 400-1,000Ω, and between each lead and ground should be more than 70,000Ω. Repair as necessary, reconnect all connectors and repeat STEP 1.

If the meter oscillates, the problem is proba-bly in the power feed to the module (red wire) or in the module itself: proceed to STEP 7.

STEP 7

1. Remove all meters and jumpers and plug in all connectors.

2. Turn the ignition switch to the RUN posi-

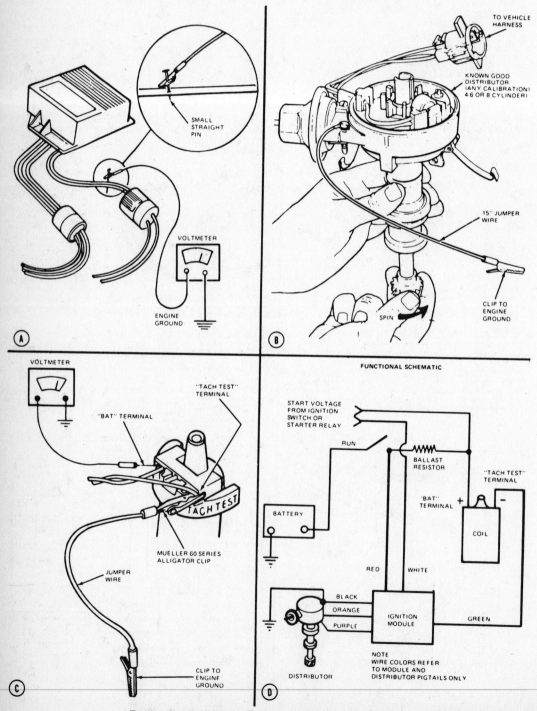

Testing the Dura Spark ignition on models without EEC

tion and measure voltage between the battery positive terminal and engine ground. It should be 12 volts.

3. Next, measure voltage between the red lead of the module and engine ground. To mark this measurement, it will be necessary to pierce the red wire with a straight pin and connect the voltmeter to the straight pin and to ground. DO NOT ALLOW THE STRAIGHT PIN TO GROUND ITSELF!

4. The two readings should be within one volt of each other. If not within one volt, the problem is in the power feed to the red lead. Check for shorts, open, or high resistance and correct as necessary. After repairs, repeat Step 1.

If the readings are within one volt, the problem is probably in the module. Replace it with a good module and repeat STEP 1. If this corrects the problem, reconnect the old module and repeat STEP 1. If the problem returns, permanently install the new module.

Start Mode Spark Test

NOTE: *The wire colors given here are the main colors of the wires, not the dots or hashmarks.*

1. Remove the coil wire from the distributor cap. Install the modified spark plug mentioned under Special Tools, above, in the coil wire and ground it to engine metal either by its spring clip (Spark Tester) or by holding the spark plug shell against the engine block with insulated pliers.

NOTE: *See CAUTION under STEP 6 of Run Mode Spark Test, above.*

2. Have an assistant crank the engine using the ignition switch and check for spark. If there is good spark, the problem is probably in distributor cap, rotor, ignition cables or spark plugs. If there is no spark, proceed to Step 3.

3. Measure the battery voltage. Next, measure the voltage at the white wire of the module while cranking the engine. To mark this measurement, it will be necessary to pierce the white wire with a straight pin and connect the voltmeter to the straight pin and to ground. DO NOT ALLOW THE STRAIGHT PIN TO GROUND ITSELF. The battery voltage and the voltage at the white wire should be within 1 volt of each other. If the readings are not within 1 volt of each other, check and repair the feed through the ignition switch to the white wire. Recheck for spark (Step 1). If the readings are within 1 volt of each other, or if there is still no spark after the power feed to white wire is repaired, proceed to Step 4.

4. Measure the coil BAT terminal voltage while cranking the engine. The reading should be within 1 volt of battery voltage. If the read-

ings are not within 1 volt of each other, check and repair the feed through the ignition switch to the coil. If the readings are within 1 volt of each other, the problem is probably in the ignition module. Substitute another module and repeat the test for spark (Step 1).

TFI SYSTEM TESTING

NOTE: *If the engine operates but has no power, the problem could be in the EEC system. Check the initial timing, if the engine is operating at a fixed 10° BTDC the system is in fail-safe mode. Have the EEC system check with necessary diagnostic equipment.*

After performing any test which requires piercing a wire with a straight pin, remove the straight pin and seal the holes in the wire with silicone sealer.

Ignition Coil Secondary Voltage

1. Disconnect the secondary (high voltage) coil wire from the distributor cap and install a spark tester (see Special Tools, located with the DuraSpark Troubleshooting) between the coil wire and ground.

2. Crank the engine. A good, strong spark should be noted at the spark tester. If spark is noted, but the engine will not start, check the spark plugs, spark plug wiring, and fuel system. If there is no spark at the tester:

a. Check the ignition coil secondary wire resistance; it should be no more than $5,000\Omega$ per inch.

b. Inspect the ignition coil for damage and/or carbon tracking.

c. With the distributor cap removed, verify that the distributor shaft turns with the engine; if it does not, repair the engine as required.

d. If the fault was not found in a, b, or c, proceed to the next test.

Ignition Coil Primary Circuit Switching

1. Insert a small straight pin in the wire which runs from the coil negative (–) terminal to the TFI module, about 1" (25.4mm) from the module.

CAUTION: *The pin must not touch ground.*

2. Connect a 12VDC test lamp between the straight pin and an engine ground.

3. Crank the engine, noting the operation of the test lamp. If the test lamp flashes, proceed to the next test. If the test lamp lights but does not flash, proceed to the Wiring Harness test. If the test lamp does not light at all, proceed to the Primary Circuit Continuity test.

Ignition Coil Resistance

Replace the ignition coil if the resistance is out of the specification range.

Wiring Harness

1. Disconnect the wiring harness connector from the TFI module; the connector tabs must be PUSHED to disengage the connector. Inspect the connector form damage, dirt, and corrosion.

2. Attach the negative lead of a voltmeter to the base of the distributor. Attach the other voltmeter lead to a small straight pin.

   a. With the ignition switch in the RUN position, insert the straight pin onto the NO.1 terminal of the TFI module connector. Note the voltage reading and proceed to b.

   b. With the ignition switch in the RUN position, move the straight pin to the No. 2 connector terminal. Again, note the voltage reading, then proceed to c.

   c. Move the straight pin to the No. 3 connector terminal, then turn the ignition switch to the START position. Note the voltage reading then turn the Ignition OFF.

3. The voltage readings from a, b, and c should all be at least 90% of the available battery voltage. If the readings are okay, proceed to the Stator Assembly and Module test. If any reading is less than 90% of the battery voltage, inspect the wiring, connectors, and/or ignition switch for defects. If the voltage is low only at the No. 1 terminal, proceed to the ignition coil primary voltage test.

Stator Assembly and Module

1. Remove the distributor from the engine.

2. Remove the TFI module from the distributor.

3. Inspect the distributor terminals, ground screw, and stator wiring for damage. Repair as necessary.

4. Measure the resistance of the stator assembly, using an ohmmeter. If the ohmmeter reading is 800-975Ω, the stator is okay, but the TFI module must be replaced. If the ohmmeter reading is less than 800Ω or more than 975Ω; the TFI module is okay, but the stator assembly must be replaced.

5. Reinstall the TFI module and the distributor.

Primary Circuit Continuity

This test is performed in the same manner as the previous Wiring Harness test, but only the NO. 1 terminal conductor is tested (ignition switch in RUN position). If the voltage is less than 90% of the available battery voltage, proceed to the next test.

Ignition Coil Primary Voltage

1. Attach the negative lead of a voltmeter to the distributor base.

2. Turn the ignition switch ON and connect the positive voltmeter lead to the negative (–) ignition coil terminal. Note the voltage reading and turn the ignition OFF. If the voltmeter reading is less than 90% of the available battery voltage, inspect the wiring between the ignition module and the negative (–) coil terminal, then proceed to the last test, which follows.

Ignition Coil Supply Voltage

1. Attach the negative lead of a voltmeter to the distributor base.

2. Turn the ignition switch ON and connect the positive voltmeter lead to the positive (+) ignition coil terminal.

NOTE: *Note the voltage reading then turn the ignition OFF.*

If the voltage reading is at least 90% of the battery voltage, yet the engine will still not run: check the ignition coil connector and terminals for corrosion, dirt, and/or damage. Replace the ignition switch if the connectors and terminals are okay.

3. Connect any remaining wiring.

GENERAL TESTING – ALL SYSTEMS

Ignition Coil Test

The ignition coil must be diagnosed separately from the rest of the ignition system.

1. Primary resistance is measured between the two primary (low voltage) coil terminals, with the coil connector disconnected and the ignition switch off. Primary resistance must be 0.71-0.77Ω for DuraSpark I. For DuraSpark II, it must be 1.13-1.23Ω. For TFI systems, the primary resistance should be 0.3-1.0Ω.

2. On DuraSpark ignitions, the secondary resistance is measured between the BATT and high voltage (secondary) terminals of the ignition coil with the ignition off, and wiring from the coil disconnected. Secondary resistance must be 7,350-8,250Ω on DuraSpark I systems. DuraSpark II figure is 7,700-9,300Ω. For TFI systems, the primary resistance should be 8,000-11,500Ω.

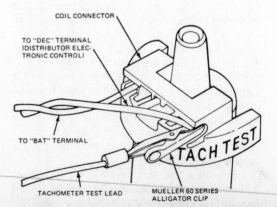

COIL CONNECTOR

TO "DEC" TERMINAL
(DISTRIBUTOR ELEC-
TRONIC CONTROL)

TO "BAT" TERMINAL

TACH TEST

TACHOMETER TEST LEAD   MUELLER 60 SERIES
ALLIGATOR CLIP

Attaching tachometer lead to coil connector

Connector Terminal	Wire Circuit	Ign Switch Position
Term 2	To ign coil neg (−) term	Run
Term 3	Run circuit	Run & Start
Term 4	Start circuit	Start

3. If resistance tests are all right, but the coil is still suspected, test the coil on a coil tester by following the test equipment manufacturer's instructions for a standard coil. If the reading differs from the original test, check for a defective harness.

Resistance Wire Test

Replace the resistance wire if it doesn't show a resistance of 1.05-1.15Ω for DuraSpark II. The resistance wire isn't used on DuraSpark I or TFI systems.

Spark Plug Wire Resistance

Resistance on these wires must not exceed 5,000Ω per inch. To properly measure this, remove the wires from the plugs, and remove the distributor cap. Measure the resistance through the distributor cap at that end. Do not pierce any ignition wire for any reason. Measure only from the two ends.

NOTE: *Silicone grease must be re-applied to the spark plug wires whenever they are removed.*

When removing the wires from the spark plugs, a special tool such as the one pictured should be used. Do not pull on the wires. Grasp and twist the boot to remove the wire.

Whenever the high tension wires are removed from the plugs, coil, or distributor, silicone grease must be applied to the boot before reconnection. Use a clean small screwdriver blade to coat the entire interior surface with Ford silicone grease D7AZ-19A331-A, Dow Corning #111, or General Electric G-627.

Adjustments.

The air gap between the armature and magnetic pick-up coil in the distributor is not adjustable, nor are there any adjustments for the amplifier module. Inoperative components are simply replaced. Any attempt to connect components outside the vehicle may result in component failure.

IGNITION TIMING

Ignition timing is the measurement, in degrees of crankshaft rotation, of the point at which the spark plugs fire in each of the cylinders. It is measured in degrees before or after Top Dead Center (TDC) of the compression stroke. Ignition timing is controlled by turning the distributor body in the engine.

Ideally, the air/fuel mixture in the cylinder will be ignited by the spark plug just as the piston passes TDC of the compression stroke. If this happens, the piston will be beginning the power stroke just as the compressed and ignited air/fuel mixture starts to expand. The expansion of the air/fuel mixture starts to expand. The expansion of the air/fuel mixture then forces the piston down on the power stroke and turns the crankshaft.

Because it takes a fraction of a second for the spark plug to ignite the mixture in the cylinder, the spark plug must fire a little before the piston reaches TDC. Otherwise, the mixture will not be completely ignited as the piston passes TDC and the full power of the explosion will not be used by the engine.

The timing measurement is given in degrees of crankshaft rotation before the piston reaches TDC (BTDC). If the setting for the ignition timing is 5° BTDC, each spark plug must fire 5° before each piston reaches TDC. This only holds true, however, when the engine is at idle speed.

As the engine speed increases, the pistons go faster. The spark plugs have to ignite the fuel even sooner if it is to be completely ignited when the piston reaches TDC. To do this, the distributor has a means to advance the timing of the spark as the engine speed increases. This is accomplished by centrifugal weights within the distributor and a vacuum diaphragm mounted on the side of the distributor. It is necessary to disconnect the vacuum lines from the diaphragm when the ignition timing is being set.

If the ignition is set too far advanced (BTDC), the ignition and expansion of the fuel in the cylinder will occur too soon and tend to force the piston down while it is still traveling up. This causes engine ping. If the ignition spark is set tool far retarded after TDC (ATDC), the piston will have already passed TDC and started on its way down when the fuel is ignited. This will cause the piston to be forced down for only a portion of its travel. This will result in poor engine performance and lack of power.

The timing is best checked with a timing light. This device is usually connected in series with the No. 1 spark plug. The current that fires the spark plug also causes the timing light to flash.

There is a notch on the crankshaft pulley on 6-200 engines. A scale of degrees of crankshaft rotation is attached to the engine block in such a position that the notch will pass close by the scale. On the V6 and V8 engines, the scale is located on the crankshaft pulley and a pointer is attached to the engine block so that the scale will pass close by. When the engine is running, the timing light is aimed at the mark on the crankshaft pulley and the scale.

ADJUSTMENT

NOTE: *Some engines have monolithic timing set at the factory. The monolithic system uses a timing receptacle on the front of the engine which can be connected to digital read-out equipment, which electronically determines timing. Timing can also be adjusted in the conventional way. Many 1980 and later models are equipped with EEC engine controls. All ignition timing is controlled by the EEC module. Initial ignition timing is not adjustable and no attempt at adjustment should be made on EEC-III models, or models equipped with an indexed distributor base. For a description of EEC systems, refer to the Unit Repair sections on Electronic Ignition Systems and on Engine Controls. Requirements vary from model to model. Always refer to the Emissions Specification Sticker for exact timing procedures.*

1. Locate the timing marks and pointer on the lower engine pulley and engine's front cover.

2. Clean the marks and apply chalk or brightly colored paint to the pointer.

3. On 1981 and later models, if the ignition module has (-12A224-) as a basic part number, disconnect the two wire connector (yellow and black wires). On engines equipped with the EEC-IV system, disconnect the single white (Black on some models) wire connector near the distributor.

4. Attach a timing light and tachometer according to manufacturer's specifications.

5. Disconnect and plug all vacuum lines leading to the distributor.

6. Start the engine, allow it to warm to normal operating temperature, then set the idle to the specifications given on the underhood sticker (for timing).

7. On 1981 and later models equipped with the module mentioned in Step 3, jumper the pins in the module connector for the yellow and black wires.

8. Aim the timing light at the timing mark and pointer on the front of the engine. If the marks align when the timing light flashes, remove the timing light, set the idle to its proper specification, and connect the vacuum lines at the distributor. If the marks do not align when the light flashes, turn the engine off and loosen the distributor holddown clamp slightly.

9. Start the engine again, and observe the alignment of the timing marks. To advance the timing, turn the distributor counterclockwise

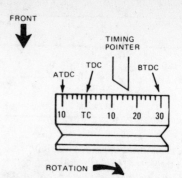

Crankshaft timing marks—4 cyl. 140 engine

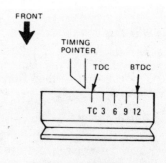

Crankshaft timing marks V6 170 engine

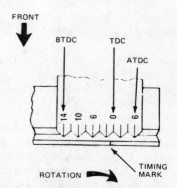

Crankshaft timing marks 6 cyl. 200 engine

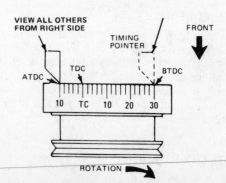

Crankshaft timing marks V6 232 and V8 255, 302 engines

on 6-200 engines, and clockwise, for the 6-232 and V8 engines. When altering the timing, it is wise to tap the distributor lightly with a wooden hammer handle to move it in the desired direction. Grasping the distributor with your hand may result in a painful electric shock. When the timing marks are aligned, turn the engine off and tighten the distributor holddown clamp. Remove the test equipment, reconnect the vacuum hoses and white (black) single wire connector (EEC-IV).

10. On 1981 and later models equipped with the module mentioned in Step 3, remove the jumper connected in Step 7 and reconnect the two wire connector. Test the module operation as follows:

    a. Disconnect and plug the vacuum source hose to the ignition timing vacuum switch.

    b. Using an external vacuum source, apply vacuum greater than 12 in. Hg to the switch, and compare the ignition timing with the requirements below.

- 4-cylinder: per specifications less 32-40°
- 6-cylinder: per specifications less 21-27°
- 8-cylinder: per specifications less 16-20°

TACHOMETER CONNECTION

The coil connector used with DuraSpark is provided with a cavity for connection of a tachometer, so that the connector doesn't have to be removed to check engine rpm.

Install the tach lead with an alligator clip on its end into the cavity marked TACH TEST and connect the other lead to a good ground.

If the coil connector must be removed, pull it out horizontally until it is disengaged from the coil terminal.

FIRING ORDERS

To avoid confusion, replace spark plug wires one at a time, or, using and indelible marker, number the wires for reference purposes.

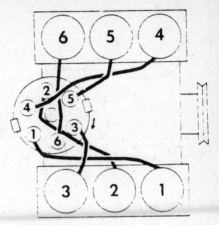

FORD MOTOR CO, 2800cc V6
Engine firing order: 1-4-2-5-3-6
Distributor rotation: Clockwise

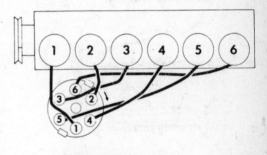

FORD MOTOR CO. 200
Engine firing order: 1-5-3-6-2-4
Distributor rotation: clockwise

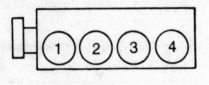

FORD MOTOR CO. 2300 cc 4-cyl.
Engine firing order: 1-3-4-2
Distributor rotation: clockwise

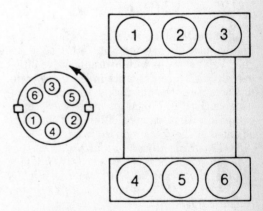

FORD MOTOR CO. 232 V6
Engine firing order: 1-4-2-5-3-6
Distributor rotation: counterclockwise

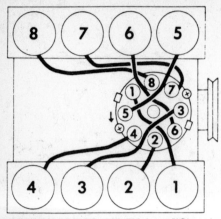

FORD MOTOR CO. 255,302 (exc. HO)
V8 Engine firing order: 1-5-4-2-6-3-7-8
Distributor rotation: counterclockwise

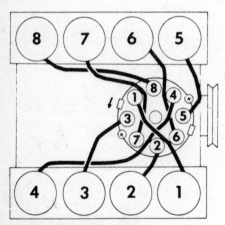

FORD MOTOR CO. 302HO
Engine firing order: 1-3-7-2-6-5-4-8
Distributor rotation: counterclockwise

VALVE ADJUSTMENT

All of the Mustang and Capri engines use hydraulic valve lifters except the V6 170 cu in. engine. Valve systems with hydraulic valve lifters operate with zero clearance in the valve train, and because of this the rocker arms are nonadjustable. The V6 170 cu in. engine however, is equipped with mechanical lifters and should be adjusted at the recommended interval.

NOTE: *While all valve adjustments must be as accurate as possible, it is better to have the valve adjustment slightly loose than slightly tight, as burnt valves may result from overly tight adjustments.*

6-170 ENGINE

1. Remove the air cleaner assembly and disconnect the negative battery cable.

Adjusting valve lash, 2.8L V6

2. Remove the Thermactor® air by-pass valve and its mounting bracket.

3. Remove the two engine lifting eyes; remove the alternator drive belt, loosen the alternator mounting bolts and wing the alternator toward the fender.

4. Remove the plug wires and remove the rocker arms.

5. When removing the rocker covers, remove or reposition any wires or hoses which might block the removal of the rocker covers.

6. Torque the rocker arm support bolts to 46 ft. lbs.

7. Reconnect the battery cable, place the transmission in Neutral (manual) or Park (automatic), and apply the parking brake.

8. Place a finger on the adjusting screw of the intake valve rocker arm for cylinder No.5 Cylinder numbering is shown under Firing Order at the start of the section. Valve arrangement, from front to rear, on the left bank is I-E-E-I-E-I; on the right it is I-E-I-E-E-I. You will able to feel the rocker arm begin to move.

9. Use a remote starter switch to turn the engine over until you can just feel the valve begin to open. Now the cam is in position to adjust

Valve Clearance Adjustment V6 170 Cu. In. Engine

Intake Valve Just Opening for Cyl.:	Adjust Both Valves For This Cylinder (Intake—0.016 in.; Exhaust—0.018 in.)
5	1
3	4
6	2
1	5
4	3
2	6

the intake and exhaust valves on the No.1 cylinder.

10. Adjust the No.1 intake valve so that a 0.016" feeler gauge has a slight drag, while a 0.017" feeler gauge is a tight fit. To decrease lash, turn the adjusting screw clockwise. There are no lockbolts to tighten as the adjusting screws are self-tightening.

CAUTION: *Do not use a step-type "go-no go" feeler gauge. When checking lash, you must insert the feeler gauge and move it parallel with the crankshaft. Do not move it in and out perpendicular with the crankshaft as this will give an erroneous feel which will result in overtightened valves.*

11. Adjust the exhaust valve the same way so that a 0.018" feeler gauge is a tight fit.

12. The rest of the valves are adjusted in the same way, in their firing order (1-4-2-5-3-6), by positioning the cam according to the following chart:

13. Remove all the old gasket material from the cylinder heads and rocker cover gasket surfaces, and disconnect the negative cable from the battery.

14. Remove the spark plug wires and reinstall the rocker arm covers.

15. Reinstall any hoses and wires which were removed previously.

16. Reinstall the spark plug wires, the alternator drive belt, and the Termactor® air bypass valve and its mounting bracket.

17. Reconnect the battery cable, replace the air cleaner assembly, start the engine, and check for leaks.

IDLE SPEED AND MIXTURE ADJUSTMENTS

This section contains only carburetor adjustments as they normally apply to engine tune-up. Descriptions of the carburetor and complete adjustment procedures can be found in Chapter 5, under Fuel System.

Carbureted Engines

NOTE: *Since the design of the 2700VV and 7200VV carburetor is different from all other Motorcraft carburetors in many respects, the adjusting procedures are necessarily different as well. Although the idle speed adjustment alone is identical, there is further information you will need to know in order to adjust the 2700VV and 7200VV properly. Refer to Chapter 4 for an explanation.*

In order to limit exhaust emissions, plastic caps have been installed on the idle fuel mixture screw(s), which prevent the carbure- *tor from being adjusted on an overly rich idle fuel mixture. Under no circumstances should these limiters be modified or removed. A satisfactory idle should be obtained within the range of the limiter(s).*

Refer to the procedures following this one for models equipped with fuel injection or for models equipped with an Automatic Overdrive Transmission (AOD).

ADJUSTMENT

1. Start the engine and run it at idle until it reaches operating temperature (about 10-20 minutes, depending on outside temperatures). Stop the engine.

2. Check the ignition timing as outlined earlier in this chapter.

3. Remove the air cleaner, taking note of the hose locations, and check that the choke plate is in the open position (plate in vertical position). Check the accompanying illustrations to see where the carburetor adjustment locations are. If you cannot reach them with the air cleaner installed, leave it off temporarily. Otherwise, reinstall the air cleaner assembly including all the hose connections.

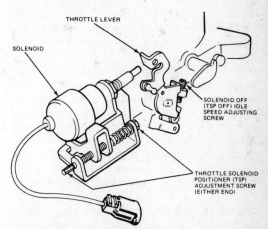

Location of idle speed adjustment—Motorcraft 2150, (all with TSP)

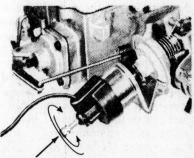

Location of idle speed adjustment—Motorcraft 2150 with solenoid dashpot TSP

NOTE: *Leaving the air cleaner removed will affect the idle speed, therefore, adjust the curb idle speed to a setting 50-100 rpm higher than specified, if the air cleaner is off. When the air cleaner is reinstalled the idle speed should be to specifications.*

4. Attach a tachometer to the engine, with the positive wire connected to the distributor side of the ignition coil, and the negative wire connected to a good ground, such as an engine mount. In order to attach an alligator clip to the distributor side (terminal) of the coil (primary connection), it will be necessary to lift off the connector and slide a female loop type connector (commercially available) sown the rubber connector over the loop connector and connect the alligator clip of your tachometer. On late models a tach connector is provided.

5. All idle speed adjustments are made with the headlights off (unless otherwise specified on the engine decal), with the air conditioning off (if so equipped), with all vacuum hoses connected, with the throttle solenoid positioner activated (connected, if so equipped), and with the air cleaner on. (See Note after Step 3.) Finally, all idle speed adjustments are made in Neutral on cars with manual transmission, and in Drive on cars equipped with automatic transmission.

CAUTION: *Whenever performing these adjustments, block all four wheels and set the parking brake.*

6a. On cars not equipped with a throttle solenoid positioner, the idle speed is adjusted with the curb idle speed adjusting screw. Start the engine. Turn the curb idle speed adjusting screw inward or outward until the correct idle speed (see Tune-Up Specifications chart) is reached, remembering to make the 50-100 rpm allowance if the air cleaner is removed.

6b. On cars equipped with a throttle solenoid positioner, the idle speed is adjusted with solenoid adjusting screw (nut), in two stages. Start the engine. The higher speed is adjusted with the solenoid connected. Turn the solenoid adjusting screw (nut) on 1 or 4 barrel carburetors, or the entire bracket on 2 barrel carburetors inward or outward until the correct higher idle speed (see Tune-Up Specifications chart) is reached, remembering to make the 50-100 rpm allowance if the air cleaner is removed. After making this adjustment on cars equipped with 2-barrel carburetors, tighten the solenoid adjusting locknut. The lower idle speed is adjusted with the solenoid lead wire disconnected near the harness (not at the carburetor). Place automatic transmission equipped cars in Neutral for this adjustment. Using the curb idle speed adjusting screw on the carburetor, turn the idle speed adjusting screw inward or outward until the correct lower idle speed (see Tune-Up Speci-

fications chart) is reached, remembering again to make the 50-100 rpm allowance if the air cleaner is removed. Finally, reconnect the solenoid, slightly depress the throttle lever and allow the solenoid plunger to fully extend.

7. If removed, install the air cleaner. Recheck the idle speed. If it is not correct, Step 6 will have to be repeated and the approximate corrections made.

8. To adjust the idle mixture, turn the idle mixture screw(s) inward to obtain the smoothest idle possible within the range of the limiter(s).

9. Turn off the engine and disconnect the tachometer.

NOTE: *If any doubt exists as to the proper idle mixture setting for your car, have the exhaust emission level checked at a diagnostic center or garage with an exhaust (HC/CO) analyzer or an air/fuel ratio meter.*

Fuel Injected Engines

NOTE: *Prior to adjusting the curb idle speed, set the parking brake and block all four wheels. Make all adjustments with the engine at normal operating temperature. Have all accessories turned off. If the underhood Emissions Sticker gives different specs and procedures than those following, always follow the sticker as it will reflect production changes and calibration differences.*

Vehicles equipped with EEC-IV, curb idle speed (RPM) is controlled by the EEC-IV processor and the idle speed control device. If the control system is operating properly, these speeds are self compensating and cannot be changed by traditional adjustment techniques.

ADJUSTMENT

6-232 Central Fuel Injection (CFI)

NOTE: *The EEC-IV system and an idle speed motor control the curb idle speed on models equipped with the V6 engine. The idle speed is not adjustable except for minimum and maximum throttle stop adjustment screw clearance. Too little clearance will prevent the throttle from closing as required thus causing a faster than normal idle speed. Any other problems with the system must be checked by EEC-IV system diagnosis.*

The exact sequence must be followed when checking the adjustment.

1. Adjustment is checked with the idle speed motor plunger fully retracted. Run the engine until normal operating temperature is reached, shut the engine off. Remove the air cleaner.

2. Locate the self test connector and self test

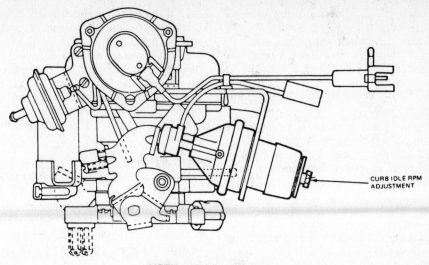

VOTM curb idle adjustment

input connector. Both are under the hood by the driver's side strut tower.

3. Connect a jumper wire between the single input connector and the signal return pin of the self test connector. The signal return pin is on the upper right of the plug when the plug is held straight on with the four prongs on the bottom facing you.

4. The motor plunger should retract when the jumper wire is connected and the ignition key turned to the Run position. If not, the EEC-IV system requires testing and service.

5. Wait about ten seconds until the plunger is fully retracted. Turn the key Off and remove the jumper.

6. If the idle speed was too high, remove the throttle stop adjusting screw and install a new one. With the throttle plates completely closed, turn the throttle stop adjusting screw in until a gap of 0.005" (0.127mm) is present between the screw tip and the throttle lever contact surface. Turn the screw in an additional 1½ turns to complete the adjustment.

7. If the speed was too low, remove the dust cover from the motor tip. Push the tip back toward the motor to remove any play. Measure the clearance between the motor tip and throttle lever by passing a $\frac{9}{32}$" (7mm) drill bit between the tip and lever. A slight drag should be felt.

8. If adjustment is required, turn the motor bracket adjusting screw until proper clearance is obtained. Tighten the lock and install the dust cover.

V8 through 1985 w/Central Fuel Injection (CFI)

1. Connect a tachometer, start the engine and allow it to reach normal operating temperature.

2. Shut the engine Off and restart it. Run the engine at about 2,000 rpm for a minute. Allow the engine to return to idle and stabilize for about 30 seconds. Place the gear selector in Reverse. (Parking brake ON and all four wheels blocked).

3. Adjust the curb idle as required using the saddle bracket adjusting screw.

4. If the rpm figure is too low, turn off the

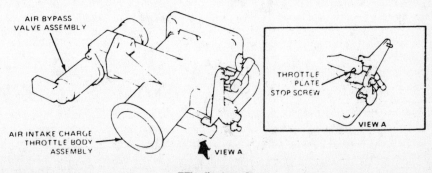

EFI adjustment

engine and turn the adjusting screw one full turn. If the speed is too high, turn off the engine and turn the screw counterclockwise.

5. Repeat Steps 2 and 4 until correct idle speed is obtained.

1986–88 V8 with Sequential Electronic Fuel Injection

1. Apply the parking brake, block the drive wheels and place the vehicle in neutral.

2. Start the engine and let it run until it reaches normal operating temperature, then turn the engine off. Connect a suitable tachometer.

3. Turn off all accessories and place the transmission in park or neutral. Check the throttle linkage for freedom of movement and correct as necessary.

4. Check for vacuum leaks. Place the transmission in neutral and operate the engine at 1,800 rpm for at least 30 seconds. Place the transmission in drive (AT) or leave in neutral for (MT) and allow the engine to stabilize.

5. Check the idle speed and if the curb idle speed falls into specification, do not adjust. If the curb idle speed does not meet specifications, turn the engine off and disconnect the positive terminal of the battery for five minutes and ten reconnect it. Repeat STEPS 4 and 5.

6. If the curb idle speed is still out of specifications, the problem could be with the EEC-IV system and the diagnostic check of the system should be made.

7. If the curb idle speed is still out specifications, back out the throttle screw until the idle speed reaches 575 ± 20 rpm (base 8-302 AT) 625 ± 20 rpm (8-302 H.O. AT) 700 ± 20 rpm (8-302 H.O. MT) then back out the throttle plate stop screw ½ additional turn to bring the throttle plate linkage into the normal operating range of the ISC system.

8. Shut off the engine and remove all test equipment.

4-140 EFI Turbo

NOTE: *Idle speed is controlled by the EEC-IV system and a air by-pass valve. If the following procedure does not correct idle rpm, EEC-IV system diagnosis is required.*

1. Run the engine until normal operating temperature is reached. Turn off all accessories.

2. Turn Off the engine. Disconnect the power lead to the idle speed by-pass control valve. Connect a tachometer to the engine.

3. Start the engine and run at 2,000 rpm for two minutes. If the electric cooling fan comes on, disconnect the wiring harness connector.

4. Let the engine return to normal idling rpm and check speed on the tachometer.

5. Adjust the rpm if necessary with the throttle plate stop screw.

6. Turn the engine Off and reconnect the by-pass valve lead and cooling fan harness.

7. Restart the engine and check the idle speed.

ENGINE ELECTRICAL

Understanding the Engine Electrical System

The engine electrical system can be broken down into three separate and distinct systems:
1. The starting system.
2. The charging system.
3. The ignition system.

BATTERY AND STARTING SYSTEM

Basic Operating Principles

The battery is the first link in the chain of mechanisms which work together to provide cranking of the automobile engine. In most modern cars, the battery is a lead/acid electrochemical device consisting of six 2v subsections connected in series so the unit is capable of producing approximately 12v of electrical pressure. Each subsection, or cell, consists of a series of positive and negative plates held a short distance apart in a solution of sulfuric acid and water. The two types of plates are of dissimilar metals. This causes a chemical reaction to be set up, and it is this reaction which produces current flow from the battery when its positive and negative terminals are connected to an electrical appliance such as a lamp or motor. The continued transfer of electrons would eventually convert the sulfuric acid in the electrolyte to water, and make the two plates identical in chemical composition. As electrical energy is removed from the battery, its voltage output tends to drop. Thus, measuring battery voltage and battery electrolyte composition are two ways of checking the ability of the unit to supply power. During the starting of the engine, electrical energy is removed from the battery. However, if the charging circuit is in good condition and the operating conditions are normal, the power removed from the battery will be replaced by the generator (or alternator)

which will force electrons back through the battery, reversing the normal flow, and restoring the battery to its original chemical state.

The battery and starting motor are linked by very heavy electrical cables designed to minimize resistance to the flow of current. Generally, the major power supply cable that leaves the battery goes directly to the starter, while other electrical system needs are supplied by a smaller cable. During starter operation, power flows from the battery to the starter and is grounded through the car's frame and the battery's negative ground strap.

The starting motor is a specially designed, direct current electric motor capable of producing a very great amount of power for its size. One thing that allows the motor to produce a great deal of power is its tremendous rotating speed. It drives the engine through a tiny pinion gear (attached to the starter's armature), which drives the very large flywheel ring gear at a greatly reduced speed. Another factor allowing it to produce so much power is that only intermittent operation is required of it. This, little allowance for air circulation is required, and the windings can be built into a very small space.

The starter solenoid is a magnetic device which employs the small current supplied by the starting switch circuit of the ignition switch. This magnetic action moves a plunger which mechanically engages the starter and electrically closes the heavy switch which connects it to the battery. The starting switch circuit consists of the starting switch contained within the ignition switch, a transmission neutral safety switch or clutch pedal switch, and the wiring necessary to connect these in series with the starter solenoid or relay.

A pinion, which is a small gear, is mounted to a one-way drive clutch. This clutch is splined to the starter armature shaft. When the ignition switch is moved to the **start** position, the solenoid plunger slides the pinion toward the flywheel ring gear via a collar and spring. If the teeth on the pinion and flywheel match properly, the pinion will engage the flywheel immediately. If the gear teeth butt one another, the spring will be compressed and will force the gears to mesh as soon as the starter turns far enough to allow them to do so. As the solenoid plunger reaches the end of its travel, it closes the contacts that connect the battery and starter and then the engine is cranked.

As soon as the engine starts, the flywheel ring gear begins turning fast enough to drive the pinion at an extremely high rate of speed. At this point, the one-way clutch begins allowing the pinion to spin faster than the starter shaft so that the starter will not operate at excessive speed. When the ignition switch is released from the starter position, the solenoid is de-energized, and a spring contained within the solenoid assembly pulls the gear out of mesh and interrupts the current flow to the starter.

Some starter employ a separate relay, mounted away from the starter, to switch the motor and solenoid current on and off. The relay thus replaces the solenoid electrical switch, buy does not eliminate the need for a solenoid mounted on the starter used to mechanically engage the starter drive gears. The relay is used to reduce the amount of current the starting switch must carry.

THE CHARGING SYSTEM

Basic Operating Principles

The automobile charging system provides electrical power for operation of the vehicle's ignition and starting systems and all the electrical accessories. The battery services as an electrical surge or storage tank, storing (in chemical form) the energy originally produced by the engine driven generator. The system also provides a means of regulating generator output to protect the battery from being overcharged and to avoid excessive voltage to the accessories.

The storage battery is a chemical device incorporating parallel lead plates in a tank containing a sulfuric acid/water solution. Adjacent plates are slightly dissimilar, and the chemical reaction of the two dissimilar plates produces electrical energy when the battery is connected to a load such as the starter motor. The chemical reaction is reversible, so that when the generator is producing a voltage (electrical pressure) greater than that produced by the battery, electricity is forced into the battery, and the battery is returned to its fully charged state.

The vehicle's generator is driven mechanically, through V-belts, by the engine crankshaft. It consists of two coils of fine wire, one stationary (the stator), and one movable (the rotor). The rotor may also be known as the armature, and consists of fine wire wrapped around an iron core which is mounted on a shaft. The electricity which flows through the two coils of wire (provided initially by the battery in some cases) creates an intense magnetic field around both rotor and stator, and the interaction between the two fields creates voltage, allowing the generator to power the accessories and charge the battery.

There are two types of generators: the earlier is the direct current (DC) type. The current produced by the DC generator is generated in the armature and carried off the spinning armature by stationary brushes contacting the commutator. The commutator is a series of smooth metal contact plates on the end of the armature. The commutator is a series of smooth metal contact plates on the end of the armature. The commutator plates, which are separated from one another by a very short gap, are connected to the armature circuits so that current will flow in one directions only in the wires carrying the generator output. The generator stator consists of two stationary coils of wire which draw some of the output current of the generator to form a powerful magnetic field and create the interaction of fields which generates the voltage. The generator field is wired in series with the regulator.

Newer automobiles use alternating current generators or alternators, because they are more efficient, can be rotated at higher speeds, and have fewer brush problems. In an alternator, the field rotates while all the current produced passes only through the stator winding. The brushes bear against continuous slip rings rather than a commutator. This causes the current produced to periodically reverse the direction of its flow. Diodes (electrical one-way switches) block the flow of current from traveling in the wrong direction. A series of diodes is wired together to permit the alternating flow of the stator to be converted to a pulsating, but unidirectional flow at the alternator output. The alternator's field is wired in series with the voltage regulator.

The regulator consists of several circuits. Each circuit has a core, or magnetic coil of wire, which operates a switch. Each switch is connected to ground through one or more resistors. The coil of wire responds directly to system voltage. When the voltage reaches the required level, the magnetic field created by the winding of wire closes the switch and inserts a resistance into the generator field circuit, thus reducing the output. The contacts of the switch cycle open and close many times each second to precisely control voltage.

Charging System Diagnosis

Condition	Possible Cause	Resolution
Battery does not stay charged— engine starts OK	1. Battery 2. Loose or worn alternator belt 3. Defective wiring or cables 4. Alternator 5. Regulator 6. Other vehicle electrical systems	1. Test battery, replace if necessary 2. Adjust or replace belt 3. Service as required 4. Test and/or replace components as required 5. Test, replace if necessary 6. Check other systems for current draw. Service as required
Alternator noisy	1. Loose or worn alternator belt 2. Bent pulley flanges 3. Alternator	1. Adjust or replace belt 2. Replace pulley 3. Service or replace alternator
Battery uses excessive water— lights and/or fuses burn out frequently	1. Defective wiring 2. Alternator regulator 3. Battery	1. Service as required 2. Replace if necessary 3. Test, replace if necessary
Charge indicator light stays on after engine starts	1. Loose or worn alternator belt 2. Alternator 3. Regulator	1. Adjust or replace 2. Service or replace 3. Replace
Charge indicator lights flickers while vehicle is being driven	1. Loose or worn alternator belt 2. Loose or improper wiring connections 3. Alternator 4. Regulator	1. Adjust or replace belt 2. Service as required 3. Service or replace 4. Service or replace
Charge indicator gauge shows discharge. (If constant high reading, see "Battery uses excessive water").	1. Loose or worn alternator belt 2. Defective wiring (Battery to alternator for ground or open) 3. Alternator 4. Regulator 5. Charge indicator gauge wiring and connections 6. Defective gauge 7. Other vehicle electrical systems malfunction	1. Adjust or replace belt 2. Service or replace wiring 3. Service or replace 4. Replace 5. Service as required 6. Replace gauge 7. Service as required

While alternators are self-limiting as far as maximum current is concerned, DC generators employ a current regulating circuit which responds directly to the total amount of current flowing through the generator circuit rather than to the output voltage. The current regulator is similar to the voltage regulator except that all system current must flow through the energizing coil on its way to the various accessories.

Ignition Coil
REMOVAL AND INSTALLATION

1. Disconnect the battery ground.
2. Disconnect the two small and one large wire from the coil.
3. Disconnect the condenser connector from the coil, if equipped.
4. Unbolt and remove the coil.
5. Installation is the reverse of removal.

Ignition Module
REMOVAL AND INSTALLATION

Removing the module, on all models, is a matter of simply removing the fasteners that attach it to the fender or firewall and pulling apart the connectors. When unplugging the connectors, pull them apart with a firm, straight pull. NEVER PRY THEM APART! To pry them will cause damage. When reconnect-

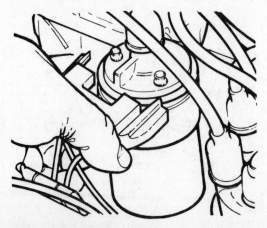

Typical coil connector removal

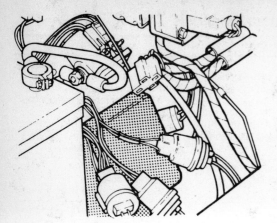

Typical control module

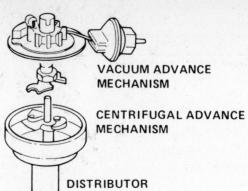

VACUUM ADVANCE
MECHANISM

CENTRIFUGAL ADVANCE
MECHANISM

DISTRIBUTOR

Dual advance distributor (typical)

ing them, coat the mating ends with silicone dielectric grease to waterproof the connection. Press the connectors together firmly to overcome any vacuum lock caused by the grease.

NOTE: *If the locking tabs weaken or break, don't replace the unit. Just secure the connection with electrical tape or tie straps.*

Distributor

REMOVAL AND INSTALLATION

1. Remove the air cleaner on V6 and V8 engines. On 4- and 6-cylinder in-line engines, removal of a Thermactor® (air) pump mounting bolt and drive belt will allow the pump to be moved to the side and permit access to the distributor. If necessary, disconnect the Thermactor® air filter and lines as well.

2. Remove the distributor cap and position the cap and ignition wires to the side.

3. Disconnect the wire harness plug from the distributor connector. Disconnect and plug the vacuum hoses from the vacuum diaphragm assembly. (DuraSpark®III systems are not equipped with a vacuum diaphragm).

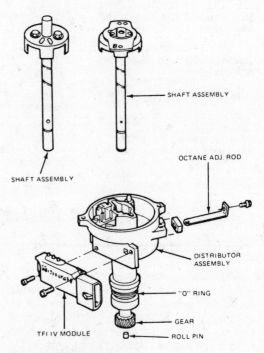

SHAFT ASSEMBLY

SHAFT ASSEMBLY

OCTANE ADJ. ROD

DISTRIBUTOR
ASSEMBLY

"O" RING

GEAR

ROLL PIN

TFI IV MODULE

Universal TFI distributor

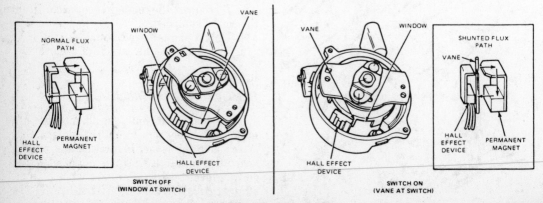

NORMAL FLUX
PATH

WINDOW

VANE

HALL
EFFECT
DEVICE

PERMANENT
MAGNET

HALL EFFECT
DEVICE

SWITCH OFF
(WINDOW AT SWITCH)

VANE

WINDOW

SHUNTED FLUX
PATH

VANE

HALL
EFFECT
DEVICE

PERMANENT
MAGNET

HALL EFFECT
DEVICE

SWITCH ON
(VANE AT SWITCH)

Hall Effect-On/Off switching

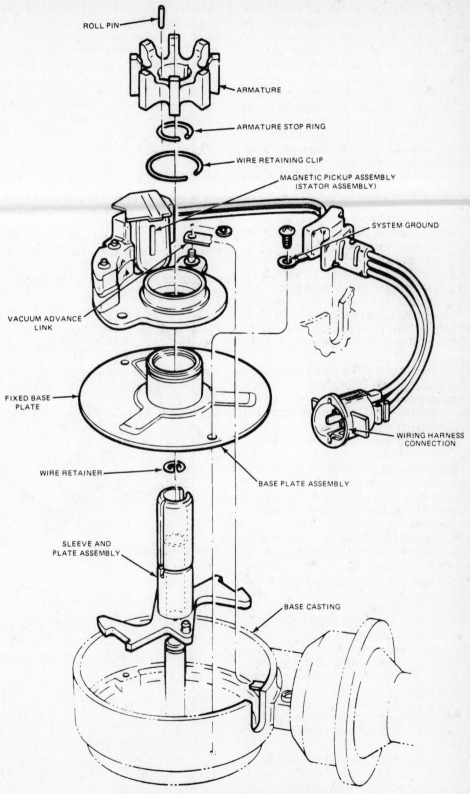

ROLL PIN

ARMATURE

ARMATURE STOP RING

WIRE RETAINING CLIP

MAGNETIC PICKUP ASSEMBLY
(STATOR ASSEMBLY)

SYSTEM GROUND

VACUUM ADVANCE
LINK

FIXED BASE
PLATE

WIRING HARNESS
CONNECTION

WIRE RETAINER

BASE PLATE ASSEMBLY

SLEEVE AND
PLATE ASSEMBLY

BASE CASTING

Exploded view of breakerless V8 distributor

4. Rotate the engine (in normal direction of rotation) until No. 1 piston is on TDC (Top Dead Center) of the compression stroke. The TDC mark on the crankshaft pulley and the pointer should align. Rotor tip pointing at No. 1 position on distributor cap.

5. On DuraSpark®I or II, turn the engine a slight bit more (if required) to align the stator (pick-up coil) assembly pole with an (closest) armature pole. On DuraSpark®III, the distributor sleeve groove (when looking down from the top) and the cap adaptor alignment slot should align. On models equipped with EEC-IV (1984 and later), remove the rotor (2 screws) and note the position of the polarizing square and shaft plate for reinstallation reference.

6. Scribe a mark on the distributor body and engine black to indicate the position of the rotor tip and position of the distributor in the engine. DuraSpark®III and some EEC-IV system distributors are equipped with a notched base and will only locate at one position on the engine.

7. Remove the holddown bolt and clamp located at the base of the distributor. (Some DuraSpark®III and EEC-IV system distributors are equipped with a special holddown bolt that requires a Torx® Head Wrench for removal). Remove the distributor from the engine. Pay attention to the direction the rotor tip points when the drive gear disengages. For reinstallation purposes, the rotor should be at this position to insure proper gear mesh and timing.

8. Avoid turning the engine, if possible, while the distributor is removed. If the engine is turned from TDC position, TDC timing marks will have to be reset before the distributor is installed; Steps 4 and 5.

9. Position the distributor in the engine with the rotor aligned to the marks made on the distributor, or to the place the rotor pointed when the distributor was removed. The stator and armature or polarizing square and shaft plate should also be aligned. Engage the oil pump intermediate shaft and insert the distributor until fully seated on the engine, if the distributor does not fully seat, turn the engine slightly to fully engage the intermediate shaft.

10. Follow the above procedures on models equipped with an indexed distributor base. Make sure when positioning the distributor that the slot in the distributor base will engage the block tab and the sleeve/adaptor slots are aligned.

11. After the distributor has been fully seated on the block install the holddown bracket and bolt. On models equipped with an indexed base, tighten the mounting bolt. On other models, snug the mounting bolt so the distributor can be turned for ignition timing purposes.

12. The rest of the installation is in the reverse order of removal. Check and reset the ignition timing on applicable models.

NOTE: *A silicone compound is used on rotor tips, distributor cap contacts and on the inside of the connectors on the spark plugs cable and module couplers. Always apply silicone dielectric compound after servicing any component of the ignition system. Various models use a multi-point rotor which do not require the application of dielectric compound.*

Alternator

The alternator charging system consists of the alternator, voltage regulator, warning light, battery, and fuse link wire.

A failure of any component of the charging system can cause the entire system to stop functioning. Because of this, the charging system can be very difficult to troubleshoot when problems occur.

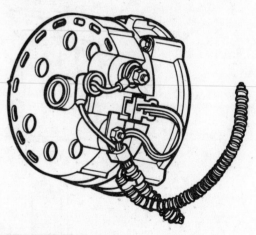

Side terminal alternator

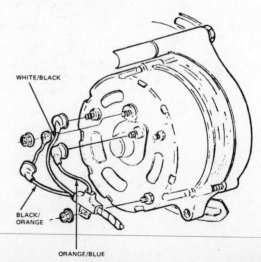

WHITE/BLACK

BLACK/ORANGE

ORANGE/BLUE

Rear terminal alternator

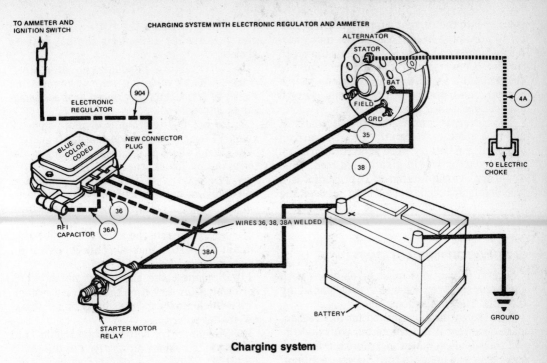

Charging system

When the ignition key is turned on, current flows from the battery, through the charging system indicator light on the instrument panel, to the voltage regulator, and to the alternator. Since the alternator is not producing any current, the alternator warning light comes on. When the engine is started, the alternator begins to produce current and turns the alternator light off. As the alternator turns and produces current, the current is divided in two ways: part to the battery to charge the battery and power the electrical components of the vehicle, and part is returned to the alternator to enable it to increase its output. In this situation, the alternator is receiving current from the battery and from itself. A voltage regulator

Troubleshooting Basic Charging System Problems

Problem	Cause	Solution
Noisy alternator	• Loose mountings • Loose drive pulley • Worn bearings • Brush noise • Internal circuits shorted (High pitched whine)	• Tighten mounting bolts • Tighten pulley • Replace alternator • Replace alternator • Replace alternator
Squeal when starting engine or accelerating	• Glazed or loose belt	• Replace or adjust belt
Indicator light remains on or ammeter indicates discharge (engine running)	• Broken fan belt • Broken or disconnected wires • Internal alternator problems • Defective voltage regulator	• Install belt • Repair or connect wiring • Replace alternator • Replace voltage regulator
Car light bulbs continually burn out— battery needs water continually	• Alternator/regulator overcharging	• Replace voltage regulator/alternator
Car lights flare on acceleration	• Battery low • Internal alternator/regulator problems	• Charge or replace battery • Replace alternator/regulator
Low voltage output (alternator light flickers continually or ammeter needle wanders)	• Loose or worn belt • Dirty or corroded connections • Internal alternator/regulator problems	• Replace or adjust belt • Clean or replace connections • Replace alternator or regulator

is wired into the current supply to the alternator to prevent it from receiving too much current which would cause it to put out too much current. Conversely, if the voltage regulator does not allow the alternator to receive enough current, the battery will not be fully charged and will eventually go dead.

The battery is connected to the alternator at all times, whether the ignition key is turned on or not. If the battery were shorted to ground, the alternator would also be shorted. This would damage the alternator. To prevent this, a fuse link is installed in the wiring between the battery and the alternator. If the battery is shorted, the fuse link is melted, protecting the alternator.

ALTERNATOR PRECAUTIONS

Several precautions must be observed with alternator equipped vehicles to avoid damaging the unit. They are as follows:

1. If the battery is removed for any reason, make sure that it is reconnected with the correct polarity. Reversing the battery connections may result in damage to the one-way rectifiers.

2. When utilizing a booster battery as a starting aid, always connect it as follows: positive to positive, and negative (booster battery) to a good ground on the engine of the car being started.

3. Never use a fast charger as a booster to start cars with alternating current (AC) circuits.

4. When servicing the battery with a fast charger, always disconnect the car battery cables.

5. Never attempt to polarize an alternator.

6. Avoid long soldering times when replacing diodes or transistors. Prolonged heat is damaging to alternators.

7. Do not use test lamps of more than 12 volts (V) for checking diode continuity.

8. Do not short across or ground any of the terminals on the alternator.

9. The polarity of the battery, alternator, and regulator must be matched and considered before making any electrical connections within the system.

10. Never separate the alternator on an open circuit. Make sure that all connections within the circuit are clean and tight.

11. Disconnect the battery terminals when performing any service on the electrical system. This will eliminate the possibility of accidental reversal of polarity.

12. Disconnect the battery ground cable if arc welding is to be done on any part of the car.

CHARGING SYSTEM TROUBLESHOOTING

There are many possible ways in which the charging system can malfunction. Often the source of a problem is difficult to diagnose, requiring special equipment and a good deal of experience. This is usually not the case, however, where the charging system fails completely and causes the dash board warning light to come on

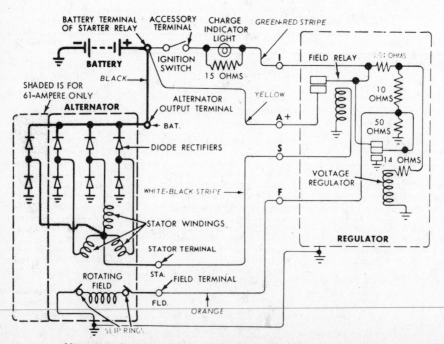

Alternator charging circuit w/indicator light—rear terminal type

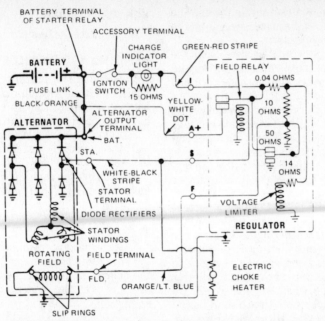

Alternator charging circuit w/indicator light—side terminal type

or the battery to become dead. To troubleshoot a complete system failure only two pieces of equipment are needed: a test light, to determine that current is reaching a certain point; and a current indicator (ammeter), to determine the direction of the current flow and its measurement in amps.

This test works under three assumptions:

1. The battery is known to be good and fully charged.

2. The alternator belt is in good condition and adjusted to the proper tension.

3. All connections in the system are clean and tight.

NOTE: *In order for the current indicator to give a valid reading, the car must be equipped with battery cables which are of the same gauge size and quality as original equipment battery cables.*

1. Turn off all electrical components on the car. Make sure the doors of the car are closed. If the car is equipped with a clock, disconnect the clock by removing the lead wire from the rear of the clock. Disconnect the positive battery cable from the battery and connect the ground wire on a test light to the disconnected positive battery cable. Touch the probe end of the test light to the positive battery post. The test light should not light. If the test light does light, there is a short or open circuit on the car.

2. Disconnect the voltage regulator wiring harness connector at the voltage regulator. Turn on the ignition key. Connect the wire on a test light to a good ground (engine bolt). Touch the probe end of a test light to the ignition wire connector into the voltage regulator wiring connector. This wire corresponds to the **I** terminal on the regulator. If the test light goes on, the charging system warning light circuit is complete. If the test light does not come on and the warning light on the instrument panel is on, either the resistor wire, which is parallel with the warning light, or the wiring to the voltage regulator, is defective. If the test light does not come on and the warning light is not on, either the bulb is defective or the power supply wire form the battery through the ignition switch to the bulb has an open circuit. Connect the wiring harness to the regulator.

3. Examine the fuse link wire in the wiring harness from the starter relay to the alternator. If the insulation on the wire is cracked or split, the fuse link may be melted. Connect a test light to the fuse link by attaching the ground wire on the test light to an engine bolt and touching the probe end of the light to the bottom of the fuse link wire where it splices into the alternator output wire. If the bulb in the test light does not light, the fuse link is melted.

4. Start the engine and place a current indicator on the positive battery cable. Turn off all electrical accessories and make sure the doors are closed. If the charging system is working properly, the gauge will show a draw of less than 5 amps. If the system is not working properly, the gauge will show a draw of more than 5

amps. A charge moves the needle toward the battery, a draw moves the needle away from the battery. Turn the engine off.

5. Disconnect the wiring harness from the voltage regulator at the regulator at the regulator connector. Connect a male spade terminal (solderless connector) to each end of a jumper wire. Insert one end of the wire into the wiring harness connector which corresponds to the **A** terminal on the regulator. Insert the other end of the wire into the wiring harness connector which corresponds to the **F** terminal on the regulator. Position the connector with the jumper wire installed so that it cannot contact any metal surface under the hood. Position a current indicator gauge on the positive battery cable. Have an assistant start the engine. Observe the reading on the current indicator. Have your assistant slowly raise the speed of the engine to about 2,000 rpm or until the current indicator needle stops moving, whichever comes first. Do not run the engine for more than a short period of time in this condition. If the wiring harness connector or jumper wire becomes excessively hot during this test, turn off the engine and check for a grounded wire in the regulator wiring harness. If the current indicator shows a charge of about three amps less than the output of the alternator, the alternator is working properly. If the previous tests showed a draw, the voltage regulator is defective. If the gauge does not show the proper charging rate, the alternator is defective.

REMOVAL AND INSTALLATION

1. Disconnect the negative battery cable from the battery.

2. Disconnect the wires from the alternator.

3. Loosen the alternator mounting bolts and remove the drive belt.

NOTE: *Some 1981 and later cars are equipped with a ribbed, K-section belt and automatic tensioner. A special tool must be made to remove the tension from the tensioner arm. Loosen the idler pulley pivot and adjuster bolts before using the tool. See the accompanying illustration for tool details.*

4. Remove the alternator mounting bolts and spacer (if equipped), and remove the alternator.

5. To install, position the alternator on its brackets and install the attaching bolts and spacer (if so equipped).

6. Connect the wires to the alternator.

7. Position the drive belt on the alternator pulley. Adjust the belt tension as outlined in Chapter 1.

8. Connect the negative battery cable.

Voltage Regulator

A completely solid-state regulator is used.

REMOVAL AND INSTALLATION

1. Remove the battery ground cable. On models with the regulator mounted behind the battery, it is necessary to remove the battery holddown, and to move the battery.

2. Remove the regulator mounting screws.

3. Disconnect the regulator from the wiring harness.

4. Mount the regulator to the regulator mounting plate. The radio suppression condenser mounts under one mounting screw; the ground lead under the other mounting screw. Tighten the mounting screws.

5. If the battery was moved to gain access to the regulator, position the battery and install the holddown. Connect the battery ground cable, and test the system for proper voltage regulation.

Starter

All engines use a positive engagement starter

The positive engagement starter system employs a starter relay, usually mounted inside the engine compartment on a fender wall, to transfer battery current to the starter. The relay is activated by the ignition switch and, when engaged, it creates a direct current from the battery to the starter windings. Simultaneously, the armature begins to turn the starter drive is pushed out to engage the flywheel.

In the solenoid actuated starter system, battery current is first directed to a solenoid assembly which is mounted on the starter case. The current closes the solenoid contacts, which engages the drive pinion and directs current to the coil windings, causing the armature to rotate. While this system does not need a starter relay, some models were nevertheless equipped with one in order to simplify assembly procedures. These vehicles also have a connector link attached to the solenoid, which provides a hook up for the relay wire.

REMOVAL AND INSTALLATION

1. Disconnect the negative battery cable.

2. Raise the front of the car and install jackstands beneath the frame. Firmly apply the parking brake and place blocks in back of the rear wheels.

3. Tag and disconnect the wiring at the starter.

4. Turn the front wheels fully to the right. On some later models it will be necessary to remove the frame brace. On many models, it will be necessary to remove the two bolts retaining

Troubleshooting Basic Starting System Problems

Problem	Cause	Solution
Starter motor rotates engine slowly	• Battery charge low or battery defective	• Charge or replace battery
	• Defective circuit between battery and starter motor	• Clean and tighten, or replace cables
	• Low load current	• Bench-test starter motor. Inspect for worn brushes and weak brush springs.
	• High load current	• Bench-test starter motor. Check engine for friction, drag or coolant in cylinders. Check ring gear-to-pinion gear clearance.
Starter motor will not rotate engine	• Battery charge low or battery defective	• Charge or replace battery
	• Faulty solenoid	• Check solenoid ground. Repair or replace as necessary.
	• Damage drive pinion gear or ring gear	• Replace damaged gear(s)
	• Starter motor engagement weak	• Bench-test starter motor
	• Starter motor rotates slowly with high load current	• Inspect drive yoke pull-down and point gap, check for worn end bushings, check ring gear clearance
	• Engine seized	• Repair engine
Starter motor drive will not engage (solenoid known to be good)	• Defective contact point assembly	• Repair or replace contact point assembly
	• Inadequate contact point assembly ground	• Repair connection at ground screw
	• Defective hold-in coil	• Replace field winding assembly
Starter motor drive will not disengage	• Starter motor loose on flywheel housing	• Tighten mounting bolts
	• Worn drive end busing	• Replace bushing
	• Damaged ring gear teeth	• Replace ring gear or driveplate
	• Drive yoke return spring broken or missing	• Replace spring
Starter motor drive disengages prematurely	• Weak drive assembly thrust spring	• Replace drive mechanism
	• Hold-in coil defective	• Replace field winding assembly
Low load current	• Worn brushes	• Replace brushes
	• Weak brush springs	• Replace springs

the steering idler arm to the frame to gain access to the starter.

5. Remove the starter mounting bolts and remove the starter.

6. Reverse the above procedure to install. Torque the mounting bolts to 12-15 ft. lbs. on starters with 3 mounting bolts and 15-20 ft. lbs. on starters with 2 mounting bolts. Torque the idler arm retaining bolts to 28-35 ft. lbs. (if removed). Make sure that the nut securing the heavy cable to the starter is snugged down tightly.

OVERHAUL

Brush Replacement

1. Remove the starter from the engine as previously outlined.

2. Remove the starter drive plunger lever cover and gasket.

3. Loosen and remove the brush cover band and remove the brushes from their holder.

4. Remove the two through-bolts from the starter frame.

5. Separate the drive-end housing, starter frame and brush end plate assemblies.

6. Remove the starter drive plunger lever and pivot pin, and remove the armature.

7. Remove the ground brush retaining screws from the frame and remove the brushes.

8. Cut the insulated brush leads from the field coils, as close to the field connection point as possible.

9. Clean and inspect the starter motor.

10. Replace the brush end plate if the insulator between the field brush holder and the end plate is cracked or broken.

11. Position the new insulated field brushes lead on the field coil connection. Position and crimp the clip provided with the brushes to hold

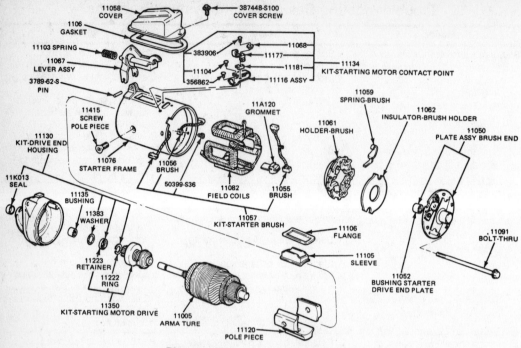

Disassembled view of starter typical

the brush lead to the connection. Solder the lead, clip, and connection together using resin core solder. Use a 300 watt soldering iron.

12. Install the ground brush leads to the frame with the retaining screws.

13. Install the starter drive plunger lever and pivot pin, and install the armature.

14. Assemble the drive-end housing, starter frame and brush end plate assemblies.

15. Install the two through-bolts in the starter frame. Torque the through-bolts to 55-75 in.lb.

16. Install the brushes in their holders and install the brush cover band.

17. Install the starter drive plunger lever cover and gasket.

22. Install the starter on the engine as previously outlined.

Drive Replacement

1. Remove the starter as outlined previously.

2. Remove the starter drive plunger lever and gasket and the brush cover band.

3. Remove the two through-bolts from the starter frame.

4. Separate the drive end housing from the starter frame.

5. The starter drive plunger lever return spring may fall out after detaching the drive end housing. If not, remove it.

6. Remove the pivot pin which attaches the starter drive plunger lever to the starter frame and remove the lever.

7. Remove the stop ring retainer and stop ring from the armature shaft.

8. Slide the starter drive off the armature shaft.

9. Examine the wear pattern on the starter drive teeth. There should be evidence of full contact between the starter drive teeth and the flywheel ring gear teeth. If there is evidence of irregular wear, examine the flywheel ring gear for damage and replace if necessary.

10. Apply a thin coat of white grease to the armature shaft before installing the drive gear. Place a small amount of grease in the drive end housing bearing. Slide the starter drive on the armature shaft.

11. Install the stop ring retainer and stop ring on the armature shaft.

12. Install the starter drive plunger lever on the starter frame and install the pin.

13. Assemble the drive end housing on the starter frame.

14. install the two through-bolts in the starter frame. Tighten the starter through bolts to 55-75 in.lb.

15. Install the starter drive plunger lever and gasket and the brush cover band.

16. Install the starter as outlined previously.

Battery

REMOVAL AND INSTALLATION

1. Remove the holddown screws from the battery box. Loosen the nuts that secure the ca-

ble ends to the battery terminals. Lift the battery cables from the terminals with a twisting motion.

2. If there is a battery cable puller available, make use of it. Lift the battery from the vehicle.

3. Before installing the battery in the vehicle, make sure that the battery terminals are clean and free from corrosion. Use a battery terminal cleaner on the terminals and on the inside of the battery cable ends. If a cleaner is not available, use a heavy sandpaper to remove the corrosion. A mixture of baking soda and water will neutralize any acid. Place the battery in the vehicle. Install the cables on the terminals. Tighten the nuts on the cable ends. Smear a light coating of grease on the cable ends and the tops of the terminals. This will prevent buildup of oxidized acid on the terminals and the cable ends. Install and tighten the nuts of the battery box.

ENGINE MECHANICAL

Design
4-140 ENGINE

This overhead camshaft engine is of lightweight iron construction. The crankshaft is supported by five main bearings and the camshaft rides in four bearings. All shaft bearings are replaceable.

The camshaft is driven via a cogged rubber belt by the crankshaft. The belt also turn the auxiliary shaft, which in turn operates the oil pump, fuel pump (on non-turbocharged engines) and distributor.

Cam belt tension is maintained by a locked idler pulley bearing on the outside of the belt.

The water pump is separately driven by a conventional V-belt, via the crankshaft. This belt also drives the alternator.

The valves are operated via rocker arms and valve lash is maintained by hydraulic lash adjusters which require no adjustment.

Most fasteners used on this engine are metric.

6-200 ENGINES

The 200 cu. in. 6-cylinder engine is of an inline, overhead valve design.

The exhaust manifold, mounted under the intake manifold, supplies heat to the intake manifold to help vaporize the incoming fuel mixture. To prevent carburetor icing, and to further vaporize the fuel, a spacer connected with the cooling system is installed under the carburetor. Hot coolant circulates through the spacer, warming the incoming fuel mixture.

The cylinder head carries the intake and exhaust valve assemblies and mechanism. Water passages in the cylinder head help keep the valves cool.

The distributor, located on the left side of the engine, is gear driven from the camshaft and also drives the oil pump through an intermediate shaft.

The crankshaft is mounted on 4 main bearings with crankshaft end thrust controlled by the flanged No. 3 bearing.

The camshaft is mounted on 4 bearings and is driven by a sprocket and chain connection with the crankcase. An integral eccentric on the camshaft operates the fuel pump. The intake and exhaust valves are the rotating type. The valve tappets are of the hydraulic type wit solid type tappets installed in early 170 cu. in. engines.

The engines are pressure lubricated by a rotor type oil pump equipped with a pressure relief valve. Oil reaches the rocker arm shaft through No. 6 valve rocker arm shaft support at the rear of the engine.

The engines re equipped with either an open or closed positive crankcase ventilation system. In either case, crankcase fumes are channeled to the intake manifold. The engines are equipped with the Thermactor® exhaust emission control system, otherwise known as the air injection system.

6-232 ENGINES

The V6 engine is of the standard, two-bank, V-design with the banks of cylinders opposed to each other at a 90° angle.

This engine design is based on the V8 and the engines are very similar.

Canadian engines, through 1986, employ a Motorcraft 2150 carburetor, while all other engines employ Central Fuel Injection (CFI).

The crankshaft is supported by 4 main bearings. The number 3 bearing takes up the thrust.

The camshaft rides in 4 bearings.

The configuration of the valve train is identical to that of the V8 engines. The rocker arms are pedestal mounted and pivot on fulcrums bolted to the cylinder head.

Most of the mating surfaces are sealed with RTV silicone gasket material which replaces conventional gaskets.

Most engine-mounted accessories are driven by the crankshaft via a single, flat serpentine belt. The Thunderbird and Cougar use an additional V-belt to drive the air conditioning compressor off of the power steering pump. Tension on the serpentine belt is maintained by an idler pulley.

8-255, 8-302

The V8 engines are of the standard, two-bank, V-design with the banks of cylinders opposed to each other at a 90° angle.

The 8-255, and 8-302 share the same design characteristics, being variations on one-another. The **W** stands for Windsor (Ontario) where the engines were first made.

To assist in the vaporization of the incoming fuel mixture, the intake manifold contains water passages and an exhaust gas crossover passage. The intake manifold has two separate fuel passages, each with its own inlet passage to the carburetor. One of the fuel passages feeds Nos. 1, 4, 6 and 7 cylinders and the other passage feeds No. 2, 3, 5 and 8 cylinders.

The crankshaft is supported by 5 main bearings, with crankshaft end thrust controlled by the flanged No. 3 bearing.

The camshaft, which is located in the center of the V design of the engine, is mounted on 5 bearings and is driven by a sprocket and chain which are connected to a sprocket on the crankshaft. An eccentric bolted to the front of the camshaft operates the fuel pump. A gear on the front of the camshaft drives the distributor, which drives the oil pump through an intermediate shaft. The oil pump is located in the left front of the oil pan.

The engine is equipped with hydraulic valve lifters.

The engine is equipped with either an open or closed positive crankcase ventilation system which directs crankcase fumes to the intake manifold.

The engine is equipped with the Thermactor® exhaust emission control system, otherwise known as the air injection system.

Engine Overhaul Tips

Most engine overhaul procedures are fairly standard. In addition to specific parts replacement procedures and complete specifications for your individual engine, this chapter also is a guide to accept rebuilding procedures. Examples of standard rebuilding practice are shown and should be used along with specific details concerning your particular engine.

Competent and accurate machine shop services will ensure maximum performance, reliability and engine life.

In most instances it is more profitable for the do-it-yourself mechanic to remove, clean and inspect the component, buy the necessary parts and deliver these to a shop for actual machine work.

On the other hand, much of the rebuilding work (crankshaft, block, bearings, piston rods, and other components) is well within the scope of the do-it-yourself mechanic.

TOOLS

The tools required for an engine overhaul or parts replacement will depend on the depth of your involvement. With a few exceptions, they will be the tools found in a mechanic's tool kit (see Chapter 1). More in-depth work will require any or all of the following:
  • a dial indicator (reading in thousandths) mounted on a universal base
  • micrometers and telescope gauges
  • jaw and screw-type pullers
  • scraper
  • valve spring compressor
  • ring groove cleaner
  • piston ring expander and compressor
  • ridge reamer
  • cylinder hone or glaze breaker
  • Plastigage®
  • engine stand

The use of most of these tools is illustrated in this chapter. Many can be rented for a one-time use from a local parts jobber or tool supply house specializing in automotive work.

Occasionally, the use of special tools is called for. See the information on Special Tools and Safety Notice in the front of this book before substituting another tool.

INSPECTION TECHNIQUES

Procedures and specifications are given in this chapter for inspecting, cleaning and assessing the wear limits of most major components. Other procedures such as Magnaflux® and Zyglo® can be used to locate material flaws and stress cracks. Magnaflux® is a magnetic process applicable only to ferrous materials. The Zyglo® process coats the material with a fluorescent dye penetrant and can be used on any material Check for suspected surface cracks can be more readily made using spot check dye. The dye is sprayed onto the suspected area, wiped off and the area sprayed with a developer. Cracks will show up brightly.

OVERHAUL TIPS

Aluminum has become extremely popular for use in engines, due to its low weight. Observe the following precautions when handling aluminum parts:
  • Never hot tank aluminum parts (the caustic hot tank solution will eat the aluminum.
  • Remove all aluminum parts (identification tag, etc.) from engine parts prior to the tanking.
  • Always coat threads lightly with engine oil or anti-seize compounds before installation, to prevent seizure.

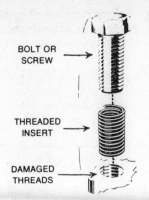

BOLT OR SCREW

THREADED INSERT

DAMAGED THREADS

Damaged bolt holes can be repaired with thread repair inserts

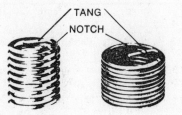

TANG

NOTCH

Standard thread repair insert (left) and spark plug thread insert (right)

Drill out the damaged threads with specified drill. Drill completely through the hole or to the bottom of a blind hole

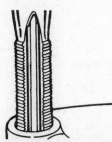

With the tap supplied, tap the hole to receive the thread insert. Keep the tap well oiled and back it out frequently to avoid clogging the threads

● Never overtorque bolts or spark plugs especially in aluminum threads.

Stripped threads in any component can be repaired using any of several commercial repair kits (Heli-Coil®, Microdot®, Keenserts®, etc.).

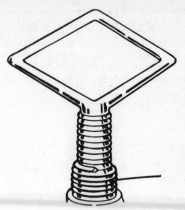

Screw the threaded insert onto the installation tool until the tang engages the slot. Screw the insert into the tapped hole until it is ¼–½ turn below the top surface. After installation break off the tang with a hammer and punch

When assembling the engine, any parts that will be frictional contact must be prelubed to provide lubrication at initial start-up. Any product specifically formulated for this purpose can be used, but engine oil is not recommended as a prelube.

When semi-permanent (locked, but removable) installation of bolts or nuts is desired, threads should be cleaned and coated with Loctite® or other similar, commercial non-hardening sealant.

REPAIRING DAMAGED THREADS

Several methods of repairing damaged threads are available. Heli-Coil® (shown here), Keenserts® and Microdot® are among the most widely used. All involve basically the same principle – drilling out stripped threads, tapping the hole and installing a prewound insert – making welding, plugging and oversize fasteners unnecessary.

Two types of thread repair inserts are usually supplied: a standard type for most Inch Coarse, Inch Fine, Metric Course and Metric Fine thread sizes and a spark lug type to fit most spark plug port sizes. Consult the individual manufacturer's catalog to determine exact applications. Typical thread repair kits will contain a selection of prewound threaded inserts, a tap (corresponding to the outside diameter threads of the insert) and an installation tool. Spark plug inserts usually differ because they require a tap equipped with pilot threads and a combined reamer/tap section. Most manufacturers also supply blister-packed thread repair inserts separately in addition to a master kit containing a variety of taps and inserts plus installation tools.

Before effecting a repair to a threaded hole, remove any snapped, broken or damaged bolts

Standard Torque Specifications and Fastener Markings

In the absence of specific torques, the following chart can be used as a guide to the maximum safe torque of a particular size/grade of fastener.

- There is no torque difference for fine or coarse threads.
- Torque values are based on clean, dry threads. Reduce the value by 10% if threads are oiled prior to assembly.
- The torque required for aluminum components or fasteners is considerably less.

U.S. Bolts

SAE Grade Number	1 or 2			5			6 or 7		
Number of lines always 2 less than the grade number.									
Bolt Size (Inches)—(Thread)	Maximum Torque			Maximum Torque			Maximum Torque		
	Ft./Lbs.	Kgm	Nm	Ft./Lbs.	Kgm	Nm	Ft./Lbs.	Kgm	Nm
¼—20	5	0.7	6.8	8	1.1	10.8	10	1.4	13.5
—28	6	0.8	8.1	10	1.4	13.6			
5/16—18	11	1.5	14.9	17	2.3	23.0	19	2.6	25.8
—24	13	1.8	17.6	19	2.6	25.7			
3/8—16	18	2.5	24.4	31	4.3	42.0	34	4.7	46.0
—24	20	2.75	27.1	35	4.8	47.5			
7/16—14	28	3.8	37.0	49	6.8	66.4	55	7.6	74.5
—20	30	4.2	40.7	55	7.6	74.5			
½—13	39	5.4	52.8	75	10.4	101.7	85	11.75	115.2
—20	41	5.7	55.6	85	11.7	115.2			
9/16—12	51	7.0	69.2	110	15.2	149.1	120	16.6	162.7
—18	55	7.6	74.5	120	16.6	162.7			
5/8—11	83	11.5	112.5	150	20.7	203.3	167	23.0	226.5
—18	95	13.1	128.8	170	23.5	230.5			
¾—10	105	14.5	142.3	270	37.3	366.0	280	38.7	379.6
—16	115	15.9	155.9	295	40.8	400.0			
7/8—9	160	22.1	216.9	395	54.6	535.5	440	60.9	596.5
—14	175	24.2	237.2	435	60.1	589.7			
1—8	236	32.5	318.6	590	81.6	799.9	660	91.3	894.8
—14	250	34.6	338.9	660	91.3	849.8			

Metric Bolts

Relative Strength Marking	4.6, 4.8			8.8		
Bolt Markings						
Bolt Size Thread Size x Pitch (mm)	Maximum Torque			Maximum Torque		
	Ft./Lbs.	Kgm	Nm	Ft./Lbs.	Kgm	Nm
6 x 1.0	2–3	.2–.4	3–4	3–6	.4–.8	5–8
8 x 1.25	6–8	.8–1	8–12	9–14	1.2–1.9	13–19
10 x 1.25	12–17	1.5–2.3	16–23	20–29	2.7–4.0	27–39
12 x 1.25	21–32	2.9–4.4	29–43	35–53	4.8–7.3	47–72
14 x 1.5	35–52	4.8–7.1	48–70	57–85	7.8–11.7	77–110
16 x 1.5	51–77	7.0–10.6	67–100	90–120	12.4–16.5	130–160
18 x 1.5	74–110	10.2–15.1	100–150	130–170	17.9–23.4	180–230
20 x 1.5	110–140	15.1–19.3	150–190	190–240	26.2–46.9	160–320
22 x 1.5	150–190	22.0–26.2	200–260	250–320	34.5–44.1	340–430
24 x 1.5	190–240	26.2–46.9	260–320	310–410	42.7–56.5	420–550

or studs. Penetrating oil can be used to free frozen threads. The offending item can be removed with locking pliers or with a screw or stud extractor. After the hole is clear, the thread can be repaired, as shown in the series of accompanying illustrations.

Checking Engine Compression

A noticeable lack of engine power, excessive oil consumption and/or poor fuel mileage measured over an extended period are all indicators of internal engine war. Worn piston rings, scored or worn cylinder bores, blown head gaskets, sticking or burnt valves and worn valve seats are all possible culprits here. A check of each cylinder's compression will help you locate the problems.

As mentioned in the Tools and Equipment section of Chapter 1, a screw-in type compression gauge is more accurate that the type you simply hold against the spark plug hole, although it takes slightly longer to use. It's worth it to obtain a more accurate reading. Follow the procedures below.

1. Warm up the engine to normal operating temperature.

2. Remove all the spark plugs.

3. Disconnect the high tension lead from the ignition coil.

4. On fully open the throttle either by operating the carburetor throttle linkage by hand or by having an assistant floor the accelerator pedal.

5. Screw the compression gauge into the no.1 spark plug hole until the fitting is snug.

WARNING: *Be careful not to crossthread the plug hole. On aluminum cylinder heads use extra care, as the threads in these heads are easily ruined.*

6. Ask an assistant to depress the accelerator pedal fully on both carbureted and fuel injected vehicles. Then, while you read the compression gauge, ask the assistant to crank the engine two

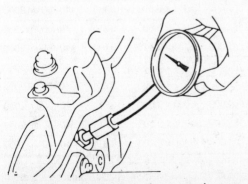

The screw-in type compression gauge is more accurate

or three times in short bursts using the ignition switch.

7. Read the compression gauge at the end of each series of cranks, and record the highest of these readings. Repeat this procedure for each of the engine's cylinders. Compare the highest reading of each cylinder to the compression pressure specification in the Tune-Up Specifications chart in Chapter 2. The specs in this chart are maximum values.

A cylinder's compression pressure is usually acceptable if it is not less than 80% of maximum. The difference between any two cylinders should be no more than 12–14 pounds.

8. If a cylinder is unusually low, pour a tablespoon of clean engine oil into the cylinder through the spark plug hole and repeat the compression test. If the compression comes up after adding the oil, it appears that the cylinder's piston rings or bore are damaged or worn. If the pressure remains low, the valves may not be seating properly (a valve job is needed), or the head gasket may be blown near that cylinder. If compression in any two adjacent cylinders is low, and if the addition of oil doesn't help the compression, there is leakage past the head gasket. Oil and coolant water in the combustion chamber can result from this problem. There may be evidence of water droplets on the engine dipstick when a head gasket has blown.

Engine

REMOVAL AND INSTALLATION

WARNING: *Disconnect the negative battery cable before beginning any work. Always label all disconnected hoses, vacuum lines and wires, to prevent incorrect reassembly. Do not disconnect any air conditioning lines unless you are thoroughly familiar with A/C systems and the hazards involved; escaping refrigerant (Freon®) will freeze any surface it contacts, including skin and eyes. Have the system discharged professionally before required repairs are started.*

1. Scribe the hood hinge outline on the underhood, disconnect the hood and remove.

2. Drain the entire cooling system and crankcase.

CAUTION: *When draining the coolant, keep in mind that cats and dogs are attracted by the ethylene glycol antifreeze, and are quite likely to drink any that is left in an uncovered container or in puddles on the ground. This will prove fatal in sufficient quantity. Always drain the coolant into a sealable container. Coolant should be reused unless it is contaminated or several years old.*

3. Remove the air cleaner, disconnect the battery at the cylinder head. On automatic

transmission equipped cars, disconnect the fluid cooler lines at the radiator. On the 4-140, remove the exhaust manifold shroud.

4. Remove the upper and lower radiator hoses and remove the radiator. If equipped with air conditioning, unbolt the compressor and position compressor out of way with refrigerant lines intact. Unbolt and lay the refrigerant condenser forward without disconnecting the refrigerant lines.

NOTE: *If there is not enough slack in the refrigerant lines to position the compressor out of the way, the refrigerant in the system must* *be evacuated (using proper safety precautions) before the lines can be disconnected from the compressor.*

5. Remove the fan, fan belt and upper pulley. On models equipped with an electric cooling fan, disconnect the power lead and remove the fan and shroud as an assembly.

6. Disconnect the heater hoses from the engine. On the 4-140, disconnect the heater hose from the water pump and choke fittings.

7. Disconnect the alternator wires at the alternator, the starter cable at the starter, the accelerator rod at the carburetor.

General Engine Specifications

Year	Engine Displacement Cu. In.	Carburetor Type	Horsepower (@ rpm)	Torque @ rpm (ft. lbs.)	Bore x Stroke (in.)	Compression Ratio	Oil Pressure @ rpm (psi)
1979	4-140	2 bbl.	88 @ 4800	118 @ 2800	3.781 x 3.126	9.0:1	50 @ 2000
	4-140 (Turbo)	2 bbl.	—	—	3.781 x 3.126	9.0:1	55 @ 2000
	6-170	2 bbl.	109 @ 4800	142 @ 2800	3.66 x 2.70	8.7:1	40–55 @ 1500
	8-302	2 bbl.	140 @ 3600	250 @ 1800	4.00 x 3.00	8.4:1	40–60 @ 2000
	8-302 (Calif.)	2 bbl.	143 @ 3600	243 @ 2200	4.00 x 3.00	8.1:1	40–60 @ 2000
1980–81	4-140	2 bbl.	88 @ 4600	119 @ 2600	3.781 x 3.126	9.0:1	50 @ 2000
	4-140 (Calif.)	2 bbl.	89 @ 4800	122 @ 2600	3.781 x 3.126	9.0:1	50 @ 2000
	4-140 (Turbo)	2 bbl.	—	—	3.781 x 3.126	9.0:1	55 @ 2000
	6-200	2 bbl.	90 @ 3800	160 @ 1600	3.68 x 3.126	8.6:1	30–50 @ 2000
	8-255	VV	118 @ 3800	193 @ 2200	3.68 x 3.00	8.8:1	40–60 @ 2000
1982	4-140	2 bbl.	88 @ 4600	118 @ 2600	3.781 x 3.126	9.0:1	50 @ 2000
	4-140 (Turbo) ①	2 bbl.	—	—	3.781 x 3.126	9.0:1	55 @ 2000
	6-200	1 bbl.	88 @ 3800	158 @ 1400	3.68 x 3.126	8.6:1	30–50 @ 2000
	8-255	2 bbl.	111 @ 3400	205 @ 2600	3.68 x 3.00	8.2:1	40–60 @ 2000
	8-302	2 bbl.	155 @ 4200	235 @ 2400	4.00 x 3.00	8.4:1	40–60 @ 2000
1983	4-140	1 bbl.	88 @ 4600	118 @ 2800	3.781 x 3.126	9.0:1	40–60 @ 2000
	6-200	1 bbl.	87 @ 3800	154 @ 1400	3.680 x 3.130	8.6:1	30–50 @ 2000
	6-232	CFI	112 @ 4000	175 @ 2600	3.810 x 3.390	8.7:1	40–60 @ 2000
	8-302	4 bbl.	140 @ 3400	265 @ 2000	4.000 x 3.000	8.4:1	40–60 @ 2000
'84–'88	4-140	1 bbl.	88 @ 4600	118 @ 2800	3.781 x 3.126	9.0:1	40–60 @ 2000
	4-140	EFI①	145 @ 3800	180 @ 3600	3.781 x 3.126	8.0:1	40–60 @ 2000
	6-232	CFI	—	—	3.810 x 3.390	8.6:1	40–60 @ 2000
	8-302	2 bbl.	155 @ 3600	265 @ 2000	4.000 x 3.000	8.4:1	40–60 @ 2000
	8-302	CFI	140 @ 3200	250 @ 1600	4.000 x 3.000	8.4:1	40–60 @ 2000
	8-302	4 bbl	175 @ 4000	245 @ 2200	4.000 x 3.000	8.3:1	40–60 @ 2000

■Horsepower and torque are SAE net figures. They are measured at the rear of the transmission with all accessories installed and operating. Since the figures vary when a given engine is installed in different models, some are representative rather than

① Merkur w/manual trans: HP-175 @ 5000 Torque—200 @ 3000

Valve Specifications

Year	Engine Displacement cu. in.	Seat Angle (deg.)	Face Angle (deg.)	Spring Test Pressure (lbs. @ in.)	Spring Installed Height (in.)	Stem to Guide Clearance (in.)		Stem Diameter (in.)	
						Intake	Exhaust	Intake	Exhaust
1979	4-140	45	45	159–175 @ 1.16	1⁹⁄₁₆	.0010–.0027	.0015–.0032	.3420	.3415
	V6-170	45	45	138–149 @ 1.22	1¹⁹⁄₃₂	.0008–.0025	.0018–.0035	.3163	.3153
	8-302	45	45	①	②	.0010–.0027	.0015–.0032	.3420	.3429
1980–88	4-140	45	44	⑥	1⁹⁄₁₆	.0010–.0027	.0015–.0032	.3420	.3415
	6-200	45	44	148–156 @ 1.21	1¹⁹⁄₃₂	.0008–.0025	.0010–.0027	.3104	.3104
	8-255	45	44	200 @ 1.30	④	.0010–.0027	.0015–.0032	.3400	.3415
	8-302	45	44	⑤	②	.0010–.0027	.0015–.0032	.3420	.3415
	6-232	45	44	215 @ 1.79	1¾	.0010–.0027	.0015–.0032	.3420	.3415

① Intake: 200 @ 1.31
  Exhaust: 200 @ 1.20
② Intake: 1¹¹⁄₁₆
  Exhaust: 1⅝
③ Intake: 200 @ 1.30
  Exhaust: 200 @ 1.20
④ Intake: 1⁴⁴⁄₆₄
  Exhaust: 1³⁸⁄₆₄

⑤ 194–214 @ 1.36
  Exhaust: 190–210 @ 1.20
⑥ 1979–81: Intake 71–79 @ 1.56
  Exhaust: 159–175 @ 1.16
  1982: 167 @ 1.16
  1983: 149 @ 1.12
  1984/85: 154 @ 1.12
  1985 Merkur—71–79 @ 1.52

8. Disconnect and plug the fuel tank line at the fuel pump on models equipped with fuel injection, depressurize the fuel system.

9. Disconnect the coil primary wire at the coil. Disconnect the wires at the oil pressure and water temperature sending units. Discon-

nect the brake booster vacuum line, if so equipped.

10. Remove the starter and dust seal.

11. On cars with manual transmission, remove the clutch retracting spring. Disconnect the clutch equalizer shaft and arm bracket at

Torque Specifications
All readings in ft. lbs.

Year	Engine Displacement cu. in. (cc)	Cylinder Head Bolts	Rod Bearing Bolts	Main Bearing Bolts	Crankshaft Pulley Bolt	Flywheel-to-Crankshaft Bolts	Manifolds
1979	4-140	80–90	30–36	80–90	100–120	54–64	①
	V6-170	65–80	21–25	65–75	92–103	47–51	②
	8-302	65–72	19–24	60–70	70–90	75–85	19–27
1980–88	4-140	80–90 ⑤	30–36	80–90	100–120	54–64	①
	6-200	70–75	19–24	60–70	85–100	75–85	—
	6-232	⑥	⑦⑧	85–100	75–85	18.4	15–22
	8-255	65–72 ④	19–24	60–70	70–90	75–85	19–27 ③
	8-302	65–72 ④	19–24	60–70	70–90	75–85	19–27 ③

① Two steps: 5–7, then 14–21
② Four steps: 3–6, 6–11, 11–15, 15–18
③ After assembly retorque with engine hot
④ Torque in 2 steps:
  First step 55–62 ft. lbs.
  Second step 65–72 ft. lbs.
⑤ Torque in two steps: First 50–60. Second 80–90
⑥ Soak bolts in oil, torque in sequence to 68–81 ft. lbs. Loosen two turns then retorque to 65–81 ft. lbs.
⑦ Soak nuts in oil, torque to 30–36 ft. lbs. Loosen two turns then retorque to 30–36 ft. lbs.
⑧ Soak bolts in oil, torque to 62–81 ft. lbs. Loosen two turns then retorque to 62–81 ft. lbs.

Crankshaft and Connecting Rod Specifications
All measurements are given in inches

Year	Engine No. Cyl. Displacement (cu. in.)	Crankshaft					Connecting Rod		
		Main Brg. Journal Dia	Main Brg. Oil Clearance	Shaft End-Play	Thrust on No.	Journal Diameter	Oil Clearance	Side Clearance
'78–'88	6-200	2.2482–2.2490	.0005–.0022 ①	.004–.008	5	2.1232–2.1240	.0008–.0015	.0035–.0105
	8-255, 302	2.2482–2.2490	.0005–.0015 ②	.004–.008	3	2.1228–2.1236	.0008–.0026 ③	.010–.020
'79–'88	4-140	2.3990–2.3982	.0008–.0015	.004–.008	3	2.0464–2.0472	.0008–.0015	.0035–.0105
'78–'79	V6-170	2.2433–2.2441	.0008–.0015	.004–.008	3	2.1252–2.1260	.0006–.0015	.004–.011
'82–'88	V6-232	2.5190	.0001–.001	.004–.008	3	2.3103–2.3111	.0008–.0026	.0047–.0114

① .0008–.0015 in. in 1977–81
② .0001–.0015 No. 1 bearing only
③ .0008–.0015 in. in thru 81

Piston and Ring Specifications
(All measurements in inches)

Engine Displacement (cu. in)	Piston Clearance	Ring Gap			Ring Side Clearance			Wear Limit
		Top Compression	Bottom Compression	Oil ① Control	Top Compression	Bottom Compression	Oil Control	
4-140 (2.3L)	0.0014–0.0022	.010–.020	.010–.020	.015–.055	.002–.004	.002–.004	Snug	.006
4-140 (2.3L) ('79–'82 Turbo)	0.0034–0.0042	.010–.020	.010–.020	.015–.055	.002–.004	.002–.004	Snug	.006
4-140 (2.3L) ('83–'85 Turbo)	0.0030–0.0038	.010–.020	.010–.020	.015–.055	.002–.004	.002–.004	Snug	.006
6-170 (2.8L)	0.0011–0.0019	.015–.023	.015–.023	.015–.055	.002–.0033	.002–.0033	Snug	.006
6-200 (3.3L)	0.0013–0.0021	.008–.016	.008–.016	.015–.055	.002–.004	.002–.004	Snug	.006
6-232 (3.8L)	0.0014–0.0028	.010–.020	.010–.020	0.15–.055	.002–.004	.002–.004	Snug	.006
8-255 (4.2L) 302 (5.0L)	0.0018–0.0026	.010–.020	.010–.020	.015–.055	.002–.004	.002–.004	Snug	.006

① Steel rails

Camshaft Specifications
(All measurements in inches)

Engine	Journal Diameter					Bearing Clearance	Lobe Lift		Endplay
	1	2	3	4	5		Intake	Exhaust	
4-140 (2.3L)	1.7713–1.7720	1.7713–1.7720	1.7713–1.7720	1.7713–1.7720	—	.001–.003	.2437 ①	.2437 ①	.001–.007
6-200 (3.3L)	1.8095–1.8105	1.8095–1.8105	1.8095–1.8105	1.8095–1.8105	—	.001–.003	.245	.245	.001–.007
6-232 (3.8L)	2.0505–2.0515	2.0505–2.0515	2.0505–2.0515	2.0505–2.0515	—	.001–.003	.240	.241	②
8-255 (4.2L)	2.0805–2.0815	2.0655–2.0665	2.0505–2.0515	2.0355–2.0365	2.0205–2.0215	.001–.003	.2375	.2375	.001–.007
8-302 (5.0L)	2.0805–2.0815	2.0655–2.0665	2.0505–2.0515	2.0355–2.0365	2.0205–2.0215	.001–.003	.2375 ③	.2474 ③	.001–.003

① '84 and later: .2381
② Endplay controlled by button and spring on camshaft end.
③ HO engine: Intake—.2600; Exhaust—.2780

Engine Weights*
1979 and Later

Engine	Weight (lbs.)
2.3L 4-cylinder	341 (308) ①
2.3L Turbo	370 (337) ①
2.8L V6	433 (390) ①
3.3L 6-cylinder	397 (348) ①
4.2L V8	431 ①
5.0L V8	550

*Weights are "dry", without oil or water
① Automatic transmission

the underbody rail and remove the arm bracket and equalizer shaft.

12. Raise the car and safely support on jackstands. Remove the flywheel or converter housing upper retaining bolts.

13. Disconnect the exhaust pipe or pipes at the exhaust manifold. Disconnect the right and left motor mount at the underbody bracket. Remove the flywheel or converter housing cover. On models so equipped, disconnect the engine roll damper on the left front of the engine from the frame.

14. On cars with manual transmission, remove the lower wheel housing bolts.

15. On models with automatic transmission, disconnect the throttle valve vacuum line at the intake manifold and disconnect the converter from the flywheel. Remove the converter housing lower retaining bolts. On models with power steering, disconnect the power steering pump from the cylinder head. Remove the drive belt and wire steering pump out of the way. Do not disconnect the hoses.

16. Lower the car. Support the transmission and flywheel or converter housing with a jack.

17. Attach an engine lifting hook. Lift the engine up and out of the compartment and onto a workstand.

18. Place a new gasket on the exhaust pipe flange.

19. Attach an engine sling and lifting device. Lift the engine from the workstand.

20. Lower the engine into the engine compartment. Be sure the exhaust manifold(s) is in proper alignment with the muffler inlet pipe(s), and the dowels in the block engage the holes in the flywheel housing.

On cars with automatic transmission, start the converter pilot into the crankshaft, making sure that the converter studs align with the flexplate holes.

On cars with manual transmission, start the transmission main drive gear into the clutch disc. If the engine hangs up after the shaft enters, rotate the crankshaft slowly (with transmission in gear) until the shaft and clutch disc splines mesh. Rotate 4-140 engines clockwise only, when viewed from the front.

21. Install the flywheel or converter housing upper bolts.

22. Install the engine support insulator to bracket retaining nuts. Disconnect the engine lifting sling and remove the lifting brackets.

23. Raise the front of the car. Connect the exhaust line(s) and tighten the attachments.

24. Install the starter.

25. On cars with manual transmission, install the remaining flywheel housing-to-engine bolts. Connect the clutch release rod. Position the clutch equalizer bar and bracket, and install the retaining bolts. Install the clutch pedal retracting spring.

26. On cars with automatic transmission, remove the retainer holding the converter in the housing. Attach the converter to the flywheel. Install the converter housing inspection cover and the remaining converter housing retaining bolts.

27. Remove the support from the transmission and lower the car.

28. Connect the engine ground strap and coil primary wire.

29. Connect the water temperature gauge wire and the heater hose at the coolant outlet housing. Connect the accelerator rod at the bellcrank.

30. On cars with automatic transmission, connect the transmission filler tube bracket. Connect the throttle valve vacuum line.

31. On cars with power steering, install the drive belt and power steering pump bracket. Install the bracket retaining bolts. Adjust the drive belt to proper tension.

32. Remove the plug from the fuel tank line. Connect the flexible fuel line and the oil pressure sending unit wire.

33. Install the pulley, belt, spacer, and fan. Adjust the belt tension.

34. Tighten the alternator adjusting bolts. Connect the wires and the battery ground cable. On the 4-140, install the exhaust manifold shroud.

35. Install the radiator. Connect the radiator hoses. On air conditioned cars, install the compressor and condenser.

36. On cars with automatic transmission, connect the fluid cooler lines. On cars with power brakes, connect the brake booster line.

37. Install the oil filter. Connect the heater hose at the water pump and carburetor choke (4-140).

38. Bring the crankcase to the full level with the correct grade of oil. Run the engine at fast idle and check for leaks. Install the air cleaner and make the final engine adjustments.

39. Install and adjust the hood.

Valve Rocker Arm Cover
REMOVAL AND INSTALLATION
4-140
6-200

1. Remove the air cleaner assembly and mounting brackets.

2. Label for identification and remove all wires and vacuum hoses interfering with valve cover removal. Remove the PCV valve with hose. Remove the accelerator control cable bracket if necessary.

NOTE: *4-140 Turbocharged models require removal of the air intake tube and air throttle body. Refer to the Fuel Injection section of Chapter 4 for procedures.*

3. Remove the valve cover retaining bolts. On 4-140 models, the front bolts equipped with rubber sealing washers must be installed in the same location to prevent oil leakage.

4. Remove the valve cover. Clean all old gasket material from the valve cover and cylinder head gasket surfaces.

5. Installation is the reverse of removal. Use oil resistant sealing compound and a new valve

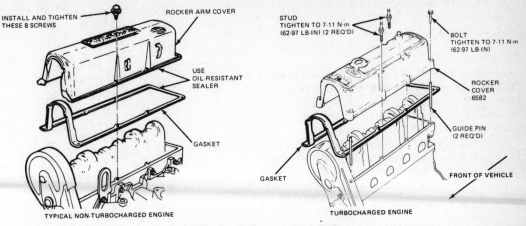

4-140 rocker arm cover installation

cover gasket. When installing the valve cover gasket, make sure all the gasket locating tangs are engaged into the cover notches provided.

V6 and V8 Engines

NOTE: *When disconnecting wires and vacuum lines, label them for reinstallation identification.*

1. Remove the air cleaner assembly.
2. On the right side:

   a. Disconnect the automatic choke heat chamber hose from the inlet tube near the right valve cover if equipped.

   b. Remove the automatic choke heat tube if equipped and remove the PCV valve and hose from the valve cover. Disconnect the EGR valve hoses.

   c. Remove the Thermactor® bypass valve and air supply hoses as necessary to gain clearance.

   d. Disconnect the spark plug wires from the plugs with a twisting pulling motion; twist and pull on the boots only, never on the wire; position the wires and mounting bracket out of the way.

   e. Remove the valve cover mounting bolts; remove the valve cover.

3. On the left side:

   a. Remove the spark plug wires and bracket.

   b. Remove the wiring harness and any vacuum hose from the bracket.

   c. Remove the valve cover mounting bolts and valve cover.

4. Clean all old gasket material from the valve cover and cylinder head mounting surfaces.

NOTE: *Some 6-232 engines were not equipped with valve cover gaskets in production. Rather, RTV silicone gasket material was originally used. Scrape away the old*
RTV sealant and clean the cover. Spread an even bead $\frac{3}{16}$" (4mm) wide of RTV sealant on the valve covers and reinstall, or install with gaskets.

5. Installation is the reverse of removal. Use oil resistant sealing compound and a new valve cover gasket. When installing the valve cover gasket, make sure all the gasket tangs are engaged into the cover notches provided.

Rocker Arm (Cam Follower) and Hydraulic Lash Adjuster

REMOVAL AND INSTALLATION

4-140 Engine

NOTE: *A special tool is required to compress the lash adjuster.*

1. Remove the valve cover and associated parts as required.

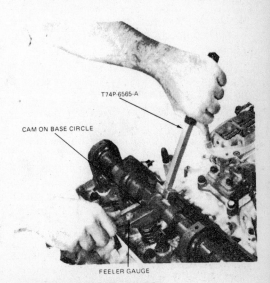

4-140 valve lash adjustment

2. Rotate the camshaft so that the base circle of the cam is against the cam follower you intend to remove.

3. Remove the retaining spring from the cam follower, if so equipped.

4. Using special tool T74P-6565-B or a valve spring compressor tool, collapse the lash adjuster and/or depress the valve spring, as necessary, and slide the cam follower over the lash adjuster and out from under the camshaft.

5. Install the cam follower in the reverse order of removal. Make sure that the lash adjuster is collapsed and released before rotating the camshaft.

Rocker Arm Shaft/Rocker Arms
REMOVAL AND INSTALLATION
6-170 and 6-200

1. Remove the rocker arm (valve) cover (see previous section).

2. Remove the rocker arm shaft mounting bolts, two turns at a time for each bolt. Start at the end of the rocker shaft and work toward the middle.

3. Lift the rocker arm shaft assembly from the engine. Remove the pin and washer from each end of the shaft. Slide the rocker arms, spring and supports off the shaft. Keep all parts in order or label them for position.

4. Clean and inspect all parts, replace as necessary.

5. Assemble the rocker shaft parts in reverse order of removal. Be sure the oil holes in the shaft are pointed downward. Reinstall the rocker shaft assembly on the engine.

NOTE: *Lubricate all parts with motor oil before installation.*

V6 and V8 Engines

1. On the right side, remove:
   a. Disconnect the automatic choke heat chamber air inlet hose.

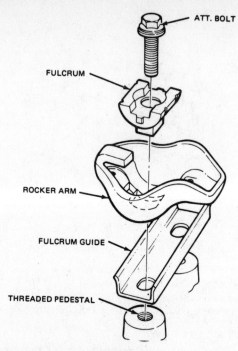

Valve rocker arms—V8 engines

b. Remove the air cleaner and duct.
   c. Remove the automatic choke heat tube (6-232, 8-302).
   d. Remove the PCV fresh air tube from the rocker cover, and disconnect the EGR vacuum amplifier hoses.

2. Remove the Thermactor® by-pass valve and air supply hoses.

3. Disconnect the spark plug wires.

4. On the left side, remove:
   a. Remove the wiring harness from the clips.
   b. Remove the rocker arm cover.

5. Remove the rocker arm stud nut or bolt, fulcrum seat and rocker arm.

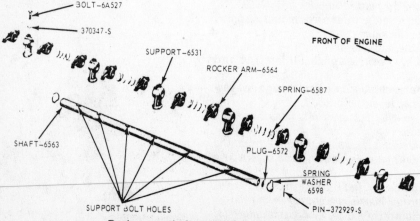

Rocker arm shaft assembly on the 6-200

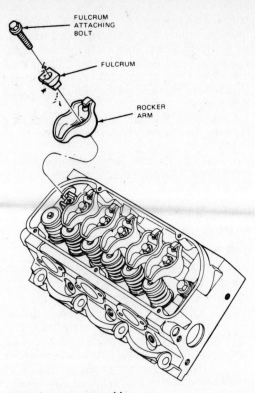

V6 rocker arm assembly

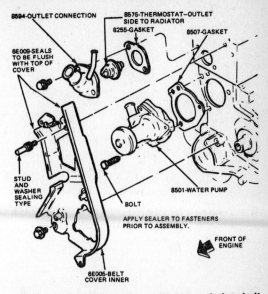

Water pump, thermostat, and inner timing belt installation—4 cyl. engine

6. Lubricate all parts with heavy SF oil before installation. When installing, rotate the crankshaft until the lifter is on the base of the cam circle (all the way down) and assemble the rocker arm. Torque the nut or bolt to 17-23 ft. lbs.

NOTE: *Some later engines use RTV sealant instead of valve cover gaskets.*

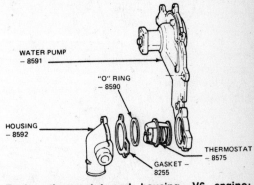

Engine thermostat and housing—V6 engine; water pumps on other engines similar

Thermostat

REMOVAL AND INSTALLATION

CAUTION: *When draining the coolant, keep in mind that cats and dogs are attracted by the ethylene glycol antifreeze, and are quite likely to drink any that is left in an uncovered container or in puddles on the ground. This will prove fatal in sufficient quantity. Always drain the coolant into a sealable container. Coolant should be reused unless it is contaminated or several years old.*

1. Open the drain cock and drain the radiator so the coolant level is below the coolant outlet elbow which houses the thermostat.

NOTE: *On some models it will be necessary to remove the distributor cap, rotor and vacuum diaphragm in order to gain access to the thermostat housing mounting bolts.*

2. Remove the outlet elbow retaining bolts and position the elbow sufficiently clear of the

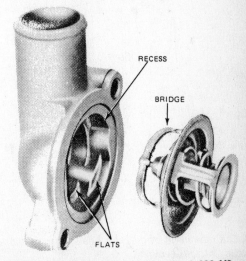

Engine thermostat and housing—6 cyl. 200, V8 engines

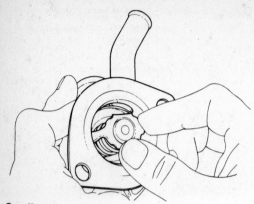

On all engines, turn thermostat clockwise to lock it into position on the flats in the outlet elbow

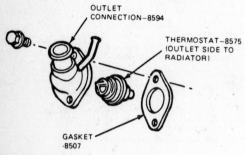

OUTLET CONNECTION–8594

THERMOSTAT–8575 (OUTLET SIDE TO RADIATOR)

GASKET ·8507

4-140 thermostat

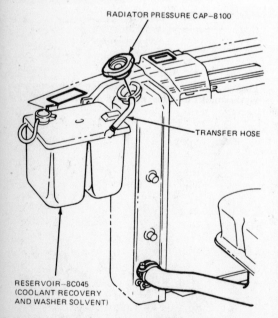

RADIATOR PRESSURE CAP–8100

TRANSFER HOSE

RESERVOIR–8C045 (COOLANT RECOVERY AND WASHER SOLVENT)

Coolant Recovery System—Typical

intake manifold or cylinder head to provide access to the thermostat.

3. Remove the thermostat and the gasket.

4. Clean the mating surfaces of the outlet el-

bow and the engine to remove all old gasket material and sealer. Coat the new gasket with water-resistant sealer. Position the gasket on the engine, and install the thermostat in the coolant elbow. The thermostat must be rotated clockwise to lock it in position on all 8-255 and 8-302.

5. Install the outlet elbow and retaining bolts on the engine. Torque the bolts to 12-15 ft. lbs.

6. Refill the radiator. Run the engine at operating temperature and check for leaks. Recheck the coolant level.

Intake Manifold
REMOVAL AND INSTALLATION
4-140 Engine

NOTE: *For engines with fuel injection, refer to the illustration provided.*

1. Drain the cooling system.

CAUTION: *When draining the coolant, keep in mind that cats and dogs are attracted by the ethylene glycol antifreeze, and are quite likely to drink any that is left in an uncovered container or in puddles on the ground. This will prove fatal in sufficient quantity. Always drain the coolant into a sealable container. Coolant should be reused unless it is contaminated or several years old.*

2. Remove the air cleaner and disconnect the throttle linkage from the carburetor.

3. Disconnect the fuel and vacuum lines from the carburetor.

4. Disconnect the carburetor solenoid wire at the quick-disconnect.

5. Remove the choke water housing and thermostatic spring from the carburetor.

6. Disconnect the water outlet and crankcase ventilation hoses from the intake manifold.

7. Disconnect the deceleration valve-to-carburetor hose (if equipped) at the carburetor.

8. Starting from each end and working towards the middle, remove the intake manifold attaching bolts and remove the manifold.

9. Clean all old gasket material from the manifold and cylinder head.

10. Apply water-resistant sealer to the intake manifold gasket and position it on the cylinder head.

11. Install the intake manifold attaching nuts. Follow the sequence given in the illustrations.

12. Connect the water and crankcase ventilation hoses to the intake manifold.

13. Connect the deceleration valve-to-carburetor hose to the carburetor.

14. Position the choke water housing and thermostatic spring on the carburetor and engage the end of the spring coil in the slot and

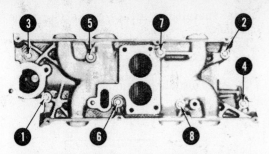

Intake manifold torque sequence—V6 170 engine

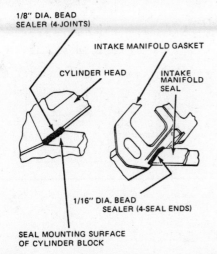

Applying a non-hardening sealer to the intake manifold

the choke adjusting lever. Align the tab on the spring housing. Tighten the choke water housing attaching screws.

15. Connect the carburetor solenoid wire.

16. Connect the fuel and vacuum lines to the carburetor.

17. Connect the throttle linkage to the carburetor.

18. Install the air cleaner and fill the cooling system.

6-200

On 6-cylinder inline engines, the intake manifold is integral with the cylinder head and cannot be removed.

V6 and V8 Engines

1. Drain the cooling system and disconnect the negative battery cable. Remove the air cleaner assembly.

CAUTION: *When draining the coolant, keep in mind that cats and dogs are attracted by the ethylene glycol antifreeze, and are quite likely to drink any that is left in an uncovered container or in puddles on the ground. This will prove fatal in sufficient quantity. Always*

drain the coolant into a sealable container. Coolant should be reused unless it is contaminated or several years old.

2. Disconnect the upper radiator hose and water pump by-pass hose from the thermostat housing and/or intake manifold. Disconnect the temperature sending unit wire connector. Remove the heater hose from the choke housing bracket and disconnect the hose from the intake manifold.

3. Disconnect the automatic choke heat chamber air inlet tube and electric wiring connector from the carburetor. Remove the crankcase ventilation hose, vacuum hoses and EGR hose and coolant lines (if equipped). Label the various hoses and wiring for reinstallation identification.

4. Disconnect the Thermactor® air supply hose at the check valve. Loosen the hose clamp at the check valve bracket and remove the air by-pass valve from the bracket and position to one side.

CAUTION: *On CFI (fuel injected) engines. System pressure must be released before disconnecting the fuel lines. See Chapter 5 for pressure release and fuel line procedures.*

5. Remove all carburetor and automatic transmission linkage attached to the carburetor or intake manifold. Remove the speed control servo and bracket, if equipped. Disconnect the fuel line and any remaining vacuum hoses or wiring from the carburetor, CFI unit, solenoids, sensors, or intake manifold.

6. On V8 engines, disconnect the distributor vacuum hoses from the distributor. Remove the distributor cap and mark the relative position of the rotor on the distributor housing. Disconnect the spark plug wires at the spark plugs and the wiring connector at the distributor. Remove the distributor holddown bolt and remove the distributor. (See Distributor Removal and Installation).

NOTE: *Distributor removal is not necessary on 6-232 engines.*

7. If your car is equipped with air conditioning and the compressor or mounting brackets interfere with manifold removal, remove the brackets and compressor and position them out of the way. Do not disconnect any compressor lines.

8. Remove the intake manifold mounting bolts. Lift off the intake manifold and carburetor, or CFI unit, as an assembly.

WARNING: *The manifold on 6-232 engines is sealed at each end with an RTV type sealer. If prying at the front of the manifold is necessary to break the seal, take care not to damage the machined surfaces.*

9. Clean all gasket mounting surfaces. 6-232 engines have aluminum cylinder heads and in-

take manifold; exercise care when cleaning the old gasket material or RTV sealant from the machined surfaces.

10. End seals are not used on 6-232 engines. Apply a ⅛" (3mm) bead of RTV sealant at each end of the engine where the intake manifold

seats. Install the intake gaskets and the manifold.

11. On V8 engines, make sure the intake gaskets interlock with the end seals. Use silicone rubber sealer (RTV) on the end seals.

12. After installing the intake manifold, run a

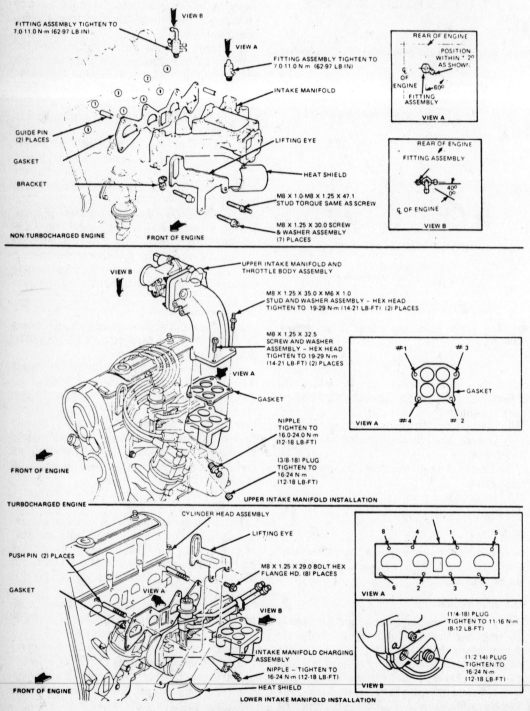

Intake manifold installation 2.3L engine

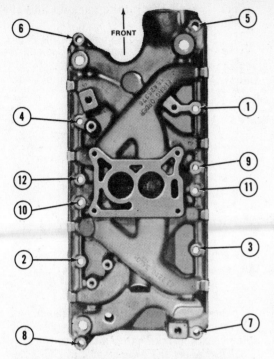

Intake manifold torque sequence—V8 engines

FRONT

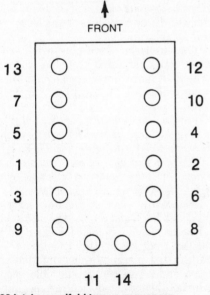

13	○	○	12
7	○	○	10
5	○	○	4
1	○	○	2
3	○	○	6
9	○	○	8
	○ ○		
	11 14		

6-232 intake manifold torque sequences

finger along the manifold ends to spread the RTV sealer and to make sure the end seals have not slipped out of place.

13. Torque the manifold mounting bolts to the required specifications in the proper sequence. Recheck the torque after the engine has reached normal operating temperature.

14. Install the brackets and compressor.

15. On V8 engines, connect the distributor vacuum hoses to the distributor.

16. Install the distributor cap.

17. Connect the spark plug wires at the spark plugs and the wiring connectors at the distributor.

18. Install the distributor. (See Distributor Removal and Installation).

19. install all carburetor and automatic transmission linkage attached to the carburetor or intake manifold.

20. Install the speed control servo and bracket, if equipped.

21. Connect the fuel line and any remaining vacuum hoses or wiring at the carburetor, CFI unit, solenoids, sensors, or intake manifold.

22. Connect the Thermactor® air supply hose at the check valve.

23. Install the air by-pass valve on its bracket.

24. Connect the automatic choke heat chamber air inlet tube and electric wiring connector at the carburetor.

25. Install the crankcase ventilation hose, vacuum hoses and EGR hose and coolant lines (if equipped).

26. Connect the upper radiator hose and water pump by-pass hose at the thermostat housing and/or intake manifold.

27. Connect the temperature sending unit wire connector.

28. Install the heater hose on the choke housing bracket and connect the hose at the intake manifold.

29. Fill the cooling system and connect the negative battery cable.

30. Install the air cleaner assembly.

Exhaust Manifold

NOTE: *Although, in most cases, the engine does not have exhaust manifold gasket installed by the factory, aftermarket gaskets are available from parts stores.*

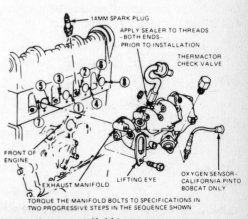

4-140 exhaust manifold torque sequence

REMOVAL AND INSTALLATION

4-140 Engine

1. Remove the air cleaner.
2. Remove the heat shroud from the exhaust manifold. On turbocharged models, remove the turbocharger.
3. Place a block of wood under the exhaust pipe and disconnect the exhaust pipe from the exhaust manifold.
4. Remove the exhaust manifold attaching nuts and remove the manifold.
5. Install a light coat of graphite grease on the exhaust manifold mating surface and position the manifold on the cylinder head.
6. Install the exhaust manifold attaching nuts and tighten them in the sequence shown in the illustration to 12-15 ft. lbs.
7. Connect the exhaust pipe to the exhaust manifold and remove the wood support from under the pipe.
8. Install the air cleaner.

6-200

1. Remove the air cleaner and heat duct body.
2. Disconnect the muffler inlet pipe and remove the choke hot air tube from the manifold.
3. Remove the EGR tube and any other emission components which will interfere with manifold removal.
4. Bend the exhaust manifold attaching bolt lock tabs back, remove the bolts and the manifold.
5. Clean all manifold mating surfaces and place a new gasket on the muffler inlet pipe.
6. Re-install the manifold by reversing the removal procedure. Torque the attaching bolts in the sequence shown. After installation, warm the engine to operating temperature and re-torque the bolts to specifications.

V6, V8 Engines

1. If removing the right side exhaust manifold, remove the air cleaner and related parts and the heat stove, if so equipped.

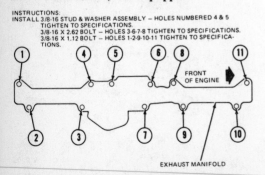

INSTRUCTIONS:
INSTALL 3/8-16 STUD & WASHER ASSEMBLY – HOLES NUMBERED 4 & 5 TIGHTEN TO SPECIFICATIONS.
3/8-16 X 2.62 BOLT – HOLES 3-6-7-8 TIGHTEN TO SPECIFICATIONS.
3/8-16 X 1.12 BOLT – HOLES 1-2-9-10-11 TIGHTEN TO SPECIFICATIONS.

FRONT OF ENGINE

EXHAUST MANIFOLD

Exhaust manifold torque sequence—6 cyl. 200 engine

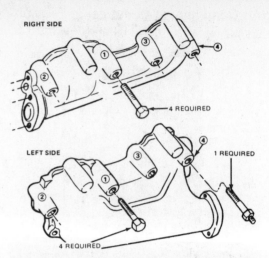

RIGHT SIDE

4 REQUIRED

LEFT SIDE

1 REQUIRED

4 REQUIRED

Typical V6 engine exhaust manifold showing torque sequence

2. On 6-232, 8-255, and 8-302, dipstick and tube removal may be required. Remove any speed control brackets that interfere.
3. Disconnect the exhaust manifold(s) from the muffler (or converter) inlet pipe(s).
NOTE: *On certain vehicles with automatic transmission and column shift it may be necessary to disconnect the selector lever cross-shaft for clearance.*
4. Disconnect the spark plug wires and remove the spark plugs and heat shields. Disconnect the EGR sensor (models so equipped), and heat control valve vacuum line (models so equipped).
NOTE: *On some engines the spark plug wire heat shields are removed with the manifold. Transmission dipstick tube and Thermactor® air tube removal may be required on certain models. Air tube removal is possible by cutting the tube clamp at the converter.*
5. Remove the exhaust manifold attaching bolts and washers, and remove the manifold(s).
6. Inspect the manifold(s) for damaged gasket surfaces, cracks, or other defects.
7. Clean the mating surfaces of the manifold(s), cylinder head and muffler inlet pipe(s).
8. Install the manifold(s) in reverse order of removal. Torque the mounting bolts to the value listed in the Torque Specifications chart. Start with the centermost bolt and work outward in both directions.
WARNING: *Slight warpage may occur on 6-232 manifolds. Elongate the holes in the manifold as necessary. Do not, however, elongate the lower front No. 5 cylinder hole on the left side, nor the lower rear No. 2 cylinder hole on the right side. These holes are used as alignment pilots.*

Air Conditioning Compressor
REMOVAL AND INSTALLATION

2-Cylinder York or Tecumseh Compressor

1. Discharge the system and disconnect the two hoses from the compressor. Cap the openings immediately! See Chapter 1.

2. Energize the clutch and remove the clutch mounting bolt.

3. Install a ⅝–11 bolt in the clutch driveshaft hole. With the cltuch still energized, tighten the bolt to remove the clutch from the shaft.

4. Disconnect the clutch wire at the connector.

5. Loosen the idler pulley or alternator and remove the drive belt and clutch, then remove the mounting bolts and compressor.

6. Installation is the reverse of removal. Prior to installation, if a new compressor is being installed, drain the oil from the old compressor into a calibrated container, then drain the oil from the new compressor into a clean container and refill the new compressor with the same amount of oil that was in the old one. Install the clutch and bolt finger-tight, install the compressor on the mounting bracket and install those bolts finger-tight. Connect the clutch wire and energize the clutch. Tighten the clutch bolt to 23 ft. lbs. Tighten the compressor mounting bolts to 30 ft. lbs. Make all other connections and evacuate, charge and leak test the system. See Chapter 1.

FS-6 6-Cylinder Axial Compressor
6-232 ENGINE

1. Discharge the refrigerant system. See Chapter 1.

2. Disconnect the two refrigerant lines from the compressor. Cap the openings immediately!

3. Remove tension from the drive belt. Remove the belt

4. Disconnect the clutch wire at the connector.

5. Remove the bolt attaching the support brace to the front brace and the nut attaching the support brace to the intake manifold. Remove the support brace.

6. Remove the two bolts attaching the rear support to the bracket.

7. Remove the bolt attaching the compressor tab to the front brace and the two bolts attaching the compressor front legs to the bracket.

8. Remove the compressor.

9. Installation is the reverse of removal. Use new O-rings coated with clean refrigerant oil at all fittings. New, replacement compressors contain 10 oz. of refrigerant oil. Prior to installation, pour off 4 oz. of oil. This will maintain the oil charge in the system. Evacuate, charge and leak test the system.

6-200 ENGINE

1. Discharge the refrigerant system. See Chapter 1.

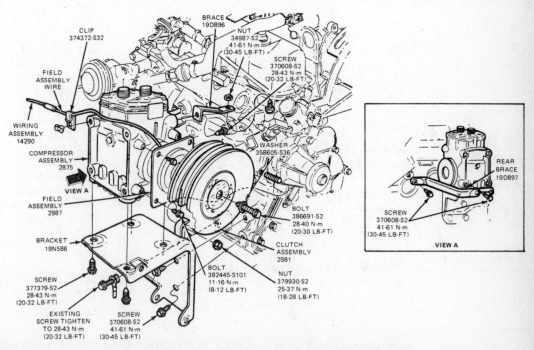

Air conditioning compressor installation on the 1981 6-200

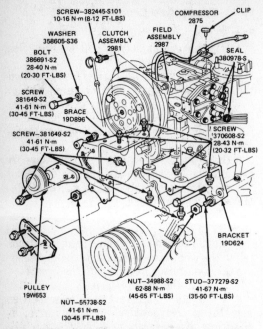

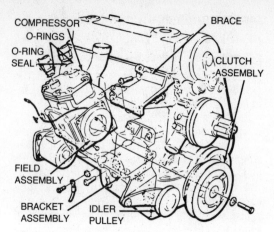

Air conditioning compressor installation on the 1981–82 4-140 for use in 49 states with manual transmission and in California with both manual and automatic transmissions

Air conditioning compressor installation on 1980–83 V8s with automatic transmission

2. Disconnect the two refrigerant lines from the compressor. Cap the openings immediately!

3. Remove tension from the drive belt. Remove the belt

4. Disconnect the clutch wire at the connector.

5. Remove the bolt attaching the support brace to the compressor upper mounting lug.

6. Remove the two bolts attaching the bracket to the compressor lower front mounting lugs.

7. Remove the compressor from the engine.

8. Installation is the reverse of removal. Use new O-rings coated with clean refrigerant oil at all fittings. New, replacement compressors contain 10 oz. of refrigerant oil. Prior to installation, pour off 4 oz. of oil. This will maintain the oil charge in the system. Evacuate, charge and leak test the system.

V8 ENGINES

1. Discharge the refrigerant system. See Chapter 1.

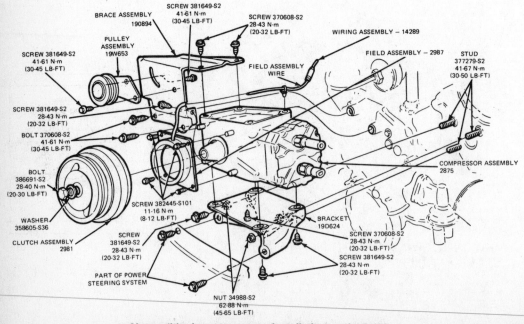

Air conditioning compressor installation on the 8-255

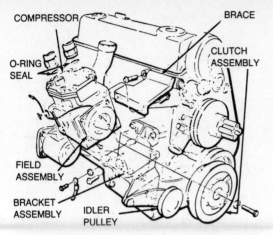

Air conditioning compressor installation on the 1981–82 4-140 for use in 49 states and Canada with manual transmission

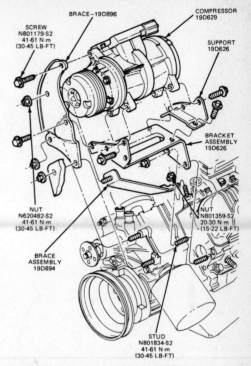

Air conditioning compressor installation on the 6-232 with the FS-6 6-cylinder compressor

2. Disconnect the two refrigerant lines from the compressor. Cap the openings immediately!

3. Remove tension from the drive belt. Remove the belt

4. Disconnect the clutch wire at the connector.

5. Remove the two nuts from the rear support bracket. Remove the three bolts from the front bosses on the bracket. On 1985-86 models, remove one bolt from the front of the tubular brace and remove the tubular brace.

6. Rotate the compressor towards the left side of the engine compartment until the compressor upper boss clears the support.

7. Remove the compressor and rear support as an assembly.

8. Installation is the reverse of removal. Use new O-rings coated with clean refrigerant oil at all fittings. New, replacement compressors con-

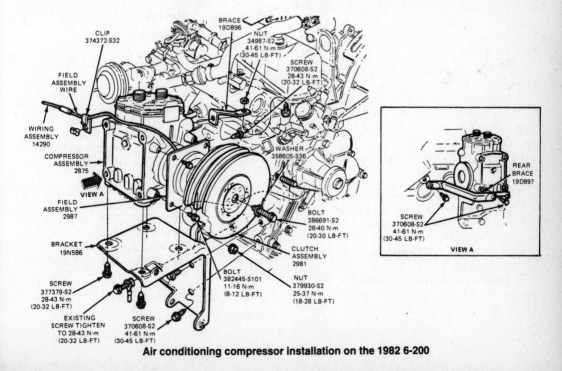

Air conditioning compressor installation on the 1982 6-200

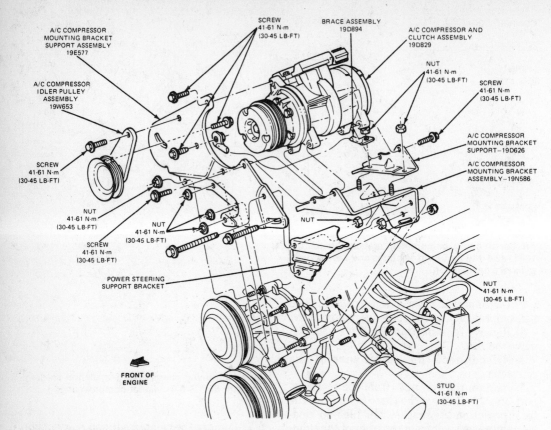

Air conditioning compressor installation on 1984–87 cars with the 8-302 and manual air conditioning

tain 10 oz. of refrigerant oil. Prior to installation, pour off 4 oz. of oil. This will maintain the oil charge in the system. Evacuate, charge and leak test the system.

MODELS WITH AUTOMATIC TEMPERATURE CONTROL AND THE 8-302 ENGINE

1. Discharge the refrigerant system. See Chapter 1.
2. Disconnect the two refrigerant lines from the compressor. Cap the openings immediately!
3. Remove tension from the drive belt. Remove the belt
4. Disconnect the clutch wire at the connector.
5. Remove the two bolts attaching the rear compressor brace to the power steering pump support. Remove the three bolts attaching the front bosses of the compressor to the power steering pump and the compressor brace.
6. Remove the compressor and rear support as an assembly.
7. Installation is the reverse of removal. Install all bolts finger-tight before tightening any of them. Use new O-rings coated with clean refrigerant oil at all fittings. New, replacement compressors contain 10 oz. of refrigerant oil. Prior to installation, pour off 4 oz. of oil. This

will maintain the oil charge in the system. Evacuate, charge and leak test the system.

HR-980 Radial Compressor

4-140 and 6-232 ENGINES AND MANUAL AIR CONDITIONING

1. Discharge the refrigerant system. See Chapter 1.
2. Disconnect the two refrigerant lines from the compressor. Cap the openings immediately!
3. Remove the bolt and washer from the adjusting bracket and remove the drive belts.
4. Remove the bolt attaching the compressor bracket to the compressor lower mounting lug.
5. Remove the compressor.
6. Installation is the reverse of removal. If a new compressor is being installed, it contains 8 fl.oz. of refrigerant oil. Prior to installing the compressor, drain 4 oz. of the oil from the compressor. This will maintain the oil charge in the system. Evacuate, charge and leak test the system.

6P148 3-Cylinder Axial Compressor

6-232 ENGINE

1. Discharge the refrigerant system. See Chapter 1.

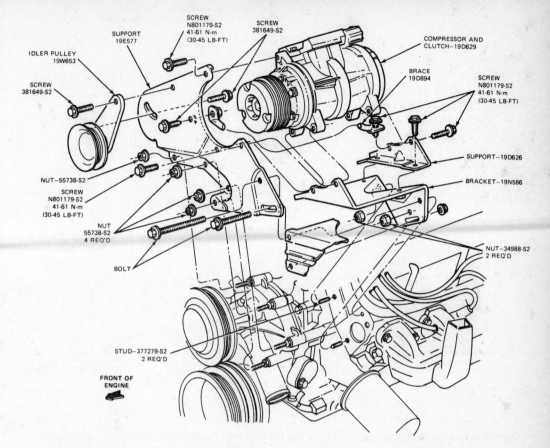

Air conditioning compressor installation 1985–87 cars with the 8-302 and automatic temperature control

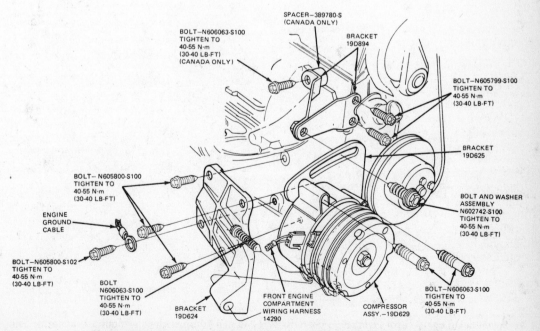

Air conditioning compressor installation on 1984–87 4-140 Turbo engines

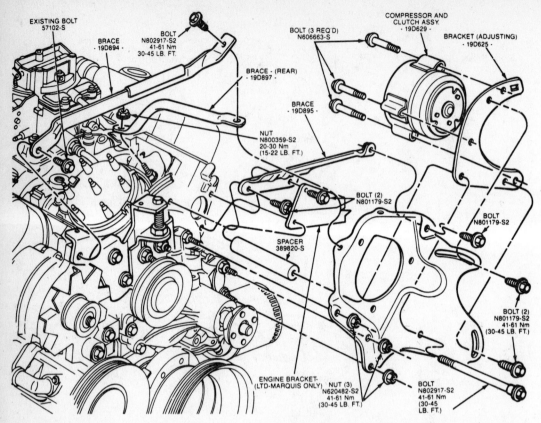

Air conditioning compressor installation on the 1982–87 6-232 with the HR-980 radial compressor

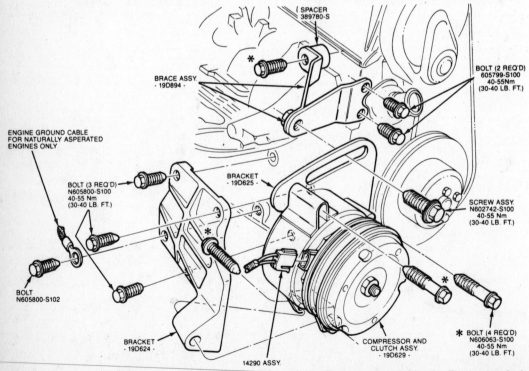

Air conditioning compressor installation on 1984–87 4-140 non-Turbo engines without a Thermactor® air pump

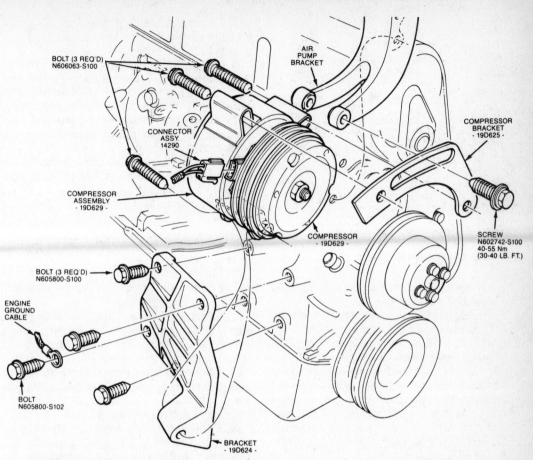

Air conditioning compressor installation on 1984–87 4-140 non-Turbo engines with a Thermactor® air pump

2. Disconnect the two refrigerant lines from the compressor. Cap the openings immediately!

3. Remove tension from the drive belt. Remove the belt

4. Disconnect the clutch wire at the connector.

5. Unbolt and remove the compressor.

6. Installation is the reverse of removal. Evacuate, charge and leak test the system.

Nippondenso 10P15

MERKUR

1. Disconnect the battery ground cable.

2. Discharge the refrigerant system. See Chapter 1.

3. Unplug the electrical connector at the compressor clutch.

4. Loosen the compressor bolts and remove the drive belt.

5. Disconnect the refrigerant lines at the compressor. Cap all openings at once! Always use a back-up wrench when loosening or tightening the connections!

6. Remove the 3 mounting bolts and lift out the compressor.

To install:

7. When installing a new compressor, add 20-25cc of refrigerant oil to the new compressor.

8. Position the compressor on its brackets and install the mounting bolts loosely.

9. Install and adjust the drive belt.

10. Torque the mounting bolts to 44 ft. lbs.

11. Reconnect the refrigerant lines. Use new O-rings coated with clean refrigerant oil.

12. Evacuate, charge and leak test the system.

Turbocharger

NOTE: *The turbocharger is serviced by replacement only.*

REMOVAL AND INSTALLATION

NOTE: *Before starting removal/service procedures, clean the area around the turbocharger with a non-caustic solution. Cover the openings of component connections to prevent the entry of dirt and foreign materials. Exercise care when handling the turbocharg-*

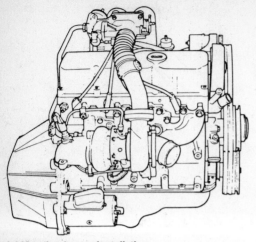

4-140 turbocharger installation

er not to nick, bend or in any way damage the compressor wheel blades.

1. Disconnect the negative battery cable.
2. Drain the cooling system.

CAUTION: *When draining the coolant, keep in mind that cats and dogs are attracted by the ethylene glycol antifreeze, and are quite likely to drink any that is left in an uncovered container or in puddles on the ground. This will prove fatal in sufficient quantity. Always drain the coolant into a sealable container. Coolant should be reused unless it is contaminated or several years old.*

3. Loosen the upper clamp on the turbocharger inlet hose. Remove the two bolts mounting the throttle body discharge tube to the turbo.
4. Label for identification and location all vacuum hoses and tubes to the turbo and disconnect them.

5. Disconnect the PCV tube from the turbo air inlet elbow. Remove the throttle busy discharge tube and hose as an assembly.
6. Disconnect the ground wire from the air inlet elbow. Remove (disconnect) the water outlet connection (and fitting if a new turbo unit is to be installed) from the turbo center housing.
7. Remove the turbo oil supply feed line. Disconnect the oxygen sensor connector at the turbocharger.
8. Raise and support the front of the vehicle on jackstands. Disconnect the exhaust pipe from the turbocharger.
9. Disconnect the oil return line from the bottom of the turbocharger. Take care not to damage or kink the line.
10. Disconnect the water inlet tube at the turbo center housing.
11. Remove the lower turbo mounting bracket-to-engine bolt. Lower the vehicle from the stands.
12. Remove the lower front mounting nut. Remove the three remaining mounting nuts evenly while sliding the turbocharger away from mounting.
13. Position a new turbocharger mounting gasket in position with the bead side facing outward. Install the turbocharger in position over the four mounting studs.
14. Position the lower mounting bracket over the two bottom studs. Using new nuts, start the two lower then the two upper mountings. Do not tighten them completely at this time; allow for slight turbo movement.
15. Raise and support the front of the vehicle on jackstands.
16. Install and tighten the lower gasket and connect the return line. Tighten the mounting bolts to 14-21 ft. lbs.

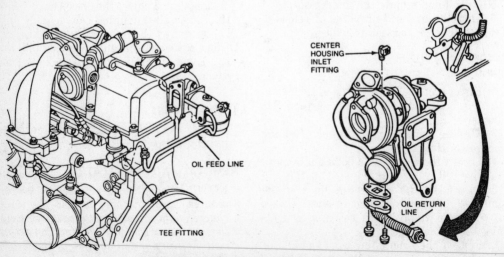

Turbo oil supply and return lines—4-140 engine

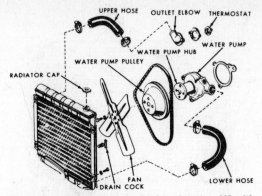

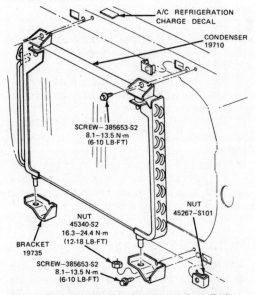

Typical cooling system and related parts—V8 with downflow radiator shown

1982–87 air conditioning condenser installation

17. Connect the water inlet tube assembly. Install the exhaust pipe on turbo. Tighten the mounting nuts to 25-35 ft. lbs.

18. Lower the vehicle. Tighten the turbo mounting nut to 28-40 ft. lbs.

19. Connect the water outlet assembly to the turbocharger, tighten the fasteners to 11-14 ft. lbs. Hold the fitting with a wrench when tightening the line.

20. Install the air inlet tube to the turbo inlet elbow (15-22 ft. lbs.). Tighten the clamp.

21. Connect the PCV tube and all vacuum lines.

22. Connect the oxygen sensor and other wiring and lines.

23. Connect the oil supply line. Connect the intake tube. Fill the cooling system.

24. Connect the negative battery cable. Start the engine and check for coolant leaks. Check vehicle operation.

WARNING: *When installing the turbocharger, or after an oil and filter change, disconnect the distributor feed harness and crank the engine with the starter motor until the oil pressure light on the dash goes out. Oil pressure must be up before starting the engine.*

Radiator

REMOVAL AND INSTALLATION

Mustang and Capri

1. Drain the cooling system.
CAUTION: *When draining the coolant, keep in mind that cats and dogs are attracted by the ethylene glycol antifreeze, and are quite likely to drink any that is left in an uncovered container or in puddles on the ground. This will prove fatal in sufficient quantity. Always drain the coolant into a sealable container. Coolant should be reused unless it is contaminated or several years old.*

2. Disconnect the upper, lower and overflow hoses at the radiator.

3. On automatic transmission equipped cars, disconnect the fluid cooler lines at the radiator.

4. Depending on the model, remove the two top mounting bolts and remove the radiator and shroud assembly, or remove the shroud mounting bolts and position the shroud out of the way, or remove the side mounting bolts. If the air conditioner condenser is attached to the radiator, remove the retaining bolts and position the condenser out of the way. DO NOT disconnect the refrigerant lines.

5. Remove the radiator attaching bolts or top brackets and lift out the radiator.

6. If a new radiator is to be installed, transfer the petcock from the old radiator to the new one. On cars equipped with automatic transmissions, transfer the fluid cooler line fittings from the old radiator.

7. Position the radiator and install, but do not tighten, the radiator support bolts. On cars equipped with automatic transmissions, connect the fluid cooler lines. Then, tighten the radiator support bolts or shroud and mounting bolts.

8. Connect the radiator hoses. Close the radiator petcock. Fill and bleed the cooling system.

9. Start the engine and bring it to operating temperature. Check for leaks.

10. On cars equipped with automatic transmissions, check the cooler lines for leaks and interference. Check the transmission fluid level.

Merkur

1. Drain the cooling system.
CAUTION: *When draining the coolant, keep in mind that cats and dogs are attracted by the ethylene glycol antifreeze, and are quite*

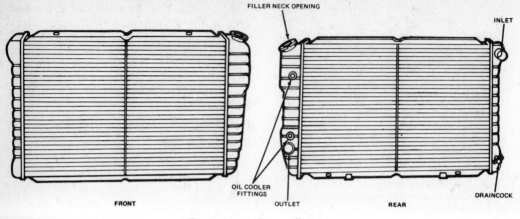

Typical crossflow radiator

likely to drink any that is left in an uncovered container or in puddles on the ground. This will prove fatal in sufficient quantity. Always drain the coolant into a sealable container. Coolant should be reused unless it is contaminated or several years old.

2. Disconnect the upper hose(s) at the radiator. Cars with a manual transmission have a vent hose at the top of the radiator.

3. Remove the 2 upper radiator frame nuts.

4. Disconnect the cooling fan wiring harness connector and cut the retaining strap to release the harness.

5. Raise and support the front end on jackstands.

6. On cars with an automatic transmission, disconnect the cooling lines.

7. Disconnect the lower radiator hose.

8. On cars with a manual transmission, release the fill tube brackets from the bottom edge of the radiator by removing the 2 retaining screws. Disconnect the fill tube connector hose from the bottom of the radiator left end tank.

9. Remove the screws securing the radiator end tank mounting brackets to the frame side rails. There are insulating bushings and washers above and below each bracket. Tip the radiator clear of the upper frame mounting studs and lower it from the car.

10. If necessary, the electric cooling fan can be removed from the radiator by removing the attaching screws and pulling the fan out of the lower retaining clips.

To install:

11. Install the electric cooling fan.

12. Position the radiator in the car.

13. Install the screws securing the radiator end tank mounting brackets to the frame side rails. There are insulating bushings and washers above and below each bracket.

14. On cars with a manual transmission, in-

stall the fill tube brackets. Connect the fill tube connector hose from the bottom of the radiator left end tank.

15. Connect the lower radiator hose.

16. On cars with an automatic transmission, connect the cooling lines.

17. Connect the cooling fan wiring harness connector and use a new retaining strap on the harness.

18. Install the 2 upper radiator frame nuts.

19. Connect the upper hose(s) at the radiator. Cars with a manual transmission have a vent hose at the top of the radiator.

20. Fill the cooling system.

Electro-Drive Cooling Fan

Various models, are equipped with a bracket-mounted electric cooling fan that replaces the conventional water pump mounted fan.

Operation of the fan motor is dependent on engine coolant temperature and air conditioner compressor clutch engagement. The fan will run only when the coolant temperature is approximately 180° or higher, or when the compressor clutch is engaged. The fan, motor and mount can be removed as an assembly after disconnecting the wiring harnesses and mounting bolts.

CAUTION: The cooling fan is automatic and may come on at any time without warning even if the ignition is switched OFF. To avoid possible injury, always disconnect the negative battery cable when working near the electric cooling fan.

REMOVAL AND INSTALLATION

Mustang and Capri

1. Disconnect the battery ground.

2. Remove the fan wiring harness from the clip.

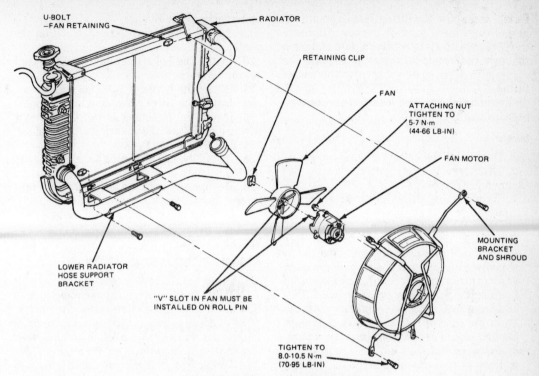

Gasoline engine electric cooling fan

3. Unplug the harness at the fan motor connector.

4. Remove the 4 mounting bracket attaching screws and remove the fan assembly from the car.

5. Remove the retaining clip from the end of the motor shaft and remove the fan.

6. Installation is the reverse of removal.

Merkur

1. Disconnect the battery ground cable.

2. Disconnect the cooling fan wiring connector.

3. Remove the screws attaching the top of the fan shroud to the radiator.

4. Pull straight up on the fan and shroud assembly to release it from the lower retining clips and remove it from the car.

5. Installation is the reverse of removal.

Air Conditioning Condenser

REMOVAL AND INSTALLATION

Mustang and Capri

1979-81

1. Discharge the system. See Chapter 1.

2. Remove the 6 attaching screws and remove the grille.

3. Move the ambient cutoff switch away from the front of the radiator and condenser.

4. Remove the battery.

5. Disconnect the refrigerant lines at the condenser and cap all openings immediately!

6. Remove the 4 bolts securing the condenser to the supports and remove the condenser.

7. Installation is the reverse of removal. Always use new O-rings coated with clean refrigerant oil at the pipe fittings. Evacuate, charge and leak test the system. See Chapter 1.

1982-88

1. Discharge the system. See Chapter 1.

2. Remove the battery.

3. Disconnect the refrigerant lines at the condenser and cap all openings immediately!

NOTE: *The fittings are spring-lock couplings and a special tool, T81P-19623-G, should be used. The larger opening end of the tool is for ½" discharge lines; the smaller end for ⅜" liquid lines.*

To operate the tool, close the tool and push the tool into the open side of the cage to expand the garter spring and release the female fitting. If the tool is not inserted straight, the garter spring will cock and not release.

After the garter spring is released, pull the fittings apart.

4. Remove the 4 bolts securing the condenser to the supports and remove the condenser.

5. Installation is the reverse of removal. Always use new O-rings coated with clean refrigerant oil at the pipe fittings.

To connect the couplings, check to ensure that the garter spring is in the cage of the male fitting, make sure the fittings are clean, install new O-rings made for this purpose, lubricate the O-rings with clean refrigerant oil and push the male and female fittings together until the garter springs snaps into place over the female fitting.

Evacuate, charge and leak test the system. See Chapter 1.

Merkur

1. Disconnect the battery ground cable.
2. Discharge the refrigerant system. See Chapter 1.
3. Remove the grille opening panel. See Chapter 10.
4. Drain the cooling system.

CAUTION: *When draining the coolant, keep in mind that cats and dogs are attracted by the ethylene glycol antifreeze, and are quite likely to drink any that is left in an uncovered container or in puddles on the ground. This will prove fatal in sufficient quantity. Always drain the coolant into a sealable container. Coolant should be reused unless it is contaminated or several years old.*

5. Remove the attaching screw, disconnect the wiring and lift out the electric cooling fan.
6. Raise and support the front end on jackstands.
7. Remove the lower radiator attaching bolts.
8. Remove the bolts retaining the right and left horn brackets, and position the horns out of the way.
9. Remove the bolts retaining the condenser mounting brackets.
10. Disconnect the refrigerant lines at the compressor and receiver/drier. Cap all openings at once!
11. Disconnect the wiring at the limit switch on the receiver/drier.
12. Working through the radiator support opening, push forward on the plastic of the two outer tabs to release the condenser.
13. Disconnect the front fan lead at the connector.
14. Swing the radiator towards the engine, lower the air conditioning fan, condenser and receiver/drier through the access opening.

To install:

15. Raise the air conditioning fan, condenser and receiver/drier through the access opening.
16. Connect the front fan lead at the connector.
17. Working through the radiator support opening, snap the condenser into place.
18. Connect the wiring at the limit switch on the receiver/drier.
19. Connect the refrigerant lines at the compressor and receiver/drier. Always use a back-

up wrench on the fittings. Always use new O-rings coated with clean refrigerant oil on the joints.

20. Install the bolts retaining the condenser mounting brackets.
21. Install the horns.
22. Install the lower radiator attaching bolts.
23. Install the attaching screw, Connect the wiring and lift out the electric cooling fan.
24. Fill the cooling system.
25. Install the grille opening panel. See Chapter 10.
26. Evacuate, charge and leak test refrigerant system. See Chapter 1.
27. Connect the battery ground cable.

Water Pump
REMOVAL AND INSTALLATION

1. Drain the cooling system.

CAUTION: *When draining the coolant, keep in mind that cats and dogs are attracted by the ethylene glycol antifreeze, and are quite likely to drink any that is left in an uncovered container or in puddles on the ground. This will prove fatal in sufficient quantity. Always drain the coolant into a sealable container. Coolant should be reused unless it is contaminated or several years old.*

2. Disconnect the negative battery cable.
3. On cars with power steering, remove the drive belt.
4. If the vehicle is equipped with air conditioning, remove the idler pulley bracket and air conditioner drive belt.
5. On engines with a Thermactor®, remove the belt.
6. Disconnect the lower radiator hose and heater hose from the water pump.
7. On cars equipped with a fan shroud, remove the retaining screws and position the shroud rearward.
8. Remove the fan, fan clutch and spacer from the engine, and if the car is equipped with an electric motor driven fan, remove the fan as an assembly for working clearance.
9. On the 4-140, remove the cam belt outer cover.
10. On cars equipped with a water pump mounted alternator, loosen the alternator mounting bolts, remove the alternator belt and remove the alternator adjusting arm bracket from the water pump. If interference is encountered, remove the air pump pulley and pivot bolts. Remove the air pump adjusting bracket. Swing the upper bracket aside. Detach the air conditioner compressor and lay it aside. Do not disconnect any of the A/C lines. Remove any accessory mounting brackets from the water pump.

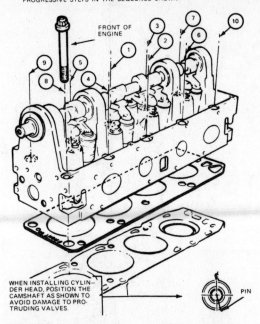

TORQUE THE CYLINDER HEAD BOLTS TO SPECIFICATIONS IN TWO PROGRESSIVE STEPS IN THE SEQUENCE SHOWN

FRONT OF ENGINE

WHEN INSTALLING CYLINDER HEAD, POSITION THE CAMSHAFT AS SHOWN TO AVOID DAMAGE TO PROTRUDING VALVES.

PIN

Cylinder head installation—4 cyl. 140 engine

11. Loosen the by-pass hose at the water pump, if so equipped.

12. Remove the water pump retaining screws and remove the pump from the engine.

13. Clean any gasket material from the pump mounting surface. On engines equipped with a water pump backing plate, remove the plate, clean the gasket surfaces, install a new gasket and plate on the water pump.

14. Remove the heater hose fitting from the old pump and install it on the new pump.

15. Coat both sides of the new gasket with a water-resistant sealer, then install the pump reversing the procedure.

Cylinder Head

REMOVAL AND INSTALLATION

NOTE: *On cars with air conditioning, remove the mounting bolts and the drive belt, and position the compressor out of the way. Remove the compressor upper mounting bracket from the cylinder head.*

CAUTION: *If the compressor refrigerant lines do not have enough slack to permit repositioning of the compressor without first disconnecting the refrigerant lines, the air conditioning system will have to be evacuated. See Chapter 1.*

4-140 Engine

NOTE: *Set the engine at TDC position for No. 1 piston, if possible prior to head removal.*

1. Drain the cooling system.

CAUTION: *When draining the coolant, keep in mind that cats and dogs are attracted by the ethylene glycol antifreeze, and are quite likely to drink any that is left in an uncovered container or in puddles on the ground. This will prove fatal in sufficient quantity. Always drain the coolant into a sealable container. Coolant should be reused unless it is contaminated or several years old.*

2. Remove the air cleaner. Disconnect the negative battery cable.

3. Remove the valve cover. Note the location of the valve cover attaching screws that have rubber grommets.

4. Remove the intake and exhaust manifolds from the head. See the procedures for intake manifold, exhaust manifold, and turbocharger removal.

5. Remove the camshaft drive belt cover. Note the location of the belt cover attaching screws that have rubber grommets.

6. Loosen the drive belt tensioner and remove the belt.

7. Remove the water outlet elbow from the cylinder head with the hose attached.

8. Remove the cylinder head attaching bolts.

9. Remove the cylinder head from the engine.

10. Clean all gaskets material and carbon from the top of the cylinder block and pistons and from the bottom of the cylinder head.

11. Position a new cylinder head gasket on the engine. Rotate the camshaft so that the hear locating pin is at the five o'clock position to avoid damage to the valves and pistons.

NOTE: *If you encounter difficulty in positioning the cylinder head on the engine block, it may be necessary to install guide studs in the block to correctly align the head and the block. To fabricate guide studs, obtain two new cylinder head bolts and cut their heads off with a hack saw. Install the bolts in the holes in the engine block which correspond with cylinder head bolt holes Nos. 3 and 4, as identified in the cylinder head bolt tightening sequence illustration. Then, install the head gasket and head over the bolts. Install the cylinder head attaching bolts, replacing the studs with the original head bolts.*

12. Using a torque wrench, tighten the head bolts in the sequence shown in the illustration.

13. Install the camshaft drive belt. See Camshaft Drive Belt Installation.

14. Install the camshaft drive belt cover and its attaching bolts. Make sure the rubber grommets are installed on the bolts. Tighten the bolts to 6-13 ft. lbs.

15. Install the water outlet elbow and a new gasket on the engine and tighten the attaching bolts to 12-15 ft. lbs.

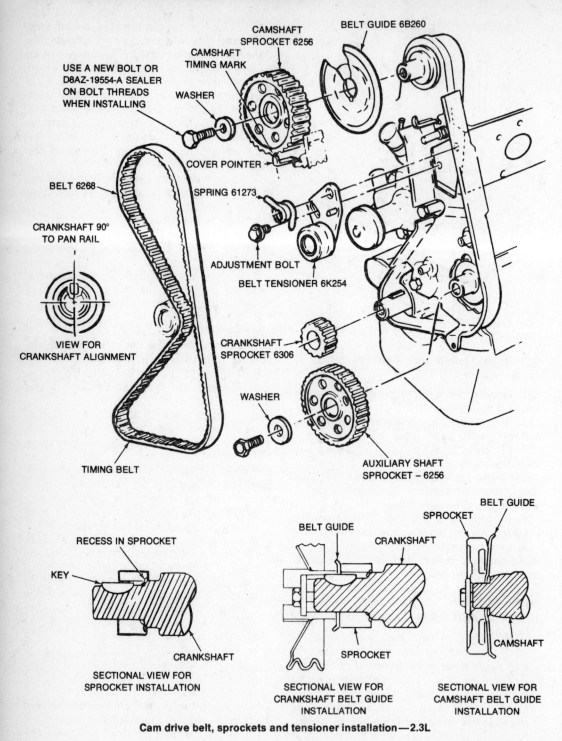

USE A NEW BOLT OR D8AZ-19554-A SEALER ON BOLT THREADS WHEN INSTALLING

WASHER

CAMSHAFT TIMING MARK

CAMSHAFT SPROCKET 6256

BELT GUIDE 6B260

COVER POINTER

BELT 6268

SPRING 61273

CRANKSHAFT 90° TO PAN RAIL

ADJUSTMENT BOLT

BELT TENSIONER 6K254

VIEW FOR CRANKSHAFT ALIGNMENT

CRANKSHAFT SPROCKET 6306

WASHER

TIMING BELT

AUXILIARY SHAFT SPROCKET – 6256

RECESS IN SPROCKET

KEY

CRANKSHAFT

SECTIONAL VIEW FOR SPROCKET INSTALLATION

BELT GUIDE

CRANKSHAFT

SPROCKET

SECTIONAL VIEW FOR CRANKSHAFT BELT GUIDE INSTALLATION

SPROCKET

BELT GUIDE

CAMSHAFT

SECTIONAL VIEW FOR CAMSHAFT BELT GUIDE INSTALLATION

Cam drive belt, sprockets and tensioner installation—2.3L

16. Install the intake and exhaust manifolds. See the procedures for intake and exhaust manifold installation.

17. Install the air cleaner and the valve cover.

18. Fill the cooling system.

V6-170

1. Remove the air cleaner assembly and disconnect the battery and accelerator linkage. Drain the cooling system.

CAUTION: *When draining the coolant, keep*

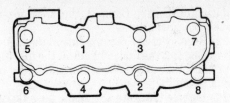

Cylinder head bolt torque sequence—V6 170 engine

in mind that cats and dogs are attracted by the ethylene glycol antifreeze, and are quite likely to drink any that is left in an uncovered container or in puddles on the ground. This will prove fatal in sufficient quantity. Always drain the coolant into a sealable container. Coolant should be reused unless it is contaminated or several years old.

2. Remove the distributor cap with the spark plug wires attached. Remove the distributor vacuum line and distributor. Remove the hose from the water pump to the water outlet which is on the carburetor.

3. Remove the valve covers, fuel line and filter, carburetor, and the intake manifold.

4. Remove the rocker arm shaft and oil baffles. Remove the pushrods, keeping them in the proper sequence for installation.

5. Remove the exhaust manifold, referring to the appropriate procedures.

6. Remove the cylinder head retaining bolts and remove the cylinder heads and gaskets.

7. Remove all gasket material and carbon from the engine block and cylinder heads.

8. Place the head gaskets on the engine block.

NOTE: *The left and right gaskets are not interchangeable.*

9. Install guide studs in the engine block. Install the cylinder head assemblies on the engine block one at a time. Tighten the cylinder head bolts in sequence, and in steps, 65-80 lbs.

10. Install the intake and exhaust manifolds.

11. Install the pushrods in the proper sequence. Install the oil baffles and the rocker arm shaft assemblies. Adjust the valve clearances.

12. Install the valve covers with new gaskets.

13. Install the distributor and set the ignition timing.

14. Install the carburetor and the distributor cap with the spark plug wires.

15. Connect the accelerator linkage, fuel line, with fuel filter installed, and distributor vacuum line to the carburetor. Fill the cooling system.

6-200

CAUTION: *When draining the coolant, keep in mind that cats and dogs are attracted by*

the ethylene glycol antifreeze, and are quite likely to drink any that is left in an uncovered container or in puddles on the ground. This will prove fatal in sufficient quantity. Always drain the coolant into a sealable container. Coolant should be reused unless it is contaminated or several years old.

1. Drain the cooling system, remove the air cleaner and disconnect the negative battery cable.

WARNING: *On cars with air conditioning, remove the mounting bolts and the drive belt, and position the compressor out of the way of the left cylinder head. Remove the compressor upper mounting bracket from the cylinder head.*

If the compressor refrigerant lines do not have enough slack to permit repositioning of the compressor without first disconnecting the refrigerant lines, the air conditioning system will have to be evacuated. See Chapter 1.

2. Disconnect the exhaust pipe at the manifold end, swing the exhaust pipe down and remove the flange gasket.

3. Disconnect the fuel and vacuum lines from the carburetor. Disconnect the intake manifold line at the intake manifold.

4. Disconnect the accelerator and retracting spring at the carburetor. Disconnect the transmission kickdown linkage, if equipped.

5. Disconnect the carburetor spacer outlet line at the spacer. Disconnect the radiator upper hose and the heater hose at the water outlet elbow. Disconnect the radiator lower hose and the heater hose at the water pump.

6. Disconnect the distributor vacuum control line at the distributor. Disconnect the gas filter line on the inlet side of the filter.

7. Disconnect and label the spark plug wires and remove the plugs. Disconnect the temperature sending unit wire.

8. Remove the rocker arm cover.

9. Remove the rocker arm shaft attaching bolts and the rocker arm and shaft assembly. Remove the valve pushrods, keep them in order for installation in their original positions.

10. Remove the remaining cylinder head bolts and lift off the cylinder head. Do not pry under

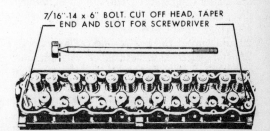

7/16"-14 x 6" BOLT, CUT OFF HEAD, TAPER END AND SLOT FOR SCREWDRIVER

Cylinder head guide stud fabrication

Cylinder head torque sequence—6 cyl. 200 engine

the cylinder head as damage to the mating surfaces can easily occur.

To help in installation of the cylinder head, two 6″ x $^7/_{16}$–14 bolts with their heads cut off and the head end slightly tapered and slotted, for installation and removal with a screwdriver, will reduce the possibility of damage during head replacement.

11. Clean the cylinder head and block surfaces. Be sure of flatness and no surface damage.

12. Apply cylinder head gasket sealer to both sides of the new gasket and slide the gasket down over the two guide studs in the cylinder block.

WARNING: *Apply gasket sealer only to steel shim head gaskets. Steel/asbestos composite head gaskets are to be installed without any sealer.*

13. Carefully lower the cylinder head over the guide studs. Place the exhaust pipe flange on the manifold studs (new gasket).

14. Coat the threads of the end bolts for the right side of the cylinder head with a small amount of water-resistant sealer. Install, but do not tighten, two head bolts at opposite ends to hold the head gasket in place. Remove the guide studs and install the remaining bolts.

15. Cylinder head torquing should proceed in three steps and in the prescribed order. Tighten them first to 55 ft. lbs., then give them a second tightening to 65 ft. lbs. The final step is to 75 ft. lbs., at which they should remain undisturbed.

16. Lubricate both ends of the pushrods and install them in their original locations.

17. Apply lubricant to the rocker arm pads and the valve stem tips and position the rocker arm shaft assembly on the head. Be sure the oil holes in the shaft are in a down position.

18. Tighten all the rocker shaft retaining bolts to 30-35 ft. lbs. and do a preliminary valve adjustment (make sure there are no tight valve adjustments).

19. Hook up the exhaust pipe.

20. Reconnect the heater and radiator hoses.

21. Reposition the distributor vacuum line, the carburetor gas line and the intake manifold vacuum line on the engine. Hook them up to their respective connections and reconnect the battery cable to the cylinder head.

22. Connect the accelerator rod and retracting spring. Connect the choke control cable and adjust the choke. Connect the transmission kickdown linkage.

23. Reconnect the vacuum line at the distributor. Connect the fuel inlet line at the fuel filter and the intake manifold vacuum line at the vacuum pump.

24. Lightly lubricate the spark plug threads and install them. Connect spark plug wires and be sure the wires are all the way down in their sockets. Connect the temperature sending unit wire.

25. Fill the cooling system. Run the engine to stabilize all engine part temperatures.

26. Adjust engine idle speed and idle fuel air adjustment.

27. Coat one side of a new rocker cover gasket with oil-resistant sealer. Lay the treated side of the gasket on the cover and install the cover. Be sure the gasket seals evenly all around the cylinder head.

6-232

1. Drain the cooling system.
CAUTION: *When draining the coolant, keep in mind that cats and dogs are attracted by the ethylene glycol antifreeze, and are quite likely to drink any that is left in an uncovered container or in puddles on the ground. This will prove fatal in sufficient quantity. Always drain the coolant into a sealable container. Coolant should be reused unless it is contaminated or several years old.*

2. Disconnect the cable from the battery negative terminal.

3. Remove the air cleaner assembly including air intake duct and heat tube.

4. Loosen the accessory drive belt idler. Remove the drive belt.

5. If the left cylinder head is being removed:

a. If equipped with power steering, remove the pump mounting brackets' attaching bolts, leaving the hoses connected, place the pump/bracket assembly aside in a position to prevent the fluid from leaking out.

b. If equipped with air conditioning, remove the mounting brackets' attaching bolts, leaving the hoses connected, and position the compressor aside.

6. If the right cylinder head is being removed:

a. Disconnect the Thermactor® diverter valve and hose assembly at the by-pass valve and downstream air tube.

b. Remove the assembly.

c. Remove the accessory drive idler.

d. Remove the alternator.

e. Remove the Thermactor® pump pulley. Remove the Thermactor® pump.

f. Remove the alternator bracket.

g. Remove the PCV valve.

7. Remove the intake manifold.

8. Remove the valve rocker arm cover attaching screws. Loosen the silicone rubber gasketing material by inserting a putty knife under the cover flange. Work the cover loosen and remove. The plastic rocker arm covers will break if excessive prying is applied.

9. Remove the exhaust manifold(s).

10. Loosen the rocker arm fulcrum attaching bolts enough to allow the rocker arm to be lifted off the pushrod and rotated to one side.

11. Remove the pushrods. Label the pushrods since they should be installed in the original position during assembly.

12. Remove the cylinder head attaching bolts. Remove the cylinder head(s).

13. Remove and discard the old cylinder head gasket(s). Discard the cylinder head bolts.

14. Lightly oil all bolt and stud bolt threads before installation except those specifying special sealant.

15. Clean the cylinder head, intake manifold, valve rocker arm cover and cylinder head gasket surfaces. If the cylinder head was removed for a cylinder head gasket replacement, check the flatness of the cylinder head and block gasket surfaces.

16. Position new head gasket(s) on the cylinder block using the dowels for alignment.

17. Position the cylinder heads to the block.

18. Apply a thin coating of pipe sealant or equivalent to the threads of the short cylinder head bolts (nearest to the exhaust manifold). Do not apply sealant to the long bolts. Lightly oil the cylinder head bolt flat washers. Install the flat washers and cylinder head bolts (Eight each side).

CAUTION: *Always use new cylinder head bolts to assure a leak tight assembly. Torque retention with used bolts can vary, which may result in coolant or compression leakage at the cylinder head mating surface area.*

19. Tighten the attaching bolts in sequence. Back off the attaching bolts 2-3 turns. Repeat tightening sequence.

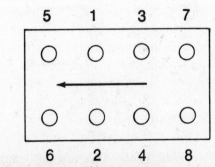

6-232 cylinder head torque sequence

NOTE: *When the cylinder head attaching bolts have been tightened using the above sequential procedure, it is not necessary to retighten the bolts after extended engine operation. However, the bolts can be checked for tightness if desired.*

20. Dip each pushrod end in heavy engine oil. Install the push rods in their original position. For each valve rotate the crankshaft until the tappet rests on the heel (base circle) of the camshaft lobe.

21. Position the rocker arms over the pushrods, install the fulcrums, and tighten the fulcrum attaching bolts to 61-132 in.lb.

WARNING: *Fulcrums must be fully seated in cylinder head and pushrods must be seated in rocker arm sockets prior to final tightening.*

22. Lubricate all rocker arm assemblies with heavy engine oil. Finally tighten the fulcrum bolts to 19-25 ft. lbs. For final tightening, the camshaft may be in any position.

NOTE: *If the original valve train components are being installed, a valve clearance check is not required. If a component has been replaced, perform a valve clearance check.*

23. Install the exhaust manifold(s).

24. Apply a 1/8-3/16" (3-4mm) bead of RTV silicone sealant to the rocker arm cover flange. make sure the sealer fills the channel in the cover flange. The rocker arm cover must be installed within 15 minutes after the silicone sealer application. After this time, the sealer may start to set-up, and its sealing effectiveness may be reduced.

25. Position the cover on the cylinder head and install the attaching bolts. Note the location of the wiring harness routing clips and spark plug wire routing clip stud bolts. Tighten the attaching bolts to 36-60 in.lb. torque.

26. Install the intake manifold.

27. Install the spark plugs, if necessary.

28. Connect the secondary wires to the spark plugs.

29. Install the oil fill cap. If equipped with air conditioning, install the compressor mounting and support brackets.

30. On the right cylinder head:

   a. Install the PCV valve.

   b. Install the alternator bracket. Tighten attaching nuts to 30-40 ft. lbs.

   c. Install the Thermactor® pump and pump pulley.

   d. Install the alternator.

   e. Install the accessory drive idler.

   f. Install the Thermactor® diverter valve and hose assembly. Tighten the clamps securely.

31. Install the accessory drive belt and tighten to the specified tension.

32. Connect the cable to the battery negative terminal.

33. Fill the cooling system with the specified coolant.

WARNING: *This engine has an aluminum cylinder head and requires a compatible coolant formulation to avoid radiator damage.*

34. Start the engine and check for coolant, fuel, and oil leaks.

35. Check and, if necessary, adjust the curb idle speed.

36. Install the air cleaner assembly including the air intake duct and heat tube.

V8 Engines

1. Drain the cooling system.

CAUTION: *When draining the coolant, keep in mind that cats and dogs are attracted by the ethylene glycol antifreeze, and are quite likely to drink any that is left in an uncovered container or in puddles on the ground. This will prove fatal in sufficient quantity. Always drain the coolant into a sealable container. Coolant should be reused unless it is contaminated or several years old.*

2. Remove the intake manifold and the carburetor or CFI unit as an assembly.

3. Disconnect the spark plug wires, marking them as to placement. Position them out of the way of the cylinder head. Remove the spark plugs.

4. Disconnect the exhaust pipes at the manifolds.

5. Remove the rocker arm covers.

6. On cars with air conditioning, remove the mounting bolts and the drive belt, and position the compressor out of the way of the left cylinder head. Remove the compressor upper mounting bracket from the cylinder head.

NOTE: *If the compressor refrigerant lines do not have enough slack to permit repositioning of the compressor without first disconnecting the refrigerant lines, the air conditioning system will have to be evacuated by a trained air conditioning serviceman. Under no circumstances should an untrained person attempt to disconnect the air conditioning refrigerant lines.*

7. In order to remove the left cylinder head, on cars equipped with power steering, it may be necessary to remove the steering pump and bracket, remove the drive belt, and wire or tie the pump out of the way, but in such a way as to prevent the loss of its fluid.

8. In order to remove the right head it may be necessary to remove the alternator mounting bracket bolt and spacer, the ignition coil, and the air cleaner inlet duct from the right cylinder head.

9. In order to remove the left cylinder head on a car equipped with a Thermactor® air pump system, disconnect the hose from the air manifold on the left cylinder head.

10. If the right cylinder head is to be removed on a car equipped with a Thermactor® system, remove the Thermactor® air pump and its mounting bracket. Disconnect the hose from the air manifold on the right cylinder head.

11. Loosen the rocker arm stud nuts enough to rotate the rocker arms to the side, in order to facilitate the removal of the pushrods. Remove the pushrods in sequence, so that they may be installed in their original positions. Remove the exhaust valve stem caps, if equipped.

12. Remove the cylinder head attaching bolts, noting their positions, Lift the cylinder head off the block. Remove and discard the old cylinder head gasket. Clean all mounting surfaces.

13. Position the new cylinder head gasket over the dowels on the block. Position new gaskets on the muffler inlet pipes at the exhaust manifold flange.

14. Position the cylinder head on the block, and install the head bolts, each in its original position. On engines on which the exhaust manifold has been removed from the head to facilitate removal, it is necessary to properly guide the exhaust manifold studs into the muffler inlet pipe flange when installing the head.

15. Step-torque the cylinder head retaining bolts first to 50 ft. lbs. then to 60 ft. lbs., and finally to the torque specification listed in the Torque Specifications chart. Tighten the exhaust manifold-to-cylinder head attaching bolts to specifications.

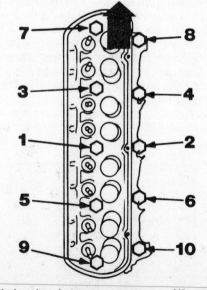

Cylinder head torque sequence—V8 engine. Arrow points to front

16. Tighten the nuts on the exhaust manifold studs at the muffler inlet flanges to 18 ft. lbs.

17. Clean and inspect the pushrods one at a time. Clean the oil passage within each pushrod with solvent and blow the passage out with compressed air. Check the ends of the pushrods for nicks, grooves, roughness, or excessive wear. Visually inspect the pushrods for straightness, and replace any bent ones. Do not attempt to straighten pushrods.

18. Install the pushrods in their original positions. Apply Lubriplate® or a similar product to the valve stem tips and to the pushrod guides in the cylinder head. Install the exhaust valve stem caps.

19. Apply Lubriplate® or a similar product to the fulcrum seats and sockets. Turn the rocker arms to their proper position and tighten the stud nuts enough to hold the rocker arms in position. Make sure that the lower ends of the pushrods have remained properly seated in the valve lifters. Tighten the stud nuts 17-23 ft. lbs. in order given under the preliminary valve adjustment.

20. Install the valve covers.

21. Install the intake manifold and carburetor, following the procedure under Intake Manifold Installation.

22. Reinstall all other items removed.

PRELIMINARY VALVE ADJUSTMENT

V6 and V8 Engine Only

This adjustment is actually part of the installation procedure for the individually mounted rocker arms found on the V-type engine, and is necessary to achieve an accurate torque value for each rocker arm nut.

By its nature, an hydraulic valve lifter will expand when it is not under load. Thus, when the rocker arms are removed and the pressure via the pushrod is taken off the lifter, the lifter expands to its maximum. If the lifter happens to be at the top of the camshaft lobe when the rocker arm is being reinstalled, a large amount of torque would be necessary when tighten the rocker arm nut just to overcome the pressure of the expanded lifter. This makes it very difficult to get an accurate torque setting with individually mounted rocker arms. For this reason, the rocker arms are installed in a certain sequence which corresponds to the low points of the camshaft lobes.

1. Turn the engine until the No. 1 cylinder is at TDC of the compression stroke and the timing pointer is aligned with the mark on the crankshaft damper.

2. Scribe a mark on the damper at this point.

3. Scribe two additional marks on the damper of a V8; a single line on a V6. (see the illustration).

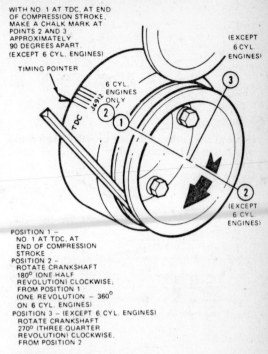

WITH NO. 1 AT TDC, AT END OF COMPRESSION STROKE, MAKE A CHALK MARK AT POINTS 2 AND 3 APPROXIMATELY 90 DEGREES APART (EXCEPT 6 CYL. ENGINES)

TIMING POINTER

6 CYL. ENGINES ONLY

(EXCEPT 6 CYL ENGINES)

(EXCEPT 6 CYL. ENGINES)

POSITION 1 –
NO. 1 AT TDC, AT END OF COMPRESSION STROKE
POSITION 2 –
ROTATE CRANKSHAFT 180° (ONE-HALF REVOLUTION) CLOCKWISE, FROM POSITION 1 (ONE REVOLUTION – 360° ON 6 CYL. ENGINES)
POSITION 3 – (EXCEPT 6 CYL. ENGINES) ROTATE CRANKSHAFT 270° (THREE-QUARTER REVOLUTION) CLOCKWISE, FROM POSITION 2

Crankshaft pulley marking for preliminary valve adjustment

4. With the timing pointer aligned with Mark 1 on the damper, tighten the following valves to the specified torque:

- 6-232 No. 1 intake and exhaust; No. 3 intake and exhaust; No. 4 exhaust and No. 6 intake.
- 8-255, 8-302 (Exc. HO) No. 1, 7 and 8 Intake; No. 1, 5, and 4 Exhaust.
- 8-302HO No. 1, 4 and 8 Intake; No. 1, 3 and 7 Exhaust.

5. Rotate the crankshaft 180° to point 2 and tighten the following valves:

- 6-232 No. 2 intake; No. 3 exhaust; No. 4 intake; No. 5 intake and exhaust; No. 6 exhaust.
- 8-255, 8-302 (Exc. HO) No. 5 and 4 Intake; No. 2 and 6 Exhaust
- 8-302HO No. 3 and 7 Intake; No. 2 and 6 Exhaust

6. Rotate the crankshaft 270° to point 3 and tighten the following valves:

- 8-302 (Exc. HO) No. 2, 3, and 6 Intake; No. 7, 3 and 8 Exhaust
- 8-302HO No. 2, 5 and 6 Intake; No. 4, 5 and 8 Exhaust

7. Rocker arm tighten specifications are:

- 6-232, 8-255, and 8-302: Tighten nut until it contacts the rocker shoulder, then torque to 18-20 ft. lbs.

CYLINDER HEAD OVERHAUL

1. Remove the cylinder head(s) from the car engine (see Cylinder Head Removal and Instal-

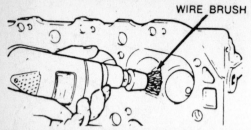

Remove the carbon from the cylinder head with a wire brush and electric drill

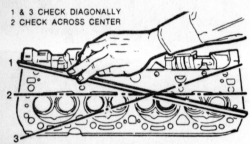

Check the cylinder head for warpage

lation). Place the head(s) on a workbench and remove any manifolds that are still connected. Remove all rocker arm retaining parts and the rocker arms, if still installed. On the 4-140, remove the camshaft (see Camshaft Removal).

2. Turn the cylinder head over so that the mounting surface is facing up and support it evenly on wood blocks.

CAUTION: *6-232 engines use aluminum cylinder heads; exercise care when cleaning.*

3. Use a scraper and remove all of the gasket material stuck to the head mounting surface. Mount a wire carbon removal brush in an electric drill and clean away the carbon on the valves and head combustion chambers.

CAUTION: *When scraping or decarbonizing the cylinder head, take care not to damage or nick the gasket mounting surface.*

4. Number the valve heads with a permanent felt-tip marker for cylinder location.

Resurfacing

If the cylinder head is warped resurfacing by a machine shop is required. Place a straightedge across the gasket surface of the head. Using feeler gauges, determine the clearance at the center and along the length between the head and straightedge. Measure clearance at the center and along the length between the head and straightedge. Measure clearance at the center and along the lengths of both diagonals. If warpage exceeds 0.003" (0.08mm) in a 6" (152mm) span, or 0.006" (0.15mm) over the total length the cylinder head must be resurfaced.

Valves and Springs

REMOVAL AND INSTALLATION

1. Block the head on its side, or install a pair of head-holding brackets made especially for valve removal.

2. Use a socket slightly larger than the valve stem and keepers, place the socket over the valve stem and gently hit the socket with a plastic hammer to break loose any varnish buildup.

3. Remove the valve keepers, retainer, spring shield and valve spring using a valve spring compressor (the locking C-clamp type is the easiest kind to use).

4. Put the parts in a separate container numbered for the cylinder being worked on; do not mix them with other parts removed.

5. Remove and discard the valve stem oil seals. A new seal will be used at assembly time.

6. Remove the valves from the cylinder head and place them, in order, through numbered holes punched in a stiff piece of cardboard or wood valve holding stick.

NOTE: *The exhaust valve stems, on some engines, are equipped with small metal caps. Take care not to lose the caps. Make sure to reinstall them at assembly time. Replace any caps that are worn.*

7. Use an electric drill and rotary wire brush to clean the intake and exhaust valve ports, combustion chamber and valve seats. In some cases, the carbon will need to be chipped away. Use a blunt pointed drift for carbon chipping. Be careful around the valve seat areas.

8. Use a wire valve guide cleaning brush and safe solvent to clean the valve guides.

9. Clean the valves with a revolving wires brush. Heavy carbon deposits may be removed with the blunt drift.

NOTE: *When using a wire brush to clean carbon on the valve ports, valves etc., be sure that the deposits are actually removed, rather than burnished.*

10. Wash and clean all valve springs, keepers, retaining caps etc., in safe solvent.

11. Clean the head with a brush and some safe solvent and wipe dry.

12. Check the head for cracks. Cracks in the cylinder head usually start around an exhaust valve seat because it is the hottest part of the combustion chamber. If a crack is suspected but cannot be detected visually have the area checked with dye penetrant or other method by the machine shop.

13. After all cylinder head parts are reasonably clean, check the valve stem-to-guide clearance. If a dial indicator is not on hand, a visual inspection can give you a fairly good idea if the guide, valve stem or both are worn.

14. Insert the valve into the guide until slight-

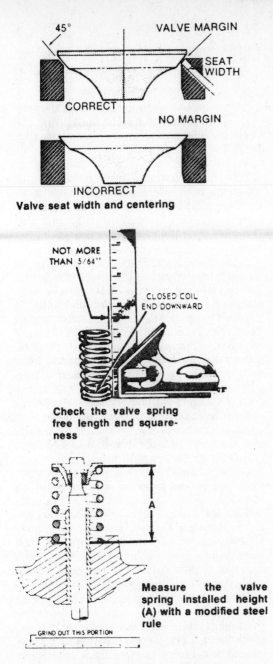

Valve seat width and centering

Check the valve spring free length and square-ness

Measure the valve spring installed height (A) with a modified steel rule

ly away from the valve seat. Wiggle the valve sideways. A small amount of wobble is normal, excessive wobble means a worn guide or valve stem. If a dial indicator is on hand, mount the indicator so that the stem of the valve is at 90° to the valve stem, as close to the valve guide as possible. Move the valve off the seat, and measure the valve guide-to-stem clearance by rocking the stem back and forth to actuate the dial indicator. Measure the valve stem using a micrometer and compare to specifications to determine whether stem or guide wear is causing excessive clearance.

15. The valve guide, if worn, must be repaired before the valve seats can be resurfaced. Ford supplies valves with oversize stems to fit valve guides that are reamed to oversize for repair. The machine shop will be able to handle the guide reaming for you. In some cases, if the guide is not too badly worn, knurling may be all that is required.

16. Reface, or have the valves and valve seats refaced. The valve seats should be a true 45° angle. Remove only enough material to clean up any pits or grooves. Be sure the valve seat is not too wide or narrow. Use a 60° grinding wheel to remove material from the bottom of the seat for raising and a 30° grinding wheel to remove material from the top of the seat to narrow.

17. After the valves are refaced by machine, hand lap them to the valve seat. Clean the grinding compound off and check the position of face-to-seat contact. Contact should be close to the center of the valve face. If contact is close to the top edge of the valve, narrow the seat; if too close to the bottom edge, raise the seat.

18. Valves should be refaced to a true angle of 44°. Remove only enough metal to clean up the valve face or to correct runout. If the edge of a valve head, after machining, is $1/32''$ (0.8mm) or less replace the valve. The tip of the valve stem should also be dressed on the valve grinding machine, however, do not remove more than $0.010''$ (0.254mm).

19. After all valve and valve seats have been machined, check the remaining valve train parts (springs, retainers, keepers, etc.) for wear. Check the valve springs for straightness and tension.

20. Install the valves in the cylinder head and metal caps.

21. Install new valve stem oil seals.

22. Install the valve keepers, retainer, spring shield and valve spring using a valve spring compressor (the locking C-clamp type is the easiest kind to use).

23. Check the valve spring installed height, shim or replace as necessary.

CHECKING VALVE SPRINGS

Place the valve spring on a flat surface next to a carpenter's square. Measure the height of the spring, and rotate the spring against the edge of the square to measure distortion. If the spring height varies (by comparison) by more than $1/16''$ (1.6mm) or if the distortion exceeds $1/16''$ (1.6mm), replace the spring.

Have the valve springs tested for spring pressure at the installed and compressed (installed height minus valve lift) height using a valve spring tester. Springs should be within one pound, plus or minus each other. Replace springs as necessary.

VALVE SPRING INSTALLED HEIGHT

After installing the valve spring, measure the distance between the spring mounting pad and the lower edge of the spring retainer. Compare the measurement to specifications. If the installed height is incorrect, add shim washers between the spring mounting pad and the spring. Use only washers designed for valve springs, available at most parts houses.

VALVE STEM OIL SEALS

Umbrella type oil seals fitting on the valve stem over the top of the valve guide are used on the 6-200. The 4-140 and 6-232 use a positive valve stem seal using a Teflon® insert. Teflon® seals are available for other engines but usually require valve guide machining. Consult your automotive machine shop for advice on having positive valve stem oil seals installed.

When installing valve stem oil seals, ensure that a small amount of oil is able to pass the seal to lubricate the valve stems and guide walls, otherwise, excessive wear will occur.

VALVE SEATS

If the valve seat is damaged or burnt and cannot be serviced by refacing, it may be possible to have the seat machined and an insert installed. Consult an automotive machine shop for their advice.

NOTE: *The aluminum heads on 6-232 engines are equipped with inserts.*

VALVE GUIDES

Worn valve guides can, in most cases, be reamed to accept a valve with an oversized stem. Valve guides that are not excessively worn or distorted may, in some cases, be knurled rather than reamed. However, if the valve stem is worn reaming for an oversized valve stem is the answer since a new valve would be required.

Knurling is a process in which metal is displaced and raised, thereby reducing clearance. Knurling also produces excellent oil control. The possibility of knurling instead of reaming the valve guides should be discussed with a machinist.

HYDRAULIC VALVE CLEARANCE

Hydraulic valve lifters operate with zero clearance in the valve train, and because of this the rocker arms are nonadjustable. The only means by which valve system clearances can be altered is by installing over or undersize pushrods; but, because of the hydraulic lifter's natural ability to compensate for slack in the valve train, all components of all the valve system should be checked for wear if there is excessive play in the system.

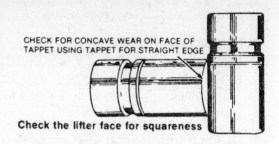

CHECK FOR CONCAVE WEAR ON FACE OF TAPPET USING TAPPET FOR STRAIGHT EDGE

Check the lifter face for squareness

When a valve in the engine is in the closed position, the valve lifter is resting on the base circle of the camshaft lobe and the pushrod is in its lowest position. To remove this additional clearance from the valve train, the valve lifter expands to maintain zero clearance in the valve system. When a rocker arm is loosened or removed from the engine, the lifter expands to it fullest travel. When the rocker arm is reinstalled on the engine, the proper valve setting is obtained by tightening the rocker arm to a specified limit. But with the lifter fully expanded, if the camshaft lobe is on a high point it will require excessive torque to compress the lifter and obtain the proper setting. Because of this, when any component of the valve system has been removed, a preliminary valve adjustment procedure must be followed to ensure that when the rocker arm is reinstalled on the engine and tightened, the camshaft lobe for that cylinder is in the low position.

To determine whether a shorter or loner push rod is necessary, make the following check:

Mark the crankshaft pulley as described under Preliminary Valve Adjustment procedure. Follow each step in the procedure. As each valve is positioned, mount a suitable hydraulic lifter compressor tool on the rocker arm. Slowly apply pressure to bleed down the lifter until the plunger is completely bottomed. Take care to avoid excessive pressure that might bend the pushrod. Hold the lifter in bottom position and check the available clearance between the rocker arm and the valve stem tip with a feeler gauge. If the clearance is less than specified, install an undersized pushrod. If the clearance is greater than specified, install an oversized pushrod. When compressing the valve spring to remove the pushrods, be sure the piston in the individual cylinder is below TDC to avoid contact between the valve and the piston. To replace a pushrod, it will be necessary to remove the valve rocker arm shaft assembly on in-line engines. Upon replacement of a valve pushrod, valve rocker arm shaft assembly or hydraulic valve lifter, the engine should not be cranked or rotated until the hydraulic lifters have had an opportunity to leak down to their normal operation position. The leak down rate can be accelerated by using the tool shown on the valve rocker arm and applying pressure in a direction to collapse the lifter.

Collapsed tappet gap

4-140
6-200
- Allowable: 0.085-0.209″ (2.159-5.309mm)
- Desired: 0.110-0.184″ (2.794-4.673mm)

6-232
- Allowable: 0.088-0.189″ (2.235-4.800mm)

V8 Engines
- 8-255 cu.in.
  Allowable: 0.098-0.198″ (2.489-5.029mm)
  Desired: 0.123-0.173″ (3.124-4.394mm)
- 8-302 cu.in.
  Allowable: 0.089-0.193″ (2.260-4.902mm)
  Desired: 0.096-0.163″ (2.438-4.140mm)

VALVE CLEARANCE W/HYDRAULIC VALVE LASH ADJUSTERS

4-140 Engine

Hydraulic valve lash adjusters are used in the valve train. These units are placed at the fulcrum point of the cam followers (or rocker arms). Their action is similar to the hydraulic tappets used in push rod engines.

1. Position the camshaft so that the base circle of the lobe is facing the cam follower of the valve to be checked.
2. Using the tool shown in the illustration, slowly apply pressure to the cam follower until the lash adjuster is completely collapsed. Hold the follower in this position and insert a 0.045″ (1.14mm) feeler gauge between the base circle of the cam and the follower.
NOTE: *The minimum gap is 0.035″ (0.89mm) and the maximum is 0.055″ (1.39mm). The desired gap is between 0.040-0.050″ (1.02-1.27mm).*
3. If the clearance is excessive, remove the cam follower and inspect it for damage.
4. If the cam follower seems OK, measure the valve spring assembled height to be sure the valve is not sticking. See the Valve Specifications chart in this chapter.
5. If the valve spring assembled height is OK, check the dimensions of the camshaft.
6. If the camshaft dimensions are OK, the lash adjuster should be cleaned and tested.
7. Replace any worn parts as necessary.
NOTE: *For any repair that includes removal of the camshaft follower (rocker arm), each affected hydraulic lash adjuster must be collapsed after installation of the camshaft fol-*

lower, and then released. This step must be taken prior to any rotation of the camshaft.

HYDRAULIC VALVE LIFTER INSPECTION

Remove the lifters from their bores and remove any gum and varnish with safe solvent. Check the lifters for concave wear. If the bottom of the lifter is worn concave or flat, replace the lifter. Lifters are built with a convex bottom, flatness indicates wear. If a worn lifter is detected, carefully check the camshaft for wear.
NOTE: *Mark lifters for cylinder and position location. Lifters must be reinstalled in the same bore from which they were removed.*
To test lifter leak down, submerge the lifter in a container of kerosene. Chuck a used pushrod or its equivalent into a drill press. Position the container of kerosene so the pushrod acts on the lifter plunger. Pump the lifter with the drill press until resistance increases. Pump several more times to bleed any air from the lifter. Apply very firm, constant pressure to the lifter and observe the rate which fluid bleeds out of the lifter. If the lifter bleeds down very quickly (less than 15 seconds), the lifter should be replaced. If the time exceeds 60 seconds, the lifter is sticking and should be cleaned or replaced. If the lifter is operating properly (leak down time 15-60 seconds) and not worn, lubricate and reinstall it in the engine.

Oil Pan

REMOVAL AND INSTALLATION

NOTE: *Always raise and safely support the vehicle safely on jackstands. When raising the engine, place a piece of wood between the jack and jacking point, make sure the hood is opened and the fan blades do not touch the radiator or that radiator hoses or transmission lines are not stretched.*

4-140 Engine

1. Disconnect the negative battery cable.
2. Drain the crankcase and cooling system.
CAUTION: *When draining the coolant, keep in mind that cats and dogs are attracted by the ethylene glycol antifreeze, and are quite likely to drink any that is left in an uncovered container or in puddles on the ground. This will prove fatal in sufficient quantity. Always drain the coolant into a sealable container. Coolant should be reused unless it is contaminated or several years old.*
3. Remove the right and left engine support bolts and nuts or through-bolts. Disconnect the hydraulic damper if so equipped. Disconnect the hydraulic damper if so equipped. Disconnect the upper and lower radiator hoses.
4. Using a jack, raise the engine as far as it

will go. Place blocks of wood between the mounts and the chassis brackets. Remove the jack.

5. Remove the steering gear retaining nuts and bolts. Remove the bolt retaining the steering flex coupling to the steering gear. Position the steering gear forward and down.

6. Remove the shake brace and starter.

7. Remove the engine rear support-to-cross-member nuts.

8. Position a jack under the transmission and take up its weight.

9. Remove the oil pan retaining bolts. Remove the oil pan. It may be necessary to turn the crankshaft when removing the pan to avoid interference.

10. Position the new oil pan gasket and end seal on the cylinder block with gasket cement.

11. Position the oil pan on the cylinder block and install its retaining bolts.

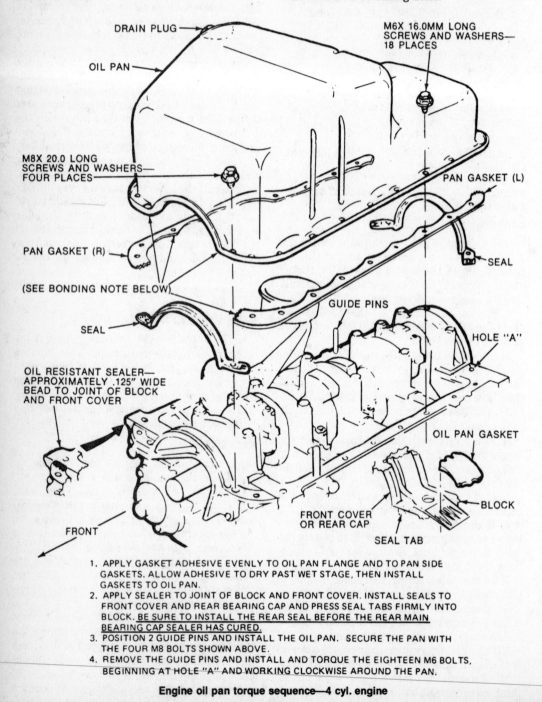

1. APPLY GASKET ADHESIVE EVENLY TO OIL PAN FLANGE AND TO PAN SIDE GASKETS. ALLOW ADHESIVE TO DRY PAST WET STAGE, THEN INSTALL GASKETS TO OIL PAN.

2. APPLY SEALER TO JOINT OF BLOCK AND FRONT COVER. INSTALL SEALS TO FRONT COVER AND REAR BEARING CAP AND PRESS SEAL TABS FIRMLY INTO BLOCK. BE SURE TO INSTALL THE REAR SEAL BEFORE THE REAR MAIN BEARING CAP SEALER HAS CURED.

3. POSITION 2 GUIDE PINS AND INSTALL THE OIL PAN. SECURE THE PAN WITH THE FOUR M8 BOLTS SHOWN ABOVE.

4. REMOVE THE GUIDE PINS AND INSTALL AND TORQUE THE EIGHTEEN M6 BOLTS, BEGINNING AT HOLE "A" AND WORKING CLOCKWISE AROUND THE PAN.

Engine oil pan torque sequence—4 cyl. engine

12. Lower the jack under the transmission and install the crossmember nuts.

13. Replace the oil filter.

14. Position the flex coupling on the steering gear and install the retaining bolt.

15. Install the steering gear.

16. Install the shake brace. Install the starter.

17. Raise the engine enough to remove the wood blocks. Lower the engine and remove the jack. Install the engine support bolts and nuts. Connect the radiator hoses.

18. Lower the vehicle and fill the crankcase with oil and the cooling system with coolant.

19. Connect the battery.

20. Start the engine and check for leaks.

6-200

1. Disconnect the two oil cooler lines at the radiator.

2. Remove the two radiator top support bolts. Remove or position the fan shroud back over the fan.

3. Remove the oil level dipstick. Drain the crankcase.

4. Remove the four bolts and nuts attaching the sway bar to the chassis and allow the sway bar to hang down.

5. Remove the K-brace.

6. Lower the front steering rack and pinion, or the center link and linkage, if necessary for clearance.

7. Remove the starter.

8. Remove the two nuts attaching the engine mounts to the support brackets.

9. Loosen the two rear insulator-to-crossmember attaching bolts.

10. Raise the engine and place a 1¼" (3.175mm) spacer between the engine support insulator and the chassis brackets.

11. Position a jack under the transmission and raise it slightly.

12. Remove the oil pan attaching bolts and lower pan to the crossmember. Position the transmission cooler lines out of the way and remove the oil pan, rotating the crankshaft if required.

13. The oil pan has a two piece gasket. Coat the block surface and the oil pan gasket surfaces with oil resistant sealer, and position the gaskets on the cylinder block.

14. Position the oil pan seals in the cylinder front cover and rear bearing cap.

15. Insert the gasket tabs under the front and rear seals.

16. Position the oil pan on the cylinder block and install the attaching bolts.

17. Connect the transmission cooler lines.

18. Lower the jack from under transmission.

19. Raise the engine to remove the spacers and lower the engine on the chassis.

20. Tighten the two nuts attaching the rear support insulator to the crossmember.

21. Install the two engine support-to-chassis through-bolts and nuts.

22. Install the starter motor and the sway bar.

23. Install the K-brace, and fill the crankcase with oil.

24. Connect the oil cooler lines to the radiator and install the upper radiator support.

25. Lower the vehicle, start the engine and check for leaks.

6-232 Engine

1. Remove the air cleaner assembly including the air intake duct. Drain the cooling system.

CAUTION: *When draining the coolant, keep in mind that cats and dogs are attracted by the ethylene glycol antifreeze, and are quite likely to drink any that is left in an uncovered container or in puddles on the ground. This will prove fatal in sufficient quantity. Always drain the coolant into a sealable container. Coolant should be reused unless it is contaminated or several years old.*

2. Remove the fan shroud attaching bolts and position the shroud back over the fan.

3. Remove the oil level dipstick.

4. Remove the screws attaching the vacuum solenoids to the dash panel. Lay the solenoids on the engine without disconnecting the vacuum hoses or electrical connectors.

5. Remove the exhaust manifold to exhaust pipe attaching nuts. Disconnect the radiator hoses from the radiator.

6. Drain the crankcase.

7. Remove the oil filter.

8. Remove the bolts attaching the shift linkage bracket to the transmission bell housing. Remove the starter motor for more clearance if necessary.

9. Disconnect the transmission cooler lines at the radiator. Remove power steering hose retaining clamp from frame.

10. Remove the converter cover.

11. On models equipped with rack and pinion steering, proceed with the following steps.

   a. Remove the engine damper-to-No. 2 crossmember bracket attaching bolt. The damper must be disconnected from the crossmember.

   b. Disconnect the steering flex coupling. Remove the two bolts attaching the steering gear to the main crossmember and let the steering gear rest on the frame away from the oil pan.

12. Remove the nut and washer assembly attaching the front engine insulator to the chassis.

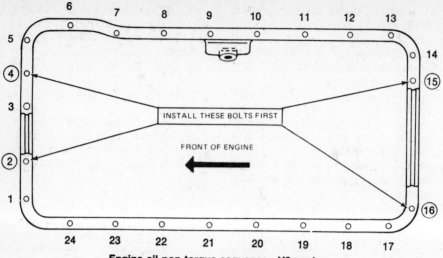

Engine oil pan torque sequence—V6 engine

13. Raise the engine 2-3″ (51-76mm) or higher on some models and insert wood blocks between the engine mounts and the vehicle frame.

NOTE: *Watch the clearance between the transmission dipstick tube and the Thermactor® downstream air tube. If the*

tubes contact before adequate pan-to-crossmember clearance is provided, lower the engine and remove the transmission dipstick tube and the downstream air tube.

14. Remove the oil pan attaching bolts. Work the oil pan loose and remove it.

15. On models with limited clearance, lower the oil pan onto the crossmember. Remove the oil pickup tube attaching nut. Lower the pickup tube/screen assembly into the pan and remove the oil pan through the front of the vehicle.

16. Remove the oil pan seal from the main bearing cap.

17. Clean the gasket surfaces on the cylinder block, oil pan and oil pick-up tube.

18. Apply an 8mm bead of RTV sealer to all matching surfaces of the oil pan and the engine front cover.

19. Install the oil pan.

NOTE: *On models with limited clearance place the oil pick-up tube/screen assembly in the oil pan.*

20. Remove the wood blocks between the engine mounts and the vehicle frame and lower the engine onto the mounts.

21. Install the nut and washer assembly attaching the front engine insulator to the chassis.

22. On models equipped with rack and pinion steering, proceed with the following steps.

   a. Connect the steering flex coupling.

   b. Install the two bolts attaching the steering gear to the main crossmember.

   c. Install the engine damper-to-No. 2 crossmember bracket attaching bolt. The damper must be connected to the crossmember.

23. Install the converter cover.

24. Connect the transmission cooler lines at the radiator.

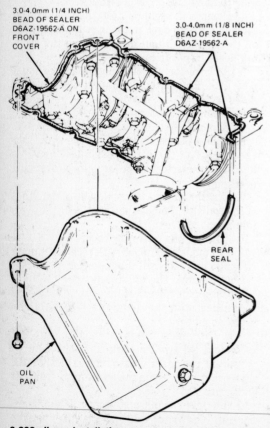

3.0-4.0mm (1/4 INCH) BEAD OF SEALER D6AZ-19562-A ON FRONT COVER

3.0-4.0mm (1/8 INCH) BEAD OF SEALER D6AZ-19562-A

REAR SEAL

OIL PAN

6-232 oil pan installation

25. Install the power steering hose retaining clamp to the frame.

26. Install the starter motor for more clearance if necessary.

27. Install the bolts attaching the shift linkage bracket to the transmission bell housing.

28. Install the oil filter.

29. Fill the crankcase.

30. Install the exhaust manifold to exhaust pipe attaching nuts.

31. Connect the radiator hoses at the radiator.

32. Install the vacuum solenoids to the dash panel.

33. Install the oil level dipstick.

34. Install the fan shroud.

35. Install the air cleaner assembly including the air intake duct.

36. Fill the cooling system.

37. Start the engine and check the fluid levels in the transmission.

38. Check for engine oil, and transmission fluid leaks.

V8 Engines

WARNING: *On vehicles equipped with a dual sump oil pan, both drain plugs must be removed to thoroughly drain the crankcase.*

When raising the engine for oil pan removal clearance, drain the cooling system, disconnect the hoses, check the fan-to-radiator clearance when jacking. Remove the radiator if clearance is inadequate.

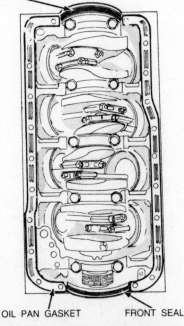

REAR SEAL

OIL PAN GASKET FRONT SEAL

Typical oil pan gasket and seal installation

CAUTION: *When draining the coolant, keep in mind that cats and dogs are attracted by the ethylene glycol antifreeze, and are quite likely to drink any that is left in an uncovered container or in puddles on the ground. This will prove fatal in sufficient quantity. Always drain the coolant into a sealable container. Coolant should be reused unless it is contaminated or several years old.*

1. Remove the fan shroud attaching bolts, positioning the fan shroud back over the fan. Remove the dipstick and tube assembly. Disconnect the negative battery cable.

2. Drain the crankcase.

3. On rack and pinion models disconnect the steering flex coupling. Remove the two bolts attaching the steering gear to the main crossmember and let the steering gear rest on the frame away from the oil pan. Disconnect the power steering hose retaining clamp from the frame.

4. Remove the starter motor.

5. Remove the idler arm bracket retaining bolts (models equipped) and pull the linkage down and out of the way.

6. Disconnect and plug the fuel line from the gas tank at the fuel pump. Disconnect and lower the exhaust pipe/converter assemblies if they will interfere with pan removal/installation. Raise the engine and place two wood blocks between the engine mounts and the vehicle frame. Remove the converter inspection cover.

WARNING: *On fuel injected models, depressurize the system prior to line disconnection.*

7. Remove the rear K-brace (four bolts).

8. Remove the oil pan attaching bolts and lower the oil pan on the frame.

9. Remove the oil pump attaching bolts and the inset tube attaching nut from the No.3 main bearing cap stud and lower the oil pump into the oil pan.

10. Remove the oil pan, rotating the crankshaft as necessary to clear the counterweights.

11. Clean the gasket mounting surfaces thoroughly. Coat the surfaces on the block and pan with sealer. Position the pan side gaskets on the engine block. Install the front cover oil seal on the cover, with the tabs over the pan side gaskets. Install the rear main cap seal with the tabs over the pan side gaskets.

12. Position the oil pump and inlet tube into the oil pan. Slide the oil pan into position under the engine. With the oil pump intermediate shaft in position in the oil pump, position the oil pump on the cylinder block, and the inlet tube on the stud on the No. 3 main bearing cap attaching bolt. Install the attaching bolts and nut and tighten to specification.

Position the oil pan on the engine and install

the attaching bolts. Tighten the bolts (working from the center toward the ends) 9-11 ft. lbs. for $\frac{5}{16}$" bolts and 7-9 ft. lbs. for $\frac{1}{4}$" bolts.

13. Position the steering gear on the main crossmember. Install the two attaching bolts and tighten them to specification. Connect the steering flex coupling.

14. Position the rear K-braces and install the four attaching bolts.

15. Raise the engine and remove the wood blocks.

16. Lower the engine and install the engine mount attaching bolts. Tighten them to specification. Install the converter inspection cover.

17. Install the oil dipstick and tube assembly, and fill crankcase with the specified engine oil. Install the idler arm.

18. Connect the transmission oil cooler lines. Connect the battery cable.

19. Position the shroud on the radiator and install the two attaching bolts. Start the engine and check for leaks.

Oil Pump

REMOVAL AND INSTALLATION

Except 6-232

1. Remove the oil pan.
2. Remove the oil pump inlet tube and screen assembly.
3. Remove the oil pump attaching bolts and remove the oil pump gasket and the intermediate shaft.
4. Prime the oil pump by filling the inlet and outlet ports with engine oil and rotating the shaft of pump to distribute it.

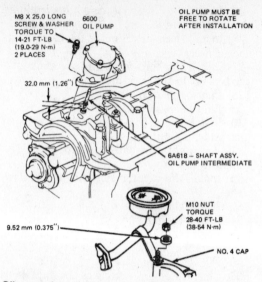

Oil pump installation—4 cyl. engine; others similar location

5. Position the intermediate driveshaft into the distributor socket.

6. Position a new gasket on the pump body and insert the intermediate driveshaft into the pump body.

7. Install the pump and intermediate shaft as an assembly.

WARNING: *Do not force the pump if it does not seat readily. The driveshaft may be misaligned with the distributor shaft. To align, rotate the intermediate driveshaft into a new position.*

8. Install and torque the oil pump attaching screws to:

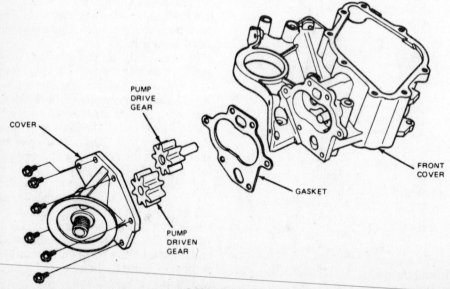

6-232 oil pump

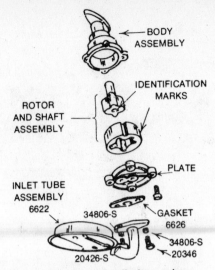

Oil pump used on 6 and 8 cylinder engines

- 4-140, 6-200 — 12-15 ft. lbs.;
- 8-302 — 22-32 ft. lbs.;
9. Install the oil pan.

6-232 Engines

NOTE: *The oil pump is mounted in the front cover assembly. Oil pan removal is necessary for pick-up tube/screen replacement or service.*

1. Raise and safely support the vehicle on jackstands.

2. Remove the oil filter.

3. Remove the cover/filter mount assembly.

4. Lift the two pump gears from their mounting pocket in the front cover.

5. Clean all gasket mounting surfaces.

6. Inspect the mounting pocket for wear. If excessive wear is present, complete timing cover assembly replacement is necessary.

7. Inspect the cover/filter mounting gasket-to-timing cover surface for flatness. Place a straightedge across the flat and check the clearance with a feeler gauge. If the measured clearance exceeds 0.004″ (0.102mm), replace the cover/filter mount.

8. Replace the pump gears if wear is excessive.

9. Remove the plug from the end of the pressure relief valve passage using a small drill and slide hammer. Use caution when drilling.

10. Remove the spring and valve from the bore. Clean all dirt, gum and metal chips from the bore and valve. Inspect all parts for wear. Replace as necessary.

11. Install the valve and spring after lubricating them with engine oil. Install a new plug flush with the machined surfaces.

12. Install the pump gears and fill the pocket with petroleum jelly. Install the cover/filter

mount using a new mounting gasket. Tighten the mounting bolts to 18-22 ft. lbs. Install the oil filter, add necessary oil for correct level.

Crankshaft Pulley (Vibration Damper)

REMOVAL AND INSTALLATION

1. Remove the fan shroud, as required. If necessary, drain the cooling system and remove the radiator. Remove drive belts from pulley.

CAUTION: *When draining the coolant, keep in mind that cats and dogs are attracted by the ethylene glycol antifreeze, and are quite likely to drink any that is left in an uncovered container or in puddles on the ground. This will prove fatal in sufficient quantity. Always drain the coolant into a sealable container. Coolant should be reused unless it is contaminated or several years old.*

2. On those engines with a separate pulley, remove the retaining bolts and separate the pulley from the vibration damper.

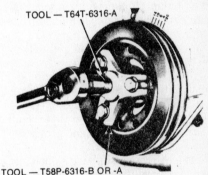

6-200 crankshaft damper removal

Using a puller to remove the vibration damper on the V6 and V8

3. Remove the vibration damper/pulley retaining bolt from the crankshaft end.

4. Using a puller, remove the damper/pulley from the crankshaft.

5. Upon installation, align the key slot of the pulley hub to the crankshaft key. Complete the assembly in the reverse order of removal. Torque the retaining bolts to specifications.

Timing Cover and Chain
REMOVAL AND INSTALLATION
6-200

1. Drain the cooling system and crankcase. CAUTION: *When draining the coolant, keep in mind that cats and dogs are attracted by the ethylene glycol antifreeze, and are quite likely to drink any that is left in an uncovered container or in puddles on the ground. This will prove fatal in sufficient quantity. Always drain the coolant into a sealable container. Coolant should be reused unless it is contaminated or several years old.*

2. Disconnect the upper radiator hose from the intake manifold and the lower hose from the water pump. On cars with automatic transmission, disconnect the cooler lines from the radiator.

3. Remove the radiator, fan and pulley, and engine drive belts. On models with air conditioning, remove the condenser retaining bolts and position the condenser forward. Do not disconnect the refrigerant lines.

4. Remove the cylinder front cover retaining bolts and front oil pan bolts and gently pry the cover away from the block.

5. Remove the crankshaft pulley bolt and use a puller to remove the vibration damper.

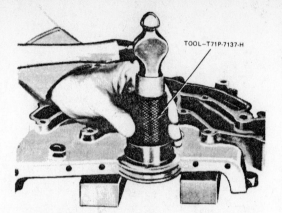

TOOL–T71P-7137-H

Installing front cover oil seal; a large socket can be used in place of tool shown

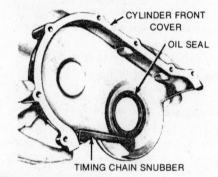

CYLINDER FRONT COVER

OIL SEAL

TIMING CHAIN SNUBBER

6-200 timing gear cover

6. With a socket wrench of the proper size on the crankshaft pulley bolt, gently rotate the crankshaft in a clockwise direction until all slack is removed from the lift side of the timing chain. Scribe a mark on the engine block parallel to the present position on the left side of the chain. Next, turn the crankshaft in a counter-clockwise direction to remove all the slack from the right side of the chain. Force the left side of the chain outward with your fingers and measure the distance between the reference point and the present position of the chain. If the distance exceeds ½″ (12.7mm), replace the chain and sprockets.

7. Crank the engine until the timing marks are aligned as shown in the illustration. Remove the bolt, slide the sprocket and chain forward and remove them as an assembly.

8. Position the sprockets and chain on the engine, making sure that the timing marks are aligned, dot-to-dot.

9. Reinstall the front cover, applying oil resistant sealer to the new gasket. Trim away the exposed portion of the old oil pan gasket flush with front of the engine block. Cut and position the required portion of a new gasket to the oil pan, applying sealer to both sides of it.

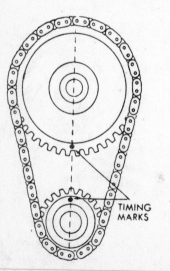

TIMING MARKS

Timing mark alignment—6 cyl. 200 eng., all V8 engines

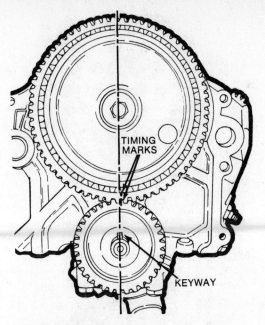

TIMING
MARKS

KEYWAY

6-170 timing gear alignment

10. Install the fan, pulley and belts. Adjust the belt tension.

11. Install the radiator, connect the radiator hoses and transmission cooling lines. If equipped with air conditioning, install the condenser.

12. Fill the crankcase and cooling system. Start the engine and check for leaks.

6-232

1. Disconnect the negative battery cable from the battery. Drain the cooling system.

CAUTION: *When draining the coolant, keep in mind that cats and dogs are attracted by the ethylene glycol antifreeze, and are quite likely to drink any that is left in an uncovered container or in puddles on the ground. This will prove fatal in sufficient quantity. Always drain the coolant into a sealable container. Coolant should be reused unless it is contaminated or several years old.*

2. Remove the air cleaner and air duct assemblies.

3. Remove the radiator fan shroud and position it back over the water pump. Remove the fan clutch assembly and shroud.

4. Remove all drive belts. If equipped with power steering, remove the pump with the hoses attached and position it out of the way. Be sure to keep the pump upright to prevent fluid leakage.

5. If your car is equipped with air conditioning, remove the front compressor mounting bracket. It is not necessary to remove the compressor.

6. Disconnect the coolant by-pass hose and the heater hose at the water pump.

7. Disconnect the upper radiator hose at the thermostat housing. Remove the distributor.

8. If your car is equipped with a tripminder, remove the flow meter support bracket and allow the meter to be supported by the hoses.

9. Raise the front of the car and support on jackstands.

10. Remove the crankshaft pulley using a suitable puller. Remove the fuel pump shield.

11. Disconnect the fuel line from the carburetor at the fuel pump. Remove the mounting bolts and the fuel pump. Position pump out of the way with tank line still attached.

12. Drain the engine oil and remove the oil filter.

13. Disconnect the lower radiator hose at the water pump.

14. Remove the oil pan mounting bolts and lower the oil pan.

NOTE: *The front cover cannot be removed unless the oil pan is lowered.*

15. Lower the car from the jackstands.

16. Remove the front cover mounting bolts.

NOTE: *Water pump removal is not necessary. A front cover mounting bolt is located behind the oil filter adapter. If the bolt is not removed and the cover is pried upon breakage will occur.*

17. Remove the timing indicator. Remove the front cover and water pump assembly.

18. Remove the camshaft thrust button and spring from the end of the camshaft. Remove the camshaft sprocket attaching bolts.

19. Remove the camshaft sprocket, crankshaft sprocket and timing chain by pulling forward evenly on both sprockets. If the crankshaft sprocket is difficult to remove, position two small prybars, one on each side, behind the sprocket and pry forward.

20. Clean all gasket surfaces on the front cover, cylinder block, fuel pump and oil pan.

21. Install a new front cover oil seal. If a new front cover is to be installed:

  a. Install the oil pump, oil filter adapter and intermediate shaft from the old cover.

  b. Remove the water pump from the old cover.

  c. Clean the mounting surface, install a new mounting gasket and the pump on the new front cover. Pump attaching bolt torque is 13-22 ft. lbs.

22. Rotate the crankshaft, if necessary, to bring No. 1 piston to TDC with the crankshaft keyway at the 12 o'clock position.

23. Lubricate the timing chain with motor oil. Install the chain over the two gears making sure the marks on both gears are positioned across from each other. Install the gears and

chain on the cam and crankshaft. Install the camshaft mounting bolts. Tighten the bolts to 15-22 ft. lbs.

24. Install the camshaft thrust button and spring. Lubricate the thrust button with polyethylene grease before installation.

WARNING: *The thrust button and spring must be bottomed in the camshaft seat and must not be allowed to fall out during front cover installation.*

25. Position a new cover gasket on the front of the engine and install the cover and water pump assemblies. Install the timing indicator. Torque the front cover bolts to 15-22 ft. lbs.

26. Install the oil pan.

27. Connect the lower radiator hose at the water pump.

28. Install the oil filter.

29. Fill the crankcase.

30. Install the fuel pump.

31. Connect the fuel line at the carburetor and at the fuel pump.

WARNING: *When installing the fuel pump, turn the crankshaft 180° to position the fuel pump drive eccentric away from the fuel pump arm. Failure to turn the drive eccentric away from the pump arm can cause stress on the pump mounting threads and strip them out when installing the pump.*

32. Install the crankshaft pulley.

33. Install the fuel pump shield.

34. Lower the front of the car.

35. If your car is equipped with a tripminder, install the flow meter support bracket.

36. Connect the upper radiator hose at the thermostat housing.

37. Install the distributor.

38. Connect the coolant by-pass hose and the heater hose at the water pump.

39. If your car is equipped with air conditioning, install the front compressor mounting bracket.

40. If equipped with power steering, install the pump. Be sure to keep the pump upright to prevent fluid leakage.

41. Install all drive belts.

42. Install the fan clutch assembly.

43. Install the radiator fan shroud.

44. Install the air cleaner and air duct assemblies.

45. Connect the negative battery cable at the battery.

46. Fill the cooling system.

V8 Engines

1. Drain the cooling system, remove the air cleaner and disconnect the battery.

CAUTION: *When draining the coolant, keep in mind that cats and dogs are attracted by the ethylene glycol antifreeze, and are quite*

REFERENCE POINT

Measuring timing chain deflection—typical

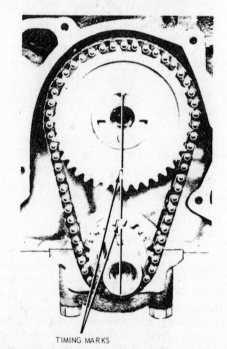

TIMING MARKS

6-232 and V8 timing mark alignment

likely to drink any that is left in an uncovered container or in puddles on the ground. This will prove fatal in sufficient quantity. Always drain the coolant into a sealable container. Coolant should be reused unless it is contaminated or several years old.

2. Disconnect the transmission cooler lines and radiator hoses and remove the radiator.

3. Disconnect the heater hose at water pump. Slide the water pump by-pass hose clamp toward the pump.

4. Loosen the alternator mounting bolts at the alternator. Remove the alternator support bolt at the water pump. Remove the

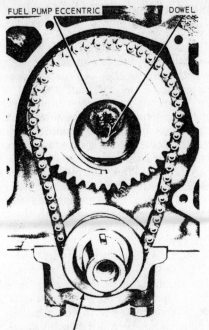

FUEL PUMP ECCENTRIC   DOWEL

CRANKSHAFT FRONT OIL SLINGER

Fuel pump eccentric and front oil slinger installed on the 8-255, 302

Thermactor® pump on all engines so equipped. If equipped with power steering or air conditioning, unbolt the component, remove the belt, and lay the pump or compressor aside with the lines attached.

5. Remove the fan, spacer, pulley, and drive belt.

6. Drain the crankcase.

7. Remove the pulley from the crankshaft pulley adapter. Remove the capscrew and washer from the front end of the crankshaft. Remove the crankshaft pulley adapter with a puller.

8. Disconnect the fuel pump outlet line at the pump. Remove the fuel pump retaining bolts and lay the pump to the side. Remove the engine oil dipstick.

9. Remove the front cover attaching bolts.

10. Remove the crankshaft oil slinger if so equipped.

11. Check timing chain deflection, using the procedure outlined in Step 6 of the 6-200 Cylinder Cover and Chain Removal.

12. Rotate the engine until the sprocket timing marks are aligned as shown in the valve timing illustration.

13. Remove the crankshaft sprocket capscrew, washers, and fuel pump eccentric. Slide both sprockets and chain forward and off as an assembly.

14. Position the sprockets and chain on the camshaft and crankshaft with both timing marks dot-to-dot on a centerline. Install the fuel pump eccentric, washers and sprocket attaching bolt. Torque the sprocket attaching bolt to 40-45 ft. lbs.

15. Install the crankshaft front oil slinger.

16. Clean the front cover and mating surfaces of old gasket material. Install a new oil seal in the cover. Use a seal driver tool, if available.

17. Coat a new cover gasket with sealer and position it on the block.

NOTE: *Trim away the exposed portion of the oil pan gasket flush with the cylinder block. Cut and position the required portion of a new gasket to the oil pan, applying sealer to both sides of it.*

18. Install the front cover, using a crankshaft-to-cover alignment tool. Coat the threads of the attaching bolts with sealer. Torque the attaching bolt to 12-15 ft. lbs.

19. Install the fuel pump and connect the fuel pump outlet tube.

20. Install the crankshaft pulley adapter and torque the attaching bolt. Install the crankshaft pulley.

21. Install the water pump pulley, drive belt, spacer and fan.

22. Install the alternator support bolt at the water pump. Tighten the alternator mounting bolts. Adjust the drive belt tension. Install the Thermactor® pump if so equipped.

23. Install the radiator and connect all coolant and heater hoses. Connect the battery cables.

24. Refill the cooling system and the crankcase. Install the dipstick.

25. Start the engine and operate it at fast idle.

26. Check for leaks, install the air cleaner. Adjust the ignition timing and make all final adjustments.

Timing Cover
REMOVAL AND INSTALLATION
6-170

1. Remove the oil pan.

2. Drain the coolant and remove the radiator and shroud.

CAUTION: *When draining the coolant, keep in mind that cats and dogs are attracted by the ethylene glycol antifreeze, and are quite likely to drink any that is left in an uncovered container or in puddles on the ground. This will prove fatal in sufficient quantity. Always drain the coolant into a sealable container. Coolant should be reused unless it is contaminated or several years old.*

3. Remove the air conditioning compressor and bracket.

4. Remove the alternator, thermactor pump and drive belts.

5. Remove the water pump and fan.

6. Remove the drive pulley from the crankshaft.

7. Remove the front cover retaining bolts. Tap the cover lightly to break the gasket seal. Remove the front cover. It may be necessary to remove the 2 screws and cover plate for replacement of the cover plate gasket.

8. If necessary, remove the guide sleeves from the cylinder block.

9. Installation is the reverse of removal. Make sure that all gasket surfaces are clean. Coat all gasket surfaces with sealer.

Front Cover Oil Seal

REMOVAL AND INSTALLATION

Except 4-140

It is recommended to replace the cover seal any time the front cover is removed.

NOTE: *On 6-232 engines, the seal may be removed, after the crank pulley is off without removing the cover.*

1. With the cover removed from the car, drive the old seal from the rear of cover with a pinpunch. Clean out the recess in the cover.

2. Coat the new seal with grease and drive it into the cover until it is fully seated. Check the seal after installation to be sure the spring is properly positioned in the seal.

4-140 Camshaft Drive Belt and Cover

The correct installation and adjustment of the camshaft drive belt is mandatory if the engine is to run properly. The camshaft controls the opening of the camshaft and the crankshaft. When any given piston is on the intake stroke the corresponding intake valve must be open to admit air/fuel mixture into the cylinder. When the same piston is on the compression and power strokes, both valves in that cylinder must be closed. When the piston is on the exhaust stroke, the exhaust valve for that cylinder must be open. If the opening and closing of the valves is not coordinated with the movements of the pistons, the engine will run very poorly, if at all.

The camshaft drive belt also turns the engine auxiliary shaft. The distributor is driven by the engine auxiliary shaft. Since the distributor controls ignition timing, the auxiliary shaft must be coordinated with the camshaft and crankshaft, since both valves in any given cylinder must be closed and the piston in that cylinder near the top of the compression stroke when the spark plug fires.

Due to this complex interrelationship between the camshaft, the crankshaft and the auxiliary shaft, the cogged pulleys on each com-

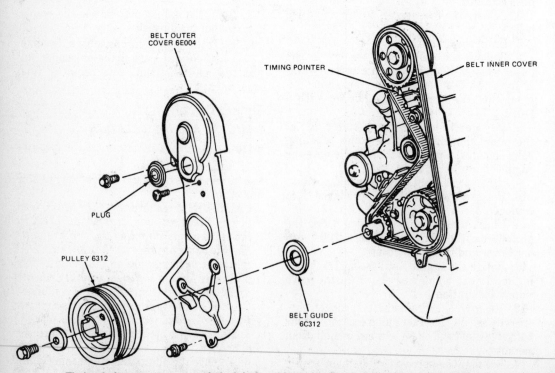

Timing belt outer cover, crankshaft belt guide and pulley installation—4 cyl. engine

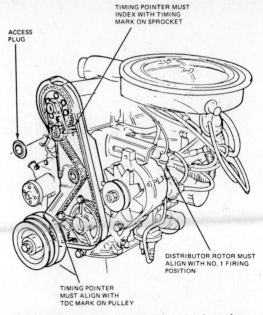

TIMING POINTER MUST INDEX WITH TIMING MARK ON SPROCKET

ACCESS PLUG

DISTRIBUTOR ROTOR MUST ALIGN WITH NO. 1 FIRING POSITION

TIMING POINTER MUST ALIGN WITH TDC MARK ON PULLEY

Camshaft drive train installation—4 cyl. engine

ponent must be aligned when the camshaft drive belt is installed.

TROUBLESHOOTING

Should the camshaft drive belt jump timing by a tooth or two, the engine could still run; but very poorly. To visually check for correct timing of the crankshaft, auxiliary shaft, and the camshaft follow this procedure:

NOTE: *There is an access plug provided in the cam drive belt cover so that the camshaft timing can be checked without moving the drive belt cover.*

1. Remove the access plug.
2. Turn the crankshaft until the timing marks on the crankshaft indicate TDC.
3. Make sure that the timing mark on the camshaft drive sprocket is aligned with the pointer on the inner belt cover. Also, the rotor of the distributor must align with the No. 1 cylinder firing position.

WARNING: *Never turn the crankshaft of any of the overhead cam engines in the opposite direction of normal rotation. Backward rotation of the crankshaft may cause the timing belt to slip and alter the timing.*

REMOVAL AND INSTALLATION

1. Set the engine to TDC as described in the troubleshooting section. The crankshaft and camshaft timing marks should align with their respective pointers and the distributor rotor should point to the No. 1 plug tower.
2. Loosen the adjustment bolts on the alternator and accessories and remove the drive

belts. To provide clearance for removing the camshaft belt, remove the fan and pulley.

3. Remove the belt outer cover.
4. Remove the distributor cap from the distributor and position it out of the way.
5. Loosen the belt tensioner adjustment and pivot bolts. Lever the tensioner away from the belt and retighten the adjustment bolt to hold it away.
6. Remove the crankshaft bolt and pulley. Remove the belt guide behind the pulley.
7. Remove the camshaft drive belt.
8. Install the new belt over the crankshaft pulley first, then counterclockwise over the auxiliary shaft sprocket and the camshaft sprocket. Adjust the belt fore and aft so that it is centered on the sprockets.
9. Loosen the tensioner adjustment bolt, allowing it to spring back against the belt.
10. Rotate the crankshaft two complete turns in the normal rotation direction to remove any belt slack. Turn the crankshaft until the timing check marks are lined up. If the timing has slipped, remove the belt and repeat the procedure.
11. Tighten the tensioner adjustment bolt to 14-21 ft. lbs., and the pivot bolt to 28-40 ft. lbs.
12. Replace the belt guide and crankshaft pulley, distributor cap, belt outer cover, fan and pulley, drive belts and accessories. Adjust the accessory drive belt tension. Start the engine and check the ignition timing.

Camshaft
REMOVAL AND INSTALLATION
4-140 Engine

NOTE: *The following procedure covers camshaft removal and installation with the cylinder head on or off the engine. If the cylinder head has been removed start at Step 9.*

1. Drain the cooling system. Remove the air cleaner assembly and disconnect the negative battery cable.

CAUTION: *When draining the coolant, keep in mind that cats and dogs are attracted by the ethylene glycol antifreeze, and are quite likely to drink any that is left in an uncovered container or in puddles on the ground. This will prove fatal in sufficient quantity. Always drain the coolant into a sealable container. Coolant should be reused unless it is contaminated or several years old.*

2. Remove the spark plug wires from the plugs, disconnect the retainer from the valve cover and position the wires out of the way. Disconnect the rubber vacuum lines as necessary
3. Remove all drive belts. Remove the alternator mounting bracket-to-cylinder head

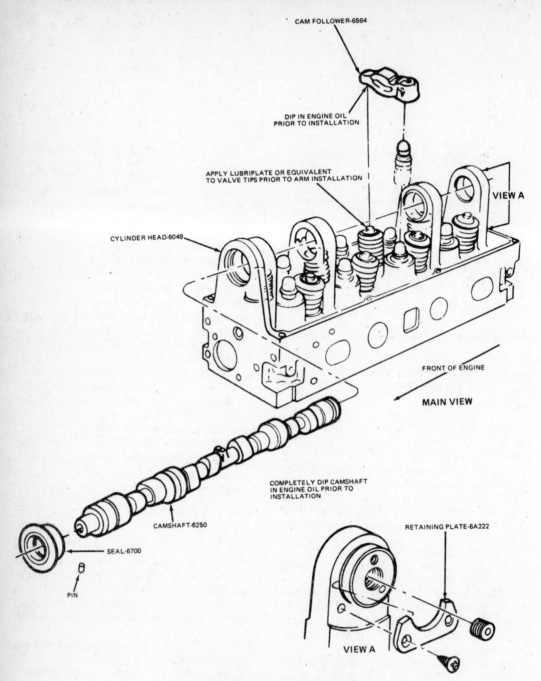

CAM FOLLOWER-6564

DIP IN ENGINE OIL
PRIOR TO INSTALLATION

APPLY LUBRIPLATE OR EQUIVALENT
TO VALVE TIPS PRIOR TO ARM INSTALLATION

CYLINDER HEAD-6049

VIEW A

FRONT OF ENGINE

MAIN VIEW

COMPLETELY DIP CAMSHAFT
IN ENGINE OIL PRIOR TO
INSTALLATION

CAMSHAFT-6250

SEAL-6700

PIN

RETAINING PLATE-6A222

VIEW A

Camshaft installation—4 cyl. engine

mounting bolts, position the bracket and alternator out of the way.

4. Disconnect and remove the upper radiator hose. Disconnect the radiator shroud.

5. Remove the fan blades and water pump pulley and fan shroud. Remove the cam belt and valve covers.

6. Align the engine timing marks at TDC. Remove the cam drive belt.

7. Jack up the front of the car and support it on jackstands. Remove the front motor mount bolts. Disconnect the lower radiator hose from the radiator. Disconnect and plug the automatic transmission cooler lines.

8. Position a piece of wood on a floor jack and raise the engine carefully as far as it will go. Place blocks of wood between the engine mounts and crossmember pedestals.

9. Remove the rocker arms as described earlier in this chapter.

10. Remove the camshaft drive gear and belt guide using a suitable puller. Remove the front oil seal with a sheet metal screw and slide hammer.

11. Remove the camshaft retainer located on the rear mounting stand, by unbolting the two bolts.

12. Remove the camshaft by carefully withdrawing it toward the front of the engine. Caution should be used to prevent damage to the cam bearings, lobes and journals.

13. Check the camshaft journals and lobes for wear. Inspect the cam bearings. If they are worn, the cylinder head must be removed for new bearings to be installed by a machine shop.

14. Install the camshaft. Caution should be used to prevent damage to the cam bearings, lobes and journals. Coat the camshaft with heavy SF oil before sliding it into the cylinder head.

15. Install the camshaft retainer located on the rear mounting stand.

16. Install a new front oil seal.

17. Install the camshaft drive gear and belt guide. Apply a coat of sealer or Teflon® tape to the cam drive gear bolt before installation.

18. Install the rocker arms as described earlier in this chapter.

19. Remove the blocks of wood between the engine mounts and crossmember pedestals and lower the engine onto the mounts.

20. Lower the front of the car.

21. Install the front motor mount bolts.

22. Connect the lower radiator hose at the radiator.

23. Connect the automatic transmission cooler lines.

24. Align the engine timing marks at TDC.

25. Install the cam drive belt.

26. Install the cam belt and valve covers.

27. Install the fan blades and water pump pulley and fan shroud.

28. Connect and install the upper radiator hose.

29. Install the alternator and mounting bracket on the cylinder head.

30. Install all drive belts.

31. Install the spark plug wires on the plugs.

32. Connect the plug wires to the retainer on the valve cover.

33. Connect the rubber vacuum lines as necessary.

34. Fill the cooling system.

35. Install the air cleaner assembly.

36. Connect the negative battery cable.

WARNING: *After any procedure requiring removal of the rocker arms, each lash adjuster must be fully collapsed after assembly, then released. This must be done before the camshaft is turned. See Valve Clearance — Hydraulic Valve Lash Adjusters.*

6-200

1. Remove the cylinder head.

2. Remove the cylinder front cover, timing chain and sprockets as outlined in the preceding section.

3. Disconnect and remove the radiator, condenser and grille. Remove the gravel deflector.

4. Using a magnet, remove the valve lifters and keep them in order so that they can be installed in their original positions.

5. Remove the camshaft thrust plate and remove the camshaft by pulling it from the front of the engine. Use care not to damage the camshaft lobes or journals while removing the cam from the engine.

6. Before installing the camshaft, coat the lobes with engine assembly lubricant and the journals and all valve parts with heavy oil. Clean the oil passage at the rear of the cylinder block with compressed air.

6-232 and V8 Engines

1. Remove or reposition the radiator, A/C condenser and grille components as necessary to provide clearance to remove the camshaft.

2. Remove the cylinder front cover and timing chain as previously described in this chapter.

3. Remove the intake manifold and related parts described earlier in this chapter.

4. Remove the crankcase ventilation valve

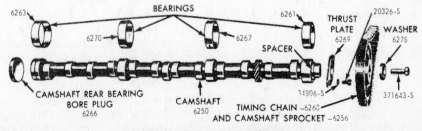

6-200 camshaft and related parts

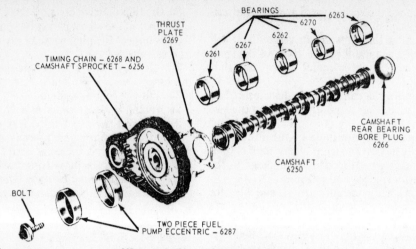

V8 camshaft and related parts

and tubes from the valve rocker covers. Remove the EGR cooler, if so equipped.

5. Remove the rocker arm covers and loosen the valve rocker arm fulcrum bolts and rotate the rocker arms to the side.

6. Remove the valve pushrods and identify them so that they can be installed in their original positions.

7. Remove the valve lifters and place them in a rack so that they can be installed in their original bores.

8. Remove the camshaft thrust plate or button and spring and carefully remove the camshaft by pulling toward the front of the engine. Be careful not to damage the camshaft bearings.

9. Before installing, oil the camshaft journals with heavy engine oil SF and apply Lubriplate® or equivalent to the lobes. Carefully slide the camshaft through the bearings.

10. Install the camshaft thrust plate with the groove towards the cylinder block.

11. Lubricate the lifters with heavy SF engine oil and install in their original bores.

12. Apply Lubriplate® or equivalent to the valve stem tips and each end of the pushrods. Install the pushrods in their original position.

13. Lubricate the rocker arms and fulcrum seats with heavy SF engine oil and position the rocker arms over the push rods.

14. Install all other parts previously removed.

15. Fill the crankcase and cooling system and adjust the timing.

Camshaft and Gears
REMOVAL AND INSTALLATION
6-170

1. Drain the coolant.
CAUTION: *When draining the coolant, keep in mind that cats and dogs are attracted by the ethylene glycol antifreeze, and are quite likely to drink any that is left in an uncovered container or in puddles on the ground. This will prove fatal in sufficient quantity. Always drain the coolant into a sealable container. Coolant should be reused unless it is contaminated or several years old.*

2. Remove the radiator, fan, spacer, water pump pulley and drive belt.

3. Remove the distributor.

4. Remove the alternator.

5. Remove the Thermactor pump.

6. Remove the rocker arm covers.

7. Remove the fuel line and filter.

8. Remove the carburetor.

9. Remove the EGR tube.

10. Remove the intake manifold.

11. Drain the crankcase.
CAUTION: *The EPA warns that prolonged contact with used engine oil may cause a number of skin disorders, including cancer! You should make every effort to minimize your exposure to used engine oil. Protective gloves should be worn when changing the oil. Wash your hands and any other exposed skin areas as soon as possible after exposure to used engine oil. Soap and water, or waterless hand cleaner should be used.*

12. Remove the rocker arm and shaft assemblies.

13. Mark and remove the pushrods.

14. Remove the oil pan.

15. Remove the crankshaft drive sprocket attaching bolt and slide the sprocket off the shaft.

16. Remove the engine front cover and water pump as an assembly.

17. Remove the camshaft gear retaing bolt and slide the gear off the shaft.

18. Remove the camshaft thrust plate.

19. Remove the valve lifters with a magnet. Keep them in order.

20. Carefully and slowly, pull the camshaft from the block. Take care to avoid banging the lobes into the bearing surfaces.

21. Remove the key and spacer from the camshaft.

To install:

22. Coat the camshaft with an engine assembly oil or gear oil.

23. Carefully slide the camshaft into the block.

24. Install the spacer with the chamfered side inward. Install the key.

25. Install the thrust plate so that it covers the main oil gallery.

26. Check the camshaft endplay. See the Camshaft Specification Chart. The spacer and thrust plate are available in different thicknesses to adjust endplay.

27. Rotate the camshaft and cranshaft to align the timing marks and install the timing gears. Make sure that the timing marks are aligned. Torque the camshaft gear bolt to 34 ft. lbs.

28. Install the lifters in their original locations.

29. Install the front cover and water pump.

30. Install the belt drive pulley.

31. Install the oil pan.

32. Apply a light coating of chassis lube to both ends of the pushrods and install them in their original locations.

33. Install the intake manifold.

34. Install the oil baffles and rocker arm assemblies. Tighten the bolts to 45 ft. lbs. Adjust the valves.

35. Install the pump pulley, fan spacer, fan and drive belt. Adjust the belt tension.

36. Install the:
- carburetor
- EGR tube
- fuel line
- fuel filter
- alternator
- Thermactor pump
- distributor
- radiator.

37. Fill the cooling system.

38. Adjust the timing.

39. Install the rocker covers.

40. Start the engine and check the idle speed.

41. Let the engine run to normal operating temperature and check for leaks.

Checking the Camshaft

Degrease the camshaft using safe solvent, clean all oil grooves. Visually inspect the cam lobes and bearing journals for excessive wear. If a lobe is questionable, check all lobes and journals with a micrometer.

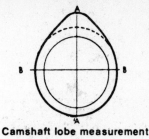

Camshaft lobe measurement

Measure the lobes from nose to base and again at 90°. The lift is determined by subtracting the second measurement from the first. If all exhaust lobes and all intake lobes are not identical, the camshaft must be reground or replaced. Measure the bearing journals and compare to specifications. If a journal is worn there is a good chance that the cam bearings are worn too, requiring replacement.

If the lobes and journals appear intact, place the front and rear cam journals in V-blocks and rest a dial indicator on the center journal. Rotate the camshaft to check for straightness, if deviation exceeds 0.001" (0.025mm), replace the camshaft.

Auxiliary Shaft

REMOVAL AND INSTALLATION

4-140 Engine

1. Remove the camshaft drive belt cover.

2. Remove the drive belt. Remove the auxiliary shaft sprocket. A puller may be necessary to remove the sprocket.

3. Remove the distributor and fuel pump.

4. Remove the auxiliary shaft cover and thrust plate.

5. Withdraw the auxiliary shaft from the block.

WARNING: *The distributor drive gear and the fuel pump eccentric on the auxiliary shaft must not be allowed to touch the auxiliary shaft bearings during removal and installation. Completely coat the shaft with oil before sliding it into place.*

6. Slide the auxiliary shaft into the housing and insert the thrust plate to hold the shaft.

7. Install a new gasket and auxiliary shaft cover.

NOTE: *The auxiliary shaft cover and cylinder front cover share a gasket. Cut off the old gasket around the cylinder cover and use half of the new gasket on the auxiliary shaft cover.*

8. Fit a new gasket into the fuel pump and install the pump.

9. Insert the distributor and install the auxiliary shaft sprocket.

10. Align the timing marks and install the drive belt.

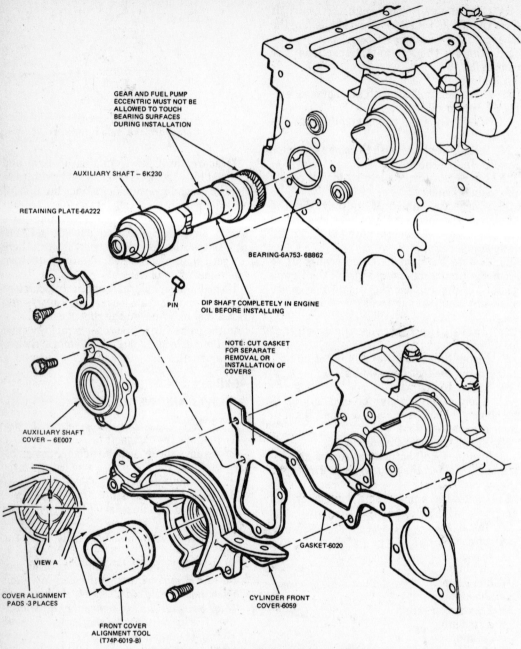

GEAR AND FUEL PUMP
ECCENTRIC MUST NOT BE
ALLOWED TO TOUCH
BEARING SURFACES
DURING INSTALLATION

AUXILIARY SHAFT — 6K230

RETAINING PLATE-6A222

BEARING-6A753- 6B862

PIN

DIP SHAFT COMPLETELY IN ENGINE
OIL BEFORE INSTALLING

NOTE: CUT GASKET
FOR SEPARATE
REMOVAL OR
INSTALLATION OF
COVERS

AUXILIARY SHAFT
COVER — 6E007

GASKET-6020

VIEW A

COVER ALIGNMENT
PADS -3 PLACES

CYLINDER FRONT
COVER-6059

FRONT COVER
ALIGNMENT TOOL
(T74P-6019-B)

Auxiliary shaft installation—4 cyl. engine

11. Install the drive belt cover.
12. Check the ignition timing.

Crankshaft/Intermediate Shaft Front Oil Seal

REMOVAL AND INSTALLATION

1. Remove the engine front cover.
2. Using an arbor press, press the old seal(s) out of the front cover.
3. Position the new seals on the front cover and install, using T84P-6019-B for crankshaft seal, or T84P-6020-A or equivalent for the intermediate shaft seal.
4. Lubricate the seal lips with engine oil.
5. Install the engine front cover.

Pistons and Connection Rods

REMOVAL AND INSTALLATION

NOTE: *Although, in most cases, the pistons and connecting rods can be removed from the engine (after the cylinder head and oil pan are removed) while the engine is still in the car, it is far easier to remove the engine from the car. If removing pistons with the engine still installed, disconnect the radiator hoses, automatic transmission cooler lines and radiator shroud. Unbolt front mounts before jacking up the engine. Block the engine in position with wooden blocks between the mounts.*

1. Remove the engine from the car. Remove the cylinder head(s), oil pan and front cover (if necessary).

2. Because the top piston ring does not travel to the very top of the cylinder bore, a ridge is built up between the end of the travel and the

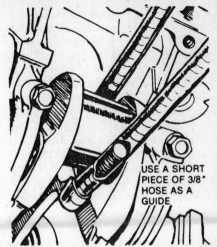

USE A SHORT PIECE OF 3/8" HOSE AS A GUIDE

Use lengths of vacuum hose or rubber tubing to protect the crankshaft journals and cylinder walls during piston installation

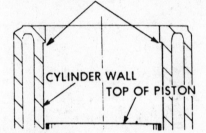

RIDGE CAUSED BY CYLINDER WEAR

CYLINDER WALL
TOP OF PISTON

Cylinder bore ridge

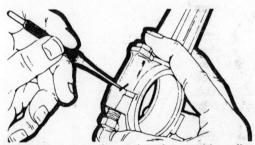

Match the connecting rod and cap with scribe marks

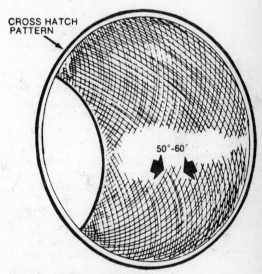

CROSS HATCH PATTERN

50°-60°

Cylinder bore after honing

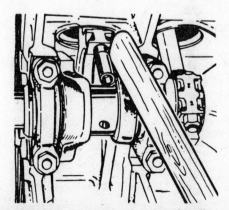

Push the piston out with a hammer handle

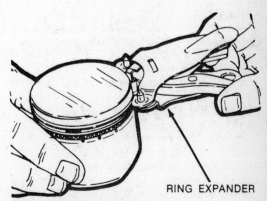

RING EXPANDER

Remove the piston rings

top of the cylinder. Pushing the piston and connecting rod assembly past the ridge is difficult and may cause damage to the piston. If new rings are installed and the ridge has not been removed, ring breakage and piston damage can occur when the ridge is encountered at engine speed.

3. Turn the crankshaft to position the piston at the bottom of the cylinder bore. Cover the top of the piston with a rag. Install a ridge reamer in the bore and follow the manufacturer's instructions to remove the ridge. Use caution; avoid cutting too deeply or into the ring travel area. Remove the rag and cuttings from

the top of the piston. Remove the ridge from all cylinders.

4. Check the edges of the connecting rod and bearing cap for numbers or matchmarks, if none are present mark the rod and cap numerically and in sequence from front to back of engine. The numbers or marks not only tell from which cylinder the piston cam from but also ensures that the rod caps are installed in the correct matching position.

5. Turn the crankshaft until the connecting rod is at the bottom of travel. Remove the two attaching nuts and the bearing cap. Take two pieces of rubber tubing and cover the rod bolts

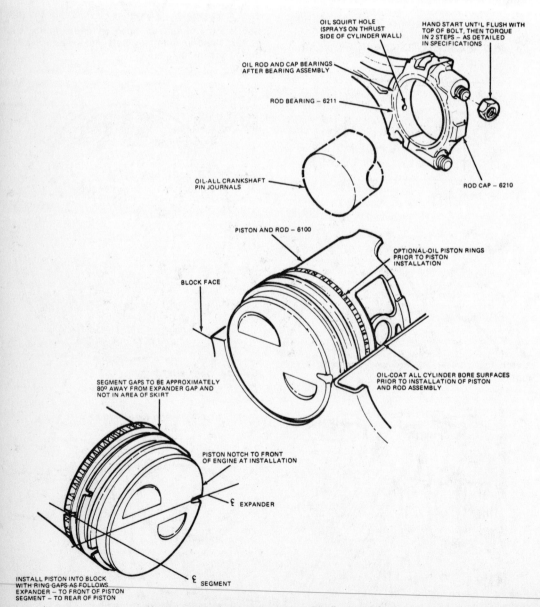

Pistons, rings and connecting rods—4 cyl. engine

to prevent crank or cylinder scoring. Use a wooden hammer handle to help push the piston and rod up and out of the cylinder. Reinstall the rod cap in proper position. Remove all pistons and connecting rods. Inspect cylinder walls and deglaze or hone as necessary.

6. Installation is in the reverse order of removal. Lubricate each piston, rod bearing and

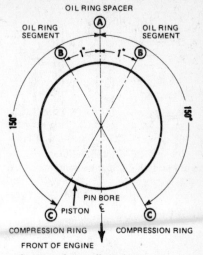

Piston ring spacing—all engines

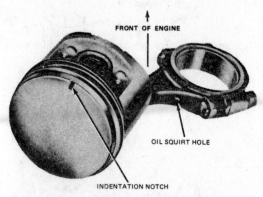

Piston and connecting rod positioning (notch to the front of the engine)—6 cyl. 200 engine

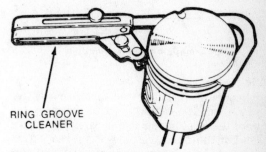

Clean the piston ring grooves

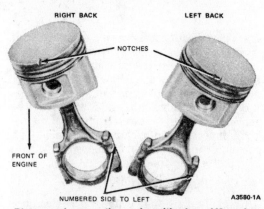

Piston and connecting rod positioning—V6 engine

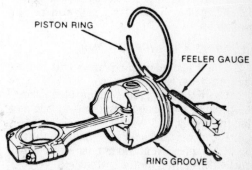

Check the piston ring side clearance

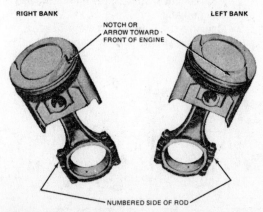

Piston and connecting rod positioning—V8 engines

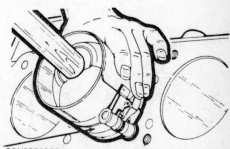

Install the piston using a ring compressor

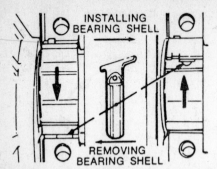

Remove or install the upper bearing insert using a roll-out pin

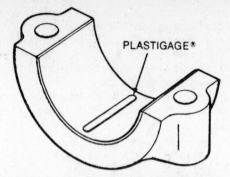

Plastigage® installed on the lower bearing shell

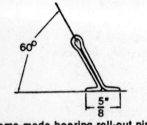

Home-made bearing roll-out pin

Check the connecting rod side clearance with a feeler gauge

cylinder wall. Install a ring compressor over the piston, position the piston with the mark toward the front of engine and carefully install. Position the connecting rod with the bearing insert installed over the crank journal. Install the rod cap with the bearing in its proper position. Secure with rod nuts and torque to the proper specifications. Install all rod and piston assemblies.

CLEANING AND INSPECTION

1. Use a piston ring expander and remove the rings from the piston.
2. Clean the ring grooves using an appropriate cleaning tool, exercising care to avoid cutting too deeply.
3. Clean all varnish and carbon from the piston with a safe solvent. Do not use a wire brush or caustic solution on the pistons.
4. Inspect the pistons for scuffing, scoring, cracks, pitting or excessive ring groove wear. If wear is evident, the piston must be replaced.
5. Have the piston and connecting rod assembly checked by a machine shop for correct alignment, piston pin wear and piston diameter. If the piston has collapsed it will have to be replaced or knurled to restore original diameter. Connecting rod bushing replacement, piston pin fitting and piston changing can be handled by the machine shop.

MEASURING THE OLD PISTONS

Check used piston-to-cylinder bore clearance as follows:

1. Measure the cylinder bore diameter with a telescope gauge.
2. Measure the piston diameter. When measuring the pistons for size or taper, measure-

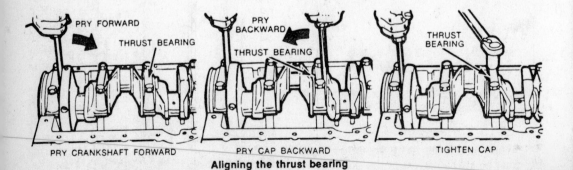

Aligning the thrust bearing

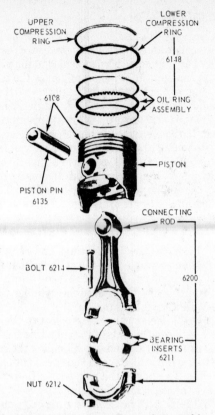

Typical piston and connecting rod assembly

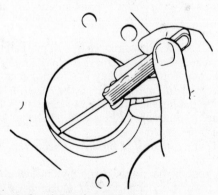

Check the piston ring end gap

ments must be made with the piston pin removed.

3. Subtract the piston diameter from the cylinder bore diameter to determine piston-to-bore clearance.

4. Compare the piston-to-bore clearances obtained with those clearances recommended. Determine if the piston-to-bore clearance is in the acceptable range.

5. When measuring taper, the largest reading must be at the bottom of the skirt.

SELECTING NEW PISTONS

1. If the used piston is not acceptable, check the service piston size and determine if a new piston can be selected. (Service pistons are available in standard, high limit and standard oversize.

2. If the cylinder bore must be reconditioned, measure the new piston diameter, then hone the cylinder bore to obtain the preferred clearance.

3. Select a new piston and mark the piston to identify the cylinder for which it was fitted. (On some vehicles, oversize pistons may be found. These pistons will be 0.254mm [0.010″] oversize).

CYLINDER HONING

1. When cylinders are being honed, follow the manufacturer's recommendations for the use of the hone.

2. Occasionally, during the honing operation, the cylinder bore should be thoroughly cleaned and the selected piston checked for correct fit.

3. When finish-honing a cylinder bore, the hone should be moved up and down at a sufficient speed to obtain a very fine uniform surface finish in a cross-hatch pattern of approximately 45–65° included angle. The finish marks should be clean but not sharp, free from imbedded particles and torn or folded metal.

4. Permanently mark the piston for the cylinder to which it has been fitted and proceed to hone the remaining cylinders.

WARNING: *Handle the pistons with care. Do not attempt to force the pistons through the cylinders until the cylinders have been honed to the correct size. Pistons can be distorted through careless handling.*

5. Thoroughly clean the bores with hot water and detergent. Scrub well with a stiff bristle brush and rinse thoroughly with hot water. It is extremely essential that a good cleaning operation be performed. If any of the abrasive material is allowed to remain in the cylinder bores, it will rapidly wear the new rings and cylinder bores. The bores should be swabbed several times with light engine oil and a clean cloth and then wiped with a clean dry cloth. CYLINDERS SHOULD NOT BE CLEANED WITH KEROSENE OR GASOLINE. Clean the remainder of the cylinder block to remove the excess material spread during the honing operation.

PISTON PIN REMOVAL AND INSTALLATION

Use care at all times when handling and servicing connecting rods and pistons. To prevent possible damage to these units, do not clamp the rod or piston in a vise since they may become distorted. Do not allow the pistons to strike against one another, against hard objects or bench surfaces, since distortion of the piston contour or nicks in the soft aluminum material may result.

1. Remove the piston rings using a suitable piston ring remover.

2. Remove the piston pin lockring, if used. Install the guide bushing of the piston pin removing and installing tool.

3. Install the piston and connecting rod assembly on a support, and place the assembly in an arbor press. Press the pin out of the connecting rod, using the appropriate piston pin tool.

4. Assembly is the reverse of disassembly. Use new lockrings where needed.

Connecting Rods and Bearings

Wash connecting rods in cleaning solvent and dry with compressed air. Check for twisted or bent rods and inspect for nicks or cracks. Replace connecting rods that are damaged.

Inspect journals for roughness and wear. Slight roughness may be removed with a fine grit polishing cloth saturated with engine oil. Burrs may be removed with a fine oil stone by moving the stone on the journal circumference. Do not move the stone back and forth across the journal. If the journals are scored or ridged, the crankshaft must be replaced.

The connecting rod journals should be checked for out-of-round and correct size with a micrometer.

NOTE: *Crankshaft rod journals will normally be standard size. If any undersized bearings are used, the size will be stamped on a counterweight.*

If plastic gauging material is to be used:

1. Clean oil from the journal bearing cap, connecting rod and outer and inner surfaces of the bearing inserts. Position the insert so that the tang is properly aligned with the notch in the rod and cap.

2. Place a piece of plastic gauging material in the center of lower bearing shell.

3. Remove the bearing cap and determine the bearing clearances by comparing the width of the flattened plastic gauging material at its widest point with the graduation on the container. The number within the graduation on the envelope indicates the clearance in thousandths of an inch or millimeters. If this clearance is excessive, replace the bearing and recheck the clearance with the plastic gauging material. Lubricate the bearing with engine oil before installation. Repeat the procedure on the remaining connecting rod bearings. All rods must be connected to their journals when rotating the crankshaft, to prevent engine damage.

CYLINDER BORE

Check the cylinder bore for wear using a telescope gauge and a micrometer, measure the cylinder bore diameter perpendicular to the piston pin at the point 2½" (63.5mm) below the top of the engine block. Measure the piston skirt perpendicular to the piston pin. The difference between the two measurement is the piston clearance. If the clearance is within specifications, finish honing or glaze breaking is all that is required. If clearance is excessive a slightly oversized piston may be required. If greatly oversize, the engine will have to be bored and 0.010" (0.254mm) or larger oversized pistons installed.

FITTING AND POSITIONING PISTON RINGS

1. Take the new piston rings and compress them, one at a time into the cylinder that they will be used in. Press the ring about 1" (25.4mm) below the top of the cylinder block using an inverted piston.

2. Use a feeler gauge and measure the distance between the ends of the ring; this is called measuring the ring end-gap. Compare the reading to the one called for in the specification table. File the ends of the ring with a fine file to obtain the necessary clearance.

WARNING: *If inadequate ring end-gap exists, ring breakage will result.*

3. Inspect the ring grooves on the piston for excessive wear or taper. If necessary, have the grooves recut for use with a standard ring and spacer. The machine shop can handle the job for you.

4. Check the ring grooves by rolling the new piston ring around the groove to check for burrs or carbon deposits. If any are found, remove them with a fine file. Hold the ring in the groove and measure side clearance with a feeler gauge. If clearance is excessive, spacer(s) will have to be added.

NOTE: *Always add the spacer above the piston ring.*

5. Install the rings on the piston, lower oil ring first. Use a ring installing tool on the compression rings. Consult the instruction sheet that comes with the rings to be sure they are installed with the correct side up. A mark on the ring usually faces upward.

6. When installing the oil rings, first install the expanding ring in the groove. Hold the ends of the ring butted together (they must not overlap) and install the bottom rail (scraper) with the end about 1" (25.4mm) away from the butted end of the control ring. Install the top rail about 1" (25.4mm) away from the butted end of the control but on the opposite side from the lower rail.

7. Install the two compression rings.

8. Consult the illustration for ring positioning, arrange the rings as shown, install a ring compressor and insert the piston and rod assembly into the engine.

Rear Main Oil Seal

REMOVAL AND INSTALLATION

NOTE: *Refer to the build dates listed below to determine if the engine is equipped with a split-type or one piece rear main oil seal. Engines after the dates indicated have a one-piece oil seal.*

4-140 OHC after 9/28/81
6-232 after 4/1/83
8-302 after 12/1/82
Engines prior to the date indicated are equipped with a split type seal.

Split-Type Seal

NOTE: *The rear oil seal installed in these engines is a rubber type (split-lip) seal.*

1. Remove the oil pan, and, if required, the oil pump.

2. Loosen all the main bearing caps allowing the crankshaft to lower slightly.

WARNING: *The crankshaft should not be allowed to drop more than $\frac{1}{32}$" (0.8mm).*

3. Remove the rear main bearing cap and remove the seal from the cap and block. Be very careful not to scratch the sealing surface. Remove the old seal retaining pin from the cap, if equipped. It is not used with the replacement seal.

4. Carefully clean the seal grooves in the cap and block with solvent.

5. Soak the new seal halves in clean engine oil.

6. Install the upper half of the seal in the block with the undercut side of the seal toward the front of the engine. Slide the seal around the crankshaft journal until $\frac{3}{8}$" (9.5mm) protrudes beyond the base of the block.

7. Tighten all the main bearing caps (except the rear main bearing) to specifications.

8. Install the lower seal into the rear cap, with the undercut side facing the front of the engine. Allow $\frac{3}{8}$" (9.5mm) of the seal to pro-

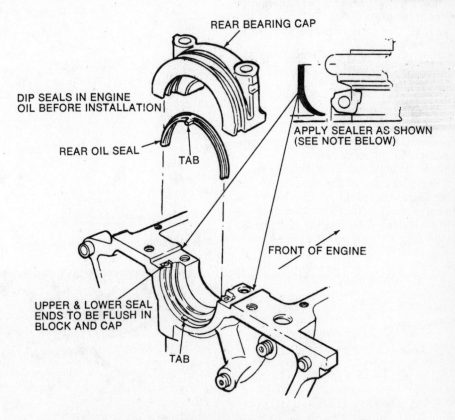

REAR BEARING CAP

DIP SEALS IN ENGINE OIL BEFORE INSTALLATION

REAR OIL SEAL

TAB

APPLY SEALER AS SHOWN (SEE NOTE BELOW)

FRONT OF ENGINE

UPPER & LOWER SEAL ENDS TO BE FLUSH IN BLOCK AND CAP

TAB

NOTE: CLEAN THE AREA WHERE SEALER IS TO BE APPLIED BEFORE INSTALLING THE SEALS. AFTER THE SEALS ARE IN PLACE, APPLY A 1/16 INCH BEAD OF SEALER AS SHOWN. *SEALER MUST NOT TOUCH SEALS*

Replacement of the crankcase rear main oil seal—4 cyl. engine

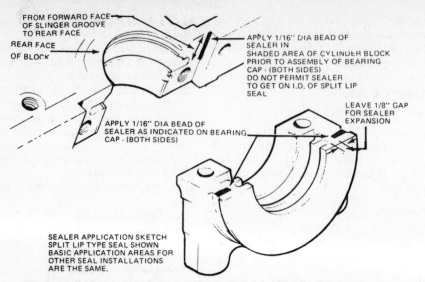

FROM FORWARD FACE
OF SLINGER GROOVE
TO REAR FACE

REAR FACE
OF BLOCK

APPLY 1/16" DIA BEAD OF
SEALER IN
SHADED AREA OF CYLINDER BLOCK
PRIOR TO ASSEMBLY OF BEARING
CAP - (BOTH SIDES)
DO NOT PERMIT SEALER
TO GET ON I.D. OF SPLIT LIP
SEAL

LEAVE 1/8" GAP
FOR SEALER
EXPANSION

APPLY 1/16" DIA BEAD OF
SEALER AS INDICATED ON BEARING
CAP - (BOTH SIDES)

SEALER APPLICATION SKETCH
SPLIT LIP TYPE SEAL SHOWN
BASIC APPLICATION AREAS FOR
OTHER SEAL INSTALLATIONS
ARE THE SAME.

Rear main bearing cap sealer installation—6 cyl. 200 eng., V8 engines

trude above the surface, at the opposite end
from the block seal.

9. Squeeze a $\frac{1}{16}$" (1.6mm) bead of silicone
sealant onto the areas shown.

10. Install the rear cap and torque to
specifications.

11. Install the oil pump and pan. Fill the
crankcase with oil, start the engine, and check
for leaks.

One-Piece Seal

1. Remove the transmission, clutch and flywheel or driveplate after referring to the appropriate section for instructions.

2. Punch two holes in the crankshaft rear oil
seal on opposite sides of the crankshaft just
above the bearing cap to the cylinder block split
line. Install a sheet metal screw in each of the
holes or use a small slide hammer, and pry the
crankshaft rear main oil seal from the block.

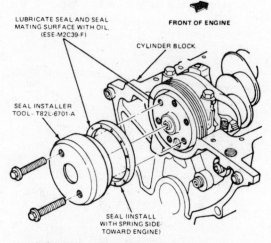

LUBRICATE SEAL AND SEAL
MATING SURFACE WITH OIL.
(ESE-M2C39-F)

FRONT OF ENGINE

CYLINDER BLOCK

SEAL INSTALLER
TOOL - T82L-6701-A

SEAL (INSTALL
WITH SPRING SIDE
TOWARD ENGINE)

NOTE: REAR FACE OF SEAL MUST BE WITHIN
0.127mm (0.005 INCH) OF THE REAR FACE OF THE BLOCK

One piece rear main oil seal installation

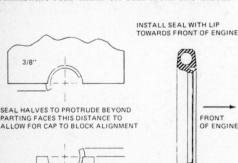

INSTALL SEAL WITH LIP
TOWARDS FRONT OF ENGINE

3/8"

SEAL HALVES TO PROTRUDE BEYOND
PARTING FACES THIS DISTANCE TO
ALLOW FOR CAP TO BLOCK ALIGNMENT

FRONT
OF ENGINE

3/8"

REAR FACE OF REAR
MAIN BEARING CAP
AND CYLINDER BLOCK

VIEW LOOKING AT PARTING
FACE OF SPLIT, LIP-TYPE
CRANKSHAFT SEAL

**Rear main seal installation—except 4 cyl. and V6
engines**

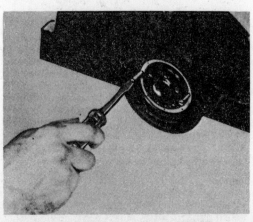

Removing crankshaft rear oil seal, 1979 V6

WARNING: *Use extreme caution not to scratch the crankshaft oil seal surface.*

3. Clean the oil seal recess in the cylinder block and main bearing cap.

4. Coat the seal and all of the seal mounting surfaces with oil and install the seal in the recess, driving it into place with an oil seal installation tool or a large socket.

5. Install the driveplate or flywheel and clutch, and transmission in the reverse order of removal.

Crankshaft and Bearings
REMOVAL AND INSTALLATION

1. Rod bearings can be installed when the pistons have been removed for servicing (rings etc.) or, in most cases, while the engine is still in the car. Bearing replacement, however, is far easier with the engine out of the car and disassembled.

2. For in car service, remove the oil pan, spark plugs and front cover is necessary. Turn the engine until the connecting rod to be serviced is at the bottom of travel. Remove the bearing cap, place two pieces of rubber hose over the rod cap bolts and push the piston and rod assembly up the cylinder bore until enough room is gained for bearing insert removal. Take care not to push the rod assembly up too far or the top ring will engage the cylinder ridge or come out of the cylinder and require head removal for reinstallation.

3. Clean the rod journal, the connecting rod end and the bearing cap after removing the old bearing inserts. Install the new inserts in the rod and bearing cap, lubricate them with oil. Position the rod over the crankshaft journal and install the rod cap. Make sure the cap and rod numbers match, torque the rod nuts to specifications.

4. Main bearings may be replaced while the engine is still in the car by rolling them out and in.

5. Special roll out pins are available from automotive parts houses or can be fabricated from a cotter pin. The roll out pin fits in the oil hole of the main bearing journal. When the crankshaft is rotated opposite the direction of the bearing lock tab, the pin engages the end of the bearing and rolls out the insert.

6. Remove the main bearing cap and roll out the upper bearing insert. Remove the insert from the main bearing cap. Clean the inside of the bearing cap and crankshaft journal.

7. Lubricate and roll the upper insert into position, making sure the lock tab is anchored and the insert is not cocked. Install the lower bearing insert into the cap, lubricate it and install it on the engine. Make sure the main bearing cap is installed facing in the correct direction and torque it to specifications.

8. With the engine out of the car. Remove the intake manifold, cylinder heads, front cover, timing gears and/or chain, oil pan, oil pump and flywheel.

9. Remove the piston and rod assemblies. Remove the main bearing caps after marking them for position and direction.

10. Remove the crankshaft, bearing inserts and rear main oil seal. Clean the engine block and cap bearing saddles. Clean the crankshaft and inspect it for wear. Check the bearing journals with a micrometer for out-of-round condition and to determine what size rod and main bearing inserts to install.

11. Install the main bearing upper inserts and rear main oil seal half into the engine block.

12. Lubricate the bearing inserts and the crankshaft journals. Slowly and carefully lower the crankshaft into position.

13. Install the bearing inserts and rear main seal into the bearing caps. Install the caps working from the middle out. Torque the cap bolts to specifications in stages, rotating the crankshaft after each torque stage. Note the illustration for thrust bearing alignment.

14. Remove the bearing caps, one at a time, and check the oil clearance with Plastigage®. Reinstall if clearance is within specifications. Check the crankshaft end-play. If it is within specifications, install the connecting rod and piston assemblies with new rod bearing inserts. Check the connecting rod bearing oil clearance and side play. If they are correct assemble the rest of the engine.

BEARING OIL CLEARANCE

Remove the cap from the bearing to be checked. Using a clean, dry rag, thoroughly clean all oil from the crankshaft journal and bearing insert.

NOTE: *Plastigage® is soluble in oil, therefore, oil on the journal or bearing could result in erroneous readings.*

Place a piece of Plastigage® along the full width of the bearing insert, reinstall cap, and torque to specification.

NOTE: *Specifications are given in the Engine Specifications Chart earlier in this chapter.*

Remove the bearing cap, and determine the bearing clearance by comparing the width of the Plastigage® to the scale on the Plastigage® envelope. Journal taper is determined by comparing the width of the bearing insert. Install the cap, and torque it to specifications.

NOTE: *Do not rotate the crankshaft with the Plastigage® installed. If the bearing insert and journal appear intact, and are within tol-*

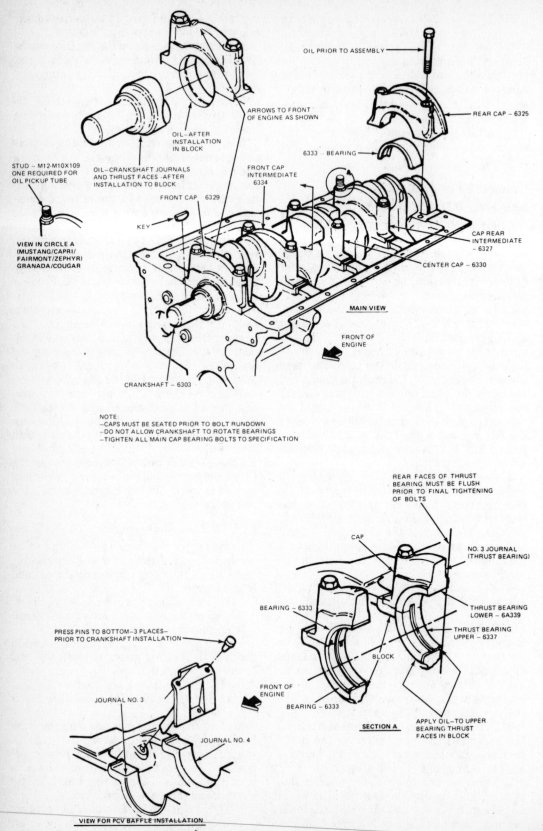

OIL PRIOR TO ASSEMBLY

REAR CAP – 6325

ARROWS TO FRONT OF ENGINE AS SHOWN

6333 – BEARING

OIL –AFTER INSTALLATION IN BLOCK

STUD –- M12-M10X109 ONE REQUIRED FOR OIL PICKUP TUBE

OIL–CRANKSHAFT JOURNALS AND THRUST FACES -AFTER INSTALLATION TO BLOCK

FRONT CAP INTERMEDIATE 6334

FRONT CAP 6329

CAP REAR INTERMEDIATE – 6327

VIEW IN CIRCLE A (MUSTANG/CAPRI/ FAIRMONT/ZEPHYR) GRANADA/COUGAR

KEY

CENTER CAP – 6330

MAIN VIEW

FRONT OF ENGINE

CRANKSHAFT – 6303

NOTE:
–CAPS MUST BE SEATED PRIOR TO BOLT RUNDOWN
–DO NOT ALLOW CRANKSHAFT TO ROTATE BEARINGS
–TIGHTEN ALL MAIN CAP BEARING BOLTS TO SPECIFICATION

REAR FACES OF THRUST BEARING MUST BE FLUSH PRIOR TO FINAL TIGHTENING OF BOLTS

CAP

NO. 3 JOURNAL (THRUST BEARING)

BEARING – 6333

THRUST BEARING LOWER – 6A339

THRUST BEARING UPPER – 6337

PRESS PINS TO BOTTOM–3 PLACES– PRIOR TO CRANKSHAFT INSTALLATION

BLOCK

FRONT OF ENGINE

JOURNAL NO. 3

BEARING – 6333

APPLY OIL–TO UPPER BEARING THRUST FACES IN BLOCK

JOURNAL NO. 4

SECTION A

VIEW FOR PCV BAFFLE INSTALLATION

4-140 crankshaft and main bearing installation

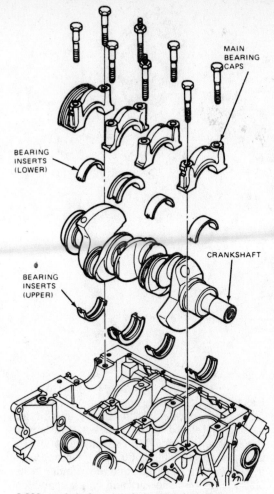

6-232 crankshaft and main bearing installation

erances, no further main bearing service is required. If the bearing or journal appear defective, the cause of failure should be determined before replacement.

CRANKSHAFT END-PLAY/CONNECTING ROD SIDE PLAY

Place a pry bar between a main bearing cap and crankshaft casting taking care not to damage any journals. Pry backward and forward, measuring the distance between the thrust bearing and crankshaft with a feeler gauge. Compare the reading with specifications. If too great a clearance is determined, a main bearing with a larger thrust surface or crank machining may be required. Check with an automotive machine shop for their advice.

Connecting rod clearance between the rod and crankthrow casting can be checked with a feeler gauge. Pry the rod carefully to one side as far as possible and measure the distance on the other side of the rod.

CRANKSHAFT REPAIRS

If a journal is damaged on the crankshaft, repair is possible by having the crankshaft machined to a standard undersize.

In most cases, however, since the engine must be removed from the car and disassembled, some thought should be given to replacing the damaged crankshaft with a reground shaft kit. A reground crankshaft kit contains the necessary main and rod bearings for installation. The shaft has been ground and polished to un-

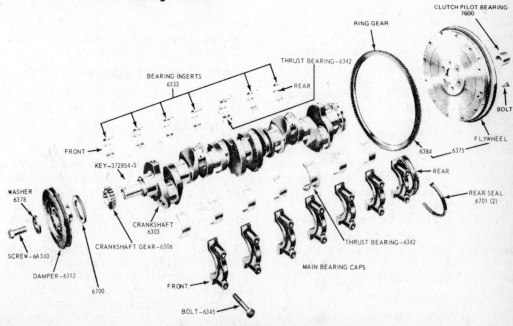

6-200 crankshaft and related parts

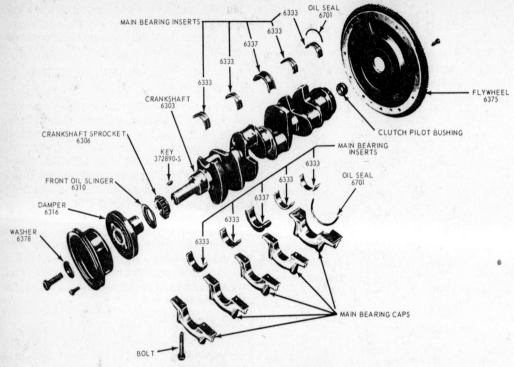

V8 crankshaft and related parts

dersize specifications and will usually hold up well if installed correctly.

COMPLETING THE REBUILDING PROCESS

Fill the oil pump with oil, to prevent cavitating (sucking air) on initial engine start up. Install the oil pump and the pickup tube on the engine. Coat the oil pan gasket as necessary, and install the gasket and the oil pan. Mount the flywheel and the crankshaft vibration damper or pulley on the crankshaft.

NOTE: *Always use new bolts when installing the flywheel. Inspect the clutch shaft pilot bushing in the crankshaft. If the bushing is excessively worn, remove it with an expanding puller and a slide hammer, and tap a new bushing into place.*

Position the engine, cylinder head side up. Lubricate the lifters, and install them into their bores. Install the cylinder head, and torque it as specified. Insert the pushrods (where applicable), and install the rocker shaft(s) (if so equipped) or position the rocker.

Install the intake and exhaust manifolds, the carburetor(s), the distributor and spark plugs. Mount all accessories and install the engine in the car. Fill the radiator with coolant, and the crankcase with high quality engine oil.

BREAK-IN PROCEDURE

Start the engine, and allow it to run at low speed for a few minutes, while checking for leaks. Stop the engine, check the oil level, and fill as necessary. Restart the engine, and fill the cooling system to capacity. Check and adjust the ignition timing. Run the engine at low to medium speed (800-2,500 rpm) for approximately ½ hour, and retorque the cylinder head bolts. Road test the car, and check again for leaks.

NOTE: *Some gasket manufacturers recommend not retorquing the cylinder head(s) due to the composition of the head gasket. Follow the directions in the gasket set.*

Flywheel/Flex Plate and Ring Gear

NOTE: *Flex plate is the term for a flywheel mated with an automatic transmission.*

REMOVAL AND INSTALLATION

All Engines

NOTE: *The ring gear is replaceable only on engines mated with a manual transmission. Engines with automatic transmissions have ring gears which are welded to the flex plate.*

1. Remove the transmission and transfer case.

2. Remove the clutch, if equipped, or torque converter from the flywheel. The flywheel bolts should be loosened a little at a time in a cross pattern to avoid warping the flywheel. On cars with manual transmissions, replace the pilot bearing in the end of the crankshaft if removing the flywheel.

3. The flywheel should be checked for cracks and glazing. It can be resurfaced by a machine shop.

4. If the ring gear is to be replaced, drill a hole in the gear between two teeth, being careful not to contact the flywheel surface. Using a cold chisel at this point, crack the ring gear and remove it.

6. Polish the inner surface of the new ring gear and heat it in an oven to about 600°F (316°C). Quickly place the ring gear on the flywheel and tap it into place, making sure that it is fully seated.

WARNING: *Never heat the ring gear past 800°F (426°C), or the tempering will be destroyed.*

7. Position the flywheel on the end of the crankshaft. Torque the bolts a little at a time, in a cross pattern, to the torque figure shown in the Torque Specifications Chart.

8. Install the clutch or torque converter.

9. Install the transmission and transfer case.

EXHAUST SYSTEM

CAUTION: *When working on exhaust systems, ALWAYS wear protective goggles! Avoid working on a hot exhaust system!*

Muffler

REMOVAL AND INSTALLATION

NOTE: *The following applies to exhaust systems using clamped joints. Some models, use welded joints at the muffler. These joints will, of course, have to be cut.*

1979

1. Raise and support the rear end on jackstands placed under the frame, allowing the rear axle to lower to the full length of its travel.

2. Remove the U-bolt clamping the inlet pipe to the muffler.

3. Unbolt the rear suppoprt bracket from the muffler.

4. Unbolt the intermediate support bracket from the muffler.

5. Remove the muffler outlet clamp and remove the muffler.

6. Installation is the reverse of removal. Always use new clamps. Always install all parts loosely until they are aligned and all clearances are satisfied. Torque the support bracket bolts to 14 ft. lbs.; the flange nuts to 30 ft. lbs.

1980-81 V8 System with a Single Converter

1. Raise and support the car on jackstands placed under the frame, to allow the rear axle to lower to the full limit of its travel.

2. Unbolt the muffler inlet flange from the converter outlet flange.

3. Remove the tailpipe support bracket.

4. Slide the muffler rearward and off of the converter flange.

5. Installation is the reverse of removal. Always use new clamps. Always install all parts loosely until they are aligned and all clearances are satisfied. Torque the support bracket bolts to 14 ft. lbs.; the flange nuts to 30 ft. lbs.

1980-81 V8 System with a Double Converter

1. Raise and support the car on jackstands placed under the frame, to allow the rear axle to lower to the full limit of its travel.

2. Unbolt the muffler inlet flange from the Y-pipe.

3. Remove the tailpipe support bracket.

4. Separate the muffler from the Y-pipe.

5. Installation is the reverse of removal. Always use new clamps. Always install all parts loosely until they are aligned and all clearances are satisfied. Torque the support bracket bolts to 14 ft. lbs.; the clamp nuts to 35 ft. lbs.

1981-82 4-140 Engine
1981-82 6-200 Engine

1. Raise and support the car on jackstands placed under the frame, to allow the rear axle to lower to the full limit of its travel.

2. Unbolt the muffler flange from the converter.

3. Remove the tailpipe support bracket.

4. Slide the muffler rearward and off of the converter.

5. Remove the intermediate hanger bolts.

6. Installation is the reverse of removal. Always use new clamps. Always install all parts loosely until they are aligned and all clearances are satisfied. Torque the support bracket bolts to 14 ft. lbs.; the flange nuts to 30 ft. lbs.

1982 Cars with the V6 or V8 Engines

1. Raise and support the car on jackstands placed under the frame, to allow the rear axle to lower to the full limit of its travel.

2. Unbolt the muffler inlet flange from the converter outlet flange.

3. Remove the tailpipe support bracket.

4. Remove the muffler support bracket attaching screws.

5. Separate the muffler from the converter.

6. Installation is the reverse of removal. Always use new clamps. Always install all parts loosely until they are aligned and all clearances are satisfied. Torque the support bracket bolts to 14 ft. lbs.; the clamp nuts to 35 ft. lbs.

1983-88 Cars with the V6 or V8 Engines

1. Disconnect both rear shock absorber lower mounting bolts.

2. Raise and support the car on jackstands placed under the frame, to allow the rear axle to lower to the full limit of its travel, WITHOUT STRETCHING THE BRAKE HOSE.

3. Unbolt the muffler inlet flange from the converter outlet flange.

4. Remove the tailpipe support bracket.

5. Remove the muffler support bracket attaching screws.

6. Separate the muffler from the converter.

7. Installation is the reverse of removal. Always use new clamps. Always install all parts loosely until they are aligned and all clearances are satisfied. Torque the support bracket bolts to 14 ft. lbs.; the clamp nuts to 35 ft. lbs.

1984-88 4-140

1. Raise and support the car on jackstands placed under the frame, disconnect the lower shock absorber mountings and allow the rear axle to lower to the full limit of its travel, WITHOUT STRETCHING THE BRAKE HOSE.

2. Unbolt the muffler flange from the converter.

3. Remove the tailpipe support bracket.

4. Slide the muffler rearward and off of the converter.

5. Remove the intermediate hanger bolts.

6. Installation is the reverse of removal. Always use new clamps. Always install all parts loosely until they are aligned and all clearances are satisfied. Torque the support bracket bolts to 14 ft. lbs.; the flange nuts to 30 ft. lbs.

Front Exhaust Pipe

REMOVAL AND INSTALLATION

1979

1. Raise and support the front end on jackstands.

2. On cars equipped with and exhaust shield, remove the shield(s).

3. Support the muffler.

4. Remove the muffler inlet clamp.

5. Unbolt the front pipe from the catalytic converter.

6. Remove the heat shield brackets.

7. Separate the front pipe from the muffler slip joint connection. It may be necessary to remove the rear hanger connections for clearance purposes.

8. Unbolt the pipe ends from the exhaust manifolds.

9. Installation is the reverse of removal. Always use new clamps. Always relpace the pipe ends-to-manifold packings. Always install all parts loosely and align the system so that clearances between the system components and surrounding parts are adequate. Torque the sup-

port bracket bolts to 14 ft. lbs.; the clamp nuts to 35 ft. lbs.; the flange nuts to 30 ft. lbs.

1980-81 V8 System with a Single Converter

1. Raise and support the front end on jackstands.

2. Support the muffler with wire.

3. Unbolt the converter inlet pipe from the Y-pipe.

4. Unbolt the Y-pipe from the exhaust manifold and remove the pipe.

5. Installation is the reverse of removal. Always use new clamps. Always replace the pipe ends-to-manifold packings. Always install all parts loosely and align the system, making sure the clearances between system components and surrounding parts are adequate. Torque the clamp nuts to 35 ft. lbs.; the flange nuts to 30 ft. lbs.

1980-81 V8 System with a Double Converter

1. Raise and support the front end on jackstands.

2. Remove the clamp attaching the Y-pipe to the muffler inlet pipe.

3. Remove the heat shields.

4. Unbolt the Y-pipe flanges from the converters.

5. Lower the Y-pipe until the inlet flanges clear the converters. It may be necessary to remove the muffler support bracket for clearance purposes.

6. Support the muffler and remove the Y-pipe.

7. Installation is the reverse of removal. Always use new clamps. Always replace the pipe ends-to-manifold packings. Always install all parts loosely and align the system, making sure that all clearances between the system parts and surrounding components are adequate. Torque the clamp nuts to 35 ft. lbs.; the flange nuts to 30 ft. lbs.

1981-82 4-140
1981-82 6-200
1984-88 4-140

1. Raise and support the front end on jackstands.

2. Support the muffler with a wire.

3. Inbolt the inlet pipe from the converter inlet flange.

4. Remove the inlet pipe-to-exhaust manifold flange.

5. Installation is the reverse of removal. Always use new clamps. Always replace the pipe ends-to-manifold packings. Always install all parts loosely and align the system, making sure that all clearances between the system parts and surrounding components are adequate.

Torque the clamp nuts to 35 ft. lbs.; the flange nuts to 30 ft. lbs.

1982-88 Models with the V6 or V8 Engine

1. Raise and support the front end on jackstands.
2. Remove the clamp attaching the Y-pipe to the converter inlet pipe.
3. Unbolt the Y-pipe flanges from the exhaust manifolds.
4. Remove the Y-pipe.
5. Installation is the reverse of removal. Always use new clamps. Always replace the pipe ends-to-manifold packings. Always install all parts loosely and align the system, making sure that all clearances between the system parts and surrounding components are adequate. Torque the clamp nuts to 35 ft. lbs.; the flange nuts to 30 ft. lbs.

Catalytic Converter

REMOVAL AND INSTALLATION

1979

1. Raise and support the car on jackstands.
2. Remove the heat shield(s).
3. Support the inlet pipe with a length of wire at the #3 crossmember.
4. Remove thd discard the inlet pipe-to-converter flange bolts.
5. Remove the heat shield brackets.
6. Remove the converter-to-manifold flage nuts.
7. Slide the inlet pipes rearward until the converter can be removed.
8. Installation is the reverse of removal. Always use new clamps. Always replace the pipe ends-to-manifold packings. Always install all parts loosely and align the system, making sure that all clearances between the system parts and surrounding components are adequate. Torque the flange nuts to 30 ft. lbs.; the manifold nuts to 35 ft. lbs.

1980-81 V8 System with a Single Converter

1. Raise and support the car on jackstands.
2. Remove the heat shield.
3. Unbolt the Y-pipe from the converter flange.
4. Unbolt the muffler at the converter flange.
5. Separate the flanges and remove the converter.
6. Installation is the reverse of removal. Always use new clamps. Always replace the pipe ends-to-manifold packings. Always install all parts loosely and align the system, making sure that all clearances between the system parts and surrounding components are adequate.

Torque the flange nuts to 30 ft. lbs.; the manifold nuts to 35 ft. lbs.

1980-81 V8 System with a Double Converter

1. Raise and support the car on jackstands.
2. Remove the heat shields.
3. Support the Y-pipe with a wire.
4. Unbolt the Y-pipe flanges from the converter flanges.
5. Unbolt the converter flange at the manifolds.
6. Slide the inlet pipe rearward until the converters can be removed. Separate the flanges and remove the converters.
7. Installation is the reverse of removal. Always use new clamps. Always replace the pipe ends-to-manifold packings. Always install all parts loosely and align the system, making sure that all clearances between the system parts and surrounding components are adequate. Torque the flange nuts to 30 ft. lbs.; the manifold nuts to 35 ft. lbs.

1981-82 4-140 Engine

1. Raise and support the front end on jackstands.
2. Remove the upper and lower heat shields from the converter.
3. Remove the front and rear converter flange bolts.
4. Separate the converter and remove it.
5. Installation is the reverse of removal. Always use new clamps. Always replace the pipe ends-to-manifold packings. Always install all parts loosely and align the system, making sure that all clearances between the system parts and surrounding components are adequate. Torque the flange nuts to 30 ft. lbs.; the manifold nuts to 35 ft. lbs.

1981-82 6-200 Engine

UNDERBODY CONVERTER

1. Raise and support the front end on jackstands.
2. Remove the upper and lower heat shields from the converter.
3. Remove the front and rear converter flange bolts.
4. Separate the converter and remove it.
5. Installation is the reverse of removal. Always use new clamps. Always replace the pipe ends-to-manifold packings. Always install all parts loosely and align the system, making sure that all clearances between the system parts and surrounding components are adequate. Torque the flange nuts to 30 ft. lbs.; the manifold nuts to 35 ft. lbs.

LIGHT-OFF CONVERTER

1. Raise and support the front end on jackstands.

2. Unbolt the light-off converter from the underbody converter.

3. Loosen the U-clamp which attach the air injection tube to the light-off converter outlet pipe.

4. Remove the air injection tube from the light-off converter pipe muzzle connection.

5. Remove the four nuts securing the light-off converter to the exhaust manifold.

6. Installation is the reverse of removal. Always use new clamps. Always replace the pipe ends-to-manifold packings. Always install all parts loosely and align the system, making sure that all clearances between the system parts and surrounding components are adequate. Torque the flange nuts to 30 ft. lbs.; the manifold nuts to 35 ft. lbs.; the clamp nuts to 13 ft. lbs.

1982-83 Cars with the V6 or V8 Engine

1. Raise and support the car on jackstands.

2. If the converters are the air-injected, dual type, disconnect the air injection tube from the cover.

3. Unbolt the Y-pipe flanges from the converter flanges.

4. Unbolt the converter flange at the manifolds.

5. Slide the inlet pipe rearward until the converters can be removed. Separate the flanges and remove the converters.

6. Installation is the reverse of removal. Always use new clamps. Always replace the pipe ends-to-manifold packings. Always install all parts loosely and align the system, making sure that all clearances between the system parts and surrounding components are adequate. Torque the flange nuts to 30 ft. lbs.; the manifold nuts to 35 ft. lbs.

1984-87 4-140

1. Disconnect the downstream injection air hose at the check valve.

2. Raise and support the front end on jackstands.

3. Remove the nuts attaching the converter inlet pipe to the exhaust manifold.

4. Remove the nuts attaching the converter outlet flange to the muffler.

5. Remove the upper and lower heat shields.

6. Remove the converter.

7. Installation is the reverse of removal. Always use new clamps. Always replace the pipe ends-to-manifold packings. Always install all parts loosely and align the system, making sure that all clearances between the system parts and surrounding components are adequate. Torque the flange nuts to 30 ft. lbs.; the manifold nuts to 35 ft. lbs.

1984-85 V6
1986-87 V8 Except the 8-302 HO

1. Raise and support the front end on jackstands.

2. Remove the bolts attaching the Y-pipe to the converter inlet flange.

3. Remove the nuts attaching the muffler inlet pipe to the converter outlet flange.

4. Separate the catalytic converter inlet and outlet flange connections.

5. Remove the converter.

6. Installation is the reverse of removal. Always use new clamps. Always replace the pipe ends-to-manifold packings. Always install all parts loosely and align the system, making sure that all clearances between the system parts and surrounding components are adequate. Torque the flange nuts to 30 ft. lbs.; the manifold nuts to 35 ft. lbs.

1984-85 V8
1986-88 8-302 HO

1. Raise and support the car on jackstands.

2. Disconnect the air injection tube from the cover.

3. Unbolt the Y-pipe flanges from the converter flanges.

4. Unbolt the converter flange at the muffler.

5. Slide the inlet pipe rearward until the converters can be removed. Separate the flanges and remove the converters.

6. Installation is the reverse of removal. Always use new clamps. Always replace the pipe ends-to-manifold packings. Always install all parts loosely and align the system, making sure that all clearances between the system parts and surrounding components are adequate. Torque the flange nuts to 30 ft. lbs.; the manifold nuts to 35 ft. lbs.

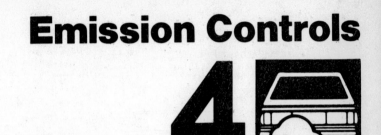

Emission Controls

EMISSION CONTROLS

There are three basic sources of automotive pollution in the modern internal combustion engine. They are the crankcase with its accompanying blow-by vapors, the fuel system with its evaporation of unburned gasoline, and the combustion chambers with their resulting exhaust emissions. Pollution arising from the incomplete combustion of fuel generally falls into three categories: hydrocarbons (HC), carbon monoxide (CO), and oxides of nitrogen (NOx).

Positive Crankcase Ventilation System

All models covered in this book are equipped with a positive crankcase ventilation (PCV) system to control crankcase blow-by vapors. The system consists of a PCV valve and oil separator mounted on top of the valve cover, a non-ventilated oil filler cap, and a pair of hoses supplying filtered intake air to the valve cover and delivering the crankcase vapors from the valve cover to the intake manifold (6-cylinder) or carburetor (V8).

The system functions as follows:

When the engine is running, a small portion of the gases which are formed in the combustion chamber leak by the piston rings and enter the crankcase. Since these gases are under pressure, they tend to escape from the crankcase and enter the atmosphere. If these gases are allowed to remain in the crankcase for any period of time, they contaminate the engine oil and cause sludge to build up in the crankcase. If the gases are allowed to escape into the atmosphere, they pollute the air, with unburned hydrocarbons. The job of the crankcase emission control equipment is to recycle the gases back into the engine combustion chamber where they are unburned.

REMOVAL AND INSTALLATION

Since the PCV valve works under severe load it is very important that it be replaced at the interval specified in the maintenance chart (see Chapter 1). Replacement involves removing the valve from the grommet in the rocker arm cover and install a new valve. Do not attempt to clean a used valve.

Fuel Evaporative Control System

This system is designed to prevent the evaporation of unburned gasoline. The system consists of a vacuum/pressure relief fuel filler cap, an expansion area at the top of the fuel tank, a foam-filled vapor separator mounted on top of the fuel tank, a carbon canister which stores fuel vapors and a number of hoses which connect the various components. The system functions as follows:

Changes in ambient temperature cause the gasoline in fuel tanks to expand or contract. If this expansion and consequent vaporization takes place in a conventional fuel tank, the fuel

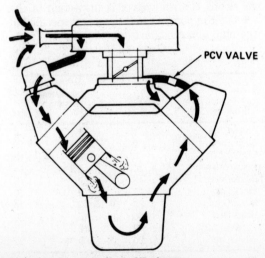

PCV VALVE

PCV system operation—V8 shown

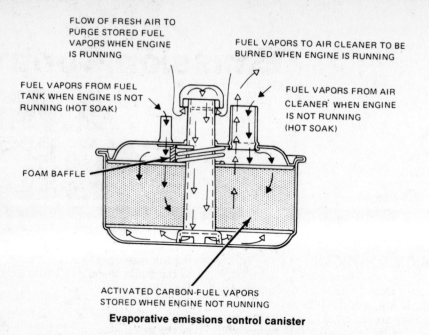

FLOW OF FRESH AIR TO PURGE STORED FUEL VAPORS WHEN ENGINE IS RUNNING

FUEL VAPORS TO AIR CLEANER TO BE BURNED WHEN ENGINE IS RUNNING

FUEL VAPORS FROM FUEL TANK WHEN ENGINE IS NOT RUNNING (HOT SOAK)

FUEL VAPORS FROM AIR CLEANER WHEN ENGINE IS NOT RUNNING (HOT SOAK)

FOAM BAFFLE

ACTIVATED CARBON-FUEL VAPORS STORED WHEN ENGINE NOT RUNNING

Evaporative emissions control canister

vapors escape through the filler cap or vent hose and pollute the atmosphere. The fuel evaporation emission control system prevents this by routing the gasoline vapors to the engine where they are burned.

As the gasoline in the fuel tank of a parked car begins to expand due to heat, the vapor that forms moves to the top of the fuel tank. The fuel tanks are enlarged so that there exists an area representing 10-20% of the total fuel tank volume above the level of the fuel tank filler tube where these gases may collect. The vapors then travel upward into the vapor separator which prevents liquid gasoline from escaping from the fuel tank. The fuel vapor is then drawn through the vapor separator outlet hose, then to the charcoal canister in the engine compartment. The vapor enters the canister, passes through a charcoal filter, and then exits through the canister's grated bottom. As the vapor passes through the charcoal, it is

cleansed of hydrocarbons, so that the air that passes out of the bottom of the canister is free of pollutants.

When the engine is started, vacuum from the carburetor draws fresh air into the canister. As the entering air passes through the charcoal in the canister, it picks up the hydrocarbons that were deposited there by the fuel vapors. This mixture of hydrocarbons and fresh air is then carried through a hose to the air cleaner. In the carburetor, it combines with the incoming air/fuel mixture and enters the combustion chambers of the engine where it is burned.

SERVICE

The only required service for the evaporative emissions control system is inspection of the various components at the interval specified in the maintenance chart (see Chapter 1). If the

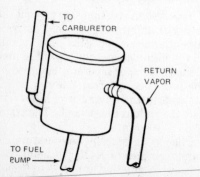

TO CARBURETOR

RETURN VAPOR

TO FUEL PUMP

Vapor separator

Valve Color	ID #	Time Delay (seconds)	
		Min.	Max.
Black/Gray	1	1	4
Black/Brown	2	2	5
Black/White	5	4	12
Black/Yellow	10	5.8	14
Black/Blue	15	7	16
Black/Green	20	9	20
Black/Orange	30	13	24
Black/Red	40	15	28
White/Brown*	2	2	5
White/Green*	20	9	20

* Dual delay, all others are single delay

charcoal element in the canister is gummed up the entire canister should be replaced. Disconnect the canister purge hose from the air cleaner fitting, loosen the canister retaining bracket, lift out the canister. Installation is the reverse of removal.

Thermactor® System

This system is found in most models sold in the 50 states.

The Thermactor® emission control system makes use of a belt-driven air pump to inject fresh air into the hot exhaust stream through the engine exhaust ports. The result is the extended burning of those fumes which were not completely ignited in the combustion chamber, and the subsequent reduction of some of the hydrocarbon and carbon monoxide content of the exhaust emissions into harmless carbon dioxide and water.

The Thermactor® system is composed of the following components:

1. Air supply pump (belt-driven)
2. Air by-pass valve
3. Check valves
4. Air manifolds (internal or external)
5. Air supply tubes (on external manifolds only).

Air for the Thermactor® system is cleaned by means of a centrifugal filter fan mounted on the air pump driveshaft. The air filter does not require a replaceable element.

To prevent excessive pressure, the air pump is equipped with a pressure relief valve which uses a replaceable plastic plug to control the pressure setting.

The Thermactor® air pump has sealed bearings which are lubricated for the life of the unit, and preset rotor vane and bearing clearances, which do not require any periodic adjustments.

The air supply from the pump is controlled by the air by-pass valve, sometimes called a dump valve. During deceleration, the air by-pass valve opens, momentarily diverting the air supply through a silencer and into the atmosphere, thus preventing backfires within the exhaust system.

A check valve is incorporated in the air inlet side of the air manifolds. Its purpose is to prevent exhaust gases from backing up into the Thermactor® system. This valve is especially important in the event of drive belt failure, and during deceleration, when the air by-pass valve is dumping the air supply.

The air manifolds and air supply tubes channel the air from the Thermactor® air pump into the exhaust ports of each cylinder, thus completing the cycle of the Thermactor® system.

SERVICE

The entire Thermactor® system should be checked periodically according to the maintenance chart in Chapter 1. Use the following procedure to determine if the system is functioning properly.

NOTE: *See Chapter 1 for belt adjustment and replacement procedures.*

1. Remove air cleaner, if necessary.
2. Inspect all components of the Thermactor® system for any loose connections or other abnormal conditions. Repair or replace them as necessary.
3. Inspect the air pump drive belt for wear and tension. Adjust or replace them as necessary.
4. With the transmission in neutral or park and the parking brake on, start engine and bring to normal operating temperature.
5. Stop the engine. Connect a tachometer to the engine. Remove the air supply hose at the check valve. If the engine has two check valves, remove both air supply hoses at the check valves and plug off one hose. Position the open hose so that the air blast emitted is harmlessly dissipated.
6. Start the engine and accelerate to 1,500 rpm. Place hand over the open hose. Air flow should be heard and felt. If not air flow is noted, the air bypass valve is defective and should be replaced. The procedure is outlined later in this section.
7. Let the engine speed return to normal idle. Pinch off and remove the vacuum hose from the bypass valve. Accelerate the engine to 1,500 rpm. With hand held over the open end of the check valve hose (same as Step 6), virtually no air flow should be felt or heard.

If air flow is noted, the bypass valve is defective and is to be replaced.

8. Let the engine speed return to normal idle and reinstall the vacuum hose on the by-pass valve vacuum hose nipple. Check hose routing to be sure it is not pinched or restricting normal vacuum signal flow.
9. With hand held over the open end of the

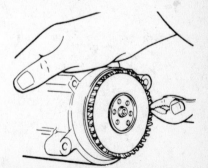

Thermactor air pump filter fan removal

check valve hose (same as Step 6), rapidly increase the engine speed to approximately 2,500 rpm. Immediately release the throttle for the engine to return to normal idle. Air flow should be felt and/or heard to momentarily diminish or go to zero during the deceleration. If the air flow does not momentarily diminish or go to zero repeat the above using an engine speed of 3,000-3,200 rpm.

If air flow does not momentarily diminish or stop during the deceleration from 3,000-3,200 rpm, the vacuum differential control valve should be replaced. Omit this step if the system is not equipped with a differential vacuum valve.

10. Accelerate the engine to 1,500 rpm and check for any exhaust gas leakage at the check valve. There should be virtually no pressure felt or heard when hand is held over the open end of the check valve for approximately 15 seconds. If excessive leakage is noted, replace the check valve(s).

CAUTION: *The check valve may be hot and capable of causing a burn if the hands are not protected.*

11. If the engine is equipped with two check valves, repeat step 10 on the second valve.

12. Stop the engine and remove all the test equipment. Reconnect all the related components. Reinstall the air cleaner, if removed.

REMOVAL AND INSTALLATION
Thermactor® Air Pump

1. Disconnect the air outlet hose at the air pump.

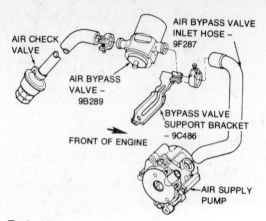

Typical Thermactor (air pump) system

2. Loosen the pump belt tension adjuster.
3. Disengage the drive belt.
4. Remove the mounting bolt and air pump.
5. To install, position the air pump on the mounting bracket and install the mounting bolt.
6. Place drive belt in pulleys and attach the adjusting arm to the air pump.
7. Adjust the drive belt tension to specifications and tighten the adjusting arm and mounting bolts.
8. Connect the air outlet hose to the air pump.

Thermactor® Air Pump Filter Fan

1. Loosen the air pump adjusting arm bolt and mounting bracket bolt to relieve drive belt tension.

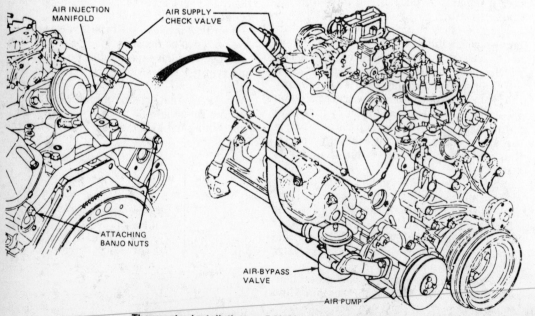

Thermactor installation on 5.0L Mustangs and Capris

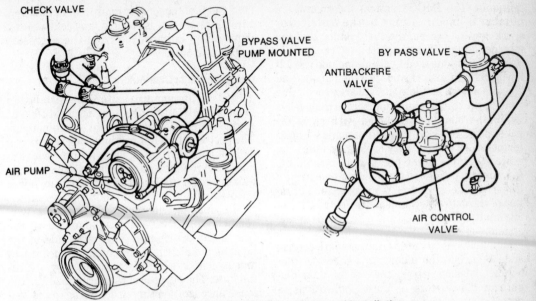

3.3L six cylinder showing Thermactor and installation

2. Remove the drive pulley attaching bolts and pull the drive pulley off the air pump shaft.

3. Pry the outer disc loose, then pull off the centrifugal filter fan with slip-joint pliers.

CAUTION: *Do not attempt to remove the metal drive hub.*

4. Install a new filter fan by drawing it into position, using the pulley and bolts as an installer. Draw the fan evenly by alternately tightening the bolts, making certain that the outer edge of the fan slips into the housing.

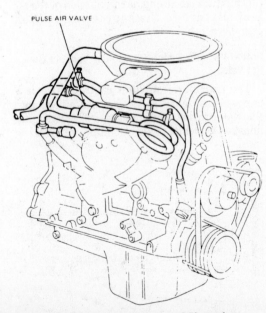

Typical Thermactor II system on 2.3L engine

NOTE: *A slight interference with the housing bore is normal. After a new fan is installed, it may squeal upon initial operation, until its outer diameter sealing lip has worn in, which may require 20 to 30 miles of operation.*

Thermactor® Check Valve

1. Disconnect the air supply hose at the valve. (Use a 1¼″ crowfoot wrench, the valve has a standard, right hand pipe thread.

2. Clean the threads on the air manifold adapter (air supply tube on 8-302 engine) with a wire brush. Do not blow compressed air through the check valve in either direction.

3. Install the check valve and tighten.

4. Connect the air supply hose.

Thermactor® Air By-Pass Valve

1. Disconnect the air and vacuum hoses at the air by-pass valve body.

2. Position the air by-pass valve, and connect the respective hoses.

Vacuum Differential Control Valve

1. Remove the hose connections.

2. Unbolt the valve at its mounting bracket.

3. Install in reverse order.

Improved Combustion System (IMCO®)

All models are equipped with the Improved Combustion (IMCO®) System. The IMCO® system controls emissions arising from the incomplete combustion of the air/fuel mixture in the cylinders. The IMCO® system incorporates a number of modifications to the distributor spark control system, the fuel system, and the internal design of the engine.

Internal engine modifications include the following: elimination of surface irregularities and crevices as well as a low surface area-to-volume ratio in the combustion chambers, a high velocity intake manifold combined with short exhaust ports, selective valve timing and a higher temperature and capacity cooling system.

Modifications to the fuel system include the following: recalibrated carburetors to achieve a leaner air/fuel mixture, more precise calibration of the choke mechanism, the installation of idle mixture limiter caps and a heated air intake system.

Modifications to the distributor spark control system include the following: a modified centrifugal advance curve, the use of dual diaphragm distributors in most applications, a ported vacuum switch, a deceleration valve and a spark delay valve.

SYSTEM DESCRIPTION

Heated Air Intake System

The heated air intake portion of the air cleaner consists of a thermostat, or bimetal switch and vacuum motor, and a spring-loaded temperature control door in the snorkel of the air cleaner. The temperature control door is located between the end of the air cleaner snorkel which draws in air from the engine compartment and the duct that carries heated air up from the exhaust manifold. When underhood temperature is below 90°F (32°C), the temperature control door blocks off underhood air from entering the air cleaner and allows only heated air from the exhaust manifold to be drawn into the air cleaner. When underhood temperature rises above 130°F (54°C), the temperature control door blocks off heated air from the exhaust manifold and allows only underhood air to be drawn into the air cleaner.

By controlling the temperature of the engine intake air this way, exhaust emissions are low-

ered and fuel economy is improved. In addition, throttle plate icing is reduced, and cold weather driveability is improved from the necessary leaner mixtures.

Dual Diaphragm Distributors

Dual diaphragm distributors are installed in most models and appear in many different engine/transmission/equipment combinations. The best way to tell if you have one is to take a look at your distributor. One vacuum hose running from the vacuum capsule indicates a single diaphragm distributor. Two vacuum hoses means that you have a dual diaphragm unit.

The dual distributor diaphragm is a two-chambered housing which is mounted on the side of the distributor. The outer side of the housing is a distributor vacuum advance mechanism, connected to the carburetor by a vacuum hose. The purpose of the vacuum advance is to advance ignition timing according to the conditions under which the engine is operating. This device has been used on automobiles for many years now and its chief advantage is economical engine operation. The second side of the dual diaphragm is the side that has been added to help control engine exhaust emissions at idle and during deceleration.

The inner side of the dual diaphragm is connected by a vacuum hose to the intake manifold. When the engine is idling or decelerating, intake manifold vacuum is high and carburetor vacuum is low. Under these conditions, intake manifold vacuum, applied to the inner side of the dual diaphragm, retards ignition timing to promote more complete combustion of the air fuel mixture in the engine combustion of the air fuel mixture in the engine combustion chambers.

Ported Vacuum Switch (distributor Vacuum Control Valve)

The distributor vacuum control valve is a temperature sensitive valve which screws into the water jacket of the engine. Three vacuum lines are attached to the vacuum control valve:

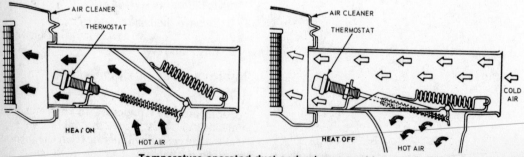

Temperature-operated duct and valve assembly

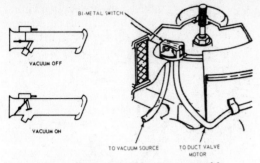

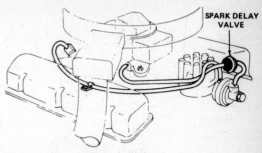

Vacuum-operated duct and valve assembly

Spark delay valve installation

one which runs from the carburetor to the control valve, one which runs from the control valve to the distributor vacuum advance (outer) chamber, and one which runs from the intake manifold to the distributor vacuum control valve.

During normal engine operation, vacuum from the carburetor passes through the top nipple of the distributor control valve, through the valve to the second nipple on the valve, and out the second nipple on the valve to the distributor vacuum advance chamber. When the engine is idling however, carburetor vacuum is very low, so that there is little, if any, vacuum in the passageways described above.

If the engine should begin to overheat while idling, a check ball inside the distributor vacuum control which normally blocks off the third nipple of the valve (intake manifold vacuum) moves upward to block off the first nipple (carburetor vacuum). This applies intake manifold

vacuum (third nipple) to the distributor vacuum advance chamber (second nipple). Since intake manifold vacuum is very high while the engine is idling, ignition timing is advanced by the application of intake manifold vacuum to the distributor vacuum advance chamber. This raises the engine idle speed and helps to cool the engine.

Spark Delay Valve

The spark delay valve is a plastic, spring-loaded, color-coded valve which is installed in the vacuum line to the distributor advance diaphragm on many models. Under heavy throttle applications, the valve will close, blocking normal carburetor vacuum to the distributor. After the designated period of closed time, the valve opens, restoring the carburetor vacuum to the distributor.

3-PORT PVS OPERATION

- **EGR/CSC** – switches EGR vacuum from EGR system to distributor advance with cold engine.
- **Cold Start Spark Advance (CSSA)** – supplies manifold vacuum to distributor below 125° F. coolant temperature.
- **Coolant Spark Control (CSC)** – cuts off distributor advance below hot engine temperature.
- **Cooling PVS** – switches advance vacuum from spark port to manifold vacuum if engine overheats.

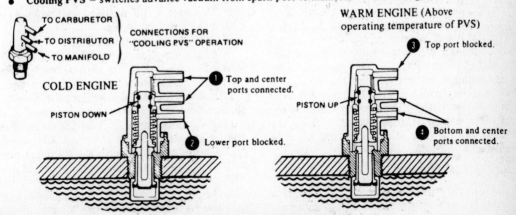

Ported vacuum switch (PVS) operation

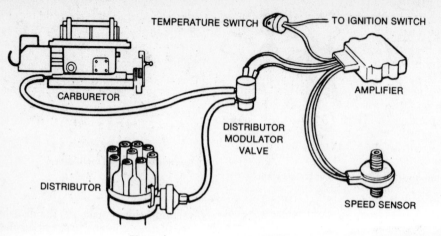

TEMPERATURE SWITCH — TO IGNITION SWITCH

AMPLIFIER

CARBURETOR

DISTRIBUTOR
MODULATOR
VALVE

DISTRIBUTOR

SPEED SENSOR

Electronic spark control system

TESTING IMCO® SYSTEM COMPONENTS

Heated Air Intake System

DUCT AND VALVE ASSEMBLY TEST

1. Either start with a cold engine or remove the air cleaner from the engine for at least half an hour. While cooling the air cleaner, leave the engine compartment hood open.

2. Tape a thermometer, of known accuracy, to the inside of the air cleaner so that is is near the temperature sensor unit. Install the air cleaner on the engine but do not fasten its securing nut.

3. Start the engine. With the engine cold and the outside temperature less than 90°F (32°C), the door should in the **HEAT ON position (closed to outside air).**

4. Operate the throttle lever rapidly to ½-¾ of its opening and release it. The air door should open to allow outside air to enter and then close again.

5. Allow the engine to warm up to normal temperature. Watch the door. When it opens to the outside air, remove the cover from the air cleaner. The temperature should be over 90°F (32°C) and no more than 130°F (54°C); 105°F (41°C) is about normal. If the door does not work within these temperature ranges, or fails to work at all, check for linkage or door binding.

If binding is not present and the air door is not working, proceed with the vacuum tests given below. If these indicate no faults in the vacuum motor and the door is not working, the temperature sensor is defective and must be replaced.

VACUUM MOTOR TEST

NOTE: *Be sure that the vacuum hose that runs between the temperature switch and the vacuum motor is not pinched by the retaining*

clip under the air cleaner. This could prevent the air door from closing.

1. Check all the vacuum lines and fittings for leaks. Correct any leaks. If none are found, proceed with the test.

2. Remove the hose which runs from the sensor to the vacuum motor. Run a hose directly from the manifold vacuum source to the vacuum motor.

3. If the motor closes the air door, it is functioning properly and the temperature sensor is defective.

4. If the motor does not close the door and no binding is present in its operation, the vacuum motor is defective and must be replaced.

NOTE: *If an alternator vacuum source is applied to the motor, insert a vacuum gauge in the line by using a T-fitting. Apply at least 9 in.Hg of vacuum in order to operate the motor.*

Dual Diaphragm Distributor Advance and Retard Mechanisms Test

1. Connect a timing light to the engine. Check the ignition timing.

WARNING: *Before proceeding with the tests, disconnect any spark control devices, distributor vacuum valves, etc. If these are left connected, inaccurate results may be obtained.*

2. Remove the retard hose from the distributor and plug it. Increase the engine speed. The timing should advance. If it fails to do so, then the vacuum unit if faulty and must be replaced.

3. Check the timing with the engine at normal idle speed. Unplug the retard hose and connect it to the vacuum unit. The timing should instantly be retarded 4-10°. If this does not occur, the retard diaphragm has a leak and the vacuum unit must be replaced.

Ported Vacuum Switch (Distributor Vacuum Control Valve) Test

1. Check the routing and connection of all vacuum hoses.
2. Attach a tachometer to the engine.
3. Bring the engine up to normal operating temperature. The engine must not be overheated.
4. Note the engine rpm, with the transmission in neutral, and the throttle in the curb idle position.
5. Disconnect the vacuum hose from the intake manifold at the temperature sensing valve. Plug or clamp the hose.
6. Note the idle rpm with the hose disconnected. If there is no change in rpm, the valve is good. If there is a drop of 100 or more rpm, the valve should be replaced. Replace the vacuum line.
7. Check to make sure that the all-season cooling mixture meets specifications, and that the correct radiator cap is in place and functioning.
8. Block the radiator air flow to induce a higher-than-normal temperature condition.
9. Continue to operate until the engine temperature or heat indicator shows above normal.

If engine speed by this time has increased 100 or more rpm, the temperature sensing valve is satisfactory. If not, it should be replaced.

Spark Delay Valve Test

NOTE: *If the distributor vacuum line contains a cut-off solenoid, it must be open during this test.*

1. Detach the vacuum line from the distributor at the spark delay valve end. Connect a vacuum gauge to the valve, in its place.
2. Connect a tachometer to the engine. Start the engine and rapidly increase its speed to 2,000 rpm with the transmission in neutral.
3. As soon as the engine speed is increased, the vacuum gauge reading should drop to zero.
4. Hold the engine speed at a steady 2,000 rpm. It should take longer than two seconds for the gauge to register 6 in.Hg. If it takes lass than two seconds, the valve is defective and must be replaced.
5. If it takes longer than the number of seconds specified in the application chart for the gauge to reach 6 in.Hg, disconnect the vacuum gauge from the spark delay valve. Disconnect the hose which runs from the spark delay valve to the carburetor at the valve end. Connect the vacuum gauge to this hose.
6. Start the engine and increase its speed to 2,000 rpm. The gauge should indicate 10-16 in.Hg. If it does not, there is a blockage in the carburetor vacuum port or else the hose itself is

plugged or broken. If the gauge reading is within specification, the valve is defective.
7. Reconnect all vacuum lines and remove the tachometer, once testing is completed.

REMOVAL AND INSTALLATION OF IMCO® SYSTEM COMPONENTS

Temperature Operated Duct and Valve Assembly (Heated Air Intake System)

1. Remove the hex-head cap screws which secure the air intake duct and valve assembly to the air cleaner.
2. Remove the air intake duct and valve assembly from the engine.
3. If inspection reveals that the valve plate is sticking or the thermostat is malfunctioning, remove the thermostat and valve plates as follows:
   a. Detach the valve plate tension spring from the valve plate using long-nose pliers.
   b. Loosen the thermostat locknut and unscrew the thermostat from the mounting bracket.
   c. Grasp the valve plate and withdraw it from the cut.
4. Install the air intake duct and valve assembly on the shroud tube.
5. Connect the air intake duct and valve assembly the air cleaner and tighten the hex-head retaining cap screws.
6. If it was necessary to disassemble the thermostat and air duct and valve, assembly the unit as follows: Install the locknut on the thermostat, and screw the thermostat into the mounting bracket. Install the valve plate tension spring on the valve plate and duct.
7. Install the vacuum override motor (if applicable) and check for proper operation.

Vacuum Operated Duct and Valve Assembly (Heated Air Intake System)

1. Disconnect the vacuum hose at the vacuum motor.
2. Remove the hex-head cap screws which secure the air intake duct and valve assembly to the air cleaner.
3. Remove the duct and valve assembly from the engine.
4. Position the duct and valve assembly to the air cleaner and heat stove tube. Install the attaching cap screws.
5. Connect the vacuum line at the vacuum motor.

Ported Vacuum Switch (Distributor Vacuum Control Valve)

1. Drain about one gallon of coolant out of the radiator.
CAUTION: *When draining the coolant, keep in mind that cats and dogs are attracted by*

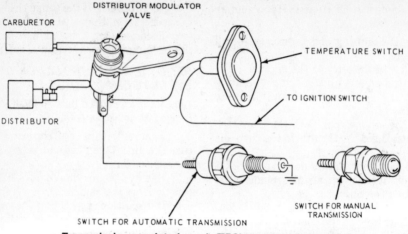

Transmission regulated spark (TRS) system schematic

the ethylene glycol antifreeze, and are quite likely to drink any that is left in an uncovered container or in puddles on the ground. This will prove fatal in sufficient quantity. Always drain the coolant into a sealable container. Coolant should be reused unless it is contaminated or several years old.

2. Tag the vacuum hoses that attach to the control valve and disconnect them.

3. Unscrew and remove the control valve.

4. Install the new control valve.

5. Connect the vacuum hoses.

6. Fill the cooling system.

Spark Delay Valve

1. Locate the spark delay valve in the distributor vacuum line and disconnect it from the line.

2. Install a new spark delay valve in line, making sure that the black end of the valve is connected to the line from the carburetor and the color coded end is connected to the line from the spark delay valve to the distributor.

Exhaust Gas Recirculation System

All models are equipped with an exhaust gas recirculation (EGR) system to control oxides of nitrogen.

On V8 engines, exhaust gases travel through the exhaust gas crossover passage in the intake manifold. On 6-200 engines, an external tube carries exhaust manifold gases to a carburetor spacer. On spacer entry equipped engines, a portion of these gases are diverted into a spacer which is mounted under the carburetor. On floor entry models, a regulated portion of exhaust gases enters the intake manifold through a pair of small holes drilled in the floor of the intake manifold riser. The EGR control valve, which is attached to the rear of the spacer or intake manifold, consists of a vacuum diaphragm with an attached plunger which normally blocks exhaust gases from entering the intake manifold.

On all models, the EGR valve is controlled by a vacuum line from the carburetor which passes through a ported vacuum switch. The EGR ported vacuum switch provides vacuum to the EGR valve at coolant temperatures above 125°F (52°C). The vacuum diaphragm then opens the EGR valve permitting exhaust gases to flow through the carburetor spacer and enter the combustion chambers. The exhaust gases are relatively oxygen-free, and tend to dilute the combustion charge. This lowers peak combustion temperature thereby reducing oxides of nitrogen.

EGR SYSTEM TEST

1. Allow the engine to warm up, so that the coolant temperature has reached at least 125°F (52°C).

2. Disconnect the vacuum hose which runs from the temperature cut-in valve to the EGR valve at the EGR valve end. Connect a vacuum gauge to this hose with a T-fitting.

3. Increase engine speed. The gauge should indicate a vacuum. If no vacuum is present, check the following:

   a. The carburetor — look for a clogged vacuum port.

   b. The vacuum hoses — including the vacuum hoses to the transmission modulator.

   c. The temperature cut-in valve — if no vacuum is present at its outlet with the engine temperature above 125°F (52°C) and vacuum available from the carburetor, the valve is defective.

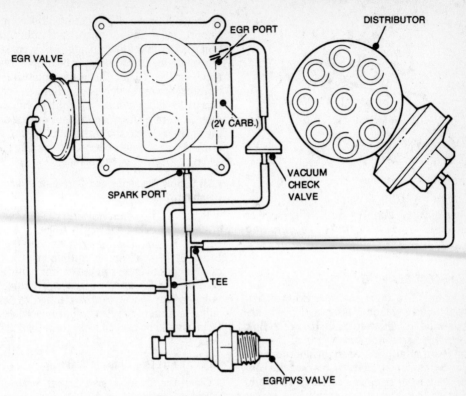

Typical EGR valve installation

4. If all the above tests are positive, check the EGR valve itself.

5. Connect an outside vacuum source and a vacuum gauge to the valve.

6. Apply vacuum to the EGR valve. The valve should open at 3-10 in.Hg, the engine idle speed should slow down and the idle quality should become more rough.

7. If this does not happen, i.e., the EGR valve remains closed, the EGR valve is defective and must be replaced.

8. If the valve stem moves but the idle remains the same, the valve orifice is clogged and must be cleaned.

NOTE: *If an outside vacuum source is not available, disconnect the hose which runs between the EGR valve and the temperature cut-in valve and plug the hose connections on*

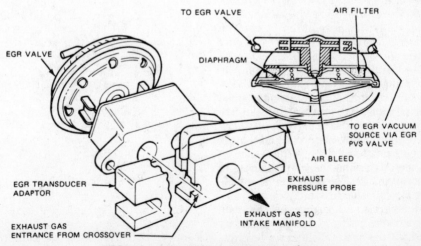

EGR valve exhaust backpressure tranducer

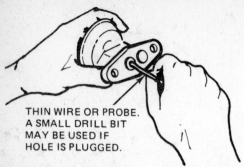

THIN WIRE OR PROBE.
A SMALL DRILL BIT
MAY BE USED IF
HOLE IS PLUGGED.

Cleaning EGR valve orifice

the cut-in valve. Connect the EGR valve hose to a source of intake manifold vacuum and watch the idle. The results should be the same as in steps 6-7, above.

EGR SYSTEM SERVICE

Since the EGR system channels exhaust gases through quite narrow passages, deposits are likely to build up and eventually block the flow of gases. this necessitates servicing of the system at the interval specified in the maintenance chart (see Chapter 1). EGR system service consists of cleaning or replacing the EGR valve and cleaning all the exhaust gas channels.

EGR VALVE CLEANING

Remove the EGR valve for cleaning. Do not strike or pry on the valve diaphragm housing or supports, as this may damage the valve operating mechanism and/or change the valve calibration. Check orifice hole in the EGR valve body for deposits. A small hand drill of no more than 0.060″ (1.5mm) diameter may be used to clean the hole if plugged. Extreme care must be taken to avoid enlarging the hole or damaging the surface of the orifice plate.

NOTE: *The remainder of this procedure refers only to EGR valves which can be disassembled. Valves which are riveted or otherwise permanently assembled cannot be cleaned and should be replaced if highly contaminated.*

Separate the diaphragm section from the main mounting body. Clean the valve plates, stem, and the mounting plate, using a small power-driven rotary type wire brush. Take care not to damage the parts. Remove deposits between stem and valve disc by using a steel blade or shim approximately 0.028″ (0.7mm) thick in a sawing motion around the stem shoulder at both sides of the disc. The poppet must wobble and move axially before assembly.

Clean the cavity and passages in the main body of the valve with a power-driven rotary wire brush. If the orifice plate has a hole less than 0.050″ (1.27mm) it must be removed for

cleaning. Remove all loosened debris using shop compressed air. Reassemble the diaphragm section on the main body using a new gasket between them. Torque the attaching screws to specification. Clean the orifice plate and the counterbore in the valve body. Reinstall the orifice plate using a small amount of contact cement to retain the plate in place during assembly of the valve to the carburetor spacer. Apply cement only to outer edges of the orifice plate to avoid restriction of the orifice.

EGR Supply Passages and Carburetor Space Cleaning

Remove the carburetor and carburetor spacer on engines so equipped. Clean the supply tube with a small power-driven rotary type wire brush or blast cleaning equipment. Clean the exhaust gas passages in the spacer using a suitable wire brush and/or scraper. The machined holes in the spacer can be cleaned by using a suitable round wire brush. hard encrusted material should be probed loose first, then brushed out.

EGR Exhaust Gas Channel Cleaning

Clean the exhaust gas channel, where applicable, in the intake manifold, using a suitable carbon scraper. Clean the exhaust gas entry

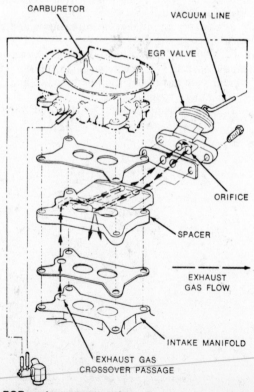

CARBURETOR

VACUUM LINE

EGR VALVE

ORIFICE

SPACER

EXHAUST GAS FLOW

INTAKE MANIFOLD

EXHAUST GAS CROSSOVER PASSAGE

EGR system spacer entry

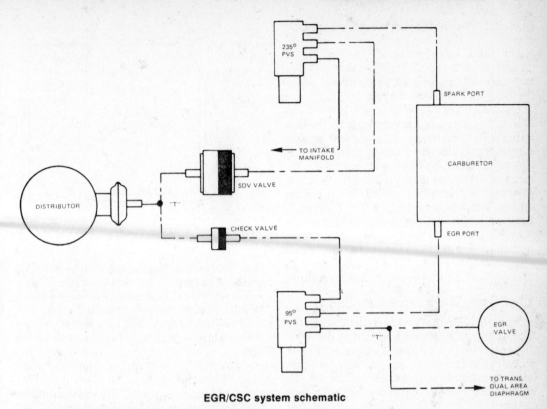

EGR/CSC system schematic

port in the intake manifold by hand passing a suitable drill bit through the holes to auger out the deposits. do not use a wire brush. The manifold riser bore(s) should be suitably plugged during the above action to prevent any of the residue from entering the induction system.

Venturi Vacuum Amplifier System

Many models use a venturi vacuum amplifier in conjunction with the EGR system. The amplifier is used to boost a relatively weak venturi vacuum signal in the throat of the carburetor into a strong intake manifold vacuum signal to operate the EGR valve. This device improves driveability by more closely matching venturi airflow and EGR flow.

The amplifier features a vacuum reservoir and check valve to maintain an adequate vacuum supply regardless of variations in engine manifold vacuum. Also used in conjunction with the amplifier, is a relief valve, which will cancel the output EGR vacuum signal whenever the venturi vacuum signal is equal to, or greater than, the intake manifold vacuum. Thus, the EGR valve may close at or near wide-open throttle acceleration, when maximum power is needed.

EGR/Coolant Spark Control

The EGR/CSC system is used on most models. It regulates both distributor spark advance and the EGR valve operation according to coolant temperature by sequentially switching vacuum signals.

The major EGR/CSC system components are:
1. 95°F (35°C) EGR-PVS valve.
2. Spark Delay Valve (SDV).
3. Vacuum check valve.

When the engine coolant temperature is below 82°F (28°C), the EGR-PVS valve admits carburetor EGR port vacuum (occurring at about 2,500 rpm) directly to the distributor advance diaphragm, through the one-way check valve.

At the same time, the EGR-PVS valve shuts off carburetor EGR vacuum to the EGR valve and transmission diaphragm.

When engine coolant temperature is 95°F (35°C) and above, the EGR-PVS valve is actuated and directs carburetor EGR vacuum to the EGR valve and transmission instead of the distributor. At temperatures between 82-95°F (28-35°C), the EGR-PVS valve may be opened, closed, or in mid-position.

The SDV valve delays carburetor spark vacuum to the distributor advance diaphragm by restricting the vacuum signal through the SDV valve for a predetermined time. During normal acceleration, little or no vacuum is admitted to the distributor advance diaphragm until acceleration is completed, because of (1) the time delay of the SDV valve and (2) the rerouting of the

EGR port vacuum if the engine coolant temperature if 95°F (35°C) or higher.

The check valve blocks off vacuum signal from the SDV to the EGR-PVS so that carburetor spark vacuum will not be dissipated when the EGR-PVS is actuated above 95°F (35°C).

The 235°F (113°C) PVS is not part of the EGR/CSC system, but is connected to the distributor vacuum advance to prevent engine overheating while idling (as on previous models). At idle speed, no vacuum is generated at either the carburetor spark port or EGR port and engine timing is fully retarded. When engine coolant temperatures reaches 235°F (113°C), however, the valve is actuated to admit intake manifold vacuum to the distributor advance diaphragm. This advances the engine timing and speeds up the engine. The increase in coolant flow and fan speed lowers engine temperature.

Cold Start Spark Advance (CSSA)

Many 1977-78 models are equipped with the CSSA System. It is a modification of the existing spark control system to aid in cold start driveability. The system uses a coolant temperature sensing vacuum switch located on the thermostat housing. When the engine is cold (below 125°F [113°C]), it permits full manifold vacuum to the distributor advance diaphragm. After the engine warms up, normal spark control (retard) resumes.

Vacuum Operated Heat Control Valve (VOHV)

To further aid cold start driveability during engine warmup, most engines use a VOHV located between the exhaust manifold and the exhaust inlet (header) pipe.

When the engine is first started, the valve is closed, blocking exhaust gases from existing from one bank of cylinders. These gases are

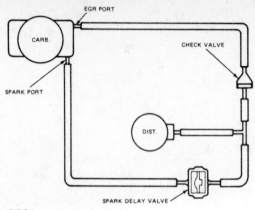

DSSA system schematic

then diverted back through the intake manifold crossover passage under the carburetor. The result is quick heat to the carburetor. The result is quick heat to the carburetor and choke.

The VOHV is controlled by a ported vacuum switch which uses manifold vacuum to keep the vacuum motor on the valve closed until the coolant reaches a predetermined warm-up valve. When the engine is warmed-up, the PVS shuts off vacuum to the VOHV, and a strong return spring opens the VOHV butterfly.

Dual Signal Spark Advance (DSSA) System

The DSSA system is used on many engines. It incorporates a spark delay valve (SDV) and a one-way check valve to provide improved spark and EGR function during mild acceleration.

The check valve prevents spark port vacuum from reaching the EGR valve and causing excessive EGR valve flow. It also prevents EGR port vacuum, which could result in improper spark advance due to weakened signal. The SDV permits application of full EGR vacuum to the distributor vacuum advance diaphragm during mild acceleration. During steady speed or cruise conditions, EGR port vacuum is applied to the EGR valve and spark port vacuum is applied to the distributor vacuum advance diaphragm.

Catalytic Converter System

All models are equipped with a catalytic converter system to meet 1975 Federal and California emission control standards. California models are equipped with two converters, while models sold in the other 49 states have only one unit.

Catalytic converters convert noxious emissions of hydrocarbons (HC) and carbon monoxide (CO) into harmless carbon dioxide and water. The reaction takes place inside the reac-

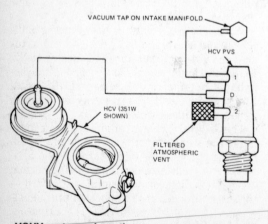

VOHV system schematic

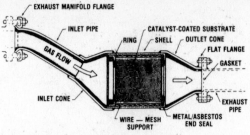

EXHAUST MANIFOLD FLANGE
INLET PIPE
RING
GAS FLOW
CATALYST-COATED SUBSTRATE
SHELL **OUTLET CONE**
FLAT FLANGE
GASKET
INLET CONE
EXHAUST PIPE
WIRE — MESH SUPPORT
METAL/ASBESTOS END SEAL

Sectional view of catalytic converter

tor(s) at great heat using platinum or palladium metals as the catalyst. The 5″ (127mm) diameter units are installed in the exhaust system ahead of the mufflers. They are designed, if the engine is properly tuned, to last 50,000 miles before replacement.

NOTE: *Lead-free gasoline must be used on all converter equipped vehicles.*

Ford Electronic Engine Control System

EEC-I

Designed to precisely control ignition timing, EGR and Thermactor (air pump) flow, the system consists of Electronic Control Assembly (ECA), seven monitoring sensors, a DuraSpark®II ignition module and coil, a special distributor assembly, and an EGR system designed to operate on air pressure.

The ECA is a solid state micro computer, consisting of a processor assembly and a calibration assembly. The processor continuously receives inputs from the seven sensors, which it converts to usable information for the calculating section of the computer. It also performs ignition timing, Thermactor® and EGR flow calculations, processes the information and sends out signals to the ignition module and control

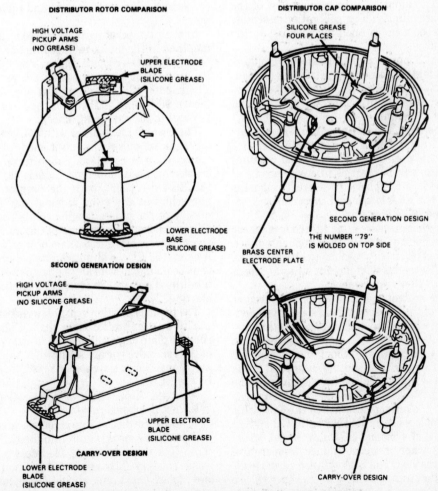

DISTRIBUTOR ROTOR COMPARISON

HIGH VOLTAGE PICKUP ARMS (NO GREASE)
UPPER ELECTRODE BLADE (SILICONE GREASE)
LOWER ELECTRODE BASE (SILICONE GREASE)

SECOND GENERATION DESIGN

HIGH VOLTAGE PICKUP ARMS (NO SILICONE GREASE)
UPPER ELECTRODE BLADE (SILICONE GREASE)
CARRY-OVER DESIGN
LOWER ELECTRODE BLADE (SILICONE GREASE)

DISTRIBUTOR CAP COMPARISON

SILICONE GREASE FOUR PLACES
SECOND GENERATION DESIGN
THE NUMBER "79" IS MOLDED ON TOP SIDE
BRASS CENTER ELECTRODE PLATE
CARRY-OVER DESIGN

Comparison of early and later model EEC distributor caps

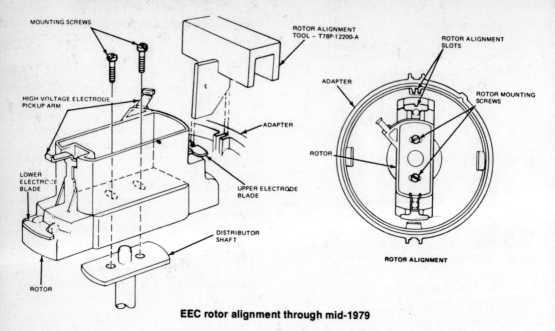

EEC rotor alignment through mid-1979

solenoids to adjust the timing and flow of the system accordingly. The calibration assembly contains the memory and programming for the processor.

Processor inputs come from sensors monitoring manifold pressure, barometric pressure, engine coolant temperature, inlet air temperature, crankshaft position, throttle position, and EGR valve position.

The manifold absolute pressure sensor determines changes in intake manifold pressure (barometric pressure minus manifold vacuum) which result from changes in engine load and speed, or in atmospheric pressure. It signal is used by the ECA to set part throttle spark advance and EGR flow rate.

Barometric pressure is monitored by a sensor mounted on the firewall. Measurements taken are converted into a usable electrical signal. The ECA uses this reference for altitude-dependent EGR flow requirements.

Engine coolant temperature is measured at the rear of the intake manifold by a sensor consisting of a brass housing containing a thermistor (resistance decreases as temperature rises). When reference voltage (about 9 volts, supplied by the processor to all sensors) is applied to the sensor, the resistance can be measured by the resulting voltage drop. Resistance is then interpreted as coolant temperature by the ECA. This sensor replaces both the PVS and EGR PVS in conventional systems. EGR flow is cut off by the ECA when a predetermined temperature value is reached. The ECA will also advance initial ignition timing to increase idle speed if the coolant overheats due to prolonged idle. A fast-

er idle speed increases coolant and radiator air flow.

Inlet air temperature is measured by a sensor mounted in the air cleaner. It functions in the same way as the coolant sensor. The ECA uses its signal for proper spark advance and Thermactor® flow. At high inlet temperatures (above 90°F [32°C]) the ECA modifies timing advance to prevent spark knock.

The crankshaft is fitted with a 4-lobed powdered metal pulse ring, positioned 10°BTDC. Its position is constantly monitored by the crankshaft position sensor. Signals are sent to the ECA describing both the position of the crankshaft at any given moment, and the frequency of the pulses (engine rpm). These signals are used to determine optimum ignition timing advance. If either the sensor or wiring is broken, the ECA will not receive a signal, and thus be unable to send any signal to the ignition module. This will prevent the engine from starting.

The throttle position sensor is a rheostat connected to the throttle plate shaft. Changes in throttle plate angle change the resistance valve of the reference voltage supplied by the processor. Signals are interpreted in one of three ways by the ECA.
- Closed throttle (idle or deceleration)
- Part throttle (cruise)
- Full throttle (maximum acceleration)

A position sensor is built into the EGR valve. The ECA uses its signal to determine EGR valve position. The valve and position sensor are replaced as a unit, should either fail.

CAUTION: *Because of the complicated na-*

ture of this system, special diagnostic tools are necessary for troubleshooting. Any troubleshooting without these tools must be limited to mechanical checks of connectors and wiring.

The distributor is locked in place during engine manufacture; no rotational adjustment is possible for initial ignition timing, since all timing is controlled by the ECA. There are no mechanical advance mechanisms or adjustments under the rotor, thus there is no need to remove it except for replacement.

EEC-II

The second generation EEC-II system was introduced in 1979. It is based on the EEC-I system, but some changes have been made to reduce complexity and cost, increase the number of controlled functions, and improve reliability and performance.

In general, the EEC-II system operates in the same manner as EEC-I. An Electronic Control Assembly (ECA) monitors reports from six sensors, and adjusts the EGR flow, ignition timing, Thermactor® (air pump) air flow, and carburetor air/fuel mixture in response to the incoming signals. Although there are only six sensors, seven conditions are monitored. The sensors are: (1) Engine Coolant Temperature, (2) Throttle Position, (3) Crankshaft Position, (4) Exhaust Gas Oxygen, (5) Barometric and Manifold Absolute Pressure, and (6) EGR Valve Position. These sensors function in the same manner as the EEC-I sensors, and are described in the EEC-I section. Note that inlet air temperature is not monitored in the EEC-II system, and that the barometric and manifold pressure sensors have been combined into one unit. One more change from the previous system is in the location of the crankshaft sensor: it is mounted on the front of the engine, behind the vibration damper and crankshaft pulley.

The biggest difference between EEC-I and EEC-II is that the newer system is capable of continually monitoring and adjusting the carburetor air/fuel ratio. Monitoring is performed by the oxygen sensor installed in the right exhaust manifold. Adjustment is made via an electric stepper motor installed on the model 7200 VV carburetor.

The stepper motor has four separate armature windings, which can be sequentially energized by the ECA. As the motor varies the position of the carburetor metering valve, the amount of control vacuum exposed to the fuel bowl in correspondingly altered. Increased vacuum reduces pressure in the fuel bowl, causing a leaner air/fuel mixture, and vice-versa. During engine starting and immediately after, the ECA sets the motor at a point dependent on its initial position. Thereafter, the motor position is changed in response to the ECA calculations of the six input signals.

EEC-II is also capable of controlling purging of vapors from the evaporative emission control storage canister. A canister purge solenoid, a combination solenoid and valve, is located in the line between the intake manifold purge fitting and the carbon canister. It controls the flow of vapors from the canister to the intake manifold, opening and closing in response to signals from the ECA.

CAUTION: *As in the case with EEC-I, diagnosis and repair of the system requires special tools and equipment.*

The distributor is locked in place during engine manufacture; no rotational adjustment is possible for initial ignition timing, since all timing is controlled by the ECA. There are no mechanical advance mechanisms or adjustments under the ignition rotor, and thus there is no need to remove it except for replacement.

Air/fuel mixture is entirely controlled by the ECA; no adjustments are possible.

EEC-III

EEC-III was introduced in 1980. It is a third generation system developed entirely from EEC-II. The only real differences between EEC-II and III are contained within the Electronic Control Assembly (ECA) and the DuraSpark® ignition module. The EEC-III system uses a separate program module which plugs into the main ECA module. This change allows various programming calibrations for specific applications to be made to the program module, while allowing the main ECA module to be standardized. Additionally, EEC-III uses a DuraSpark®III ignition module, which contains fewer electronic functions than the DuraSpark®II module. The functions have been incorporated into the main ECA module. There is no interchangeability between the DuraSpark®II and III models.

NOTE: *Since late 1979 emission controls and air/fuel mixtures have been controlled by various electronic methods. An electronically controlled feedback carburetor is used to precisely calibrate fuel metering, many vacuum check valves, solenoids and regulators have been added and the electronic control boxes (ECU and MCU) can be calibrated and programmed in order to be used by different engines and under different conditions.*

EEC-IV

All 1984 and later engines use the EEC-IV system. The heart of the EEC-IV system is a micro-processor called an electronic control assembly (ECA). The ECA receives data from a number of sensors and other electronic components (switches, relay, etc.). Based on information received and information programmed in the ECA's memory, it generates output signals to control various relay, solenoids and other actuators. The ECA in the EEC-IV system has calibration modules located inside the assembly that contain calibration specifications for optimizing emissions, fuel economy and drive ability. The calibration module is called a PROM.

A potentiometer senses the position of the vane airflow meter in the engine's air induction system and generates a voltage signal that varies with the amount of air drawn into the engine. A sensor in the area of the vane airflow meter measures the temperature of the incoming air and transmits a corresponding electrical signal. Another temperature sensor inserted in the engine coolant tells if the engine is cold or warmed up. And a switch that senses throttle plate position produces electrical signals that tell the control unit when the throttle is closed or wide open.

A special probe (oxygen sensor) in the exhaust manifold measures the amount of oxygen in the exhaust gas, which is in indication of combustion efficiency, and sends a signal to the control unit. The sixth signal, crankshaft posi-

tion information, is transmitted by a sensor integral with the new-design distributor.

The EEC-IV microcomputer circuit processes the input signals and produces output control signals to the fuel injectors to regulate fuel discharged to the injectors. It also adjusts ignition spark timing to provide the best balance between driveability and economy.

NOTE: *Because of the complicated nature of the Ford system, special tools and procedures are necessary for testing and troubleshooting.*

The following emission control devices described can be tested and maintained. Any not mentioned should be serviced by qualified mechanics using the required equipment.

Oxygen Sensor
REMOVAL AND INSTALLATION

The oxygen sensor is located in the exhaust headpipe. To replace it, unplug the connector and unscrew the sensor.

Replacement senors will be packaged with anti-sieze compound for the threads. If not, or if you are reinstalling the old unit, the threads MUST be coated with anti-sieze compound! Torque the sensor to 12 ft.lb.

Fuel System

FUEL SYSTEM

Mechanical Fuel Pump

A single-action, diaphragm-type, mechanical fuel pump, driven by the camshaft is found on all carbureted models.

The mechanical fuel pump is located at the lower left side of the engine block on the 6-200, at the lower left side of the cylinder front cover on 6-170 and V8 models and the right side front on the 6-232.

TESTING

No adjustments may be made to the fuel pump. Before removing and replacing the old fuel pump, the following test may be made while the pump is still installed on the engine.

1. If a fuel pressure gauge is available, connect the gauge to the engine and operate the engine until the pressure stops rising. Stop the engine and take the reading. If the reading is within the specifications given in the Tune-Up Specifications chart in Chapter 2, the malfunctions is not in the fuel pump. Also check the pressure drop after the engine is stopped. A large pressure drop below the minimum specification indicates leaky valves. If the pump proves to be satisfactory, check the tank and inlet line.

2. If a fuel pressure gauge is not available, disconnect the fuel line at the pump outlet, place a vessel beneath the pump outlet, and crank the engine. A good pump will force the fuel out of the outlet in steady spurts. One pint in 25-30 seconds is a good flow. A worn diaphragm spring may not provide proper pumping action.

3. As a further test, disconnect and plug the fuel line from the tank at the pump, and hold your thumb over the pump inlet. If the pump is functioning properly, a suction indicates that

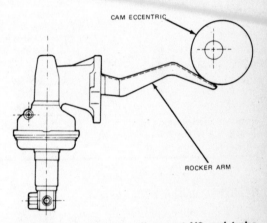

Mechanical fuel pump; all except V6 and turbo automatic

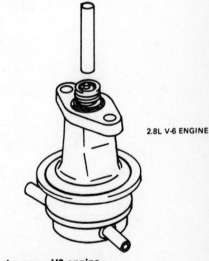

Fuel pump—V6 engine

the pump diaphragm is leaking, or that the diaphragm linkage is worn.

4. Check the crankcase for gasoline. A ruptured diaphragm may leak fuel into the engine.

Troubleshooting Basic Fuel System Problems

Problem	Cause	Solution
Engine cranks, but won't start (or is hard to start) when cold	• Empty fuel tank • Incorrect starting procedure • Defective fuel pump • No fuel in carburetor • Clogged fuel filter • Engine flooded • Defective choke	• Check for fuel in tank • Follow correct procedure • Check pump output • Check for fuel in the carburetor • Replace fuel filter • Wait 15 minutes; try again • Check choke plate
Engine cranks, but is hard to start (or does not start) when hot— (presence of fuel is assumed)	• Defective choke	• Check choke plate
Rough idle or engine runs rough	• Dirt or moisture in fuel • Clogged air filter • Faulty fuel pump	• Replace fuel filter • Replace air filter • Check fuel pump output
Engine stalls or hesitates on acceleration	• Dirt or moisture in the fuel • Dirty carburetor • Defective fuel pump • Incorrect float level, defective accelerator pump	• Replace fuel filter • Clean the carburetor • Check fuel pump output • Check carburetor
Poor gas mileage	• Clogged air filter • Dirty carburetor • Defective choke, faulty carburetor adjustment	• Replace air filter • Clean carburetor • Check carburetor
Engine is flooded (won't start accompanied by smell of raw fuel)	• Improperly adjusted choke or carburetor	• Wait 15 minutes and try again, without pumping gas pedal • If it won't start, check carburetor

REMOVAL AND INSTALLATION

NOTE: *Before removing the pump, rotate the engine so that the low point of the cam lobe is against the pump arm. This can be determined by rotating the engine with the fuel pump mounting bolts loosened slightly.*

When tension (resistance) is removed from the arm, proceed.

1. Disconnect and plug the inlet and outlet lines at the fuel pump.

2. Remove the fuel pump retaining bolts and carefully pull the pump and old gasket away from the block.

3. Discard the old gasket. Clean the mating

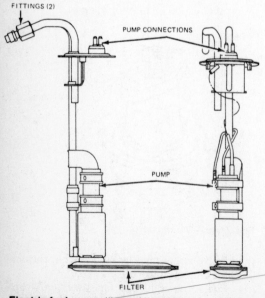

Electric fuel pump, "in tank" location

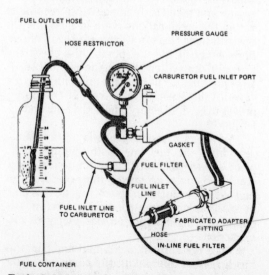

Typical fuel pump pressure and capacity test equipment

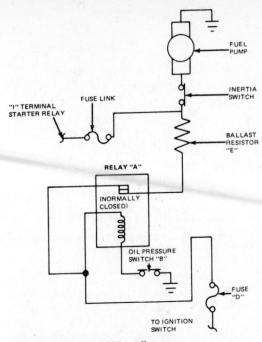

Electric fuel pump wiring diagram

engine lose oil pressure, the pump is automatically disconnected, stopping the engine.

All 1984 models equipped with a high output injected or turbocharged injected engine are equipped with two electric pumps. A low pressure pump is mounted in the tank and a high pressure pump is externally mounted.

All 1985-88 models are equipped with a single, in-tank, high pressure fuel pump.

CAUTION: *Before servicing any part of the fuel injection it is necessary to depressurize the system. A special tool is available for testing and bleeding the system.*

1980-84 Low Pressure In-Tank Pump

1. Disconnect the negative battery cable.
2. Depressurize the system and drain as much gas from the tank by pumping out through the filler neck.
3. Raise and support the rear end on jackstands.

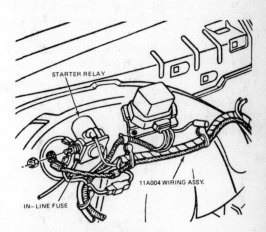

In-line-fuse—electric fuel pump

surfaces on the block and position a new gasket on the block, using oil-resistant sealer.

4. Mount the fuel pump and gasket to the engine block, being careful to insert the pump lever (rocker arm) in the engine block, aligning it correctly above the camshaft lobe.

NOTE: *If resistance is felt while positioning the fuel pump on the block, the camshaft bole is probably on the high position. To ease installation, connect a remote engine starter switch to the engine and tap the switch until resistance fades.*

5. While holding the pump securely against the block, install the retaining bolts. On 6-cylinder engines, torque the bolts to 12-15 ft. lbs., and on V8, 20-24 ft. lbs.

6. Unplug and reconnect the fuel line at the pump.

7. Start the engine and check for fuel leaks. Also check for oil leaks where the fuel pump attaches to the block.

Electric Fuel Pump

REMOVAL AND INSTALLATION

All 1980-83 models equipped with automatic transmissions are equipped with an electric fuel pump located in the fuel tank. The circuit is equipped with an interlock system that provides power to the pump during start-up, through the starter relay, and provides operating voltage during engine operation. Should the

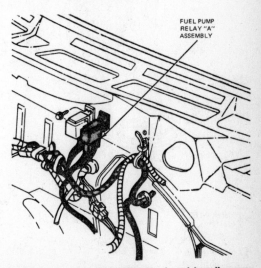

Relay "A" location identified in the wiring diagram

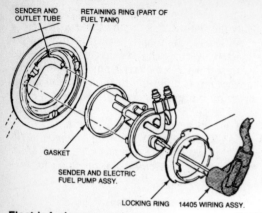

Electric fuel pump, exploded view

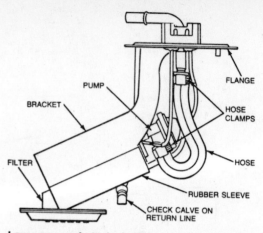

Low pressure in-tank electric fuel pump used with the 6-232 and 8-302 engines

4. Disconnect the fuel supply, return and vent lines at the right and left side of the frame.

5. Disconnect the wiring to the fuel pump.

6. Support the gas tank, loosen and remove the mounting straps. Remove the gas tank.

7. Disconnect the lines and harness at the pump flange.

8. Clean the outside of the mounting flange and retaining ring. Turn the fuel pump lock ring counterclockwise and remove.

9. Remove the fuel pump.

10. Clean the mounting surfaces. Put a light coat of grease on the mounting surfaces and on the new sealing ring. Install the new fuel pump.

11. Installation is in the reverse order of removal. If you have a single high pressure pump system, fill the tank with at least 10 gals. of gas. Turn the ignition key ON for three seconds. Repeat 6 or 7 times until the fuel system is pressurized. Check for any fitting leaks. Start the engine and check for leaks.

1984 High Pressure External Pump

1. Disconnect the negative battery cable.

2. Depressurize the fuel system.

3. Raise and support the rear of the vehicle on jackstands.

4. Disconnect the inlet and outlet fuel lines.

5. Disconnect the electrical harness connection.

6. Bend down the retaining tab and remove the pump from the mounting bracket ring.

7. Install in reverse order, make sure the pump is indexed correctly in the mounting bracket insulator.

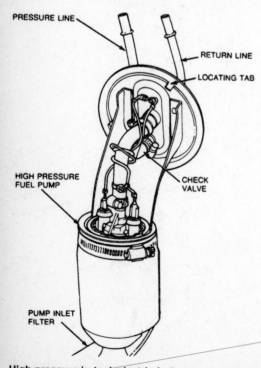

High pressure in-tank electric fuel pump

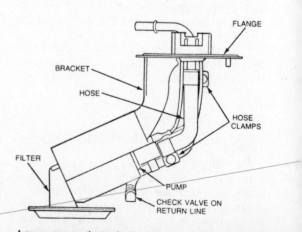
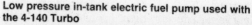

Low pressure in-tank electric fuel pump used with the 4-140 Turbo

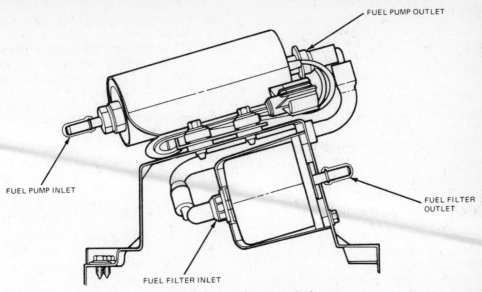

FUEL PUMP OUTLET

FUEL PUMP INLET

FUEL FILTER OUTLET

FUEL FILTER INLET

High pressure in-line electric fuel pump

1985-88 High Pressure In-Tank Pump

1. Depressurize the system.
2. Disconnect the negative battery cable.
3. Drain as much gas from the tank by pumping out through the filler neck.
4. Raise and support the rear end on jackstands.
5. Disconnect the filler hose, fuel supply, return and vent lines at the right and left side of the frame.
6. Disconnect the wiring to the fuel pump.
7. Support the gas tank, loosen and remove the mounting straps. Remove the gas tank.
8. Disconnect the lines and harness at the pump flange.
9. Clean the outside of the mounting flange and retaining ring. Turn the fuel pump lock ring counterclockwise and remove.
10. Remove the fuel pump.
11. Clean the mounting surfaces. Put a light coat of grease on the mounting surfaces and on the new sealing ring. Install the new fuel pump.
12. Installation is in the reverse order of removal. If you have a single high pressure pump system, fill the tank with at least 10 gals. of gas. Turn the ignition key ON for three seconds. Repeat 6 or 7 times until the fuel system is pressurized. Check for any fitting leaks. Start the engine and check for leaks.

Quick-Connect Fuel Line Fittings
REMOVAL AND INSTALLATION

NOTE: *Quick-Connect (push) type fuel fittings are used on most models equipped with a pressurized fuel system. The fittings must be disconnected using proper procedures or*

the fitting may be damaged. Two types of retainers are used on the push connect fittings. Line sizes of ⅜" and ⁵⁄₁₆" use a hairpin clip retainer, ¼" line connectors use a duck bill clip retainer.

Hairpin Clip

1. Clean all dirt and/or grease from the fitting. Spread the two clip legs about ⅛" (3mm) each to disengage from the fitting and pull the clip outward from the fitting. Use finger pressure sure only, do not use any tools.

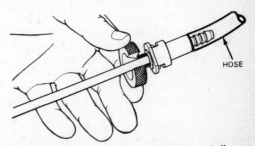

HOSE

Connector removal using a push-connect disconnection tool

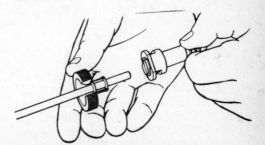

Pulling off the push-connect fitting

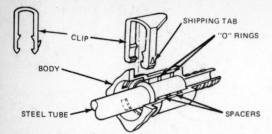

Push-connect type fitting with a hairpin clip

2. Grasp the fitting and hose assembly and pull away from the steel line. Twist the fitting and hose assembly slightly while pulling, if necessary, when a sticking condition exists.

3. Inspect the hairpin clip for damage, replace the clip if necessary. Reinstall the clip in position on the fitting.

4. Inspect the fitting and inside of the connector to insure freedom of dirt or obstruction. Install fitting into the connector and push together. A click will be heard when the hairpin clip snaps into proper connection. Pull on the line to insure full engagement.

Duck Bill Clip

1. A special tool is available from Ford for removing the retaining clips (Ford Tool No. T82L-9500-AH). If the tool is not on hand see Step 2. Align the slot on the push connector disconnect tool with either tab on the retaining clip. Insert the tool to disengage the clip. Pull the line from the connector.

2. If the special clip tool is not available, use a pair of narrow 6" (152mm) locking pliers with a jaw width of 0.2" (5mm) or less. Align the jaws of the pliers with the openings of the fitting case and compress the part of the retaining clip that engages the case. Compressing the retaining clip will release the fitting which may be pulled from the connector. Both sides of the clip must be compressed at the same time to disengage.

3. Inspect the retaining clip, fitting end and connector. Replace clip if any damage is apparent.

4. Push the line into the steel connector until a click is heard, indicating clip is in place. Pull on line to check engagement.

Electric Choke

All carbureted models use an electrically assisted choke to reduce exhaust emissions of carbon monoxide during warm-up. The system consists of a choke cap, a thermostatic spring, a bimetal sensing disc (switch) and a ceramic positive temperature coefficient (PTC) heater.

The choke is powered from the center tap of the alternator, so that current is constantly applied to the temperature sensing disc. The system is grounded through the carburetor body. At temperatures below approximately 60°F (16°C), the switch is open and no current is supplied to the ceramic heater, thereby resulting in normal unassisted thermostatic spring choke action. When the temperature rises above 60°F (16°C), the temperature sensing disc closes and current is supplied to the heater, which in turn, acts on the thermostatic spring. Once the heater starts, it causes the thermostatic spring to pull the choke plate(s) open within 1½ minutes, which is sooner than it would open if non-assisted.

OPERATIONAL TEST

1. Detach the electrical lead from the choke cap.

2. Use a jumper lead to connect the terminal on the choke cap and the wire terminal, so that the electrical circuit is still completed.

3. Start the engine.

4. Hook up a test light between the connector on the choke lead and ground.

5. The test light should glow. If it does not, current is not being supplied to the electrically assisted choke.

6. Connect the test light between the terminal on the alternator and the terminal on the choke cap. If the light now glows, replace the lead, since it is not passing current to the choke assist.

CAUTION: *Do not ground the terminal on the alternator while performing Step 6.*

7. If the light still does not glow, the fault lies somewhere in the electrical system. Check the system out.

If the electrically assisted choke receives power but still does not appear to be functioning properly, reconnect the choke lead and proceed with the rest of the test.

8. Tape the bulb end of the thermometer to the metallic portion of the choke housing.

9. If the electrically assisted choke operates below 55°F (13°C), it is defective and must be replaced.

10. Allow the engine to warm up to 80-100°F (27-38°C); at these temperatures the choke should operate for about 1½ minutes.

11. If it does not operate for this length of time, check the bimetallic spring to see if it is connected to the tang on the choke lever.

12. If the spring is connected and the choke is not operating properly, replace the cap assembly.

Carburetors

THROTTLE SOLENOID (ANTI-DIESELING SOLENOID) TEST

1. Turn the ignition key on and open the throttle. The solenoid plunger should extend (solenoid energize).

2. Turn the ignition off. The plunger should retract, allowing the throttle to close.

WARNING: *With the anti-dieseling de-energized, the carburetor idle speed adjusting screw must make contact with the throttle shaft to prevent the throttle plates from jamming in the throttle bore when the engine is turned off.*

3. If the solenoid is functioning properly and the engine is still dieseling, check for one of the following:

   a. High idle or engine shut off speed.
   b. Engine timing not set to specification.
   c. Binding throttle linkage.
   d. Too low an octane fuel being used.

Correct any of these problems as necessary.

4. If the solenoid fails to function as outlined in Steps 1-2, disconnect the solenoid leads; the solenoid should de-energize. If it does not, it is jammed and must be replaced.

5. Connect the solenoid to a 12 V power source and to ground. Open the throttle so that the plunger can extend. If it does not, the solenoid is defective.

6. If the solenoid is functioning correctly and no other source of trouble can be found, the fault probably lies in the wiring between the solenoid and the ignition switch or in the ignition switch itself. Remember to reconnect the solenoid when finished testing.

CARBURETOR REMOVAL AND INSTALLATION

1. Remove the air cleaner.

2. Disconnect the throttle cable or rod at the throttle lever. Disconnect the distributor vacuum line, exhaust gas recirculation line (1973 and later models), inline fuel filter, choke heat tube and the positive crankcase ventilation hose at the carburetor.

3. Disconnect the throttle solenoid (if so equipped) and electric choke assist at their connectors.

4. Remove the carburetor retaining nuts. Lift off the carburetor carefully, taking care not to spill any fuel. Remove the carburetor mounting gasket and discard it. Remove the carburetor mounting spacer, if so equipped, from the intake manifold.

5. Prior to installation, clean the gasket mounting surfaces of the intake manifold, spacer (if so equipped), and carburetor. When using a spacer, use two new gaskets, sandwiching the spacer between the gaskets. If a spacer is not used, only one new carburetor mounting gasket is required.

6. Place the new gasket(s) and spacer (if so equipped) on the carburetor mounting studs. Position the carburetor on top of the gasket and hand tighten the retaining nuts. Then tighten the nuts in a crisscross pattern to 10-15 ft. lbs.

7. Connect the throttle linkage, the distributor vacuum line, exhaust gas recirculation line, inline fuel filter, choke heat tube, positive crankcase ventilation hose, throttle solenoid (if so equipped) and electric choke assist.

8. Perform the preliminary adjustments of idle speed and mixture settings as outlined in Chapter 2.

OVERHAUL

All Types Except 2700 VV and 7200 VV

WARNING: *The 2700 VV and 7200 VV are part of the extremely sophisticated EEC system. Do not attempt to overhaul these units.*

Efficient carburetion depends greatly on careful cleaning and inspection during overhaul, since dirt, gum, water, or varnish in or on the carburetor parts are often responsible for poor performance.

Overhaul your carburetor in a clean, dust free area. Carefully disassemble the carburetor, referring often to the exploded views. Keep all similar and look-alike parts segregated during the disassembly and cleaning to avoid accidental interchange during assembly. Make a note of all jet sizes.

When the carburetor is disassembled, wash all parts (except diaphragms, electric choke units, pump plunger, and any other plastic, leather, fiber, or rubber parts) in clean carburetor solvent. Do not leave parts in the solvent any longer than is necessary to sufficiently loosen the deposits. Excessive cleaning may remove the special finish from the float bowl and choke valve bodies, leaving these parts unfit for service. Rinse all parts in clean solvent and blow them dry with compressed air or allow them to air dry. Wipe clean all cork, plastic, leather, and fiber parts with a clean, lint-free cloth.

Blow out all passages and jets with compressed air and be sure that there are no restrictions or blockages. never use wire of similar tools to clean jets, fuel passages, or air bleeds. Clean all jets and valves separately to avoid accidental interchange.

Check all parts for wear or damage. If wear or damage is found, replace the defective parts. Especially check the following:

1. Check the float needle and seat for wear. If wear is found, replace the complete assembly.

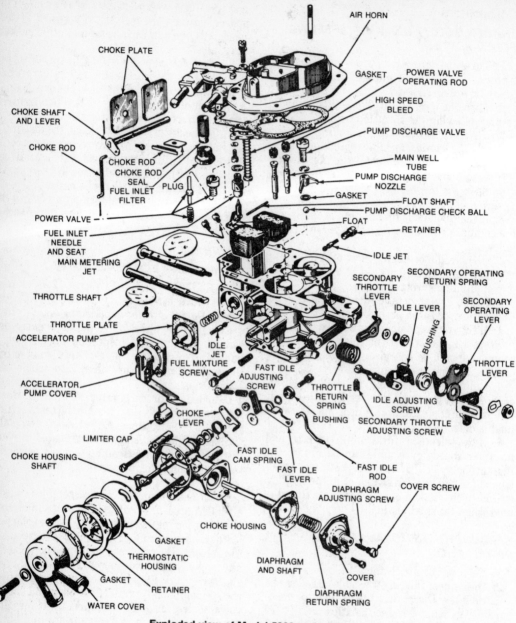

Exploded view of Model 5200 carburetor

2. Check the float hinge pin for wear and the float(s) for dents or distortion. Replace the float if fuel has leaked into it.

3. Check the throttle and choke shaft bores for wear or an out-of-round condition. Damage or wear to the throttle arm, shaft, or shaft bore will often require replacement of the throttle body. These parts require a close tolerance of fit; wear may allow air linkage, which could affect starting and idling.

NOTE: *Throttle shafts and bushings are not included in overhaul kits. They can be purchased separately.*

4. Inspect the idle mixture adjusting needles for burrs for grooves. Any such condition requires replacement of the needle, since you will not be able to obtain a satisfactory idle.

5. Test the accelerator pump check valves. They should pass air one way but on the other. Test for proper seating by blowing and sucking on the valve. Replace the valve is necessary. If the valve is satisfactory, wash the valve again to remove breath moisture.

6. Check the bowl cover for warped surfaces with a straightedge.

7. Closely inspect the valves and seats for

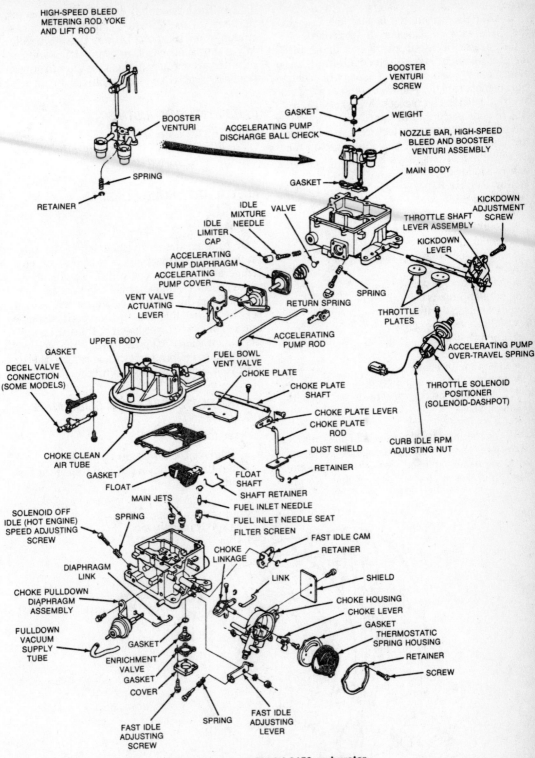

HIGH-SPEED BLEED
METERING ROD YOKE
AND LIFT ROD

BOOSTER
VENTURI
SCREW

GASKET

WEIGHT

BOOSTER
VENTURI

ACCELERATING PUMP
DISCHARGE BALL CHECK

NOZZLE BAR, HIGH-SPEED
BLEED AND BOOSTER
VENTURI ASSEMBLY

SPRING

GASKET

MAIN BODY

RETAINER

IDLE
MIXTURE
NEEDLE

VALVE

KICKDOWN
ADJUSTMENT
SCREW

THROTTLE SHAFT
LEVER ASSEMBLY

IDLE
LIMITER
CAP

KICKDOWN
LEVER

ACCELERATING
PUMP DIAPHRAGM
ACCELERATING
PUMP COVER

RETURN SPRING

SPRING

VENT VALVE
ACTUATING
LEVER

THROTTLE
PLATES

ACCELERATING
PUMP ROD

ACCELERATING PUMP
OVER-TRAVEL SPRING

GASKET

UPPER BODY

DECEL VALVE
CONNECTION
(SOME MODELS)

FUEL BOWL
VENT VALVE

CHOKE PLATE

THROTTLE SOLENOID
POSITIONER
(SOLENOID-DASHPOT)

CHOKE PLATE
SHAFT

CHOKE PLATE LEVER

CHOKE PLATE
ROD

CURB IDLE RPM
ADJUSTING NUT

DUST SHIELD

RETAINER

CHOKE CLEAN
AIR TUBE

GASKET

FLOAT

FLOAT
SHAFT

SHAFT RETAINER

MAIN JETS

FUEL INLET NEEDLE

SOLENOID OFF
IDLE (HOT ENGINE)
SPEED ADJUSTING
SCREW

SPRING

FUEL INLET NEEDLE SEAT

FILTER SCREEN

FAST IDLE CAM

CHOKE
LINKAGE

RETAINER

DIAPHRAGM
LINK

LINK

SHIELD

CHOKE PULLDOWN
DIAPHRAGM
ASSEMBLY

CHOKE HOUSING

CHOKE LEVER

FULLDOWN
VACUUM
SUPPLY
TUBE

GASKET

GASKET
THERMOSTATIC
SPRING HOUSING

ENRICHMENT
VALVE
GASKET

RETAINER

SCREW

COVER

FAST IDLE
ADJUSTING
SCREW

SPRING

FAST IDLE
ADJUSTING
LEVER

Exploded view of Model 2150 carburetor

wear and damage, replacing as necessary.

8. After the carburetor is assembled, check the choke valve for freedom of operation.

Carburetor overhaul kits are recommended for each overhaul. These kits contain all gaskets and new parts to replace those which deteriorate most rapidly. Failure to replace all parts supplied with the kit (especially gaskets) can result in poor performance later.

Some carburetor manufacturers supply overhaul kits of three basic types: minor repair; major repair; and gasket kits. Basically, they contain the following:

Minor Repair Kits:
- All gasket
- Float needle valve
- Volume control screw
- All diaphragms
- Spring for the pump diaphragm

Major Repair Kits:
- All jets and gaskets
- All diaphragms
- Float needle valve
- Volume control screw
- Pump ball valve
- Float
- Complete intermediate rod
- Intermediate pump lever
- Some cover holddown screws and washers

Gasket Kits:
- All gaskets

After cleaning and checking all components, reassemble the carburetor, using new parts and referring to he exploded view. When reassembling, make sure that all screws and jets are tight in their seats, but do not overtighten as the tops will be distorted. Tighten all screws gradually, in rotation. Do not tighten needle valves into their seats; uneven jetting will result. Always use new gaskets. Be sure to adjust the float level when reassembling.

CARBURETOR ADJUSTMENTS

NOTE: *Adjustments for the 2700VV and 7200VV, are covered following adjustments for all other carburetors.*

AUTOMATIC CHOKE HOUSING ADJUSTMENT

All carburetors

By rotating the spring housing of the automatic choke, the reaction of the choke to engine temperature can be controlled. To adjust, remove the air cleaner assembly, loosen the thermostatic spring housing retaining screws and set the spring housing to the specified index mark. The marks are shown in the accompanying illustration. After adjusting the setting, tighten the retaining screws and replace the air cleaner assembly to the carburetor.

CHOKE PLATE PULLDOWN CLEARANCE ADJUSTMENT

Motorcraft 2150

1. Remove the air cleaner assembly.
2. Set the throttle on the stop step of the fast idle cam.

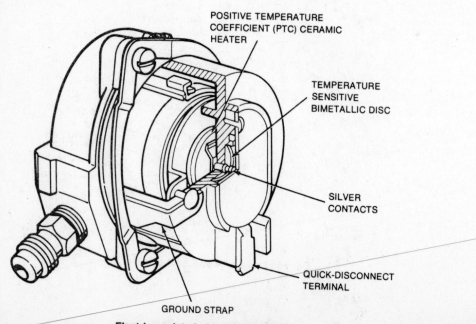

POSITIVE TEMPERATURE COEFFICIENT (PTC) CERAMIC HEATER

TEMPERATURE SENSITIVE BIMETALLIC DISC

SILVER CONTACTS

QUICK-DISCONNECT TERMINAL

GROUND STRAP

Electric assist choke—Model 2150

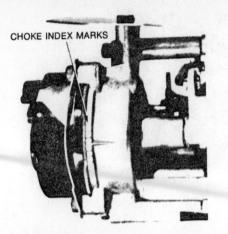

CHOKE INDEX MARKS

Automatic choke thermostatic spring housing adjustment—Model 2150

3. Noting the position of the choke housing cap, loosen the retaining screws and rotate the cap 90° in the rich (closing) direction.

4. Activate the pulldown motor by manually forcing the pulldown control diaphragm link in the direction of applied vacuum or by applying vacuum to the external vacuum tube.

5. Using a drill gauge of the specified diameter, measure the clearance between the choke plate and the center of the air horn wall nearest the fuel bowl.

6. To adjust, reset the diaphragm stop on the end of the choke pulldown diaphragm.

7. After adjusting, reset the choke housing cap to the specified notch. Check and reset fast idle speed, if necessary. Install the air cleaner.

Holley 1946

NOTE: *On these carburetors, this adjustment is preset at the factory and protected by a tamper-proof plug.*

Holley 4180

1. Remove the choke thermostat housing, gasket and retainer.

2. Insert a piece of wire into the choke piston bore to move the piston down against the stop screw.

3. Measure the gap between the lower edge of the choke plate and the air horn wall.

4. Turn the adjustment screw to specifications.

5. Reinstall the choke thermostat housing, gasket and retainer.

Motorcraft 5200

1. Remove the choke thermostatic spring cover.

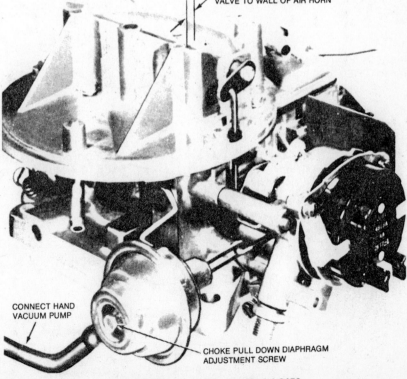

MEASURE CLEARANCE
BOTTOM EDGE OF CHOKE
VALVE TO WALL OF AIR HORN

CONNECT HAND
VACUUM PUMP

CHOKE PULL DOWN DIAPHRAGM
ADJUSTMENT SCREW

Adjusting plate pulldown—Model 2150

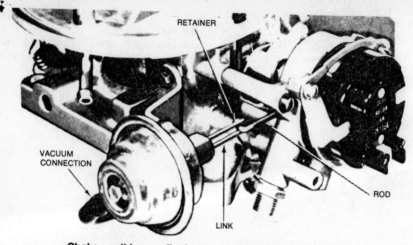

Choke pulldown diaphragm assembly—Model 2150

2. Pull the coolant cover and the thermostatic spring cover assembly, or electric assist assembly out of the way.

3. Set the fast idle cam on the second step.

4. Push the diaphragm stem against its top and insert the specified gauge between the wall and the lower edge of the choke plate.

5. Apply sufficient pressure against the upper edge of the choke plate to take up any slack in the linkage.

6. Turn the adjusting screw in or out of get the proper clearance.

Carter YFA

PISTON TYPE CHOKE

NOTE: *This adjustment requires that the thermostatic spring housing and gasket (choke cap) are removed. Refer to the Choke Cap removal procedure below.*

1. Remove the air cleaner assembly, then the choke cap.

2. Bend a 0.026″ (0.66mm) diameter wire gauge at a 90° angle approximately ⅛″ (3mm) from one end. Insert the bent end of the gauge

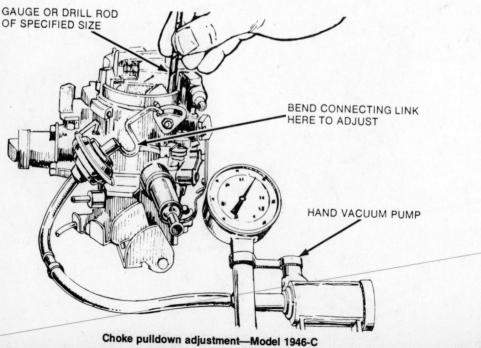

Choke pulldown adjustment—Model 1946-C

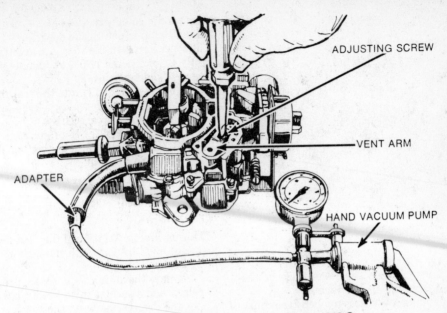

External fuel bowl vent adjustment—Model 1946-C

between the choke piston slot and the right hand slot in the choke housing. Rotate the choke piston lever counterclockwise until the gauge is shut in the piston slot.

3. Apply light pressure on the choke piston lever to hold the gauge in place. Then measure the clearance between the lower edge of the choke plate and the carburetor bore using a drill with the diameter equal to the specified pulldown clearance.

4. Bend the choke piston lever to obtain the proper clearance.

5. Install the choke cap.

DIAPHRAGM TYPE CHOKE

1. Activate the pulldown motor by applying an external vacuum source.

2. Close the choke plate as far as possible without forcing it.

3. Using a drill of the specified size, measure

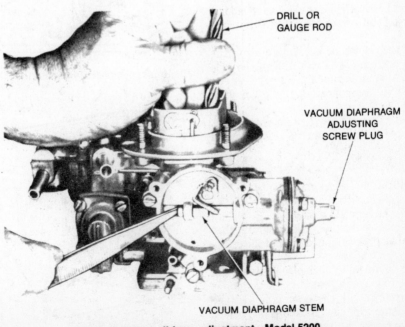

Choke vacuum pulldown adjustment—Model 5200

Measuring choke plate pulldown, 5200

the clearance between the lower edge of the choke plate and the air horn wall.

4. If adjustment is necessary, bend the choke diaphragm link as required.

CHOKE CAP REMOVAL

NOTE: *The automatic choke has two rivets and a screw, retaining the choke cap in place. There is a locking and indexing plate to prevent misadjustment.*

1. Remove the air cleaner assembly from the carburetor.

2. Check the choke cap retaining ring rivets to determine if the mandrel is well below the rivet head. If the mandrel appears to be at or within the rivet head thickness, drive it down or out with an $1/16$" (1.6mm) diameter punch.

3. Use a $1/8$" diameter of No. 32 drill. for drilling the rivet heads. Drill into the rivet head until the rivet head comes loose from the rivet body.

4. After the rivet head is removed, drive the remaining portion of the rivet out of the hole with an $1/8$" diameter punch.

NOTE: *This procedure must be followed to retain the hole size.*

5. Repeat Steps 1-4 for the remaining rivet.

6. Remove the screw in the conventional manner.

CHOKE CAP INSTALLATION

1. Install the choke cap gasket.
2. Install the locking and indexing plate.
3. Install the notched gasket.
4. Install the choke cap, making certain that the bimetal loop is positioned around the choke lever tang.
5. While holding the cap in place, actuate the choke plate to make certain the bimetal loop is properly engaged with the lever tang. Set the retaining clamp over the choke cap and orient the clamp to match the holes in the casting (the

holes are not equally spaced). Make sure the retaining clamp is not upside down.

6. Place a rivet in the rivet gun and trigger it lightly to retain the rivet ($1/8$" diameter x $1/2$" long x $1/4$" diameter head).

7. Press the rivet fully into the casting after passing through the retaining clamp and pop the rivet (mandrel breaks off).

8. Repeat this step for the remaining rivet.

9. Install the screw in the conventional manner. Tighten to 17-20 in. lbs.

FLOAT LEVEL ADJUSTMENT

Autolite (Motorcraft) 2150

DRY ADJUSTMENT

This preliminary setting of the float level adjustment must be done with the carburetor removed from the engine.

1. Remove the air horn and see that the float is raised and the fuel inlet needle is seated. Check the distance between the top surface of the main body (with the gasket removed) and the top surface of the float. Depress the float

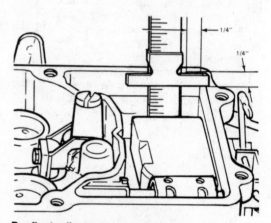

Dry float adjustment—model 2150

Model 2150 float adjustment—wet

tab to seat the fuel inlet needle. Take a measurement near the center of the float, at a point ⅛" (3mm) from the free end. If you are using a prefabricated float gauge, place the gauge in the corner of the enlarged end section of the fuel bowl. The gauge should touch the float near the end, but not on the end radius.

2. If necessary, bend the tab on the end of the float to bring the setting within the specified limits.

WET ADJUSTMENT

1. Bring the engine to its normal operating temperature, park the car on as nearly level a surface as possible, and stop the engine.

2. Remove the air cleaner assembly from the carburetor.

3. Remove the air horn retaining screws and the carburetor identification tag. Leave the air horn and gasket in position on the carburetor main body. Start the engine, let it idle for several minutes, rotate the air horn out of the way, and remove the gasket to provide access to the float assembly.

4. With the engine idling, use a standard depth scale to measure the vertical distance from the top machined surface of the carburetor main body to the level of the fuel in the fuel bowl. This measurement must be made at least ¼" (6mm) away from any vertical surface in order to assure an accurate reading.

5. Stop the engine before making any adjustment to the float level. Adjustment is accomplished by bending the float tab (with contacts the fuel inlet valve) up or down as required to raise or lower the fuel level. After making an adjustment, start the engine, and allow it to idle for several minutes before repeating the fuel level check. Repeat as necessary until the proper fuel level is attained.

6. Reinstall the air horn with a new gasket and secure it with the screw. Include the installation of the identification tag in its proper location.

7. Check the idle speed, fuel mixture, and dashpot adjustments. Install the air cleaner assembly.

Holley 4180

To perform a preliminary dry float adjustment on both the primary and secondary fuel bowl float assemblies, remove the fuel bowls and invert them allowing the float to rest on the fuel inlet valve and set assembly. the fuel inlet valve and seat can be rotated until the float is parallel with the fuel bowl floor (actually the top of the fuel bowl chamber inverted). Note that this is an initial dry float setting which must be rechecked with the carburetor assem-

bled and on the engine to obtain the proper wet fuel level.

This carburetor has an externally adjustable needle and seat assembly which allows the fuel level to be checked and adjust without removing the carburetor from the engine.

1. Run the engine with the vehicle resting on a level surface until the engine temperature has normalized.

2. Remove the air cleaner assembly.

3. Place a suitable container or an absorbent cloth below the fuel level sight plug in the fuel bowl.

4. Stop the engine and remove the sight plug and gasket on the primary float bowl. The fuel level in the bowl should be at the lower edge of the sight plug hole, plus or minus ¹⁄₁₆".

CAUTION: *Never loosen the lockscrew or nut, or attempt to adjust the fuel level with the sight plug removed or the engine running, since fuel will spray out creating a fire hazard!*

5. To adjust the fuel level, install the sight plug and gasket, loosen one on the lower fuel bowl retaining screws and drain the fuel from the bowl only if the level is too high. Loosen the lockscrew on top of the fuel bowl just enough to allow the adjusting nut to be turned. Turn the adjusting nut about ½ of a turn in to lower the fuel level and out to raise the fuel level. By turning the adjusting nut ⁵⁄₃₂ of a turn, the fuel level will change ¹⁄₃₂" at the sight plug.

6. Start the engine and allow the fuel level to stabilize. Check the fuel level as outlined in Step 4.

7. Repeat the procedure for the secondary float bowl adjustment.

8. Install the air cleaner assembly if no further adjustments are necessary.

Motorcraft 5200

1. Remove the float bowl cover and hold it upside down.

2. With the float tang resting lightly on the spring loaded fuel inlet needle, measure the clearance between the edge of the float and the bowl cover.

3. To adjust the float, bend the float tang. Make sure that both floats are adjusted equally.

Holley 1946

1. Remove the air horn and place a finger over the hinge pin retainer and catch the accelerator pump ball when it falls out.

2. Lay a ruler across the housing under the floats. The lowest point of the floats should be just touching the ruler for all except California models. For California models, the ruler should just contact the heel (raised step) of the float.

3. Bend the tang of the float to adjust.

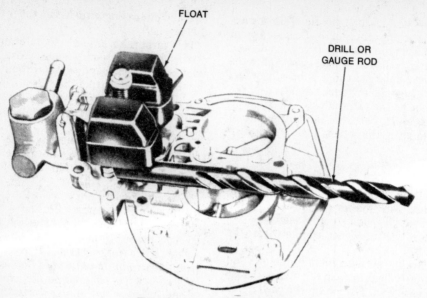

Float level check—Model 5200

Float adjustment—Model 5200

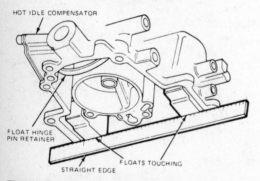

Float adjustment—Model 1946-C

Carter YFA

1. Invert the air horn assembly and check the clearance from the top of the float to the surface of the air horn with a T-scale. The air horn should be held at eye level when gauging

and the float arm should be resting on the needle pin.

2. Do not exert pressure on the needle valve when measuring or adjusting the float. Bend the float arm as necessary to adjust the float level.

CAUTION: *Do not bend the tab at the end of the float arm as it prevents the float from striking the bottom of the fuel bowl when empty and keeps the needle in place.*

DECHOKE CLEARANCE ADJUSTMENT

Holley 1946

1. With the engine off, hold the throttle in the wide open position.

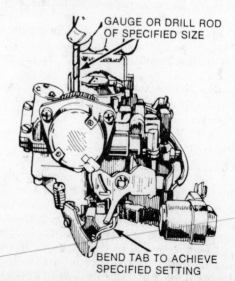

Dechoke clearance adjustment—Model 1946-C

2. Insert the specified gauge between the upper edge of the choke plate and the air horn wall.

3. With a slight pressure against the choke shaft, a slight drag should be felt when the gauge is withdrawn.

4. To adjust, bend the unloader tab on the throttle lever.

Motorcraft 5200

1. Hold the throttle wide open. Remove all slack from the choke linkage by applying pressure to the upper edge of the choke plate.

2. Measure the distance between the lower edge of the choke plate and the air horn wall.

3. Adjust by bending the tab on the fast idle lever where it touches the cam.

Carter YFA

1. Remove the air cleaner assembly.

2. Hold the throttle plate fully open and close the choke plate as far as possible without forcing it. Use a drill of the proper diameter to check the clearance between the choke plate and air horn.

3. If the clearance is not within specification, adjust by bending the arm on the choke lever of the throttle lever. Bending the arm downward will decrease the clearance, and bending it upward will increase the clearance. Always recheck the clearance after making any adjustment.

ACCELERATOR PUMP LEVER ADJUSTMENT

Holley 4180

1. Hold the primary throttle plates in the wide open position.

2. Using a feeler gauge, check the clearance accelerator pump operating lever adjustment screw head and the pump arm while depressing the pump arm with your finger. The clearance should be $1/64''$ (0.015''; 0.381mm).

3. To make an adjustment, hold the adjusting screw locknut and turn the adjusting screw inward to increase, or outward to decrease, the adjustment. $1/2$ turn will change the clearance by $1/64''$.

ACCELERATOR PUMP STROKE ADJUSTMENT

Autolite (Motorcraft) 2150

In order to keep the exhaust emission level of the engine within the specified limits, the accelerating pump stroke has been preset at the factory. The additional holes are provided for differing engine-transmission-body applications only. The primary throttle shaft lever (overtravel lever) has four holes to control the

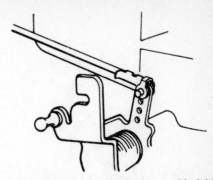

Accelerator pump stroke adjustment—Model 2150

pump stroke. The accelerating pump operating rod should be in the overtravel lever hole number listed in the Carburetor Specifications chart, and in the inboard hole (hole closest to the pump plunger) in the accelerating pump link. If the pump stroke has been changed from the specified settings, use the following procedure to correct the stroke.

1. Release the operating rod from the retaining clip by pressing the tab end of the clip toward the rod while pressing the rod away from the clip until it disengages.

2. Position the clip over the specified hole (see Carburetor Specifications chart) in the overtravel lever. Press the ends of the clip together and insert the operating rod through the clip and the overtravel lever. Release the clip to engage the rod.

ANTI-STALL DASHPOT ADJUSTMENT

All Carburetors

Having made sure that the engine idle speed and mixture are correct and that the engine is at normal operating temperature, loosen the anti-stall dashpot locking nut (see accompanying illustration). With the throttle held closed, depress the plunger with a screwdriver blade and measure the clearance between the throttle lever and the plunger tip. If the clearance is not as specified in the Carburetor Specifications chart, turn the dashpot until the proper clearance is obtained between the throttle lever and the plunger tip. After tightening the locking nut, recheck the adjustment.

FAST IDLE CAM INDEX SETTING

Motorcraft 5200

1. Insert a $5/32''$ drill between the lower edge of the choke plate and the air horn wall.

2. With the fast idle screw held on the second step of the fast idle cam, measure the clearance between the tang of the choke lever and the arm of the cam.

3. Bend the choke lever tang for adjustment.

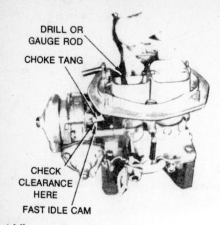

Fast idle cam clearance—Model 5200

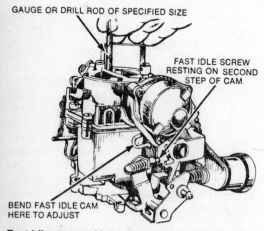

Fast idle cam position adjustment—Model 1946-C

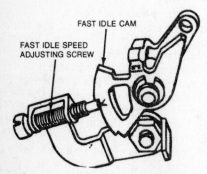

Fast idle speed adjustment—Model 2150

Holley 1946

1. Position the fast idle adjusting screw on the second step of the fast idle cam.

2. Lightly move the choke plate towards the closed position.

3. Check the fast idle cam setting by placing the specified gauge between the upper edge of the choke plate and the air horn wall.

4. Bend the fast idle cam link to adjust.

Carter YFA

1. Put the fast idle screw on the second highest step of the fast idle cam against the shoulder of the high step.

2. Adjust by bending the choke plate connecting rod to obtain the specified clearance between the lower edge of the choke plate and the air horn wall.

Holley 4180

1. Remove the spark delay valve, if so equipped, from the Distributor vacuum advance line, and route the vacuum line directly to the advance side of the distributor.

2. Trace the EGR signal vacuum line from the EGR valve to the carburetor and if there is EGR/PVS valve or temperature vacuum switch located in the vacuum line routing, disconnect the EGR vacuum line at the EGR valve and plug the line.

3. If not equipped with an EGR/PVS valve or temperature vacuum switch do not detach the EGR vacuum line.

4. Trace the purge valve vacuum line from the purge valve located on the canister, to the first point where the vacuum line can be detached from the underhood hose routing. Disconnect the vacuum line at that point, cap the open port, and plug the vacuum line.

WARNING: *To prevent damage to the purge valve do not disconnect the vacuum line at the purge valve.*

5. With the engine running at normal operating temperature, the choke plate fully opened and the manual transmission in Neutral and the automatic transmission in Park, place the fast idle level on the 2nd or kickdown step of the fast idle cam.

6. Adjust the fast idle screw to within 100 rpm of the specified speed given on the Vehicle Emission Control Decal.

7. Reconnect all vacuum lines.

VACUUM OPERATED THROTTLE MODULATOR ADJUSTMENT

Holley 4180

1. Set the parking brake, put the transmission in Park or Neutral and run the engine up to operating temperature.

2. Turn off the air conditioning and heater controls.

3. Disconnect and plug the vacuum hoses at the air control valve and EGR valve and purge control valve.

4. Place the transmission in the position specified on the underhood decal.

5. If necessary, check and adjust the curb idle rpm.

6. Place the transmission in Neutral or Park

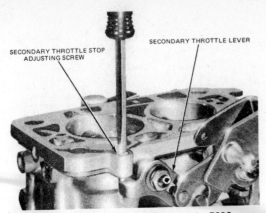

SECONDARY THROTTLE STOP
ADJUSTING SCREW

SECONDARY THROTTLE LEVER

Secondary throttle stop adjustment, 5200 carburetor

and rev the engine. Place the transmission in the specified position according to the underhood decal and recheck the curb idle rpm. Readjust if necessary.

7. Connect an external vacuum source which provides a minimum of 10″ of vacuum to the VOTM (Vacuum Operated Throttle Modulator) kicker.

8. Place the transmission in the specified position.

9. Adjust the VOTM (throttle kicker) locknut if necessary to obtain the proper idle rpm.

10. Reconnect all vacuum hoses.

THROTTLE AND DOWNSHIFT LINKAGE ADJUSTMENT

With Manual Transmission

Throttle linkage adjustments are not normally required, unless the carburetor or linkage have been removed from the car or otherwise disturbed. In all cases, the car is first brought to operating temperature, with the choke open the off the fast idle cam. The idle speed is then set to specifications (see Chapter 2).

SECONDARY THROTTLE PLATE ADJUSTMENT

Holley 4180

1. Remove the carburetor.
2. Hold the secondary throttle plates closed.
3. Turn the secondary throttle shaft lever stop screw out until the secondary throttle plates seat in the throttle bores.
4. Turn the screw back in until the screw just touches the lever, then ⅜ turn more.

Motorcraft 2700VV and 7200VV
DESIGN

Since the design of the 2700VV (variable venturi) carburetor differs considerably from the other carburetors in the Ford lineup, an expla-

nation in the theory and operation is presented here.

In exterior appearance, the variable venturi carburetor is similar to conventional carburetor and, like a conventional carburetor, it uses a normal float and fuel bowl system. However, the similarity end there. In place of the normal choke plate and fixed area venturis, the 2700VV carburetor has a pair of small oblong castings in the top of the upper carburetor body where you would normally expect to see the choke plate. These castings slide back and forth across the top of the carburetor in response to fuel-air demands. Their movement is controlled by a spring-loaded diaphragm valve regulated by a vacuum signal taken below the venturis in the throttle bores. As the throttle is opened, the strength of the vacuum signal increases, opening the venturis and allowing more air to enter the carburetor.

Fuel is admitted into the venturi area by means of tapered metering rods that fit into the main jets. These rods are attached to the venturis, and, as the venturis open or close in response to air demand, the fuel needed to maintain the proper mixture increase or decreases as the metering rods slide in the jets. In comparison to a conventional carburetor with fixed venturis and a variable air supply, this system provides much more precise control of the fuel-air supply during all modes of operation. Because of the variable venturi principle, there are fewer fuel metering systems and fuel passages. The only auxiliary fuel metering systems required are an idle trim, accelerator pump (similar to a conventional carburetor), starting enrichment, and cold running enrichment.

NOTE: *Adjustment, assembly and disassembly of this carburetor require special tools for some of the operations. These tools are available (see the Tools and Equipment Section). Do not attempt any operations on this carburetor without first checking to see if you need the special tools for that particular operation. The adjustment and repair procedures given here mention when and if you will need the special tools.*

The Motorcraft model 7200 variable venturi (VV) carburetor shares most of its design features with the model 2700VV. The major difference between the two is that the 7200VV is designed to work with Ford's EEC (electronic engine control) feedback system. The feedback system precisely controls the air/fuel ration by varying signals to the feedback control monitor located on the carburetor, which opens or closes the metering valve in response. This expands or reduces the amount of control vacuum above the fuel bowl, leaning or richening the mixture accordingly.

FLOAT LEVEL ADJUSTMENT

1. Remove and invert the upper part of the carburetor, with the gasket in place.
2. Measure the vertical distance between the carburetor body, outside the gasket, and the bottom of the float.
3. To adjust, bend the float operating lever that contacts the needle valve. Make sure that the float remains parallel to the gasket surface.

FLOAT DROP ADJUSTMENT

1. Remove and hold upright the upper part of the carburetor.
2. Measure the vertical distance between the carburetor body, outside the gasket, and the bottom of the float.
3. Adjust by bending the stop tab on the float lever that contacts the hinge pin.

FAST IDLE SPEED ADJUSTMENT

1. With the engine warmed up and idling, place the fast idle lever on the step of the fast idle cam specified on the engine compartment sticker or in the specifications chart. Disconnect and plug the EGR vacuum line.
2. Make sure the high speed cam positioner lever is disengaged.
3. Turn the fast idle speed screw to adjust to the specified speed.

FAST IDLE CAM ADJUSTMENT

You will need a special tool for this job: Ford calls it a stator cap (#T77L-9848-A). It fits over the choke thermostatic lever when the choke cap is removed.

1. Remove the choke coil cap. On 1980 and later California models, the choke cap is riveted in place. The top rivets will have to be drilled out. The bottom rivet will have to be driven out from the rear. New rivets must be used upon installation.
2. Place the fast idle lever in the corner of the

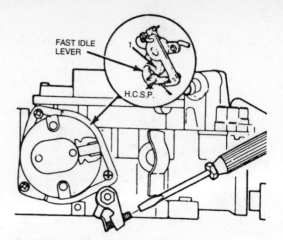

Fast idle speed adjustment—Model 2700 VV

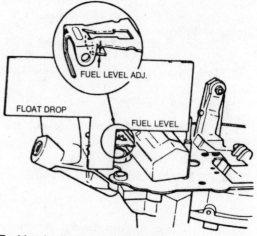

Fuel level adjustment—Model 2700 VV

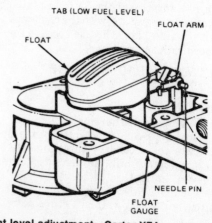

Float level adjustment—Carter YFA

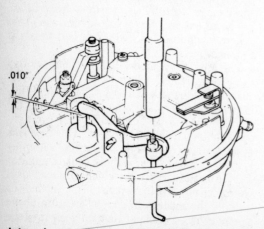

Internal vent adjustment—Model 2700 VV

specified step of the fast idle cam (the highest step is first) with the high speed cam positioner retracted.

3. If the adjustment is being made with the

carburetor removed, hold the throttle lightly close with a rubber band.

4. Turn the stator cap clockwise until the lever contacts the fast idle cam adjusting screw.

5. Turn the fast idle cam adjusting screw until the index mark on the cap lines up with the specified mark on the casting.

6. Remove the stator cap. Install the choke coil cap and set it to the specified housing mark.

COLD ENRICHMENT METERING ROD ADJUSTMENT

A dial indicator and the stator cap are required for this adjustment.

1. Remove the choke coil cap. See Step 1 of the Fast idle Cam Adjustment.

2. Attach a weight to the choke coil mechanism to seat the cold enrichment rod.

3. Install and zero a dial indicator with the tip of top of the enrichment rod. Raise and release the weight to verify zero on the dial indicator.

4. With the stator cap at the index position, the dial indicator should read the specified dimension. Turn the adjusting nut to correct it.

5. Install the choke cap at the correct setting.

CONTROL VACUUM ADJUSTMENT

1979 Only

1. Make sure the idle speed is correct.

2. Using a $5/32''$ Allen wrench, turn the venturi valve diaphragm adjusting screw clockwise until the valve is firmly closed.

3. Connect a vacuum gauge to the vacuum tap on the venturi valve cover.

4. Idle the engine and use a $1/8''$ Allen wrench to turn the venturi by-pass adjusting screw to the specified vacuum setting. You may have to correct the idle speed.

5. Turn the venturi valve diaphragm adjusting screw counterclockwise until the vacuum drops to the specified setting. You will have to work the throttle to get the vacuum to drop.

6. Reset the idle speed.

1980-82

This adjustment is necessary only on non-feedback systems.

1. Remove the carburetor. Remove the venturi valve diaphragm plug with a center-punch.

2. If the carburetor has a venturi valve by-pass, remove it be removing the two cover retaining screw; invert and remove the by-pass screw plug from the cover with a drift. Install the cover.

3. Install the carburetor. Start the engine and allow it to reach normal operating temperature. Connect a vacuum gauge to the venturi valve cover. Set the idle speed to 500 rpm with the transmission in Drive.

4. Push and hold the venturi valve closed. Adjust the bypass screw to obtain a reading of 8 in. H_2O on the vacuum gauge. Make sure the idle speed remains constant. Open and close the throttle and check the idle speed.

5. With the engine idling, adjust the venturi valve diaphragm screw to obtain a reading of 6 in. H_2O. Set the curb idle to specification. Install new venturi valve bypass and diaphragm plugs.

VENTURI VALVE LIMITER ADJUSTMENT

1. Remove the carburetor. Take off the venturi valve cover and the two rollers.

2. Use a center punch to loosen the expansion plug at the rear of the carburetor main body on the throttle side. Remove it.

3. Use an Allen wrench to remove the venturi valve wide open stop screw.

4. Hold the throttle wide open.

5. Apply a light closing pressure on the venturi valve and check the gap between the valve and the air horn wall. To adjust, move the venturi valve to the wide open position and insert an Allen wrench into the stop screw hole. Turn clockwise to increase the gap. Remove the wrench and check the gap again.

6. Replace the wide open stop screw and turn it clockwise until it contact the valve.

7. Push the venturi valve wide open and check the gap. Turn the stop screw to bring the gap to specifications.

8. Reassemble the carburetor with a new expansion plug.

CONTROL VACUUM REGULATOR ADJUSTMENT

The cold enrichment metering rod adjustment must be checked and set before making this adjustment.

1. After adjusting the cold enrichment metering rod, leave the dial indicator in place but remove the stator cap. Do not re-zero the dial indicator.

2. Press down on the C.V.R. rod until it bottoms on its seat. Measure this amount of travel with the dial indicator.

3. If the adjustment is incorrect, hold the $3/8''$ C.V.R. adjusting nut with a box wrench to prevent it from turning. Use a $3/32''$ Allen wrench to turn the C.V.R. rod; turning counterclockwise will increase the travel, and vice-versa.

HIGH SPEED CAM POSITIONER ADJUSTMENT

1979 Only

1. Place the high speed cam positioner in the corner of the specified cam step, counting the highest step as the first.

2. Place the fast idle lever in the corner of the positioner.

3. Hold the throttle firmly closed.

4. Remove the diaphragm cover. Adjust the diaphragm assembly clockwise until it lightly bottoms. Turn it counterclockwise ½-1½ turns until the vacuum port and diaphragm hole line up.

5. Replace the cover.

DISASSEMBLY

WARNING: *Special tools are required. If you have any doubts about your ability to successfully complete this procedure, leave it to a professional service person.*

Upper Body

1. Remove the fuel inlet fitting, fuel filter, gasket and spring.

2. Remove the screws retaining the upper body assembly and remove the upper body.

3. Remove the float hinge pin and float assembly.

4. Remove the fuel inlet valve, seat and gasket.

5. Remove the accelerator pump rod and the choke control rod.

6. Remove the accelerator pump link retaining pin and the link.

7. Remove the accelerator pump swivel and the retaining nut.

8. Remove the E-ring on the choke hinge pin and slide the pin out of the casting.

9. Remove the cold enrichment rod adjusting nut, lever and swivel; remove the control vacuum nut and regulator as an assembly.

10. Remove the cold enrichment rod.

11. Remove the venturi valve cover plate and roller bearings. Remove the venturi valve cover plate and roller bearings. Remove the venturi air bypass screw.

12. Using special tool T77P-9928-A, press the tapered plugs out of the venturi valve pivot pins.

13. Remove the venturi valve pivot pins, bushings and the venturi valve.

14. Remove the metering rod pivot pins, springs and metering rods. Be sure to mark the rods so that you know on which side they belong. Also, keep the venturi valve blocked open when working on the jets.

15. Using tool T77L-9533-B, remove the cup plugs.

16. Using tool T77L-9533-A, turn each main metering jet clockwise, counting the number of turns until they bottom in the casting. You will need to know the number of turns when you reassemble the carburetor. Remove the jets and mark them so that you know on which side they belong. Don't lose the O-rings.

17. Remove the accelerator pump plunger assembly.

18. Remove the idle trim screws. Remove the venturi valve limiter adjusting screw.

19. Assembly is the reverse of disassembly.

Main Body

1. Remove the cranking enrichment solenoid and the O-ring seal.

2. Remove the venturi valve cover, spring guide, and spring. Remove the venturi valve.

3. Remove the throttle body.

4. Remove the choke heat shield.

5. Assembly is in the reverse order.

FUEL INJECTION

Central Fuel Injection

DESCRIPTION

Central Fuel Injection (CFI) is a throttle body injection system in which two fuel injectors are mounted in a common throttle body, spraying fuel down through the throttle valves at the bottom of the body and into the intake manifold.

OPERATION

Fuel is supplied from the fuel tank by a high pressure, in-tank fuel pump. The fuel passes through a filter and is sent to the throttle body where a regulator keeps the fuel delivery pressure at a constant 39 psi. The two fuel injectors are mounted vertically above the throttle plates and are connected in line with the fuel pressure regulator. Excess fuel supplied by the pump, but not needed by the engine, is returned to the fuel tank by a steel fuel return line.

The fuel injection system is linked with and controlled by the Electronic Engine Control (EEC) system.

Air and Fuel Control

The throttle body assembly is comprised of six individual components which perform the job of mixing the air and fuel to the ideal ratio for controlling exhaust emissions and providing performance and economy. The six components are: air control, fuel injector nozzles, fuel pressure regulator, fuel pressure diagnostic valve, cold engine speed control, and throttle position sensor.

Air Control

Air flow to the engine is controlled by two butterfly valves mounted in a two piece, die-cast aluminum housing called the throttle body. The butterfly valves, or throttle valves, are identical in design to the throttle plates of a conventional carburetor and are actuated by a similar linkage and pedal cable arrangement.

Fuel Injector Nozzles

The fuel injector nozzles are mounted in the throttle body and are electro-mechanical de- vices which meter and atomize the fuel deliv- ered to the engine. The injector valve bodies consist of a solenoid actuated pintle and needle valve assembly. An electrical control signal from the EED electronic processor activates the solenoid causing the pintle to move inward off

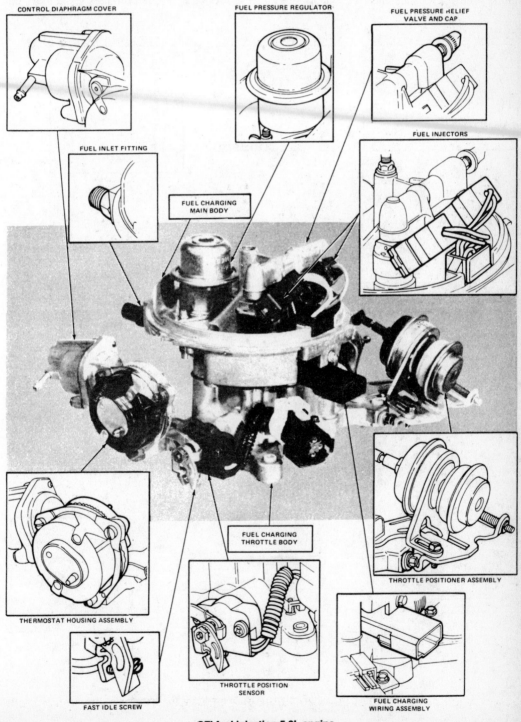

CFI fuel injection 5.0L engine

its seat and allowing fuel to flow. the fuel flow through the injector is controlled by the amount of time the injector solenoid holds the pintle off its seat.

Fuel Pressure Regulator

The fuel pressure regulator is mounted on the throttle body. The regulator smooths out fuel pressure drops from the fuel pump. It is not sensitive to back pressure in the return line to the tank.

A second function of the pressure regulator is to maintain fuel supply pressure upon engine and fuel pump shut down. The regulator acts as a check valve and traps fuel between itself and the fuel pump. This promotes rapid start ups

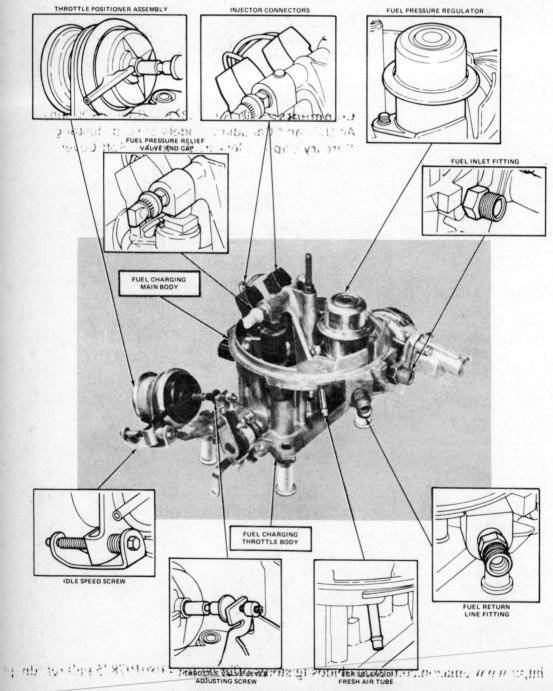

THROTTLE POSITIONER ASSEMBLY

INJECTOR CONNECTORS

FUEL PRESSURE REGULATOR

FUEL PRESSURE RELIEF VALVE AND CAP

FUEL INLET FITTING

FUEL CHARGING MAIN BODY

FUEL CHARGING THROTTLE BODY

IDLE SPEED SCREW

FUEL RETURN LINE FITTING

THROTTLE VALVE LEVER ADJUSTING SCREW

EGR SOLENOID FRESH AIR TUBE

CFI fuel injection 5.0L engine left side view

and helps prevent fuel vapor formation in the lines, or vapor lock. The regulator makes sure that the pressure of the fuel at the injector nozzles stays at a constant 39 psi.

Fuel Pressure Diagnostic Valve

A Schrader-type diagnostic pressure valve is located at the top of the throttle body. This valve can be used by service personnel to monitor fuel pressure, bleed down the system pressure prior to maintenance and to bleed out air which may have been introduced during assembly or filter servicing. A special Ford Tool (T80L-9974-A) is used to accomplish these procedures.

CAUTION: *Under no circumstances should compressed air be forced into the fuel system using the diagnostic valve.*

Cold Engine Speed Control

The cold engine speed control serves the same purpose as the fast idle speed device on a carbureted engine, which is to raise engine speed during cold engine idle. A throttle stop cam positioner is used. the cam is positioned by a bimetal spring and an electric heating element. The cold engine speed control is attached to the throttle body. As the engine heats up, the fast idle cam on the cold engine speed control is gradually repositioned by the bimetal spring, heating element and EEC computer until normal idle speed is reached. The EEC computer automatically kicks down the fast idle cam to a lower step (lower engine speed) by supplying vacuum to the automatic kickdown motor which physically moves the high speed cam a predetermined time after the engine starts.

Throttle Position Sensor

This sensor is attached to the throttle body and is used to monitor changes in throttle plate position. the throttle position sensor sends this information to the computer, which uses it to select proper air/fuel mixture, spark timing and EGR control under different engine operating conditions.

Fuel System Inertia Switch

In the event of a collision, the electrical contacts in the inertia switch open and the fuel pump automatically shuts off. The fuel pump will shut off even if the engine does not stop running. The engine, however, will stop a few seconds after the fuel pump stops. It is not possible to restart the engine until the inertia switch is manually reset. The switch is located in the luggage compartment on the left hinge support on all models. To reset, depress both buttons on the switch at the same time.

CAUTION: *Do not reset the inertia switch*

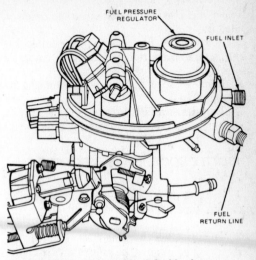

CFI fuel injection 3.8L engine left side view

until the complete fuel system has been inspected for leaks.

FUEL CHARGING ASSEMBLY REMOVAL AND INSTALLATION

1. Remove the air cleaner.
2. Release the pressure from the fuel system at the diagnostic valve using Tool T80L-9974-A or its equivalent.
3. Disconnect the throttle cable and transmission throttle valve lever.
4. Disconnect the fuel, vacuum and electrical

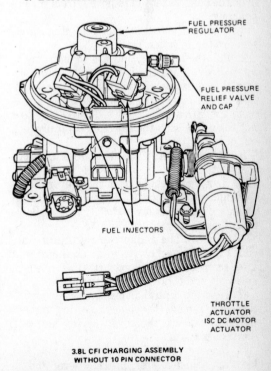

3.8L CFI CHARGING ASSEMBLY
WITHOUT 10 PIN CONNECTOR

CFI fuel injection 3.8L engine

connections. Use care to prevent combustion of spilled fuel.

5. Remove the fuel charging assembly retaining nuts then remove the fuel charging assembly.

6. Remove the mounting gasket from the intake manifold.

7. Installation is the reverse of removal. Tighten the fuel charging assembly nuts to 120 in. lbs.

THROTTLE BODY DISASSEMBLY AND ASSEMBLY

1. Remove the air cleaner mounting stud in order to separate the upper body from the throttle body.

2. Turn the fuel charging assembly (throttle body) over and remove the four screws from the bottom of the throttle body.

3. Separate the throttle body (lower half) from the main body (upper half).

4. Remove the old gasket. If it is stuck and scraping is necessary, use only a plastic or wood scraper. Take care not to damage the gasket surfaces.

5. Remove the three pressure regulator mounting screws. Remove the pressure regulator.

6. Disconnect the electrical connectors at each injector by pulling outward on the connector and not on the wire. Loosen but do not remove the wiring harness retaining screw. Push in on the harness tabs to remove it from the upper body.

7. Remove the fuel injector retaining screw. Remove the injection retainer.

8. Pull the injectors, one at a time, from the upper body. Mark the injectors for identification, they must be reinstalled in the same position (choke or throttle side). Each injector is equipped with a small O-ring. If the O-ring does not come out with the injector, carefully pick out of body.

9. Remove the fuel diagnostic valve assembly.

10. Remove the choke cover by drilling the retaining rivets. A ⅛″ or No. 30 drill is required. A choke mounting kit for installation is available from Ford.

11. Remove the choke cap retaining ring, choke cap and gasket. Remove the thermostat lever screw and lever. Remove the fast idle cam assembly and control rod positioner.

12. Hold the control diaphragm cover in position and remove the two mounting screws. Carefully remove the cover, spring and pull down diaphragm.

13. Remove the fast idle retaining nut, fast idle cam adjuster lever, fast idle lever and E-clip.

14. Remove the potentiometer (sensor) connector bracket retaining screw. Mark the throttle body and throttle position sensor for correct installation position. Remove the throttle sensor retaining screws and slide the sensor off of the throttle shaft. Remove the throttle positioner retaining screw and remove the throttle positioner.

15. Perform any necessary cleaning or repair.

16. Assemble the upper body by first installing the fuel diagnostic fuel pressure valve assembly.

17. Lubricate the new injector O-rings with a light grade oil. Install the O-rings on each injector. Install the injectors in their appropriate choke or throttle side position. Use a light, twisting, pushing motion to install the injectors.

18. Install the injector retainer and tighten the retaining screw to 30-60 in. lbs.

19. Install the injector wiring harness and snap into position. Tighten the harness retaining screw to 8-10 in. lbs.

20. Snap the electrical connectors into position on the injectors. Lubricate the fuel pressure regulator O-ring with light oil. Install the O-ring and new gasket on the regulator, install the regulator and tighten retaining screws to 27-40 in. lbs.

21. Install the throttle positioner onto the throttle body. Tighten the retaining screw to 32-44 in. lbs.

22. hold the throttle sensor (potentiometer) with the location identification mark (see step 14) in the 12 o'clock position. The two rotary tangs should be at 3 o'clock and 9 o'clock positions.

23. Slide the sensor onto the throttle shaft with the identification mark still in the 12 o'clock position. Hold the sensor firmly against the throttle body.

24. Rotate the sensor until the identification marks on the sensor and body are aligned. Install the retaining screws and tighten to 13-18 in. lbs.

25. Install the sensor wiring harness bracket retaining screw, tighten to 18-22 in. lbs. Install the E-clip, fast idle lever, fast idle adjustment lever and fast idle retaining nut. Tighten the retaining nut to 16-20 in. lbs.

26. Install the pull down diaphragm, spring and cover. Hold the cover in position and tighten the retaining screws to 13-19 in. lbs.

27. Install the fast idle control rod positioner, fast idle cam and the thermostat lever. Tighten the retaining screw to 13-19 in. lbs.

28. Install the choke cap gasket, bimetal spring, cap and retaining ring. Install new rivets and snug them with the rivet gun. do not break rivets, loosely install so choke cover can

rotate. Index choke and break rivets to tighten.

29. Install the gasket between the main body and the throttle body. Place the throttle body in position. Install the four retaining screws loosely. Install the air cleaner stud and tighten to 70-95 in. lbs. Tighten the four retaining screws.

30. The rest of the assembly is in the reverse order of disassembly.

ELECTRONIC CONTROL SYSTEM

Electronic Control Assembly (ECA)

The Electronic Control Assembly (ECA) is a solid-state micro-computer consisting of a processor assembly and a calibration assembly. It is located under the instrument panel or passenger's seat and is usually covered by a kick panel. 1981-82 models use an EEC-III engine control system, while 1983 and later models use the EEC-IV. Although the two systems are similar in appearance and operation, the ECA units are not interchangeable. A multipin connector links the ECA with all system components. The processor assembly is housed in an aluminum case. It contains circuits designed to continuously sample input signals from the engine sensors. It then calculates and sends out proper control signals to adjust air/fuel ratio, spark timing and emission system operation. The processor also provides a continuous reference voltage to the B/MAP, EVP, and TPS sensors. EEC-III reference voltage is 8-10 volts, while EEC-IV systems use a 5 volt reference signal. The calibration assembly is contained in a black plastic housing which plugs into the top of the processor assembly. It contains the memory and programming information used by the processor to determine optimum operating conditions. different calibration information is used in different vehicle applications, such as California or Federal models. For this reason, careful identification of the engine, year, model and type of electronic control system is essential to insure correct component replacement.

ENGINE SENSORS

Air Charge Temperature Sensor (ACT)

The ACT is threaded into the intake manifold air runner. It is located behind the distributor on V6 engines and directly below the accelerator linkage on V8 engines. The ACT monitors air/fuel charge temperature and sends an appropriate signal to the ECA. This information is used to correct fuel enrichment for variations in intake air density due to temperature changes.

Barometric & Manifold Absolute Pressure Sensors (B/MAP)

The B/MAP sensor on V8 engines is located on the right fender panel in the engine com-partment. The MAP sensor used on V6 engines is separate from the barometric sensor and is located on the left fender panel in the engine compartment. The barometric sensor signals the ECA of changes in atmospheric pressure and density to regulate calculated air flow into the engine. The MAP sensor monitors and signals the ECA of changes in intake manifold pressure which result from engine load, speed and atmospheric pressure changes.

Crankshaft Position (CP) Sensor

The purpose of the CP sensor is to provide the ECA with an accurate ignition timing reference (when the piston reaches 10°BTDC) and injector operation information (twice each crankshaft revolution). The crankshaft vibration damper is fitted with a 4 lobe pulse ring. As the crankshaft rotates, the pulse ring lobes interrupt the magnetic field at the tip of the CP sensor.

EGR Valve Position Sensor (EVP)

This sensor, mounted on EGR valve, signals the computer of EGR opening so that it may subtract EGR flow from total air flow into the manifold. In this way, EGR flow is excluded from air flow information used to determine mixture requirements.

Engine Coolant Temperature Sensor (ECT)

The ECT is threaded into the intake manifold water jacket directly above the water pump bypass hose. The ECT monitors coolant temperature and signals the ECA, which then uses these signals for mixture enrichment (during cool operation), ignition timing and EGR operation. The resistance value of the ECT increases with temperature, causing a voltage signal drop as the engine warms up.

Exhaust Gas Oxygen Sensor (EGO)

The EGO is mounted in the right side exhaust manifold on V8 engines, in the left and right side exhaust manifolds on V6 models. The EGO monitors oxygen content of exhaust gases and sends a constantly changing voltage signal to the ECA. The ECA analyzes this signal and adjusts the air/fuel mixture to obtain the optimum (stoichiometric) ratio.

Knock Sensor (KS)

This sensor is used on various models equipped with the 6-232 engine. It is attached to the intake manifold in front of the ACT sensor. The KS detects engine vibrations caused by preignition or detonation and provides information to the ECA, which then retards the timing to eliminate detonation.

Thick Film Integrated Module Sensor (TFI)

The TFI module sensor plugs into the distributor just below the distributor cap and replaces the CP sensor on some engines. Its function is to provide the ECA with ignition timing information, similar to what the CP sensor provides.

Throttle Position Sensor (TPS)

The TPS is mounted on the right side of the throttle body, directly connected to the throttle shaft. The TPS senses the throttle movement and position and transmits an appropriate electrical signal to the ECA. These signals are used by the ECA to adjust the air/fuel mixture, spark timing and EGR operation according to engine load at idle, part throttle, or full throttle. The TPS is nonadjustable.

ON-CAR SERVICE

NOTE: *Diagnostic and test procedures on the EEC-III and EEC-IV electronic control system require special test equipment. Have the testing done by a professional.*

Fuel Pressure Tests

The diagnostic pressure valve (Schrader type) is located at the top of the Fuel charging main body. This valve provides a convenient point for service personnel to monitor fuel pressure, bleed down the system pressure prior to maintenance, and to bleed out air which may become trapped in the system during filter replacement. A pressure gauge with a adapter is required to perform pressure tests.

CAUTION: *Under no circumstances should compressed air be forced into the fuel system using the diagnostic valve. Depressing the pin in the diagnostic valve will relieve system pressure by expelling fuel into the throttle body.*

System Pressure Test

Testing fuel pressure requires the use of a special pressure gauge (T80L-9974-A or equivalent) that attaches to the diagnostic pressure tap on the fuel charging assembly. Depressurize the fuel system before disconnecting any lines.

1. Disconnect the fuel return line at the throttle body (in-tank high pressure pump) and connect the hose to a 1 quart calibrated container. Connect a pressure gauge.

2. Disconnect the electrical connector at the fuel pump. The connector is located ahead of fuel tank (in-tank high pressure pump) or just forward of pump outlet (in-line high pressure pump). Connect an auxiliary wiring harness to the connector of the fuel pump. Energize the pump for 10 seconds by applying 12 volts to the auxiliary harness connector, allowing the fuel

to drain into the calibrated container. Note the fuel volume and pressure gauge reading.

3. Correct fuel pressure should be 35-45 psi (241-310 kPa). Fuel volume should be 10 oz. in 10 seconds (minimum) and fuel pressure should maintain a minimum of 30 psi (206 kPa) immediately after pump cut-off.

If the pressure condition is met, but the fuel flow is not, check for blocked filter(s) and fuel supply lines. After correcting the problem, repeat the test procedure. If the fuel flow is still inadequate, replace the high pressure pump. If the flow specification is met but the pressure is not, check for a worn or damaged pressure regulator valve on the throttle body. If both the pressure and fuel flow specifications are met, but the pressure drops excessively after de-energizing, check for a leaking injector valve(s) and/or pressure regulator valve. If the injector valves and pressure regulator valve are okay, replace the high pressure pump. If no pressure or flow is seen in the fuel system, check for blocked filters and fuel lines. If no trouble is found, replace the in-line fuel pump, in-tank fuel pump and the fuel filter inside the tank.

Fuel Injector Pressure Test

1. Connect pressure gauge T80L-9974-A, or equivalent, to the fuel pressure test fitting. Disconnect the coil connector from the coil. Disconnect the electrical lead from one injector and pressurize the fuel system. Disable the fuel pump by disconnecting the inertia switch or the fuel pump relay and observe the pressure gauge reading.

2. Crank the engine for 2 seconds. Turn the ignition OFF and wait 5 seconds, then observe the pressure drop. If the pressure drop is 2-16 psi (14-110 kPa), the injector is operating properly. Reconnect the injector, activate the fuel pump, then repeat the procedure for other injector.

3. If the pressure drop is less than 2 psi (14 kPa) or more than 16 psi (110 kPa), switch the electrical connectors on injectors and repeat the test. If the pressure drop is still incorrect, replace the disconnected injector with one of the same color code, then reconnect both injectors properly and repeat the test.

4. Disconnect and plug the vacuum hose at EGR valve. It may be necessary to disconnect the idle speed control (6-232) or the throttle kicker solenoid (8-302) and use the throttle body stop screw to set the engine speed. Start and run the engine at 1,800 rpm (2,000 rpm on 1984 and later models). Disconnect the left injector electrical connector. Note the rpm after the engine stabilizes (around 1,200 rpm). Reconnect the injector and allow the engine to return to high idle.

5. Perform the same procedure for the right injector. Note the difference between the rpm readings of the left and right injectors. If the difference is 100 rpm or less, check the oxygen sensor. If the difference is more than 100 rpm, replace both injectors.

CFI COMPONENT TESTS

NOTE: *Complete CFT system diagnosis requires the use of special test equipment. Have the system tested professionally.*

Before beginning any component testing, always check the following:

- Check the ignition and fuel systems to ensure there is fuel and spark.
- Remove the air cleaner assembly and inspect all vacuum and pressure hoses for proper connection to fittings. Check for damaged or pinched hoses.
- Inspect all sub-system wiring harnesses for proper connections to the EGR solenoid valves, injectors, sensors, etc.
- Check for loose or detached connectors and broken or detached wires. Check that all terminals are seated firmly and are not corroded. Look for partially broken or frayed wires or any shorting between the wires.
- Inspect the sensors for physical damage. Inspect the vehicle electrical system. Check the battery for full charge and cable connections for tightness.
- Inspect the relay connector and make sure the ECA power relay is securely attached and making a good ground connection.

High Pressure In-Tank Pump

Disconnect the electrical connector just forward of the fuel tank. Connect a voltmeter to the body wiring harness connector. Turn the key ON while watching the voltmeter. Voltage should rise to battery voltage, then return to zero after about 1 second. Momentarily turn the key to the **START** position. Voltage should rise to about 8 volts while cranking. If voltage is not specified, check electrical system.

High Pressure In-Line & Low Pressure In-Tank Pumps

Disconnect the electrical connector at the fuel pumps. Connect a voltmeter to the body wiring harness connector. Turn the key **ON** while watching the voltmeter. The voltage should rise to battery voltage, then return to zero after about 1 second. If the voltage is not as specified, check the inertia switch and the electrical system. Connect an ohmmeter to the in-line pump wiring harness connector. If no continuity is present, check the continuity directly at the in-line pump terminals. If no continuity at the in-line pump terminals, replace the in-line pump. If continuity is present, service or replace the wiring harness.

Connect an ohmmeter across the body wiring harness connector. If continuity is present (about 5 ohms), the low pressure pump circuit is OK. If no continuity is present, remove the fuel tank and check for continuity at the in-tank pump flange terminals on top of the tank. If continuity is absent at the in-tank pump flange terminals, replace the assembly. If continuity is present at the in-tank pump but not in the harness connector, service or replace the wiring harness at the in-tank pump.

Solenoid and Sensor Resistance Tests

All CFI components must be disconnected from the circuit before testing the resistance with a suitable ohmmeter. Replace any component whose measured resistance does not agree with the specifications chart. Shorting the wiring harness across a solenoid valve can burn out the circuitry in the ECA that control the solenoid valve actuator. Exercise caution when testing the solenoid valves to avoid accidental damage to ECA.

Electronic Multi-Point Injection (EFI)

DESCRIPTION

The Electronic Fuel Injector System (EFI) is classified as a multi-point, pulse time, mass air flow fuel injection system. Fuel is metered into the intake air stream in accordance with engine demand through four injectors mounted on a tuned intake manifold. A blow-through turbocharger system is utilized to reduce fuel delivery time and increase power.

An on board vehicle electronic engine control (EEC) computer accepts inputs from various engine sensors to compute the required fuel flow rate necessary to maintain a prescribed air/fuel ration throughout the entire engine operational range. The computer then outputs a command to the fuel injectors to meter the approximate quantity of fuel.

OPERATION

The fuel delivery sub-system consists of a high pressure, chassis mounted, electric fuel pump delivering fuel from the fuel tank through a 20 micron fuel filter to a fuel charging manifold assembly.

The fuel charging manifold assembly incorporates electrically actuated fuel injectors directly above each of the engine's four intake ports. The injectors, when energized, spray a metered quantity of fuel into the intake air stream.

A constant fuel pressure drop is maintained across the injector nozzles by a pressure regulator. The regulator is connected in series with the fuel injectors and positioned down stream from them. Excess fuel supplied by the pump, but not required by the engine, passes through the regulator and returns to the fuel tank through a fuel return line.

All injectors are energized simultaneously, once every crankshaft revolution. The period of time that the injectors are energized (injector on-time or the pulse width) is controlled by the vehicles' Engine Electronic Control (EEC) computer. Air entering the engine is measured by a vane air flow meter located between the air cleaner and the fuel charging manifold assembly. This air flow information and input from various other engine sensors is used to compute the required fuel flow rate necessary to maintain a prescribed air/fuel ratio for the given engine operation. The computer determines the needed injector pulse width and outputs a commend to the injector to meter the exact quantity of fuel.

COMPONENT DESCRIPTION

Fuel Injectors

The four fuel injector nozzles are electro-mechanical devices which both meter and atomize fuel delivered to the engine. The injectors are mounted in the lower intake manifold and are positioned so that their tips are directing fuel just ahead of the engine intake valves. The injector bodies consist of a solenoid actuated pintle and needle valve assembly. An electrical control signal from the Electronic Engine Control unit activates the injector solenoid causing the pintle to move inward off the seat, allowing fuel to flow. Since the injector flow orifice is fixed and the fuel pressure drop across the injector tip is constant, fuel flow to the engine is regulated by how long the solenoid is energized. Atomization is obtained by contouring the pintle at the point where the fuel separates.

Fuel Pressure Regulator

The fuel pressure regulator is attached to the fuel supply manifold assembly downstream of the fuel injectors. It regulates the fuel pressure supplied to the injectors. The regulator is a diaphragm operated relief valve in which one side of the diaphragm senses fuel pressure and the other side is subjected to intake manifold pressure. The nominal fuel pressure is established by a spring preload applied to the diaphragm. Balancing one side of the diaphragm with manifold pressure maintains a constant fuel pressure drop across the injectors. Fuel, in excess of that used by the engine, is bypassed through the regulator and returns to the fuel tank.

Air Vane Meter Assembly

The air vane meter assembly is located between the air cleaner and the throttle body and is mounted on a bracket near the left shock tower. The vane air meter contains two sensors which furnish input to the Electronic Control Assembly: a vane airflow sensor and a vane air temperature. The air vane meter measures the mass of air flow to the engine. Air flow through the body moves a vane mounted on a pivot pin. This vane is connected to a variable resistor (potentiometer) which in turn is connected to a 5 volt reference voltage. The output of this potentiometer varies depending on the volume of air flowing through the sensor. The temperature sensor in the air vane meter measures the incoming air temperature. These two inputs, air volume and temperature, are used by the Electronic Control Assembly to compute the mass air flow. This valve is then used to compute the fuel flow necessary for the optimum air/fuel ratio which is fed to the injectors.

Air Throttle Body Assembly

The throttle body assembly controls air flow to the engine through a single butterfly-type valve. The throttle position is controlled by conventional cable/cam throttle linkage. The body is a single piece die casting made of aluminum. It has a single bore with an air bypass channel around the throttle plate. This by-pass channel controls both cold and warm engine idle air flow control as regulated by an air bypass valve assembly mounted directly to the throttle body. The valve assembly is an electromechanical device controlled by the EEC computer. It incorporates a linear actuator which positions a variable area metering valve.

Other features of the air throttle body assembly include:

- An adjustment screw to set the throttle plate at a minimum idle airflow position.
- A preset stop to locate the WOT position.
- A throttle body mounted throttle position sensor.
- A PCV fresh air source located upstream of the throttle plate.
- Individual ported vacuum taps (as required) for PCV and EVAP control signals.

Fuel Supply Manifold Assembly

The fuel supply manifold assembly is the component that delivers high pressure fuel from the vehicle fuel supply line to the four fuel injectors. The assembly consists of a single preformed tube or stamping with four injector connector, a mounting flange for the fuel pressure regulator, a pressure relief valve for diagnostic testing or field service fuel system pressure

CHILTON'S
FUEL ECONOMY
& TUNE-UP TIPS

Tune-up • Spark Plug Diagnosis • Emission Controls

Fuel System • Cooling System • Tires and Wheels

General Maintenance

55 WAYS TO IMPROVE FUEL ECONOMY

CHILTON'S FUEL ECONOMY & TUNE-UP TIPS

Fuel economy is important to everyone, no matter what kind of vehicle you drive. The maintenance-minded motorist can save both money and fuel using these tips and the periodic maintenance and tune-up procedures in this Repair and Tune-Up Guide.

There are more than 130,000,000 cars and trucks registered for private use in the United States. Each travels an average of 10-12,000 miles per year, and, and in total they consume close to 70 billion gallons of fuel each year. This represents nearly ⅔ of the oil imported by the United States each year. The Federal government's goal is to reduce consumption 10% by 1985. A variety of methods are either already in use or under serious consideration, and they all affect you driving and the cars you will drive. In addition to "down-sizing", the auto industry is using or investigating the use of electronic fuel delivery, electronic engine controls and alternative engines for use in smaller and lighter vehicles, among other alternatives to meet the federally mandated Corporate Average Fuel Economy (CAFE) of 27.5 mpg by 1985. The government, for its part, is considering rationing, mandatory driving curtailments and tax increases on motor vehicle fuel in an effort to reduce consumption. The government's goal of a 10% reduction could be realized — and further government regulation avoided — if every private vehicle could use just 1 less gallon of fuel per week.

How Much Can You Save?

Tests have proven that almost anyone can make at least a 10% reduction in fuel consumption through regular maintenance and tune-ups. When a major manufacturer of spark plugs sur-

TUNE-UP

1. Check the cylinder compression to be sure the engine will really benefit from a tune-up and that it is capable of producing good fuel economy. A tune-up will be wasted on an engine in poor mechanical condition.

2. Replace spark plugs regularly. New spark plugs alone can increase fuel economy 3%.

3. Be sure the spark plugs are the correct type (heat range) for your vehicle. See the Tune-Up Specifications.

Heat range refers to the spark plug's ability to conduct heat away from the firing end. It must conduct the heat away in an even pattern to avoid becoming a source of pre-ignition, yet it must also operate hot enough to burn off conductive deposits that could cause misfiring.

The heat range is usually indicated by a number on the spark plug, part of the manufacturer's designation for each individual spark plug. The numbers in bold-face indicate the heat range in each manufacturer's identification system.

Manufacturer	Typical Designation
AC	R **45** TS
Bosch (old)	WA **145** T30
Bosch (new)	HR **8** Y
Champion	RBL **15** Y
Fram/Autolite	**4**15
Mopar	P-**62** PR
Motorcraft	BRF-**42**
NGK	BP **5** ES-15
Nippondenso	W **16** EP
Prestolite	14GR **5** 2A

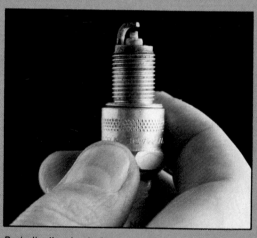

Periodically, check the spark plugs to be sure they are firing efficiently. They are excellent indicators of the internal condition of your engine.

On AC, Bosch (new), Champion, Fram/Autolite, Mopar, Motorcraft and Prestolite, a higher number indicates a hotter plug. On Bosch (old), NGK and Nippondenso, a higher number indicates a colder plug.

4. Make sure the spark plugs are properly gapped. See the Tune-Up Specifications in this book.

5. Be sure the spark plugs are firing efficiently. The illustrations on the next 2 pages show you how to "read" the firing end of the spark plug.

6. Check the ignition timing and set it to specifications. Tests show that almost all cars have incorrect ignition timing by more than 2°.

veyed over 6,000 cars nationwide, they found that a tune-up, on cars that needed one, increased fuel economy over 11%. Replacing worn plugs alone, accounted for a 3% increase. The same test also revealed that 8 out of every 10 vehicles will have some maintenance deficiency that will directly affect fuel economy, emissions or performance. Most of this mileage-robbing neglect could be prevented with regular maintenance.

Modern engines require that all of the functioning systems operate properly for maximum efficiency. A malfunction anywhere wastes fuel. You can keep your vehicle running as efficiently and economically as possible, by being aware of your vehicle's operating and performance characteristics. If your vehicle suddenly develops performance or fuel economy problems it could be due to one or more of the following:

PROBLEM	POSSIBLE CAUSE
Engine Idles Rough	Ignition timing, idle mixture, vacuum leak or something amiss in the emission control system.
Hesitates on Acceleration	Dirty carburetor or fuel filter, improper accelerator pump setting, ignition timing or fouled spark plugs.
Starts Hard or Fails to Start	Worn spark plugs, improperly set automatic choke, ice (or water) in fuel system.
Stalls Frequently	Automatic choke improperly adjusted and possible dirty air filter or fuel filter.
Performs Sluggishly	Worn spark plugs, dirty fuel or air filter, ignition timing or automatic choke out of adjustment.

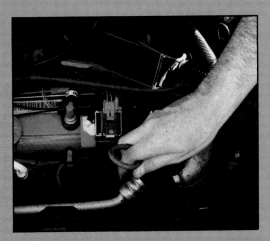

Check spark plug wires on conventional point type ignition for cracks by bending them in a loop around your finger.

Be sure that spark plug wires leading to adjacent cylinders do not run too close together. (Photo courtesy Champion Spark Plug Co.)

7. If your vehicle does not have electronic ignition, check the points, rotor and cap as specified.

8. Check the spark plug wires (used with conventional point-type ignitions) for cracks and burned or broken insulation by bending them in a loop around your finger. Cracked wires decrease fuel efficiency by failing to deliver full voltage to the spark plugs. One misfiring spark plug can cost you as much as 2 mpg.

9. Check the routing of the plug wires. Misfiring can be the result of spark plug leads to adjacent cylinders running parallel to each other and too close together. One wire tends to pick up voltage from the other causing it to fire "out of time".

10. Check all electrical and ignition circuits for voltage drop and resistance.

11. Check the distributor mechanical and/or vacuum advance mechanisms for proper functioning. The vacuum advance can be checked by twisting the distributor plate in the opposite direction of rotation. It should spring back when released.

12. Check and adjust the valve clearance on engines with mechanical lifters. The clearance should be slightly loose rather than too tight.

SPARK PLUG DIAGNOSIS

Normal

APPEARANCE: This plug is typical of one operating normally. The insulator nose varies from a light tan to grayish color with slight electrode wear. The presence of slight deposits is normal on used plugs and will have no adverse effect on engine performance. The spark plug heat range is correct for the engine and the engine is running normally.

CAUSE: Properly running engine.

RECOMMENDATION: Before reinstalling this plug, the electrodes should be cleaned and filed square. Set the gap to specifications. If the plug has been in service for more than 10-12,000 miles, the entire set should probably be replaced with a fresh set of the same heat range.

Oil Deposits

APPEARANCE: The firing end of the plug is covered with a wet, oily coating.

CAUSE: The problem is poor oil control. On high mileage engines, oil is leaking past the rings or valve guides into the combustion chamber. A common cause is also a plugged PCV valve, and a ruptured fuel pump diaphragm can also cause this condition. Oil fouled plugs such as these are often found in new or recently overhauled engines, before normal oil control is achieved, and can be cleaned and reinstalled.

RECOMMENDATION: A hotter spark plug may temporarily relieve the problem, but the engine is probably in need of work.

Incorrect Heat Range

APPEARANCE: The effects of high temperature on a spark plug are indicated by clean white, often blistered insulator. This can also be accompanied by excessive wear of the electrode, and the absence of deposits.

CAUSE: Check for the correct spark plug heat range. A plug which is too hot for the engine can result in overheating. A car operated mostly at high speeds can require a colder plug. Also check ignition timing, cooling system level, fuel mixture and leaking intake manifold.

RECOMMENDATION: If all ignition and engine adjustments are known to be correct, and no other malfunction exists, install spark plugs one heat range colder.

Carbon Deposits

APPEARANCE: Carbon fouling is easily identified by the presence of dry, soft, black, sooty deposits.

CAUSE: Changing the heat range can often lead to carbon fouling, as can prolonged slow, stop-and-start driving. If the heat range is correct, carbon fouling can be attributed to a rich fuel mixture, sticking choke, clogged air cleaner, worn breaker points, retarded timing or low compression. If only one or two plugs are carbon fouled, check for corroded or cracked wires on the affected plugs. Also look for cracks in the distributor cap between the towers of affected cylinders.

RECOMMENDATION: After the problem is corrected, these plugs can be cleaned and reinstalled if not worn severely.

MMT Fouled

APPEARANCE: Spark plugs fouled by MMT (Methycyclopentadienyl Maganese Tricarbonyl) have reddish, rusty appearance on the insulator and side electrode.

CAUSE: MMT is an anti-knock additive in gasoline used to replace lead. During the combustion process, the MMT leaves a reddish deposit on the insulator and side electrode.

RECOMMENDATION: No engine malfunction is indicated and the deposits will not affect plug performance any more than lead deposits (see Ash Deposits). MMT fouled plugs can be cleaned, regapped and reinstalled.

High Speed Glazing

APPEARANCE: Glazing appears as shiny coating on the plug, either yellow or tan in color.

CAUSE: During hard, fast acceleration, plug temperatures rise suddenly. Deposits from normal combustion have no chance to fluff-off; instead, they melt on the insulator forming an electrically conductive coating which causes misfiring.

RECOMMENDATION: Glazed plugs are not easily cleaned. They should be replaced with a fresh set of plugs of the correct heat range. If the condition recurs, using plugs with a heat range one step colder may cure the problem.

Ash (Lead) Deposits

APPEARANCE: Ash deposits are characterized by light brown or white colored deposits crusted on the side or center electrodes. In some cases it may give the plug a rusty appearance.

CAUSE: Ash deposits are normally derived from oil or fuel additives burned during normal combustion. Normally they are harmless, though excessive amounts can cause misfiring. If deposits are excessive in short mileage, the valve guides may be worn.

RECOMMENDATION: Ash-fouled plugs can be cleaned, gapped and reinstalled.

Detonation

APPEARANCE: Detonation is usually characterized by a broken plug insulator.

CAUSE: A portion of the fuel charge will begin to burn spontaneously, from the increased heat following ignition. The explosion that results applies extreme pressure to engine components, frequently damaging spark plugs and pistons.

Detonation can result by over-advanced ignition timing, inferior gasoline (low octane) lean air/fuel mixture, poor carburetion, engine lugging or an increase in compression ratio due to combustion chamber deposits or engine modification.

RECOMMENDATION: Replace the plugs after correcting the problem.

Photos Courtesy Champion Spark Plug Co.

EMISSION CONTROLS

13. Be aware of the general condition of the emission control system. It contributes to reduced pollution and should be serviced regularly to maintain efficient engine operation.

14. Check all vacuum lines for dried, cracked or brittle conditions. Something as simple as a leaking vacuum hose can cause poor performance and loss of economy.

15. Avoid tampering with the emission control system. Attempting to improve fuel econ-

FUEL SYSTEM

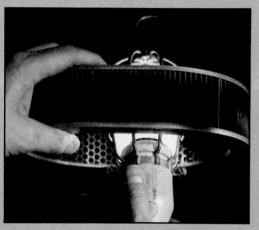

Check the air filter with a light behind it. If you can see light through the filter it can be reused.

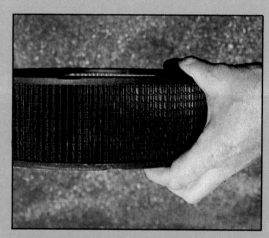

Extremely clogged filters should be discarded and replaced with a new one.

18. Replace the air filter regularly. A dirty air filter richens the air/fuel mixture and can increase fuel consumption as much as 10%. Tests show that ⅓ of all vehicles have air filters in need of replacement.

19. Replace the fuel filter at least as often as recommended.

20. Set the idle speed and carburetor mixture to specifications.

21. Check the automatic choke. A sticking or malfunctioning choke wastes gas.

22. During the summer months, adjust the automatic choke for a leaner mixture which will produce faster engine warm-ups.

COOLING SYSTEM

29. Be sure all accessory drive belts are in good condition. Check for cracks or wear.

30. Adjust all accessory drive belts to proper tension.

31. Check all hoses for swollen areas, worn spots, or loose clamps.

32. Check coolant level in the radiator or expansion tank.

33. Be sure the thermostat is operating properly. A stuck thermostat delays engine warm-up and a cold engine uses nearly twice as much fuel as a warm engine.

34. Drain and replace the engine coolant at least as often as recommended. Rust and scale

TIRES & WHEELS

38. Check the tire pressure often with a pencil type gauge. Tests by a major tire manufacturer show that 90% of all vehicles have at least 1 tire improperly inflated. Better mileage can be achieved by over-inflating tires, but never exceed the maximum inflation pressure on the side of the tire.

39. If possible, install radial tires. Radial tires deliver as much as ½ mpg more than bias belted tires.

40. Avoid installing super-wide tires. They only create extra rolling resistance and decrease fuel mileage. Stick to the manufacturer's recommendations.

41. Have the wheels properly balanced.

omy by tampering with emission controls is more likely to worsen fuel economy than improve it. Emission control changes on modern engines are not readily reversible.

16. Clean (or replace) the EGR valve and lines as recommended.

17. Be sure that all vacuum lines and hoses are reconnected properly after working under the hood. An unconnected or misrouted vacuum line can wreak havoc with engine performance.

23. Check for fuel leaks at the carburetor, fuel pump, fuel lines and fuel tank. Be sure all lines and connections are tight.

24. Periodically check the tightness of the carburetor and intake manifold attaching nuts and bolts. These are a common place for vacuum leaks to occur.

25. Clean the carburetor periodically and lubricate the linkage.

26. The condition of the tailpipe can be an excellent indicator of proper engine combustion. After a long drive at highway speeds, the inside of the tailpipe should be a light grey in color. Black or soot on the insides indicates an overly rich mixture.

27. Check the fuel pump pressure. The fuel pump may be supplying more fuel than the engine needs.

28. Use the proper grade of gasoline for your engine. Don't try to compensate for knocking or "pinging" by advancing the ignition timing. This practice will only increase plug temperature and the chances of detonation or pre-ignition with relatively little performance gain.

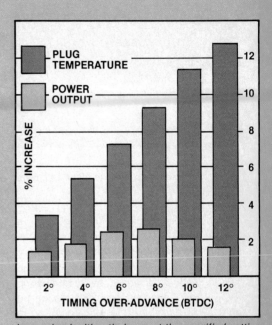

Increasing ignition timing past the specified setting results in a drastic increase in spark plug temperature with increased chance of detonation or preignition. Performance increase is considerably less. (Photo courtesy Champion Spark Plug Co.)

that form in the engine should be flushed out to allow the engine to operate at peak efficiency.

35. Clean the radiator of debris that can decrease cooling efficiency.

36. Install a flex-type or electric cooling fan, if you don't have a clutch type fan. Flex fans use curved plastic blades to push more air at low speeds when more cooling is needed; at high speeds the blades flatten out for less resistance. Electric fans only run when the engine temperature reaches a predetermined level.

37. Check the radiator cap for a worn or cracked gasket. If the cap does not seal properly, the cooling system will not function properly.

42. Be sure the front end is correctly aligned. A misaligned front end actually has wheels going in differed directions. The increased drag can reduce fuel economy by .3 mpg.

43. Correctly adjust the wheel bearings. Wheel bearings that are adjusted too tight increase rolling resistance.

Check tire pressures regularly with a reliable pocket type gauge. Be sure to check the pressure on a cold tire.

GENERAL MAINTENANCE

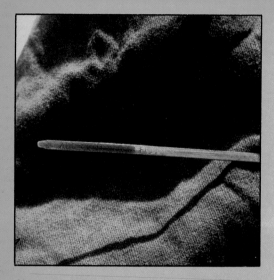

Check the fluid levels (particularly engine oil) on a regular basis. Be sure to check the oil for grit, water or other contamination.

A vacuum gauge is another excellent indicator of internal engine condition and can also be installed in the dash as a mileage indicator.

44. Periodically check the fluid levels in the engine, power steering pump, master cylinder, automatic transmission and drive axle.

45. Change the oil at the recommended interval and change the filter at every oil change. Dirty oil is thick and causes extra friction between moving parts, cutting efficiency and increasing wear. A worn engine requires more frequent tune-ups and gets progressively worse fuel economy. In general, use the lightest viscosity oil for the driving conditions you will encounter.

46. Use the recommended viscosity fluids in the transmission and axle.

47. Be sure the battery is fully charged for fast starts. A slow starting engine wastes fuel.

48. Be sure battery terminals are clean and tight.

49. Check the battery electrolyte level and add distilled water if necessary.

50. Check the exhaust system for crushed pipes, blockages and leaks.

51. Adjust the brakes. Dragging brakes or brakes that are not releasing create increased drag on the engine.

52. Install a vacuum gauge or miles-per-gallon gauge. These gauges visually indicate engine vacuum in the intake manifold. High vacuum = good mileage and low vacuum = poorer mileage. The gauge can also be an excellent indicator of internal engine conditions.

53. Be sure the clutch is properly adjusted. A slipping clutch wastes fuel.

54. Check and periodically lubricate the heat control valve in the exhaust manifold. A sticking or inoperative valve prevents engine warm-up and wastes gas.

55. Keep accurate records to check fuel economy over a period of time. A sudden drop in fuel economy may signal a need for tune-up or other maintenance.

Ford Electronic Fuel Injection Troubleshooting

Symptom	Possible Problem Areas
Surging, backfire, misfire, runs rough	1. EEC distributor rotor registry ① 2. EGR solenoid(s) defective 3. Distributor, cap, body, rotor, ignition wires, plugs, coil defective 4. Pulse ring behind vibration damper misaligned or damaged 5. Spark plug fouling
Stalls on deceleration	1. EGR solenoid(s) or valve defective 2. EEC distributor rotor registry ①
Stalls at idle	1. Idle speed wrong 2. Throttle kicker not working
Hesitates on acceleration	1. Acceleration enrichment system defective 2. Fuel pump ballast bypass relay not working
Fuel pump noisy	1. Fuel pump ballast bypass relay not working
Engine won't start	1. Fuel pump power relay defective, no spark, EGR system defective, no or low fuel pressure 2. Crankshaft position sensor not sealed, clearance wrong, defective 3. Pulse ring behind vibration damper misaligned, sensor tabs damaged 4. Power and ground wires open or shorted, poor electrical connections 5. Inertia switch tripped
Engine starts and stalls or runs rough	1. Fuel pump ballast wire defective 2. Manifold absolute pressure (MAP) sensor circuit not working 3. Low fuel pressure 4. EGR system problem 5. Microprocessor and calibration assembly faulty
Starts hard when cold	1. Cranking signal circuit faulty

bleed down and mounting attachments which locate the fuel manifold assembly and provide fuel injector retention.

Air Intake Manifold

The air intake manifold is a two piece (upper and lower intake manifold) aluminum casting. Runner lengths are turned to optimize engine torque and power output. The manifold provides mounting flanges for the air throttle body assembly, fuel supply manifold and accelerator control bracket and the EGR valve and supply tube. Vacuum taps are provided to support various engine accessories. Pockets for the fuel injectors are machined to prevent both air and fuel leakage. The pockets, in which the injectors are mounted, are placed to direct the injector fuel spray immediately in front of each engine intake valve.

COMPONENT REMOVAL AND INSTALLATION

Fuel Charging Assembly

WARNING: *If any of the sub-assemblies are to be serviced and/or removed, with the fuel charging assembly mounted to the engine, the following steps must be taken.*

1. Make sure the ignition key is in the off position.
2. Drain the coolant from the radiator.
CAUTION: *When draining the coolant, keep in mind that cats and dogs are attracted by the ethylene glycol antifreeze, and are quite likely to drink any that is left in an uncovered container or in puddles on the ground. This will prove fatal in sufficient quantity. Always drain the coolant into a sealable container. Coolant should be reused unless it is contaminated or several years old.*
3. Disconnect the negative battery cable.
4. Remove the fuel cap to relieve fuel tank pressure.
5. Relieve the pressure from the fuel system at the pressure relief valve. Special tool T80L-9974-A or its equal is needed for this procedure.
6. Disconnect the fuel supply line.
7. Identify and disconnect the fuel return lines and vacuum connections.
8. Disconnect the injector wiring harness by disconnecting the ECT sensor in the heater supply tube, under the lower intake manifold.
9. Disconnect the air by-pass connector from EEC harness.
NOTE: *Not all assemblies may be serviceable*

while on the engine. In some cases, removal of the fuel charging assembly may facilitate service of the various sub-assemblies. To remove the entire fuel charging assembly, the following should be observed.

10. Remove the engine air cleaner outlet tube between the vane air meter and air throttle body by loosening two the clamps.

11. Disconnect and remove the accelerator and speed control cables (if so equipped) from the accelerator mounting bracket and throttle lever.

12. Disconnect the top manifold vacuum fitting connections by disconnecting:

a. Rear vacuum line at the dash panel vacuum tree.

b. Front vacuum line at the air cleaner and fuel pressure regulator.

13. Disconnect the PCV system by removing the following:

a. Two large forward facing connectors on the throttle body and intake manifold.

b. Throttle body port hose at the straight plastic connector.

c. Canister purge line at the straight plastic connector.

d. PCV hose at the valve cover.

e. Unbolt the PCV separator support bracket from the cylinder head and remove the PCV system.

14. Disconnect the EGR tube from the upper intake manifold by removing the two flange nuts.

15. Disconnect the EGR tube from the upper intake manifold by removing the two flange nuts.

1. Spring—carburetor throttle return
2. Bushing—accelerator pump overtravel spring (2)
3. Lever—engine throttle
4. Screw—M4 × .7 × 8
5. Plate—air intake charge throttle
6. Shaft—air intake charge throttle
7. Spring—secondary throttle return
8. E-ring
9. Hub—throttle control
10. Spacer
11. Washer—nylon (2)
12. Lever—throttle control
13. Rod—engine secondary throttle control
14. Body—air intake charge throttle
14A. Bolt M8 × 1.25 × 30 hex flange head (2 req'd)
15. Nut—M8 (2 req'd)
16. Stud—M8 × 42.5 (2 req'd)
17A. Screw throttle stop
17B. Spring—throttle return control
18. Gasket—air charge control to intake manifold
19. Gasket—air bypass valve
20. Seal—throttle control shaft
21. Bushing—carburetor throttle shaft
22. Valve assembly—throttle air bypass
23. Bolt—M6 × 1.0 × 20 hex head flange
24. Valve assembly—throttle air bypass (alt.)
25. Potentiometer throttle position

26. Screw and washer assembly M4 × 22
27. Screw—M4 × 0.7 × 14.0 hex. washer tap
28. Manifold—intake upper
29. Gasket T.P.S.
1. Wiring harness—fuel charging
2. Regulator assembly—fuel pressure
3. Cap—fuel pressure relief
4. Valve assembly—fuel pressure relief
5. Manifold assembly—fuel injection fuel supply
6. Screw—M5 × 0.8 × 10 socket head (3 req'd)
7. Seal—5/16 × .070 o-ring
8. Bolt (2 req'd)
9. Injector assembly—fuel (4 req'd)
10. Manifold—intake lower
11. Plug

EFI fuel injection 2.3L engine

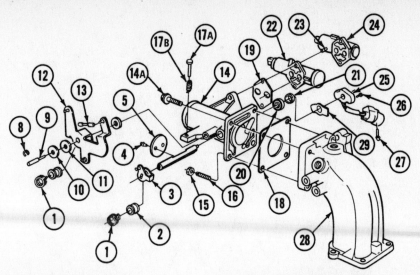

1. Spring—carburetor throttle return
2. Bushing—accelerator pump overtravel spring (2)
3. Lever—engine throttle
4. Screw—m4 × .7 × 8
5. Plate—air intake charge throttle
6. Shaft—air intake charge throttle
7. Spring—secondary throttle return
8. E-ring
9. Hub—throttle control
10. Spacer
11. Washer—nylon (2)
12. Lever—throttle control
13. Rod—engine secondary throttle control
14. Body—air intake charge throttle
14A. Bolt m8 × 1.25 × 30 hex flange head 2 req'd
15. Nut—m8 2 req'd

16. Stud—m8 × 42.5 2 req'd
17A. Screw throttle stop
17B. Spring—throttle return control
18. Gasket—air charge control to intake manifold
19. Gasket—air bypass valve
20. Seal—throttle control shaft
21. Bushing—carburetor throttle shaft
22. Valve assy—throttle air bypass
23. Bolt—m6 × 1.0 × 20 hex head flange
24. Valve assy—throttle air bypass (alt.)
25. Potentiometer throttle position
26. Screw and washer assy m4 × 22
27. Screw—m4 × 0.7 × 14.0 hex. washer tap
28. Manifold—intake upper
29. Gasket tps

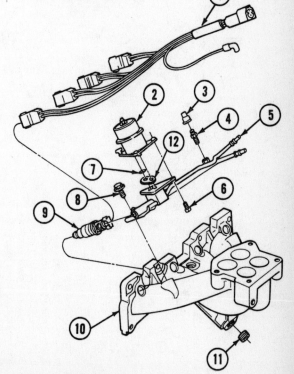

1. Wiring harness—fuel charging
2. Regulator assy—fuel pressure
3. Cap—fuel pressure relief
4. Valve assy—fuel pressure relief
5. Manifold assy—fuel injection fuel supply
6. Screw—m5 × 0.8 × 10 socket head 3 req'd
7. Seal—5/16 × .070 O-ring
8. Bolt (2 req'd)
9. Injector assy—fuel 4 req'd
10. Manifold—intake lower
11. Plug
12. Gasket—fuel pressure regulator

EFI components used on the 1985–86 4-140

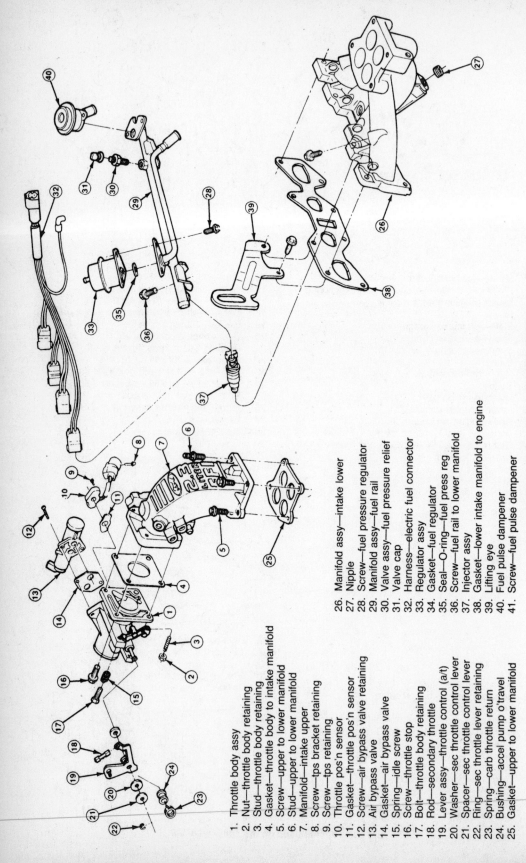

EFI components used on the 1987 4-140 Turbo

1. Throttle body assy
2. Nut—throttle body retaining
3. Stud—throttle body retaining
4. Gasket—throttle body to intake manifold
5. Screw—upper to lower manifold
6. Stud—upper to lower manifold
7. Manifold—intake upper
8. Screw—tps bracket retaining
9. Screw—tps retaining
10. Throttle pos'n sensor
11. Gasket—throttle pos'n sensor
12. Screw—air bypass valve retaining
13. Air bypass valve
14. Gasket—air bypass valve
15. Spring—idle screw
16. Screw—throttle stop
17. Bolt—throttle body retaining
18. Rod—secondary throttle
19. Lever assy—throttle control (a/t)
20. Washer—sec throttle control lever
21. Spacer—sec throttle control lever
22. Ring—sec throttle lever retaining
23. Spring—carb throttle return
24. Bushing—accel pump o'travel
25. Gasket—upper to lower manifold
26. Manifold assy—intake lower
27. Nipple
28. Screw—fuel pressure regulator
29. Manifold assy—fuel rail
30. Valve assy—fuel pressure relief
31. Valve cap
32. Harness—electric fuel connector
33. Regulator assy
34. Gasket—fuel regulator
35. Seal—O-ring—fuel press reg
36. Screw—fuel rail to lower manifold
37. Injector assy
38. Gasket—lower intake manifold to engine
39. Lifting eye
40. Fuel pulse dampener
41. Screw—fuel pulse dampener

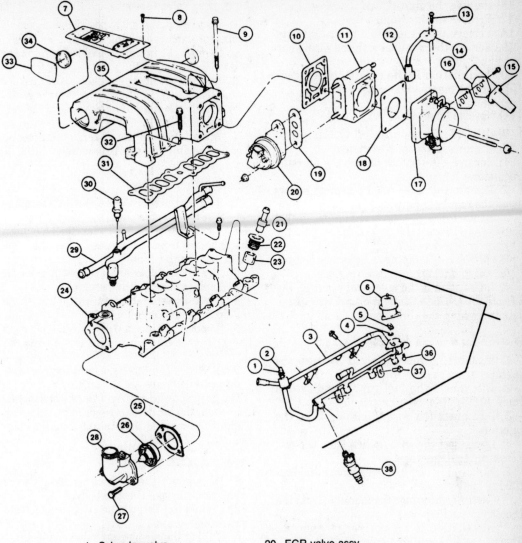

1. Schrader valve
2. Cap-Schrader valve
3. Fuel rail assy
4. Seal O-ring ⁵⁄₁₆-18 × 6.07 inch
5. Gasket, fuel pressure regulator
6. Fuel pressure regulator
7. Cover, upper manifold
8. Screw
9. Bolt ⁵⁄₁₆-18 × 6.07 inch
10. Gasket, EGR spacer
11. EGR spacer
12. Connector, tp sensor (pia tps)
13. Screw
14. Sensor, throttle position
15. Throttle air bypass valve
16. Gasket, throttle air bypass valve
17. Throttle body assy
18. Gasket, throttle body
19. Gasket, EGR valve
20. EGR valve assy
21. PCV valve assy
22. PCV grommet
23. Element, crankcase vent
24. Lower intake manifold
25. Gasket, thermostat housing
26. Thermostat
27. Bolt ⁵⁄₁₆-18 × 3.50 inch
28. Connector assy, engine coolant outlet
29. Tube, heater water supply and return
30. Sensor, EEC coolant temperature
31. Gasket, upper to lower manifold
32. Bolt ⁵⁄₁₆-18 × 1.62 inch
33. Cover, decorative end
34. Plug—cap 1.75 inch dia.
35. Upper intake manifold
36. Screw—socket head 5.0 × 0.8 × 1.0
37. Botl, att rail assy to lower manifold
38. Fuel injector

Fuel injection components used on the 1987 8-302

16. Remove the dipstick and its tube.

17. Remove the fuel return line.

18. Remove the six manifold mounting nuts.

19. Remove the manifold with the wiring harness and gasket.

20. Installation is the reverse of removal. Tighten the manifold bolt 12-15 ft. lbs.

Fuel Pressure Regulator

WARNING: *Before attempting this procedure depressurize the fuel system.*

1. Remove the vacuum line at the pressure regulator.

2. Remove the three Allen retaining screws from the regulator housing.

3. Remove the pressure regulator, gasket and O-ring. Discard the gasket and inspect the O-ring for deterioration.

WARNING: *If scraping is necessary be careful not to damage the gasket surface.*

4. Installation is the reverse of removal. Lubricate the O-ring with light oil prior to installation. Tighten the three screws 27-40 in. lbs.

Fuel Injector Manifold Assembly

1. Remove the fuel tank cap. Release the pressure from the fuel system.

2. Disconnect the fuel supply and return lines.

3. Disconnect the wiring harness from the injectors.

4. Disconnect the vacuum line from the fuel pressure regulator valve.

5. Remove the two fuel injector manifold retaining bolts.

6. Carefully disengage the manifold from the fuel injectors. Remove the manifold.

7. Installation is the reverse of removal. Torque the fuel manifold bolts 15-22 ft. lbs.

Pressure Relief Valve

1. If the fuel charging assembly is mounted on the engine, the fuel system must be depressurized.

2. Using an open end wrench or suitable deep well socket, remove the pressure relief valve from the injection manifold.

3. Installation is the reverse of removal. Torque the valve 48-84 in. lbs.

Throttle Position Sensor

1. Disconnect the throttle position sensor from the wiring harness.

2. Remove the two retaining screws.

3. Remove the throttle position sensor.

4. Installation is the reverse of removal. Torque the sensor screws 11-16 in. lbs.

NOTE: *This throttle position sensor is not adjustable.*

Air By-pass Valve Assembly

1. Disconnect the air bypass valve assembly connector from the wiring harness.

2. Remove the two air bypass valve retaining screws.

3. Remove the air bypass valve and gasket.

WARNING: *If necessary to remove the gasket by scraping, be careful not to damage the gasket surface.*

4. Installation is the reverse of removal. Torque the air bypass valve assembly 71-102 in. lbs.

Air Intake Throttle Body

1. Remove the four throttle body nuts. Make sure that the throttle position sensor connector and the air by-pass valve connector have been disconnected from the harness. Disconnect the air cleaner outlet tube.

2. Identify and disconnect the vacuum hoses.

3. Remove the throttle bracket.

4. Carefully separate the throttle body from the upper intake manifold.

5. Remove and discard the gasket between the throttle body and the upper intake manifold.

WARNING: *If scraping is necessary, be careful not to damage the gasket surfaces, or allow any material to drop into the manifold.*

6. Installation is the reverse of removal. Tighten the throttle body-to-upper intake manifold nuts 12-15 ft. lbs.

Upper Intake Manifold

1. Disconnect the air cleaner outlet tube from the air intake throttle body.

2. Unplug the throttle position sensor from the wiring harness.

3. Unplug the air by-pass valve connector.

4. Remove the three upper manifold retaining bolts.

5. Remove the upper manifold assembly.

6. Remove and discard the gasket from the lower manifold assembly.

WARNING: *If scraping is necessary, be careful not to damage gasket surfaces, or allow any material to drop into the lower manifold.*

7. Installation is the reverse of removal. Tighten the upper intake manifold bolts 15-22 ft. lbs. Use a new gasket between the manifolds.

Fuel Injector

WARNING: *The fuel system must be depressurized prior to starting this procedure.*

1. Disconnect the fuel supply and return lines.

2. Remove the vacuum line from the fuel pressure regulator.

3. Disconnect the wiring harness.

4. Remove the fuel injector manifold assembly.

5. Carefully remove the connectors from the individual injectors.

6. Grasping the injectors body, pull up while gently rocking the injector from side to side.

7. Inspect the injector O-rings (two per injector) for signs of deterioration. Replace as needed.

8. Inspect the injector plastic hat (covering the injector pintle) and washer for signs of deterioration. Replace as needed. If a hat is missing, look for it in the intake manifold.

9. Installation is the reverse of removal. Lubricate all O-rings with a light oil. Carefully seat the fuel injector manifold assembly on the four injectors and secure the manifold with the attaching bolts. Torque the bolts 15-22 ft. lbs.

Vane Air Meter

1. Loosen the hose clamp which secures engine air cleaner outlet hose to the vane meter assembly.

2. Remove air intake and outlet tube from the air cleaner.

3. Disengage four spring clamps and remove air cleaner front cover and air cleaner filter panel.

4. Remove the two screw and washer assemblies which secure the air meter to its bracket. Remove the vane air meter assembly.

5. Installation is the reverse of removal.

FUEL TANK

CAUTION: *NEVER SMOKE AROUND OR NEAR GASOLINE! GASOLINE VAPORS ARE EXTREMELY FLAMMABLE! EVEN THE PROXIMITY OF LIGHTED SMOKING MATERIAL CAN CAUSE AN EXPLOSION AND FIRE!*

REMOVAL AND INSTALLATION

NOTE: *On engines with fuel injection, before disconnecting any fuel line, relieve the pressure from the fuel system. On 6-232 and 8-302 engines with CFI, relieve the system pressure at the pressure relief valve mounted on the throttle body. Special tool T80L-9974-A, or its equivalent, is needed for this procedure.*

On the 4-140 turbocharged engine with EFI this valve is located in the flexible fuel supply tube approximately 12" (305mm) back from where it connects to the engine fuel rail on the driver's side of the engine compartment.

On the 8-302 with EFI, the valve is located in the metal engine fuel line at the left front corner of the engine.

Before opening the fuel system on EFI engines:

1. Remove the fuel tank cap.

2. Disconnect the vacuum hose from the fuel pressure regulator located on the engine fuel rail.

Motorcraft 2150 Specifications

Year	(9510) * Carburetor Identification	Dry Float Level (in.)	Wet Float Level (in.)	Pump Setting Hole # ①	Choke Plate Pulldown (in.)	Fast Idle Cam Linkage Clearance (in.)	Fast Idle (rpm)	Dechoke (in.)	Choke Setting
1979	D9AE-AHA	7/16	13/16	3	0.147	①	②	0.250	3 Rich
	D9AE-AJA	7/16	13/16	3	0.147	①	②	0.250	3 Rich
	D9AE-ANB	7/16	13/16	3	0.129	①	②	—	1 Rich
	D9AE-APB	7/16	13/16	3	0.129	①	②	—	1 Rich
	D9AE-AVB	7/16	13/16	3	0.129	①	②	—	1 Rich
	D9AE-AYA	7/16	13/16	3	0.129	①	②	—	1 Rich
	D9AE-AYB	7/16	13/16	3	0.129	①	②	—	1 Rich
	D9AE-TB	7/16	13/16	3	0.129	①	②	—	2 Rich
	D9AE-UB	7/16	13/16	3	0.129	①	②	—	2 Rich
	D9BE-VB	7/16	13/16	3	0.153	①	②	0.250	2 Rich
	D9BE-YB	7/16	13/16	3	0.153	①	②	—	2 Rich
	D9DE-NB	7/16	13/16	3	0.153	①	②	0.250	2 Rich
	D9DE-RA	7/16	13/16	2	0.125	①	②	0.115	3 Rich
	D9DE-RB	7/16	13/16	2	0.125	①	②	0.115	3 Rich
	D9DE-RD	7/16	13/16	2	0.125	①	②	—	3 Rich

Motorcraft 2150 Specifications *(cont.)*

Year	(9510) * Carburetor Identification	Dry Float Level (in.)	Wet Float Level (in.)	Pump Setting Hole # ①	Choke Plate Pulldown (in.)	Fast Idle Cam Linkage Clearance (in.)	Fast Idle (rpm)	Dechoke (in.)	Choke Setting
1979	D9DE-SA	7/16	13/16	2	0.125	①	②	0.250	3 Rich
	D9DE-SC	7/16	13/16	2	0.125	①	②	—	3 Rich
	D9ME-BA	7/16	13/16	2	0.136	①	②	0.115	Index
	D9ME-CA	7/16	13/16	2	0.136	①	②	0.115	Index
	D9OE-CB	7/16	13/16	3	0.132	①	②	0.115	3 Rich
	D9OE-DB	7/16	13/16	3	0.132	①	②	—	3 Rich
	D9OE-EA	7/16	13/16	3	0.132	①	②	0.115	2 Rich
	D9OE-FA	7/16	13/16	3	0.132	①	②	0.115	2 Rich
	D9SE-GA	7/16	13/16	3	0.150	①	②	0.250	2 Rich
	D9VE-LC	7/16	13/16	3	0.145	①	②	0.250	3 Rich
	D9VE-SA	7/16	13/16	3	0.147	①	②	—	3 Rich
	D9VE-UB	7/16	13/16	3	0.155	①	②	0.250	3 Rich
	D9VE-VA	3/8	3/4	3	0.145	①	②	—	3 Rich
	D9VE-YB	3/8	3/4	2	0.145	①	②	0.250	3 Rich
	D9WE-CB	7/16	13/16	3	0.132	①	②	—	3 Rich
	D9WE-DB	7/16	13/16	3	0.132	①	②	—	3 Rich
	D9WE-EB	7/16	13/16	3	0.132	①	②	—	2 Rich
	D9WE-FB	7/16	13/16	3	0.132	①	②	—	2 Rich
	D9WE-JA	7/16	13/16	3	0.150	①	②	0.250	2 Rich
	D9WE-MB	7/16	13/16	3	0.132	①	②	—	1 Rich
	D9WE-NB	7/16	13/16	3	0.132	①	②	—	1 Rich
	D9YE-EA	7/16	13/16	3	0.118	①	②	0.115	1 Rich
	D9YE-FA	7/16	13/16	3	0.118	①	②	0.115	1 Rich
	D9YE-AB	7/16	13/16	3	0.118	①	②	0.115	Index
	D9YE-BB	7/16	13/16	3	0.118	①	②	0.115	Index
	D9YE-CA	7/16	13/16	2	0.118	①	②	0.115	Index
	D9YE-DA	7/16	13/16	2	0.118	①	②	0.115	Index
	D9ZE-AYA	7/16	13/16	3	0.138	①	②	0.115	Index
	D9ZE-BFB	7/16	13/16	2	0.125	①	②	—	3 Rich
	D9ZE-BGB	7/16	13/16	2	0.125	①	②	—	3 Rich
	D9ZE-BHB	7/16	13/16	2	0.125	①	②	0.250	3 Rich
	D9ZE-BJB	7/16	13/16	2	0.125	①	②	—	3 Rich
1980	EO4E-PA, RA	—	13/16	2	0.104	①	②	1/4	③
	EOBE-AUA	—	13/16	3	0.116	①	②	1/4	③
	EODE-SA, TA	—	13/16	2	0.104	①	②	1/4	③
	EOKE-CA, DA	—	13/16	3	0.116	①	②	1/4	③
	EOKE-GA, HA	—	13/16	3	0.116	①	②	1/4	③
	EOKE-JA, KA	—	13/16	3	0.116	①	②	1/4	③
	D84E-TA, UA	—	13/16	2	0.125	①	②	1/4	③

Motorcraft 2150 Specifications (cont.)

Year	(9510) * Carburetor Identification	Dry Float Level (in.)	Wet Float Level (in.)	Pump Setting Hole # ①	Choke Plate Pulldown (in.)	Fast Idle Cam Linkage Clearance (in.)	Fast Idle (rpm)	Dechoke (in.)	Choke Setting
1980 (cont.)	EO4E-ADA, AEA	—	13/16	2	0.104	①	②	¼	③
	EO4E-CA	—	13/16	2	0.104	①	②	¼	③
	EO4E-EA, FA	—	13/16	2	0.104	①	②	¼	③
	EO4E-JA, KA	—	13/16	2	0.137	①	②	¼	③
	EO4E-SA, TA	—	13/16	2	0.104	①	②	¼	③
	EO4E-VA, YA	—	13/16	2	0.104	①	②	¼	③
	EODE-TA, VA	—	13/16	2	0.104	①	②	¼	③
	EOSE-GA, HA	—	13/16	2	0.104	①	②	¼	③
	EOSE-LA, MA	—	13/16	2	0.104	①	②	¼	③
	EOSE-NA	—	13/16	2	0.104	①	②	¼	③
	EOSE-PA	—	13/16	2	0.137	①	②	¼	③
	EOVE-FA	—	13/16	2	0.104	①	②	¼	③
	EOWE-BA, CA	—	13/16	2	0.137	①	②	¼	③
	D9AE-ANA, APA	—	13/16	3	0.129	①	②	¼	③
	D9AE-AVA, AYA	—	13/16	3	0.129	①	②	¼	③
	EOAE-AGA	—	13/16	3	0.159	①	②	¼	③
1981	EIKE-CA	7/16	0.810	3	0.124	①	②	0.250	③
	EIKE-EA	7/16	0.810	3	0.124	①	②	0.250	③
	EIKE-DA	7/16	0.810	3	0.124	①	②	0.250	③
	EIKE-FA	7/16	0.810	3	0.124	①	②	0.250	③
	EIWE-FA	7/16	0.810	2	0.120	①	②	0.250	③
	EIWE-EA	7/16	0.810	2	0.120	①	②	0.250	③
	EIWE-CA	7/16	0.810	2	0.120	①	②	0.250	③
	EIWE-DA	7/16	0.810	2	0.120	①	②	0.250	③
	EIAE-YA	7/16	0.810	3	0.124	①	②	0.250	③
	EIAE-ZA	7/16	0.810	3	0.124	①	②	0.250	③
	EIAE-ADA	7/16	0.810	3	0.124	①	②	0.250	③
	EIAE-AEA	7/16	0.810	3	0.124	①	②	0.250	③
	EIAE-TA	—	0.810	2	0.104	①	②	0.250	③
	EIAE-UA	—	0.810	2	0.104	①	②	0.250	③
1982	E2ZE-BAA	13/32	0.780	2	0.172	①	1400	0.250	③
	E2ZE-BBA	13/32	0.780	2	0.172	①	1400	0.250	③
	E3CE-LA	7/16	0.810	3	0.103	①	2200	0.250	③
	E3CE-MA	7/16	0.810	3	0.103	①	2200	0.250	③
	E3CE-JA	7/16	0.810	3	0.103	①	2200	0.250	③
	E3CE-KA	7/16	0.810	3	0.103	①	2200	0.250	③
	E3CE-NA	7/16	0.810	3	0.120	①	2100	0.250	③
	E3CE-PA	7/16	0.810	3	0.120	①	2100	0.250	③

① With link in inbound hole of pump lever   ② See underhood sticker   ③ Opposite V notch

Model 1946

Year	Part Number	Float Level (in.)	Choke Pulldown (in.)	Dechoke (in.)	Fast Idle Cam (in.)	Accelerator Pump Stroke Slot
1980	E0ZE-GA	.69	.110	.150	.05–.09	#2
	E0ZE-BBA	.69	.120	.150	.086	#2
	E0BE-CA	.69	.100	.150	.070	#2
	E0BE-AA	.69	.100	.150	.070	#2
	E0BE-AAA	.69	.115	.150	.090	#1
	E0BE-ZA	.69	.115	.150	.090	#1
	E0ZE-EA	.69	.110	.150	.070	#2
	E0ZE-DA	.69	.110	.150	.070	#2
1981	EIBE-AFA	.69	.113	.150	.082	#2
	EIBE-AKA	.69	.113	.150	.082	#2
	E0BE-CA	.69	.100	.150	.070	#2
	E0BE-AA	.69	.100	.150	.070	#2
1982	EIBE-AGA	.69	.120	.150	.086	#2
	E2BE-CA	.69	.110	.150	.078	#2
	E2BE-BA	.69	.110	.150	.078	#2
	E2BE-JA	.69	.110	.150	.078	#2
	E2BE-HA	.69	.110	.150	.078	#2
	E2BE-TA	.69	.110	.150	.078	#2
	E2BE-SA	.69	.110	.150	.078	#2
1983	E2BE-CA	.69	.110	.150	.078	#2
	E2BE-BA	.69	.110	.150	.078	#2
	E2BE-TA	.69	.110	.150	.078	#2
	E2BE-SA	.69	.110	.150	.078	#2
	E3SE-CA	.69	.105	.150	.078	#2
	E3SE-DA	.69	.105	.150	.078	#2
	E3SE-AA	.69	.095	.150	.078	#2
	E3SE-BA	.69	.095	.150	.078	#2

Holley 4180 Specifications

Year	(9510) * Carburetor Identification	Dry Float Level (in.)	Wet Float Level (in.)	Pump Setting Hole	Choke Plate Pulldown (in.)	Fast Idle Cam Linkage Clearance (in.)	Fast Idle (rpm)	Dechoke (in.)	Choke Setting
1983	E3ZE-AUA	②	①	#1	.195–.215	NA	③	.300	3 Rich
	E3ZE-BGA	②	①	#1	.195–.215	NA	③	.300	3 Rich
1984	E4ZE-SA	②	①	#1	.195–.215	NA	③	.300	1 Lean

① Bottom of sight plug
② See text
③ See Underhood sticker
NA—not available

Carter YFA Specifications

Year	Model ①	Float Level (in.)	Fast Idle Cam (in.)	Choke Plate Pulldown (in.)	Unloader (in.)	Dechoke (in.)	Choke
1983	E3ZE-LA	0.650	0.140	0.260	—	0.220	—
	E3ZE-MA	0.650	0.140	0.260	—	0.220	—
	E3ZE-TB	0.650	0.140	0.240	—	0.220	—
	E3ZE-UA	0.650	0.140	0.240	—	0.220	—
	E3ZE-VA	0.650	0.140	0.260	—	0.220	—
	E3ZE-YA	0.650	0.140	0.260	—	0.220	—
	E3ZE-NB	0.650	0.160	0.260	—	0.220	—
	E3ZE-PB	0.650	0.160	0.260	—	0.220	—
	E3ZE-ASA	0.650	0.160	0.260	—	0.220	—
	E3ZE-APA	0.650	0.140	0.240	—	0.220	—
	E3ZE-ARA	0.650	0.140	0.240	—	0.220	—
	E3ZE-ADA	0.650	0.140	0.260	—	0.220	—
	E3ZE-AEA	0.650	0.140	0.260	—	0.220	—
	E3ZE-ACA	0.650	0.140	0.260	—	0.220	—
	E3ZE-ATA	0.650	0.160	0.260	—	0.220	—
	E3ZE-ABA	0.650	0.140	0.260	—	0.220	—
	E3ZE-UB	0.650	0.140	0.240	—	0.220	—
	E3ZE-TC	0.650	0.140	0.240	—	0.220	—
1984–87	E4ZE-HC, DB	0.650	0.140	0.260	—	0.270	—
	E4ZE-MA, NA	0.650	0.140	0.240	—	0.270	—
	E4ZE-PA, RA	0.650	0.140	0.260	—	0.270	—
	E5ZE-CA	0.650	0.140	0.260	—	0.270	—
	E4ZE-PB, RB	0.650	0.140	0.240	—	0.270	—

① Model number located on the tag or casting

Motorcraft Model 2700 VV Specifications

Year	Model	Float Level (in.)	Float Drop (in.)	Fast Idle Cam Setting (notches)	Cold Enrichment Metering Rod (in.)	Control Vacuum (in. H₂O)	Venturi Valve Limiter (in.)	Choke Cap Setting (notches)	Control Vacuum Regulator Setting (in.)
1979	D9ZE-LB	1³⁄₆₄	1¹⁵⁄₃₂	1 Rich/2nd step	.125	①	②	Index	.230
	D84E-KA	1³⁄₆₄	1¹⁵⁄₃₂	1 Rich/3rd step	.125	5.5	6¹⁄₆₄	Index	—
1980	All	1³⁄₆₄	1¹⁵⁄₃₂	1 Rich/4th step	.125	③	④	⑤	.075
1981	EIAE-AAA	1.015–1.065	1.435–1.485	—	—	③	④	⑤	—

① Venturi Air Bypass 6.8–7.3
  Venturi Valve Diaphragm 4.6–5.1
② Limiter Setting .38–.42
  Limiter Stop Setting .73–.77
③ See text
④ Opening gap: 0.99–1.01
  Closing gap: 0.94–0.98
⑤ See underhood decal

Holley Model 5200

Year	(9510) *Carburetor Identification	Fast Idle Cam	Acc. Pump Stroke	Dechoke Clearance	Choke Pulldown	Choke Cap Setting (notches)	Float Adjustment
1979	D9BE-AAA/ADA	3.0 mm	No. 2	6.0 mm	6.0 mm	2 Rich	.41–.51
	D9BE-ABA/ACA	3.0 mm	No. 2	6.0 mm	6.0 mm	2 Rich	.41–.51
	D9EE-ANA/APA	3.0 mm	No. 2	6.0 mm	6.0 mm	2 Rich	.41–.51
	D9ZE-BCA/BDA	—	—	—	—	—	—
	D9ZE-MD/ND	3.0 mm	No. 3	6.0 mm	6.0 mm	2 Rich	.41–.51
	D9ZE-SB/TB	—	—	—	—	—	—
1980	D9EE-APA/ANA	2.5–3.5 mm	No. 2	6.0 mm	5.5–6.5 mm	—	.41–.51 in.①
	E0EE-GA/RA	2.0 mm	No. 2	5.0 mm	5.0 mm	—	.46 in.①
	E0EE-JA/TA	2.0 mm	No. 2	5.0 mm	5.0 mm	—	.46 in.①
	E0EE-NA/VA	3.0 mm	No. 2	10.0 mm	6.0 mm	—	.46 in.①
	E0ZE-SB	—	—	—	—	—	—
	E0ZE-AFB	—	—	—	—	—	—
	E0ZE-AAA	4.0 mm	No. 3	6.0 mm	7.0 mm	—	.46 in.①
	E0ZE-ACA	4.0 mm	No. 2	6.0 mm	7.0 mm	—	.46 in.①
1981	E1ZE-YA	.080	No. 2	.200	.200	—	.41–.51
	E0EE-RB	.080	No. 2	.200	.200	—	.41–.51
	E1ZE-VA	.080	No. 2	.200	.200	—	.41–.51

① Dry Setting
*Basic carburetor number for Ford products

3. Using a hand vacuum pump, apply about 25 in.Hg to the pressure regulator. Fuel pressure will be released into the fuel tank through the fuel return hose.

1. Raise and support the rear end on jackstands.

2. Disconnect the battery ground cable.

3. Siphon off as much gasoline as possible into an approved container.

NOTE: *On cars with fuel injection, the fuel tank has small reservoirs inside to maintain the fuel level at or near the fuel pick-up. These reservoirs are difficult to drain in as much as they may block the siphoning hose. You'll have to try different angle and repeated attempts with the siphoning hose. Be patient.*

4. Place a pan under the fuel fill hose and disconnect the fuel filler hose at the tank. Pour any drained fuel into an approved container.

5. Place a floor jack, cushioned with a length of wood, under the fuel tank.

6. Remove the fuel tank strap nuts and lower the fuel tank just enough to disconnect the fuel liquid and vapor lines, and the fuel sending unit wire.

Remove the air deflector from the tank retaining straps. The deflector is retained with pop rivets.

On cars cars equipped with a metal retainer which fastens the filler pipe to the tank, remove the screw attaching the retainer to the fuel tank flange.

7. Continue lowering the tank once all lines are disconnected, and remove it from the car.

8. Installation is the reverse of removal. The fuel vapor line should be retaped in position in the ribbed channel atop the tank.

Chassis Electrical

6

UNDERSTANDING AND TROUBLESHOOTING ELECTRICAL SYSTEMS

At the rate with which both import and domestic manufacturers are incorporating electronic control systems into their production lines, it won't be long before every new vehicle is equipped with one or more on-board computer. These electronic components (with no moving parts) should theoretically last the life of the vehicle, provided nothing external happens to damage the circuits or memory chips.

While it is true that electronic components should never wear out, in the real world malfunctions do occur. It is also true that any computer-based system is extremely sensitive to electrical voltages and cannot tolerate careless or haphazard testing or service procedures. An inexperienced individual can literally do major damage looking for a minor problem by using the wrong kind of test equipment or connecting test leads or connectors with the ignition switch ON. When selecting test equipment, make sure the manufacturers instructions state that the tester is compatible with whatever type of electronic control system is being serviced. Read all instructions carefully and double check all test points before installing probes or making any test connections.

The following section outlines basic diagnosis techniques for dealing with computerized automotive control systems. Along with a general explanation of the various types of test equipment available to aid in servicing modern electronic automotive systems, basic repair techniques for wiring harnesses and connectors is given. Read the basic information before attempting any repairs or testing on any computerized system, to provide the background of information necessary to avoid the most common and obvious mistakes that can cost both time and money. Although the replacement and testing procedures are simple in themselves, the systems are not, and unless one has a thorough understanding of all components and their function within a particular computerized control system, the logical test sequence these systems demand cannot be followed. Minor malfunctions can make a big difference, so it is important to know how each component affects the operation of the overall electronic system to find the ultimate cause of a problem without replacing good components unnecessarily. It is not enough to use the correct test equipment; the test equipment must be used correctly.

Safety Precautions

CAUTION: *Whenever working on or around any computer based microprocessor control system, always observe these general precautions to prevent the possibility of personal injury or damage to electronic components.*

• Never install or remove battery cables with the key ON or the engine running. Jumper cables should be connected with the key OFF to avoid power surges that can damage electronic control units. Engines equipped with computer controlled systems should avoid both giving and getting jump starts due to the possibility of serious damage to components from arcing in the engine compartment when connections are made with the ignition ON.

• Always remove the battery cables before charging the battery. Never use a high output charger on an installed battery or attempt to use any type of "hot shot" (24 volt) starting aid.

• Exercise care when inserting test probes into connectors to insure good connections without damaging the connector or spreading the pins. Always probe connectors from the rear (wire) side, NOT the pin side, to avoid accidental shorting of terminals during test procedures.

• Never remove or attach wiring harness connectors with the ignition switch ON, especially to an electronic control unit.

• Do not drop any components during service procedures and never apply 12 volts directly to any component (like a solenoid or relay) unless instructed specifically to do so. Some component electrical windings are designed to safely handle only 4 or 5 volts and can be destroyed in seconds if 12 volts are applied directly to the connector.

• Remove the electronic control unit if the vehicle is to be placed in an environment where temperatures exceed approximately 176°F (80°C), such as a paint spray booth or when arc or gas welding near the control unit location in the car.

ORGANIZED TROUBLESHOOTING

When diagnosing a specific problem, organized troubleshooting is a must. The complexity of a modern automobile demands that you approach any problem in a logical, organized manner. There are certain troubleshooting techniques that are standard:

1. Establish when the problem occurs. Does the problem appear only under certain conditions? Were there any noises, odors, or other unusual symptoms?

2. Isolate the problem area. To do this, make some simple tests and observations; then eliminate the systems that are working properly. Check for obvious problems such as broken wires, dirty connections or split or disconnected vacuum hoses. Always check the obvious before assuming something complicated is the cause.

3. Test for problems systematically to determine the cause once the problem area is isolated. Are all the components functioning properly? Is there power going to electrical switches and motors? Is there vacuum at vacuum switches and/or actuators? Is there a mechanical problem such as bent linkage or loose mounting screws? Doing careful, systematic checks will often turn up most causes on the first inspection without wasting time checking components that have little or no relationship to the problem.

4. Test all repairs after the work is done to make sure that the problem is fixed. Some causes can be traced to more than one component, so a careful verification of repair work is important to pick up additional malfunctions that may cause a problem to reappear or a different problem to arise. A blown fuse, for example, is a simple problem that may require more than another fuse to repair. If you don't look for a problem that caused a fuse to blow, for example, a shorted wire may go undetected.

Experience has shown that most problems tend to be the result of a fairly simple and obvious cause, such as loose or corroded connectors or air leaks in the intake system; making careful inspection of components during testing essential to quick and accurate troubleshooting. Special, hand held computerized testers designed specifically for diagnosing the EEC-IV system are available from a variety of aftermarket sources, as well as from the vehicle manufacturer, but care should be taken that any test equipment being used is designed to diagnose that particular computer controlled system accurately without damaging the control unit (ECU) or components being tested.

NOTE: *Pinpointing the exact cause of trouble in an electrical system can sometimes only be accomplished by the use of special test equipment. The following describes commonly used test equipment and explains how to put it to best use in diagnosis. In addition to the information covered below, the manufacturer's instructions booklet provided with the tester should be read and clearly understood before attempting any test procedures.*

TEST EQUIPMENT

Jumper Wires

Jumper wires are simple, yet extremely valuable, pieces of test equipment. Jumper wires are merely wires that are used to bypass sections of a circuit. The simplest type of jumper wire is merely a length of multistrand wire with an alligator clip at each end. Jumper wires are usually fabricated from lengths of standard automotive wire and whatever type of connector (alligator clip, spade connector or pin connector) that is required for the particular vehicle being tested. The well equipped tool box will have several different styles of jumper wires in several different lengths. Some jumper wires are made with three or more terminals coming from a common splice for special purpose testing. In cramped, hard-to-reach areas it is advisable to have insulated boots over the jumper wire terminals in order to prevent accidental grounding, sparks, and possible fire, especially when testing fuel system components.

Jumper wires are used primarily to locate open electrical circuits, on either the ground (-) side of the circuit or on the hot (+) side. If an electrical component fails to operate, connect the jumper wire between the component and a good ground. If the component operates only with the jumper installed, the ground circuit is open. If the ground circuit is good, but the component does not operate, the circuit between the power feed and component is open. You can sometimes connect the jumper wire directly from the battery to the hot terminal of the component, but first make sure the component uses 12 volts in operation. Some electrical components, such as fuel injectors, are designed to operate on about 4 volts and running 12 volts directly to the injector terminals can burn out the wiring. By inserting an inline fuseholder between a set of test leads, a fused jumper wire can be used for bypassing open circuits. Use a 5 amp fuse to provide protection against voltage spikes. When in doubt, use a voltmeter to check the voltage input to the component and measure how much voltage is being applied normally. By moving the jumper wire successively back from the lamp toward the power source, you can isolate the area of the circuit where the open is located. When the component stops functioning, or the power is cut off, the open is in the segment of wire between the jumper and the point previously tested.

CAUTION: *Never use jumpers made from wire that is of lighter gauge than used in the circuit under test. If the jumper wire is of too small gauge, it may overheat and possibly melt. Never use jumpers to bypass high resistance loads (such as motors) in a circuit. Bypassing resistances, in effect, creates a short circuit which may, in turn, cause damage and fire. Never use a jumper for anything other than temporary bypassing of components in a circuit.*

12 Volt Test Light

The 12 volt test light is used to check circuits and components while electrical current is flowing through them. It is used for voltage and ground tests. Twelve volt test lights come in different styles but all have three main parts; a ground clip, a probe, and a light. The most commonly used 12 volt test lights have pick-type probes. To use a 12 volt test light, connect the ground clip to a good ground and probe wherever necessary with the pick. The pick should be sharp so that it can penetrate wire insulation to make contact with the wire, without making a large hole in the insulation. The wrap-around light is handy in hard to reach areas or where it is difficult to support a wire to push a probe pick into it. To use the wrap around light, hook the wire to probed with the hook and pull the trigger. A small pick will be forced through the wire insulation into the wire core.

CAUTION: *Do not use a test light to probe electronic ignition spark plug or coil wires. Never use a pick-type test light to probe wiring on computer controlled systems unless specifically instructed to do so. Any wire insulation that is pierced by the test light probe should be taped and sealed with silicone after testing.*

Like the jumper wire, the 12 volt test light is used to isolate opens in circuits. But, whereas the jumper wire is used to bypass the open to operate the load, the 12 volt test light is used to locate the presence of voltage in a circuit. If the test light glows, you know that there is power up to that point; if the 12 volt test light does not glow when its probe is inserted into the wire or connector, you know that there is an open circuit (no power). Move the test light in successive steps back toward the power source until the light in the handle does glow. When it does glow, the open is between the probe and point previously probed.

NOTE: *The test light does not detect that 12 volts (or any particular amount of voltage) is present; it only detects that some voltage is present. It is advisable before using the test light to touch its terminals across the battery posts to make sure the light is operating properly.*

Self-Powered Test Light

The self-powered test light usually contains a 1.5 volt penlight battery. One type of self-powered test light is similar in design to the 12 volt test light. This type has both the battery and the light in the handle and pick-type probe tip. The second type has the light toward the open tip, so that the light illuminates the contact point. The self-powered test light is dual purpose piece of test equipment. It can be used to test for either open or short circuits when power is isolated from the circuit (continuity test). A powered test light should not be used on any computer controlled system or component unless specifically instructed to do so. Many engine sensors can be destroyed by even this small amount of voltage applied directly to the terminals.

Open Circuit Testing

To use the self-powered test light to check for open circuits, first isolate the circuit from the vehicle's 12 volt power source by disconnecting the battery or wiring harness connector. Connect the test light ground clip to a good ground and probe sections of the circuit sequentially with the test light. (start from either end of the circuit). If the light is out, the open is between the probe and the circuit ground. If the light is on, the open is between the probe and end of the circuit toward the power source.

Short Circuit Testing

By isolating the circuit both from power and from ground, and using a self-powered test light, you can check for shorts to ground in the circuit. Isolate the circuit from power and ground. Connect the test light ground clip to a good ground and probe any easy-to-reach test point in the circuit. If the light comes on, there is a short somewhere in the circuit. To isolate the short, probe a test point at either end of the isolated circuit (the light should be on). Leave the test light probe connected and open connectors, switches, remove parts, etc., sequentially, until the light goes out. When the light goes out, the short is between the last circuit component opened and the previous circuit opened.

NOTE: *The 1.5 volt battery in the test light does not provide much current. A weak battery may not provide enough power to illuminate the test light even when a complete circuit is made (especially if there are high resistances in the circuit). Always make sure that the test battery is strong. To check the battery, briefly touch the ground clip to the probe; if the light glows brightly the battery is strong enough for testing. Never use a self-powered test light to perform checks for opens or shorts when power is applied to the electrical system under test. The 12 volt vehicle power will quickly burn out the 1.5 volt light bulb in the test light.*

Voltmeter

A voltmeter is used to measure voltage at any point in a circuit, or to measure the voltage drop across any part of a circuit. It can also be used to check continuity in a wire or circuit by indicating current flow from one end to the other. Voltmeters usually have various scales on the meter dial and a selector switch to allow the selection of different voltages. The voltmeter has a positive and a negative lead. To avoid damage to the meter, always connect the negative lead to the negative (-) side of circuit (to ground or nearest the ground side of the circuit) and connect the positive lead to the positive (+) side of the circuit (to the power source or the nearest power source). Note that the negative voltmeter lead will always be black and that the positive voltmeter will always be some color other than black (usually red). Depending on how the voltmeter is connected into the circuit, it has several uses.

A voltmeter can be connected either in parallel or in series with a circuit and it has a very high resistance to current flow. When connected in parallel, only a small amount of current will flow through the voltmeter current path; the rest will flow through the normal circuit current path and the circuit will work normally. When the voltmeter is connected in series with a circuit, only a small amount of current can flow through the circuit. The circuit will not work properly, but the voltmeter reading will show if the circuit is complete or not.

Available Voltage Measurement

Set the voltmeter selector switch to the 20V position and connect the meter negative lead to the negative post of the battery. Connect the positive meter lead to the positive post of the battery and turn the ignition switch ON to provide a load. Read the voltage on the meter or digital display. A well charged battery should register over 12 volts. If the meter reads below 11.5 volts, the battery power may be insufficient to operate the electrical system properly. This test determines voltage available from the battery and should be the first step in any electrical trouble diagnosis procedure. Many electrical problems, especially on computer controlled systems, can be caused by a low state of charge in the battery. Excessive corrosion at the battery cable terminals can cause a poor contact that will prevent proper charging and full battery current flow.

Normal battery voltage is 12 volts when fully charged. When the battery is supplying current to one or more circuits it is said to be "under load". When everything is off the electrical system is under a "no-load" condition. A fully charged battery may show about 12.5 volts at no load; will drop to 12 volts under medium load; and will drop even lower under heavy load. If the battery is partially discharged the voltage decrease under heavy load may be excessive, even though the battery shows 12 volts or more at no load. When allowed to discharge further, the battery's available voltage under load will decrease more severely. For this reason, it is important that the battery be fully charged during all testing procedures to avoid errors in diagnosis and incorrect test results.

Voltage Drop

When current flows through a resistance, the voltage beyond the resistance is reduced (the larger the current, the greater the reduction in voltage). When no current is flowing, there is no voltage drop because there is no current flow. All points in the circuit which are connected to the power source are at the same voltage as the power source. The total voltage drop always equals the total source voltage. In a long circuit with many connectors, a series of small, unwanted voltage drops due to corrosion at the connectors can add up to a total loss of voltage which impairs the operation of the normal loads in the circuit.

INDIRECT COMPUTATION OF VOLTAGE DROPS

1. Set the voltmeter selector switch to the 20 volt position.

2. Connect the meter negative lead to a good ground.

3. Probe all resistances in the circuit with the positive meter lead.

4. Operate the circuit in all modes and observe the voltage readings.

DIRECT MEASUREMENT OF VOLTAGE DROPS

1. Set the voltmeter switch to the 20 volt position.

2. Connect the voltmeter negative lead to the ground side of the resistance load to be measured.

3. Connect the positive lead to the positive side of the resistance or load to be measured.

4. Read the voltage drop directly on the 20 volt scale.

Too high a voltage indicates too high a resistance. If, for example, a blower motor runs too slowly, you can determine if there is too high a resistance in the resistor pack. By taking voltage drop readings in all parts of the circuit, you can isolate the problem. Too low a voltage drop indicates too low a resistance. If, for example, a blower motor runs too fast in the MED and/or LOW position, the problem can be isolated in the resistor pack by taking voltage drop readings in all parts of the circuit to locate a possibly shorted resistor. The maximum allowable voltage drop under load is critical, especially if there is more than one high resistance problem in a circuit because all voltage drops are cumulative. A small drop is normal due to the resistance of the conductors.

HIGH RESISTANCE TESTING

1. Set the voltmeter selector switch to the 4 volt position.

2. Connect the voltmeter positive lead to the positive post of the battery.

3. Turn on the headlights and heater blower to provide a load.

4. Probe various points in the circuit with the negative voltmeter lead.

5. Read the voltage drop on the 4 volt scale. Some average maximum allowable voltage drops are:

FUSE PANEL—7 volts
IGNITION SWITCH—5volts
HEADLIGHT SWITCH—7 volts
IGNITION COIL (+)—5 volts
ANY OTHER LOAD—1.3 volts
NOTE: *Voltage drops are all measured while a load is operating; without current flow, there will be no voltage drop.*

Ohmmeter

The ohmmeter is designed to read resistance (ohms) in a circuit or component. Although there are several different styles of ohmmeters, all will usually have a selector switch which permits the measurement of different ranges of re-

sistance (usually the selector switch allows the multiplication of the meter reading by 10, 100, 1000, and 10,000). A calibration knob allows the meter to be set at zero for accurate measurement. Since all ohmmeters are powered by an internal battery (usually 9 volts), the ohmmeter can be used as a self-powered test light. When the ohmmeter is connected, current from the ohmmeter flows through the circuit or component being tested. Since the ohmmeter's internal resistance and voltage are known values, the amount of current flow through the meter depends on the resistance of the circuit or component being tested.

The ohmmeter can be used to perform continuity test for opens or shorts (either by observation of the meter needle or as a self-powered test light), and to read actual resistance in a circuit. It should be noted that the ohmmeter is used to check the resistance of a component or wire while there is no voltage applied to the circuit. Current flow from an outside voltage source (such as the vehicle battery) can damage the ohmmeter, so the circuit or component should be isolated from the vehicle electrical system before any testing is done. Since the ohmmeter uses its own voltage source, either lead can be connected to any test point.

NOTE: *When checking diodes or other solid state components, the ohmmeter leads can only be connected one way in order to measure current flow in a single direction. Make sure the positive (+) and negative (-) terminal connections are as described in the test procedures to verify the one-way diode operation.*

In using the meter for making continuity checks, do not be concerned with the actual resistance readings. Zero resistance, or any resistance readings, indicate continuity in the circuit. Infinite resistance indicates an open in the circuit. A high resistance reading where there should be none indicates a problem in the circuit. Checks for short circuits are made in the same manner as checks for open circuits except that the circuit must be isolated from both power and normal ground. Infinite resistance indicates no continuity to ground, while zero resistance indicates a dead short to ground.

RESISTANCE MEASUREMENT

The batteries in an ohmmeter will weaken with age and temperature, so the ohmmeter must be calibrated or "zeroed" before taking measurements. To zero the meter, place the selector switch in its lowest range and touch the two ohmmeter leads together. Turn the calibration knob until the meter needle is exactly on zero.

NOTE: *All analog (needle) type ohmmeters*

must be zeroed before use, but some digital ohmmeter models are automatically calibrated when the switch is turned on. Self-calibrating digital ohmmeters do not have an adjusting knob, but its a good idea to check for a zero readout before use by touching the leads together. All computer controlled systems require the use of a digital ohmmeter with at least 10 meagohms impedance for testing. Before any test procedures are attempted, make sure the ohmmeter used is compatible with the electrical system or damage to the onboard computer could result.

To measure resistance, first isolate the circuit from the vehicle power source by disconnecting the battery cables or the harness connector. Make sure the key is OFF when disconnecting any components or the battery. Where necessary, also isolate at least one side of the circuit to be checked to avoid reading parallel resistances. Parallel circuit resistances will always give a lower reading than the actual resistance of either of the branches. When measuring the resistance of parallel circuits, the total resistance will always be lower than the smallest resistance in the circuit. Connect the meter leads to both sides of the circuit (wire or component) and read the actual measured ohms on the meter scale. Make sure the selector switch is set to the proper ohm scale for the circuit being tested to avoid misreading the ohmmeter test value.

CAUTION: *Never use an ohmmeter with power applied to the circuit. Like the self-powered test light, the ohmmeter is designed to operate on its own power supply. The normal 12 volt automotive electrical system current could damage the meter.*

Ammeters

An ammeter measures the amount of current flowing through a circuit in units called amperes or amps. Amperes are units of electron flow which indicate how fast the electrons are flowing through the circuit. Since Ohms Law dictates that current flow in a circuit is equal to the circuit voltage divided by the total circuit resistance, increasing voltage also increases the current level (amps). Likewise, any decrease in resistance will increase the amount of amps in a circuit. At normal operating voltage, most circuits have a characteristic amount of amperes, called "current draw" which can be measured using an ammeter. By referring to a specified current draw rating, measuring the amperes, and comparing the two values, one can determine what is happening within the circuit to aid in diagnosis. An open circuit, for example, will not allow any current to flow so the ammeter reading will be zero. More current flows

through a heavily loaded circuit or when the charging system is operating.

An ammeter is always connected in series with the circuit being tested. All of the current that normally flows through the circuit must also flow through the ammeter; if there is any other path for the current to follow, the ammeter reading will not be accurate. The ammeter itself has very little resistance to current flow and therefore will not affect the circuit, but it will measure current draw only when the circuit is closed and electricity is flowing. Excessive current draw can blow fuses and drain the battery, while a reduced current draw can cause motors to run slowly, lights to dim and other components to not operate properly. The ammeter can help diagnose these conditions by locating the cause of the high or low reading.

Multimeters

Different combinations of test meters can be built into a single unit designed for specific tests. Some of the more common combination test devices are known as Volt/Amp testers, Tach/Dwell meters, or Digital Multimeters. The Volt/Amp tester is used for charging system, starting system or battery tests and consists of a voltmeter, an ammeter and a variable resistance carbon pile. The voltmeter will usually have at least two ranges for use with 6, 12 and 24 volt systems. The ammeter also has more than one range for testing various levels of battery loads and starter current draw and the carbon pile can be adjusted to offer different amounts of resistance. The Volt/Amp tester has heavy leads to carry large amounts of current and many later models have an inductive ammeter pickup that clamps around the wire to simplify test connections. On some models, the ammeter also has a zero-center scale to allow testing of charging and starting systems without switching leads or polarity. A digital multimeter is a voltmeter, ammeter and ohmmeter combined in an instrument which gives a digital readout. These are often used when testing solid state circuits because of their high input impedance (usually 10 megohms or more).

The tach/dwell meter combines a tachometer and a dwell (cam angle) meter and is a specialized kind of voltmeter. The tachometer scale is marked to show engine speed in rpm and the dwell scale is marked to show degrees of distributor shaft rotation. In most electronic ignition systems, dwell is determined by the control unit, but the dwell meter can also be used to check the duty cycle (operation) of some electronic engine control systems. Some tach/dwell meters are powered by an internal battery, while others take their power from the car battery in use. The battery powered testers usually require calibration much like an ohmmeter before testing.

Special Test Equipment

A variety of diagnostic tools are available to help troubleshoot and repair computerized engine control systems. The most sophisticated of these devices are the console type engine analyzers that usually occupy a garage service bay, but there are several types of aftermarket electronic testers available that will allow quick circuit tests of the engine control system by plugging directly into a special connector located in the engine compartment or under the dashboard. Several tool and equipment manufacturers offer simple, hand held testers that measure various circuit voltage levels on command to check all system components for proper operation. Although these testers usually cost about $300-500, consider that the average computer control unit (or ECM) can cost just as much and the money saved by not replacing perfectly good sensors or components in an attempt to correct a problem could justify the purchase price of a special diagnostic tester the first time it's used.

These computerized testers can allow quick and easy test measurements while the engine is operating or while the car is being driven. In addition, the on-board computer memory can be read to access any stored trouble codes; in effect allowing the computer to tell you where it hurts and aid trouble diagnosis by pinpointing exactly which circuit or component is malfunctioning. In the same manner, repairs can be tested to make sure the problem has been corrected. The biggest advantage these special testers have is their relatively easy hookups that minimize or eliminate the chances of making the wrong connections and getting false voltage readings or damaging the computer accidentally.

NOTE: *It should be remembered that these testers check voltage levels in circuits; they don't detect mechanical problems or failed components if the circuit voltage falls within the preprogrammed limits stored in the tester PROM unit. Also, most of the hand held testers are designed to work only on one or two systems made by a specific manufacturer.*

A variety of aftermarket testers are available to help diagnose different computerized control systems. Owatonna Tool Company (OTC), for example, markets a device called the OTC Monitor which plugs directly into the assembly line diagnostic link (ALDL). The OTC tester makes diagnosis a simple matter of pressing the correct buttons and, by changing the internal PROM or inserting a different diagnosis cartridge, it will work on any model from full size to subcompact, over a wide range of years. An adapter is supplied with the tester to allow connection to all types of ALDL links, regardless of the number of pin terminals used. By inserting an updated PROM into the OTC tester, it can be easily updated to diagnose any new modifications of computerized control systems.

Wiring Harnesses

The average automobile contains about ½ mile of wiring, with hundreds of individual connections. To protect the many wires from damage and to keep them from becoming a confusing tangle, they are organized into bundles, enclosed in plastic or taped together and called wire harnesses. Different wiring harnesses serve different parts of the vehicle. Individual wires are color coded to help trace them through a harness where sections are hidden from view.

A loose or corroded connection or a replacement wire that is too small for the circuit will add extra resistance and an additional voltage drop to the circuit. A ten percent voltage drop can result in slow or erratic motor operation, for example, even though the circuit is complete. Automotive wiring or circuit conductors can be in any one of three forms:

1. Single strand wire
2. Multistrand wire
3. Printed circuitry

Single strand wire has a solid metal core and is usually used inside such components as alternators, motors, relays and other devices. Multistrand wire has a core made of many small strands of wire twisted together into a single conductor. Most of the wiring in an automotive electrical system is made up of multistrand wire, either as a single conductor or grouped together in a harness. All wiring is color coded on the insulator, either as a solid color or as a colored wire with an identification stripe. A printed circuit is a thin film of copper or other conductor that is printed on an insulator backing. Occasionally, a printed circuit is sandwiched between two sheets of plastic for more protection and flexibility. A complete printed circuit, consisting of conductors, insulating material and connectors for lamps or other components is called a printed circuit board. Printed circuitry is used in place of individual wires or harnesses in places where space is limited, such as behind instrument panels.

Wire Gauge

Since computer controlled automotive electrical systems are very sensitive to changes in resistance, the selection of properly sized wires is critical when systems are repaired. The wire gauge number is an expression of the cross section area of the conductor. The most common system for expressing wire size is the American Wire Gauge (AWG) system.

Wire cross section area is measured in circular mils. A mil is $\frac{1}{1000}''$ (0.001''); a circular mil is the area of a circle one mil in diameter. For example, a conductor ¼'' in diameter is 0.250 in. or 250 mils. The circular mil cross section area of the wire is 250 squared (250^2) or 62,500 circular mils. Imported car models usually use metric wire gauge designations, which is simply the cross section area of the conductor in square millimeters (mm^2).

Gauge numbers are assigned to conductors of various cross section areas. As gauge number increases, area decreases and the conductor becomes smaller. A 5 gauge conductor is smaller than a 1 gauge conductor and a 10 gauge is smaller than a 5 gauge. As the cross section area of a conductor decreases, resistance increases and so does the gauge number. A conductor with a higher gauge number will carry less current than a conductor with a lower gauge number.

NOTE: *Gauge wire size refers to the size of the conductor, not the size of the complete wire. It is possible to have two wires of the same gauge with different diameters because one may have thicker insulation than the other.*

12 volt automotive electrical systems generally use 10, 12, 14, 16 and 18 gauge wire. Main power distribution circuits and larger accessories usually use 10 and 12 gauge wire. Battery cables are usually 4 or 6 gauge, although 1 and 2 gauge wires are occasionally used. Wire length must also be considered when making repairs to a circuit. As conductor length increases, so does resistance. An 18 gauge wire, for example, can carry a 10 amp load for 10 feet without excessive voltage drop; however if a 15 foot wire is required for the same 10 amp load, it must be a 16 gauge wire.

An electrical schematic shows the electrical current paths when a circuit is operating properly. It is essential to understand how a circuit works before trying to figure out why it doesn't. Schematics break the entire electrical system down into individual circuits and show only one particular circuit. In a schematic, no attempt is made to represent wiring and components as they physically appear on the vehicle; switches and other components are shown as simply as possible. Face views of harness connectors show the cavity or terminal locations in all multi-pin connectors to help locate test points.

If you need to backprobe a connector while it is on the component, the order of the terminals must be mentally reversed. The wire color code can help in this situation, as well as a keyway, lock tab or other reference mark.

NOTE: *Wiring diagrams are not included in this book. As trucks have become more complex and available with longer option lists, wiring diagrams have grown in size and complexity. It has become almost impossible to provide a readable reproduction of a wiring diagram in a book this size. Information on ordering wiring diagrams from the vehicle manufacturer can be found in the owner's manual.*

WIRING REPAIR

Soldering is a quick, efficient method of joining metals permanently. Everyone who has the occasion to make wiring repairs should know how to solder. Electrical connections that are soldered are far less likely to come apart and will conduct electricity much better than connections that are only "pig-tailed" together. The most popular (and preferred) method of soldering is with an electrical soldering gun. Soldering irons are available in many sizes and wattage ratings. Irons with higher wattage ratings deliver higher temperatures and recover lost heat faster. A small soldering iron rated for no more than 50 watts is recommended, especially on electrical systems where excess heat can damage the components being soldered.

There are three ingredients necessary for successful soldering; proper flux, good solder and sufficient heat. A soldering flux is necessary to clean the metal of tarnish, prepare it for soldering and to enable the solder to spread into tiny crevices. When soldering, always use a resin flux or resin core solder which is non-corrosive and will not attract moisture once the job is finished. Other types of flux (acid core) will leave a residue that will attract moisture and cause the wires to corrode. Tin is a unique metal with a low melting point. In a molten state, it dissolves and alloys easily with many metals. Solder is made by mixing tin with lead. The most common proportions are 40/60, 50/50 and 60/40, with the percentage of tin listed first. Low priced solders usually contain less tin, making them very difficult for a beginner to use because more heat is required to melt the solder. A common solder is 40/60 which is well suited for all-around general use, but 60/40 melts easier, has more tin for a better joint and is preferred for electrical work.

Soldering Techniques

Successful soldering requires that the metals to be joined be heated to a temperature that will melt the solder—usually 360-460°F (182-238°C). Contrary to popular belief, the purpose of the soldering iron is not to melt the solder itself, but to heat the parts being soldered to a temperature high enough to melt the solder when it is touched to the work. Melting flux-cored solder on the soldering iron will usually destroy the effectiveness of the flux.

NOTE: *Soldering tips are made of copper for good heat conductivity, but must be "tinned" regularly for quick transference of heat to the project and to prevent the solder from sticking to the iron. To "tin" the iron, simply heat it and touch the flux-cored solder to the tip; the solder will flow over the hot tip. Wipe the excess off with a clean rag, but be careful as the iron will be hot.*

After some use, the tip may become pitted. If so, simply dress the tip smooth with a smooth file and "tin" the tip again. An old saying holds that "metals well cleaned are half soldered." Flux-cored solder will remove oxides but rust, bits of insulation and oil or grease must be removed with a wire brush or emery cloth. For maximum strength in soldered parts, the joint must start off clean and tight. Weak joints will result in gaps too wide for the solder to bridge.

If a separate soldering flux is used, it should be brushed or swabbed on only those areas that are to be soldered. Most solders contain a core of flux and separate fluxing is unnecessary. Hold the work to be soldered firmly. It is best to solder on a wooden board, because a metal vise will only rob the piece to be soldered of heat and make it difficult to melt the solder. Hold the soldering tip with the broadest face against the work to be soldered. Apply solder under the tip close to the work, using enough solder to give a heavy film between the iron and the piece being soldered, while moving slowly and making sure the solder melts properly. Keep the work level or the solder will run to the lowest part and favor the thicker parts, because these require more heat to melt the solder. If the soldering tip overheats (the solder coating on the face of the tip burns up), it should be retinned. Once the soldering is completed, let the soldered joint stand until cool. Tape and seal all soldered wire splices after the repair has cooled.

Wire Harness and Connectors

The on-board computer (ECM) wire harness electrically connects the control unit to the various solenoids, switches and sensors used by the control system. Most connectors in the engine compartment or otherwise exposed to the elements are protected against moisture and dirt which could create oxidation and deposits on the terminals. This protection is important because of the very low voltage and current levels used by the computer and sensors. All connectors have a lock which secures the male and female terminals together, with a secondary lock holding the seal and terminal into the connector. Both terminal locks must be released when disconnecting ECM connectors.

These special connectors are weather-proof and all repairs require the use of a special terminal and the tool required to service it. This tool is used to remove the pin and sleeve terminals. If removal is attempted with an ordinary pick, there is a good chance that the terminal will be bent or deformed. Unlike standard blade type terminals, these terminals cannot be straightened once they are bent. Make certain that the connectors are properly seated and all of the sealing rings in place when connecting leads. On some models, a hinge-type flap proides a backup or secondary locking feature for the terminals. Most secondary locks are used to improve the connector reliability by retaining the terminals if the small terminal lock tangs are not positioned properly.

Molded-on connectors require complete replacement of the connection. This means splicing a new connector assembly into the harness. All splices in on-board computer systems should be soldered to insure proper contact. Use care when probing the connections or replacing terminals in them as it is possible to short between opposite terminals. If this happens to the wrong terminal pair, it is possible to damage certain components. Always use jumper wires between connectors for circuit checking and never probe through weatherproof seals.

Open circuits are often difficult to locate by sight because corrosion or terminal misalignment are hidden by the connectors. Merely wiggling a connector on a sensor or in the wiring harness may correct the open circuit condition. This should always be considered when an open circuit or a failed sensor is indicated. Intermittent problems may also be caused by oxidized or loose connections. When using a circuit tester for diagnosis, always probe connections from the wire side. Be careful not to damage sealed connectors with test probes.

All wiring harnesses should be replaced with identical parts, using the same gauge wire and connectors. When signal wires are spliced into a harness, use wire with high temperature insulation only. With the low voltage and current levels found in the system, it is important that the best possible connection at all wire splices be made by soldering the splices together. It is seldom necessary to replace a complete harness. If replacement is necessary, pay close attention to insure proper harness routing. Secure the harness with suitable plastic wire clamps to prevent vibrations from causing the harness to wear in spots or contact any hot components.

NOTE: *Weatherproof connectors cannot be*

replaced with standard connectors. Instructions are provided with replacement connector and terminal packages. Some wire harnesses have mounting indicators (usually pieces of colored tape) to mark where the harness is to be secured.

In making wiring repairs, it's important that you always replace damaged wires with wires that are the same gauge as the wire being replaced. The heavier the wire, the smaller the gauge number. Wires are color-coded to aid in identification and whenever possible the same color coded wire should be used for replacement. A wire stripping and crimping tool is necessary to install solderless terminal connectors. Test all crimps by pulling on the wires; it should not be possible to pull the wires out of a good crimp.

Wires which are open, exposed or otherwise damaged are repaired by simple splicing. Where possible, if the wiring harness is accessible and the damaged place in the wire can be located, it is best to open the harness and check for all possible damage. In an inaccessible harness, the

Troubleshooting Basic Lighting Problems

Problem	Cause	Solution
Lights		
One or more lights don't work, but others do	· Defective bulb(s) · Blown fuse(s) · Dirty fuse clips or light sockets · Poor ground circuit	· Replace bulb(s) · Replace fuse(s) · Clean connections · Run ground wire from light socket housing to car frame
Lights burn out quickly	· Incorrect voltage regulator setting or defective regulator · Poor battery/alternator connections	· Replace voltage regulator · Check battery/alternator connections
Lights go dim	· Low/discharged battery · Alternator not charging · Corroded sockets or connections · Low voltage output	· Check battery · Check drive belt tension; repair or replace alternator · Clean bulb and socket contacts and connections · Replace voltage regulator
Lights flicker	· Loose connection · Poor ground · Circuit breaker operating (short circuit)	· Tighten all connections · Run ground wire from light housing to car frame · Check connections and look for bare wires
Lights "flare"—Some flare is normal on acceleration—if excessive, see "Lights Burn Out Quickly"	· High voltage setting	· Replace voltage regulator
Lights glare—approaching drivers are blinded	· Lights adjusted too high · Rear springs or shocks sagging · Rear tires soft	· Have headlights aimed · Check rear springs/shocks · Check/correct rear tire pressure
Turn Signals		
Turn signals don't work in either direction	· Blown fuse · Defective flasher · Loose connection	· Replace fuse · Replace flasher · Check/tighten all connections
Right (or left) turn signal only won't work	· Bulb burned out · Right (or left) indicator bulb burned out · Short circuit	· Replace bulb · Check/replace indicator bulb · Check/repair wiring
Flasher rate too slow or too fast	· Incorrect wattage bulb · Incorrect flasher	· Flasher bulb · Replace flasher (use a variable load flasher if you pull a trailer)
Indicator lights do not flash (burn steadily)	· Burned out bulb · Defective flasher	· Replace bulb · Replace flasher
Indicator lights do not light at all	· Burned out indicator bulb · Defective flasher	· Replace indicator bulb · Replace flasher

Troubleshooting Basic Turn Signal and Flasher Problems

Most problems in the turn signals or flasher system, can be reduced to defective flashers or bulbs, which are easily replaced. Occasionally, problems in the turn signals are traced to the switch in the steering column, which will require professional service.
F = Front   R = Rear   • = Lights off   ○ = Lights on

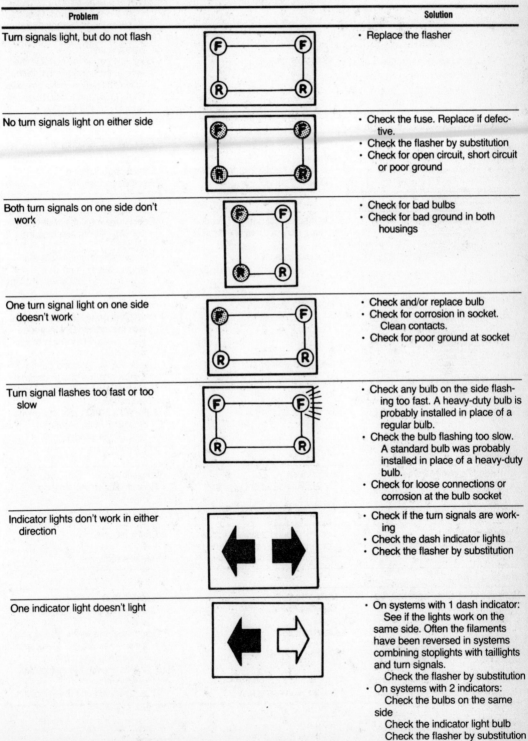

Problem	Solution
Turn signals light, but do not flash	• Replace the flasher
No turn signals light on either side	• Check the fuse. Replace if defective. • Check the flasher by substitution • Check for open circuit, short circuit or poor ground
Both turn signals on one side don't work	• Check for bad bulbs • Check for bad ground in both housings
One turn signal light on one side doesn't work	• Check and/or replace bulb • Check for corrosion in socket. Clean contacts. • Check for poor ground at socket
Turn signal flashes too fast or too slow	• Check any bulb on the side flashing too fast. A heavy-duty bulb is probably installed in place of a regular bulb. • Check the bulb flashing too slow. A standard bulb was probably installed in place of a heavy-duty bulb. • Check for loose connections or corrosion at the bulb socket
Indicator lights don't work in either direction	• Check if the turn signals are working • Check the dash indicator lights • Check the flasher by substitution
One indicator light doesn't light	• On systems with 1 dash indicator: See if the lights work on the same side. Often the filaments have been reversed in systems combining stoplights with taillights and turn signals. Check the flasher by substitution • On systems with 2 indicators: Check the bulbs on the same side Check the indicator light bulb Check the flasher by substitution

Troubleshooting Basic Dash Gauge Problems

Problem	Cause	Solution
Coolant Temperature Gauge		
Gauge reads erratically or not at all	· Loose or dirty connections · Defective sending unit	· Clean/tighten connections · Bi-metal gauge: remove the wire from the sending unit. Ground the wire for an instant. If the gauge registers, replace the sending unit.
	· Defective gauge	· Magnetic gauge: disconnect the wire at the sending unit. With ignition ON gauge should register COLD. Ground the wire; gauge should register HOT.
Ammeter Gauge—Turn Headlights ON (do not start engine). Note reaction		
Ammeter shows charge Ammeter shows discharge Ammeter does not move	· Connections reversed on gauge · Ammeter is OK · Loose connections or faulty wiring · Defective gauge	· Reinstall connections · Nothing · Check/correct wiring · Replace gauge
Oil Pressure Gauge		
Gauge does not register or is inaccurate	· On mechanical gauge, Bourdon tube may be bent or kinked	· Check tube for kinks or bends preventing oil from reaching the gauge
	· Low oil pressure	· Remove sending unit. Idle the engine briefly. If no oil flows from sending unit hole, problem is in engine.
	· Defective gauge	· Remove the wire from the sending unit and ground it for an instant with the ignition ON. A good gauge will go to the top of the scale.
	· Defective wiring	· Check the wiring to the gauge. If it's OK and the gauge doesn't register when grounded, replace the gauge.
	· Defective sending unit	· If the wiring is OK and the gauge functions when grounded, replace the sending unit
All Gauges		
All gauges do not operate	· Blown fuse · Defective instrument regulator	· Replace fuse · Replace instrument voltage regulator
All gauges read low or erratically	· Defective or dirty instrument voltage regulator	· Clean contacts or replace
All gauges pegged	· Loss of ground between instrument voltage regulator and car · Defective instrument regulator	· Check ground · Replace regulator
Warning Lights		
Light(s) do not come on when ignition is ON, but engine is not started	· Defective bulb · Defective wire	· Replace bulb · Check wire from light to sending unit
	· Defective sending unit	· Disconnect the wire from the sending unit and ground it. Replace the sending unit if the light comes on with the ignition ON.
Light comes on with engine running	· Problem in individual system · Defective sending unit	· Check system · Check sending unit (see above)

Troubleshooting the Heater

Problem	Cause	Solution
Blower motor will not turn at any speed	• Blown fuse • Loose connection • Defective ground • Faulty switch • Faulty motor • Faulty resistor	• Replace fuse • Inspect and tighten • Clean and tighten • Replace switch • Replace motor • Replace resistor
Blower motor turns at one speed only	• Faulty switch • Faulty resistor	• Replace switch • Replace resistor
Blower motor turns but does not circulate air	• Intake blocked • Fan not secured to the motor shaft	• Clean intake • Tighten security
Heater will not heat	• Coolant does not reach proper temperature • Heater core blocked internally • Heater core air-bound • Blend-air door not in proper position	• Check and replace thermostat if necessary • Flush or replace core if necessary • Purge air from core • Adjust cable
Heater will not defrost	• Control cable adjustment incorrect • Defroster hose damaged	• Adjust control cable • Replace defroster hose

Troubleshooting Basic Windshield Wiper Problems

Problem	Cause	Solution
Electric Wipers		
Wipers do not operate— Wiper motor heats up or hums	• Internal motor defect • Bent or damaged linkage • Arms improperly installed on linking pivots	• Replace motor • Repair or replace linkage • Position linkage in park and reinstall wiper arms
Wipers do not operate— No current to motor	• Fuse or circuit breaker blown • Loose, open or broken wiring • Defective switch • Defective or corroded terminals • No ground circuit for motor or switch	• Replace fuse or circuit breaker • Repair wiring and connections • Replace switch • Replace or clean terminals • Repair ground circuits
Wipers do not operate— Motor runs	• Linkage disconnected or broken	• Connect wiper linkage or replace broken linkage
Vacuum Wipers		
Wipers do not operate	• Control switch or cable inoperative • Loss of engine vacuum to wiper motor (broken hoses, low engine vacuum, defective vacuum/fuel pump) • Linkage broken or disconnected • Defective wiper motor	• Repair or replace switch or cable • Check vacuum lines, engine vacuum and fuel pump • Repair linkage • Replace wiper motor
Wipers stop on engine acceleration	• Leaking vacuum hoses • Dry windshield • Oversize wiper blades • Defective vacuum/fuel pump	• Repair or replace hoses • Wet windshield with washers • Replace with proper size wiper blades • Replace pump

wire must be bypassed with a new insert, usually taped to the outside of the old harness.

When replacing fusible links, be sure to use fusible link wire, NOT ordinary automotive wire. Make sure the fusible segment is of the same gauge and construction as the one being replaced and double the stripped end when crimping the terminal connector for a good contact. The melted (open) fusible link segment of the wiring harness should be cut off as close to the harness as possible, then a new segment spliced in as described. In the case of a damaged fusible link that feeds two harness wires, the harness connections should be replaced with two fusible link wires so that each circuit will have its own separate protection.

NOTE: *Most of the problems caused in the wiring harness are due to bad ground connections. Always check all vehicle ground connections for corrosion or looseness before performing any power feed checks to eliminate the chance of a bad ground affecting the circuit.*

Repairing Hard Shell Connectors

Unlike molded connectors, the terminal contacts in hard shell connectors can be replaced. Weatherproof hard-shell connectors with the leads molded into the shell have non-replaceable terminal ends. Replacement usually involves the use of a special terminal removal tool that depress the locking tangs (barbs) on the connector terminal and allow the connector to be removed from the rear of the shell. The connector shell should be replaced if it shows any evidence of burning, melting, cracks, or breaks. Replace individual terminals that are burnt, corroded, distorted or loose.

NOTE: *The insulation crimp must be tight to prevent the insulation from sliding back on the wire when the wire is pulled. The insulation must be visibly compressed under the crimp tabs, and the ends of the crimp should be turned in for a firm grip on the insulation.*

The wire crimp must be made with all wire strands inside the crimp. The terminal must be fully compressed on the wire strands with the ends of the crimp tabs turned in to make a firm grip on the wire. Check all connections with an ohmmeter to insure a good contact. There should be no measurable resistance between the wire and the terminal when connected.

Mechanical Test Equipment

Vacuum Gauge

Most gauges are graduated in inches of mercury (in.Hg), although a device called a manometer reads vacuum in inches of water (in. H_2O). The normal vacuum reading usually varies between 18 and 22 in.Hg at sea level. To test engine vacuum, the vacuum gauge must be connected to a source of manifold vacuum. Many engines have a plug in the intake manifold which can be removed and replaced with an adapter fitting. Connect the vacuum gauge to the fitting with a suitable rubber hose or, if no manifold plug is available, connect the vacuum gauge to any device using manifold vacuum, such as EGR valves, etc. The vacuum gauge can be used to determine if enough vacuum is reaching a component to allow its actuation.

Hand Vacuum Pump

Small, hand-held vacuum pumps come in a variety of designs. Most have a built-in vacuum gauge and allow the component to be tested without removing it from the vehicle. Operate the pump lever or plunger to apply the correct amount of vacuum required for the test specified in the diagnosis routines. The level of vacuum in inches of Mercury (in.Hg) is indicated on the pump gauge. For some testing, an additional vacuum gauge may be necessary.

Intake manifold vacuum is used to operate various systems and devices on late model vehicles. To correctly diagnose and solve problems in vacuum control systems, a vacuum source is necessary for testing. In some cases, vacuum can be taken from the intake manifold when the engine is running, but vacuum is normally provided by a hand vacuum pump. These hand vacuum pumps have a built-in vacuum gauge that allow testing while the device is still attached to the component. For some tests, an additional vacuum gauge may be necessary.

HEATING AND AIR CONDITIONING

Heater Core
Non-Air Conditioned Cars
REMOVAL AND INSTALLATION
Mustang and Capri

It is not necessary to remove the heater case for access to the heater core.

1. Drain enough coolant from the radiator to drain the heater core.

CAUTION: *When draining the coolant, keep in mind that cats and dogs are attracted by the ethylene glycol antifreeze, and are quite likely to drink any that is left in an uncovered container or in puddles on the ground. This will prove fatal in sufficient quantity. Always drain the coolant into a sealable container. Coolant should be reused unless it is contaminated or several years old.*

2. Loosen the heater hose clamps on the engine side of the firewall and disconnect the heater hoses. Cap the heater core tubes.
3. Remove the glove box lines.
4. Remove the instrument panel-to-cowl brace retaining screws and remove the brace.
5. Move the temperature lever to **WARM**.
6. Remove the heater core cover screws. Remove the cover through the glove box.
7. Loosen the heater case mounting nuts on the engine side of the firewall.
8. Push the heater core tubes and seals toward the interior of the car to loosen the core.

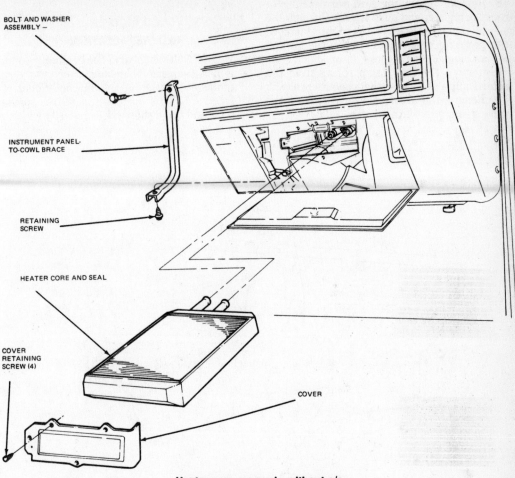

BOLT AND WASHER
ASSEMBLY —

INSTRUMENT PANEL-
TO-COWL BRACE

RETAINING
SCREW

HEATER CORE AND SEAL

COVER
RETAINING
SCREW (4)

COVER

Heater core removal—without a/c

9. Remove the heater core through the glove box opening.

10. Service these components as necessary, installation is the reverse of removal.

Blower Motor
Non-Air Conditioned Models
REMOVAL AND INSTALLATION

Mustang and Capri

The right side ventilator assembly must be removed for access to the blower motor and wheel.

1. Remove the retaining screw from the right register duct mounting bracket.

2. Remove the screws holding the control cable lever assembly to the instrument panel.

3. Remove the glove box liner.

4. Remove the plastic rivets securing the grille to the floor outlet, and remove the grille.

5. Remove the right register duct and register assembly:

a. Remove the register duct bracket retaining screw on the lower edge of the instrument panel, and disengage the duct from the opening and remove them through the glove box opening.

b. Insert a thin blade under the retaining tab and pry the tab toward the louvers until retaining tab pivot clears the hole in the register opening. Pull the register assembly end out from the housing only enough to prevent the pivot from going back into the pivot hole. Pry the other retaining tab loose and remove the register assembly from the opening.

6. Remove the retaining screws securing the ventilator assembly to the blower housing. The upper right screw can be reached with a long extension through the register opening; the upper left screw can be reached through the glove box opening. The other two screws are on the bottom of the assembly.

7. Slide the assembly to the right, then down and out from under the instrument panel.

8. Remove the motor lead wire connector from the register and push it back through the hole in the case. Remove the right side cowl trim panel for access, and remove the ground terminal lug retaining screw.

9. Remove the hub clamp spring from the motor shaft and remove the blower wheel.

10. Remove the blower motor bolts from the housing and remove the motor.

Heater Core
Air Conditioned Models
REMOVAL AND INSTALLATION

WARNING: Removal of the heater/air conditioner (evaporator) housing, if necessary, requires evacuation of the air conditioner refrigerant. This operation requires special tools and and a thorough familiarity with au-

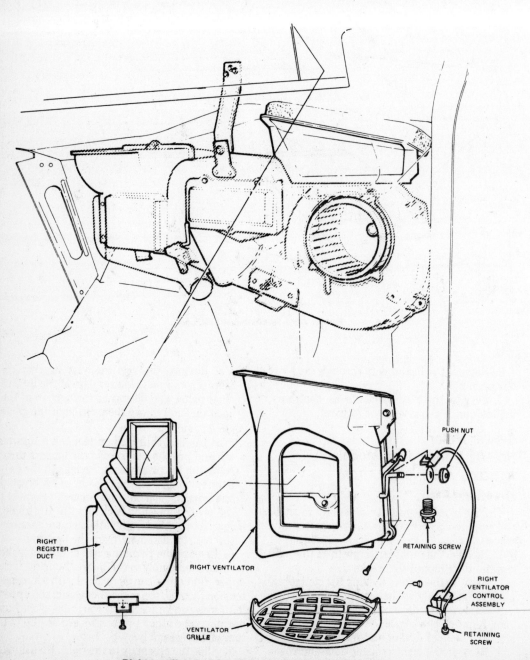

RIGHT REGISTER DUCT

RIGHT VENTILATOR

VENTILATOR GRILLE

PUSH NUT

RETAINING SCREW

RIGHT VENTILATOR CONTROL ASSEMBLY

RETAINING SCREW

Right ventilator and register duct removal—without a/c

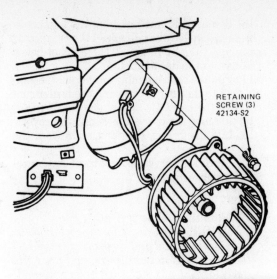

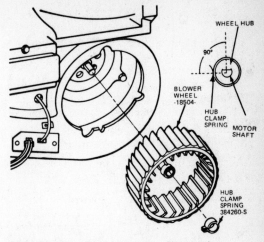

Blower motor wheel removal—without a/c

Blower motor and wheel assembly removal—without a/c

tomotive refrigerant systems. Failure to follow proper safety precautions may cause personal injury. If you are not familiar with these systems, it is recommended that discharging and charging of the A/C system be performed by an experienced professional mechanic. For discharging, evacuating and charging procedures, see Chapter 1.

Mustang and Capri

The instrument panel must be removed for access to the heater core.

1. Disconnect the battery ground cable.
2. Remove the instrument panel pad:
   a. Remove the screws attaching the instrument cluster trim panel to the pad.
   b. Remove the screw attaching the pad to the panel at each defroster opening.
   c. Remove the screws attaching the edge of the pad to the panel.
3. Remove the steering column opening cover.
4. Remove the nuts and bracket retaining the steering column to the instrument panel and lay the column against the seat.

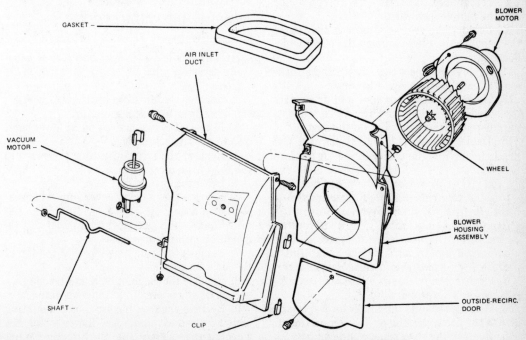

Air inlet duct and blower housing (disassembled)—with a/c

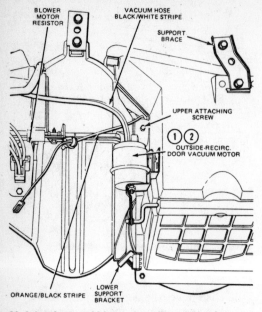

Air inlet duct and blower housing—with a/c

5. Remove the instrument panel to brake pedal support screw at the column opening.

6. Remove the screws attaching the lower brace to the panel below the radio, and below the glove box.

7. Disconnect the temperature cable from the door and case bracket.

8. Unplug the 7-port vacuum hose connectors at the evaporator case.

9. Disconnect the resistor wire connector and the blower feed wire.

10. Remove the screws attaching the top of the panel to the cowl. Support the panel while doing this.

11. Remove the one screw at each end attaching the panel to the cowl side panels.

12. Move the panel rearward and disconnect the speedometer cable and any wires preventing the panel from lying flat on the seat.

13. Drain the coolant and disconnect the heater hoses from the heater core. Plug the core tubes.

CAUTION: *When draining the coolant, keep in mind that cats and dogs are attracted by the ethylene glycol antifreeze, and are quite likely to drink any that is left in an uncovered container or in puddles on the ground. This will prove fatal in sufficient quantity. Always drain the coolant into a sealable container. Coolant should be reused unless it is contaminated or several years old.*

14. Remove the nuts retaining the evaporator case to the firewall in the engine compartment.

15. Remove the case support bracket screws and air inlet duct support bracket.

16. Remove the nut retaining the bracket to the dash panel at the left side of the evaporator case, and the nut retaining the bracket below the case to the dash panel.

17. Pull the case assembly away from the panel to get to the screws retaining the heater core cover to the case.

18. Remove the cover screws and the cover.

19. Lift the heater core and seals from the evaporator case.

20. Service as required. Reinstall in the reverse order of removal.

Merkur

1. Drain the cooling system.

CAUTION: *When draining the coolant, keep in mind that cats and dogs are attracted by the ethylene glycol antifreeze, and are quite likely to drink any that is left in an uncovered container or in puddles on the ground. This will prove fatal in sufficient quantity. Always drain the coolant into a sealable container. Coolant should be reused unless it is contaminated or several years old.*

2. Disconnect the heater hoses at the core tubes in the engine compartment.

3. Place protective covers on the carpeting.

4. In the passenger compartment, remove the 2 core-to-case screws and pull the core out of the case.

5. Installation is the reverse of removal.

Blower Motor
Air Conditioned Models
REMOVAL AND INSTALLATION
Mustang and Capri

NOTE: *The air inlet duct and blower housing assembly must be remove for access to the blower motor.*

1. Remove the glove box liner and disconnect the hose from the vacuum motor.

2. Remove the instrument panel lower right side to cowl attaching bolt.

3. Remove the screw attaching the brace to the top of the air inlet duct.

4. Disconnect the motor wire.

5. Remove the housing lower support bracket to case nut.

6. Remove the side cowl trim panel and remove the ground wire screw.

7. Remove the attaching screw at the top of the air inlet duct.

8. Remove the air inlet duct and housing assembly down an away from the evaporator case.

9. Remove the four blower motor mounting plate screws and remove the blower motor and wheel as an assembly from the housing. Do not remove the mounting plate from the motor.

Evaporator

REMOVAL AND INSTALLATION

Mustang and Capri

1. Discharge the system at the service access port on the underside of the combination valve. See Chapter 1.

2. Remove the instrument panel and lay it on the front seat.

3. Drain the cooling system and disconnect the heater hoses at the core tubes.

CAUTION: *When draining the coolant, keep in mind that cats and dogs are attracted by the ethylene glycol antifreeze, and are quite likely to drink any that is left in an uncovered container or in puddles on the ground. This will prove fatal in sufficient quantity. Always drain the coolant into a sealable container.*

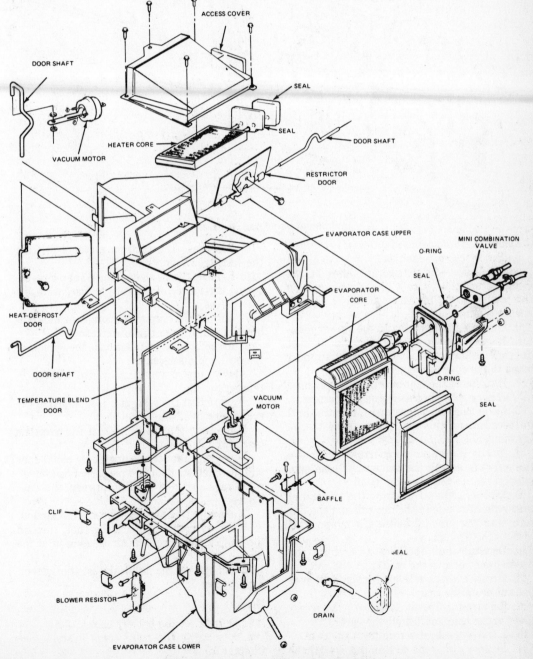

Evaporator case assembly—disassembled

INSTRUMENT
PANEL PAD —

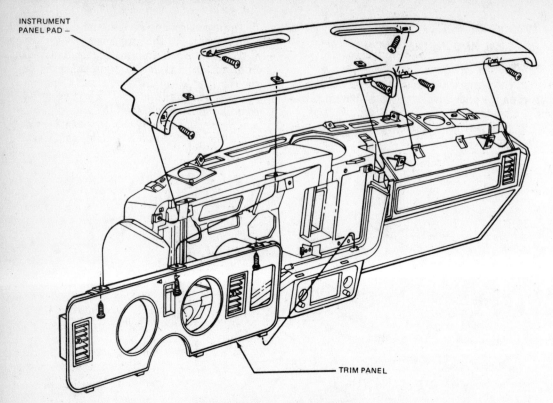

TRIM PANEL

Instrument panel pad removal

Coolant should be reused unless it is contaminated or several years old.

4. Disconnect the refrigerant lines at the combination valve. Use a back-up wrench on the suction throttling valve manifold. Cap all openings immediately!.

5. Disconnect the wiring at the blower resistor. Remove the screw attaching the air inlet duct and blower housing assembly support brace to the cowl top panel.

6. Disconnect the black vacuum supply hose at the check valve, in the engine compartment.

7. In the engine compartment, remove the 2 nuts retaining the evaporator case to the firewall.

8. In the passenger compartment, remove the screw attaching the evaporator case support bracket to the cowl top panel.

9. Remove the nut retaining the left end of the evaporator case to the firewall and the nut retaining the bracket below the evaporator case, to the dash panel.

10. Carefully pull the case away from the firewall and remove the case from the car.

11. Remove the air inlet duct and blower housing from the case.

12. Remove the 5 screws retaining the access cover to the case and lift off the cover.

13. Remove the heater core from the case.

14. Remove the 2 nuts retaining the restrictor door vacuum motor to the mounting bracket.

15. Disengage the vacuum motor arm from the restrictor door.

16. Remove the 11 screws and 6 snap-clips securing the halves of the case and separate the case halves.

17. Lift out the evaporator core, seal and combination valve from the lower case half.

18. Assembly and installation is the reverse of removal and disassembly.

Always use new O-rings coated with clean refrigerant oil.

Be sure that the restrictor is installed in the evaporator inlet line.

Make sure that the core seal fits over the case lower half edge.

Make sure that the temperature blend door and heat/defrost door are properly positioned.

Always use new sealer between the case halves.

Make sure that the drain hose is not kinked.

When everything is back together, turn on the blower and check for air leaks around the case.

Evacuate, charge and leak test the system. See Chapter 1.

Merkur

1. Disconnect the battery cables.

2. Discharge the refrigerant system. See Chapter 1.

3. Remove the engine valve cover.

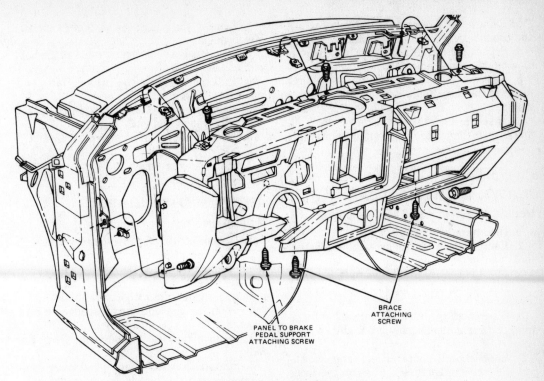

BRACE
ATTACHING
SCREW

PANEL TO BRAKE
PEDAL SUPPORT
ATTACHING SCREW

Instrument panel removal

4. Remove the cowl insulator cover.

5. Pull the water valve out of its retaining clip and remove the clip.

6. Remove the battery shield.

7. Remove the EGR valve.

8. Remove the air conditioning hose plate and seal from the firewall.

9. Disconnect the wiring harness at the partition.

10. Unbolt the refrigerant lines at the expansion valve (#30 Torx® bolt).

11. Disconnect the suction and liquid lines from the valve. Cap all openings at once.

12. Remove the weatherstripping at the upper edge of the partition.

13. Remove the partition.

14. Remove the right and left drainage valves.

15. Disconnect the deicing switch wiring.

16. Disconnect the evaporator ground wire.

17. Remove the evaporator-to-firewall screws.

18. Remove the cowl grille panel.

19. Disconnect the wiper linkage at the wiper motor arm.

20. Slide the evaporator case upward and forward out of the engine compartment.

To install:

21. Position the evaporator case in the engine compartment.

22. Connect the wiper linkage at the wiper motor arm.

23. Install the cowl grille panel.

24. Install the evaporator-to-firewall screws.

25. Connect the evaporator ground wire.

26. Connect the deicing switch wiring.

27. Install the right and left drainage valves.

28. Install the partition.

29. Install the weatherstripping at the upper edge of the partition.

30. Connect the suction and liquid lines from the valve.

31. Secure the refrigerant lines at the expansion valve (#30 Torx® bolt).

32. Connect the wiring harness at the partition.

33. Install the air conditioning hose plate and seal at the firewall.

34. Install the EGR valve.

35. Install the battery shield.

36. Install the water valve and clip.

37. Install the cowl insulator cover.

38. Install the engine valve cover.

39. Evacuate, charge and leak test the refrigerant system. See Chapter 1.

40. Connect the battery cables.

Evaporator Core/Blower Motor

REMOVAL AND INSTALLATION

Merkur

1. Remove the evaporator case.

2. Remove the 3 access cover retaining screws and pry open the cover.

3. Remove the 2 screws on the blower scrolls and the 2 deice thermostat screws.

4. Separate the evaporator case halves by removing the connecting clips.

5. Remove the screw retaining the blower motor to the case. Remove the core and blower motor.

6. Installation is the reverse of removal. Make sure that the deice switch is properly positioned.

Control Panel

REMOVAL AND INSTALLATION

Mustang and Capri without Air Conditioning

1. Disconnect the battery ground.
2. Remove the 4 control assembly-to-instrument panel screws.
3. Pull the control panel towards you.
4. Disconnect the wiring from the panel connectors.
5. Disconnect the vacuum harness and the temperature control cable from the control panel.
6. Installation is the reverse of removal. Adjust the cables as necessary. Push on the vacuum harness retaining nut, DO NOT TRY TO SCREW IT ON!

Mustang and Capri with Air Conditioning

1. Disconnect the battery ground.
2. Remove the instrument cluster trim panel (3 screws).
3. Disconnect the temperature cable at the evaporator case.
4. Remove the 4 screws attaching the control panel to the instrument panel.
5. Pull the control panel from the instrument panel.
6. Remove the pushnut retaining the cable to the control arm and disconnect the cable.
7. Disconnect the wire connectors from the control panel.
8. Remove the pushnuts retaining the vacuum harness to the control panel and pull off the vacuum harness.
9. Installation is the reverse of removal. Adjust the cable as necessary.

Merkur

1. Disconnect the battery ground cable.
2. Remove the steering column shroud halves.
3. Remove the instrument cluster.
4. Remove the console.
5. Remove the left side cowl trim panel.
6. Pull off the fan switch and bezel.
7. Disconnect the glove compartment light and cigar lighter.
8. Remove the left lower dash panel.

9. Remove the passenger side lower instrument panel.

10. Disconnect the 2 control cable at the bottom of the heater.

11. Pull the hoses off the vacuum valve and remove the 3 control unit screws.

12. Push the control unit through the panel and pull it down and out.

13. Installation is the reverse of removal.

RADIO

REMOVAL AND INSTALLATION

Mustang and Capri

1. Disconnect the negative battery cable.
2. Disconnect the electrical, speaker, and antenna leads from the radio.
3. Remove the knobs, discs, and control shaft nuts and washers from the radio shafts.
4. Remove the ash tray receptacle and bracket.
5. Remove the rear support nut from the radio.
6. Remove the instrument panel lower reinforcement and the heater or air conditioning floor ducts.
7. Remove the radio fro the rear support, and drop the radio down and out from behind the instrument panel.
8. To install, reverse the removal procedure.

Merkur

1. Disconnect the battery ground.
2. Insert 2 radio removing tools, T85M-19061-A, into the sides of the radio access holes until they click into position.
3. Apply an outward pressure to release the locking tangs and slide the radio from the dash.
4. Disconnect the wiring.
5. Installation is the reverse of removal.

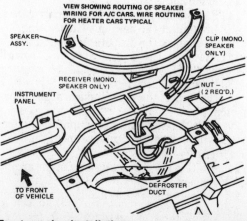

Front speaker installation

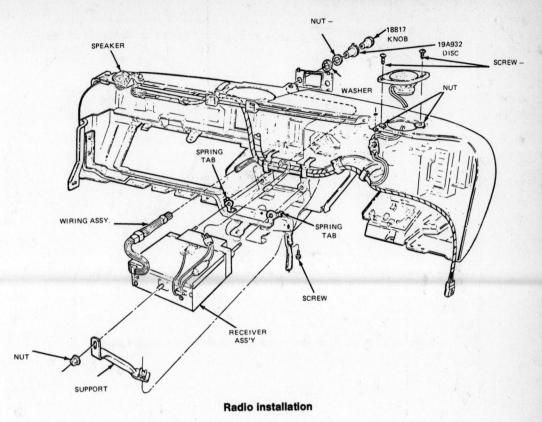

Radio installation

WINDSHIELD WIPERS

Motor
REMOVAL AND INSTALLATION
Mustang and Capri

1. Remove the retaining clip and disconnect the linkage from the motor arm.

2. Remove the 3 motor mounting screws and lower the motor away from the left underside of the instrument panel.

3. Disconnect the wiring and remove the motor.

4. Installation is the reverse of removal.

Merkur

1. Turn the wipers on and when the blades are at the vertical position, turn the key off.

2. Remove the wiper arms.

3. Disconnect the battery ground.

4. Remove the locknut from the motor shaft and remove the arm from the shaft.

5. Remove the 3 mounting bolts and remove the motor. Disconnect the wiring.

6. Installation is the reverse of removal. Torque the motor mounting bolts to 108 in. lbs.; the motor arm locknut to 15 ft. lbs.

Linkage
REMOVAL AND INSTALLATION
Mustang and Capri

1. Disconnect the battery ground.

2. Remove the cowl top grille attaching screws and the grille.

3. Remove the clip and ddisconnect the linkage arm from the motor crank pin.

4. Remove the 2 bolts retaining the right pivot shaft to the cowl, and remove the large nut, washer and spacer from the left pivot shaft.

5. Installation is the reverse of removal. Before installing the arms, make sure that the motor is in the PARK position. Install the arms so that the blade parks 1.8-3.0″ above the lower moulding on the driver's side and 2.3-3.5″ above the moulding on the passenger's side.

Merkur

1. Disconnect the battery ground.

2. Remove the wiper arms.

3. Disconnect the washer hoses.

4. Remove the cowl top panel.

5. Remove the bolts securing the wiper motor bracket to the body.

6. Remove the linkage and wiper motor.

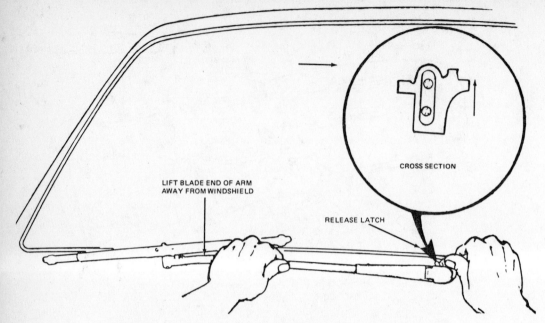

CROSS SECTION

LIFT BLADE END OF ARM
AWAY FROM WINDSHIELD

RELEASE LATCH

Installation of the wiper arm and blade assembly to the pivot shaft

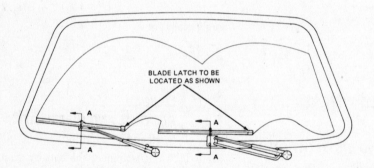

BLADE LATCH TO BE
LOCATED AS SHOWN

A

A

A

A

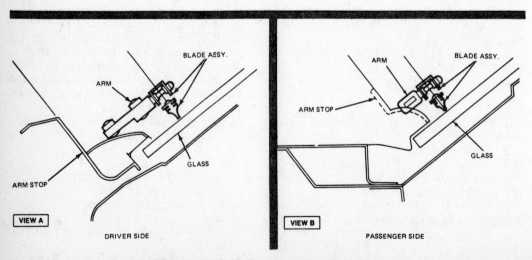

BLADE ASSY.

ARM

BLADE ASSY.

ARM

ARM STOP

ARM STOP

GLASS

GLASS

VIEW A

VIEW B

ARM STOP

DRIVER SIDE

PASSENGER SIDE

Wiper arm and blade assembly—adjustment

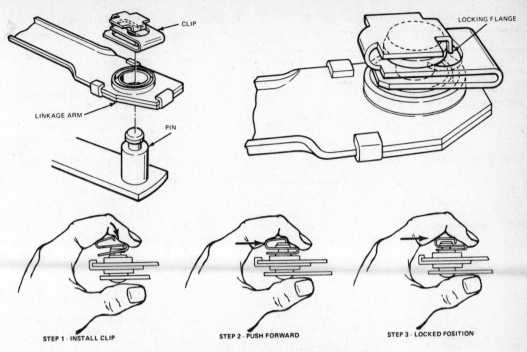

Installation of the wiper arm connecting clips

7. Remove the nut holding the motor arm to the motor and remove the arm from the shaft.

8. Remove the 3 bolts securing the motor to the bracket and separate the motor from the linkage.

9. Installation is the reverse of removal. Torque the motor mounting bolts to 108 in. lbs.; The arm locknut to 15 ft. lbs.

Rear Wiper Motor and Linkage
REMOVAL AND INSTALLATION

Merkur

1. Turn the ignition switch OFF.
2. Pull the wiper arm from the pivot shaft.
3. Remove the pivot shaft nut and spacers.
4. Open the hatch and remove the inner trim panel.
5. Disconnect the wiper motor wiring.
6. Remove the motor and bracket attaching screws and remove the motor.
7. Installation is the reverse of removal.

INSTRUMENTS AND SWITCHES

Instrument Cluster
REMOVAL AND INSTALLATION

WARNING: *Extreme care must be exercised during the removal and installation of the instrument cluster and dash components to avoid damage or breakage. Wooden paddles should be used to separate dash components, if required. Tape or cover dash areas that may be damaged by the removal and installation of the dash components.*

During the removal and installation procedures, slight variations may be required from the general outline, to facilitate the removal and installation of the instrument panel and cluster components, due to slight changes from model year to model year.

Mustang and Capri

1. Disconnect the battery ground cable.
2. Remove the 3 upper retaining screws from the cluster trim cover and remove the cover.
3. Remove the 2 upper and 2 lower screws retaining the cluster to the instrument panel.
4. Pull the cluster away from the panel and disconnect the speedometer cable and wiring connectors.
5. Remove the cluster.
6. Installation is the reverse of removal.

Merkur

1. Remove the upper steering column shroud.
2. Remove the instrument panel illumination control and intermittant wiper control rheostats.
3. Remove the 4 bezel retaining screws and remove the bezel.

Troubleshooting Electrical—Instruments and Accessories

Condition	Possible Cause	Resolution
Cigar lighter—knob pops out before adequate heating	• Defective element • Defective socket	• Replace element • Replace socket
Cigar lighter—element stays in, won't heat up	• Fuse burnt out • Open in wiring • Defective socket • Defective element	• Replace fuse. If fuse blows again, check for short circuit • Service wiring • Replace socket • Replace element
Clock does not work	• Fuse burnt out • Open in wiring • Defective clock	• Replace fuse. If fuse blows again, check for short circuit • Service wiring • Replace clock
Horn sounds continuously— vehicles without speed control	• Short circuit between column disconnect and horn(s) • Short circuit in switch or column wiring	• Service as required • Service as required
Horn sounds continuously— vehicles with speed control	• Short circuit between horn relay disconnect and horn • Grounded circuit between horn switch and horn relay • Open horn switch • Defective horn relay	• Service as required • Service as required • Replace horn switch • Replace horn relay
Horn(s) inoperative	• Fuse or C.B. burnt out • Poor horn ground • Horns out of adjustment • Defective horn • Open in wiring • Defective horn switch • Defective turn signal switch and wiring • Defective horn relay	• Replace fuse or C.B. If fuse or C.B. goes again, check for short circuit • Assure a good ground • Adjust horn • Replace horn • Service wiring • Replace horn switch • Service or replace turn signal switch and wiring • Replace horn relay
Gauge inoperative—(temp., fuel, oil pressure)	• Poor sending unit ground • Defective sending unit • Open in wiring • Open IVR • Defective gauge	• Assure good ground • Replace sending unit • Repair wiring • Replace IVR • Replace gauge
Gauge inaccurate—(temp., fuel, oil pressure)	• Defective sending unit • Defective IVR • Loose wiring	• Replace sending unit • Replace IVR • Service wiring
Oil pressure light does not go out with ignition switch on (engine running)	• Short circuit between bulb and switch • Defective switch • Low oil pressure	• Service as necessary • Replace switch • Refer to engine diagnosis section in Volume II
Oil pressure light does not light with ignition key in start or run position. (engine not running)	• Bulb burnt out • Defective sending unit • Burnt fuse • Open in wiring	• Replace bulb • Check continuity of switch unit. Check ground. Service or replace as required • Replace fuse. If fuse blows again check for short circuit • Service wiring
Hot temperature warning light does not go out (engine running) • Defective ignition switch	• Defective sending unit • Short circuit	• Replace switch unit • Check circuit to ignition prove out terminal. Service as required • Check continuity of ignition switch prove out circuit. Replace as necessary
Hot temperature warning light does not light with engine cranking	• Fuse burnt out	• Replace fuse. If fuse blows again, check for short circuit

Troubleshooting Electrical—Instruments and Accessories (cont.)

Condition	Possible Cause	Resolution
Hot temperature wrning light does not light when engine cranking (cont.) • Defective ignition switch	• Bulb burnt out • Open in wiring • Engine overheats	• Replace bulb • Check circuit to ignition prove out terminal. Service as required. • Replace ignition switch
"Engine" light does not come on with ignition switch in "run" or "start" (engine not running)	• Fuse burnt out • Defective oil pressure sending unit • Bulb burnt out • Open in wiring	• Replace fuse. If fuse blows again, check for short circuit • Replace switch unit • Replace bulb • Service wiring as required
"Engine" warning light does not go out with ignition switch on (engine running)	• Grounded circuit between bulb and switches • Defective switches • Engine problem	• Service as required • Replace switches • Refer to engine diagnosis section for engine overheating or low oil pressure in Volume II
Key warning buzzer sounds when driver door is opened with key not in ignition lock cylinder	• Short in key warning switch • Short in wiring	• Service or replace key warning switch as necessary • Service as required
Key warning buzzer inoperative	• Fuse burnt out • Drivers door courtesy light switch defective • Defective buzzer • Open in wiring • Defective key warning switch	• Replace fuse. If fuse blows again, check for short circuit • Replace switch • Replace buzzer • Service wiring • Replace key warning switch
"Headlights on" buzzer inoperative	• Improperly installed relay and wiring connections • Open circuit, short circuit or faulty connection • Improper relay ground • Defective relay	• Check and service as required • Service as required • Assure relay ground • Replace relay
Speedometer noisy	• Improper cable connection or routing • Binding sensor • Cable core kinked, burred or bent • Damaged driven gear • Defective speedometer	• Check for proper cable connections at head. Check cable for kinks or bends. Service or replace as required. • Check sensor for binding, erratic or noisy operation. Lube or replace sensor • Lube and replace as required • Replace driven gear • Replace speedometer head
Speedometer/odometer inoperative	• Cable disconnected • Cable broken • Binding in sensor and/or speedometer	• Connect cable • Replace cable • Replace sensor or speedometer
Speedometer/odometer inaccurate	• Incorrect driven gear • Incorrect drive gear • Faulty speedometer	• Check speedometer and odometer over a measured mile. Check proper cable driven gear to match axle ratio and tire size. Replace gear. • Check for proper drive gear for axle ratio and tire size. Replace gear. • Replace speedometer
Ignition switch—improper operation	• Binding lock cylinder • Binding ignition switch • Ignition slide switch out of adjustment • Open in wiring • Inoperative ignition switch	• Service or replace lock cylinder • Replace switch • Adjust slide switch • Service wiring • Replace switch (see Chapter 8)

4. Remove the 4 screws retaining the cluster to the panel and pull the cluster towards you.

5. Disconnect the speedometer cable and wiring

6. Installation is the reverse of removal.

Windshield Wiper Switch
REMOVAL & INSTALLATION
Mustang and Capri

1. Disconnect the negative battery cable.

2. Remove the split steering column cover retaining screws.

3. Separate the two halves and remove the wiper switch retaining screws.

4. Disconnect the wire connector and remove the wiper switch.

5. The installation of the wiper switch is the reverse of the removal procedure.

Merkur

1. Disconnect the battery ground cable.

2. Remove the upper and lower steering column shrouds.

3. Remove the 2 phillips screws and remove the switch from the column. Disconnect the wiring.

4. Installation is the reverse of removal.

Headlight Switch
REMOVAL AND INSTALLATION
Mustang and Capri

1. Disengage the 2 locking tabs on the left side of the switch by pushing the tabs in with a small screwdriver and pulling on the paddles.

2. Using a screwdriver, pry the right side of the switch out of the instrument panel.

3. Pull the switch completely out of the panel and disconnect the wiring.

4. Installation is the reverse of removal.

Merkur

1. Disconnect the battery ground cable.

2. Remove the upper and lower steering column shroud halves.

3. Remove the 2 screws securing the multi-switch to the steering column, disconnect the wiring connector and remove the switch.

4. Installation is the reverse of removal.

Instrument Panel
REMOVAL AND INSTALLATION
Mustang and Capri

1. Disconnect the battery ground.

2. In the engine compartment, disconnect all main wiring harness-to-instrument panel connectors.

3. Remove the rubber grommet from the firewall and feed all the wiring into the passenger compartment.

4. Remove the headlamp switch.

5. Remove the steering column extension shroud.

6. Remove the steering column cover.

7. Remove the 6 steering column support nuts and lower the column to the floor.

8. Remove the floor console.

9. Snap out the defroster grille.

10. Remove the screws from the speaker covers and snap them out.

11. Remove the 4 screws retaining the steering column reinforcement opening.

12. Remove the right and left side cowl panels.

13. Remove the cowl side retaining bolts.

14. Open the glove compartment door and bend the bin tabs inward. Let the door drop.

15. Remove the brake pedal support nut.

16. Remove the 5 cowl top screw attachments.

17. Gently push the instrument panel away from the cowl. Disconnect the air conditioning controls and wire connectors.

To install:

18. Position the panel in the car.

19. Install the 5 cowl top screw attachments.

20. Install the brake pedal support nut.

21. Assemble the glove compartment.

22. Install the cowl side retaining bolts.

23. Install the right and left side cowl panels.

24. Install the 4 screws retaining the steering column reinforcement opening.

25. Install the the speaker covers.

26. Install the defroster grille.

27. Install the floor console.

28. Install the steering column.

29. Install the steering column cover.

30. Install the steering column extension shroud.

31. Install the headlamp switch.

32. Install the wiring and rubber grommet in the firewall.

33. In the engine compartment, connect all main wiring harness-to-instrument panel connectors.

34. Connect the battery ground.

Floor Console
REMOVAL AND INSTALLATION
Mustang and Capri

1. Snap out the 2 access covers at the rear of the console to gain access to the armrest retaining bolts.

2. Remove the 4 armrest-to-floor bracket retaining bolts and snap out the armrest.

3. Snap out the shift lever opening finish panel. On cars with a manual transmission, the shift boot is attached to the bottom of the finish

panel. Remove the shift knob and slide the boot and finish panel.

4. To remove the top finish panel, position the emergency brake lever in the UP position. Remove the 4 retaining screws and lift the panel up. Disconnect the wiring.

5. Remove the 2 console-to-rear floor bracket retaining screws.

6. Insert a small screwdriver into the 2 notches at the bottom of the front upper finish panel and snap it out.

7. There are 3 combinations of radio cover finish panels:

    a. Radio opening cover plate with storage bin. Pry the finish cover out of the console.

    b. Radio storage bin. Remove the radio.

    c. Radio with graphic equalizer. Remove the radio.

8. Open the glove compartment door and remove the glove compartment assembly.

9. Remove the remote fuel filler door switch, if so equipped.

10. Remove the 2 console-to-panel screws.

11. Remove the 4 console-to-bracket screws.

12. Remove the console.

To install:

13. Install the console.

14. Install the 4 console-to-bracket screws.

15. Install the 2 console-to-panel screws.

16. Install the remote fuel filler door switch, if so equipped.

17. Install the glove compartment assembly.

18. Install the radio or cover panel.

19. Install the front upper finish panel.

20. Install the 2 console-to-rear floor bracket retaining screws.

21. Install the top finish panel. Connect the wiring.

22. Install the shift lever opening finish panel.

23. Install the shift knob and slide the boot and finish panel.

24. Install the armrest.

Speedometer Cable

REMOVAL AND INSTALLATION

NOTE: *Depending on year and model, some dash panels or the instrument cluster may require removal to gain access to the rear of the speedometer.*

1. Reach up behind the speedometer and depress the flat, quick-disconnect tab, while pulling back on the cable.

2. If the inner cable is broken, raise and support the car and remove the cable-to-transmission clamp and pull the cable from the transmission.

3. Pull the core from the cable.

4. Installation is the reverse of removal. Lu-

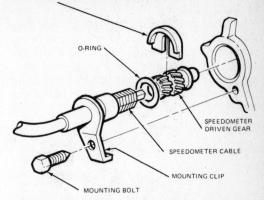

SPEEDOMETER DRIVEN GEAR RETAINER

O-RING

SPEEDOMETER DRIVEN GEAR

SPEEDOMETER CABLE

MOUNTING CLIP

MOUNTING BOLT

Speedometer cable to transmission mounting

bricate the core with speedometer cable lubricant prior to installation.

LIGHTING

Headlights

REMOVAL AND INSTALLATION

All Except Aerodynamic Headlamps

1. If the car is equipped with moveable headlamp covers, close the bypass valve to raise the headlamp covers. The valve is located in the vacuum lines near the reservoir and left fender.

2. On cars without moveable headlamp doors, remove the headlamp door retaining screws and remove the doors.

3. Remove the headlamp trim mounting screws and remove the trim.

4. Remove the retaining ring screws and remove the retaining ring from the headlamp. Pull the headlamp out and unplug it.

4. Installation is the reverse of removal.

Aerodynamic Headlamps

BULB ASSEMBLY

CAUTION: *The halogen bulb contains pressurized gas. If the bulb is dropped or scratched it will shatter. Also, avoid touching the bulb glass with your bare fingers. Grasp the bulb only by its plastic base. Oil from bare skin will cause hot spots on the glass surface and lead to premature burnout. If you do touch the glass, clean it prior to installation.*

1. Make sure that the headlamp switch is OFF.

2. Raise the hood. The bulb protrudes from the rear of the headlamp assembly.

3. Unplug the electrical connector from the bulb.

4. Rotate the bulb retaining ring ⅛ turn counterclockwise and remove it.

5. Pull the bulb straight back out of its socket. Don't rotate it.

6. When installing the bulb, push it into position, turning it slightly right or left to align the grooves in the forward part of the base with the tabs in the socket. When they are aligned, push the bulb firmly into position until the mounting flange on the base contacts the rear face of the socket.

7. Install the locking ring, turning it until a stop is felt.

8. Push the connector onto the bulb until it snaps into position.

HEADLAMP ASSEMBLY

1. Make sure that the headlamp switch is OFF.

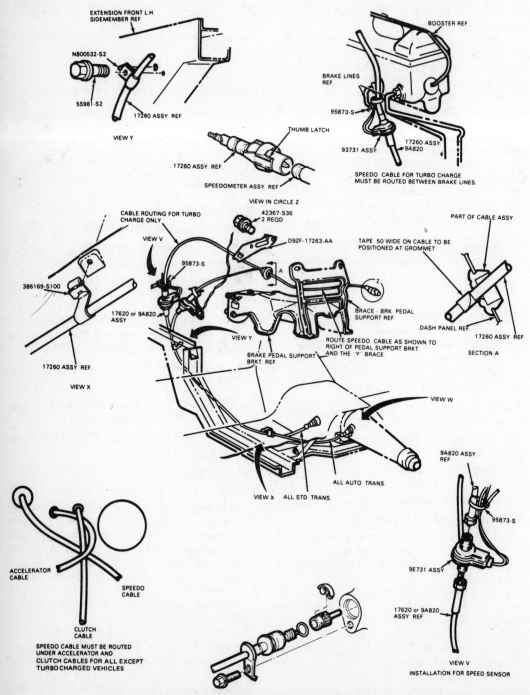

Speedometer cable and casing routing

2. Raise the hood. The bulb protrudes from the rear of the headlamp assembly.

3. Unplug the electrical connector from the bulb.

4. Remove the 3 nuts and washers from the rear of the headlamp.

5. Push forward on the headlamp at the bulb socket. It may be necessary to loosen the parking lamp and cornering lamp fasteners.

6. Remove the 3 clips which attach the headlamp to the black ring by prying them out from the base with a flat-bladed screwdriver.

7. Installation is the reverse of removal. Make sure that the black rubber shield is securely crimped on the headlamp.

Parking/Turn Signal Lights/Front Side Marker

REMOVAL AND INSTALLATION

Mustang and Capri

Reach behind the parking lamp body and remove the socket. Remove the bulb from the socket and insert a new one.

Rear Lamp/Rear Side Marker Lights

REMOVAL AND INSTALLATION

Mustang and Capri

From inside the trunk, remove the bulb socket from the lamp body and replace the bulb.

Rear Lamp Bulbs

REMOVAL AND INSTALLATION

Merkur

1. Raise the liftgate.
2. Lift up the trim cover from the lower back panel.
3. Remove the bulb holder assembly by depressing the lock tab.
4. Remove the bulb.

Front and/or Rear Side Marker Bulbs

REPLACEMENT

Merkur

From under the car, twist the bulb holder counterclockwise and pull it out of the lamp. Replace the bulb.

Parking Lamp Bulb

REPLACEMENT

Merkur

The grille opening panel must be removed. See Chapter 10. Once the grille is off, replace the bulb.

Front Turn Signal Lamp

REMOVAL AND INSTALLATION

Merkur

1. Insert a thin, flat bladed prybar between the upper edge of the front turn signal lens and the bumper trim. Gently pry the release lever upwards to release the lamp assembly.
2. Remove the bulb holder from the lamp.
3. Remove the bulb by turning it counterclockwise.
4. Installation is the reverse of removal.

High-Mount Stop Lamp

REMOVAL AND INSTALLATION

Mustang and Capri 2-Door Coupe

1. Disconnect the wiring in the luggage compartment.
2. Remove the 2 protective caps from the lamp cover.
3. Remove the 2 screws from the sides of the lamp.
4. Remove the lamp. The bulbs can be removed by turning them counterclockwise.
5. Installation is the reverse of removal.

Mustang and Capri Hatchback

1. Remove the 2 screws from the lamp.
2. Lift up the lamp and pull off the strain clip.
3. Turn the bulbs counterclockwise to remove them.
4. Installation is the reverse of removal.

Mustang Convertible

1. Remove the luggage crossbar.
2. Remove the 2 lamp screws.
3. Lift up the lamp and pull off the strain clip.
4. Turn the bulbs counterclockwise to remove them.
5. Installation is the reverse of removal.

Merkur

1. Remove the 2 screws attaching the lamp to the spoiler.
2. Pry the bulb holder out of the lamp.
3. Remove the bulb by pulling it straight out of the holder.
4. Installation is the reverse of removal.

TRAILER WIRING

Wiring the car for towing is fairly easy. There are a number of good wiring kits available and these should be used, rather than trying to design your own. All trailers will need brake lights and turn signals as well as tail lights and side marker lights. Most states require extra marker lights for overwide trailers. Also, most states have recently required back-up lights for trailers, and most trailer manufacturers have been building trailers with back-up lights for several years.

Additionally, some Class I, most Class II and just about all Class III trailers will have electric brakes.

Add to this number an accessories wire, to operate trailer internal equipment or to charge the trailer's battery, and you can have as many as seven wires in the harness.

Determine the equipment on your trailer and buy the wiring kit necessary. The kit will contain all the wires needed, plus a plug adapter set which included the female plug, mounted on the bumper or hitch, and the male plug, wired into, or plugged into the trailer harness.

When installing the kit, follow the manufacturer's instructions. The color coding of the wires is standard throughout the industry.

One point to note, some domestic vehicles, and most imported vehicles, have separate turn signals. On most domestic vehicles, the brake lights and rear turn signals operate with the same bulb. For those vehicles with separate turn signals, you can purchase an isolation unit so that the brake lights won't blink whenever the turn signals are operated, or, you can go to your local electronics supply house and buy four diodes to wire in series with the brake and turn signal bulbs. Diodes will isolate the brake and turn signals. The choice is yours. The isolation units are simple and quick to install, but far more expensive than the diodes. The diodes, however, require more work to install properly, since they require the cutting of each bulb's wire and soldering in place of the diode.

One final point, the best kits are those with a spring loaded cover on the vehicle mounted socket. This cover prevents dirt and moisture from corroding the terminals. Never let the vehicle socket hang loosely. Always mount it securely to the bumper or hitch.

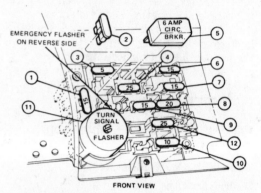

FRONT VIEW

1. Turn signal back-up lamps
   15 amp. fuse
2. Heater (std.) 15 amp. fuse
   air conditioning 30 amp. fuse
3. Instrument panel lamps 5 amp. fuse
4. Accessory-A/C clutch 25 amp. fuse
5. Windshield wiper/washer 6 amp.
   circuit breaker
6. Stop lamps-emergency warning
   amp. fuse
7. Courtesy lamps
   15 amp. fuse
8. Cigar lighter-horn
   20 amp. fuse
9. Radio 15 amp. fuse
10. Warning lamps
    10 amp. fuse
11. Turn signal flasher
12. Electric choke
    25 amp. fuse

Fuse and circuit breaker panel

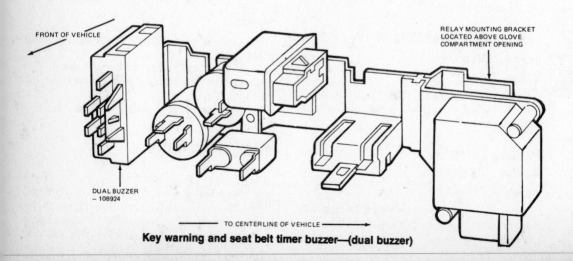

FRONT OF VEHICLE

RELAY MOUNTING BRACKET
LOCATED ABOVE GLOVE
COMPARTMENT OPENING

DUAL BUZZER
– 10B924

← TO CENTERLINE OF VEHICLE →

Key warning and seat belt timer buzzer—(dual buzzer)

REMOVE EXISTING VINYL TUBE SHIELDING
REINSTALL OVER FUSE LINK BEFORE CRIMPING
FUSE LINK TO WIRE ENDS

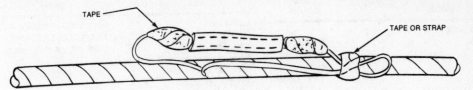

TAPE

TAPE OR STRAP

TYPICAL REPAIR USING THE SPECIAL #17 GA. (9.00″ LONG-YELLOW) FUSE LINK REQUIRED FOR THE AIR/COND.
CIRCUITS (2) #687E and #261A LOCATED IN THE ENGINE COMPARTMENT

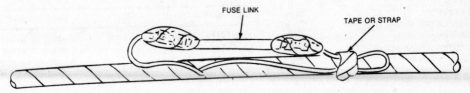

FUSE LINK

TAPE OR STRAP

TYPICAL REPAIR FOR ANY IN-LINE FUSE LINK USING THE SPECIFIED GAUGE FUSE LINK FOR THE SPECIFIC CIRCUIT

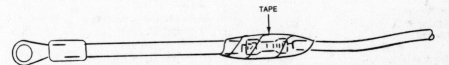

TAPE

TYPICAL REPAIR USING THE EYELET TERMINAL FUSE LINK OF THE SPECIFIED GAUGE FOR ATTACHMENT TO A CIRCUIT WIRE END

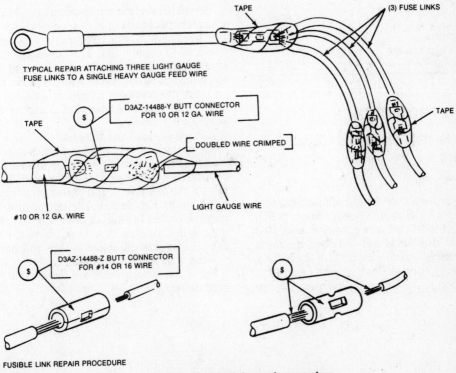

TAPE

(3) FUSE LINKS

TYPICAL REPAIR ATTACHING THREE LIGHT GAUGE
FUSE LINKS TO A SINGLE HEAVY GAUGE FEED WIRE

D3AZ-14488-Y BUTT CONNECTOR
FOR 10 OR 12 GA. WIRE

TAPE

DOUBLED WIRE CRIMPED

TAPE

LIGHT GAUGE WIRE

#10 OR 12 GA. WIRE

D3AZ-14488-Z BUTT CONNECTOR
FOR #14 OR 16 WIRE

FUSIBLE LINK REPAIR PROCEDURE

General fusible link repair procedure

Light Bulb Specifications

Function	Trade Number
Exterior illumination	
Headlamps	H4656
	Low Beam
	H4651
	High Beam
Front park/Turn lamps	1157
Front side marker lamps	194
Rear tail/Stop lamps & turn	1157
License plate lamp	168
Back-up lamp	156
Interior illumination	
Turn signal indicator	194
Electric de-ice nomenclature (opt.)	**
Heater control nomenclature	161
A/C control nomenclature (opt.)	161
Glove compartment lamp (opt.)	1816
Courtesy lamp—under instrument panel (opt.)	N.A.
Ash tray lamp (opt.)	1892
Digital clock lamp (Opt.)	194
High beam indicator	194
Warning lamps	194
Gauge illumination—all	
Dome lamp (standard)	906
Dome/Map lamp (opt.): dome	906
map	1816
Trunk compartment lamp (opt.)	89
Engine compartment lamp (opt.)	89
Automatic transmission "PRND21" indicator (floor)	1893
Radio lamps	
Dial illumination	1893
AM, AM/FM	
AM/FM/MPX/Tape	
Premium sound indicator	
Stereo indicator lamp	

CIRCUIT PROTECTION

Fuses, Fusible Links and Circuit Breakers

LOCATION

A fuse link is a short length of insulated wire, integral with the engine compartment wiring harness. It is several wire gauges smaller than the circuit it protects and is located in-line directly from the positive terminal of the battery. When heavy current flows or when a short to ground occurs in the wiring harness, the fuse

Fusible Link Location

Fuse Link	GA	Location
Lamp feed	16	Near voltage regulator
Ignition feed	16	Near voltage regulator
Charging circuit	14	Near starter motor relay
Heated backlite and power door locks	16	Near starter motor relay
Engine compartment lamp	20	Near starter motor relay

Circuit Breaker Location

Location	Size	Circuit Protected
Part of headlight switch	22 amp.	Headlights, high-beam indicator
Fuse panel	6 amp.	Windshield wiper-washer system

link burns out and protects the alternator or wiring. Production fuse links are color coded:

a. 12 gauge: Grey.
b. 14 gauge: Dark Green.
c. 16 gauge: Black.
d. 18 gauge: Brown.
e. 20 gauge: Dark Blue.

NOTE: *Replacement fuse link color coding may vary from production fuse link color coding.*

Circuit breakers are used on certain electrical components requiring high amperage, such as the headlamp circuit, electrical seats and/or windows to name a few. The advantage of the circuit breaker is its ability to open and close the electrical circuit as the lead demands, rather than the necessity of a part replacement, should the circuit be opened with another protective device in line.

A fuse panel is used to house the numerous fuses protecting the various branches of the electrical system and is normally the most accessible. the mounting of the fuse panel is usually on the left side of the passenger compartment, under the dash, either on the side kick panel or on the firewall to the left of the steering column. Certain models will have the fuse panel exposed while other models will have it covered with a removable trim cover.

Fuses are simply snapped in and out for replacement.

UNDERSTANDING THE MANUAL TRANSMISSION AND CLUTCH

Because of the way an internal combustion engine breathes, it can produce torque, or twisting force, only within a narrow speed range. Most modern, overhead valve engines must turn at about 2,500 rpm to produce their peak torque. By 4,500 rpm they are producing so little torque that continued increases in engine speed produce no power increases.

The torque peak on overhead camshaft engines is, generally, much higher, but much narrower.

The manual transmission and clutch are employed to vary the relationship between engine speed and the speed of the wheels so that adequate engine power can be produced under all circumstances. The clutch allows engine torque to be applied to the transmission input shaft gradually, due to mechanical slippage. The car can, consequently, be started smoothly from a full stop.

The transmission changes the ratio between the rotating speeds of the engine and the wheels by the use of gears. 4-speed or 5-speed transmissions are most common. The lower gears allow full engine power to be applied to the rear wheels during acceleration at low speeds.

The clutch drive plate is a thin disc, the center of which is splined to the transmission input shaft. Both sides of the disc are covered with a layer of material which is similar to brake lining and which is capable of allowing slippage without roughness or excessive noise.

The clutch cover is bolted to the engine flywheel and incorporates a diaphragm spring which provides the pressure to engage the clutch. The cover also houses the pressure plate. The driven disc is sandwiched between the pressure plate and the smooth surface of the flywheel when the clutch pedal is released,

thus forcing it to turn at the same speed as the engine crankshaft.

The transmission contains a mainshaft which passes all the way through the transmission, from the clutch to the driveshaft. This shaft is separated at one point, so that front and rear portions can turn at different speeds.

Power is transmitted by a countershaft in the lower gears and reverse. The gears of the countershaft mesh with gears on the mainshaft, allowing power to be carried from one to the other. All the countershaft gears are integral with that shaft, while several of the mainshaft gears can either rotate independently of the shaft or be locked to it. Shifting from one gear to the next causes one of the gears to be freed from rotating with the shaft and locks another to it. Gears are locked and unlocked by internal dog clutches which slide between the center of the gear and the shaft. The forward gears usually employ synchronizers; friction members which smoothly bring gear and shaft to the same speed before the toothed dog clutches are engaged.

The clutch is operating properly if:

1. It will stall the engine when released with the vehicle held stationary.

2. The shift lever can be moved freely between first and reverse gears when the vehicle is stationary and the clutch disengaged.

A clutch pedal free-play adjustment is incorporated in the linkage. If there is about 1-2″ (25-50mm) of motion before the pedal begins to release the clutch, it is adjusted properly. Inadequate free-play wears all parts of the clutch releasing mechanisms and may cause slippage. Excessive free-play may cause inadequate release and hard shifting of gears.

Some clutches use a hydraulic system in place of mechanical linkage. If the clutch fails to release, fill the clutch master cylinder with fluid to the proper level and pump the clutch pedal to fill the system with fluid. Bleed the system in

Troubleshooting the Manual Transmission

Problem	Cause	Solution
Transmission shifts hard	• Clutch adjustment incorrect • Clutch linkage or cable binding • Shift rail binding	• Adjust clutch • Lubricate or repair as necessary • Check for mispositioned selector arm roll pin, loose cover bolts, worn shift rail bores, worn shift rail, distorted oil seal, or extension housing not aligned with case. Repair as necessary.
	• Internal bind in transmission caused by shift forks, selector plates, or synchronizer assemblies • Clutch housing misalignment • Incorrect lubricant • Block rings and/or cone seats worn	• Remove, dissemble and inspect transmission. Replace worn or damaged components as necessary. • Check runout at rear face of clutch housing • Drain and refill transmission • Blocking ring to gear clutch tooth face clearance must be 0.030 inch or greater. If clearance is correct it may still be necessary to inspect blocking rings and cone seats for excessive wear. Repair as necessary.
Gear clash when shifting from one gear to another	• Clutch adjustment incorrect • Clutch linkage or cable binding • Clutch housing misalignment • Lubricant level low or incorrect lubricant • Gearshift components, or synchronizer assemblies worn or damaged	• Adjust clutch • Lubricate or repair as necessary • Check runout at rear of clutch housing • Drain and refill transmission and check for lubricant leaks if level was low. Repair as necessary. • Remove, disassemble and inspect transmission. Replace worn or damaged components as necessary.
Transmission noisy	• Lubricant level low or incorrect lubricant • Clutch housing-to-engine, or transmission-to-clutch housing bolts loose • Dirt, chips, foreign material in transmission • Gearshift mechanism, transmission gears, or bearing components worn or damaged • Clutch housing misalignment	• Drain and refill transmission. If lubricant level was low, check for leaks and repair as necessary. • Check and correct bolt torque as necessary • Drain, flush, and refill transmission • Remove, disassemble and inspect transmission. Replace worn or damaged components as necessary. • Check runout at rear face of clutch housing
Jumps out of gear	• Clutch housing misalignment • Gearshift lever loose • Offset lever nylon insert worn or lever attaching nut loose • Gearshift mechanism, shift forks, selector plates, interlock plate, selector arm, shift rail, detent plugs, springs or shift cover worn or damaged • Clutch shaft or roller bearings worn or damaged	• Check runout at rear face of clutch housing • Check lever for worn fork. Tighten loose attaching bolts. • Remove gearshift lever and check for loose offset lever nut or worn insert. Repair or replace as necessary. • Remove, disassemble and inspect transmission cover assembly. Replace worn or damaged components as necessary. • Replace clutch shaft or roller bearings as necessary

Troubleshooting the Manual Transmission(cont.)

Problem	Cause	Solution
Jumps out of gear (cont.)	• Gear teeth worn or tapered, synchronizer assemblies worn or damaged, excessive end play caused by worn thrust washers or output shaft gears • Pilot bushing worn	• Remove, disassemble, and inspect transmission. Replace worn or damaged components as necessary. • Replace pilot bushing
Will not shift into one gear	• Gearshift selector plates, interlock plate, or selector arm, worn, damaged, or incorrectly assembled • Shift rail detent plunger worn, spring broken, or plug loose • Gearshift lever worn or damaged • Synchronizer sleeves or hubs, damaged or worn	• Remove, disassemble, and inspect transmission cover assembly. Repair or replace components as necessary. • Tighten plug or replace worn or damaged components as necessary • Replace gearshift lever • Remove, disassemble and inspect transmission. Replace worn or damaged components.
Locked in one gear—cannot be shifted out	• Shift rail(s) worn or broken, shifter fork bent, setscrew loose, center detent plug missing or worn • Broken gear teeth on countershaft gear, clutch shaft, or reverse idler gear Gearshift lever broken or worn, shift mechanism in cover incorrectly assembled or broken, worn damaged gear train components	• Inspect and replace worn or damaged parts • Inspect and replace damaged part • Disassemble transmission. Replace damaged parts or assemble correctly.

the same way as a brake system. If leaks are located, tighten loose connections or overhaul the master or slave cylinder as necessary.

MANUAL TRANSMISSION

Transmission

REMOVAL AND INSTALLATION

CAUTION: *The clutch driven disc contains asbestos, which has been determined to be a cancer causing agent. Never clean clutch surfaces with compressed air! Avoid inhaling any dust from any clutch surface! When cleaning clutch surfaces, use a commercially available brake cleaning fluid.*

Mustang and Capri

1. Disconnect and remove starter and dust ring, if the clutch is to be removed. Remove the boot retainer and shifter lever.

2. On models with the ET 4-speed transmission: working under the hood, remove the upper clutch housing-to-engine bolts.

3. Raise and safely support the car.

4. Matchmark the driveshaft and axle flange for reassembly. Disconnect the driveshaft at the rear universal joint and remove the driveshaft. Plug the extension housing.

5. Disconnect the speedometer cable at the transmission extension. Disconnect the seat belt sensor wires and the back-up lamp switch wires. Remove the clutch lever boot and cable on models so equipped.

6. Disconnect the gear shift rods from the transmission shift lever. If car is equipped with a 4-speed, remove the bolts that secure the shift control bracket to the extension housing. Support the engine with a jack.

7. Remove the bolt holding the extension housing to the rear support, and remove the muffler inlet pipe bracket-to-housing bolt.

8. Remove the two rear support bracket insulator nuts from the underside of the crossmember. Remove the crossmember.

9. Place a jack (equipped with a protective piece of wood) under the rear of the engine oil pan. Raise or lower the engine slightly as necessary to provide access to the bolts.

10. Remove the flywheel housing-to-engine bolts.

11. Slide the transmission back and out of the car. It may be necessary to slide the catalytic converter bracket forward to provide clearance on some models.

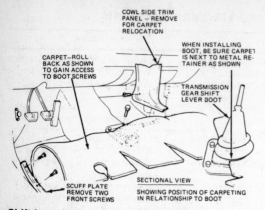

COWL SIDE TRIM PANEL — REMOVE FOR CARPET RELOCATION

WHEN INSTALLING BOOT, BE SURE CARPET IS NEXT TO METAL RETAINER AS SHOWN

CARPET — ROLL BACK AS SHOWN TO GAIN ACCESS TO BOOT SCREWS

TRANSMISSION GEAR SHIFT LEVER BOOT

SCUFF PLATE REMOVE TWO FRONT SCREWS

SECTIONAL VIEW

SHOWING POSITION OF CARPETING IN RELATIONSHIP TO BOOT

Shift lever boot removal—Model RAD

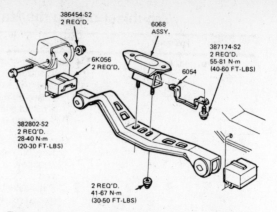

386454-S2 2 REQ'D.

6068 ASSY.

6K056 2 REQ'D.

387174-S2 2 REQ'D. 55-81 N·m (40-60 FT-LBS)

6054

382802-S2 2 REQ'D. 28-40 N·m (20-30 FT-LBS)

2 REQ'D. 41-67 N·m (30-50 FT-LBS)

Transmission crossmember—All four speeds

GEAR SHIFT LEVER

Removing or installing shift lever-Model RAD

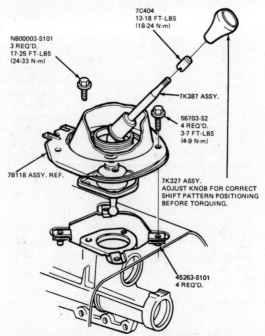

7C404 13-18 FT-LBS (18-24 N·m)

N800003-S101 3 REQ'D. 17-25 FT-LBS (24-33 N·m)

7K387 ASSY.

56703-S2 4 REQ'D. 3-7 FT-LBS (4-9 N·m)

7B118 ASSY. REF.

7K327 ASSY. ADJUST KNOB FOR CORRECT SHIFT PATTERN POSITIONING BEFORE TORQUING.

45263-S101 4 REQ'D.

Gearshift lever installation—Model 79ET, 80ET

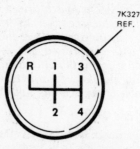

7K327 REF.

R 1 3

2 4

WITH LEVER IN NEUTRAL POSITION, INSTALL LOCKING NUT 7C404 UNTIL HAND TIGHT. THEN INSTALL KNOB 7K327 UNTIL HAND TIGHT. BACK KNOB OFF UNTIL SHIFT PATTERN ALIGNS WITH THE OF DRIVE LINE. TIGHTEN LOCKING NUT 13-18 FT-LBS (18-24 N·m) NO THREADS SHALL BE VISIBLE AFTER NUT HAS BEEN TIGHTENED. SHIFT PATTERN ALIGNMENT MUST BE WITHIN ± 15° OF OF DRIVE LINE.

Shift knob installation—Model 79ET, 80ET

12. To remove the clutch, remove the release lever retracting spring. Disconnect the pedal at the equalizer bar, or the clutch cable from the housing, as applicable.

13. Remove the bolts that secure the engine rear plate to the front lower part of the bellhousing.

14. Remove bolts that attach the bellhousing to the cylinder block and remove the housing and release lever as a unit. Remove the clutch release lever by pulling it through the window in the housing until the retainer spring disengages from the pivot.

15. Make sure the flywheel housing and engine block are clean. Any missing or damaged mounting dowels must be replaced. Install the flywheel housing and torque the attaching bolts to 38-61 ft. lbs. on all V8s, 38-55 ft. lbs. on 6-200s, and 28-38 ft. lbs. on 4-140 and 6-232s. Install the dust cover and torque the bolts to 17-20 ft. lbs.

16. Connect the release rod or cable and the retracting spring. Connect the pedal-to-equalizer rod at the equalizer bar.

17. Install starter and dust ring.

18. After moving the transmission back just far enough for the pilot shaft to clear the clutch housing, move it upward and into position on the flywheel housing. It may be necessary to put the transmission in gear and rotate the output shaft to align the input shaft and clutch splines.

19. Move the transmission forward and into place against the flywheel housing, and install the transmission attaching bolts finger-tight.

20. Tighten the transmission bolts to 37-42 ft. lbs. on all cars.

21. Install the crossmember and torque the mounting bolts to 20-30 ft. lbs. Slowly lower the engine onto the crossmember.

22. Torque the rear mount to 30-50 ft. lbs.

23. Connect the gear shift rods and the speedometer cable.

24. Remove the plug from the extension housing and install the driveshaft, aligning the marks made previously.

25. Refill transmission to proper level. On floorshift models, install the boot retainer and shift lever.

Merkur

1. Wedge a 7″ long block of wood under the clutch pedal to hold it in the fully up position. Propping it up in its above-normal position will disengage the clutch cable self-adjuster.

2. Disconnect the battery ground cable.

3. Raise and support the car on jackstands.

4. Remove the catalytic converter/inlet pipe assembly.

5. Matchmark and remove the driveshaft. Install a plug in the opening in the extension housing to keep the oil from running out.

6. Remove the starter.

7. Remove the front stabilizer bar U-brakets and the body stiffener rod.

8. Remove the transmission air baffle.

9. Position a block of wood between the stabilizer bar and the body side rail.

10. Support the transmission with a floor jack.

11. Remove the transmission-to-rear mount bolt.

12. Unbolt the rear mount from the body.

13. Loosen the engine mount nuts until just 2 or 3 threads are visible above the nut.

14. Place a block of wood on a jack, and jack up the front of the engine until the stud nuts on the engine mounts contact the crossmember. As the engine tilts downward, lower the transmission jack.

15. Disconnect the back-up switch wire.

16. Disconnect the neutral safety switch wire.

17. Unbolt and remove the shifter from the transmission extension housing. These are No.40 Torx® bolts.

18. Remove the snapring and pull the speedometer cable from the extension housing.

19. Remove the clutch release lever cover.

20. Pull rearward on the clutch cable and release it from the lever.

21. Remove the speedometer cable routing clips and position the cable out of the way.

22. Remove the flywheel cover plate.

23. Remove the upper bellhousing-to-engine bolts.

24. Remove the 4 remaining bellhousing-to-engine bolts.

25. Pull the transmission rearward until it clears the engine and lower it from the car.

To install:

26. Raise the transmission into position and push it forward until the input shaft splines enter the clutch driven disc and the bellhousing contacts the engine. You'll probably have to rock the transmission back and forth and/or up and down to get the input shaft to enter the clutch. Just be careful to avoid damage to the splines.

27. Install the bellhousing-to-engine bolts. Torque them to 35 ft. lbs.

28. Install the flywheel cover plate. Torque the bolt to 35 ft. lbs.

29. Remove the engine support jack. Raise the transmission support jack until the transmission is in its normal position.

30. Torque the engine mount nuts to 70 ft. lbs.

31. Install the shifter.

32. Connect the neutral safety switch wire.

33. Connect the back-up switch wire.

34. Install the speedometer cable.

35. Install the rear mount on the body. Torque the bolts to 35 ft. lbs.

36. Install the transmission-to-rear mount bolt. Torque the bolt to 70 ft. lbs.

37. Install the transmission air baffle.

38. Remove the block of wood from between the stabilizer bar and the body side rail.

39. Install the front stabilizer bar U-brakets and the body stiffener rod. Torque the bolts to 40 ft. lbs.

40. Connect the clutch cable to the release lever.

41. Install the clutch release lever cover.
42. Remove the transmission jack.
43. Install the starter.
44. Install the driveshaft.
45. Install the catalytic converter/inlet pipe assembly. Torque the inlet-to-turbocharger nuts to 35 ft. lbs.; the converter outlet nuts to 30 ft. lbs.
46. Lower the car.
47. Connect the battery ground cable.
48. Remove the block of wood from under the clutch pedal. Depress the pedal several times to adjust the clutch.

ET 4-Speed Overhaul

DISASSEMBLY

1. Remove the clutch release bearing and the lever, then detach the clutch housing.
2. Drain the lubricant, then remove the cover and the gasket from the case.
3. Remove the threaded plug, the spring and the shift rail detent plunger from the front of the case.
4. Drive the access plug from the rear of the case. Drive the interlock retaining pin from the case and remove the interlock plate.
5. Remove the roll pin from the selector lever arm.
6. Tap the front end of the shift rail, to displace the plug at the rear of the extension housing. Remove the shift rail from the rear of the extension housing.
7. Remove the selector arm and shift forks from the case.
8. Remove the extension housing attaching bolts. Loosen the extension housing and rotate the housing to align the countershaft with the cutaway in the extension housing flange.
9. Drive the countershaft rearward until the shaft clears the front of the case. Install a dummy shaft through the case and into the gear until the countershaft gear can be lowered to the bottom of the case. Remove the countershaft.
10. Remove the extension housing and mainshaft assembly from the case.
11. Remove the input shaft bearing retainer bolts, the bearing retainer and the input shaft from the case.
12. Remove the Reverse idler gear and shaft from the rear of the case.
13. Remove the bearing retainers, the bearings and the dummy shaft from the countershaft gear.
14. Remove the retainer and the pilot bearing from the input shaft gear.
15. Do not remove the ball bearing from the input shaft unless replacement is necessary. To remove it, take off the snapring and press the bearing off the shaft.

16. Pry the input shaft seal out of the bearing retainer.
17. Remove the 4th speed gear blocking ring from the front of the output shaft.
18. Remove the snapring from the forward end of the output shaft.
19. Support the 3rd speed gear (on press plates), the output shaft and the extension housing in a press. Push the output shaft out of the 3rd/4th synchronizer and the 3rd speed gear, while supporting the extension housing and the output shaft from beneath. Remove the snapring, the washer, the 2nd speed gear and the blocking ring from the output shaft.
20. Disassemble the synchronizer assembly by pulling the sleeve from the hub, then remove the inserts and spring.
21. Remove the output shaft bearing-to-extension housing snapring.
22. Using a plastic hammer, tap the output shaft assembly from the extension housing.
23. Measure or scribe the speedometer gear location on the output shaft and press the gear off.
24. Position press plates behind 1st speed gear and place the assembly in a press. The 1st/2nd synchronizer are serviced as an assembly.
   WARNING: *No attempt should be made to separate the hub from the shaft. The only serviceable parts are the springs and inserts. If the hub or sleeve is worn, the shaft and synchronizer must be replaced as an assembly.*
25. Using a 9/16" socket, drive the shift rail bushing from the rear of the extension housing. Do not remove serviceable bushings.
26. Pry the shift rail seal from the rear of the case.
27. Remove the remaining shift linkage from the case.

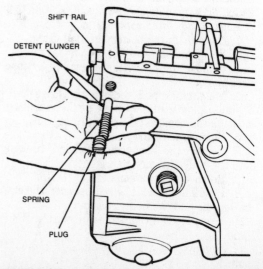

SHIFT RAIL

DETENT PLUNGER

SPRING

PLUG

82ET shift rail detent plunger

ASSEMBLY

1. Install a new shift rail seal in the rear of the case.

2. If the shift rail bushing was removed, drive a new one into position with a $^9/_{16}''$ socket.

3. Slide the synchronizer hub onto the shaft, making sure that the shift fork groove is facing the front of the shaft.

NOTE: *The sleeve and hub are select fit and must be assembled with the etched marks in the same relative locations.*

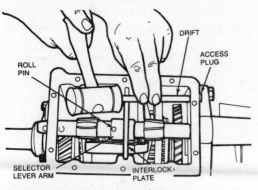

82ET interlock plate access plug

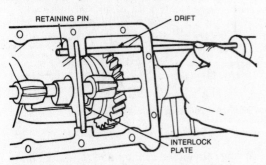

82ET interlock plate retaining pin removal

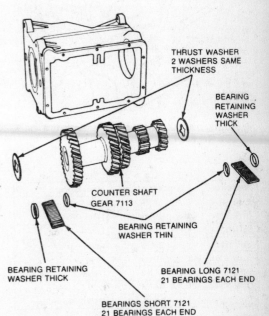

82ET countershaft disassembled

82ET input shaft disassembled

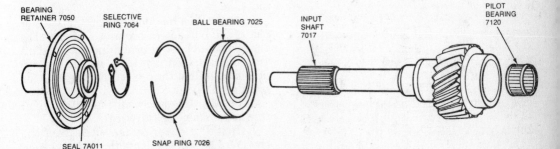

82ET output shaft disassembled

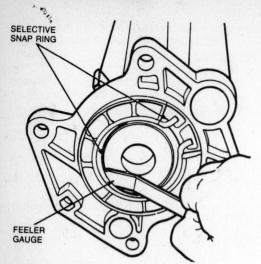

SELECTIVE
SNAP RING

FEELER
GAUGE

Measuring output shaft bearing snapring thickness on the 82ET

Part Number	Thickness (Inches)	Identification
D1FZ-7030-A	0.0679	Color Coded — Copper
D1FZ-7030-B	0.0689	Letter — W
D1FZ-7030-C	0.0699	Letter — V
D1FZ-7030-D	0.0709	Letter — U
D1FZ-7030-E	0.0719	None
D1FZ-7030-F	0.0728	Color Coded — Blue
D1FZ-7030-G	0.0738	Color Coded — Black
D1FZ-7030-H	0.0748	Color Coded — Brown

82ET output shaft bearing snapring thickness determination chart

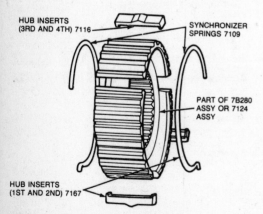

HUB INSERTS
(3RD AND 4TH) 7116

SYNCHRONIZER
SPRINGS 7109

PART OF 7B280
ASSY OR 7124
ASSY

HUB INSERTS
(1ST AND 2ND) 7167

82ET synchronizer spring installation

4. Locate an insert in each of three slots in the hub. Lubricate the parts and install an insert spring inside the sleeve; the spring tab must locate in a U-section of an insert. Fit the other spring to the opposite face, making sure that the tab locates in the same insert. Both

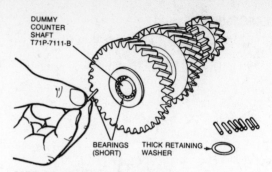

DUMMY
COUNTER
SHAFT
T71P-7111-B

BEARINGS
(SHORT)

THICK RETAINING
WASHER

82ET countershaft gear assembly

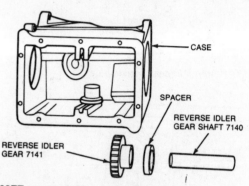

CASE

SPACER

REVERSE IDLER
GEAR SHAFT 7140

REVERSE IDLER
GEAR 7141

82ET reverse idler gear disassembled

springs should be in the same rotational direction. The tab end of one spring should be aligned with the tab of the spring on the opposite side.

5. Assemble a blocking ring on the 1st gear side of the 1st/2nd synchronizer. Lubricate the cone surface of 1st gear and the output shaft gear journals, then slide the cone onto the output shaft, so that the cone surface engages the blocking ring.

6. Position the spacer on the output shaft (the larger diameter rearward).

7. Install a snapring (selected from the chart) which will eliminate the end play from the output shaft bearing. Position the output shaft bearing on the shaft and press it into place. Secure the bearing with the thickest snapring that will fit the groove.

8. Slide the synchronizer onto the hub and locate an insert in each of three slots in the sleeve.

NOTE: *When installing the sleeve to the hub, the etched marks must be in the same relative locations.*

9. Lightly oil the parts and complete the assembly of the synchronizer by following the directions in previous Steps 3 and 4.

10. Position the 2nd speed gear and the blocking ring on the output shaft (the dog teeth must

face rearward. Install the washer and snapring, then position the 3rd speed gear onto the output shaft (the dog teeth must face forward). Lubricate the gear cones and assemble a blocking ring onto the 3rd gear cone.

11. Position the 3rd/4th synchronizer assembly on the output shaft (the hub boss must face forward).

12. Install the press plates against the boss on the synchronizer hub, then place the entire unit in a press (the extension end up) and press the synchronizer assembly onto the output shaft as far as possible.

13. Retain the 3rd/4th synchronizer assembly to the output shaft with a snapring. Pull up on the synchronizer so that the snapring is tight in the groove.

14. Lubricate the gear cone and place the blocking ring on the input shaft gear cone.

15. Press the speedometer drive gear onto the shaft to the marked location.

16. Lubricate the bearing bore of the extension housing. Install the output shaft in the housing; it may be necessary to tap the shaft while holding the synchronizer sleeves firmly. Secure the shaft to the housing with the snapring.

17. Press the bearing onto the input shaft; the snapring groove must face the front of the shaft (use the thickest snapring that will fit).

18. Slide the spacer and the dummy shaft into the countershaft gear. Position a thin bearing retaining washer on each end of the dummy shaft. Lubricate the roller bearings and install the long bearings in the small end of the gear and the short bearings in the long end of the gear (21 needle bearings are used at either end of the gear).

19. Place a thick retaining washer over each end of the dummy shaft. Grease the thrust washers and place one on each end of the dummy shaft, then lower the gear into the case.

CHILTON TIP: *When installing the thrust washers, the tabs must be in the same relative position to engage the slots in the case when the gear is lowered. Loop a piece of rope around each end of the gear and carefully install the gear and rope through the rear of the case.*

20. Lubricate the Reverse idler gear shaft. Position the selector lever relay on the pivot pin and secure with a spring clip. Hold the gear in the lever (with the long hub facing the rear of the case) and slide the Reverse idler shaft into place. Seat the shaft in the case with a brass hammer.

21. Install a new seal in the input shaft bearing retainer and the input shaft in the case with a new bearing retainer O-ring. Tap on the outer race of the bearing to seat the outer snapring.

WARNING: *Use a soft hammer and do not tap on the input shaft itself.*

22. Carefully slide the 3rd/4th synchronizer sleeve into the 4th speed position.

23. Place a new gasket on the extension housing.

24. Lubricate and install the input shaft pilot bearing on the shaft. Slide the extension housing and output shaft into place, being careful not to disturb the 3rd/4th synchronizer.

25. Align the cutaway in the extension housing flange with the countershaft bore in the rear of the case.

26. Move the countershaft gear into place and install the countershaft, making sure that the thrust washers remain in place. The flat on the countershaft should be parallel to the top of the case. Tap the shaft with a brass hammer until the front of the shaft is flush with the case.

27. Rotate the extension housing to align the bolt holes and loosely install the bolts. Apply sealer to the attaching bolts and torque to 33-36 ft. lbs.

NOTE: *When installing the extension housing-to-case, make sure that the rail slides freely in its bore. Binding is remedied by slightly rotating the extension housing to free the rail, then push the housing into the case.*

28. Place the shift forks in the synchronizer sleeves and install the interlock lever and new retaining pin. Lubricate the shift rail oil seal and slide the shift rail through the extension housing, the case and the 1st/2nd speed shift fork. Position the selector arm on the rail and slide the rail through the 3rd/4th shift fork. Slide the shift rail through the front of the case until the center detent bore is aligned with the detent plunger bore, then install a new retaining pin in the selector arm.

29. Install the detent plunger, the spring and the plug with sealer. Install a new access plug in the rear of the case. Position a new oil seal with a tension spring and lip facing in the direction of the case and drive the seal in until it bottoms.

30. Position a new O-ring in the groove in the case. Position the input shaft bearing retainer with the groove in the retainer aligned with the oil passage in the case and install the retaining bolts finger tight.

31. Install the flywheel housing, then torque the housing and the front bearing retainer bolts. Coat the retainer with grease.

32. Install the clutch release arm and the bearing.

33. Install a new extension housing plug, using sealer.

34. Install a new cover gasket and cover, with the vent facing the rear. Apply sealer to the left front cover attaching bolt and torque to 8-10 ft. lbs.

RAD 4-Speed Overhaul

TRANSMISSION CASE

Disassembly

1. Remove the lower extension housing bolt and drain the lubricant.

2. Drive the access plug from the rear of the extension housing. Remove the offset lever assembly nut and washer, then the lever assembly.

3. Remove the remaining extension housing bolts and washers, the extension from the case and discard the old gasket.

4. Remove the cover-to-case bolts, the cover, the shifter fork and the shift rod assembly, then discard the old cover gasket.

5. Remove the front bearing retainer-to-case bolts and washers, then the front bearing retainer and gasket.

6. Remove the Reverse lever assembly-to-pivot bolt spring clip, then the pivot and the Reverse lever assembly.

7. Remove the input bearing-to-input shaft snapring, the input bearing outer snapring and pull the bearing out.

8. Remove the speedometer drive gear-to-output shaft snapring, then slide the gear off and remove the lock ball from the shaft.

9. Remove the output shaft bearing-to-shaft snapring. Use the outer snapring to pull the output shaft bearing from the shaft and the case, then remove the snapring from the bearing.

10. Remove the input shaft through the front bearing hole in the case. Carefully lift the output shaft and gear train from the top of the case. Slide the Reverse idler gear shaft through the rear of the case and remove Reverse gear.

11. Insert a dummy shaft through the front of the case to drive the countershaft out through the rear of the case. Lift the countershaft gear, the thrust washers and the dummy shaft through the top of the case. Remove the cluster gear thrust washers.

12. Clean and inspect the parts. If the back up light switch is damaged, remove it.

Assembly

1. Position the Reverse idler gear and shaft in place.

2. Coat the surfaces of the countershaft thrust washers with a thin film of grease and position in the case (the plastic washer goes in front, the bronze one at the rear). Position the cluster gear assembly in the bottom of the case.

3. Place the transmission in the vertical position. Align the countershaft gear bore and the thrust washers with the case bore, then install the countershaft from the rear of the case. Re-turn the transmission to the horizontal position.

4. Position the output shaft assembly into the case through the cover opening. With the snapring groove facing rearward, place the rear bearing on the output shaft. Place the transmission in the vertical position and install the bearing. Position the 1st gear thrust washer on the roll pin, holding it tightly during bearing installation. Install the rear bearing snaprings.

5. Install the input shaft and the blocking ring through the front of the case. Make sure that the blocking ring notches engage the synchronizer insert.

6. Using a new gasket, install the front bearing retainer. Apply gasket sealer to the bolt threads and torque to 11-15 ft. lbs.

7. Install the Reverse idler gear lever assembly, taking care to insert the fork in the Reverse idler gear groove.

8. Apply gasket sealer to the Reverse lever pivot bolt threads and install the bolt. Align the lever on the pivot bolt and torque the bolt to 15-25 ft. lbs. Install the Reverse lever retaining spring clip to the Reverse gear pivot bolt. Tilt the transmission forward and pour a light coating of gear lube over the gear train.

9. Using a new cover gasket, install the cover assembly. Install the bolts and the wiring clips, then torque.

NOTE: *The two shouldered locating bolts must be installed first. Position the shift rail in the 1st or 3rd gear.*

10. Insert the speedometer drive gear lock ball into its hole. While holding the ball, slide the speedometer drive gear into place and secure it with a new snapring.

11. Using a new gasket, install the extension housing to the case. Using gasket sealer on the bolts, torque them to 18-27 ft. lbs. Take care not to damage the extension yoke seal.

12. Install the offset lever assembly onto the shift shaft, then secure the assembly with a nut and flat washer. Use sealer on the shift shaft threads and torque to 8-12 ft. lbs.

13. Install the gearshift lever and check its operation in each gear position.

14. Using a soft mallet, install the access plug into the rear of the extension housing.

COVER

Disassembly

1. Remove the detent screw, the spring and the plunger.

2. Pull the shifter shaft rod rearward while rotating it counterclockwise.

3. Remove the selector/interlock-to-shifter shaft spring pin.

4. Remove the shifter shaft from the cover (DO NOT damage the seal).

5. Remove the manual selector and interlock plate.

6. Remove the 1st-2nd speed shifter fork and the 3rd-4th speed shifter fork.

7. Clean and inspect the parts. Replace the shifter shaft seal and the welch plug, if damaged.

Assembly

1. Assemble the two plastic inserts to each shift fork; the two projections on the inside of

1	Case assembly—transmission
2	Case—transmission
3	Magnet—transmission case chip
4	Nut spring 9/64
5	Pin—3/16 diameter x 13/16 rolled spring
6	Lever assembly—transmission gearshift shaft offset
7	Lever transmission gearshift shaft offset
8	Pin—transmission gearshift shaft offset lever
9	Shaft—transmission shifter
10	Seal—O-ring
11	Gear & bush assembly—transmission reverse idler sliding
12	Gear—transmission reverse idler sliding
13	Bushing—transmission reverse idler gear
14	Pin—transmission reverse gear selector fork pivot
15	Ring—7/16 retaining
16	Pin—¼ x 1 spring
17	Shaft—transmission reverse idler gear
18	Gear—transmission countershaft
19	Roller—transmission countershaft bearing
20	Washer—208/.918 flat
21	Washer—transmission countershaft gear thrust
22	Countershaft—transmission
23	Shaft assembly—transmission output
24	Shaft—transmission output
25	Hub—transmission synchronizer 1st & 2nd gear cluster
26	Shaft and gear assembly—transmission output
27	Gear—transmission reverse sliding
28	Insert—transmission synchronizer hub
29	Spring—transmission synchronizer retaining
30	Ring—transmission synchronizer blocking
31	Ring—transmission 2nd speed gear retaining snap
32	Gear—transmission 2nd speed
33	Washer—transmission 2nd speed gear thrust
34	Pin—⅛ x ¼ rolled spring
35	Gear—transmission 3rd speed
36	Synchronizer assembly—3rd & 4th speed
37	Hub—transmission synchronizer
38	Insert—transmission synchronizer hub
39	Sleeve—transmission 3rd & 4th gear clutch hub
40	Spring—transmission synchronizer retaining
41	Ring—transmission synchronizer blocking
42	Ring—transmission m/d gear bearing shaft snap
43	Fork—transmission 1st & 2nd gear shift
44	Fork—transmission 3rd & 4th gear shift
45	Lever assembly—transmission reverse gear shaft relay

46	Retaining—transmission reverse gear shaft relay lever
47	Lever—transmission reverse gear shaft relay
48	Fork—transmission reverse gear shift
49	Spring—transmission shifter interlock
50	Plunger—transmission meshlock
51	Screw—m12 x 10 round head flat
52	Plate—transmission gear selector interlock
53	Screw & washer assembly—m10 x 30 hex head
54	Plug—¾ diameter welch type
55	Shaft—transmission input
56	Roller—transmission mainshaft bearing
57	Bearing assembly—transmission m/d gear ball
58	Ring—m/d gear bearing retaining snap
59	Ring—1.00 retaining
60	Seal—transmission shift shaft
61	Gear—transmission 1st speed
62	Clip—spark control switch wire retaining
63	Gear—speedometer drive
64	Extension assembly—transmission
65	Extension—transmission
66	Bushing—transmission extension
67	Stop—transmission gear shift lever reverse
68	Gasket—transmission extension
69	Seal assembly—transmission extension oil
70	Plug—transmission extension
71	Retainer—transmission input shaft gear bearing
72	Seal assembly—transmission input shaft oil
73	Gasket—transmission input shaft bearing retainer
74	Bolt—M8 x 20 hex head-lock
75	Gasket—transmission case cover
76	Cover—transmission case
77	Screw—m6 x 20 hex head
78	Bolt—m6 x 32 hex washer HD shoulder
79	Plug—½-14 pipe (filler)
80	Bushing—transmission gear shift damper
81	Washer—spring lock
82	Nut—hexagon
83	Switch assembly—back-up lamp
84	Switch assembly—transmission seat belt warning sensor
85	Tag—transmission service identification
86	Washer—transmission 1st gear thrust
87	Ball—.25 diameter
88	Screw & lockwasher assembly—m12 x 40
89	Arm assembly—transmission control selector
90	Arm—transmission control selector
91	Pin—transmission gear shift

RAD exploded view

the inserts fit into the blind holes in the ends of the shift forks. Insert the selector arm plates into the shift forks.

2. Install the 3rd-4th shifter fork and the 1st-2nd shifter fork into the cover, then lubricate the shifter shaft bore with grease.

3. Install the manual selector arm through the interlock plate and position the two pieces into the cover, with the wide leg of the interlock plate facing the inside of the transmission case.

4. Align the shifter shaft in the cover, then insert the shaft through the shifter forks and manual selector. Coat the shifter shaft with a light coating of grease. Make sure the detent grooves face the plunger side of the cover.

5. Align the pin holes in the manual selector arm and shifter shaft and install the spring pin flush with the surface of the selector arm.

6. Install the detent plunger, the spring and the plug. Torque the plug to 8-12 ft. lbs.

7. Check the operation of the shift forks in each gear position.

OUTPUT SHAFT

Disassembly

1. Scribe alignment marks on the synchronizer and the blocking rings. Remove the front output shaft snapring. Slide the 3rd-4th synchronizer assembly, the blocking rings and the 3rd gear off the shaft.

2. Remove the snapring and the 2nd speed gear thrust washer from the shaft. Slide 2nd speed gear and the blocking ring off the shaft, taking care not to lose the sliding gear from the 1st-2nd synchronizer assembly.

NOTE: *The 1st-2nd synchronizer hub cannot be removed from the output shaft.*

3. Remove the 1st gear thrust washer (oil slinger) from the rear of the output shaft. Remove the spring pin retaining 1st speed gear to the shaft.

4. Slide 1st speed gear off the output shaft and remove the blocking ring. Take care not to lose the sliding gear from the 1st-2nd synchronizer assembly.

5. Clean and inspect the parts.

Assembly

1. Place a blocking ring on the 1st speed gear cone, then slide the gear and ring assembly onto the output shaft.

NOTE: *Make sure that the inserts in the synchronizer engage in the blocking ring notches.*

2. Install the 1st speed gear-to-output shaft spring pin.

3. Install a blocking ring on the 2nd speed gear cone, then slide the gear and ring assembly onto the output shaft.

NOTE: *Make sure that the inserts in the synchronizer engage in the blocking ring notches.*

4. Install the 2nd speed gear thrust washer and new snapring on the shaft.

5. Install a blocking ring on the 3rd speed gear cone, then slide the gear and ring assembly onto the output shaft. Install the 3rd-4th synchronizer.

NOTE: *Make sure that the inserts in the synchronizer engage in the blocking ring notches.*

6. Install a new 3rd-4th synchronizer snapring.

7. Place the 1st gear thrust washer (oil slinger) on the shaft and on the 1st gear spring pin.

CAUTION: *The oil grooves must be positioned against the gear.*

COUNTERSHAFT GEAR BEARING

Replacement

1. Remove the dummy shaft, the bearing retainer washers and needle bearings from the countershaft gear. Clean and inspect the parts.

2. Coat the bore at each end of the countershaft gear with grease to retain the needle bearings.

3. While holding the dummy shaft in the gear, install the needle bearings and the retainer washers in each end of the gear.

INPUT SHAFT BEARING

Replacement

1. Remove the roller bearings from the input shaft.

2. Remove the input shaft bearing snapring and press the input shaft out of the bearing. Clean and inspect the parts.

3. Press the input shaft bearing onto the input shaft, making sure that the snapring groove faces the front of the shaft and install a new snapring.

4. Lightly coat the bore of the input shaft with grease.

NOTE: *If a thick film of grease, such as wheel bearing grease, is applied to the shaft, the lubrication holes may become clogged, thereby preventing transmission oil from reaching the bearings, possibly resulting in premature bearing failure.*

5. Install the roller bearings in the bore.

SYNCHRONIZER

Replacement

1. Scribe alignment marks on the hub and sleeve of the synchronizer.

2. Push the synchronizer sleeve from each synchronizer hub.

NOTE: *The 1st-2nd synchronizer hub cannot be removed from the output shaft.*

3. Separate the inserts and the springs from the hubs, taking care not to mix the 1st-2nd synchronizer parts with the 3rd-4th synchronizer. Clean and inspect the parts.

4. Position the sleeve on the hub, making sure that the alignment marks are aligned.

5. Position the three inserts on the hub. Install the insert springs, taking care not to seat the bent tab in one of the inserts. The springs must face in opposite directions.

T5 OD 5-Speed Overhaul

DISASSEMBLY

1. Remove the drain plug from the lower right side of the main case and drain any excess oil from the transmission.

2. Place the shift lever in the Neutral position, then remove the turret cover-to-transmission bolts.

3. Using a medium pry bar, pry the turret cover from the extension housing.

4. Using a $^3/_{16}$" (5mm) pin punch and a hammer, remove the offset lever-to-shifter shaft roll pin, then the damper sleeve.

WARNING: *If the extension housing is bolted in place, do not attempt to remove the offset lever; a lug, (located at the bottom of the offset lever) meshing with the detent plate, prevents rearward movement of the offset lever.*

5. Remove the extension housing-to-main case bolts. Using a medium pry bar, pry the extension housing (break the seal) from the main case. Remove the extension housing/offset lever assembly by sliding it rearward.

6. Remove the offset lever, the roll pin, the detent spring/ball from the extension housing detent plate.

7. Remove the shift cover-to-main case bolts. Using a medium pry bar, pry the shift cover from the main case, then lift it slightly and slide it towards the filler plug side of the transmission. When the shift forks clear groove in the 5th/Reverse shift lever, continue lifting the cover.

8. Using a pair of needle-nose pliers, remove the 5th/Reverse shift lever-to-lever pivot pin C-clip.

9. Using the T50 Torx® Driver tool, remove the 5th/Reverse shift lever pivot pin but do not remove the 5th/Reverse shift lever. Remove the backup lamp switch.

10. Using a pair of snapring pliers, remove the 5th gear synchronizer snapring/spacer from the rear of the countershaft.

11. Remove the 5th gear, the synchronizer, the shift fork and the shift rail by gripping the components as an assembly and pulling them rearward from the main case.

NOTE: *To disengage the 5th/Reverse shift rail, work it until it is free of the shift rail.*

12. To remove the speedometer gear, press downward on the speedometer gear retaining clip and slide the gear from the output shaft, then remove the retaining clip.

13. Remove the front bearing retainer-to-main case bolts. Using a medium pry bar, pry the bearing retainer housing from the main case.

14. To remove the input shaft, rotate it until the flat on the clutch teeth aligns with the countershaft, then pull it from the main case; be careful not to drop the roller bearings, the thrust bearing or the race from the rear of the input shaft.

15. Remove the 4th gear blocking ring from the 3rd/4th synchronizer.

16. Pull the output shaft rearward, until the 1st gear stops against the case, then remove the output shaft bearing race.

NOTE: *If the race sticks, work the shaft back and forth until it is free.*

17. Tilt the output shaft so that the gear/synchronizer assembly end may be lifted up and out of the main case.

18. From the main case, remove the 5th/Reverse shift fork, the Reverse shift fork and the inhibitor spring.

19. Using a $^3/_{16}$" (5mm) pin punch and a hammer, drive the roll pin from the Reverse idler shaft.

20. Through the back of the main case, slide out the Reverse idler shaft, then remove the Reverse idler gear and the overtravel rubber stop.

21. Using a hammer and a punch or chisel, flatten the countershaft retainer tabs (all four corners). Remove the countershaft retainer-to-main case bolts, the retainer, the shims and the bearing race.

NOTE: *If the race sticks, work the shaft back and forth until it is free.*

22. Using the Puller tool No. T81P-1104-C1 and the Puller Clamp tool No. D84L-1123-A, press the bearing from the rear of the countershaft.

23. Move the countershaft rearward, tilt the assembly upward and remove it from the case.

24. Clean all of the parts in solvent and inspect for damage or wear; replace the parts as necessary. Remove the front bearing from the countershaft.

ASSEMBLY

1. Using an arbor press and the Bearing Installation tool No. T57L-4621-B, press a new bearing onto the front of the countershaft, then position the countershaft in the main case.

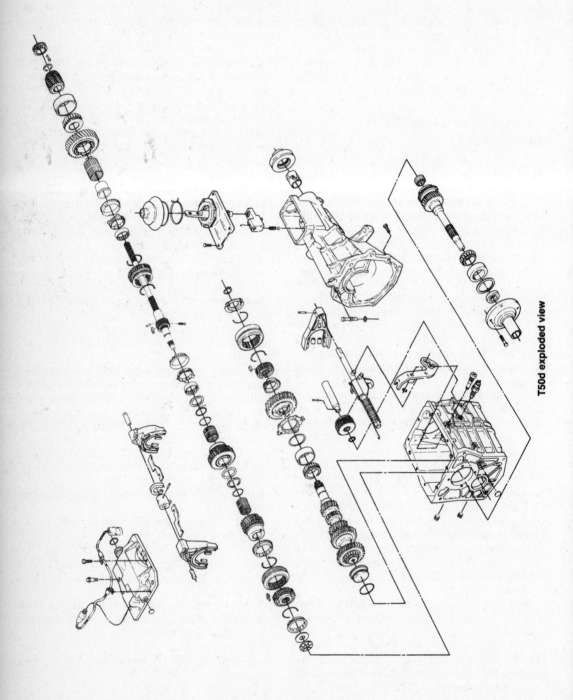

T50d exploded view

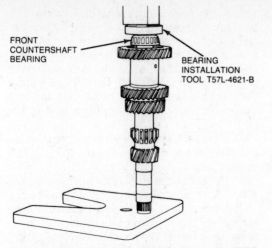

FRONT
COUNTERSHAFT
BEARING

BEARING
INSTALLATION
TOOL T57L-4621-B

Installing the front countershaft bearing on the T50D

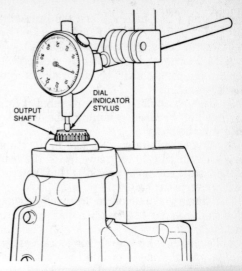

OUTPUT
SHAFT

DIAL
INDICATOR
STYLUS

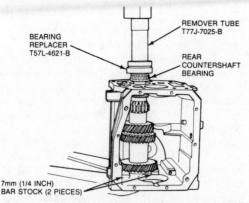

BEARING
REPLACER
T57L-4621-B

REMOVER TUBE
T77J-7025-B

REAR
COUNTERSHAFT
BEARING

7mm (1/4 INCH)
BAR STOCK (2 PIECES)

Installing the countershaft rear bearing on the T50D

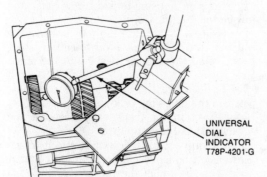

UNIVERSAL
DIAL
INDICATOR
T78P-4201-G

Dial indicator positioning

2. Using an arbor press and the Bearing In-stallation tool No. T83P-7025-AH, press the rear bearing onto the countershaft.

WARNING: *When pressing the rear bearing onto the countershaft, place two pieces of ¼" bar stock inside the main case, between the countergear front and the main case to support it.*

During installation, if the countershaft is not properly supported, permanent distor-

• Using a wood block, push upward on the in-put shaft and note the dial indicator reading.

NOTE: A shim must be installed that is the thickness of the dial indicator reading. This will provide zero end play.

CAUTION: Although zero end play is the ideal end play specification, a plus or minus .050mm (.002 inch) is an acceptable tolerance. Do not overload the bearings with too thick a shim.

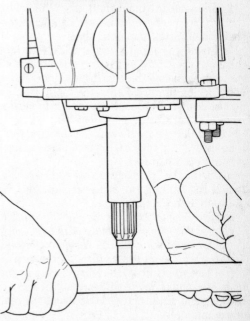

tion/damage may result to the main case.

3. Install the rear bearing race onto the countershaft. Install the countershaft bearing retainer and torque the retainer-to-main case bolts to 10-15 ft. lbs.

NOTE: *Initially, when installing the coun-tershaft bearing retainer, do not use any shims.*

4. Using a Dial Indicator and the Bracketry tool No. D78P-4201-F, measure the countergear end play; it should be 0.001-0.005" (0.0254-0.127mm). If the end play is excessive, remove the countershaft bearing retainer and install shims.

5. After reinstalling the countershaft bearing retainer, bend the retaining tabs over the mounting bolts.

6. Install the Reverse idler gear in the main case with the shift lever groove facing the rear of the case, then the Reverse idler shaft and the rubber overtravel stop.

7. Using a $\frac{3}{16}$" pin punch, drive the Reverse idler shaft roll pin into the idler shaft to secure the shaft.

8. Position the Reverse shifting fork and the 5th/Reverse shifting lever into the main case.

9. Install the output shaft assembly into the main case.

10. Using Polyethylene Grease No. D0AZ-19584-A, or equivalent, coat the input shaft roller bearings (place the bearings into the input shaft), the thrust bearing and the bearing race.

11. Install the 4th gear blocking ring; align the blocking ring notches with the inserts of the 3rd/4th synchronizer.

12. To install the input shaft, align the flat on the synchronizer teeth the with the countershaft, then install the input shaft.

13. Install the input shaft bearing race into the input shaft bearing retainer; do not install the shims. Install the bearing retainer (inner notch facing upwards) onto the main case; do not use sealant. Torque the bearing retainer-to-main case bolts to 11-20 ft. lbs.

14. Install the output shaft rear bearing race; if necessary, tap the bearing into place using a plastic tipped hammer.

15. Install the 5th gear onto the countershaft. Install the shifting rail/5th gear shifting fork assembly into the main case.

NOTE: *When installing the shifting rail/5th gear shifting fork assembly, align the shift rail fork and slide the rail through the fork, stop after the rod passes through the fork.*

16. Place the shift lever return spring in the main case and slide the shifting rail through it; the long end of the spring MUST face the rear of the main case.

17. Install the blocking ring and the 5th gear synchronizer into the 5th gear shifting fork, then slide the fork rail assembly into position.

18. Using a pair of snapring pliers, install the 5th gear synchronizer retainer and snapring.

19. Using a pair of needlenose pliers, connect the lever return spring to the front of the main case.

20. Apply Teflon® Pipe Sealant No. D8AZ-19554-A, or equivalent, to the 5th/Reverse shift lever pivot pin and the back-up light switch. Position the Reverse shift fork pin and the 5th gear shift rail pin so that they are engaged with the shift lever, then install the shift lever pivot pin. Using the T50 Torx® Driver tool, torque the pivot pin-to-shift lever to 23-32 ft. lbs. and the back-up light switch-to-transmission to 12-18 ft. lbs.

21. Install the speedometer gear onto the output shaft; make sure that the retainer clip engages a hole in the output shaft.

22. Using Silicone Rubber Sealant No. D6AZ-19562-A, or equivalent, apply a ⅛" bead to the shift cover assembly. Position the synchronizers and the shifting cover into the Neutral positions, then install the cover assembly (shifting forks engaging the synchronizers). Torque the shift cover-to-main case bolts to 6-11 ft. lbs.

23. Using Silicone Rubber Sealant No. D6AZ-19562-A, or equivalent, apply a ⅛" bead to the extension housing mating surface and the lubrication funnel in the extension housing.

24. Coat the offset lever's detent spring, the detent and the detent ball (place in the Neutral position) with petroleum jelly; position and install these parts into the extension housing (be sure to position the offset lever with the spring over the detent ball.

25. Install the extension housing and shift lever to the main case; be sure the lubrication funnel engages into the 5th gear synchronizer.

26. To install the offset lever, push it downward to compress the detent spring and to push the lever and the housing into position. Install the extension housing-to-main case bolts and torque to 20-45 ft. lbs.

27. Using a $\frac{3}{16}$" (5mm) pin punch, drive the roll pin into the offset lever-to-shifter shaft hole. Install the damper sleeve into the offset lever.

28. To measure the output shaft end play, perform the following procedures:

    a. Position the transmission so that the extension is facing upwards.

    b. Using a Dial Indicator, secure it to the extension housing and position it so that it rides on the end of the output shaft.

    c. Rotate the input and the output shafts, then zero the dial indicator.

    d. Using a wooden block, push upwards on the input shaft and note the dial indicator reading.

WARNING: *A shim must be installed that is the thickness of the dial indicator reading, which will provide a zero end play. DO NOT overload the bearings with too thick a shim; a ± 0.002" (± 0.050mm) is acceptable.*

29. Place the transmission on a level surface and remove the input bearing retainer and the

bearing race from the retainer; install the shim under the bearing race.

30. Using Silicone Rubber Sealant No. D6AZ-19562-A, or equivalent, apply a ⅛″ bead to the bearing retainer, install the retainer and check the end play.

NOTE: *When applying sealant to the bearing retainer, sealant must not cover the notch on the inner edge of the retainer. Be sure to position the retainer with the inner notch facing upwards.*

31. Using Silicone Rubber Sealant No. D6AZ-19562-A, or equivalent, apply a ⅛″ bead to the turret cover. Place the cover onto the extension housing and torque the bolts to 11-15 ft. lbs.

32. Install and torque the drain plug-to-main case to 15-30 ft. lbs.

Merkur 5-Speed Overhaul

DESCRIPTION

This transmission has 3 forward reduction gear ratios, a 1-1 4th gear ratio and an overdrive 5th gear ratio. These forward ratios are provided through helical-cut, constant mesh gears. reverse gear is provided through an idler gear that slides along a shaft to engage spur gears on the cluster gear and output shaft. All gears, except the 5th speed gears are contained in the case. The 5th speed gears are located on the back of the case in the extension housing.

3 synchronizers are used to lock the driven gears to the output shaft. 2 synchronizers provide 1st through 4th gears, while the 3rd synchronizer provides 5th gear. The synchronizers are shifted by 3 forks attached to a common shift rail. A system of interlocks on the shaft prevents the engagement of more than 1 gear at any 1 time. The shift rail extends from the shift lever mounted on the extension housing to the front of the case. At the front of the case, a spring loaded plunger contacts the shift rail to provide the shift detent. reverse gear requires an intermediate lever between the shift rail and the sliding gear. The lever is mounted on a pivot pin which is pressed into the left side of the case. A spring returns the lever to the released position when the transmission is shifted out of reverse.

The input and output shafts are supported in the case on ball bearings to provide durability and quiet operation. The rear of the cluster gear is supported in the case on a roller bearing. The front of the cluster gear is supported on 21 needle bearings installed between the countershaft and cluster gear bore.

EXTENSION HOUSING BUSHING REPLACEMENT

The extension housing bushing can be removed and replaced with the housing on the transmission, when appropriate removing and installation tools are utilized. The bushing depth must be maintained during the installation, either by measuring before removal or by a depth adapter, mounted on the installation tool.

SHIFT LEVER AND BOOT REMOVAL

1. Remove the shift knob and the bezel attaching screws at the console. Remove the bezel.
2. If equipped with power windows, raise the bezel, disconnect the wiring connections from the switches and remove the bezel.
3. Remove the shift boot and foam insulator.
4. Remove the screws attaching the shift lever boot retainer to the floor pan and remove the retainer.
5. Remove the shift lever attaching screws using a No. 40® torx socket and remove the shift lever.

SHIFT LEVER AND BOOT INSTALLATION

1. Install the shift lever and install the retaining screws. Torque to 16–19 ft. lbs. (21–26 Nm).
2. Position the boot retainer and install the attaching screws.
3. Install the shift lever boot and the foam insulator.
4. If equipped with power windows, connect the wiring connectors and position the console bezel.
5. Install the console bezel attaching screws and install the shift lever knob.

TRANSMISSION DISASSEMBLY

1. Remove the clutch release lever and bearing from the flywheel housing.
2. Remove the flywheel housing from the case.
3. If available, mount the transmission in a holding fixture. If not available, secure the case to a work surface in an upright position.
4. Remove the speedometer gear from the extension housing.
5. Remove the back-up light switch and the Neutral safety switches from the extension housing.
6. Remove the case cover retaining bolts, remove the cover with gasket, turn the transmission case over and allow the oil to drain into a suitable container.
7. Remove the shift detent bore plug and using a small magnet, remove the detent spring and detent plunger.
8. Drive the welsh plug from the extension housing, using a brass drift and light hammer.
9. Shift the transmission into reverse gear to

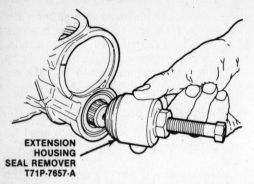

EXTENSION
HOUSING
SEAL REMOVER
T71P-7657-A

Removing the extension housing seal on the Merkur
5-speed

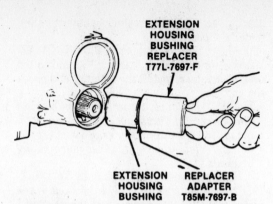

EXTENSION
HOUSING
BUSHING
REPLACER
T77L-7697-F

EXTENSION
HOUSING
BUSHING

REPLACER
ADAPTER
T85M-7697-B

Installing the extension housing bushing on the Merkur 5-speed

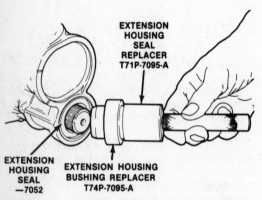

EXTENSION
HOUSING
SEAL
REPLACER
T71P-7095-A

EXTENSION
HOUSING
SEAL
—7052

EXTENSION HOUSING
BUSHING REPLACER
T74P-7095-A

Installing the extension housing seal on the Merkur
5-speed

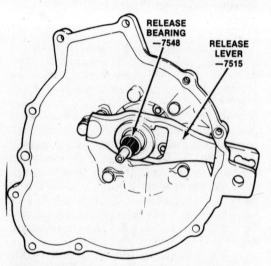

RELEASE
BEARING
—7548

RELEASE
LEVER
—7515

Clutch release lever and bearing on the Merkur 5-
speed

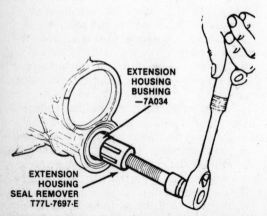

EXTENSION
HOUSING
BUSHING
—7A034

EXTENSION
HOUSING
SEAL REMOVER
T77L-7697-E

Removing the extension housing bushing on the
Merkur 5-speed

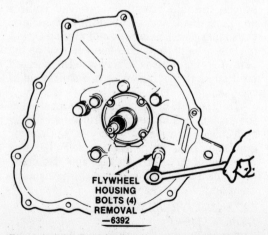

FLYWHEEL
HOUSING
BOLTS (4)
REMOVAL
—6392

Removing the flywheel housing bolts on the Merkur
5-speed

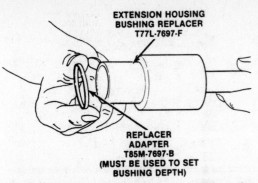

Extension housing bushing replacer adapter on the Merkur 5-speed

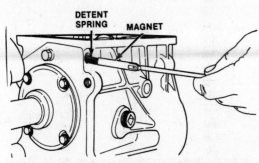

Removing the detent spring on the Merkur 5-speed

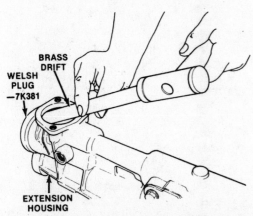

Driving out the welch plug on the Merkur 5-speed

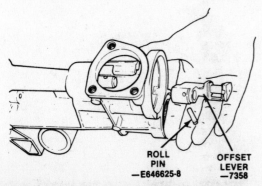

Removing the offset lever on the Merkur 5-speed

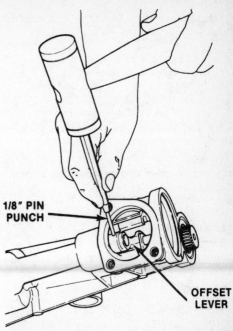

Removing the offset lever retaining pin on the Merkur 5-speed

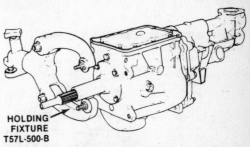

Mounting the Merkur 5-speed in a holding fixture

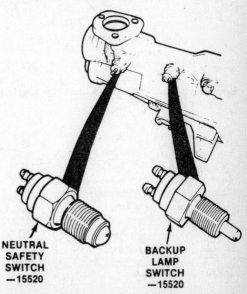

Neutral safety switch and back-up light switch on the Merkur 5-speed

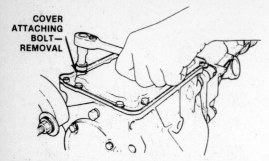

Removing the cover bolts on the Merkur 5-speed

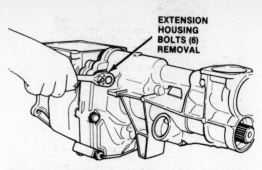

Removing the extension housing bolts on the Merkur 5-speed

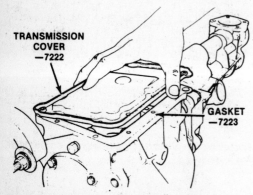

Removing the cover on the Merkur 5-speed

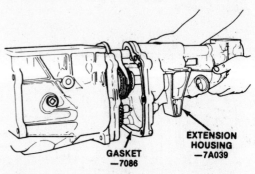

Removing the extension housing on the Merkur 5-speed

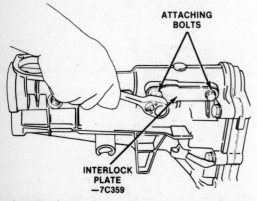

Removing the 5th gear interlock plate attaching bolts on the Merkur 5-speed

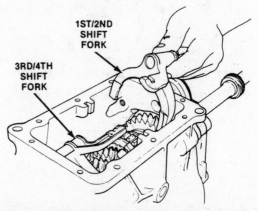

Removing the 1st/2nd shift fork on the Merkur 5-speed

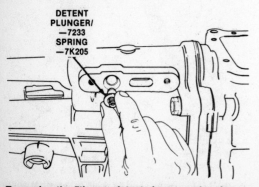

Removing the 5th gear detent plunger and spring on the Merkur 5-speed

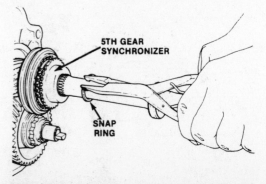

Removing the 5th gear synchronizer snapring on the Merkur 5-speed

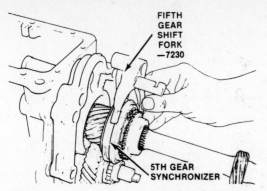

Removing the 5th gear shift fork on the Merkur 5-speed

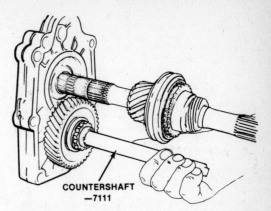

Pulling the countershaft from the cluster gear on the Merkur 5-speed

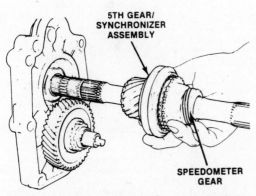

Removing the 5th gear synchronizer on the Merkur 5-speed

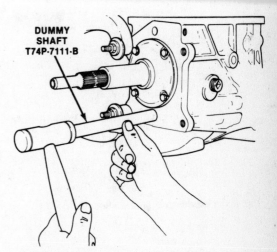

Installing a dummy shaft to hold the cluster gear on the Merkur 5-speed

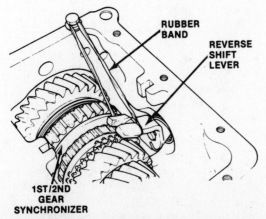

Installing a rubber band to hold the reverse idler gear in position on the Merkur 5-speed

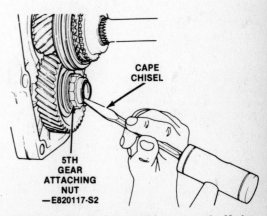

Unstaking the 5th gear attaching nut on the Merkur 5-speed

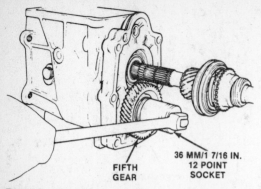

Removing the 5th gear attaching nut on the Merkur 5-speed

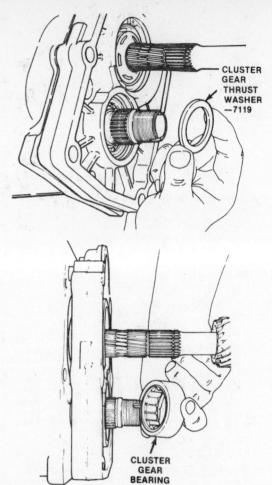

Removing the cluster gear rear bearing and thrust washer on the Merkur 5-speed

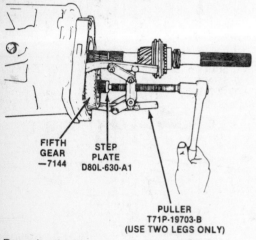

Removing the 5th gear on the Merkur 5-speed

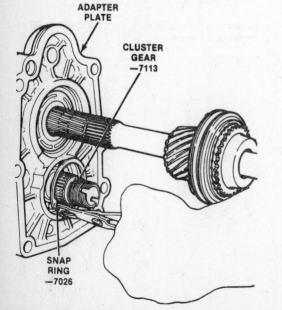

Removing the cluster gear rear bearing snapring on the Merkur 5-speed

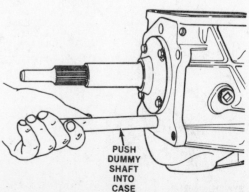

Pushing the dummy shaft into the case to allow the cluster bearing to drop, on the Merkur 5-speed

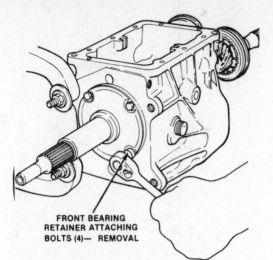

FRONT BEARING
RETAINER ATTACHING
BOLTS (4)— REMOVAL

Removing the front bearing retainer attaching bolts
on the Merkur 5-speed

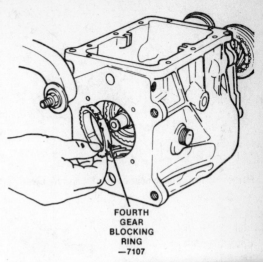

FOURTH
GEAR
BLOCKING
RING
—7107

Removing the 4th gear blocking ring on the Merkur
5-speed

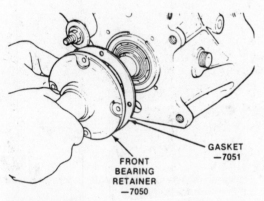

GASKET
—7051

FRONT
BEARING
RETAINER
—7050

Removing the bearing retainer and gasket on the
Merkur 5-speed

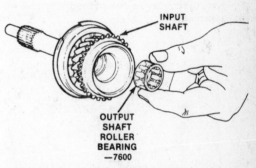

INPUT
SHAFT

OUTPUT
SHAFT
ROLLER
BEARING
—7600

Removing the output shaft front roller bearing from
the input shaft on the Merkur 5-speed

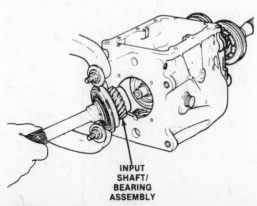

INPUT
SHAFT/
BEARING
ASSEMBLY

Removing the input shaft and bearing on the Merkur
5-speed

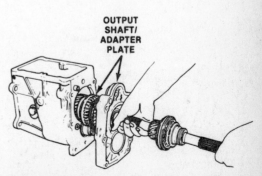

OUTPUT
SHAFT/
ADAPTER
PLATE

Removing the output shaft and adapter plate on the
Merkur 5-speed

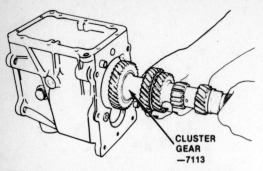

Removing the cluster gear on the Merkur 5-speed

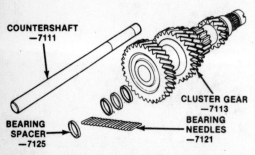

Removing the dummy shaft from the cluster gear on the Merkur 5-speed

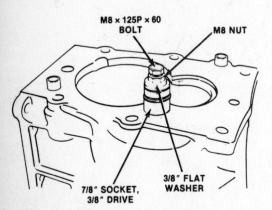

Homemade puller

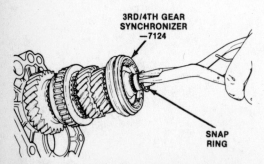

Removing the 3rd/4th gear snapring on the Merkur 5-speed

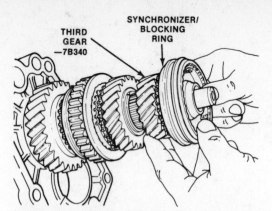

Removing the 3rd/4th gear synchronizer, blocking ring and gear on the Merkur 5-speed

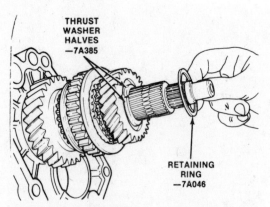

Removing the retaining ring and thrust washer halves on the Merkur 5-speed

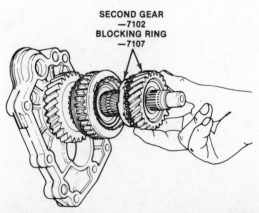

Removing the 2nd gear and blocking ring on the Merkur 5-speed

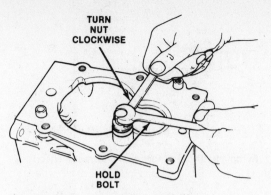

Tightening the reverse idler gear puller

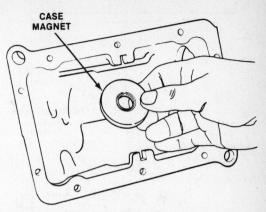

Ceramic magnet on the Merkur 5-speed

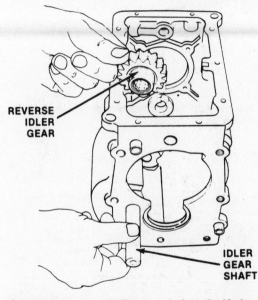

Removing the reverse idler gear shaft on the Merkur 5-speed

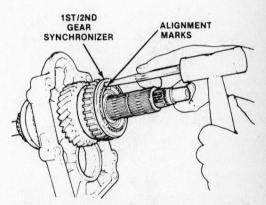

Matchmarking the 1st/2nd gear synchronizer sleeve and hub on the Merkur 5-speed

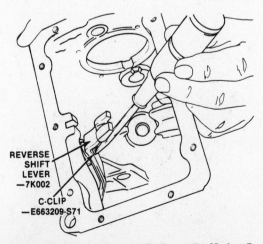

Removing the reverse lever C-clip on the Merkur 5-speed

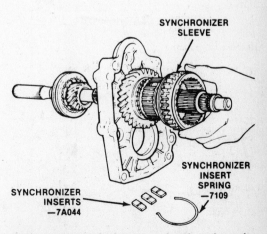

Removing the 1st/2nd gear synchronizer sleeve, inserts and spring on the Merkur 5-speed

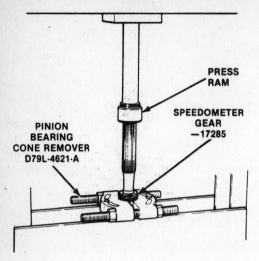

Pressing out the speedometer gear on the Merkur 5-speed

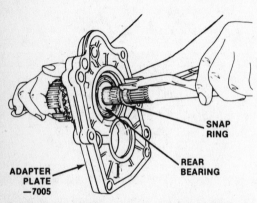

Removing the output shaft rear bearing snapring on the Merkur 5-speed

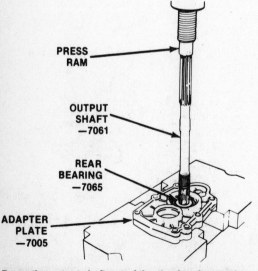

Press the output shaft out of the rear bearing on the Merkur 5-speed

Removing the oil slinger on the Merkur 5-speed

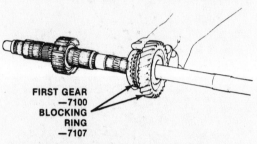

Removing the 1st gear synchronizer and blocking ring on the Merkur 5-speed

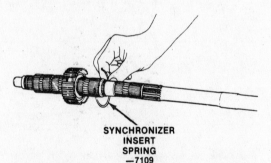

Removing the synchronizer insert spring on the Merkur 5-speed

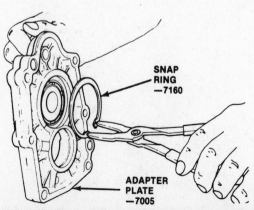

Removing the snapring from the adapter plate on the Merkur 5-speed

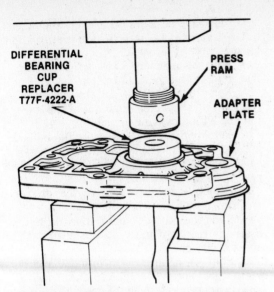

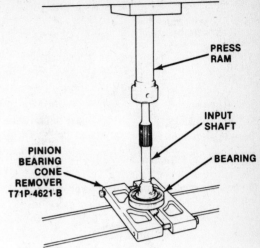

Pressing out the bearing on the Merkur 5-speed

Removing the bearing using a press and special tools on the Merkur 5-speed

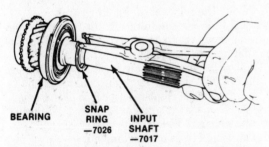

Removing the snapring from the input shaft on the Merkur 5-speed

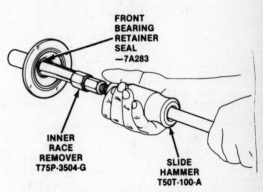

Removing the front bearing seal on the Merkur 5-speed

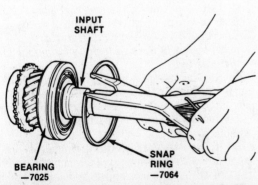

Removing the snapring from the bearing on the Merkur 5-speed

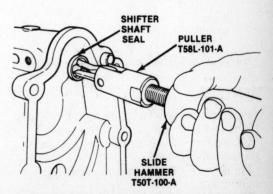

Removing the shifter seal from the extension housing on the Merkur 5-speed

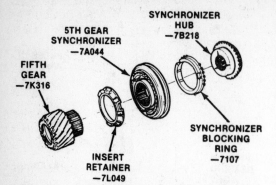

5th gear synchronizer disassembled on the Merkur 5-speed

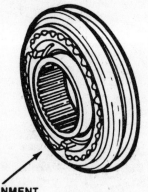

MAKE ALIGNMENT MARKS BEFORE DISASSEMBLING

Matchmarking the synchronizer on the Merkur 5-speed

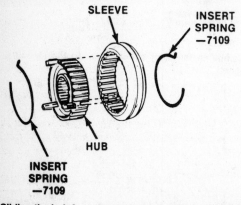

Sliding the hub from the sleeve on the Merkur 5-speed

gain access to the offset lever roll pin. Remove the pin with the use of an ⅛" pin punch.

10. Remove the offset lever and roll pin from the extension housing.

11. Remove the 5th gear interlock plate retaining bolts.

12. Remove the 5th gear interlock plate, detent spring and the detent plunger.

13. Remove the extension housing retaining bolts. Remove the extension housing and gasket.

14. With the use of an ⅛" pin punch and hammer, remove the shift rail roll pin.

15. Remove the shift rail and the 5th gear interlock. Pull the shifter shaft out of the transmission with a twisting motion.

16. Remove the shift interlock for the 1st/2nd and 3rd/4th shift forks. Remove the shift forks.

17. Remove the 5th gear shift fork from the rear of the transmission.

18. Remove the 5th gear synchronizer snapring from the output shaft.

19. Slide the 5th gear and the synchronizer assembly rearward until it stops against the speedometer gear.

20. Shift the transmission into 1st and reverse gears to prevent rotation of the mainshaft and cluster gears. To hold the reverse idler gear in position, install a cover bolt into the transmission case and stretch a rubber band from the reverse lever to the bolt.

NOTE: *The cover bolt can be left in place, since it will be needed during the assembly.*

21. Partially install a dummy shaft through the front of the case to support the cluster gear during the removal of the 5th gear.

22. Pull the countershaft out of the cluster gear from the rear of the case, allowing the dummy shaft to follow the countershaft. Do not allow the dummy shaft to move any further into the case than the point where its end is flush with the front exterior face of the case.

23. Remove the nut staking from the 5th gear retaining nut. Using the proper sized socket, remove the 5th gear attaching nut.

24. Remove the 5th gear with an appropriate puller having puller jaws that will fully engage with the underside of the 5th gear.

25. Remove the cluster gear rear bearing snapring from the adapter plate. Remove the rear bearing and the thrust bearing washer as they drop from the adapter plate.

26. Push the dummy shaft rearward until it just clears the front of the case and allows the cluster gear to drop into the bottom of the case.

CAUTION: *Guide the cluster gear assembly to the bottom of the case to prevent damage to the gear teeth.*

27. Remove the front bearing retainer attaching bolts. Remove the bearing retainer and gasket assembly.

28. Remove the input shaft and bearing as an assembly.

29. If the 4th gear blocking ring does not come out with the input shaft, remove it from the 3rd/4th gear synchronizer by hand.

30. Remove the output shaft front roller bearing from the output shaft.

31. Remove the output shaft and adapter plate as an assembly through the rear of the transmission case. Discard the adapter plate gasket.

32. Carefully remove the cluster gear from the case.

33. Remove the dummy shaft from the cluster gear. Carefully remove the spacers and bearing needles from the front end of the cluster gear.

34. A puller tool is needed to remove the reverse idler shaft from the case. A puller can be fabricated with the use of a ⅜″ drive, ⅞″ socket and the necessary bolt, washer and nut.

35. Install the bolt into the end of the reverse idler gear shaft and while holding the bolt head, turn the nut clockwise to remove the shaft.

36. Remove the reverse idler gear and shaft assembly from the case.

37. Remove the C-clip attaching the reverse lever to the lever pivot pin. Remove the reverse shift lever and return spring from the pivot pin.

38. Remove the magnet from the case carefully, as the magnet is ceramic and can easily be broken.

39. Disassemble the output shaft assembly in the following manner.

 a. Remove the snapring from the shaft that is retaining the 3rd/4th gear synchronizer.

 b. Remove the 3rd/4th synchronizer, 3rd gear belcing ring and the 3rd gear as an assembly.

 c. Remove the retaining ring and the thrust washer halves. Remove the 2nd speed gear and the blocking ring.

NOTE: *A snapring is installed on the 2nd gear to prevent the synchronizer from over-traveling. If necessary, remove the snapring from the gear.*

 d. Make an alignment mark on the 1st/2nd synchronizer sleeve and hub.

NOTE: *These marks will provide the necessary alignment references during assembly, since the synchronizer sleeve and hub are matched during the manufacture and must be assembled in the same position.*

 e. Remove the 1st/2nd synchronizer sleeve, inserts and spring.

 f. Mark the position of the speedometer gear on the output shaft and remove the gear using an appropriate puller tool and press.

 g. Remove the 5th gear synchronizer snapring from the output shaft, remove the 5th gear and synchronizer assembly from the shaft.

 h. Remove the output shaft rear bearing snapring from the output shaft.

 i. With the adapter plate and the rear bearing properly supported, press the output shaft from the rear bearing.

WARNING: *Failure to correctly support the adaptor plate and rear bearing could cause damage to the plate and bearing.*

 j. Remove the oil slinger from the shaft. Remove the 1st gear synchronizer and blocking ring. Remove the synchronizer insert ring.

40. Remove the snapring from the adapter plate and remove the rear bearing from the plate, using a press and an appropriate pressing tool.

41. To remove the bearing from the input shaft, remove the snapring from the input shaft and the snapring from the outer race of the bearing. Place the bearing in a press platform and press the input shaft from the bearing.

42. To remove the varied seals from the transmission and components, the use of a slide hammer and seal remover jaws are recommended.

43. Before disassembling a synchronizer assembly, make an alignment mark on the mated parts. The parts are matched during assembly at time of manufacture and must be assembled to their original positions.

44. The transmission components can now be inspected for damage, wear, scoring or pitting. Replace the necessary components as required.

TRANSMISSION ASSEMBLY

Synchronizer

1. Align the reference marks made during the disassembly and slide the slide of the synchronizer sleeve over the hub.

NOTE: *When assembling the 5th gear synchronizer, be sure the beveled side of the synchronizer sleeve faces the synchronizer hub.*

2. Install the inserts and springs. The hooked end of the springs engage the same insert but rotates away from the insert in the opposite directions.

NOTE: *When assembling the sleeve and hub, hold both square with each other. Do not force the hub into the sleeve since both are an extremely close fit.*

3. Install the insert retainer, gear, blocking ring and hub into the 5th gear synchronizer.

Front Bearing Retainer Seal

1. Using a socket of suitable size, install a new seal into the bearing retainer.

2. Lubricate the seal lip with appropriate lubrication.

Input Shaft Bearing

1. Install the input shaft bearing using a press and plate. To prevent damage to the synchronizer taper of the bearing bore, place a suit-

able plate between the press ram and the input shaft.

2. Install the snapring on the bearing outer race.

3. Install a new selective snapring on the input shaft.

INSTALLATION

Output Shaft Bearing

1. Install the output shaft rear bearing in the adapter plate, using a press and installer tube.

2. Install a new selective snapring in the adapter plate bore.

ASSEMBLY

Output Shaft Components

1. Assemble the 1st/2nd synchronizer.

NOTE: *Be sure the shift fork groove faces the front of the output shaft as viewed in its assembled position when in the transmission.*

2. Install the 2nd gear blocking ring and 2nd gear.

3. Install the thrust washer halves and the retaining ring. Be sure the thrust with the tang engages the hole in the output shaft.

4. Install the 3rd gear and the 3rd gear blocking ring. Install the 3rd/4th synchronizer.

5. Install a new selective fit 3rd/4th synchronizer snapring.

6. Install the 1st gear blocking ring and the 1st gear.

7. Install the oil slinger with the oil groove facing 1st gear.

8. With the use of a front cover aligning tool, Ford part No. T57L–4621–B, or equivalent, install the rear bearing and adapter plate assembly.

9. Install the new selective fit rear bearing snapring on the output shaft.

10. Install the 5th gear and 5th gear synchronizer assembly.

NOTE: *Be sure the synchronizer is assembled with the beveled side of the synchronizer sleeve facing the speedometer gear end of the output shaft.*

11. Install the new selective fit 5th gear snapring on the output shaft.

12. Install the speedometer gear with a bearing installer tool or equivalent. Press the gear onto the shaft until it aligns with the mark made during disassembly.

NOTE: *The speedometer gear should require a fair amount of force due to the interference fit between the gear and the output shaft. If the gear seems loose on the shaft, replace the gear and/or shaft. If a new output shaft has been installed, press the speedometer gear onto the shaft until the distance from the*

front face of the gear to the rear face of the 5th gear synchronizer hub measures $4^{27}/_{32}$–$4^{7}/_{8}$".

TRANSMISSION COMPONENTS ASSEMBLY

1. Install the ceramic magnet into the case.

2. Install the reverse shift lever return spring on the lever.

3. Position the return spring and the reverse shift lever on the pivot pin.

NOTE: *Be sure the spring is tensioned to return the lever to the released position and install the C-clip.*

4. Position the reverse idler gear in the case with the shoulder facing the rear of the case and with the gear engaged in the reverse shift lever.

5. Install the reverse idler gear shaft. Tap the shaft into the case with the aid of a plastic tipped hammer.

6. Position the countershaft in the cluster gear and install 3 bearing spacers in the front end of the cluster gear.

7. Install the needle bearings (21) into the cluster gear. Lubricate them with petroleum jelly to retain them in place.

8. Install the remaining bearing spacers on the cluster gear.

9. Install the cluster gear with the bottom countershaft and lay it on the bottom of the case. Push the countershaft to the front until it supports the front needle bearings. As the front of the cluster gear enters the case, pull the countershaft rearward until the front of the shaft end is flush with the end of the cluster gear.

NOTE: *Be sure the bearing spacer does not fall off the end of the countershaft while the cluster gear is being lowered into the case.*

10. With a new gasket installed on the adaptor plate, install the output shaft, adapter plate and gasket as an assembly.

11. Coat the input shaft roller bearing with transmission oil and install in the end of the input shaft.

12. Install the 4th gear blocking ring.

13. Install the input shaft.

14. Install a new gasket on the front bearing retainer. Position the bearing retainer. Position the bearing retainer on the case with the groove in the gasket and retainer, facing the bottom of the case to align with the oil drain hole.

15. Install the front bearing retainer attaching bolts and tighten to 7–8 ft. lbs. (9–11 Nm.).

16. Rotate the countershaft until the flat on the rear end of the shaft is facing up in the horizontal position.

WARNING: *The positioning of the countershaft flat is critical because it must fit into a matching flat in the extension housing. If the flat is not correct, the extension housing will not fit correctly.*

17. Raise the front of the cluster gear to align the countershaft with the countershaft bore in the case. While holding this alignment, tap the countershaft forward into the case bore.

18. Remove the 5th gear synchronizer snapring from the output shaft groove.

19. Slide the synchronizer and ssnapring rearward against the speedometer gear to allow clearance for installation of the 5th gear.

20. Install the cluster gear rear bearing.

21. Install the cluster gear bearing spacer.

22. Install the cluster gear rear bearing snapring.

23. Install the 5th gear on the cluster gear using a forcing tool assembly.

24. Position the 5th gear and the 5th gear synchronizer. Install the 5th gear synchronizer snapring.

25. If necessary, install a cover bolt into the transmission case, in order to hold the reverse idler gear into position. Using a rubber band, stretch it from the reverse lever to the cover bolt.

26. To prevent rotation of the mainshaft and cluster gear, shift the transmission into 1st and reverse gears.

27. Install the 5th gear attaching nut and washer.

28. Using a $1\frac{7}{16}''$, twelve point socket, tighten the 5th gear attaching nut to 89–111 ft. lbs. (120–150 Nm.).

29. Stake the 5th gear attaching nut, using a staking punch and light hammer.

30. Remove the rubber band and the cover bolt. Shift the transmission out of the 1st and reverse gears.

31. Install the 1st/2nd and 3rd/4th shift forks. Be sure the 3rd/4th fork is on top of the 1st/2nd fork.

32. Position the 5th gearshift fork and interlock on the 5th gear synchronizer. Slide the shift rail through the interlock and shift fork until it enters the case.

33. Position the 1st/2nd shift fork, the 2nd/3rd shift interlock and cam and the 3rd/4th shift fork. Then slide the shift rail through the shift forks and shift interlock until the shaft enters the bore at the front of the case.

NOTE: *Be sure the 5th gear interlock is correctly aligned to allow the shift rail to slide through the shifter fork. Be sure the synchronizers are in the neutral position and the shift levers forks engage the synchronizer sleeves.*

34. Align the shift rail with the shift interlock and install the roll pin.

NOTE: *To ease the installation of the pin, use the center detent on the shaft rail as the point of alignment.*

35. Apply sealant to the detent plug and install into the bore, along with the spring and detent plunger.

36. Shift the transmission into the 4th gear.

37. Install a new extension housing gasket.

38. Position a new gasket and install the extension housing. Be sure the flat on the countershaft and the matching flat on the extension housing are properly aligned.

39. Install the extension housing attaching bolts and torque to 33–36 ft. lbs. (40–49 Nm.).

NOTE: *Apply sealer to the threads of the 3 bolts entering the transmission case.*

40. Shift the transmission into the reverse gear.

41. Position the offset lever on the shifter shaft and install the roll pin with a ⅛" pin punch.

42. Install the welsh plug into the extension housing bore, using appropriate tools.

43. Install the 5th gear detent plunger and spring.

44. Tighten the lockplate retaining bolts to 16019 ft. lbs. after coating them with a sealant.

45. With the use of a new gasket, install the cover on the transmission case and torque the retaining bolts to 14–15 ft. lbs. (18–20 Nm). Be sure the cover guide engages the shift interlock.

46. Wrap the threads of the back-up light switch and the neutral start switch and the neutral start switch with teflon thread type tape and install into the extension housing.

47. Tighten the switches to 7–10 ft. lbs. (10–14 Nm).

48. Install the flywheel housing and tighten the retaining bolts to 52–67 ft. lbs. (70–90 Nm).

49. Install the clutch release bearing lever and the bearing assembly.

50. Fill the transmission with lubricant, equal to Ford specification ESD-M-2C175A or equivalent, to its proper level.

51. Install the speedometer driven gear in the extension housing.

NOTE: *The transmission lubricant is a semi-synthetic oil. When adding oil to the transmission use only lubricant equal to Ford specification ESD–M–2C175A.*

Back-Up Light Switch

REMOVAL AND INSTALLATION

1. Place the shift lever in neutral.
2. Raise and support the car on jackstands.
3. Unplug the electrical connector at the switch.
4. Unscrew the switch from the transmission extension housing.
5. Screw the new switch into place and tighten it to 60 in.lb.
6. Connect the wiring.

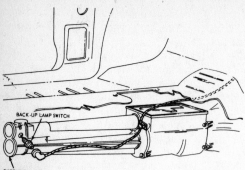

BACK-UP LAMP SWITCH

EXTENSION HOUSING

82ET back-up lamp switch

CLUTCH

NOTE: *Models through 1986 employ a mechanically actuated clutch system. Clutch release is accomplished through a cable linkage system.*

1987-88 models use a hydraulically actuated clutch with a master cylinder, plastic reservoir, and slave cylinder

Clutch Disc

REMOVAL AND INSTALLATION

CAUTION: *The clutch driven disc contains asbestos, which has been determined to be a cancer causing agent. Never clean clutch surfaces with compressed air! Avoid inhaling any dust from any clutch surface! When cleaning clutch surfaces, use a commercially available brake cleaning fluid.*

1. Remove the transmission.
2. Mark the cover and flywheel to facilitate reassembly in the same position. Loosen the six pressure plate cover attaching bolts evenly to release the spring pressure.
3. Remove the six attaching bolts while holding the pressure plate cover. Remove the pressure plate and clutch disc.

WARNING: *Do not depress the clutch pedal while the transmission is removed.*

4. Before installing the clutch, clean the flywheel surface. Inspect the flywheel and pressure plate for wear, scoring, or burn marks (blue color). Light scoring and wear may be cleaned up with emery paper; heavy wear may

Troubleshooting Basic Clutch Problems

Problem	Cause
Excessive clutch noise	Throwout bearing noises are more audible at the lower end of pedal travel. The usual causes are: • Riding the clutch • Too little pedal free-play • Lack of bearing lubrication A bad clutch shaft pilot bearing will make a high pitched squeal, when the clutch is disengaged and the transmission is in gear or within the first 2″ of pedal travel. The bearing must be replaced. Noise from the clutch linkage is a clicking or snapping that can be heard or felt as the pedal is moved completely up or down. This usually requires lubrication. Transmitted engine noises are amplified by the clutch housing and heard in the passenger compartment. They are usually the result of insufficient pedal free-play and can be changed by manipulating the clutch pedal.
Clutch slips (the car does not move as it should when the clutch is engaged)	This is usually most noticeable when pulling away from a standing start. A severe test is to start the engine, apply the brakes, shift into high gear and SLOWLY release the clutch pedal. A healthy clutch will stall the engine. If it slips it may be due to: • A worn pressure plate or clutch plate • Oil soaked clutch plate • Insufficient pedal free-play
Clutch drags or fails to release	The clutch disc and some transmission gears spin briefly after clutch disengagement. Under normal conditions in average temperatures, 3 seconds is maximum spin-time. Failure to release properly can be caused by: • Too light transmission lubricant or low lubricant level • Improperly adjusted clutch linkage
Low clutch life	Low clutch life is usually a result of poor driving habits or heavy duty use. Riding the clutch, pulling heavy loads, holding the car on a grade with the clutch instead of the brakes and rapid clutch engagement all contribute to low clutch life.

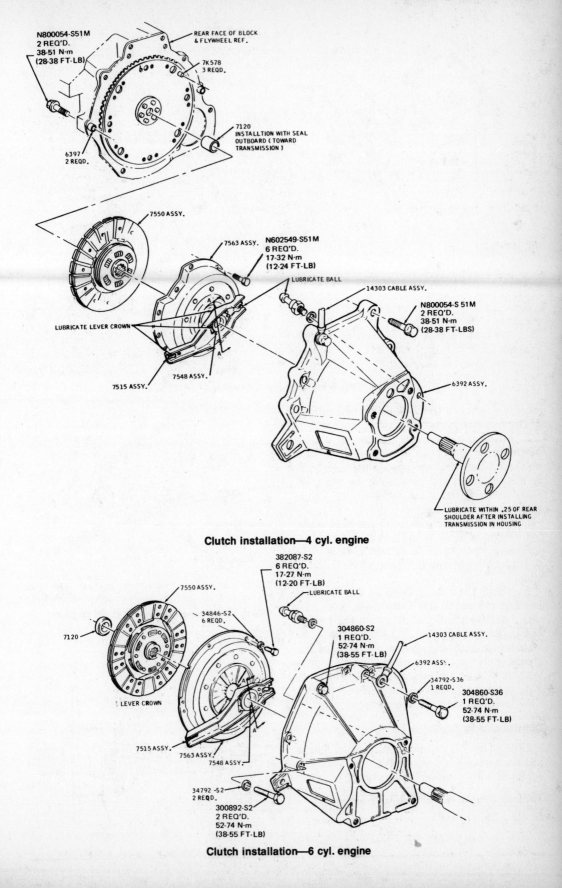

N800054-S51M
2 REQ'D.
38-51 N·m
(28-38 FT-LB)

REAR FACE OF BLOCK
& FLYWHEEL REF.

7K 578
3 REQD.

7120
INSTALLTION WITH SEAL
OUTBOARD (TOWARD
TRANSMISSION)

6397
2 REQD.

7550 ASSY.

7563 ASSY.

N602549-S51M
6 REQ'D.
17-32 N·m
(12-24 FT-LB)

LUBRICATE BALL

14303 CABLE ASSY.

N800054-S 51M
2 REQ'D.
38-51 N·m
(28-38 FT-LBS)

LUBRICATE LEVER CROWN

7548 ASSY.

7515 ASSY.

6392 ASSY.

LUBRICATE WITHIN .25 OF REAR
SHOULDER AFTER INSTALLING
TRANSMISSION IN HOUSING

Clutch installation—4 cyl. engine

7550 ASSY.

382087-S2
6 REQ'D.
17-27 N·m
(12-20 FT-LB)

LUBRICATE BALL

34846-S2
6 REQD.

7120

304860-S2
1 REQ'D.
52-74 N·m
(38-55 FT-LB)

14303 CABLE ASSY.

6392 ASSY.

34792-S36
1 REQD.

304860-S36
1 REQ'D.
52-74 N·m
(38-55 FT-LB)

LEVER CROWN

7515 ASSY.

7563 ASSY.

7548 ASSY.

34792 -S2
2 REQD.

300892-S2
2 REQ'D.
52-74 N·m
(38-55 FT-LB)

Clutch installation—6 cyl. engine

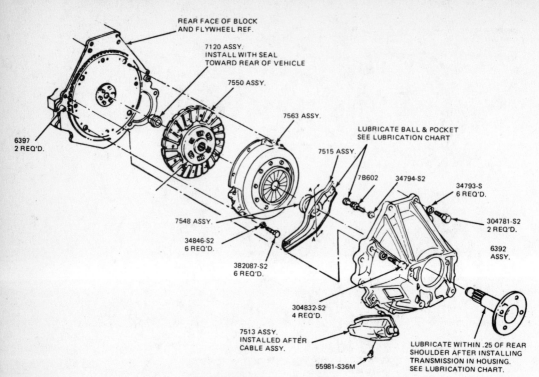

REAR FACE OF BLOCK
AND FLYWHEEL REF.

7120 ASSY.
INSTALL WITH SEAL
TOWARD REAR OF VEHICLE

7550 ASSY.

7563 ASSY.

LUBRICATE BALL & POCKET
SEE LUBRICATION CHART

7515 ASSY.

6397
2 REQ'D.

7B602   34794-S2

34793-S
6 REQ'D.

304781-S2
2 REQ'D.

7548 ASSY.

34846-S2
6 REQ'D.

6392
ASSY.

382087-S2
6 REQ'D.

304832-S2
4 REQ'D.

7513 ASSY.
INSTALLED AFTER
CABLE ASSY.

55981-S36M

LUBRICATE WITHIN .25 OF REAR
SHOULDER AFTER INSTALLING
TRANSMISSION IN HOUSING.
SEE LUBRICATION CHART.

Clutch installation—V8 engine

require refacing of the flywheel or replacement of the damaged parts.

5. Attach the clutch disc and pressure plate assembly to the flywheel. The three dowel pins on the flywheel, if so equipped, must be properly aligned. Damaged pins must be replaced. Avoid touching the clutch plate surface. Tighten the bolts finger tight.

6. Align the clutch disc with the pilot bushing. Torque cover bolts to 12-14 ft. lbs. on Mustang and Capri; 15-19 ft. lbs. on Merkur.

7. Lightly lubricate the release lever fulcrum ends.

8. Install the release lever in the flywheel housing and install the dust shield.

9. Apply very little lubricant on the release bearing retainer journal. Fill the groove in release bearing hub with grease. Clean all excess grease from the inside bore of the hub to prevent clutch disc contamination. Attach the release bearing and hub on the release lever.

10. Install the transmission.

Adjustments

1979-80 models require a clutch pedal height adjustment. 1981 and later models are equipped with a self-adjusting clutch.

1979-80 PEDAL HEIGHT ADJUSTMENT

Except 6-200 Engine

1. Raise and support the front end on jackstands.

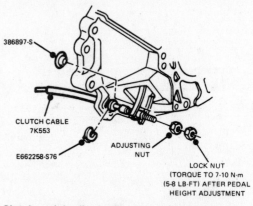

386897-S

CLUTCH CABLE
7K553

E662258-S76

ADJUSTING
NUT

LOCK NUT
(TORQUE TO 7-10 N·m
(5-8 LB-FT) AFTER PEDAL
HEIGHT ADJUSTMENT

Clutch pedal adjustment—4 cyl. V8 engines

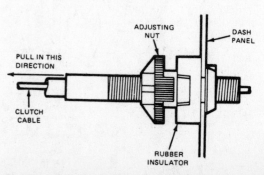

ADJUSTING
NUT

DASH
PANEL

PULL IN THIS
DIRECTION

CLUTCH
CABLE

RUBBER
INSULATOR

Clutch pedal adjustment—6 cyl. 200 engine

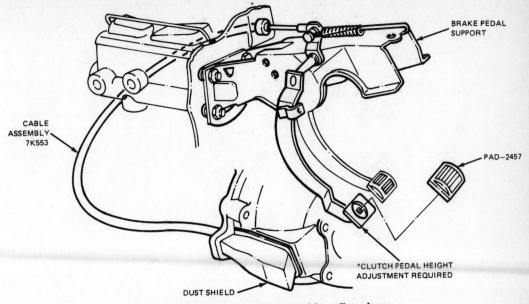

Clutch pedal and cable assembly—all engines

2. Remove the dust shield.

3. Loosen the clutch cable locknut.

4. To raise the clutch pedal, turn the adjusting nut clockwise; to lower the clutch pedal, turn the adjusting nut counterclockwise. The pedal height should be:
- 4-cylinder: 5.3″
- 8-cylinder: 6.5″

5. Tighten the locknut. When the pedal is properly adjusted, the pedal can be raised about 2¾″ on the 4-cylinder and 1½″ on the 8-cylinder, to reach the pedal stop.

6. Install the dust shield.

6-200

1. Raise and support the front end on jackstands.

2. Pull the clutch cable toward the front of the car until the adjusting nut can be rotated. In order to free the nut from the rubber insulator, it may be necessary to block the clutch release forward so the clutch is partially disengaged.

3. Rotate the adjusting nut to obtain a pedal height of 5.3″.

4. Depress the pedal a few times and recheck the adjustment. When the pedal is properly adjusted, it can be raised about 2¾″ to reach the pedal stop.

Self-Adjusting Clutch

The free play in the clutch is adjusted by a built in mechanism that allows the clutch controls to be self-adjusted during normal operation.

The self-adjusting feature should be checked every 5,000 miles. This is accomplished by insuring that the clutch pedal travels to the top of its upward position. Grasp the clutch pedal with your hand or put your foot under the clutch pedal, pull up on the pedal until it stops. Very little effort is required (about 10 lbs.) During the application of upward pressure, a click may be heard which means an adjustment was necessary and has been accomplished.

COMPONENTS

The self-adjusting clutch control mechanism is automatically adjusted by a device on the clutch pedal. The system consists of a spring loaded gear quadrant, a spring loaded pawl, and a clutch cable which is spring loaded to preload the clutch release lever bearing to compensate for movement of the release lever, as the clutch disc wears. The spring loaded pawl located at the top of the clutch pedal, engages the gear quadrant when the clutch pedal is depressed and pulls the cable through its continuously adjusted stroke. Clutch cable adjustments are not required because of this feature.

STARTER/CLUTCH INTERLOCK SWITCH

The starter/clutch switch is designed to prevent starting the engine unless the clutch pedal is fully depressed. The switch is connected between the ignition switch and the starter motor relay coil and maintains an open circuit with the clutch pedal up (clutch engaged).

The switch is designed to self-adjust automatically the first time the clutch pedal is

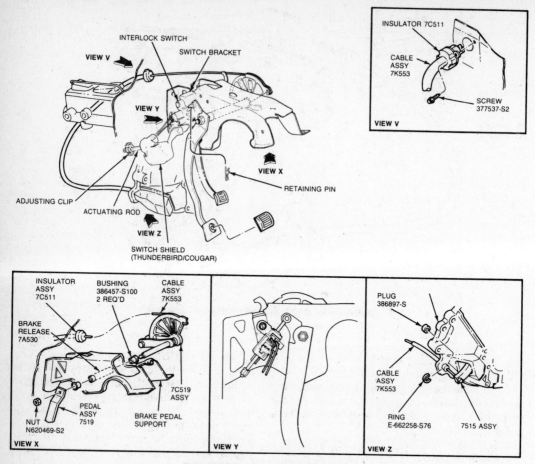

Self-adjusting clutch components

pressed to the floor. The self-adjuster consists of a two-piece clip snapped together over a serrated rod. When the plunger or rod is extended, the clip bottoms out on the switch body and allows the rod to ratchet over the serrations to a position determined by the clutch pedal travel limit. In this way, the switch is set to close the starter circuit when the clutch is pressed all the way to the floor (clutch disengaged).

Testing Continuity

1. Disconnect inline wiring connector at jumper harness.

2. Using a test lamp or continuity tester, check that switch is open with clutch pedal up (clutch engaged), and closed at approximately 1" (25.4mm) from the clutch pedal full down position (clutch disengaged).

3. If switch does not operate, check to see if

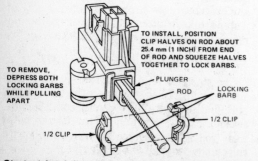

Starter/clutch interlock switch self-adjuster clip installation

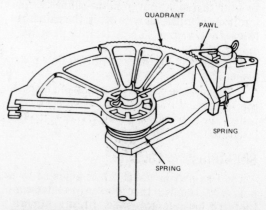

Self-adjusting clutch mechanism

Self-Adjusting Clutch Diagnosis

Condition	Possible Source	Action
Clutch does not disengage.	Pawl binding due to entrapped sound absorber	Remove contamination and free up pawl.
Clutch gears clash while shifting.	Pawl does not fully engage due to missing or weak pawl spring	Install new spring (pawl).
Pedal makes racheting noise while traveling to floor.	Teeth stripped on pawl or quadrant	Replace worn components.
Pedal travels to floor with no effort or noise.	Pawl does not engage quadrant due to missing spring	Install new spring (pawl).
Excessive pedal effort over 20 kg (45 lbs).*	Damaged or worn cable	Inspect cable. Replace if kinked or crushed.
	Clutch cable excessive wear	Disconnect cable from release lever. Check for smooth operation or binding. Replace if operation is erratic.
	Clutch pedal binding	Disconnect cable from release lever. Check for free pedal movement. Free up as required.
	Clutch release lever binding	Inspect and service as required.
	Clutch disc worn or pressure plate damaged	Service as required
Vehicle will not start with clutch pedal fully depressed.	Clutch interlock switch improperly adjusted.	Reposition self-adjusting clip or rod on press and release clutch pedal.
	Clutch interlock switch damaged.	Perform continuity test. Replace switch if necessary.
	Starter, wiring or battery damaged.	Refer to Section 28-02 and/or Section 31-02.

*NOTE: In the event of a sheared teeth condition on the pawl or quadrant, the pedal efforts are to be evaluated after installation of new components. If the pedal efforts are in excess of 45 lbs., the clutch disc, pressure plate or clutch cable may require replacement.

the self-adjusting clip is out of position on the rod. It should be near the end of the rod.

4. If the self-adjusting clip is out of position, remove and reposition the clip to about 1" (25.4mm) from the end of the rod.

5. Reset the switch by pressing the clutch pedal to the floor.

6. Repeat Step 2. If switch is damaged, replace it.

REMOVAL AND INSTALLATION

Starter/Clutch Interlock Switch

1. Disconnect the wiring connector.

2. Remove the retaining pin from the clutch pedal.

3. Remove the switch bracket attaching screw.

4. Lift the switch and bracket assembly upward to disengage tab from pedal support.

5. Move the switch outward to disengage actuating rod eyelet from clutch pedal pin and remove switch from vehicle.

WARNING: *Always install the switch with the self-adjusting clip about 1" (25.4mm) from the end of the rod. The clutch pedal must be fully up (clutch engaged). Otherwise, the switch may be misadjusted.*

6. Place the eyelet end of the rod onto the pivot pin.

7. Swing the switch assembly around to line up hole in the mounting boss with the hole in the bracket.

8. Install the attaching screw.

9. Replace the retaining pin in the pivot pin.

10. Connect the wiring connector.

Clutch Pedal Assembly

1. Remove the starter/clutch interlock switch.

2. Remove the clutch pedal attaching nut.

3. Pull the clutch pedal off the clutch pedal shaft.

4. Align the square hole of the clutch pedal

with the clutch pedal shaft and push the clutch pedal on.

5. Install the clutch pedal attaching nut and tighten to 32-50 ft. lbs.

6. Install the starter/clutch interlock switch.

Self-Adjusting Assembly

1. Disconnect the battery cable from the negative terminal of the battery.

2. Remove the steering wheel using a steering wheel puller Tool T67L-3600-A or equivalent.

3. Remove the lower dash panel section to the left of the steering column.

4. Remove the shrouds from the steering column.

5. Disconnect the brake lamp switch and the master cylinder pushrod from the brake pedal.

6. Rotate the clutch quadrant forward and unhook the clutch cable from the quadrant. Allow the quadrant to slowly swing rearward.

7. Remove the bolt holding the brake pedal support bracket lateral brace to the left side of the vehicle.

8. Disconnect all electrical connectors to the steering column.

9. Remove the 4 nuts that hold the steering column to the brake pedal support bracket and lower the steering column to the floor.

10. Remove the 4 booster nuts that hold the brake pedal support bracket to the dash panel.

11. Remove the bolt that holds the brake pedal support bracket to the underside of the instrument panel, and remove the brake pedal support bracket assembly from the vehicle.

12. Remove the clutch pedal shaft nut and the clutch pedal as outlined.

13. Slide the self-adjusting mechanism out of the brake pedal support bracket.

14. Remove the self-adjusting mechanism shaft bushings from either side of the brake pedal support bracket and replace if worn.

15. Lubricate the self-adjusting mechanism shaft with motor oil and install the mechanism into the brake pedal support bracket.

16. Position the quadrant towards the top of the vehicle. Align the flats on the shaft with the flats in the clutch pedal assembly, and install the retaining nuts. Tighten to 32-50 ft. lbs.

17. Position the brake pedal support bracket assembly beneath the instrument panel aligning the four holes with the studs in the dash panel. Install the four nuts loosely. Install the bolt through the support bracket into the instrument panel and tighten to 13-25 ft. lbs.

18. Tighten the four booster nuts that hold the brake pedal support bracket to the dash panel to 13-25 ft. lbs.

19. Connect the brake lamp switch and the master cylinder pushrod to the brake pedal.

20. Attach the clutch cable to the quadrant.

21. Position the steering column onto the four studs in the support bracket and start the four nuts.

22. Connect the steering column electrical connectors.

23. Install the steering column shrouds.

24. Install the brake pedal support lateral brace.

25. Tighten the steering column attaching nuts to 20-37 ft. lbs.

26. Install the lower dash panel section.

27. Install the steering wheel.

28. Connect the battery cable to the negative terminal on the battery.

29. Check the steering column for proper operation.

30. Depress the clutch pedal several times to adjust cable.

Quadrant Pawl, Self-Adjusting

1. Remove the self-adjusting mechanism.

2. Remove the two hairpin clips that hold the pawl and quadrant on the shaft assembly.

3. Remove the quadrant and quadrant spring.

4. Remove the pawl spring.

5. Remove the pawl.

6. Lubricate the pawl and quadrant pivot shafts with M1C75B or equivalent grease.

7. Install pawl. Position the teeth of the pawl toward the long shaft, and the spring hole at the end of the arm. Do not position the spring hole beneath the arm.

8. Insert the straight portion of the spring into the hole, with the coil up.

9. Keeping the straight portion in the hole rotate the spring 180 degrees to the left and slide the coiled portion of the spring over the boss.

10. Hook the bend portion of the spring under the arm.

11. Install the retainer clip on opposite side of spring.

12. Place the quadrant spring on the shaft with the bent portion of the spring in the hole in the arm.

13. Place the lubricated quadrant on the shaft aligning the projection at the bottom of the quadrant to a position beneath the arm of the shaft assembly. Push the pawl up so the bottom tooth of the pawl meshes with bottom tooth of quadrant.

14. Install the quadrant retainer pin.

15. Grasp the straight end of the quadrant spring with pliers and position behind the ear of the quadrant.

16. Install the self-adjusting mechanism.

17. Install the clutch pedal assembly.

Clutch Cable Assembly

1. Lift the clutch pedal to its upward most position to disengage the pawl and quadrant. Push the quadrant forward, unhook the cable from the quadrant and allow to slowly swing rearward.

2. Open the hood and remove the screw that holds the cable assembly isolator to the dash panel.

3. Pull the cable through the dash panel and into the engine compartment. On 4-140 EFI turbocharged and 8-302 engines, remove cable bracket screw from fender apron.

4. Raise the vehicle and safely support on jackstands.

5. Remove the dust cover from the bell housing.

6. Remove the clip retainer holding the cable assembly to the bell housing.

7. Slide the ball on the end of the cable assembly through the hole in the clutch release lever and remove the cable.

8. Remove the dash panel isolator from the cable.

9. Install the dash panel isolator on the cable assembly.

10. Insert the cable through the hole in the bell housing and through the hole in the clutch release lever. Slide the ball on the end of the cable assembly away from the hole in the clutch release lever.

11. Install the clip retainer that holds the cable assembly to the bell housing.

12. Install the dust shield on the bell housing.

13. Push the cable assembly into the engine compartment and lower the vehicle. On 4-140 EFI turbocharged and 8-302 engines, install cable bracket screw in fender apron.

14. Push the cable assembly into the hole in the dash panel and secure the isolater with a screw.

15. Install the cable assembly by lifting the clutch pedal to disengage the pawl and quadrant, the, pushing the quadrant forward, hook the end of the cable over the rear of the quadrant.

16. Depress clutch pedal several times to adjust cable.

Hydraulic Clutch

MASTER CYLINDER REMOVAL AND INSTALLATION

1. Remove the slave cylinder as outlined below.

2. Unbolt and remove the reservoir.

3. Turn the master cylinder 45° clockwise and slowly pull it out.

4. Installation is the reverse of removal.

SLAVE CYLINDER REMOVAL AND INSTALLATION

1. Raise and support the front end on jackstands.

2. Unbolt and remove the dust cover.

3. Unlatch the slave cylinder from the transmission housing bracket.

4. Place a drip pan under the cylinder and disconnect the fluid line. Cap the line.

5. Installation is the reverse of removal.

CLUTCH INTERLOCK SWITCH REMOVAL AND INSTALLATION

1. Remove the switch mounting bracket nuts.

2. Disconnect the wiring.

3. Remove the switch and bracket.

4. Installation is the reverse of removal.

AUTOMATIC TRANSMISSION

Understanding Automatic Transmissions

The automatic transmission allows engine torque and power to be transmitted to the rear wheels within a narrow range of engine operating speeds. The transmission will allow the engine to turn fast enough to produce plenty of power and torque at very low speeds, while keeping it at a sensible rpm at high vehicle speeds. The transmission performs this job entirely without driver assistance. The transmission uses a light fluid as the medium for the transmission of power. This fluid also works in the operation of various hydraulic control circuits and as a lubricant. Because the transmission fluid performs all of these three functions, trouble within the unit can easily travel from one part to another. For this reason, and because of the complexity and unusual operating principles of the transmission, a very sound understanding of the basic principles of operation will simplify troubleshooting.

THE TORQUE CONVERTER

The torque converter replaces the conventional clutch. It has three functions:

1. It allows the engine to idle with the vehicle at a standstill, even with the transmission in gear.

2. It allows the transmission to shift from range to range smoothly, without requiring that the driver close the throttle during the shift.

3. It multiplies engine torque to an increasing extent as vehicle speed drops and throttle opening is increased. This has the effect of mak-

ing the transmission more responsive and reduces the amount of shifting required.

The torque converter is a metal case which is shaped like a sphere that has been flattened on opposite sides. It is bolted to the rear end of the engine's crankshaft. Generally, the entire metal case rotates at engine speed and serves as the engine's flywheel.

The case contains three sets of blades. One set is attached directly to the case. This set forms the torus or pump. Another set is directly connected to the output shaft, and forms the turbine. The third set is mounted on a hub which, in turn, is mounted on a stationary shaft through a one-way clutch. This third set is known as the stator.

A pump, which is driven by the converter hub at engine speed, keeps the torque converter full of transmission fluid at all times. Fluid flows continuously through the unit to provide cooling.

Under low speed acceleration, the torque converter functions as follows:

The torus is turning faster than the turbine. It picks up fluid at the center of the converter and, through centrifugal force, slings it outward. Since the outer edge of the converter moves faster than the portions at the center, the fluid picks up speed.

The fluid then enters the outer edge of the turbine blades. It then travels back toward the center of the converter case along the turbine blades. In impinging upon the turbine blades, the fluid loses the energy picked up in the torus.

If the fluid were now to immediately be returned directly into the torus, both halves of the converter would have to turn at approximately the same speed at all times, and torque input and output would both be the same.

In flowing through the torus and turbine, the fluid picks up two types of flow, or flow in two separate directions. It flows through the turbine blades, and it spins with the engine. The stator, whose blades are stationary when the vehicle is being accelerated at low speeds, converts one type of flow into another. Instead of allowing the fluid to flow straight back into the torus, the stator's curved blades turn the fluid almost 90 degrees toward the direction of rotation of the engine. Thus the fluid does not flow as fast toward the torus, but is already spinning when the torus picks it up. This has the effect of allowing the torus to turn much faster than the turbine. This difference in speed may be compared to the difference in speed between the smaller and larger gears in any gear train. The result is that engine power output is higher, and engine torque is multiplied.

As the speed of the turbine increases, the fluid spins faster and faster in the direction of engine rotation. As a result, the ability of the stator to redirect the fluid flow is reduced. Under cruising conditions, the stator is eventually forced to rotate on its one-way clutch in the direction of engine rotation. Under these conditions, the torque converter begins to behave almost like a solid shaft, with the torus and turbine speeds being almost equal.

THE PLANETARY GEARBOX

The ability of the torque converter to multiply engine torque is limited. Also, the unit tends to be more efficient when the turbine is rotating at relatively high speeds. Therefore, a planetary gearbox is used to carry the power output of the turbine to the driveshaft.

Planetary gears function very similarly to conventional transmission gears. However, their construction is different in that three elements make up one gear system, and, in that all three elements are different from one another. The three elements are: an outer gear that is shaped like a hoop, with teeth cut into the inner surface; a sun gear, mounted on a shaft and located at the very center of the outer gear; and a set of three planet gears, held by pins in a ring-like planet carrier, meshing with both the sun gear and the outer gear. Either the outer gear or the sun gear may be held stationary, providing more than one possible torque multiplication factor for each set of gears. Also, if all three gears are forced to rotate at the same speed, the gearset forms, in effect, a solid shaft.

Most modern automatics use the planetary gears to provide either a single reduction ratio of about 1.8:1, or two reduction gears: a low of about 2.5:1, and an intermediate of about 1.5:1. Bands and clutches are used to hold various portions of the gearsets to the transmission case or to the shaft on which they are mounted. Shifting is accomplished, then, by changing the portion of each planetary gearset which is held to the transmission case or to the shaft.

THE SERVOS AND ACCUMULATORS

The servos are hydraulic pistons and cylinders. They resemble the hydraulic actuators used on many familiar machines, such as bulldozers. Hydraulic fluid enters the cylinder, under pressure, and forces the piston to move to engage the band or clutches.

The accumulators are used to cushion the engagement of the servos. The transmission fluid must pass through the accumulator on the way to the servo. The accumulator housing contains a thin piston which is sprung away from the discharge passage of the accumulator. When fluid passes through the accumulator on the way to the servo, it must move the piston against spring pressure, and this action smooths out the action of the servo.

THE HYDRAULIC CONTROL SYSTEM

The hydraulic pressure used to operate the servos comes from the main transmission oil pump. This fluid is channeled to the various servos through the shift valves. There is generally a manual shift valve which is operated by the transmission selector lever and an automatic shift valve for each automatic upshift the transmission provides: i.e., 2-speed automatics have a low/high shift valve, while 3-speeds have a 1-2 valve, and a 2-3 valve.

There are two pressures which effect the operation of these valves. One is the governor pressure which is affected by vehicle speed. The other is the modulator pressure which is affected by intake manifold vacuum or throttle position. Governor pressure rises with an increase in vehicle speed, and modulator pressure rises as the throttle is opened wider. By responding to these two pressures, the shift valves cause the upshift points to be delayed with increased

throttle opening to make the best use of the engine's power output.

Most transmissions also make use of an auxiliary circuit for downshifting. This circuit may be actuated by the throttle linkage or the vacuum line which actuates the modulator, or by a cable or solenoid. It applies pressure to a special downshift surface on the shift valve or valves.

The transmission modulator also governs the line pressure, used to actuate the servos. In this way, the clutches and bands will be actuated with a force matching the torque output of the engine.

Pan Removal and Filter Change

NOTE: *Refer to Chapter 1 for current fluid requirements.*

C3, C4, C5

1. Raise the vehicle, so that the transmission oil pan is readily accessible. Safely support on jackstands.

2. Disconnect the fluid filler tube from the

Troubleshooting Basic Automatic Transmission Problems

Problem	Cause	Solution
Fluid leakage	• Defective pan gasket	• Replace gasket or tighten pan bolts
	• Loose filler tube	• Tighten tube nut
	• Loose extension housing to transmission case	• Tighten bolts
	• Converter housing area leakage	• Have transmission checked professionally
Fluid flows out the oil filler tube	• High fluid level	• Check and correct fluid level
	• Breather vent clogged	• Open breather vent
	• Clogged oil filter or screen	• Replace filter or clean screen (change fluid also)
	• Internal fluid leakage	• Have transmission checked professionally
Transmission overheats (this is usually accompanied by a strong burned odor to the fluid)	• Low fluid level	• Check and correct fluid level
	• Fluid cooler lines clogged	• Drain and refill transmission. If this doesn't cure the problem, have cooler lines cleared or replaced.
	• Heavy pulling or hauling with insufficient cooling	• Install a transmission oil cooler
	• Faulty oil pump, internal slippage	• Have transmission checked professionally
Buzzing or whining noise	• Low fluid level	• Check and correct fluid level
	• Defective torque converter, scored gears	• Have transmission checked professionally
No forward or reverse gears or slippage in one or more gears	• Low fluid level	• Check and correct fluid level
	• Defective vacuum or linkage controls, internal clutch or band failure	• Have unit checked professionally
Delayed or erratic shift	• Low fluid level	• Check and correct fluid level
	• Broken vacuum lines	• Repair or replace lines
	• Internal malfunction	• Have transmission checked professionally

Lockup Torque Converter Service Diagnosis

Problem	Cause	Solution

No lockup	• Faulty oil pump
	• Sticking governor valve
	• Valve body malfunction
	   (a) Stuck switch valve
	   (b) Stuck lockup valve
	   (c) Stuck fail-safe valve
	• Failed locking clutch
	• Leaking turbine hub seal
	• Faulty input shaft or seal ring
		• Replace oil pump
		• Repair or replace as necessary
		• Repair or replace valve body or its internal components as necessary
		
		• Replace torque converter
		• Replace torque converter
		• Repair or replace as necessary

Will not unlock	• Sticking governor valve
	• Valve body malfunction
	   (a) Stuck switch valve
	   (b) Stuck lockup valve
	   (c) Stuck fail-safe valve
		• Repair or replace as necessary
		• Repair or replace valve body or its internal components as necessary

Stays locked up at too low a speed in direct	• Sticking governor valve
	• Valve body malfunction
	   (a) Stuck switch valve
	   (b) Stuck lockup valve
	   (c) Stuck fail-safe valve
		• Repair or replace as necessary
		• Repair or replace valve body or its internal components as necessary

Locks up or drags in low or second	• Faulty oil pump
	• Valve body malfunction
	   (a) Stuck switch valve
	   (b) Stuck fail-safe valve
		• Replace oil pump
		• Repair or replace valve body or its internal components as necessary

Sluggish or stalls in reverse	• Faulty oil pump
	• Plugged cooler, cooler lines or fittings
	• Valve body malfunction
	   (a) Stuck switch valve
	   (b) Faulty input shaft or seal ring
		• Replace oil pump as necessary
		• Flush or replace cooler and flush lines and fittings
		• Repair or replace valve body or its internal components as necessary

Loud chatter during lockup engagement (cold)	• Faulty torque converter • Failed locking clutch • Leaking turbine hub seal	• Replace torque converter • Replace torque converter • Replace torque converter
Vibration or shudder during lockup engagement	• Faulty oil pump • Valve body malfunction • Faulty torque converter • Engine needs tune-up	• Repair or replace oil pump as necessary • Repair or replace valve body or its internal components as necessary • Replace torque converter • Tune engine
Vibration after lockup engagement	• Faulty torque converter • Exhaust system strikes underbody • Engine needs tune-up • Throttle linkage misadjusted	• Replace torque converter • Align exhaust system • Tune engine • Adjust throttle linkage
Vibration when revved in neutral Overheating: oil blows out of dip stick tube or pump seal	• Torque converter out of balance • Plugged cooler, cooler lines or fittings • Stuck switch valve	• Replace torque converter • Flush or replace cooler and flush lines and fittings • Repair switch valve in valve body or replace valve body
Shudder after lockup engagement	• Faulty oil pump • Plugged cooler, cooler lines or fittings • Valve body malfunction • Faulty torque converter • Fail locking clutch • Exhaust system strikes underbody • Engine needs tune-up • Throttle linkage misadjusted	• Replace oil pump • Flush or replace cooler and flush lines and fittings • Repair or replace valve body or its internal components as necessary • Replace torque converter • Replace torque converter • Align exhaust system • Tune engine • Adjust throttle linkage

Transmission Fluid Indications

The appearance and odor of the transmission fluid can give valuable clues to the overall condition of the transmission. Always note the appearance of the fluid when you check the fluid level or change the fluid. Rub a small amount of fluid between your fingers to feel for grit and smell the fluid on the dipstick.

If the fluid appears:	It indicates:
Clear and red colored	• Normal operation
Discolored (extremely dark red or brownish) or smells burned	• Band or clutch pack failure, usually caused by an overheated transmission. Hauling very heavy loads with insufficient power or failure to change the fluid, often result in overheating. Do not confuse this appearance with newer fluids that have a darker red color and a strong odor (though not a burned odor).
Foamy or aerated (light in color and full of bubbles)	• The level is too high (gear train is churning oil) • An internal air leak (air is mixing with the fluid). Have the transmission checked professionally.
Solid residue in the fluid	• Defective bands, clutch pack or bearings. Bits of band material or metal abrasives are clinging to the dipstick. Have the transmission checked professionally.
Varnish coating on the dipstick	• The transmission fluid is overheating

pan and allow the fluid to drain into an appropriate container.

3. Remove the transmission oil pan attaching bolts, pan and gasket.

4. Clean the transmission oil pan and transmission mating surfaces.

5. Install the transmission oil pan in the reverse order of removal, torquing the attaching bolts to 12-16 ft. lbs. and using a new gasket. Fill the transmission with 3 qts. of the correct type fluid.

6. Lower the vehicle. Start the engine and move the gear selector through shift pattern. Allow the engine to reach normal operating temperature.

7. Check the transmission fluid. Add fluid, if necessary, to maintain correct level.

AOD

1. Raise the car and support on jackstands.

2. Place a drain pan under the transmission.

3. Loosen the pan attaching bolts and drain the fluid from the transmission.

4. When the fluid has drained to the level of the pan flange, remove the remaining pan bolts working from the rear and both sides of the pan to allow it to drop and drain slowly.

5. When all of the fluid has drained, remove the pan and clean it thoroughly. discard the pan gasket.

6. Place a new gasket on the pan, and install the pan on the transmission. Tighten the attaching bolts to 12-16 ft. lbs.

7. Add three quarts of fluid to the transmission through the filler tube.

8. Lower the vehicle. Start the engine and

move the gear selector through shift pattern. Allow the engine to reach normal operating temperature.

9. Check the transmission fluid. Add fluid, if necessary, to maintain correct level.

Fluid pan removal, automatic transmissions (shown upside down)

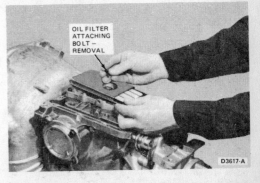

Filter element removal, automatics (shown upside down)

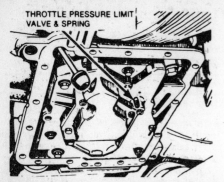

C4 throttle limit valve and spring. They are held in place by the transmission filter. The valve is installed with the large end towards the valve body, the spring fits over the valve stem.

Adjustments

SHIFT LINKAGE ADJUSTMENT

Column Shift

1. With the engine off, place the gear selector in the D (Drive) position, or D (overdrive) position (AOD). Either hang a weight on the shifter or have an assistant sit in the car and hold the selector against the stop.

2. Loosen the adjusting nut or clamp at the shift lever so that the shift rod if free to slide. On models with a shift cable, remove the nut from the transmission lever and disconnect the cable from the transmission.

3. Place the manual shift lever on the transmission in the D (Drive) or D (Overdrive) posi-

tion. This is the second detent position from the full counterclockwise position.

4. Tighten the adjusting bolt. On cars with a cable, position the cable end on the transmission lever stud, aligning the flats. Tighten the adjusting nut.

5. Check the pointer alignment and transmission operation for all selector positions. If not correct, adjust linkage.

Floor or Console Shift

1. Place the transmission shift lever in D.

2. Raise the vehicle and loosen the manual lever shift rod retaining nut. Move the transmission lever to D1 or D position. D is the fourth detent from the rear.

3. With the transmission shift lever and transmission manual lever in position, tighten the nut at point A to 10-20 ft. lbs.

4. Check transmission operation for all selector lever detent positions.

Back-up Light Switch

NOTE: *Vehicles with a floor mounted shifter incorporate the back-up light switch into the neutral start switch. For those vehicles, see the Neutral Start Switch section, below.*

REMOVAL, INSTALLATION AND ADJUSTMENT

Column Mounted Shifters

1. Working under the instrument panel, disconnect the wiring at the switch.

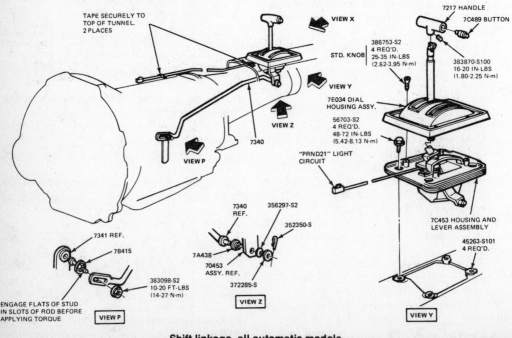

Shift linkage, all automatic models

2. On cars so equipped, disconnect the 2 parking brake release vacuum hoses.

3. Remove the 2 screws securing the switch to the steering column and remove the switch.

4. Check the column to make sure that the metal switch actuator is secured to the shift tube and that it is seated as far as possible forward against the shift tube bearing. Also check for a broken or damaged actuator.

5. When installing the new switch, align the hole in the switch with the hole in the bracket and insert a No. 43 drill through the holes.

6. Place the shift lever in the DRIVE position and hold it against the detent. Install and tighten the switch mounting screws.

7. Remove the drill bit.

8. Connect the wires.

NEUTRAL START SWITCH REMOVAL, INSTALLATION AND ADJUSTMENT

NOTE: *The neutral safety switch on C3 and AOD transmission is non-adjustable.*

1979 Floor Mounted Shifters

1. Place the shift lever in NEUTRAL.

2. Raise and support the car on jackstands.

3. Remove the nut that secures the shift rod to the transmission manual lever. Make sure that the rod is free on the selector lever grommet.

4. Remove the shift lever handle.

5. Remove the shift lever selector housing.

6. Disconnect the dial light.

7. Disconnect the back-up/neutral start switch wires and selector indicator light wires at the instrument panel.

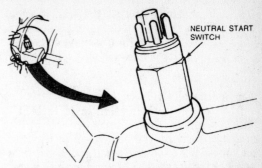

Neutral start switch used on the C3, AOD and A4LD

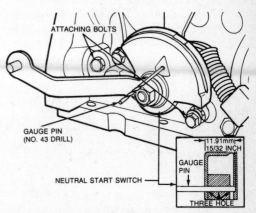

Neutral start switch adjustment on the C5

8. Remove the selector lever housing.

9. Remove the selector pointer shield.

10. Remove the 2 neutral start/back-up light switch screws and remove the switch. Push the harness plug inward and remove the switch and harness.

11. Before installing the new switch, be sure that the selector lever is against the neutral detent stop and the actuator lever is properly aligned in the neutral position.

12. Position the harness and switch in the housing. Install the two screws loosely.

13. Put the selector lever in PARK and hold it against the forward stop.

14. Move the switch to the end of its rearward travel.

15. Hold the switch in this position and tighten the two attaching screws.

16. The remainder of installation is the reverse of removal. Check the operation of the switch.

1981-84 Floor Mounted Shifter

1. Raise and support the front end on jackstands.

2. Remove the downshift linkage rod from the transmission downshift lever.

3. Apply penetrating oil to the downshift le-

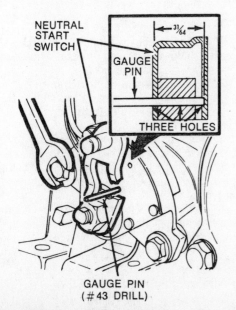

GAUGE PIN
(# 43 DRILL)

C-4 neutral start switch adjustment

ver shaft and nut. Remove the transmission downshift outer lever retaining nut and lever.

4. Remove the 2 switch attaching screws.

5. Unplug the connector and remove the switch.

6. Position the new switch on the transmission and install the bolts loosely.

7. Place the transmission lever in NEUTRAL, rotate the switch until the hole in the switch aligns with the depression in the case and insert a No. 43 drill bit through the hole and into the depression. Make sure the drill bit is fully inserted. Tighten the switch bolts to 60 in.lb. Remove the gauge pin.

8. The remainder of installation is the reverse of removal. Torque the shaft nut to 20 ft. lbs.

1985-88 C5 w/Floor Shift

1. Raise and support the front end on jackstands.

2. Remove the downshift linkage rod from the transmission downshift lever.

3. Apply penetrating oil to the downshift lever shaft and nut. Remove the transmission downshift outer lever retaining nut and lever.

4. Remove the 2 switch attaching screws.

5. Unplug the connector and remove the switch.

6. Position the new switch on the transmission and install the bolts loosely.

7. Place the transmission lever in NEUTRAL, rotate the switch until the hole in the switch aligns with the depression in the case and insert a No. 43 drill bit through the hole and into the depression. Make sure the drill bit is fully inserted. Tighten the switch bolts to 60 in.lb. Remove the gauge pin.

8. The remainder of installation is the reverse of removal. Torque the shaft nut to 20 ft. lbs.

1985-88 AOD w/Floor Shift

1. Place the selector lever in the MANUAL LOW position.

2. Diasconnect the battery ground.

3. Raise and support the car on jackstands.

4. Disconnect the switch harness by pushing the harness straight up off the switch with a long screwdriver underneath the rubber plug section.

5. Using special tool socket T74P-77247-A, or equivalent, on a ratchet extension at least 9½" (241mm) long, unscrew the switch. Once the tool is on the switch, reach around the rear of the transmission over the extension housing.

6. Installation is the reverse of removal. Use a new O-ring. Torque the switch to 11 ft. lbs.

DOWNSHIFT (THROTTLE) LINKAGE ADJUSTMENT

All Models Except AOD Transmissions

1. With the engine off, disconnect the throttle and downshift return springs, if equipped.

2. Hold the carburetor throttle lever in the wide open position against the stop.

3. Hold the transmission downshift linkage in the full downshift position against the internal stop.

4. Turn the adjustment screw on the carburetor downshift lever to obtain 0.010-0.080" (0.254-2.032mm) clearance between the screw tip and the throttle shaft lever tab.

5. Release the transmission and carburetor to their normal free positions. Install the throttle and downshift return springs, if removed.

AOD

1. With the engine off, remove the air cleaner and make sure the fast idle cam is released; the throttle lever must be at the idle stop.

2. Turn the linkage lever adjusting screw counterclockwise until the end of the screw is flush with the face of the lever.

3. Turn the linkage adjustment screw in until there is a maximum clearance of 0.005" (0.127mm) between the throttle lever and the end of the adjustment screw.

4. Turn the linkage lever adjusting screw clockwise three full turns. A minimum of one turn is permissible if the screw travel is limited.

5. If it is not possible to turn the adjusting screw at least one full turn or if the initial gap of 0.005" (0.127mm) could not be obtained, perform the linkage adjustment at the transmission.

AOD Alternate Method

If you are unable to adjust the throttle valve control linkage at the carburetor, as described above, proceed as follows.

1. At the transmission, loosen the 8 mm bolt on the throttle (TV) control rod sliding trunnion block. Make sure the trunnion block slides freely on the control rod.

2. Push up on the lower end of the TV control rod to insure that the carburetor linkage lever is held against the throttle lever. When the pressure is released, the control rod must stay in position.

3. Force the TV control lever on the transmission against its internal stop. While maintaining pressure tighten the trunnion block bolt. Make sure the throttle lever is at the idle stop.

AOD IDLE SPEED ADJUSTMENT

Whenever it is necessary to adjust the idle speed by more than 50 rpm either above or below the factory specifications, the adjustment screw on the linkage lever at the carburetor should used. 1½ turns either way will change the idle speed by 50-100 rpm; 2½ turns either way will change the idle speed by 100-150 rpm.

After making any idle speed adjustments, make sure the linkage lever and throttle lever are in contact with the throttle lever at its idle stop and verify that the shift lever is in N (neutral).

BAND ADJUSTMENTS

NOTE: *No external adjustments are possible on AOD transmissions.*

C3 Front Band

1. Wipe clean the area around the adjusting screw on the side of the transmission, near the left front corner of the transmission.
2. Remove the adjusting screw locknut and discard it.
3. Install a new locknut on the adjusting screw but do not tighten it.
4. Tighten the adjusting screw to exactly 10 ft. lbs.

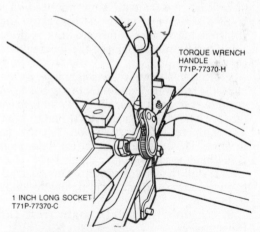

TORQUE WRENCH HANDLE T71P-77370-H

1 INCH LONG SOCKET T71P-77370-C

C3 front band adjustment

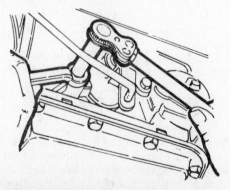

C-4, C-5 intermediate band adjustment

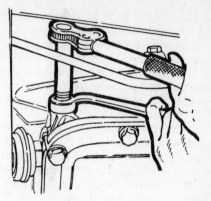

C-4, C-5 reverse band adjustment

5. Back off the adjusting screw exactly 2 turns.
6. Hold the adjusting screw so that it does not turn and tighten the adjusting screw locknut to 35-45 ft. lbs.

C4 and C5 Intermediate Band

1. Clean all the dirt from the adjusting screw and remove and discard the locknut.
2. Install a new locknut on the adjusting screw using a torque wrench, tighten the adjusting screw to 10 ft. lbs.
3. Back off the adjusting screw exactly 1¾ turns for the C4 and 4¼ turns for the C5.
4. Hold the adjusting screw steady and tighten the locknut to 35 ft. lbs.

C4, and C5 Low-Reverse Band

1. Clean all dirt from around the band adjusting screw, and remove and discard the locknut.
2. Install a new locknut of the adjusting screw. Using a torque wrench, tighten the adjusting screw to 10 ft. lbs.
3. Back off the adjusting screw exactly three full turns.
4. Hold the adjusting screw steady and tighten the locknut to 35 ft. lbs.

Transmission
REMOVAL AND INSTALLATION
C3

1. Raise and safely support the vehicle.
2. Place a drain pan under the transmission fluid pan. Starting at the rear of the pan and working toward the front, loosen the attaching bolts and allow the fluid to drain. Then remove all of the pan attaching bolts except two at the front, to allow the fluid to further drain. After all the fluid has drained, install two bolts on the rear side of the pan to temporarily hold it in place.
3. Remove the converter drain plug access

cover and adapter plate bolts from the lower end of the converter housing.

4. Remove the four flywheel to converter attaching nuts. Crank the engine to turn the converter to gain access to the nuts, using a wrench on the crankshaft pulley attaching bolt. On belt driven overheat camshaft engines, never turn the engine backwards.

5. Crank the engine until the converter drain plug is accessible and remove the plug. Place a drain pan under the converter to catch the fluid. After all the fluid has been drained from the converter, reinstall the plug and tighten to specification.

6. Remove the driveshaft and install the extension housing seal replacer tool in the extension housing.

7. Remove the speedometer cable from the extension housing.

8. Disconnect the shift rod at the transmission manual lever. Disconnect the downshift rod at the transmission downshift lever.

9. Remove the starter-to-converter housing attaching bolts and position the starter out of the way.

10. Disconnect the neutral start switch wires from the switch.

11. Remove the vacuum line from the transmission vacuum unit.

12. Position a transmission jack under the transmission and raise it slightly.

13. Remove the engine rear support-to-crossmember nut.

14. Remove the crossmember-to-frame side support attaching bolts and remove the crossmember.

15. Remove the inlet pipe steady rest from the inlet pipe and rear engine support; then disconnect the muffler inlet pipe at the exhaust manifold and secure it.

16. Lower the jack under the transmission and allow the transmission to hang.

17. Position a jack to the front of the engine and raise the engine to gain access to the two upper converter housing-to-engine attaching bolts.

18. Disconnect the oil cooler lines at the transmission. Plug all openings to keep out dirt.

19. Remove the lower converter housing-to-engine attaching bolts.

20. Remove the transmission filter tube.

21. Secure the transmission to the jack with a safety chain.

22. Remove the two upper converter housing-to-engine attaching bolts. Move the transmission to the rear and down to remove it from under the vehicle.

23. Tighten the converter drain plug to 20-30 ft. lbs. if not previously done.

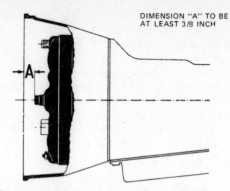

DIMENSION "A" TO BE AT LEAST 3/8 INCH

C3 converter hub-to-housing flange position

24. Position the converter to the transmission making sure the converter hub is fully engaged in the pump gear. The dimension given in the illustration is for guidance only. It does not indicate engagement.

25. With the converter properly installed, place the transmission on the jack and secure with safety chain.

26. Rotate the converter so the drive studs and drain plug are in alignment with their holes in the flywheel.

27. With the transmission mounted on a transmission jack, move the converter and transmission assembly forward into position being careful not to damage the flywheel and the converter pilot.

During this move, to avoid damage, do not allow the transmission to get into a nosed down position as this will cause the converter to move forward and disengage from the pump gear. The converter must rest squarely against the flywheel. This indicates that the converter pilot is not binding in the engine crankshaft.

28. Install the two upper converter housing-to-engine attaching bolts and tighten to 28-38 ft. lbs.

29. Remove the safety chain from the transmission.

30. Insert the filler tube in the stub tube and secure it to the cylinder block with the attaching bolt. Tighten the bolt to 28-38 ft. lbs. If the stub tube is loosened or dislodged, it should be replaced.

31. Install the oil cooler lines in the retaining clip at the cylinder block. Connect the lines to the transmission case.

32. Remove the jack supporting the front of the engine.

33. Position the muffler inlet pipe support bracket to the converter housing and install the four lower converter housing-to-engine attaching bolts. Tighten the bolts to 28-38 ft. lbs.

34. Raise the transmission. Position the crossmember to the frame side supports and in-

stall the attaching bolts. Tighten the bolts to 30-40 ft. lbs.

35. Lower the transmission and install the rear engine support-to-crossmember nut. Tighten the nut to 30-40 ft. lbs.

36. Remove the transmission jack.

37. Install the vacuum hose on the transmission vacuum unit. Install the vacuum line into the retaining clip.

38. Connect the neutral start switch plug to the switch.

39. Install the starter and tighten the attaching bolts.

40. Install the four flywheel-to-converter attaching nuts.

41. Install the converter drain plug access cover and adaptor plate bolts. Tighten the bolts to 15-20 ft. lbs.

42. Connect the muffler inlet pipe to the exhaust manifold.

43. Connect the transmission shift rod to the manual lever.

44. Connect the downshift rod to the downshift lever.

45. Connect the speedometer cable to the extension housing.

46. Install the driveshaft. Tighten the companion flange U-bolt attaching nuts to 30 ft. lbs.

47. Adjust the manual and downshift linkage as required.

48. Lower the vehicle. Fill the transmission to the proper level with Dexron®II. Pour in 5 quarts of fluid; then run the engine and add fluid as required.

49. Check the transmission, converter assembly and oil cooler lines for leaks.

C4

1. Raise and safely support the vehicle.

2. place the drain pan under the transmission fluid pan. Remove the fluid filler tube from the pan and drain the transmission fluid. On some models it may be necessary to loosen the pan attaching bolts and allow the fluid to drain. Start loosening the bolts at the rear of the pan and work toward the front. Finally remove all of the pan attaching bolts except two at the front, to allow the fluid to further drain. After the fluid has drained, install two bolts on the rear side of the pan to temporarily hold it in place.

3. Remove the converter drain plug access cover from the lower end of the converter housing.

4. Remove the converter-to-flywheel attaching nuts. Place a wrench on the crankshaft pulley attaching bolt to turn the converter to gain access to the nuts.

5. With the wrench on the crankshaft pulley attaching bolt, turn the converter to gain access to the converter drain plug. Then, remove the plug. Place a drain pan under the converter to catch the fluid. After the fluid has been drained from the converter, reinstall the plug.

6. Remove the driveshaft and install the extension housing seal replacer tool in the extension housing.

7. Remove the vacuum line hose from the transmission vacuum unit. Disconnect the vacuum line from the retaining clip. Disconnect the transmission regulated spark (T.R.S.) switch wire at the transmission, if so equipped.

8. Remove the engine support to crossmember bolts or nuts.

9. Remove the speedometer cable from the extension housing.

10. Disconnect the oil cooler lines from the transmission case.

11. Disconnect the selector rod or cable at the transmission manual lever. Disconnect the downshift rod at the transmission downshift lever.

12. On console and floor shift vehicles, disconnect the column lock rod at the transmission, if so equipped.

13. Disconnect the starter cable. Remove the starter attaching bolts and remove the starter from the converter housing.

14. Remove the bolt that secures the transmission fluid filler tube to the cylinder head and lift the fluid fitter tube from the case.

15. Position the transmission jack to support the transmission and secure the transmission to the jack with a safety chain.

16. Remove the crossmember attaching bolts and lower the crossmember.

17. Remove the five converter housing-to-engine attaching bolts. Lower the transmission and remove it from under the vehicle.

18. Torque the converter drain plug to 20-30 ft. lbs.

19. Position the converter to the transmission making sure the converter drive flats are fully engaged in the pump gear.

20. With the converter properly installed, place the transmission on the jack. Secure the transmission to the jack with a safety chain.

21. Rotate the converter so that the studs and drain plug are in alignment with their holes in the flywheel.

22. With the transmission mounted on a transmission jack, move the converter and transmission assembly forward into position, using care not to damage the flywheel and the converter pilot. The converter must rest squarely against the flywheel. This indicates that the converter pilot is not binding in the engine crankshaft.

23. Install the five converter housing-to-en-

gine attaching bolts. Torque the bolts to 23-28 ft. lbs. Remove the safety chain from the transmission.

24. Position the crossmember and install the attaching bolts. Torque the bolts to 40-50 ft. lbs.

25. Lower the transmission and install the engine support to crossmember bolts or nuts. Torque the bolts or nuts to 30-40 ft. lbs.

26. Install the flywheel to the converter attaching nuts. Torque the nuts to 23-28 ft. lbs.

27. Remove the transmission jack. Install the fluid filler tube in the transmission case or pan. Secure the tube to the cylinder head with the attaching bolt. Install the vacuum hose on the transmission vacuum unit. Install the vacuum line retaining clip. Connect the transmission regulated spark (T.R.S.) switch wires to the switch, if so equipped.

28. Connect the fluid cooling lines to the transmission case.

29. Connect the downshift rod to the downshift lever.

30. Connect the selector rod or cable to the transmission manual lever. Connect the column lock rod on console and floor shift vehicles, if so equipped.

31. Connect the speedometer cable to the extension housing.

32. Install the converter housing cover and torque the attaching bolts to 12-16 ft. lbs.

33. Install the starter and torque the attaching bolts to 25-30 ft. lbs. Connect the starter cable.

34. Install the driveshaft. Torque the companion flange U-bolts attaching nuts to 25-30 ft. lbs.

35. Lower the vehicle. Fill the transmission to the proper level with fluid. Adjust the manual and downshift linkage as required.

C5

1. Open the hood and install protective covers on the fenders.

2. Disconnect the battery negative cable.

3. On models equipped with a 6-232 engine, remove the air cleaner assembly.

4. Remove the fan shroud attaching bolts and position the shroud back over the fan.

5. On models equipped with a 6-232 engine, loosen the clamp and disconnect the Thermactor® air injection hose at the catalytic converter check valve. The check valve is located on the right side of the engine compartment near the dash panel.

6. On models equipped with a 6-232 engine, remove the two transmission-to-engine attaching bolts located at the top of the transmission bell housing. These bolts are accessible from the engine compartment.

7. Raise and safely support the vehicle.

8. Remove the driveshaft.

9. Disconnect the muffler inlet pipe from the catalytic converter outlet pipe. Support the muffler/pipe assembly by wiring it to a convenient underbody bracket.

10. Remove the nuts attaching the exhaust pipe(s) to the exhaust manifold(s).

11. Pull back on the catalytic coverts to release the converter hangers from the mounting bracket.

12. Remove the speedometer clamps bolt and pull the speedometer out of the extension housing.

13. Separate the neutral start switch harness connector.

14. Disconnect the kick down rod at the transmission lever.

15. Disconnect the shift linkage at the linkage bellcrank. On vehicles equipped with floor mounted shift, remove the shift cable routing bracket attaching bolts and disconnect the cable at the transmission lever.

16. Remove the converter dust shield.

17. Remove the torque converter to drive plate attaching nuts. To gain access to the converter nuts, turn the crankshaft and drive plate using a ratchet handle and socket on the crankshaft pulley attaching bolt.

18. Remove the starter attaching bolts.

19. Loosen the nuts attaching the rear support to the No. 3 crossmember.

20. Position a transmission jack under the transmission oil pan. Secure the transmission to the jack with a safety chain.

21. Remove the through bolts attaching the No. 3 crossmember to the body brackets.

22. Lower the transmission enough to allow access to the cooler line fittings. Disconnect the cooler lines.

23. On models with the 6-232, remove the (4) remaining transmission-to-engine attaching bolts (2 each side). On all models, remove the (6) transmission-to-engine attaching bolts.

24. Pull the transmission back to disengage the converter studs from the drive plate. Lower the transmission out of the vehicle.

25. Raise the transmission into the vehicle. As the transmission is being slowly raised into position, rotate the torque converter until the studs and drain plug are aligned with the holes in the drive plate.

26. Move the converter/transmission assembly forward against the back of the engine. Make sure the converter studs engage the drive plate and that the transmission dowels on the back of the engine engage the bolts holes in the bellhousing.

27. On models equipped with a 6-232 engine, install four transmission-to-engine attaching

bolts (2 each side). On all other models, install the (6) transmission-to-engine attaching bolts. Tighten the attaching bolts to 40-50 ft. lbs.

28. Connect the cooler lines.

29. Raise the transmission and install the No. 3 crossmember through bolts. Tighten the attaching nuts to 20-30 ft. lbs.

30. Remove the safety chain and transmission jack.

31. Tighten the rear support attaching nuts to 30-50 ft. lbs.

32. Position the starter and install the attaching bolts.

33. Install the torque converter to drive plate attaching nuts. Tighten the attaching nuts to 20-30 ft. lbs.

34. Position the dust shield and on vehicles with column mounted shift, position the linkage bellcrank bracket. Install the attaching bolts and tighten to 12-16 ft. lbs.

35. Connect the shift linkage to the linkage bellcrank. On vehicles equipped with floor mounted shift, connect the cable to the shift lever and install the routing bracket attaching bolt.

36. Connect the kick down rod to the transmission lever.

37. Connect the neutral start switch harness.

38. Install the speedometer and the clamp bolt. Tighten the clamp bolt to 35-54 in.lb.

39. Install the catalytic converts using new seal(s) at the pipe(s) to exhaust manifold connection(s).

40. Install the pipe(s) to exhaust manifold attaching nuts. Do not tighten the attaching nuts.

41. Remove the wire supporting the muffler/pipe assembly and connect the pipe to the converter outlet. Do not tighten the attaching nuts.

42. Align the exhaust system and tighten the manifold and converter outlet attaching nuts.

43. Install the driveshaft.

44. Check and if necessary, adjust the shift linkage.

45. Lower the vehicle.

46. On models equipped with a 6-232 engine, install the two transmission-to-engine attaching bolts located at the top of the transmission bellhousing.

47. On models equipped with a 6-232 engine, connect the Thermactor® air injection hose to the converter check valve.

48. Position the fan shroud and install the attaching bolts.

49. On models equipped with a 6-232 engine, install the air cleaner assembly.

50. Connect the battery negative cable.

51. Start the engine. Make sure the engine cranks only when the selector lever is positioned in the neutral (N) or Park (P) detent.

52. Fill the transmission with type H fluid.

53. Raise the vehicle and inspect for fluid leaks.

Automatic Overdrive (AOD)

1. Raise and safely support the vehicle.

2. Place the drain pan under the transmission fluid pan. Starting at the rear of the pan and working toward the front, loosen the attaching bolts and allow the fluid to drain. Finally removal all of the pan attaching bolts except two at the front, to allow the fluid to further drain. With fluid drained, install two bolts on the rear side of the pan to temporarily hold it in place.

3. Remove the converter drain plug access cover from the lower end of the converter housing.

4. Remove the converter-to-flywheel attaching nuts. place a wrench on the crankshaft pulley attaching bolt to turn the converter to gain access to the nuts.

5. Place a drain pan under the converter to catch the fluid. With the wrench on the crankshaft pulley attaching bolts, turn the converter to gain access to the converter drain plug and remove the plug. After the fluid has been drained, reinstall the plug.

6. Disconnect the driveshaft from the rear axle and slide shaft rearward from the transmission. Install a seal installation tool in the extension housing to prevent fluid leakage.

7. Disconnect the cable from the terminal on the starter motor. Remove the three attaching bolts and remove the starter motor. Disconnect the neutral start switch wires at the plug connector.

8. Remove the rear mount-to-crossmember attaching bolts and the two crossmember-to-frame attaching bolts.

9. Remove the two engine rear support-to-extension housing attaching bolts.

10. Disconnect the TV linkage rod from the transmission TV lever. Disconnect the manual rod from the transmission manual lever at the transmission.

11. Remove the two bolts securing the bellcrank bracket to the converter housing.

12. Raise the transmission with a transmission jack to provide clearance to remove the crossmember. Remove the rear mount from the crossmember and remove the crossmember from the side supports.

13. Lower the transmission to gain access to the oil cooler lines.

14. Disconnect each oil line from the fittings on the transmission.

15. Disconnect the speedometer cable from the extension housing.

16. Remove the bolt that secures the transmission fluid filler tube to the cylinder block. Lift the filler tube and the dipstick from the transmission.

17. Secure the transmission to the jack with the chain.

18. Remove the converter housing-to-cylinder block attaching bolts.

19. Carefully move the transmission and converter assembly away from the engine and, at the same time, lower the jack to clear the underside of the vehicle.

20. Remove the converter and mount the transmission in a holding fixture.

21. Tighten the converter drain plug to 20-28 ft. lbs.

22. Position the converter on the transmission, making sure the converter drive flats are fully engaged in the pump gear by rotating the converter.

23. With the converter properly installed, place the transmission on the jack. Secure the transmission to the jack with a chain.

24. Rotate the converter until the studs and drain plug are in alignment with the holes in the flywheel.

WARNING: *Lube the pilot bushing.*

25. Align the yellow balancing marks on converter and flywheel on models with the 8-302.

26. move the converter and transmission assembly forward into position, using care not to damage the flywheel and the converter pilot. The converter must rest squarely against the flywheel. This indicates that the converter pilot is not binding in the engine crankshaft.

27. Install and tighten the converter housing-to-engine attaching bolts to 40-50 ft. lbs. make sure that the vacuum tube retaining clips are properly positioned.

28. Remove the safety chain from around the transmission.

29. Install a new O-ring on the lower end of the transmission filler tube. Insert the tube in the transmission case and secure the tube to the engine with the attaching bolts.

30. Connect the speedometer cable to the extension housing.

31. Connect the oil cooler lines to the right side of the transmission case.

32. Position the crossmember on the side supports. Position the rear mount on the crossmember and install the attaching bolt and nut.

33. Secure the engine rear support to the extension housing and tighten the bolts to 35-40 ft. lbs.

34. Lower the transmission and remove the jack.

35. Secure the crossmember to the side supports with the attaching bolts and tighten them to 35-40 ft. lbs.

36. Position the bellcrank to the converter housing and install the two attaching bolts.

37. Connect the TV linkage rod to the transmission TV lever. Connect the manual linkage rod to the manual lever at the transmission.

38. Secure the converter-to-flywheel attaching nuts and tighten them to 20-30 ft. lbs.

39. Install the converter housing access cover and secure it with the attaching bolts.

40. Secure the starter motor in place with the attaching bolts. Connect the cable to the terminal on the starter. Connect the neutral start switch wires at the plug connector.

41. Connect the driveshaft to the rear axle.

42. Adjust the shift linkage as required.

43. Adjust throttle linkage.

44. Lower the vehicle.

45. Fill the transmission to the correct level with Dexron®II. Start the engine and shift the transmission to all ranges, then recheck the fluid level.

DRIVELINE

Driveshaft and U-Joints

The driveshaft is the means by which the power from the engine and transmission (in the front of the car) is transferred to the differential and rear axles, and finally to the rear wheels.

The driveshaft assembly incorporates two universal joints, one at each end, and a slip yoke at the front end of the assembly, which fits into the back of the transmission.

All driveshafts are balanced when installed in a car. It is therefore imperative that before applying undercoating to the chassis, the driveshaft and universal joint assembly be completely covered to prevent the accidental application of undercoating to the surfaces, and the subsequent loss of balance.

DRIVESHAFT REMOVAL

The procedure for removing the driveshaft assembly, complete with universal joint and slip yoke, is as follows:

1. Mark the relationship of the rear dirveshaft yoke and the drive pinion flange of the axle. If the original yellow alignment marks are visible, there is not need for new marks. The purpose of this marking is to facilitate installation of the assembly in its exact original position, thereby maintaining proper balance.

2. Remove the four bolts or U-clamps which hold the rear universal joint to the pinion flange. Wrap tape around the loose bearing caps in order to prevent them from falling off the spider.

Troubleshooting the Driveline

The Problem	Is Caused By	What to Do
Shudder as car accelerates from stop or low speed	• Loose U-joint • Defective center bearing	• Tighten U-joint or have it replaced • Have center bearing replaced
Loud clunk in driveshaft when shifting gears	• Worn U-joint	• Have U-joints replaced
Roughness or vibration at any speed	• Out-of-balance, bent or dented driveshaft • Worn U-joints • U-joint clamp bolts loose	• Have driveshaft serviced • Have U-joints serviced • Tighten U-joint clamp bolts
Squeaking noise at low speeds	• Lack of U-joint lubrication	• Lubricate U-joint; if problem persists, have U-joint serviced
Knock or clicking noise	• U-joint or driveshaft hitting frame tunnel • Worn CV joint	• Correct overloaded condition • Have CV joint replaced

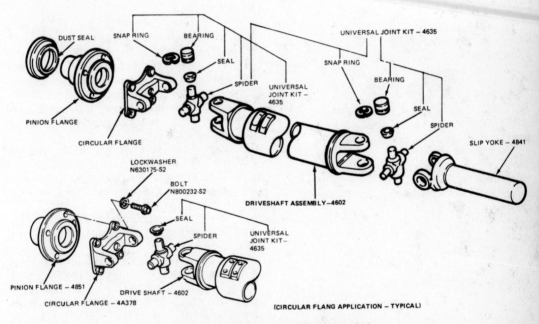

Driveshaft and U-joints disassembled

3. Pull the driveshaft toward the rear of the vehicle until the slip yoke clears the transmission housing and the seal. Plug the hole at the rear of the transmission housing or place a container under the opening to catch any fluid which might leak.

UNIVERSAL JOINT OVERHAUL

1. Position the driveshaft assembly in a sturdy vise.
2. Remove the snaprings which retain the bearings in the slip yoke (front only) and in the driveshaft (front and rear).
3. Using a large vise or an arbor press and a socket smaller than the bearing cap on one side

and a socket larger than the bearing cap on the other side, drive one of the bearings in toward the center of the universal joint, which will force the opposite bearing out.

4. As each bearing is forced far enough out of the universal joint assembly that it is accessible, grip it with a pair of pliers, and pull it from the driveshaft yoke. Drive the spider in the opposite direction in order to make the opposite bearing accessible, and pull it free with a pair of pliers. Use this procedure to remove all bearings from both universal joints.

5. After removing the bearings, lift the spider from the yoke.

6. Thoroughly clean all dirt and foreign mat-

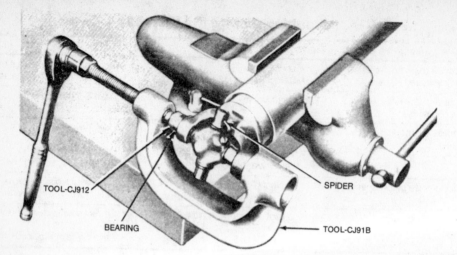

Installing bearing cap

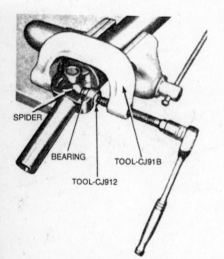

Removing U-joint bearing cap

ter from the yokes on both ends of the driveshaft.

WARNING: *When installing new bearings in the yokes, it is advisable to use an arbor press. However, if this tool is not available, the bearings should be driven into position with extreme car, as a heavy jolt on the needle bearings can easily damage or misalign them, greatly shortening their lift and hampering their efficiency.*

7. Start a new bearing into the yoke at the rear of the driveshaft.

8. Position a new spider in the rear yoke and press the new bearing ¼" (6mm) below the outer surface of the yoke.

9. With the bearing in position, install a new snapring.

10. Start a new bearing into the opposite side of the yoke.

11. Press the bearing until the opposite bearing, which you have just installed, contacts the inner surface of the snapring.

12. Install a new snapring on the second bearing. It may be necessary to grind the surface of this second snapring.

13. Reposition the driveshaft in the vise, so that the front universal joint is accessible.

14. Install the new bearings, new spider, and new snaprings in the same manner as you did for the rear universal joint.

15. Position the slip yoke on the spider. Install new bearings, nylon thrust bearings, and snaprings.

16. Check both reassembled joints for freedom of movement. If misalignment of any part is causing a bind, a sharp rap on the side of the yoke with a brass hammer should seat the bearing needle and provide the desired freedom of movement. Care should be exercised to firmly support the shaft end during this operation, as well as to prevent blows to the bearings themselves. Under no circumstances should the driveshaft be installed in a car if there is any binding in the universal joints.

DOUBLE CARDAN JOINT REPLACEMENT (REAR)

1. Working at the rear axle end of the shaft, mark the position of the spiders, the center yoke, and the centering socket yoke as related to the companion flange. The spiders must be assembled with the bosses in their original position to provide proper clearances.

2. Using a large vise or an arbor press and a socket smaller than the bearing cap on one side and a socket larger than the bearing cap on the

other side, drive one of the bearings in toward the center of the universal joint, which will force the opposite bearing out.

3. Remove the driveshaft from the vise.

4. Tighten the bearing in the vise and tap on the yoke to free the bearing from the center yoke. Do not tap on the driveshaft tube.

5. Reposition the sockets on the yoke and force the opposite bearing outward and remove it.

6. Position the sockets on one of the remaining bearings and force it outward approximately ⅜″ (9.5mm).

7. Grip the bearing in the vise and tap on the weld yoke to free the bearing from the center yoke. Do not tap on the driveshaft tube.

8. Reposition the sockets on the yoke to press out the remaining bearing.

9. Remove the spider from the center yoke.

10. Remove the bearings from the driveshaft yoke as outlined above and remove the spider from the yoke.

11. Insert a suitable tool into the centering ball socket located in the companion flange and pry out the rubber seal. Remove the retainer, three piece ball seat, washer and spring from the ball socket.

12. Inspect the centering ball socket assembly for worn or damaged parts. If any damage is evident replace the entire assembly.

13. Insert the spring, washer, three piece ball seat and retainer into the ball socket.

14. Using a suitable tool, install the centering ball socket seal.

15. Position the spider in the driveshaft yoke. Make sure the spider bosses are in the same position as originally installed. Press in the bearing cups with the sockets and vise. Install the internal snaprings provided in the repair kit.

16. Position the center yoke over the spider ends and press in the bearing cups. Install the snaprings.

17. Install the spider in the companion flange yoke. Make sure the spider bosses are in the position as originally installed. Press on the bearing cups and install the snaprings.

18. Position the center yoke over the spider ends and press on the bearing cups. Install the snaprings.

DRIVESHAFT INSTALLATION

1. Carefully inspect the rubber seal on the output shaft and the seal in end of the transmission extension housing. Replace them if they are damaged.

2. Examine the lugs on the axle pinion flange and replace the flange if the lugs are shaved or distorted.

3. Coat the yoke spline with special-purpose

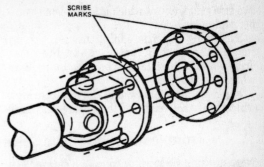

Driveshaft to axle U-joint connection, showing scribe marking

lubricant. The Ford part number for this lubricant if B8A-19589-A.

4. Remove the plug from the rear of the transmission housing.

5. Insert the yoke into the transmission housing and onto the transmission output shaft. Make sure that the yoke assembly does not bottom on the output shaft with excessive force.

6. Locate the marks which you made on the rear driveshaft yoke and the pinion flange prior to removal of the driveshaft assembly. Install the driveshaft assembly with the marks properly aligned.

7. Install the U-bolts and nuts or bolts which attach the universal joint to the pinion flange. Torque the U-bolts nuts to 8-15 ft. lbs. Flange bolts are tighten to 70-95 ft. lbs.

REAR AXLE

Understanding Drive Axles

The drive axle is a special type of transmission that reduces the speed of the drive from the engine and transmission and divides the power to the wheels. Power enters the axle from the driveshaft via the companion flange. The flange is mounted on the drive pinion shaft. The drive pinion shaft and gear which carry the power into the differential turn at engine speed. The gear on the end of the pinion shaft drives a large ring gear the axis of rotation of which is 90 degrees away from the of the pinion. The pinion and gear reduce the gear ratio of the axle, and change the direction of rotation to turn the axle shafts which drive both wheels. The axle gear ratio is found by dividing the number of pinion gear teeth into the number of ring gear teeth.

The ring gear drives the differential case. The case provides the two mounting points for the ends of a pinion shaft on which are mounted two pinion gears. The pinion gears drive the two side gears, one of which is located on the inner end of each axle shaft.

By driving the axle shafts through the arrangement, the differential allows the outer drive wheel to turn faster than the inner drive wheel in a turn.

The main drive pinion and the side bearings, which bear the weight of the differential case, are shimmed to provide proper bearing preload, and to position the pinion and ring gears properly.

WARNING: *The proper adjustment of the relationship of the ring and pinion gears is critical. It should be attempted only by those with extensive equipment and/or experience.*

Limited-slip differentials include clutches

Troubleshooting Basic Driveshaft and Rear Axle Problems

When abnormal vibrations or noises are detected in the driveshaft area, this chart can be used to help diagnose possible causes. Remember that other components such as wheels, tires, rear axle and suspension can also produce similar conditions.

BASIC DRIVESHAFT PROBLEMS

Problem	Cause	Solution
Shudder as car accelerates from stop or low speed	• Loose U-joint • Defective center bearing	• Replace U-joint • Replace center bearing
Loud clunk in driveshaft when shifting gears	• Worn U-joints	• Replace U-joints
Roughness or vibration at any speed	• Out-of-balance, bent or dented driveshaft • Worn U-joints • U-joint clamp bolts loose	• Balance or replace driveshaft • Replace U-joints • Tighten U-joint clamp bolts
Squeaking noise at low speeds	• Lack of U-joint lubrication	• Lubricate U-joint; if problem persists, replace U-joint
Knock or clicking noise	• U-joint or driveshaft hitting frame tunnel • Worn CV joint	• Correct overloaded condition • Replace CV joint

BASIC REAR AXLE PROBLEMS

First, determine when the noise is most noticeable.

Drive Noise: Produced under vehicle acceleration.

Coast Noise: Produced while the car coasts with a closed throttle.

Float Noise: Occurs while maintaining constant car speed (just enough to keep speed constant) on a level road.

Road Noise

Brick or rough surfaced concrete roads produce noises that seem to come from the rear axle. Road noise is usually identical in Drive or Coast and driving on a different type of road will tell whether the road is the problem.

Tire Noise

Tire noises are often mistaken for rear axle problems. Snow treads or unevenly worn tires produce vibrations seeming to originate elsewhere. **Temporarily** inflating the tires to 40 lbs will significantly alter tire noise, but will have no effect on rear axle noises (which normally cease below about 30 mph).

Engine/Transmission Noise

Determine at what speed the noise is most pronounced, then stop the car in a quiet place. With the transmission in Neutral, run the engine through speeds corresponding to road speeds where the noise was noticed. Noises produced with the car standing still are coming from the engine or transmission.

Front Wheel Bearings

While holding the car speed steady, lightly apply the footbrake; this will often decease bearing noise, as some of the load is taken from the bearing.

Rear Axle Noises

Eliminating other possible sources can narrow the cause to the rear axle, which normally produces noise from worn gears or bearings. Gear noises tend to peak in a narrow speed range, while bearing noises will usually vary in pitch with engine speeds.

NOISE DIAGNOSIS

The Noise Is	Most Probably Produced By
· Identical under Drive or Coast	· Road surface, tires or front wheel bearings
· Different depending on road surface	· Road surface or tires
· Lower as the car speed is lowered	· Tires
· Similar with car standing or moving	· Engine or transmission
· A vibration	· Unbalanced tires, rear wheel bearing, unbalanced driveshaft or worn U-joint
· A knock or click about every 2 tire revolutions	· Rear wheel bearing
· Most pronounced on turns	· Damaged differential gears
· A steady low-pitched whirring or scraping, starting at low speeds	· Damaged or worn pinion bearing
· A chattering vibration on turns	· Wrong differential lubricant or worn clutch plates (limited slip rear axle)
· Noticed only in Drive, Coast or Float conditions	· Worn ring gear and/or pinion gear

which tend to link each axle shaft to the differential case. Clutches may be engaged either by spring action or by pressure produced by the torque on the axles during a turn. During turning on a dry pavement, the effects of the clutches are overcome, and each wheel turns at the required speed. When slippage occurs at either wheel, however, the clutches will transmit some of the power to the wheel which has the greater amount of traction. Because of the presence of clutches, limited-slip units require a special lubricant.

Determining Axle Ratio

The drive axle is said to have a certain axle ratio. This number (usually a whole number and a decimal fraction) is actually a comparison of the number of gear teeth on the ring gear and the pinion gear. For example, a 4.11 rear means that theoretically, there are 4.11 teeth on the ring gear and one tooth on the pinion gear or, put another way, the driveshaft must turn 4.11 times to turn the wheels once. Actually, on a 4.11 rear, there might be 37 teeth on the ring gear and 9 teeth on the pinion gear. By dividing the number of teeth on the pinion gear into the number of teeth on the ring gear, the numerical axle ratio (4.11) is obtained. This also provides

a good method of ascertaining exactly what axle ratio one is dealing with.

Another method of determining gear ratio is to jack up and support the car so that both rear wheels are off the ground. Make a chalk mark on the rear wheel and the driveshaft. Put the transmission in neutral. Turn the rear wheel one complete turn and count the number of turns that the driveshaft makes. The number of turns that the driveshaft makes in one complete revolution of the rear wheel is an approximation of the rear axle ratio.

Differential Overhaul

A differential overhaul is a complex, highly technical, and time-consuming operation, which requires a great many tools, extensive knowledge of the unit and the way it works, and a high degree of mechanical experience and ability. It is highly advisable that the amateur mechanic not attempt any work on the differential unit.

Improved Traction Differentials

Ford calls their improved traction differential Traction-Lok®. In this assembly, a multiple-disc clutch is employed to control differential action. Repair procedures are the same as for conventional axles (within the scope of this book).

Pinion Oil Seal

REMOVAL AND INSTALLATION

NOTE: *Special tools are needed for this job.*
1. Raise and support the vehicle and remove the rear wheels and brake drums, or calipers.
2. Mark the driveshaft and yoke for reassembly and disconnect the driveshaft from the rear yoke.
3. With a socket on the pinion nut and an inch lb. torque wrench, rotate the drive pinion

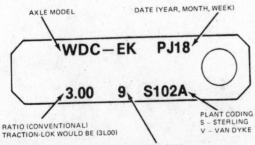

AXLE MODEL   DATE (YEAR, MONTH, WEEK)

WDC – EK   PJ18

3.00   9   S102A

RATIO (CONVENTIONAL)
TRACTION-LOK WOULD BE (3L00)

RING GEAR DIAMETER

PLANT CODING
S – STERLING
V – VAN DYKE

Rear axle identification tag

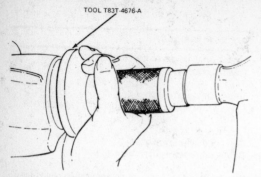

TOOL T83T-4676-A

Pinion seal installation

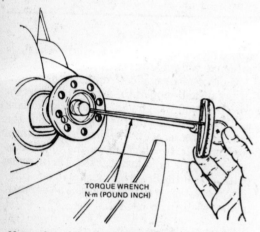

TORQUE WRENCH
N·m (POUND INCH)

Measuring pinion bearing preload

several revolutions. Check and record the torque required to turn the drive pinion.

4. Remove the pinion nut. Use a flange holding tool to hold the flange while removing the pinion nut. Discard the pinion nut.

5. Mark the yoke and the drive pinion shaft for reassembly reference.

6. Remove the rear yoke with a puller.

7. Inspect the seal surface of the yoke and replace it with a new one if the seal surface is pitted, grooved, or otherwise damaged.

8. Remove the pinion oil seal using tools 1175-AC and T50T-100A.

9. Before installing the new seal, coat the lip of the seal with rear axle lubricant.

10. Install the seal, driving it into place with a seal driver.

11. Install the yoke on the pinion shaft. Align the marks made on the pinion shaft and yoke during disassembly.

12. Install a new pinion nut. Tighten the nut until endplay is removed from the pinion bearing. Do not overtighten.

13. Check the torque required to turn the drive pinion. The pinion must be turned several revolutions to obtain an accurate reading.

14. Tighten the pinion nut to obtain the

torque reading observed during disassembly (Step 3) plus 5 in.lb. Tighten the nut minutely each time, to avoid overtightening. Do not loosen and then retighten the nut. Pinion preload should be 8-14 in.lb.

NOTE: *If the desired torque is exceeded a new collapsible pinion spacer sleeve must be installed and the pinion gear preload reset.*

15. Install the driveshaft, aligning the index marks made during disassembly. Install the rear brake drums, or calipers, and wheels.

Axle Shaft and Bearing

NOTE: *Both integral and removable carrier type axles are used. The axle type and ratio are stamped on a plate attached to a rear housing cover bolt. Axle types also indicate whether the axle shafts are retained by C-locks. To properly identify a C-lock axle, drain the lubricant, remove the rear cover and look for the C-lock on the end of the axle shaft in the differential side gear bore. If the axle has no cover (solid housing) it is not a C-lock. If the second letter of the axle model code is F, it is a Traction-Lok axle. Always refer to the axle tag code and ratio when ordering parts.*

REMOVAL AND INSTALLATION

NOTE: Bearings must be pressed on and off the shaft with an arbor press. Unless you

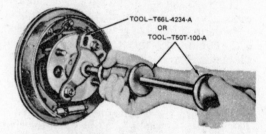

TOOL—T66L-4234-A
OR
TOOL—T50T-100-A

Axle shaft removal—all models

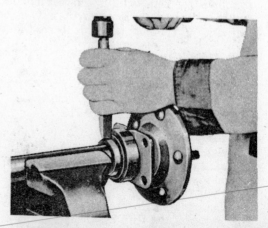

Loosening the inner retaining ring—6¾ in. axle

Axle shaft bearing removal and installation, using press

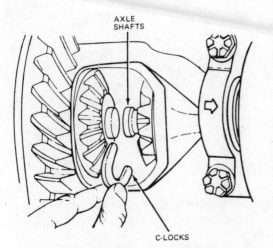

Removal and installation of C-locks and axle shafts—7½ in. ring gear

have access to one, it is inadvisable to attempt any repair work on the axle shaft bearing assemblies.

Flange Type

1. Remove the wheel, tire, and brake drum. With the disc brakes, remove the caliper, retainer, nuts and rotor. New anchor plate bolts will be needed for reassembly.

2. Remove the nuts holding the retainer plate in the backing plate, or axle shaft retainer bolts from the housing. Disconnect the brake line with drum brakes.

3. Remove the retainer and install nuts, finger-tight, to prevent the brake backing plate from being dislodged.

4. Pull out the axle shaft and bearing assembly, using a slide hammer.

On models with a tapered roller bearing, the tapered cup will normally remain in the axle housing when the shaft is removed. The cup must be removed from the housing to prevent seal damage when the shaft is reinstalled. The cup can be removed with a slide hammer and an expanding puller.

WARNING: *If end-play is found to be excessive, the bearing should be replaced. Shimming the bearing is not recommended as this ignores end-play of the bearing itself and could result in improper bearing seating.*

5. Using a chisel, nick the bearing retainer in 3 or 4 places. The retainer does not have to be cut, but merely collapsed sufficiently to allow the bearing retainer to be slid from the shaft.

6. Press off the bearing and install the new one by pressing it into position. With tapered bearings, place the lubricated seal and bearing on the axle shaft (cup rib ring facing the flange). make sure that the seal is the correct length. Disc brake seal rims are black, drum brake seal rims are grey. Press the bearing and seal onto the shaft.

7. Press on the new retainer.

NOTE: *Do not attempt to press the bearing and the retainer on at the same time.*

8. On ball bearing models, to replace the seal: remove the seal from the housing with an expanding cone type puller and a slide hammer. the seal must be replaced whenever the shaft is removed. Wipe a small amount of sealer onto the outer edge of the new seal before installation; do not put sealer on the sealing lip. Press the seal into the housing with a seal installation tool.

9. Assemble the shaft and bearing in the housing, being sure that the bearing is seated properly in the housing. On ball bearing models, be careful not to damage the seal with the shaft. With tapered bearings, first install the tapered cup on the bearing, and lubricate the outer diameter of the cup and the seal with axle lube. Then install the shaft and bearing assembly into the housing.

10. Install the retainer, drum or rotor and caliper, wheel and tire. Bleed the brakes.

C-Lock Type

1. Jack up and support the rear of the car.

2. Remove the wheels and tires from the brake drums.

3. Place a drain pan under the housing and drain the lubricant by loosening the housing cover.

4. Remove the locks securing the brake drums to the axle shaft flanges and remove the drums.

5. Remove the housing cover and gasket, if used.

6. Position jackstands under the rear frame member and lower the axle housing. This is done to give easy access to the inside of the differential.

7. Working through the opening in the differential case, remove the side gear pinion shaft lockbolt and the side gear pinion shaft.

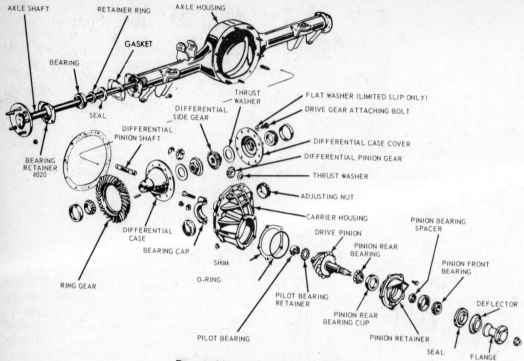

AXLE SHAFT · RETAINER RING · AXLE HOUSING · GASKET · BEARING · SEAL · BEARING RETAINER 4020 · DIFFERENTIAL PINION SHAFT · DIFFERENTIAL SIDE GEAR · THRUST WASHER · FLAT WASHER (LIMITED SLIP ONLY) · DRIVE GEAR ATTACHING BOLT · DIFFERENTIAL CASE COVER · DIFFERENTIAL PINION GEAR · THRUST WASHER · ADJUSTING NUT · CARRIER HOUSING · PINION BEARING SPACER · DRIVE PINION · PINION REAR BEARING · PINION FRONT BEARING · DEFLECTOR · DIFFERENTIAL CASE · BEARING CAP · SHIM · O-RING · PILOT BEARING RETAINER · PINION REAR BEARING CUP · PINION RETAINER · SEAL · FLANGE · RING GEAR · PILOT BEARING

Removable carrier axle assembly

8. Push the axle shafts inward and remove the C-locks from the inner end of the axle shafts. Temporarily replace the shaft and lockbolt to retain the differential gears in position.

9. Remove the axle shafts with a slide hammer. Be sure the seal is not damaged by the splines on the axle shaft.

10. Remove the bearing and oil seal from the housing. Both the seal and bearing can be removed with a slide hammer. Two types of bearings are used on some axles, one requiring a press fit and the other a loose fit. A loose fitting bearing does not necessarily indicate excessive wear.

11. Inspect the axle shaft housing and axle shafts for burrs or other irregularities. Replace any worn or damaged parts. A light yellow color on the bearing journal of the axle shaft is normal, and does not require replacement of the axle shaft. Slight pitting and wear is also normal.

12. Lightly coat the wheel bearing rollers with axle lubricant. Install the bearings in the axle housing until the bearing seats firmly against the shoulder.

13. Wipe all lubricant from the oil seal bore, before installing the seal.

14. Inspect the original seals for wear. If necessary, these may be replace with new seals, which are prepacked with lubricant and do not require soaking.

15. Install the oil seal.

CAUTION: *Installation of the seal without the proper tool can cause distortion and seal leakage. Seals may be colored coded for side identification. Do not interchange seals form side to side, if they are coded.*

16. Remove the lockbolt and pinion shaft. Carefully slide the axle shafts into place. Be careful that you do not damage the seal with the splined end of the axle shaft. Engage the splined end of the shaft with the differential side gears.

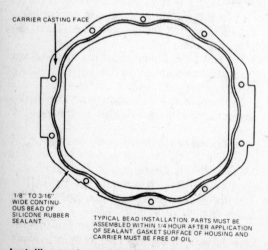

CARRIER CASTING FACE

1/8" TO 3/16" WIDE CONTINUOUS BEAD OF SILICONE RUBBER SEALANT

TYPICAL BEAD INSTALLATION. PARTS MUST BE ASSEMBLED WITHIN 1/4 HOUR AFTER APPLICATION OF SEALANT. GASKET SURFACE OF HOUSING AND CARRIER MUST BE FREE OF OIL.

Installing sealer—all models

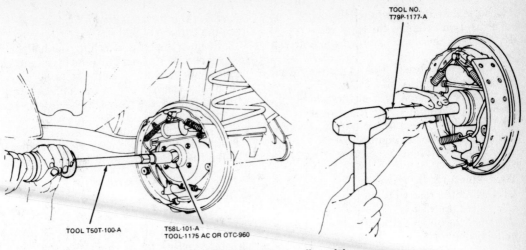

TOOL NO.
T79P-1177-A

TOOL T50T-100-A

T58L-101-A
TOOL-1175 AC OR OTC-960

Axle seal replacement—all models

17. Install the axle shaft C-locks on the inner end of the axle shafts and seat the C-locks in the counterbore of the differential side gears.

18. Rotate the differential pinion gears until the differential pinion shaft can be installed. Install the differential pinion shaft lockbolt. Tighten to 15-22 ft. lbs.

19. Install the brake drum on the axle shaft flange.

20. Install the wheel and tire on the brake drum and tighten the attaching nuts.

21. Clean the gasket surface of the rear housing and install a new cover gasket and the housing cover. Some models do not use a paper gasket. On these models, apply a bead of silicone sealer on the gasket surface. The bead should run inside the bolt holes.

22. Raise the rear axle so that it is in the running position. Add the amount of specified lubricant to bring the lubricant level to ½″ (12.7mm) below the filler hole.

AXLE SHAFT SEAL REPLACEMENT

1. Remove the axle shaft from the rear axle assembly, following the procedures previously discussed.

2. Using a two-fingered seal puller (slide hammer), remove the seal from the axle housing.

3. Thoroughly clean the recess in the rear axle housing from which the seal was removed.

4. Position a new seal on the housing and drive it into place with a seal installation tool. If this tool is not available, a wood block may be substituted.

NOTE: *Although the right and left end seals are identical, there are many different types of seals which have been used on rear axle assembles. It is advisable to have one of the old seals with you when you are purchasing new ones.*

5. When the seal is properly installed, install the axle shaft.

Axle Housing

REMOVAL AND INSTALLATION

1977-78

1. Raise the vehicle and support it on jackstands placed under the frame.

2. Remove the rear wheels.

3. Place an indexing mark on the rear yoke and driveshaft, and disconnect the shaft.

4. Disconnect the shock absorbers from the axle tubes. Disconnect the stabilizer bar at the axle bracket, on vehicles so equipped.

5. Disconnect the brake hose from the tee fitting on the axle housing. Disconnect the brake lines at the clips on the housing. Disconnect the vent tube at the axle.

6. Disconnect the parking brake cable at the frame mounting.

7. Support the rear axle with a jack.

8. Disconnect the lower control arms at the axle and swing them down out of the way.

9. Disconnect the upper control arms at the axle and swing them up out of the way.

10. Lower the axle slightly, remove the coil springs and insulators.

11. Lower the axle housing.

To install:

12. Raise the axle into position and connect the lower arms. Don't tighten the bolts yet.

13. Lower the axle slightly and install the coil springs and insulators.

14. Raise the axle and connect the upper control arms. Don't tighten the bolts yet.

15. Connect the parking brake cable at the frame mounting.

16. Connect the brake hose at the tee fitting on the axle housing.

17. Connect the vent tube at the axle. Apply thread locking compound to the threads.

18. Connect the stabilizer bar at the axle bracket, on vehicles so equipped.

19. Connect the shock absorbers from the axle tubes.

20. Connect the driveshaft.

21. Install the rear wheels.

22. Lower the vehicle.

23. Once the car is back on its wheels, observe the following torques:

Removeable carrier axles:
- Lower control arm bolts — 90 ft. lbs.
- Lower shock absorber nuts — 85 ft. lbs.
- Upper control arm bolts — 120 ft. lbs.

Integral carrier axles:
- Lower arm bolts — 100 ft. lbs.
- Lower shock absorber nuts — 55 ft. lbs.
- Upper arm bolts — 100 ft. lbs.

WARNING: *Bleed and adjust the brakes accordingly.*

MERKUR REAR HALFSHAFTS

Halfshaft

REMOVAL AND INSTALLATION

1. Raise and support the rear end on jackstands placed under the frame.

2. Place the transmission in neutral and release the parking brake.

3. Remove the bolts attaching the halfshaft to the wheel stub shaft. Turn the driveshaft as necessary to gain access to the bolts.

4. Secure the free end of the halfshaft with wire and remove the mounting bolts from the axle stub shaft.

5. Remove the halfshaft.

6. Installaion is the reverse of removal. Tighten the bolts to 28-30 ft. lbs.

Wheel Stub Shaft

REMOVAL AND INSTALLATION

1. Raise and support the rear end on jackstands placed under the frame.

2. Remove the brake drum and wheel flange.

3. Remove the bolts attaching the halfshaft to the wheel stub axle. Suspend the halfshaft with wire. DO NOT ALLOW IT TO HANG FREELY!

4. Pull the stub axle from the wheel retainer.

5. Installation is the reverse of removal.

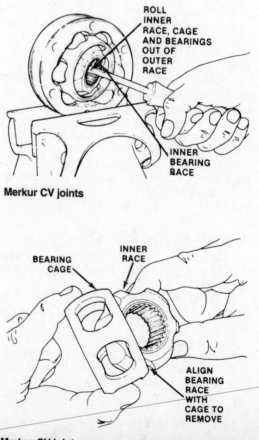

Merkur CV joints

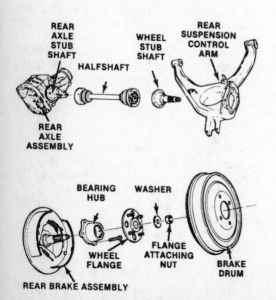

Merkur halfshafts/wheel hub assemblies

Merkur CV joint component alignment

CV-Joint

REMOVAL AND INSTALLATION

1. Remove the halfshaft and secure it in a soft-jawed vise.

2. Break and remove the boot clamps.

3. Pell the boot away from the joint flange and slide it along the shaft.

4. Remove the snapring from the end of the shaft.

5. Using a 2-jawed puller, remove the CV-joint from the shaft.

6. Clamp the joint in a soft-jawed vise.

7. Using a small, flat-tipped prybar, roll the inner race and ball cage out of the outer race.

8. The balls can now be removed by prying them out of the cage.

9. Remove the inner race by aligning one of the bearing races with the cage and then rolling the race out of the cage.

10. Inspect all parts after cleaning them. Replace any worn or damaged parts.

11. Assemble the inner race, cage and ball bearings.

12. Install the assembly in the housing with 2 of the bearings entering 2 races.

13. Pull upwards on the inner race and roll the assembly into position.

NOTE: *The narrow ends of the inner races must be aligned with the wide ends of the housing races before the race, cage and ball assembly can enter the housing.*

14. Pack the CV-joint with lubricant CLAZ-19590-B, C, D, or E, or their equivalent.

15. Install the CV-joint on the halfshaft and install the snapring. A hammer and socket can be used to mount the joint.

16. Install a new boot and clamps.

MERKUR REAR AXLE

Axle and Suspension

REMOVAL AND INSTALLATION

1. Remove the springs. See Chapter 8.

2. Disconnect the driveshaft.

3. Remove the exhaust system

4. Remove the parking brake cables. See Chapter 9.

5. Remove the stabilizer bar. See Chapter 8.

6. Position a floor jack under the rear axle and secure the crossmember to the jack with a safety chain.

7. Remove the crossmember bushing attaching bolt from both sides of the car.

8. Remove the crossmember bushing guide plate attaching bolts and the guide plate from both sides.

9. Remove the axle mount bolts.

10. Carefully lower the crossmember from the car.

To install:

11. Raise the assembly into position.

12. Install, but do not tighten, the axle mounting bolts.

13. Position the insulating guide plates.

14. Install the crossmember bushing attaching bolts and washers.

15. Tighten the guide plate attaching bolts to 35 ft. lbs.

16. Tighten the crossmember bushing bolts to 70 ft. lbs.

17. Tighten the 4 axle mount attaching bolts to 25 ft. lbs.

18. The remainder of installation is the reverse of removal.

Suspension and Steering

MUSTANG/CAPRI FRONT SUSPENSION

Springs

WARNING: *Always use extreme caution when working with coil springs. make sure the vehicle is supported sufficiently.*

REMOVAL

1. Raise the front of the vehicle and place safety stands under both sides of the jack pads just back of the lower arms.

2. Remove the wheel and tire assembly.

3. Disconnect the stabilizer bar link from the lower arm.

4. Remove the steering gear bolts, and move the steering gear out of the way.

5. Disconnect the tie rod from the steering spindle.

6. Using a spring compressor, install one plate with the pivot ball seat down into the coils of the spring. Rotate the plate, so that it is fully seated into the lower suspension arm spring seat.

7. Install the other plate with the pivot ball seat up into the coils of the spring. Insert the ball nut through the coils of the spring. Insert the ball nut through the coils of the spring, so it rests in the upper plate.

8. Insert the compression rod into the opening in the lower arm through the lower and up-

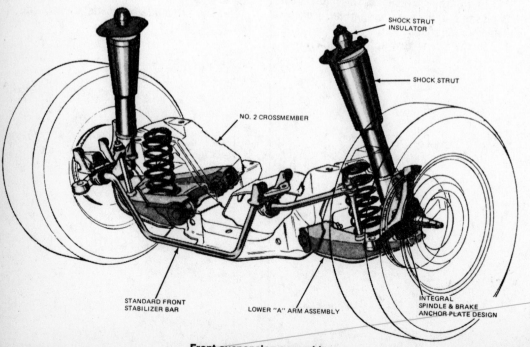

SHOCK STRUT
INSULATOR

SHOCK STRUT

NO. 2 CROSSMEMBER

STANDARD FRONT
STABILIZER BAR

LOWER "A" ARM ASSEMBLY

INTEGRAL
SPINDLE & BRAKE
ANCHOR PLATE DESIGN

Front suspension assembly

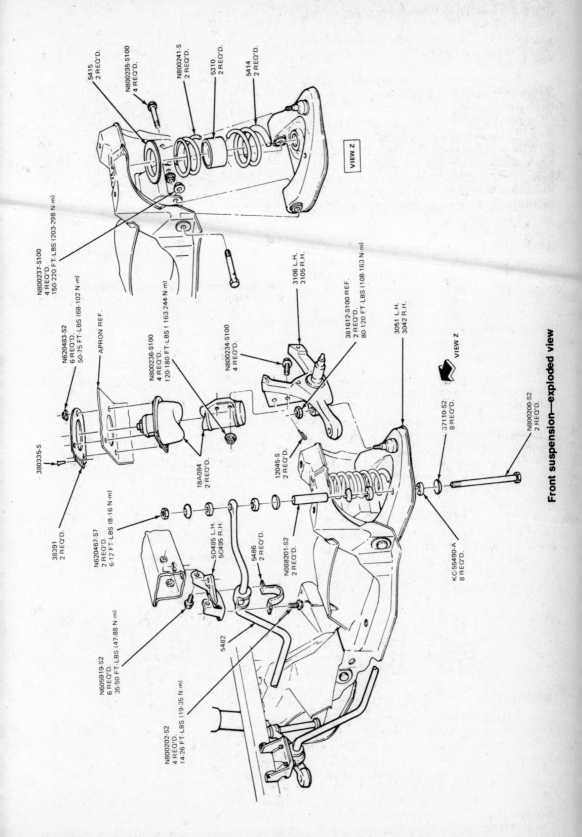

VIEW Z

5415
2 REQ'D.

N800235-S100
4 REQ'D.

N800241-S
2 REQ'D.

5310
2 REQ'D.

5414
2 REQ'D.

N800237-S100
4 REQ'D.
150-220 FT-LBS (203-298 N·m)

N620483-S2
6 REQ'D.
50-75 FT-LBS (68-102 N·m)

APRON REF.

N800236-S100
4 REQ'D.
120-180 FT-LBS (163-244 N·m)

N800234-S100
4 REQ'D.

3106 L.H.
3105 R.H.

381612-S100 REF.
2 REQ'D.
80-120 FT-LBS (108-163 N·m)

3051 L.H.
3042 R.H.

380335-S

18A084
2 REQ'D.

12045-S
2 REQ'D.

VIEW Z

37110-S2
8 REQ'D.

N800200-S2
2 REQ'D.

38391
2 REQ'D.

N620467-S7
2 REQ'D.
6-12 FT-LBS (8-16 N·m)

5D485 L.H.
5C495 R.H.

5486
2 REQ'D.

N088201-S2
2 REQ'D.

KC-55490-A
8 REQ'D.

N605919-S2
6 REQ'D.
35-50 FT-LBS (47-88 N·m)

N800202-S2
4 REQ'D.
14-26 FT-LBS (19-35 N·m)

5482

Front suspension—exploded view

per plate. Install the upper ball nut on the rod, and return the securing pin.

NOTE: *This pin can only be inserted one way into the upper ball nut because of a stepped hole design.*

9. With the upper ball nut secured turn the upper plate, so it walks up the coil until it contacts the upper spring seat.

10. Install the lower ball nut, thrust bearing and forcing nut on the compression rod.

11. Rotate the nut until the spring is compressed enough so that it is free in its seat.

12. Remove the two lower control arm pivot bolts and nuts, and disengage the lower arm from the frame crossmember and remove the spring assembly.

13. If a new spring is to be installed, mark the position of the upper and lower plates on the spring with chalk. Measure the compressed length of the spring as well as the amount of the spring curvature to assist in the compressing and installation of a new spring.

14. Loosen the nut to relieve spring tension, and remove the tools from the spring.

INSTALLATION

1. Assemble the spring compressor tool, and locate it in the same position as indicted in Step 13 of the removal procedure.

WARNING: *Before compressing the coil spring, be sure the upper ball nut securing pin is inserted properly.*

2. Compress the coil spring until the spring height reaches the dimension in Step 13.

3. Position the coil spring assembly into the lower arm.

WARNING: *Make sure that the lower end of the spring is properly positioned between the two holes in the lower arm spring pocket depression.*

4. To finish installing the coil spring reverse the removal procedure.

Ball Joints

Ball joints are not replaceable. If the ball joints are found to be defective the lower control arm assembly must be replaced.

INSPECTION

1. Support the vehicle in normal driving position with both ball joints loaded.

2. Wipe the grease fitting and checking surface, so they are free of dirt and grease. The checking surface is the round boss into which the grease fitting is threaded.

3. The checking surface should project outside the cover. If the checking surface is inside the cover, replace the lower arm assembly.

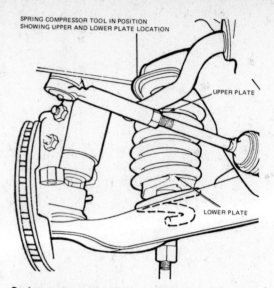

SPRING COMPRESSOR TOOL IN POSITION
SHOWING UPPER AND LOWER PLATE LOCATION

UPPER PLATE

LOWER PLATE

Spring compressor tool in position showing upper and lower plate location

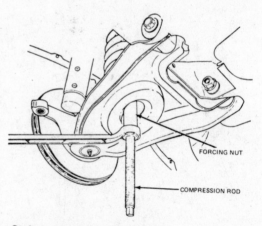

FORCING NUT

COMPRESSION ROD

Spring compressed for removal

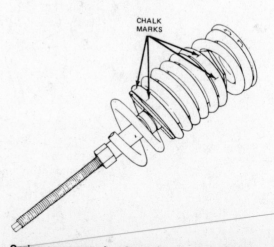

CHALK
MARKS

Spring compressed and removed from the vehicle

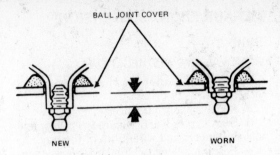

BALL JOINT COVER

NEW   WORN

CHECKING SURFACE

Inspection of lower ball joint

Shock Strut
REMOVAL

1. Place the ignition key in the unlock position to permit free movement of the front wheels.

2. Working from the engine compartment remove the nut that attaches the strut to the upper mount. A screwdriver in the slot will hold the rod stationary while removing the nut.

WARNING: *The vehicle should not be driven while the nut is removed so make sure the car is in position for hoisting purposes.*

3. Raise the front of the vehicle by the lower control arms, and place safety stands under the frame jacking pads, rearward of the wheels.

4. Remove the tire and wheel assembly.

5. Remove the brake caliper, rotor assembly, and dust shield.

6. Remove the two lower nuts and bolts attaching the strut to the spindle.

7. Lift the strut up from the spindle to compress the rod, then pull down and remove the strut.

INSTALLATION

1. With the rod half extended, place the rod through the upper mount and hand start the mount as soon as possible.

2. Extend the strut and position into the spindle.

3. Install the two lower mounting bolts and hand start the nuts.

4. Tighten the nut that attaches the strut to the upper body mount to 60-75 ft. lbs. This can be done from inside the engine compartment.

NOTE: *Position a suitable tool in the slot to hold the rod stationary while the nut is being tightened.*

5. Remove the suspension load from the lower control arms by lowering the hoist and tighten the lower mounting nuts to 150 ft. lbs.

6. Raise the suspension control arms and in-

stall the brake caliper, rotor assembly and dust shield.

7. Install the tire and wheel assembly.

8. Remove the safety stands and lower the vehicle.

Lower Control Arm
REMOVAL

1. Raise the front of the vehicle and position safety stands under both sides of the jack pads, just to the rear of the lower arms.

2. Remove the wheel and tire assembly.

3. Disconnect the stabilizer bar link from the lower arm.

4. Remove the disc brake caliper, rotor and dust shield.

5. Remove the steering gear bolts and position out of the way.

6. Remove the cotter pin from the ball joint stud nut, and loosen the ball joint nut one or two turns.

7. Tap the spindle sharply to relieve the stud pressure.

8. Remove the tie rod end from the spindle. Place a floor jack under the lower arm, supporting the arm at both bushings. Remove both lower arm bolts, lower the jack and remove the coil spring as outlined earlier in the chapter.

9. Remove the ball nut and remove the arm assembly.

INSTALLATION

1. Place the new arm assembly into the spindle and tighten the ball joint nut to 100 ft. lbs. Install the cotter pin.

2. Position the coil spring in the upper spring pocket. Make sure the insulator is on top of the spring and the lower end is properly positioned between the two holes in the depression of the lower arm.

3. Carefully raise the lower arm with the floor jack until the bushings are properly positioned in the crossmember.

4. Install the lower arm bolts and nuts, finger tight only.

5. Install and tighten the steering gear bolts.

6. Connect the tie rod end and tighten the nut to 35-47 ft. lbs.

7. Connect the stabilizer link bolt and nut and tighten to 10 ft. lbs.

8. Install the brake dust shield, rotor and caliper.

9. Install the wheel and tire assembly.

10. Remove the safety stands and lower the vehicle. After the vehicle has been lowered to the floor and at curb height, tighten the lower arm nuts to 210 ft. lbs.

Sway Bar

REMOVAL AND INSTALLATION

1. Raise and support the front end on jackstands.

2. Disconnect the stabilizer bar from the links, or the links from the lower arm.

3. Disconnect the bar from the retaining clamps.

4. Installation is the reverse of removal. Torque the bar fasteners to 25 ft. lbs.; the link-to-arm fasteners to 12 ft. lbs.

Spindle

REMOVAL AND INSTALLATION

1. Raise and support the front end on jackstands under the frame.

2. Remove the wheels.

3. Remove the calipers and suspend them out of the way.

4. Remove the hub and rotor assemblies.

5. Remove the rotor dust shields.

6. Unbolt the stabilizer links from the control arms.

7. Using a separator, disconnect the tie rod ends from the spindle.

8. Remove the cotter pin and loosen the ball joint stud nut a few turns. Don't remove it at this time!

9. Using a hammer, tap the spindle boss sharply to relieve stud pressure.

10. Support the lower control arm with a floor jack, compress the coil spring and remove the stud nut.

11. Remove the two bolts and nuts attaching the spindle to the shock strut. Compress the shock strut until working clearance is obtained.

12. Remove the spindle.

To install:

13. Place the spindle on the ball joint stud, and install the stud nut, but don't tighten it yet.

14. Lower the shock strut until the attaching holes are aligned with the holes in the spindle. Install two new bolts and nuts.

15. Tighten the ball stud nut to 80-120 ft. lbs. and install the cotter pin.

16. Torque the shock strut-to-spindle attaching nuts to 80-120 ft. lbs. for 1980-81 cars; 150-180 ft. lbs. for 1982-85 cars; 140-200 ft. lbs. for 1986-88 cars.

17. Lower the floor jack.

18. Install the stabilizer links. Torque the nuts to 12 ft. lbs.

19. Attach the tie rod ends and torque the nuts to 45 ft. lbs.

20. The remainder of installation is the reverse of removal.

MERKUR FRONT SUSPENSION

Strut

REMOVAL AND INSTALLATION

1. Raise and support the front end on jackstands.

2. Remove the front wheels.

3. See Chapter 9 and remove the caliper and anchor support and wire it out of the way.

4. Position a floor jack under the lower control arm and raise the jck until it is just below, but not touching, the arm.

5. Remove the strut-to-spindle arm pinch bolt. Using a prybar, spread the mounting flange ears and push down on the control arm to separate the arm and strut.

6. Carefully lower the jack to clear the strut, but DON'T STRETCH THE BRAKE LINE!

7. Insert a 6mm hex wrench in the top slot of the strut to hold it and remove the locknut.

8. Remove the strut.

9. Installation is the reverse of removal. Torque the strut-to-arm nut to 60-65 ft. lbs.; the strut upper nut to 32-38 ft. lbs.

Control Arm

REMOVAL AND INSTALLATION

1. Raise and support the front end on jackstands.

2. Remove the wheels.

3. Remove the cotter pin and nut and separate the control arm from the spindle.

4. Remove the pivot bolt attaching the control arm to the crossmember.

5. Remove the nut attaching the stabilizer bar to the control arm.

6. Installation is the reverse of removal. With the control arm installed, tighten all fasteners snugly but not torqued to specification.

7. Lower the car to the ground and then torque all fasteners to:

- Control arm pivot bolt: 11 ft. lbs. + 90°
- Control arm-to-spindle: 50-65 ft. lbs.
- Stabilizer nut: 52-80 ft. lbs.

Stabilizer Bar

REMOVAL AND INSTALLATION

1. Raise and support the front end on jackstands.

2. Remove the attaching nuts and front washers/covers from the ends of the stabilizer bar.

3. Remove the 4 bolts securing the 2 U-brackets and torque brace to the body.

4. Detach one control arm pivot bolt and pull the control arm out of the crossmember.

5. Pull the stabilizer bar out of the lower control arms and remove it.

6. Installation is the reverse of removal. Coat all bushings with chassis lube prior to installation. Note that the rear washer is black and has a shallower dish than the front washer. When the washer is installed, make sure that the plastic cover is in place between the dished steel washer and the bushing, and that the dished side of the steel washer faces away from the bushing.

When the bar is in place, torque the U-bolts to 50 ft. lbs., but just snug the attaching nuts. Lower the car to the ground, then torque the attaching nuts to 50-80 ft. lbs. Tighten the control arm pivot bolt to 11 ft. lbs. + 90°.

Spindle Carrier and Bearings
REMOVAL AND INSTALLATION

1. Raise and support the front end on jackstands.

2. Remove the wheels.

3. Remove the calipers and suspend them out of the way. See Chapter 9.

4. Matchmark the rotor and hub. These parts are matched and balanced and must be installed in the smae exact relationship as originally assembled.

5. Remove the retaining clip and remove the rotor from the hub.

6. Remove the cotter pin and nut and separate the tie rod end from the spindle using a separator tool.

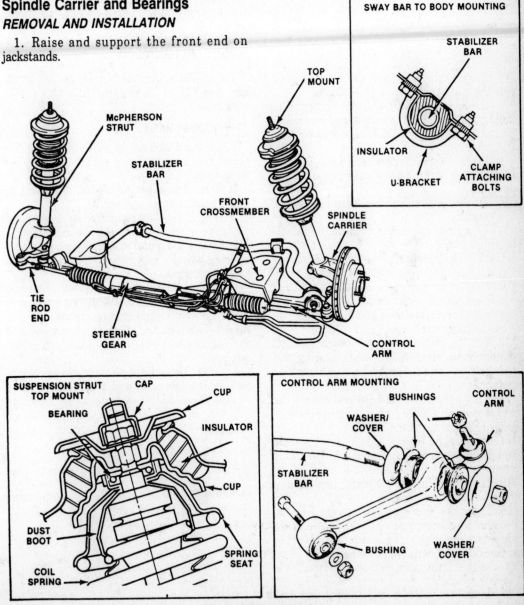

Merkur front suspension

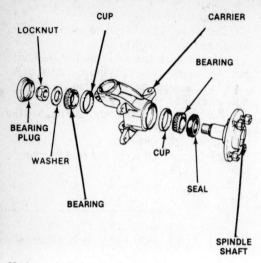

CUP   CARRIER

LOCKNUT

BEARING

BEARING
PLUG

WASHER   CUP

BEARING   SEAL

SPINDLE
SHAFT

Merkur spindle/knuckle exploded view

7. Remove the cotter pin and nut and separate the control arm from the spindle.

8. Remove the strut-to-spindle carrier pinch bolt and pry apart the spindle flange ears with a prybar and lever the spindle carrier away from the strut.

9. Place the spindle carrier and hub in a soft jawed vise with the wheel lugs facing downward.

10. Drive the bearing plug from the rear of the knuckle.

11. Using a 27mm socket, remove the spindle bearing locknut.

CAUTION: *Spindle from the right side of the car is equipped with left hand threads. Loosen the nut by turning it clockwise! The left side spindle has conventional threads. The spindle are marked with and L or R in the recessed hexagonal area.*

12. Lift the carrier and inner bearing off the spindle shaft. Remove the inner bearing and splined washer. Tag the bearing for installation.

13. Clamp the carrier in a vise and remove the grease seal using a flat prybar. Remove the outer bearing and tag it for installation.

14. Remove the bearing cups from the spindle by driving them out or pulling them with a slide hammer.

15. Clean and inspect all parts. Replace any worm or damaged parts.

16. Drive new bearing cups into the spindle. Pack the wheel bearings with high temperature wheel bearing grease. It's best to use a bearing packer but the bearings can be packed by hand if you make certain that each and every roller is thoroughly coated.

17. Install the outer bearing and grease seal in the spindle.

18. Install the spindle shaft.

19. Install the inner bearing and splined washer.

20. Install the spindle bearing locknut and tighten it to 200-230 ft. lbs..

CAUTION: *The bearing torque is extremely important! Too high or too low a torque will result in bearing failure! Make sure that the spindle is securely tightened in the vise prior to torquing the nut!*

21. Install the cover plug.

22. Install the spindle carrier in reverse order of removal.

23. Torque the spindle-to-strut pinch bolt to 60-65 ft. lbs.; the lower control arm nut to 50-63 ft. lbs.; the tie rod end nut to 15-20 ft. lbs. Use new cotter pins.

WHEEL ALIGNMENT

The caster and camber are set at the factory and cannot be changed. Only the toe is adjustable.

TOE ADJUSTMENT

Toe is the difference in width (distance), between the front and rear inside edges of the front tires.

1. Turn the steering wheel, from left to right, several times and center.

NOTE: *If car has power steering, start the engine before centering the steering wheel.*

2. Secure the centered steering wheel with a steering wheel holder, or any device that will keep it centered.

3. Release the tie rod end bellows clamps so the bellows will not twist while adjustment is made. Loosen the jam nuts on the tie rod ends. Adjust the left and right connector sleeves until each wheel has one-half of the desired toe setting.

4. After the adjustment has been made, tighten the jam nuts and secure the bellows clamps. Release the steering wheel lock and

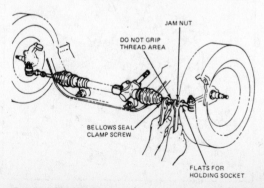

JAM NUT

DO NOT GRIP
THREAD AREA

BELLOWS SEAL
CLAMP SCREW

FLATS FOR
HOLDING SOCKET

Toe-in adjustment

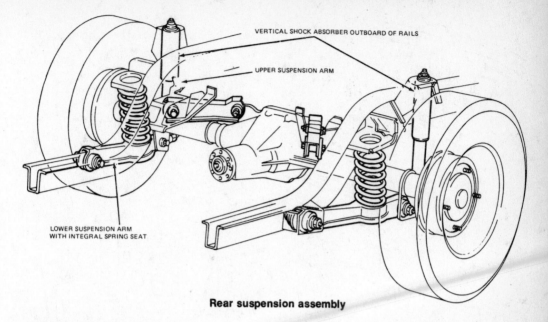

VERTICAL SHOCK ABSORBER OUTBOARD OF RAILS

UPPER SUSPENSION ARM

LOWER SUSPENSION ARM
WITH INTEGRAL SPRING SEAT

Rear suspension assembly

check for steering wheel center. Readjust, if necessary until steering wheel is centered and toe is within specs.

MUSTANG/CAPRI REAR SUSPENSION

Coil Spring

REMOVAL AND INSTALLATION

NOTE: *If one spring must be replaced, the other should be replaced also. If the car has a*

stabilizer bar, the bar must be removed first.

1. Raise and support the car at the rear crossmember, while supporting the axle with a jack.

2. Lower the axle until the shocks are fully extended.

3. Place a jack under the lower arm pivot bolt. Remove the pivot bolt and nut. Carefully and slowly lower the arm until the spring load is relieved.

4. Remove the spring and insulators.

5. To install, tape the insulator in place in the frame, and place the lower insulator in place on the arm. Install the internal damper in the spring.

6. Position the spring in place and slowly raise the jack under the lower arm. Install the

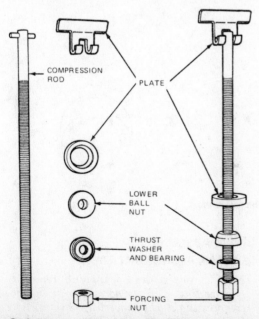

COMPRESSION ROD

PLATE

LOWER BALL NUT

THRUST WASHER AND BEARING

FORCING NUT

Spring compressor tool for MacPherson struts

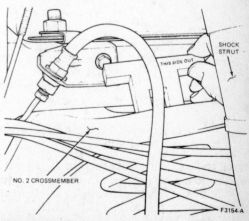

SHOCK STRUT

THIS SIDE OUT

NO. 2 CROSSMEMBER

F3154-A

Spring compressor tool—upper plate being placed into spring pocket cavity on the No. 2 crossmember

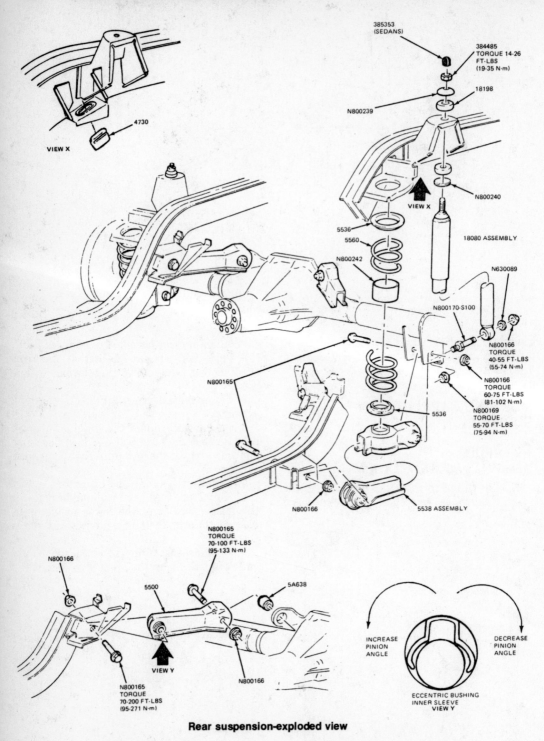

Rear suspension-exploded view

pivot bolt and nut, with the nut facing outwards. Do not tighten the nut.

7. Raise the axle to curb height, and tighten the lower pivot bolt to 70-100 ft. lbs.

8. Install the stabilizer bar, if removed. The proper torque is 20-27 ft. lbs. Remove the crossmember stands and lower the car.

Shock Absorber

REMOVAL AND INSTALLATION

NOTE: *Purge a new shock of air by repeatedly extending it in its normal position and compressing it while inverted.*

1. Remove the upper attaching nut, washer,

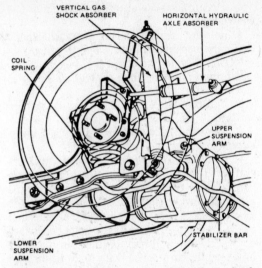

Performance handling rear suspension shock mounting

and insulator. Access is through the trunk on sedans or side panel trim covers on station wagons and hatchbacks. Sedan studs have rubber caps.

2. Raise the car. Compress the shock to clear the upper tower. Remove the lower nut and washer; remove the shock.

3. Purge the shock of air and compress. Place the lower mounting eye over the lower stud and install the washer and a new locking nut. do not tighten the nut yet.

4. Place the insulator and washer on the up-

per stud. Extend the shock, install the stud through the upper mounting hole.

5. Torque the lower mounting nut to 40-55 ft. lbs.

6. Lower the car. Install the outer insulator and washer on the upper stud, and install a new nut. Tighten to 14-26 ft. lbs. Install the trim panel on station wagons and hatchbacks or the rubber cap on sedans.

Sway (Stabilizer) Bar
REMOVAL AND INSTALLATION

1. Raise and support the rear end on jackstands.

2. Remove the 4 stabilizer bar-to-lower arm bolts.

3. Remove the stabilizer bar.

4. Installation is the reverse of removal. Torque the new bolts to 20 ft. lbs. on 1980-81 cars; 45-50 ft. lbs. on 1982-88 cars.

MERKUR REAR SUSPENSION

Springs
REMOVAL AND INSTALLATION

NOTE: *Ford recommends that springs be replaced as a set. If one is bad replace both.*

1. Raise and support the rear end on jackstands placed under the rear crossmember.

2. Remove the halfhsft-to-stubshaft attaching bolts. Suspend the halfshaft from the underbody with a length of wire.

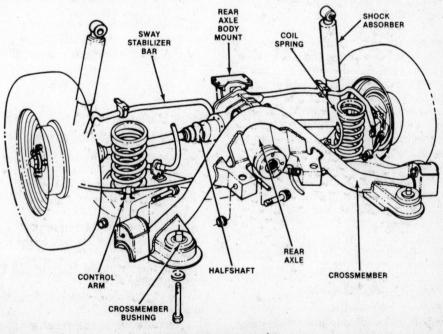

Merkur rear suspension

3. Remove the clip attaching the rear brake hose to the bracket on the control arm.

4. Disconnect the brake tube from the brake hose. Cap the openings.

5. Remove the protective cap from the bottom of the shok absorber.

6. Support the control arm with a floor jack. Raise the arm just enough to relieve the coil spring tension from the shock absorber.

7. Remove the nut and bolt attaching the lower end of the shock absorber.

8. Slowly and carefully lower the floor jack until the jack is no longer supporting the arm and the jack can be removed.

9. Support the axle housing with the floor jack.

10. Remove the bolts attaching the rear axle mount to the body and disconnect the axle vent tube.

11. Slowly and carefully lower the jack until the coil spring and seat can be removed.

NOTE: *Don't remove the spring support from the axle. Lower the axle just enough to remove the spring. Don't allow the axle to hang unsupported!*

To install:

12. Install the upper spring seat on the spring. Be sure that the spring end seats against the stop on the seat. Nake sure that the seat tabs are positioned between the first and second coils.

NOTE: *The spring and seat must be installed dry! Don't use any lubricant on them!*

13. Install the spring and seat.

14. Raise the rear axle into position and install the body mount attaching bolts.

15. Use Loctite® on the threads and torque the bolts to 15-18 ft. lbs.

16. Remove the axle support and position it under the control arm. Raise the jack until the coil spring is compressed enough to allow installation of the shock absorber lower attaching bolt. Torque the nut to 30-35 ft. lbs.

17. Remove the jack and install the protective cap.

18. Connect the brake hose and line and install the retaining clip.

19. Connect the halfshaft and stubshaft Torque the bolts to 30 ft. lbs.

20. Connect the axle vent hose.

21. Connect the stabilizer bar link.

22. Bleed the brakes.

Control Arm

REMOVAL AND INSTALLATION

1. Remove the coil spring.

2. Disengage the parking brake cable from the control arm.

3. Disconnect the stabilizer bar from the control arm.

4. Remove the rear bearing hub and suspend the brake backing plate by a length of wire.

NOTE: *The left side wheel flange nuts are left hand threads. Turn the nut clockwise to remove it.*

5. Pull the wheel stub shaft out of the control arm.

6. Remove the control arm inner and outer attaching bolts.

7. Installation is the reverse of removal. Install all fasteners snugly, but don't torque them. Lower the car to the ground and torque all fasteners with the car's weight on the wheels. Make sure that the control arm bolt heads are facing inward. If the bolts heads face outward they will rub against the parking brake cable. Torque the bolts to 70 ft. lbs.

Shock Absorber

REMOVAL AND INSTALLATION

1. Remove the rear parcel shelf.

2. Remove the shock absorber trim cover from the rear wheel housing.

3. Raise and support the front end on jackstands.

4. Support the control arm with a floor jack. Raise it enough to take spring pressure off the shock absorber.

5. Remove the upper shock absorber bolt.

6. Remove the protective lower cap.

7. Remove the nut and bolt attaching the lower end to the control arm.

8. Installation is the reverse of removal. Install the upper end first and torque the nut to 35 ft. lbs. Torque the lower end nut to 35 ft. lbs. also. The bolt heads should face inwards.

Sway Bar

REMOVAL AND INSTALLATION

1. Raise and support the rear end on jackstands.

2. Remove the wheels.

3. Disconnect the stabilizer bar links from the control arms.

4. For alignment reference, place a piece of tape on the stabilizer bar next to the U-bracket and insulator.

5. Remove the bolts attaching the U-brackets to the body.

6. Disengage the U-brackets from the body. Remove the bar.

7. Installation is the reverse of removal. Torque the attaching bolts to 15 ft. lbs.

STEERING

Steering Wheel
REMOVAL AND INSTALLATION

1. Open the hood and disconnect the negative cable from the battery.

2. On models with safety crash pads, remove the crash pad attaching screws from the underside of the steering wheel spoke and remove the pad. On all models equipped with a horn button, remove the horn button or ring by pressing down evenly and turning it counterclockwise approximately 20° and then lifting it from the steering wheel. On 1981 and later models, pull straight out on the hub cover. Disconnect the horn wires from the crash pad on models so equipped.

3. Remove and discard the nut from the end of the shaft. Install a steering wheel puller on the end of the shaft and remove the wheel.

CAUTION: *The use of a knock-off type steering wheel puller or the use of a hammer on the steering shaft will damage the collapsible column.*

4. Lubricate the upper surface of the steering shaft upper bushing with white grease. Transfer all serviceable parts to the new steering wheel.

5. Position the steering wheel on the shaft so that the alignment marks line up. Install a locknut and torque it to 30-40 ft. lbs. Connect the horn wires.

6. Install the horn button or ring by turning it clockwise or install the crash pad.

Turn Signal Switch
REPLACEMENT
Mustang and Capri

1. Remove the four screws retaining the steering column shroud.

2. Remove the turn signal lever by pulling and twisting straight out.

3. Peel back the foam shield. Disconnect the two electrical connectors.

4. Remove the two attaching screws and disengage the switch from the housing.

5. To install, position the switch to the housing and install the screws. Stick the foam to the switch.

6. Install the lever by aligning the key and pushing the lever fully home.

7. Install the two electrical connectors, test the switch, and install the shroud.

Merkur

1. Remove the steering column upper and lower shroud halves.

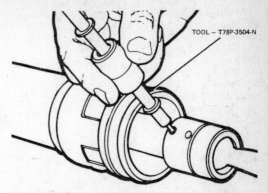

Removing the spiral pin from the ball housing

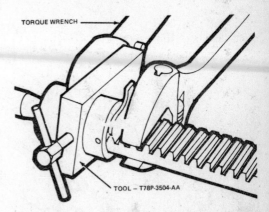

Removing or installing the tie rod ball housing assembly

2. Remove the 2 phillips screws securing the switch to the steering column and disconnect the wiring.

3. Installation is the reverse of removal.

Ignition Switch
REMOVAL AND INSTALLATION
Mustang and Capri
1979-81

1. Disconnect the battery ground.

2. On tilt columns, remove the upper extension shroud by unsnapping the shroud from the retaining clip at the 9 o'clock position.

3. Remove the trim shroud halves.

4. Disconnect the switch wiring.

5. Drill out the break-off head bolts attaching the switch to the lock cylinder with a ⅛" drill bit.

6. Remove the remainder of the bolts with a screw extractor.

7. Disengage the switch from the actuator pin.

To install:

8. Slide the switch carrier to the switch lock position. Insert a 7/16" drill bit shank through

1. Emblem assy.
2. Nut ⅝-18 hex
3. Wheel assy-stng
4. Lock cyl-(body)
5. Key-(body)
6. Ring
7. Bearing
8. Gear-stng col lock
9. Shroud-upper

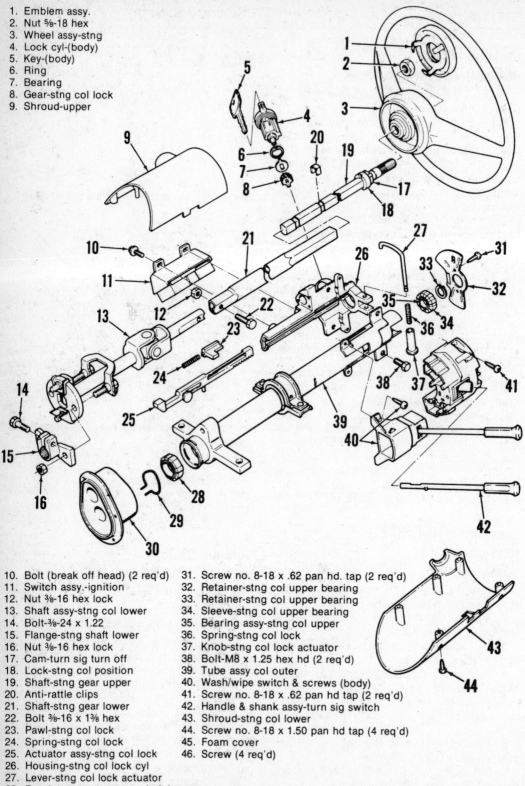

10. Bolt (break off head) (2 req'd)
11. Switch assy.-ignition
12. Nut ⅜-16 hex lock
13. Shaft assy-stng col lower
14. Bolt-⅜-24 x 1.22
15. Flange-stng shaft lower
16. Nut ⅜-16 hex lock
17. Cam-turn sig turn off
18. Lock-stng col position
19. Shaft-stng gear upper
20. Anti-rattle clips
21. Shaft-stng gear lower
22. Bolt ⅜-16 x 1⅜ hex
23. Pawl-stng col lock
24. Spring-stng col lock
25. Actuator assy-stng col lock
26. Housing-stng col lock cyl
27. Lever-stng col lock actuator
28. Bearing assy-stng gear shaft lower
29. Ring-stng gear shaft lower bearing retainer
30. Boot assy-stng col

31. Screw no. 8-18 x .62 pan hd. tap (2 req'd)
32. Retainer-stng col upper bearing
33. Retainer-stng col upper bearing
34. Sleeve-stng col upper bearing
35. Bearing assy-stng col upper
36. Spring-stng col lock
37. Knob-stng col lock actuator
38. Bolt-M8 x 1.25 hex hd (2 req'd)
39. Tube assy col outer
40. Wash/wipe switch & screws (body)
41. Screw no. 8-18 x .62 pan hd tap (2 req'd)
42. Handle & shank assy-turn sig switch
43. Shroud-stng col lower
44. Screw no. 8-18 x 1.50 pan hd tap (4 req'd)
45. Foam cover
46. Screw (4 req'd)

Standard (non-tilt) steering column assembly showing ignition switch placement

Troubleshooting the Steering Column

Problem	Cause	Solution
Will not lock	• Lockbolt spring broken or defective	• Replace lock bolt spring
High effort (required to turn ignition key and lock cylinder)	• Lock cylinder defective • Ignition switch defective • Rack preload spring broken or deformed • Burr on lock sector, lock rack, housing, support or remote rod coupling • Bent sector shaft • Defective lock rack • Remote rod bent, deformed • Ignition switch mounting bracket bent • Distorted coupling slot in lock rack (tilt column)	• Replace lock cylinder • Replace ignition switch • Replace preload spring • Remove burr • Replace shaft • Replace lock rack • Replace rod • Straighten or replace • Replace lock rack
Will stick in "start"	• Remote rod deformed • Ignition switch mounting bracket bent	• Straighten or replace • Straighten or replace
Key cannot be removed in "off-lock"	• Ignition switch is not adjusted correctly • Defective lock cylinder	• Adjust switch • Replace lock cylinder
Lock cylinder can be removed without depressing retainer	• Lock cylinder with defective retainer • Burr over retainer slot in housing cover or on cylinder retainer	• Replace lock cylinder • Remove burr
High effort on lock cylinder between "off" and "off-lock"	• Distorted lock rack • Burr on tang of shift gate (automatic column) • Gearshift linkage not adjusted	• Replace lock rack • Remove burr • Adjust linkage
Noise in column	• One click when in "off-lock" position and the steering wheel is moved (all except automatic column) • Coupling bolts not tightened • Lack of grease on bearings or bearing surfaces • Upper shaft bearing worn or broken • Lower shaft bearing worn or broken • Column not correctly aligned • Coupling pulled apart • Broken coupling lower joint • Steering shaft snap ring not seated • Shroud loose on shift bowl. Housing loose on jacket—will be noticed with ignition in "off-lock" and when torque is applied to steering wheel.	• Normal—lock bolt is seating • Tighten pinch bolts • Lubricate with chassis grease • Replace bearing assembly • Replace bearing. Check shaft and replace if scored. • Align column • Replace coupling • Repair or replace joint and align column • Replace ring. Check for proper seating in groove. • Position shroud over lugs on shift bowl. Tighten mounting screws.
High steering shaft effort	• Column misaligned • Defective upper or lower bearing • Tight steering shaft universal joint • Flash on I.D. of shift tube at plastic joint (tilt column only) • Upper or lower bearing seized	• Align column • Replace as required • Repair or replace • Replace shift tube • Replace bearings
Lash in mounted column assembly	• Column mounting bracket bolts loose • Broken weld nuts on column jacket • Column capsule bracket sheared	• Tighten bolts • Replace column jacket • Replace bracket assembly

Troubleshooting the Steering Column (cont.)

Problem	Cause	Solution
Lash in mounted column assembly (cont.)	• Column bracket to column jacket mounting bolts loose	• Tighten to specified torque
	• Loose lock shoes in housing (tilt column only)	• Replace shoes
	• Loose pivot pins (tilt column only)	• Replace pivot pins and support
	• Loose lock shoe pin (tilt column only)	• Replace pin and housing
	• Loose support screws (tilt column only)	• Tighten screws
Housing loose (tilt column only)	• Excessive clearance between holes in support or housing and pivot pin diameters	• Replace pivot pins and support
	• Housing support-screws loose	• Tighten screws
Steering wheel loose—every other tilt position (tilt column only)	• Loose fit between lock shoe and lock shoe pivot pin	• Replace lock shoes and pivot pin
Steering column not locking in any tilt position (tilt column only)	• Lock shoe seized on pivot pin	• Replace lock shoes and pin
	• Lock shoe grooves have burrs or are filled with foreign material	• Clean or replace lock shoes
	• Lock shoe springs weak or broken	• Replace springs
Noise when tilting column (tilt column only)	• Upper tilt bumpers worn	• Replace tilt bumper
	• Tilt spring rubbing in housing	• Lubricate with chassis grease
One click when in "off-lock" position and the steering wheel is moved	• Seating of lock bolt	• None. Click is normal characteristic sound produced by lock bolt as it seats.
High shift effort (automatic and tilt column only)	• Column not correctly aligned	• Align column
	• Lower bearing not aligned correctly	• Assemble correctly
	• Lack of grease on seal or lower bearing areas	• Lubricate with chassis grease
Improper transmission shifting— automatic and tilt column only	• Sheared shift tube joint	• Replace shift tube
	• Improper transmission gearshift linkage adjustment	• Adjust linkage
	• Loose lower shift lever	• Replace shift tube

Troubleshooting the Ignition Switch

Problem	Cause	Solution
Ignition switch electrically inoperative	• Loose or defective switch connector	• Tighten or replace connector
	• Feed wire open (fusible link)	• Repair or replace
	• Defective ignition switch	• Replace ignition switch
Engine will not crank	• Ignition switch not adjusted properly	• Adjust switch
Ignition switch wil not actuate mechanically	• Defective ignition switch	• Replace switch
	• Defective lock sector	• Replace lock sector
	• Defective remote rod	• Replace remote rod
Ignition switch cannot be adjusted correctly	• Remote rod deformed	• Repair, straighten or replace

Troubleshooting the Turn Signal Switch

Problem	Cause	Solution
Turn signal will not cancel	• Loose switch mounting screws • Switch or anchor bosses broken • Broken, missing or out of position detent, or cancelling spring	• Tighten screws • Replace switch • Reposition springs or replace switch as required
Turn signal difficult to operate	• Turn signal lever loose • Switch yoke broken or distorted • Loose or misplaced springs • Foreign parts and/or materials in switch • Switch mounted loosely	• Tighten mounting screws • Replace switch • Reposition springs or replace switch • Remove foreign parts and/or material • Tighten mounting screws
Turn signal will not indicate lane change	• Broken lane change pressure pad or spring hanger • Broken, missing or misplaced lane change spring • Jammed wires	• Replace switch • Replace or reposition as required • Loosen mounting screws, reposition wires and retighten screws
Turn signal will not stay in turn position	• Foreign material or loose parts impeding movement of switch yoke • Defective switch	• Remove material and/or parts • Replace switch
Hazard switch cannot be pulled out	• Foreign material between hazard support cancelling leg and yoke	• Remove foreign material. No foreign material impeding function of hazard switch—replace turn signal switch.
No turn signal lights	• Inoperative turn signal flasher • Defective or blown fuse • Loose chassis to column harness connector • Disconnect column to chassis connector. Connect new switch to chassis and operate switch by hand. If vehicle lights now operate normally, signal switch is inoperative • If vehicle lights do not operate, check chassis wiring for opens, grounds, etc.	• Replace turn signal flasher • Replace fuse • Connect securely • Replace signal switch • Repair chassis wiring as required
Instrument panel turn indicator lights on but not flashing	• Burned out or damaged front or rear turn signal bulb • If vehicle lights do not operate, check light sockets for high resistance connections, the chassis wiring for opens, grounds, etc. • Inoperative flasher • Loose chassis to column harness connection • Inoperative turn signal switch • To determine if turn signal switch is defective, substitute new switch into circuit and operate switch by hand. If the vehicle's lights operate normally, signal switch is inoperative.	• Replace bulb • Repair chassis wiring as required • Replace flasher • Connect securely • Replace turn signal switch • Replace turn signal switch
Stop light not on when turn indicated	• Loose column to chassis connection • Disconnect column to chassis connector. Connect new switch into system without removing old.	• Connect securely • Replace signal switch

Troubleshooting the Turn Signal Switch (cont.)

Problem	Cause	Solution
Stop light not on when turn indicated (cont.)	Operate switch by hand. If brake lights work with switch in the turn position, signal switch is defective.	
	• If brake lights do not work, check connector to stop light sockets for grounds, opens, etc.	• Repair connector to stop light circuits using service manual as guide
Turn indicator panel lights not flashing	• Burned out bulbs • High resistance to ground at bulb socket	• Replace bulbs • Replace socket
	• Opens, ground in wiring harness from front turn signal bulb socket to indicator lights	• Locate and repair as required
Turn signal lights flash very slowly	• High resistance ground at light sockets	• Repair high resistance grounds at light sockets
	• Incorrect capacity turn signal flasher or bulb	• Replace turn signal flasher or bulb
	• If flashing rate is still extremely slow, check chassis wiring harness from the connector to light sockets for high resistance	• Locate and repair as required
	• Loose chassis to column harness connection	• Connect securely
	• Disconnect column to chassis connector. Connect new switch into system without removing old. Operate switch by hand. If flashing occurs at normal rate, the signal switch is defective.	• Replace turn signal switch
Hazard signal lights will not flash— turn signal functions normally	• Blow fuse • Inoperative hazard warning flasher	• Replace fuse • Replace hazard warning flasher in fuse panel
	• Loose chassis-to-column harness connection	• Conect securely
	• Disconnect column to chassis connector. Connect new switch into system without removing old. Depress the hazard warning lights. If they now work normally, turn signal switch is defective.	• Replace turn signal switch
	• If lights do not flash, check wiring harness "K" lead for open between hazard flasher and connector. If open, fuse block is defective	• Repair or replace brown wire or connector as required

the switch housing and into the carrier, thereby, preventing any movement. New replacement switch already have a pin installed for this purpose.

9. Turn the key to the LOCK position and remove the key.

10. Position the switch on the actuator pin.

11. Install new break-off bolts and hand tighten them.

12. Push the switch towards the steering wheel, parallel with the column, to remove any slack between the bolts and the switch slots.

13. While holding the switch in this position, tighten the bolts until the heads break off.

14. Remove the drill bit or packaging pin.

15. Connect the wiring.

16. The remainder of installation is the reverse of removal.

1982-88

1. Disconnect the battery ground.

2. On tilt columns, remove the upper extension shroud by unsnapping the shroud from the retaining clip at the 9 o'clock position.

3. Remove the trim shroud halves.

4. Disconnect the switch wiring.

5. On 1982-85 cars, drill out the break-off head bolts attaching the switch to the lock cyl-

inder with a ⅛" drill bit. Remove the remainder of the bolts with a screw extractor.

6. On 1986-88 cars, remove the bolts securing the switch to the lock cylinder housing.

7. Disengage the switch from the actuator pin.

To install:

8. Slide the switch carrier to the ON RUN position. New replacement switches will be in this position.

9. Turn the key to the ON RUN position.

10. Position the switch on the actuator pin.

11. On 1982-85 cars, install new break-off bolts and hand tighten them.

On 1986-88 cars, install the bolts and tighten them to 50-60 in.lb.

12. Push the switch towards the steering wheel, parallel with the column, to remove any slack between the bolts and the switch slots.

13. While holding the switch in this position, tighten the bolts until the heads break off.

14. Remove the drill bit or packaging pin.

15. Connect the wiring.

16. The remainder of installation is the reverse of removal.

Merkur

The ignition switch is mounted onto the lock cylinder housing and is controlled by a lock barrel which is part of the actuator assembly.

The switch has a short harness connector acrrying connections which engage the connectors of a multiple connector.

To remove the switch, remove the steering column shroud and disconnect the switch.

Ignition Lock Cylinder

REMOVAL AND INSTALLATION
FUNCTIONAL LOCK CYLINDER

Mustang and Capri

1. Disconnect the battery ground.

2. On tilt columns, remove the upper extension shroud by unsnapping the shroud from the retaining clip at the 9 o'clock position.

3. Remove the trim shroud halves.

4. Unplug the wire connector at the key warning switch.

5. Place the shift lever in PARK and turn the key to RUN.

6. Place a ⅛" wire pin in the hole in the casting surrounding the lock cylinder and depress the retaining pin while pulling out on the cylinder.

7. When installing the cylinder, turn the lock cylinder to the RUN position and depress the retaining pin, then insert the lock cylinder into its housing in the flange casting. Assure that the cylinder is fully seated and aligned in the interlocking washer before turning the key to the OFF position. This will allow the cylinder retaining pin to extend into the cylinder cast housing hole.

8. The remainder of installation is the reverse of removal.

REMOVAL AND INSTALLATION
NON-FUNCTIONING LOCK CYLINDER

Mustang and Capri

1. Disconnect the battery ground.

2. Remove the steering wheel.

3. On tilt columns, remove the upper extension shroud by unsnapping the shroud from the retaining clip at the 9 o'clock position.

4. Remove the steering column trim shrouds.

5. Disconnect the wiring at the key warning switch.

6. Using a ⅛" drill bit, mounted in a right angle drive drill adapter, drill out the retaining pin, going no deeper than ½" (12.7mm).

7. Tilt the column to the full down position. Place a chisel at the base of the ignition lock cylinder cap and using a hammer break away the cap from the lock cylinder.

8. Using a ⅜" drill bit, drill down the center of the ignition lock cylinder key slot about 1¾" (44mm), until the lock cylinder breaks loose from the steering column cover casting.

9. Remove the lock cylinder and the drill shavings from the housing.

10. Remove the upper bearing snapring washer and steering column lock gear.

11. Carefully inspect the steering column housing for signs of damage from the previous operation. If any damage is apparent, the components should be replaced.

12. Installation is the reverse of removal.

Merkur

1. Remove the steering column shroud.

2. Insert the key in the lock and turn it to the **ACC** position.

3. Using a thin rod, depress the lock cylinder retaining spring through the hole in the lock housing. At the same time, jiggle the key back and forth until the lock barrel and key cylinder come free.

4. Remove the circlip from the lock barrel. Be sure not to damage the circlip location in the lock barrel.

5. Pull the key out about 5mm. This will cause an additional ridge to project which acts on the key cylinder chamfer causing it to be brought flush with the barrel. Remove the key.

To install:

6. Insert the key fully into the lock barrel.

7. Pull it out 5mm to bring the additional ridge flush with the barrel notch.

8. Insert the key barrel into the cylinder.

The barrel can be installed in only one position and this allows the ridge to act on the cylinder chamfer.

9. Fully insert the key and check that the key and barrel can be turned freely.

10. Turn the key to the **ACC** position and install the circlip. The open jaws of the circlip must align with the keyway register of the cylinder.

11. Insert the clyinder into the housing. Make sure that the cylinder is firmly seated in the housing so that the retaining spring fits into the undercut slot in the housing. It may be necessary to jiggle the key back and forth to proper align the unit.

12. Check key operation in all positions.

Steering Column

REMOVAL AND INSTALLATION

1. Disconnect the battery ground.

2. Unbolt the flexible coupling from the steering input shaft.

3. Disengage the safety strap and bolt from the flexible coupling.

4. Disconnect the transmission shift rod from the control selector lever.

NOTE: *Column-type automatic transmission linkage use oil impregnated plastic grommets to connect the rods and levers. Whenever a grommet-type connection is changed, the grommets should be replaced.*

5. Remove the steering wheel.

6. Remove the steering column trim shrouds.

7. Remove the steering column cover.

8. Remove the hood release lever.

9. Disconnect all electrical and vacuum connections at the column.

10. Loosen the 4 nuts securing the column to the brake pedal support bracket, allowing the column to be lowered enough to access the selector lever cable and cable. Don't lower the column too far or damage to the lever and/or cable will occur!

11. Reach between the column and instrument panel and gently lift off the selector cable from the pin on the lever.

12. Remove the cable clamp from the steering column tube.

13. Remove the 4 dust boot-to-dash panel screws.

14. Remove the 4 nuts attaching the column to the brake pedal support.

15. Lower the column to clear the 4 mounting bolts and pull the column out.

To install:

16. Position the column in the car.

17. Install the column collar-to-brake pedal support nuts loosely.

18. Install the selector cable clamp loosely.

19. Attach the cable to the lever pin.

20. Tighten the 4 column-to-brake pedal support nuts to 35 ft. lbs.

21. Move the shift selector to the DRIVE position, against the drive stop. Rotate the selector bracket clockwise or counterclockwise until the selector pointer in the cluster centers on the letter **D**. Tighten the bracket nut.

22. Connect the electrical and vacuum connectors.

23. Install the safety strap and bolt on the flange on the steering input flange.

24. Install the 2 nuts connecting the steering shaft to the flexible coupling. Tighten the nuts to 35 ft. lbs. The safety strap must be properly positioned to avoid metal-to-metal contact. The flexible coupling must not be distorted when the nuts are tightened. Pry the shaft up or down to allow a ± 1/8" (3mm) insulator flatness.

25. Connect the shift rod to the shift lever on the lower end of the steering column. Make sure the grommet is replaced.

26. The remainder of installation is the reverse of removal. Adjust the shift linkage.

MANUAL RACK AND PINION STEERING

ADJUSTMENTS

The rack and pinion gear provides two means of service adjustment. The gear must be removed from the vehicle to perform both adjustments.

Support Yoke to Rack

1. Clean the exterior of the steering gear thoroughly and mount the gear by installing two long bolts and washers through the mounting boss bushings and attaching to Bench Mounted Holding Fixture, Tool T57L-500-B or equivalent.

2. Remove the yoke cover, gasket, shims, and yoke spring.

3. Clean the cover and housing flange areas thoroughly.

4. Reinstall the yoke and cover, omitting the gasket, shims, and the spring.

5. Tighten the cover bolts lightly until the cover just touches the yoke.

6. Measure the gap between the cover and the housing flange. With the gasket, add selected shims to give a combined pack thickness 0.13-0.15mm greater than the measured gap.

7. Remove the cover.

8. Assemble the gasket next to the housing flange, then the selected shims, spring, and cover.

9. Install cover bolts, sealing the threads

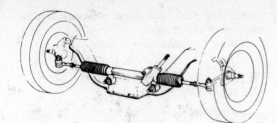

Typical rack and pinion steering gear linkage

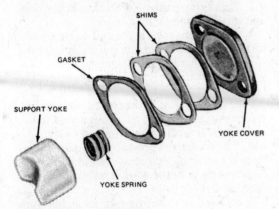

Support yoke arrangement

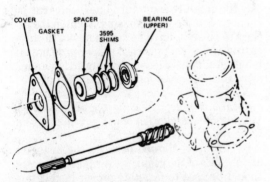

Pinion bearing cover and shim arrangement

with ESW-M46-132A or equivalent, and tighten.

10. Check to see that the gear operates smoothly without binding or slackness.

Pinion Bearing Preload

1. Clean the exterior of the steering gear thoroughly and place the gear in the bench mounted holding fixture as outlined under Support Yoke to Back Adjustment.

2. Loosen the bolts of the yoke cover to relieve spring pressure on the rack.

3. Remove the pinion cover and gasket. Clean the cover flange area thoroughly.

4. Remove the spacer and shims.

5. Install a new gasket, and fit shims between the upper bearing and the spacer until the top of the spacer is flush with the gasket. Check with a straightedge, using light pressure.

6. Add one shim, 0.0025-0.0050″ (0.0635-0.1270mm) to the pack in order to preload the bearings. The spacer must be assembled next to the pinion cover.

7. Install the cover and bolts.

Tie Rod Articulation Effort

1. Install the hook end of a pull scale through the hole in the tie rod end stud. The effort to move the tie rod should be 1-5 lb. (0.45-2.27 kg). Do not damage the tie rod end.

2. Replace the ball joint/tie rod assembly if the effort falls outside this range. Save the tie rod end for use on the new tie rod assembly.

REMOVAL AND INSTALLATION

1. Disconnect the negative battery cable from the battery.

2. Remove the one bolt retaining the flexible coupling to the input shaft.

3. Leave the ignition key in the ON position, and raise the vehicle on a hoist.

4. Remove the two tie rod end retaining cotter pins and nuts. Separate the studs from the spindle arms, using the ball joint separator tool. Do not use a hammer or similar tool as this may damage spindle arms or rod studs.

5. Support the steering gear, and remove the two nuts, insulator washers, and bolts retaining the steering gear to the No. 2 crossmember.

6. Remove the steering gear assembly from the vehicle.

7. Insert the input shaft into the flexible coupling aligning the flats and position the steering gear to the No. 2 crossmember. Install the two bolts.

8. Connect the tie rod ends to the spindle arms, and install the two retaining nuts. Tighten the nuts to specifications, and install the two cotter pins.

9. Lower the vehicle, and install the one bolt retaining the flexible coupling to the input shaft. Tighten the bolt to specifications.

10. Turn the ignition key to the OFF position.

11. Connect the negative battery cable to the battery.

12. Check the toe, and reset if necessary.

Tie Rod Ends

REMOVAL AND INSTALLATION

1. Remove the cotter pin and nut at the spindle. Separate the tie rod end stud from the spindle with a puller.

2. Matchmark the position of the locknut with paint on the tie rod. Unscrew the locknut.

Unscrew the tie rod end, counting the number of turns required to remove.

3. Install the new end the same number of turns. Attach the tie rod end stud to the spindle. Install the nut and torque to 35 ft. lbs., then continue to tighten until the cotter pin holes align. Install a new cotter pin. Check the toe and adjust if necessary, then torque the tie rod end locknut to 35 ft. lbs.

POWER RACK AND PINION STEERING

ADJUSTMENTS

The power rack and pinion steering gear provides for only one service adjustment. The gear must be removed from the vehicle to perform this adjustment.

Rack Yoke Plug Preload

1. Clean the exterior of the steering gear thoroughly.

2. Install two long bolts and washers through the bushing, and attach to the bench mounted holding fixture, Tool T57L-500-B or equivalent.

3. Do not remove the external pressure lines, unless they are leaking or damaged. If these lines are removed, they must be replaced with new lines.

4. Drain the power steering fluid by rotating the input shaft lock-to-lock twice using Tool T74P-3505-R or equivalent. Cover ports on valve housing with shop cloth while draining gear.

5. Insert an inch-pound torque wrench with maximum capacity of 30-60 in.lb. into the input shaft torque adapter, Tool T74P-3504-R or equivalent. Position the adapter and wrench on the input shaft splines.

6. Loosen the yoke plug locknut with wrench, Tool T78P-3504-H or equivalent.

7. Loosen yoke plug with a ¾" socket wrench.

8. With the rack at the center of travel, tighten the yoke plug to 45-50 in.lb. Clean the threads of the yoke plug prior to tightening to prevent a false reading.

9. Back off the yoke plug approximately ⅛ turn (44° minimum to 54° maximum) until the torque required to initiate and sustain rotation of the input shaft is 7-18 in.lb.

10. Place Tool T78P-3504-H or equivalent on the yoke plug locknut. While holding the yoke plug, tighten the locknut to 44-66 ft.lbs. Do not allow the yoke plug to move while tightening or the preload will be affected. Recheck input shaft torque after tightening locknut.

11. If the external pressure lines were re-moved, they must be replaced with new service line. Remove the copper seals from the housing ports prior to installation of new lines.

STEERING GEAR REMOVAL AND INSTALLATION

1. Disconnect the negative battery cable from the battery.

2. Remove the one bolt retaining the flexible coupling to the input shaft.

3. Leave the ignition key in the On position, and raise the vehicle on a hoist.

4. Remove the two tie rod end retaining cotter pins and nuts. Separate the studs from the spindle arms, using the ball joint separator tool.

5. Support the steering gear, and remove the two nuts, insulator, washers, and bolts retaining the steering gear to the No. 2 crossmember. Lower the gear slightly to permit access to the pressure and return line fittings.

6. Disconnect the pressure and return lines from the steering gear valve housing. Plug the lines and parts in the valve housing to prevent entry of dirt.

7. Remove the steering gear assembly from the vehicle.

8. Support and position the steering gear, so that the pressure and return line fittings can be connected to the valve housing. Tighten the fittings to 15-20 ft. lbs. The design allows the hoses to swivel when tightened properly. do not attempt to eliminate looseness by overtightening, since this can cause damage to the fittings.

NOTE: *The rubber insulators must be pushed completely inside the gear housing before the installation of the gear housing on the No. 2 crossmember.*

9. No gap is allowed between the insulator and the face of the gear boss. A rubber lubricant should be used to facilitate proper installation of the insulators in the gear housing. Insert the input shaft into the flexible coupling, and position the steering gear to the No. 2 crossmember. Install the two bolts, insulator washers, and nuts. Tighten the two nuts to 80-100 ft. lbs.

10. Connect the tie rod ends to the spindle arms, and install the two retaining nuts. Tighten the nuts to 35-45 ft. lbs., then, after tightening to specification, tighten the nuts to their nearest cotter pin castellation, and install two new cotter pins.

11. Lower the vehicle, and install the one bolt retaining the flexible coupling to the input shaft. Tighten the bolt to 18-23 ft. lbs.

12. Turn the ignition key to the Off position.

13. Connect the negative battery cable to the battery.

14. Remove the coil wire.

15. Fill the power steering pump reservoir.

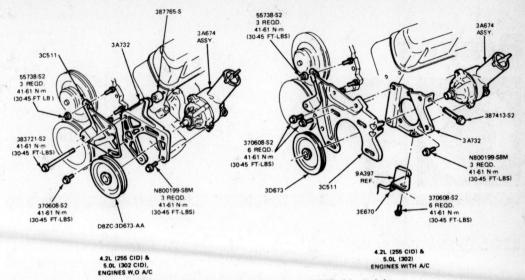

Power steering pump installation on 1980–81 models

16. Engage the starter, and cycle the steering wheel to distribute the fluid. Check the fluid level and add as required.

17. Install the coil wire, start the engine, and cycle the steering wheel. Check for fluid leaks.

18. If the tie rod ends were loosened, check the wheel alignment.

Power Steering Pump

REMOVAL AND INSTALLATION

1. Drain the fluid from the pump reservoir by disconnecting the fluid return hose at the pump. Disconnect the pressure hose from the pump.

2. Remove the mounting bolts from the front of the pump.

3. Move the pump inward to loosen the belt tension and remove the belt from the pulley. Remove the pump from the car.

4. To install the pump, position on mounting bracket and loosely install the mounting bolts and nuts. Put the drive belt over the pulley and move the pump outward against the belt until the proper belt tension is obtained. Do not pry against the pump body. Measure the belt tension with a belt tension gauge for the proper adjustment. Only in cases where a belt tension gauge is not available should the belt deflection method be used.

5. Tighten the mounting bolts and nuts.

Brakes

9

BASIC OPERATING PRINCIPLES

Hydraulic systems are used to actuate the brakes of all automobiles. The system transports the power required to force the frictional surfaces of the braking system together from the pedal to the individual brake units at each wheel. A hydraulic system is used for two reasons.

First, fluid under pressure can be carried to all parts of an automobile by small pipes and flexible hoses without taking up a significant amount of room or posing routing problems.

Second, a great mechanical advantage can be given to the brake pedal end of the system, and the foot pressure required to actuate the brakes can be reduced by making the surface area of the master cylinder pistons smaller than that of any of the pistons in the wheel cylinders or calipers.

The master cylinder consists of a fluid reservoir and a double cylinder and piston assembly. Double type master cylinders are designed to separate the front and rear braking systems hydraulically in case of a leak.

Steel lines carry the brake fluid to a point on the vehicle's frame near each of the vehicle's wheels. The fluid is then carried to the calipers and wheel cylinders by flexible tubes in order to allow for suspension and steering movements.

In drum brake systems, each wheel cylinder contains two pistons, one at either end, which push outward in opposite directions.

In disc brake systems, the cylinders are part of the calipers. One cylinder in each caliper is used to force the brake pads against the disc.

All pistons employ some type of seal, usually made of rubber, to minimize fluid leakage. A rubber dust boot seals the outer end of the cylinder against dust and dirt. The boot fits around the outer end of the piston on disc brake calipers, and around the brake actuating rod on wheel cylinders.

The hydraulic system operates as follows: When at rest, the entire system, from the piston(s) in the master cylinder to those in the wheel cylinders or calipers, is full of brake fluid. Upon application of the brake pedal, fluid trapped in front of the master cylinder piston(s) is forced through the lines to the wheel cylinders. Here, it forces the pistons outward, in the case of drum brakes, and inward toward the disc, in the case of disc brakes. The motion of the pistons is opposed by return springs mounted outside the cylinders in drum brakes, and by spring seals, in disc brakes.

Upon release of the brake pedal, a spring located inside the master cylinder immediately returns the master cylinder pistons to the normal position. The pistons contain check valves and the master cylinder has compensating ports drilled in it. These are uncovered as the pistons reach their normal position. The piston check valves allow fluid to flow toward the wheel cylinders or calipers as the pistons withdraw. Then, as the return springs force the brake pads or shoes into the released position, the excess fluid reservoir through the compensating ports. It is during the time the pedal is in the released position that any fluid that has leaked out of the system will be replaced through the compensating ports.

Dual circuit master cylinders employ two pistons, located one behind the other, in the same cylinder. The primary piston is actuated directly by mechanical linkage from the brake pedal through the power booster. The secondary piston is actuated by fluid trapped between the two pistons. If a leak develops in front of the secondary piston, it moves forward until it bottoms against the front of the master cylinder, and the fluid trapped between the pistons will operate the rear brakes. If the rear brakes develop a leak, the primary piston will move forward until direct contact with the secondary piston takes place, and it will force the secondary piston to actuate the front brakes. In either case, the brake pedal moves farther when the brakes are applied, and less braking power is available.

All dual circuit systems use a switch to warn the driver when only half of the brake system is operational. This switch is located in a valve body which is mounted on the firewall or the frame below the master cylinder. A hydraulic piston receives pressure from both circuits, each circuit's pressure being applied to one end of the piston. When the pressures are in balance, the piston remains stationary. When one circuit has a leak, however, the greater pressure in that circuit during application of the brakes will push the piston to one side, closing the switch and activating the brake warning light.

In disc brake systems, this valve body also contains a metering valve and, in some cases, a proportioning valve. The metering valve keeps pressure from traveling to the disc brakes on the front wheels until the brake shoes on the rear wheels have contacted the drums, ensuring that the front brakes will never be used alone. The proportioning valve controls the pressure to the rear brakes to lessen the chance of rear wheel lock-up during very hard braking.

Warning lights may be tested by depressing the brake pedal and holding it while opening one of the wheel cylinder bleeder screws. If this does not cause the light to go on, substitute a new lamp, make continuity checks, and, finally, replace the switch as necessary.

The hydraulic system may be checked for leaks by applying pressure to the pedal gradually and steadily. If the pedal sinks very slowly to the floor, the system has a leak. This is not to be confused with a springy or spongy feel due to the compression of air within the lines. If the system leaks, there will be a gradual change in the position of the pedal with a constant pressure.

Check for leaks along all lines and at wheel cylinders. If no external leaks are apparent, the problem is inside the master cylinder.

Disc Brakes
BASIC OPERATING PRINCIPLES

Instead of the traditional expanding brakes that press outward against a circular drum, disc brake systems utilize a disc (rotor) with brake pads positioned on either side of it. Braking effect is achieved in a manner similar to the way you would squeeze a spinning phonograph record between your fingers. The disc (rotor) is a casting with cooling fins between the two braking surfaces. This enables air to circulate between the braking surfaces making them less sensitive to heat buildup and more resistant to fade. Dirt and water do not affect braking action since contaminants are thrown off by the centrifugal action of the rotor or scraped off the by the pads. Also, the equal clamping action of the two brake pads tends to ensure uniform, straight line stops. Disc brakes are inherently self-adjusting.

There are three general types of disc brake:
1. A fixed caliper.
2. A floating caliper.
3. A sliding caliper.

The fixed caliper design uses two pistons mounted on either side of the rotor (in each side of the caliper). The caliper is mounted rigidly and does not move.

The sliding and floating designs are quite similar. In fact, these two types are often lumped together. In both designs, the pad on the inside of the rotor is moved into contact with the rotor by hydraulic force. The caliper, which is not held in a fixed position, moves slightly, bringing the outside pad into contact with the rotor. There are various methods of attaching floating calipers. Some pivot at the bottom or top, and some slide on mounting bolts. In any event, the end result is the same.

All the cars covered in this book employ the sliding caliper design.

Drum Brakes
BASIC OPERATING PRINCIPLES

Drum brakes employ two brake shoes mounted on a stationary backing plate. These shoes are positioned inside a circular drum which rotates with the wheel assembly. The shoes are held in place by springs. This allows them to slide toward the drums (when they are applied) while keeping the linings and drums in alignment. The shoes are actuated by a wheel cylinder which is mounted at the top of the backing plate. When the brakes are applied, hydraulic pressure forces the wheel cylinder's actuating links outward. Since these links bear directly against the top of the brake shoes, the tops of the shoes are then forced against the inner side of the drum. This action forces the bottoms of the two shoes to contact the brake drum by rotating the entire assembly slightly (known as servo action). When pressure within the wheel cylinder is relaxed, return springs pull the shoes back away from the drum.

Most modern drum brakes are designed to self-adjust themselves during application when the vehicle is moving in reverse. This motion causes both shoes to rotate very slightly with the drum, rocking an adjusting lever, thereby causing rotation of the adjusting screw.

Power Boosters

Power brakes operate just as non-power brake systems except in the actuation of the master cylinder pistons. A vacuum diaphragm is located on the front of the master cylinder and assists the driver in applying the brakes, reducing both the effort and travel he must put into moving the brake pedal.

The vacuum diaphragm housing is connected to the intake manifold by a vacuum hose. A check valve is placed at the point where the hose enters the diaphragm housing, so that during periods of low manifold vacuum brake assist vacuum will not be lost.

Depressing the brake pedal closes off the vacuum source and allows atmospheric pressure to enter on one side of the diaphragm. This causes the master cylinder pistons to move and apply the brakes. When the brake pedal is released, vacuum is applied to both sides of the diaphragm, and return springs return the diaphragm and master cylinder pistons to the released position. If the vacuum fails, the brake pedal rod will butt against the end of the master cylinder actuating rod, and direct mechanical application will occur as the pedal is depressed.

The hydraulic and mechanical problems that apply to conventional brake systems also apply to power brakes, and should be checked for if the tests below do not reveal the problem.

Test for a system vacuum leak as described below:

1. Operate the engine at idle without touching the brake pedal for at least one minute.
2. Turn off the engine, and wait one minute.
3. Test for the presence of assist vacuum by depressing the brake pedal and releasing it several times. Light application will produce less and less pedal travel, if vacuum was present. If there is no vacuum, air is leaking into the system somewhere.

Test for system operation as follows:

1. Pump the brake pedal (with engine off) until the supply vacuum is entirely gone.
2. Put a light, steady pressure on the pedal.
3. Start the engine, and operate it at idle. If the system is operating, the brake pedal should fall toward the floor if constant pressure is maintained on the pedal.

Power brake systems may be tested for hydraulic leaks just as ordinary systems are tested.

BRAKE SYSTEMS

BRAKE ADJUSTMENTS

Disc brakes require no adjustments

Rear Drum Brakes

1. Raise and support the rear end on jackstands.
2. Remove the rubber plug from the adjusting slot in the brake backing plate.
3. Insert a brake adjusting spoon into the slot and engage the lowest possible tooth on the star wheel. Move the end of the brake spoon downward to move the star wheel upward and expand the adjusting screw. Repeat this operation until the brakes lock the wheel.
4. Insert a small screwdriver or piece of firm wire (coat-hanger wire) into the adjusting slot

Brake Specifications
All measurements given are (in.) unless noted

Year	Model	Lug Nut Torque (ft. lbs.)	Master Cylinder Bore	Brake Disc		Brake Drum		Minimum Lining Thickness	
				Minimum Thickness	Maximum Run-Out	Max Machine O/S	Max Wear Limit	Front	Rear
1979	All	70–115	0.938	0.810	0.003	9.060	0.007	②	③
1980	All	70–115	0.875 ④	0.810	0.003	9.060	0.007	②	③
1981–82	All	80–105	0.875 ④	0.810	0.003	9.060	0.007	②	③
1983–88	Exc. Merkur	80–105	0.827 ⑤	0.810	0.003	9.060	0.007	②	③
1985–88	Merkur	75–101	0.940	0.950	0.003	10.040	0.007	②	③

NOTE: *Minimum lining thickness is as recommended by the manufacturer. Because of variations in state inspection regulations, the minimum allowable thickness may be different than recommended by the manufacturer.*
① DISC—9.3 in. outside, 6.24 in. inside
② Lining Measures ⅛ in. above metal shoe
③ Lining Measures ¹⁄₁₆" in. above rivets
④ 0.750 in. with power brakes
⑤ SVO—1.125

Troubleshooting the Brake System

Problem	Cause	Solution
Low brake pedal (excessive pedal travel required for braking action.)	• Excessive clearance between rear linings and drums caused by inoperative automatic adjusters	• Make 10 to 15 alternate forward and reverse brake stops to adjust brakes. If brake pedal does not come up, repair or replace adjuster parts as necessary.
	• Worn rear brakelining	• Inspect and replace lining if worn beyond minimum thickness specification
	• Bent, distorted brakeshoes, front or rear	• Replace brakeshoes in axle sets
	• Air in hydraulic system	• Remove air from system. Refer to Brake Bleeding.
Low brake pedal (pedal may go to floor with steady pressure applied.)	• Fluid leak in hydraulic system	• Fill master cylinder to fill line; have helper apply brakes and check calipers, wheel cylinders, differential valve tubes, hoses and fittings for leaks. Repair or replace as necessary.
	• Air in hydraulic system	• Remove air from system. Refer to Brake Bleeding.
	• Incorrect or non-recommended brake fluid (fluid evaporates at below normal temp).	• Flush hydraulic system with clean brake fluid. Refill with correct-type fluid.
	• Master cylinder piston seals worn, or master cylinder bore is scored, worn or corroded	• Repair or replace master cylinder
Low brake pedal (pedal goes to floor on first application—o.k. on subsequent applications.)	• Disc brake pads sticking on abutment surfaces of anchor plate. Caused by a build-up of dirt, rust, or corrosion on abutment surfaces	• Clean abutment surfaces
Fading brake pedal (pedal height decreases with steady pressure applied.)	• Fluid leak in hydraulic system	• Fill master cylinder reservoirs to fill mark, have helper apply brakes, check calipers, wheel cylinders, differential valve, tubes, hoses, and fittings for fluid leaks. Repair or replace parts as necessary.
	• Master cylinder piston seals worn, or master cylinder bore is scored, worn or corroded	• Repair or replace master cylinder
Decreasing brake pedal travel (pedal travel required for braking action decreases and may be accompanied by a hard pedal.)	• Caliper or wheel cylinder pistons sticking or seized	• Repair or replace the calipers, or wheel cylinders
	• Master cylinder compensator ports blocked (preventing fluid return to reservoirs) or pistons sticking or seized in master cylinder bore	• Repair or replace the master cylinder
	• Power brake unit binding internally	• Test unit according to the following procedure: (a) Shift transmission into neutral and start engine (b) Increase engine speed to 1500 rpm, close throttle and fully depress brake pedal (c) Slow release brake pedal and stop engine (d) Have helper remove vacuum check valve and hose from power unit. Observe for backward movement of brake pedal. (e) If the pedal moves backward, the power unit has an internal bind—replace power unit

Troubleshooting the Brake System (cont.)

Problem	Cause	Solution
Spongy brake pedal (pedal has abnormally soft, springy, spongy feel when depressed.)	· Air in hydraulic system	· Remove air from system. Refer to Brake Bleeding.
	· Brakeshoes bent or distorted	· Replace brakeshoes
	· Brakelining not yet seated with drums and rotors	· Burnish brakes
	· Rear drum brakes not properly adjusted	· Adjust brakes
Hard brake pedal (excessive pedal pressure required to stop vehicle. May be accompanied by brake fade.)	· Loose or leaking power brake unit vacuum hose	· Tighten connections or replace leaking hose
	· Incorrect or poor quality brakelining	· Replace with lining in axle sets
	· Bent, broken, distorted brakeshoes	· Replace brakeshoes
	· Calipers binding or dragging on mounting pins. Rear brakeshoes dragging on support plate.	· Replace mounting pins and bushings. Clean rust or burrs from rear brake support plate ledges and lubricate ledges with molydisulfide grease. **NOTE:** If ledges are deeply grooved or scored, do not attempt to sand or grind them smooth—replace support plate.
	· Caliper, wheel cylinder, or master cylinder pistons sticking or seized	· Repair or replace parts as necessary
	· Power brake unit vacuum check valve malfunction	· Test valve according to the following procedure: (a) Start engine, increase engine speed to 1500 rpm, close throttle and immediately stop engine (b) Wait at least 90 seconds then depress brake pedal (c) If brakes are not vacuum assisted for 2 or more applications, check valve is faulty
	· Power brake unit has internal bind	· Test unit according to the following procedure: (a) With engine stopped, apply brakes several times to exhaust all vacuum in system (b) Shift transmission into neutral, depress brake pedal and start engine (c) If pedal height decreases with foot pressure and less pressure is required to hold pedal in applied position, power unit vacuum system is operating normally. Test power unit. If power unit exhibits a bind condition, replace the power unit.
	· Master cylinder compensator ports (at bottom of reservoirs) blocked by dirt, scale, rust, or have small burrs (blocked ports prevent fluid return to reservoirs).	· Repair or replace master cylinder **CAUTION:** Do not attempt to clean blocked ports with wire, pencils, or similar implements. Use compressed air only.
	· Brake hoses, tubes, fittings clogged or restricted	· Use compressed air to check or unclog parts. Replace any damaged parts.
	· Brake fluid contaminated with improper fluids (motor oil, transmission fluid, causing rubber components to swell and stick in bores	· Replace all rubber components, combination valve and hoses. Flush entire brake system with DOT 3 brake fluid or equivalent.
	· Low engine vacuum	· Adjust or repair engine

Troubleshooting the Brake System (cont.)

Problem	Cause	Solution
Grabbing brakes (severe reaction to brake pedal pressure.)	• Brakelining(s) contaminated by grease or brake fluid	• Determine and correct cause of contamination and replace brakeshoes in axle sets
	• Parking brake cables incorrectly adjusted or seized	• Adjust cables. Replace seized cables.
	• Incorrect brakelining or lining loose on brakeshoes	• Replace brakeshoes in axle sets
	• Caliper anchor plate bolts loose	• Tighten bolts
	• Rear brakeshoes binding on support plate ledges	• Clean and lubricate ledges. Replace support plate(s) if ledges are deeply grooved. Do not attempt to smooth ledges by grinding.
	• Incorrect or missing power brake reaction disc	• Install correct disc
	• Rear brake support plates loose	• Tighten mounting bolts
Dragging brakes (slow or incomplete release of brakes)	• Brake pedal binding at pivot	• Loosen and lubricate
	• Power brake unit has internal bind	• Inspect for internal bind. Replace unit if internal bind exists.
	• Parking brake cables incorrrectly adjusted or seized	• Adjust cables. Replace seized cables.
	• Rear brakeshoe return springs weak or broken	• Replace return springs. Replace brakeshoe if necessary in axle sets.
	• Automatic adjusters malfunctioning	• Repair or replace adjuster parts as required
	• Caliper, wheel cylinder or master cylinder pistons sticking or seized	• Repair or replace parts as necessary
	• Master cylinder compensating ports blocked (fluid does not return to reservoirs).	• Use compressed air to clear ports. Do not use wire, pencils, or similar objects to open blocked ports.
Vehicle moves to one side when brakes are applied	• Incorrect front tire pressure	• Inflate to recommended cold (reduced load) inflation pressure
	• Worn or damaged wheel bearings	• Replace worn or damaged bearings
	• Brakelining on one side contaminated	• Determine and correct cause of contamination and replace brakelining in axle sets
	• Brakeshoes on one side bent, distorted, or lining loose on shoe	• Replace brakeshoes in axle sets
	• Support plate bent or loose on one side	• Tighten or replace support plate
	• Brakelining not yet seated with drums or rotors	• Burnish brakelining
	• Caliper anchor plate loose on one side	• Tighten anchor plate bolts
	• Caliper piston sticking or seized	• Repair or replace caliper
	• Brakelinings water soaked	• Drive vehicle with brakes lightly applied to dry linings
	• Loose suspension component attaching or mounting bolts	• Tighten suspension bolts. Replace worn suspension components.
	• Brake combination valve failure	• Replace combination valve
Chatter or shudder when brakes are applied (pedal pulsation and roughness may also occur.)	• Brakeshoes distorted, bent, contaminated, or worn	• Replace brakeshoes in axle sets
	• Caliper anchor plate or support plate loose	• Tighten mounting bolts
	• Excessive thickness variation of rotor(s)	• Refinish or replace rotors in axle sets
Noisy brakes (squealing, clicking, scraping sound when brakes are applied.)	• Bent, broken, distorted brakeshoes	• Replace brakeshoes in axle sets
	• Excessive rust on outer edge of rotor braking surface	• Remove rust

Troubleshooting the Brake System (cont.)

Problem	Cause	Solution
Noisy brakes (squealing, clicking, scraping sound when brakes are applied.) (cont.)	• Brakelining worn out—shoes contacting drum of rotor	• Replace brakeshoes and lining in axle sets. Refinish or replace drums or rotors.
	• Broken or loose holdown or return springs	• Replace parts as necessary
	• Rough or dry drum brake support plate ledges	• Lubricate support plate ledges
	• Cracked, grooved, or scored rotor(s) or drum(s)	• Replace rotor(s) or drum(s). Replace brakeshoes and lining in axle sets if necessary.
	• Incorrect brakelining and/or shoes (front or rear).	• Install specified shoe and lining assemblies
Pulsating brake pedal	• Out of round drums or excessive lateral runout in disc brake rotor(s)	• Refinish or replace drums, re-index rotors or replace

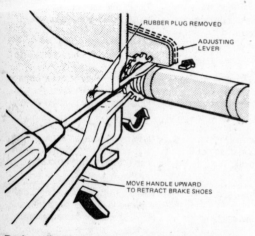

RUBBER PLUG REMOVED

ADJUSTING LEVER

MOVE HANDLE UPWARD TO RETRACT BRAKE SHOES

Brake adjustment, backing off; Move lever downward to tighten

and push the automatic adjuster lever out and free of the star wheel on the adjusting screw.

5. Holding the adjusting lever out of the way, engage the topmost tooth possible on the star wheel with a brake adjusting spoon. Move the end of the adjusting spoon upward to move the adjusting screw star wheel downward and contract the adjusting screw. Back off the adjusting screw star wheel until the wheel springs freely with a minimum of drag. Keep track of the number of turns the star wheel is backed off.

6. Repeat this operation for the other side. When backing off the brakes on the other side, the adjusting lever must be backed off the same number of turns to prevent side-to-side brake pull.

7. When both sides are adjusted, make several stops, while backing the car, to equalize both of the wheels.

8. Road test the car.

Parking Brake

WITH REAR DRUM BRAKES

The parking brake should be adjusted for proper operation every 12 months or 12,000 miles and adjusted whenever there is slack in the cables. A cable with too much slack will not hold a vehicle on an incline which presents a serious safety hazard. Usually, a rear brake adjustment will restore parking brake efficiency, but if the cables appear loose or stretched when the parking brake is released, adjust as necessary.

The procedure for adjusting the parking brake on all pedal actuated systems is as follows:

1. Fully release the parking brake.

2. Depress the parking brake pedal one notch from its normal released position. On vacuum release brakes, the first notch is approximately 2″ (51mm) of travel.

3. Taking proper safety precautions, raise the car and place the transmission in Neutral.

4. Loosen the equalizer locknut and turn the adjusting nut forward against the equalizer until moderate drag is felt when turning the rear wheels. Tighten the locknut.

5. Release the parking brake, making sure that the brake shoes return to the fully released position.

6. Lower the car and apply the parking brake. Under normal conditions, the third notch will hold the car if the brake is adjusted properly.

WITH REAR DISC BRAKES

1. Fully release the parking brake.

2. Place the transmission in Neutral. If it is necessary to raise the car to reach the adjusting nut and observe the parking brake levers, use an axle hoist or a floor jack positioned beneath

the differential. This is necessary so that the rear axle remains at the curb attitude, not stretching the parking brake cables.

CAUTION: *If you are raising the rear of the car only, block the front wheels.*

3. Locate the adjusting nut beneath the car on the driver's side. While observing the parking brake actuating levers on the rear calipers, tighten the adjusting nut until the levers just begin to move. Then, loosen the nut sufficiently for the levers to fully return to the stop position. The levers are in the stop position when a ¼" (6mm) pin can be inserted past the side of the lever into the holes in the cast iron housing.

4. Check the operation of the parking brake. Make sure the actuating levers return to the stop position by attempting to pull them rear ward. If the lever moves rearward, the cable adjustment is too tight, which will cause a dragging rear brake and consequent brake overheating and fade.

Brake Light Switch
REMOVAL AND INSTALLATION
Mustang and Capri

1. Raise the locking tab and unplug the wiring harness at the switch.

2. Remove the hairpin clip from the stud and slide the switch up and down, remove the switch and washers off of the pedal.

NOTE: *It is not necessary to remove the pushrod from the stud.*

3. Installation is the reverse of removal. Position the U-shaped side nearest the pedal and directly over/under the pin. Slide the switch up and down trapping the pushrod and bushing between the switch sideplates.

Merkur

1. Remove the lower instrument panel section.

2. Unplug the wiring connector at the switch.

3. Twist the stoplamp switch counterclockwise and remove it.

4. Installation is the reverse of removal.

HYDRAULIC SYSTEM

Master Cylinder
REMOVAL AND INSTALLATION
Mustang and Capri

1. Disconnect the brake lines from the master cylinder.

2. Remove the two nuts and lockwashers that attach the master cylinder to the brake booster.

3. Remove the master cylinder from the booster.

4. Reverse the above procedure to install. Torque the master cylinder attaching nuts to 13-25 ft. lbs.

5. Fill the master cylinder and bleed the entire brake system.

6. Refill the master cylinder.

Merkur

1. Remove the low fluid level sensor wiring at the master cylinder.

2. Remove the master cylinder reservoir cap.

3. Disconnect the brake lines from the master cylinder. Cap the lines and plug the ports.

4. Remove the nuts and lockwashers that attach the master cylinder to the brake booster.

5. Remove the master cylinder from the booster.

To install:

6. Position the master cylinder over the studs and loosely install the mounting nuts.

7. Connect the brake lines.

8. Tighten the mounting nuts to 20 ft. lbs.

9. Fill the master cylinder and bleed the entire brake system.

10. Refill the master cylinder.

OVERHAUL
Mustang and Capri

1. Remove the cylinder from the car and drain the brake fluid.

2. Mount the cylinder in a vise so that the outlets are up then remove the seal from the hub.

3. Remove the stopscrew from the bottom of the front reservoir.

4. Remove the snapring from the front of the bore and remove the rear piston assembly.

5. Remove the front piston assembly using compressed air. Cover the bore opening with a cloth to prevent damage to the piston.

6. Clean metal parts in brake fluid and discard the rubber parts.

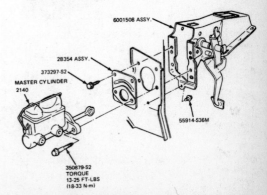

6001508 ASSY.

28354 ASSY.

373297-S2

MASTER CYLINDER
2140

55914-S36M

350879-S2
TORQUE
13-25 FT-LBS
(18-33 N·m)

Master cylinder installation—without power brake

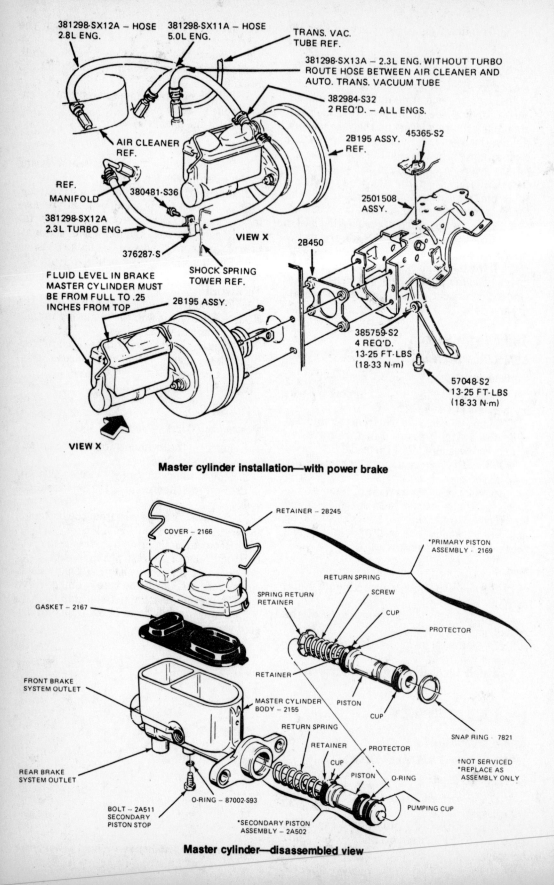

381298-SX12A – HOSE 2.8L ENG.

381298-SX11A – HOSE 5.0L ENG.

TRANS. VAC. TUBE REF.

381298-SX13A – 2.3L ENG. WITHOUT TURBO ROUTE HOSE BETWEEN AIR CLEANER AND AUTO. TRANS. VACUUM TUBE

382984-S32 2 REQ'D. – ALL ENGS.

AIR CLEANER REF.

2B195 ASSY. REF.

45365-S2

REF. MANIFOLD

380481-S36

2501508 ASSY.

381298-SX12A 2.3L TURBO ENG.

376287-S

VIEW X

2B450

SHOCK SPRING TOWER REF.

385759-S2 4 REQ'D. 13-25 FT-LBS (18-33 N·m)

FLUID LEVEL IN BRAKE MASTER CYLINDER MUST BE FROM FULL TO .25 INCHES FROM TOP

2B195 ASSY.

57048-S2 13-25 FT-LBS (18-33 N·m)

VIEW X

Master cylinder installation—with power brake

RETAINER – 2B245

COVER – 2166

*PRIMARY PISTON ASSEMBLY - 2169

RETURN SPRING

SCREW

SPRING RETURN RETAINER

CUP

GASKET – 2167

PROTECTOR

RETAINER

PISTON

CUP

FRONT BRAKE SYSTEM OUTLET

MASTER CYLINDER BODY - 2155

RETURN SPRING

SNAP RING · 7821

RETAINER

PROTECTOR

†NOT SERVICED *REPLACE AS ASSEMBLY ONLY

CUP

PISTON

O-RING

REAR BRAKE SYSTEM OUTLET

BOLT -- 2A511 SECONDARY PISTON STOP

O-RING – 87002-S93

*SECONDARY PISTON ASSEMBLY - 2A502

PUMPING CUP

Master cylinder—disassembled view

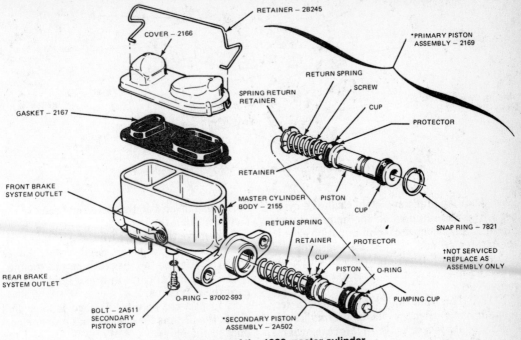

Exploded view of the 1980 master cylinder

7. Inspect the bore for damage or wear, and check the pistons for damage and proper clearance in the bore.

CAUTION: *Late models are equipped with aluminum master cylinders. DO NOT*

HONE! *If the bore is pitted or scored deeply, the master cylinder assembly must be replaced.*

8. If the bore is only slightly scored or pitted it may be honed. Always use hones that are in

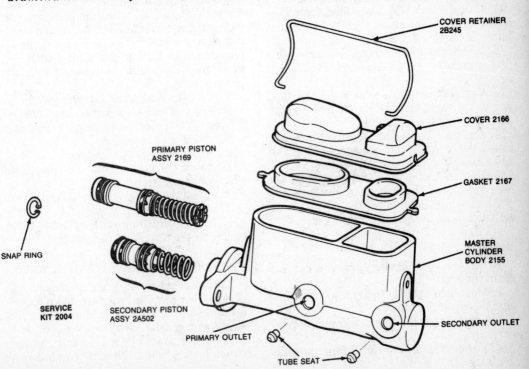

Exploded view of the 1981–86 master cylinder

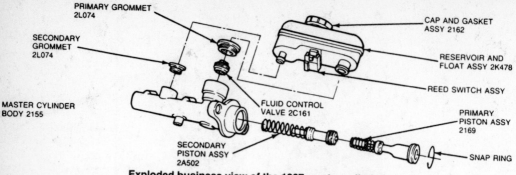

PRIMARY GROMMET
2L074

SECONDARY
GROMMET
2L074

CAP AND GASKET
ASSY 2162

RESERVOIR AND
FLOAT ASSY 2K478

REED SWITCH ASSY

MASTER CYLINDER
BODY 2155

FLUID CONTROL
VALVE 2C161

PRIMARY
PISTON ASSY
2169

SECONDARY
PISTON ASSY
2A502

SNAP RING

Exploded business view of the 1987 master cylinder

good condition and completely clean the cylinder with brake fluid when the honing is completed. If any evidence of contamination exist in the master cylinder, the entire hydraulic system should be flushed and refilled with clean brake fluid. Blow out the passages with compressed air.

NOTE: *The rebuilding kit may contain secondary and primary piston assemblies instead of just rubber seals. In this case, seal installation is not required.*

9. Install new secondary seals in the two grooves in the flat end of the front piston. The lips of the seals will be facing away from each other.

10. Install a new primary seal and the seal protector on the opposite end of the front piston with the lips of the seal facing outward.

11. Coat the seals with brake fluid. Install the spring on the front piston with the spring retainer in the primary seal.

12. Insert the piston assembly, spring end first, into the bore and use a wooden rod to seat it.

13. Coat the rear piston seals with brake fluid and install them into the piston grooves with the lips facing the spring end.

14. Assemble the spring onto the piston and install the assembly into the bore spring first. Install the snapring.

15. Hold the piston train at the bottom of the bore and install the stopscrew. Install a new seal on the hub. Bench-bleed the cylinder or install and bleed the cylinder on the car.

Merkur

1. Remove the cylinder from the car and drain the brake fluid.

2. Mount the cylinder in a soft jawed vise so that the outlets are up.

3. Carefully pry the reservoir from the cylinder body.

4. Remove the reservoir seals from the cylinder body.

5. Remove the O-ring from the front of the

bore, push inward on the piston and remove the snapring from the bore.

6. Remove the washer from the primary piston and remove the piston. Remove the cylinder from the vise and tap the secondary piston out.

7. Clean metal parts in brake fluid and discard the rubber parts.

8. Inspect the bore for damage or wear, and check the pistons for damage and proper clearance in the bore.

CAUTION: *Late models are equipped with aluminum master cylinders. DO NOT HONE! If the bore is pitted or scored deeply, the master cylinder assembly must be replaced.*

9. If the bore is only slightly scored or pitted it may be honed. Always use hones that are in good condition and completely clean the cylinder with brake fluid when the honing is completed. If any evidence of contamination exist in the master cylinder, the entire hydraulic system should be flushed and refilled with clean brake fluid. Blow out the passages with compressed air.

NOTE: *The rebuilding kit may contain secondary and primary piston assemblies instead of just rubber seals. In this case, seal installation is not required.*

10. Install new seals on pistons.

11. Install the pistons into the bore. Install the washer and snapring.

12. Install the O-ring and new reservoir seals.

13. Install the reservoir.

14. Bench bleed the master cylinder and install it on the car. Bleed the system.

Pressure Differential Warning Valve

Since the introduction of dual master cylinders to the hydraulic brake system, a pressure differential warning signal has been added. This signal consists of a warning light on the dashboard activated by a differential pressure switch located below the master cylinder. The signal indicates a hydraulic pressure differential between the front and rear brakes of 80-150

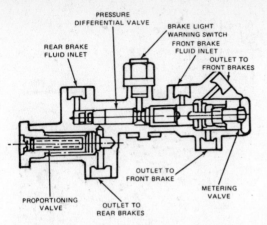

1980 and later brake control valve—aluminum

4. Turn the ignition off.

5. Prior to driving the vehicle, check the operation of the brakes and obtain a firm pedal.

Proportioning Valve

On vehicles equipped with front disc and rear drum brakes, a proportioning valve is an important part of the system. It is installed in the hydraulic line to the rear brakes. Its function is to maintain the correct proportion between line pressures to the front and rear brakes. No attempt at adjustment of this valve should be made, as adjustment is preset and tampering will result in uneven braking action.

To assure correct installation when replacing the valve, the outlet to the rear brakes is stamped with the letter **R**.

Metering Valve

On vehicles through 1980 equipped with front disc brakes, a metering valve is used. This valve is installed in the hydraulic line to the front brakes, and functions to delay pressure buildup to the front brakes on application. Its purpose is to reduce front brake pressure until rear brake pressure builds up adequately to overcome the rear brake shoe return springs. In this way disc brake pad lift is extended because it prevents the front disc brakes from carrying all or most of the braking load at low operating line pressures.

The metering valve can be checked very simply. With the car stopped, gently apply the brakes. At about 1″ (25mm) of travel, a very small change in pedal effort (like a small bump) will be felt if the valve is operating properly. Metering valves are not serviceable and must be replaced if defective.

psi, and should warn the driver that a hydraulic failure has occurred.

After repairing and bleeding any part of the hydraulic system the warning light may remain on due to the pressure differential valve remaining in the off-center position. To centralize the valve a pressure difference must be created in the opposite branch of the hydraulic system that was repaired or bled last.

NOTE: *Front wheel balancing of cars equipped with disc brakes may also cause a pressure differential in the front branch of the system.*

VALVE CENTERING PROCEDURE

1. Turn the ignition to either the **ACC** or **ON** position.

2. Check the fluid level in the master cylinder reservoirs. Fill to within ¼″ (6mm) of the top if necessary.

3. Depress the brake pedal firmly. The valve will centralize itself causing the brake warning light to go out.

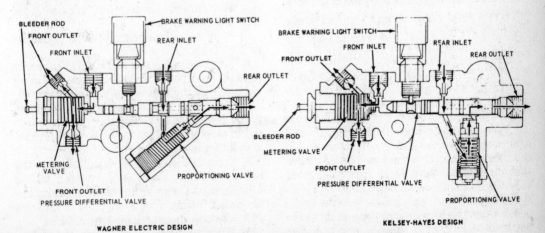

WAGNER ELECTRIC DESIGN   KELSEY-HAYES DESIGN

Brake control valve—1979 with cast iron housing

Brake Hoses and Lines
HYDRAULIC BRAKE LINE CHECK

The hydraulic brake lines and brake linings are to be inspected at the recommended intervals in the maintenance schedule. Follow the steel tubing from the master cylinder to the flexible hose fitting at each wheel. If a section of the tubing is found to be damaged, replace the entire section with tubing of the same type (steel, not copper), size, shape, and length. When installing a new section of brake tubing, flush clean brake fluid or denatured alcohol through to remove any dirt or foreign material from the line. Be sure to flare both ends to provide sound, leak-proof connections. When bending the tubing to fit the underbody contours, be careful not to kink or crack the line. Torque all hydraulic connections to 10-15 lbs.

Check the flexible brake hoses that connect the steel tubing to each wheel cylinder. Replace the hose if it shows any signs of softening, cracking, or other damage. When installing a new front brake hose, position the hose to avoid contact with other chassis parts. Place a new copper gasket over the hose fitting and thread the hose assembly into the front wheel cylinder. A new rear brake hose must be positioned clear of the exhaust pipe or shock absorber. Thread the hose into the rear brake tube connector. When installing either a new front or rear brake hose, engage the opposite end of the hose to the bracket on the frame. Install the horseshoe type retaining clip and connect the tube to the hose with the tube fitting nut.

Always bleed the system after hose or line replacement. Before bleeding, make sure that the master cylinder is topped up with high temperature, extra heavy duty fluid of at least SAE 70R3 quality.

Bleeding the Hydraulic System

NOTE: *Since the front and rear hydraulic systems are independent of each other, if it is known that only one system has air in it, only that system has to be bled.*

1. Fill the master cylinder with brake fluid.
2. Install a ⅜" box-end wrench to the bleeder screw on the right rear wheel.
3. Push a piece of small diameter rubber tubing over the bleeder screw until it is flush against the wrench. Submerge the other end of the rubber tubing in a glass jar partially filled with clean brake fluid. Make sure the rubber tube fits on the bleeder screw snugly.
4. Have a friend apply pressure to the brake pedal. Open the bleeder screw and observe the bottle of brake fluid. If bubbles appear in the glass jar; there is air in the system. When your

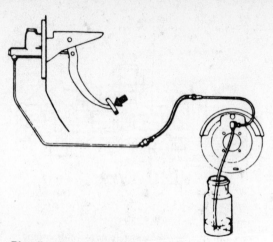

Bleeding the hydraulic brake system

friend has pushed the pedal to the floor, immediately close the bleed screw before he release the pedal.

5. Repeat this procedure until no bubbles appear in the jar. Refill the master cylinder right front and left front wheels, in that order. Periodically refill the master cylinder so it does not run dry.
6. Center the pressure differential warning valve as outlined in the Pressure Differential Warning Valve section.

Vacuum Booster
REMOVAL AND INSTALLATION

1. Working inside the car below the instrument panel, disconnect the booster valve operating rod from the brake pedal assembly.
2. Open the hood and disconnect the wires from the stop light switch at the brake master cylinder.
3. Disconnect the brake line at the master cylinder outlet fitting.
4. Disconnect the manifold vacuum hose from the booster unit.
5. Remove the four bracket-to-dash panel attaching bolts.
6. Remove the booster and bracket assembly from the dash panel, sliding the valve operating rod out from the engine side of the dash panel.
7. Mount the booster and bracket assembly to the dash panel by sliding the valve operating rod in through the hole in the dash panel, and installing the attaching bolts.
8. Connect the manifold vacuum hose to the booster.
9. Connect the brake line to the master cylinder outlet fitting.
10. Connect the stop light switch wires.
11. Working inside the car below the instrument panel, install the rubber boot on the valve

operating rod at the passenger side of the dash panel.

12. Connect the valve operating rod to the brake pedal with the bushings, eccentric shoulder bolt, and nut.

REAR DRUM BRAKES

Duo-Servo Self-Adjusting Drum Brakes

Drum brakes on all Ford cars employ single anchor, internally expanding, and self-adjusting brake assemblies. The automatic adjusting continuously maintains correct operating clearance between the linings and the drums by adjusting the brake in small increments in direct proportion to lining wear. When applying the brakes while backing up, the linings tend to follow the rotating drum counterclockwise, thus forcing the upper end of the primary shoe against the anchor pin. Simultaneously, the wheel cylinder pushes the upper end of the secondary shoe and cable guide outward, away from the anchor pin. This movement of the secondary shoe causes the cable to pull the adjusting lever upward and against the end of the tooth on the adjusting screw star wheel. As lining wear increases, the upward travel of the adjusting lever also increases. When the linings have worn sufficiently to allow the lever to move upward far enough, it passes over the end of the tooth and engages it. Upon release of the brakes, the adjusting spring pulls the adjuster level downward, turning the star wheel and expanding the brakes.

INSPECTION

CAUTION: *Brake shoes contain asbestos, which has been determined to be a cancer causing agent. Never clean the brake surfaces with compressed air! Avoid inhaling any dust from any brake surface! When cleaning brake surfaces, use a commercially available brake cleaning fluid.*

1. Raise the rear of the car and support the car with safety stands. Make sure the parking brake is not on.

2. Remove the lug nuts that attach the wheels to the axle shaft and remove the tires and wheels from the car. Using a pair of pliers, remove the Tinnerman nuts from the wheel studs. Pull the brake drum of the axle shaft. If the brakes are adjusted too tightly to remove the drum, see Step 3. If you can remove the drum, see Step 4.

3. If the brakes are too tight to remove the drum, get under the car (make sure you have safety stands under the car to support it) and remove the rubber plug from the bottom of the

brake backing plate. Shine a flashlight into the slot in the plate. You will see the top of the adjusting screw star wheel and the adjusting lever for the automatic brake adjusting mechanism. To back off on the adjusting screw, you must first inert a small, thin screwdriver or a piece of firm wire (coat hanger wire) into the adjusting slot and push the adjusting lever away from the adjusting screw. Then, insert a brake adjusting spoon into the slot and engage the top of the star wheel. Lift up on the bottom of the adjusting spoon to force the adjusting screw star wheel downward. Repeat this operation until the brake drum is free of the brake shoes and can be pulled off.

4. Clean the brake shoes and the inside of the brake drum. There must be at least $^1/_{16}"$ (1.6mm) of brake lining above the heads of the brake shoe attaching rivets. The lining should not be cracked or contaminated with grease or brake fluid. If there is grease or brake fluid on the lining it must be replaced and the source of the leak must be found and corrected. Brake fluid on the lining means leaking wheel cylinders. Grease on the brake lining means a leaking grease retainer (front wheels) or axle seal (rear brakes). If the lining is slightly glazed but otherwise in good condition, it can be cleaned up with medium sandpaper. Lift up the bottom of the wheel cylinder boots and inspect the ends of the wheel cylinders. A small amount of fluid in the end of the cylinder should be considered normal. If fluid runs out of the cylinder when the boots are lifted, however, the wheel cylinder must be rebuilt or replaced. Examine the inside of the brake drum; it should have a smooth, dull finish. If excessive brake shoe wear caused grooves to wear in the drum it must be machined or replaced. If the inside of the drum is slightly glazed, but otherwise good, it can be cleaned up with medium sandpaper.

5. If no repairs are required, install the drum and wheel. If the brake adjustment was changed to remove the drum, adjust the brakes until the drum will just fit over the brakes. After the wheel is installed it will be necessary to complete the adjustment. See Brake Adjustment later in this chapter.

Brake Shoes

REMOVAL

CAUTION: *Brake shoes contain asbestos, which has been determined to be a cancer causing agent. Never clean the brake surfaces with compressed air! Avoid inhaling any dust from any brake surface! When cleaning brake surfaces, use a commercially available brake cleaning fluid.*

WARNING: *If you are not thoroughly famil-*

Drum brake retracting spring removal

iar with the procedures involved in brake replacement, only disassembly and assemble
one side at a time, leaving the other wheel intact as a reference.

1. Remove the brake drum. See the inspection procedure.

2. Place the hollow end of the brake spring
service tool (available at auto parts stores) on
the brake shoe anchor pin and twist it to disengage one of the brake retracting springs. Repeat
this operation to remove the other spring.

CAUTION: *Be careful that the springs do*

*not slip off the tool during removal, as they
could cause personal injury.*

3. Reach behind the brake backing plate and
place a finger on the end of one of the brake
holddown spring mounting pins. Using a pair of
pliers, grasp the washer on the top of the
holddown spring that corresponds to the pin
that you are holding. Push down on the pliers
and turn them 90 degrees to align the slot in the
washer with the head on the spring mounting
pin. Remove the spring and washer and repeat
this operation on the holddown spring on the
other brake shoe.

4. Place the tip of a screwdriver on the top of
the brake adjusting screw and move the screwdriver upward to lift up on the brake adjusting
lever. When there is enough slack in the automatic adjuster cable, disconnect the loop on the
top of the cable from the anchor. Grasp the top
of each brake shoe and move it outward to disengage it from the wheel cylinder (and parking
brake link on rear wheels). When the brake
shoes are clear, lift them from the backing
plate. Twist the shoes slightly and the automatic adjuster assembly will disassemble itself.

5. Grasp the end of the brake cable spring
with a pair of pliers and, using the brake lever
as a fulcrum, pull the end of the spring away
from the lever. Disengage the cable from the
brake lever.

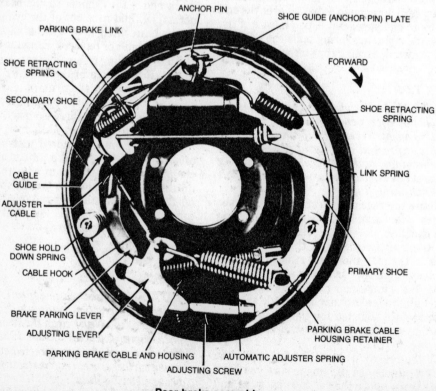

Rear brake assembly

INSTALLATION

1. The brake cable must be connected to the secondary brake shoe before the shoe is installed on the backing plate. To do this, first transfer the parking brake lever from the old secondary shoe to the new one. This is accomplished by spreading the bottom of the horseshoe clip and disengaging the lever. Position the lever on the new secondary shoe and install the spring washer and the horseshoe clip. Close the bottom of the clip after installing it. Grasp the metal tip of the parking brake cable with a pair of pliers. Position a pair of side cutter pliers on the end of the cable coil spring, and using the plier as a fulcrum, pull the coil spring back with the side cutters. Position the cable in the parking brake lever.

2. Apply a light coating of high temperature grease to the brake shoe contact points on the backing plate. Position the primary brake shoe on the front of the backing plate and install the holddown spring and washer over the mounting pin. Install the secondary shoe on the rear of the backing plate.

3. Install the parking brake link between the notch in the primary brake shoe and the notch in the parking brake lever.

4. Install the automatic adjuster cable loop end on the anchor pin. Make sure the crimped side of the loop faces the backing plate.

5. Install the return spring in the primary brake shoe and, using the tapered end of the brake spring service tool, slide the top of the spring onto the anchor pin.

CAUTION: *Be careful to make sure that the spring does not slip off the tool during installation, as it could cause injury.*

6. Install the automatic adjuster cable guide in the secondary brake shoe, making sure the flared hole in the cable guide is inside the hole in the brake shoe. Fit the cable into the groove in the top of the cable guide.

7. Install the secondary shoe return spring through the hole in the cable guide and the brake shoe. Using the brake spring tool, slide the top of the spring onto the anchor pin.

8. Clean the threads on the adjusting screw and apply a light coating of high temperature grease to the threads. Screw the adjuster closed, then open it ½ turn.

9. Install the adjusting screw between the brake shoes with the star wheel nearest to the secondary shoe. Make sure the star wheel is in a position that is accessible from the adjusting slot in the backing plate.

10. Install the short hooked end of the automatic adjuster spring in the proper hole in the primary brake shoe.

11. Connect the hooked end of the automatic adjuster cable and the free end of the automatic adjuster spring in the slot in the top of the automatic adjuster lever.

12. Pull the automatic adjuster lever (the lever will pull the cable and spring with it) downward and to the left and engage the pivot hook of the lever in the hole in the secondary brake shoe.

13. Check the entire brake assembly to make sure that everything is installed properly. Make sure that the shoes engage the wheel cylinder properly and are flush on the anchor pin. Make sure that the automatic adjuster cable is flush on the anchor pin and in the slot on the back of the cable guide. Make sure that the adjusting lever rests on the adjusting screw star wheel. Pull upward on the adjusting cable until the adjusting lever is free of the star wheel, then release the cable. The adjusting lever should snap back into place on the adjusting screw star wheel and turn the wheel one tooth.

14. Expand the brake adjusting screw until the brake drum will just fit over the brake shoes.

15. Install the wheel and drum and adjust the brakes.

Wheel Cylinders

REPLACEMENT

1. Remove the brake shoes.

2. On rear brakes, loosen the brake line on the rear of the cylinder but do not pull the line away from the cylinder or it may bend.

3. On front brakes, disconnect the metal brake line from the rubber brake hose where they join in the wheel well. Pull off the horseshoe clip that attaches the rubber brake hose to the underbody of the car. Loosen the hose at the cylinder, then turn the whole brake hose to remove it from the wheel cylinder.

4. Remove the bolts and lockwashers that attach the wheel cylinder to the backing plate and remove the cylinder.

5. Position the new wheel cylinder on the backing plate and install the cylinder attaching bolts and lockwashers.

6. Attach the metal brake line or rubber hose by reversing the procedure given in Steps 2 or 3.

7. Install the brakes.

OVERHAUL

Since the travel of the pistons in the wheel cylinder changes when new brakes shoes are installed, it is possible for previously good wheel cylinders to start leaking after new brakes are installed, Therefore, to save yourself the expense of having to replace new brakes that become saturated with brake fluid and the aggravation of having to take everything apart again,

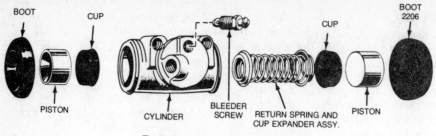

Exploded view of wheel cylinder

it is strongly recommended that wheel cylinders be rebuilt every time new brake shoes are installed. This is especially true on high mileage cars.

1. Remove the brakes.

CAUTION: *Brake shoes contain asbestos, which has been determined to be a cancer causing agent. Never clean the brake surfaces with compressed air! Avoid inhaling any dust from any brake surface! When cleaning brake surfaces, use a commercially available brake cleaning fluid.*

2. Place a bucket or old newspapers under the brake backing plate to catch the brake fluid that will run out of the wheel cylinder.

3. Remove the boots from the ends of the wheel cylinders.

4. Push one piston toward the center of the cylinder to force the opposite piston and cup out of the other end of the cylinder. Reach in the open end of the cylinder and push the spring cup, and piston out of the cylinder.

5. Remove the bleeder screw from the rear of the cylinder, on the back of the backing plate.

6. Inspect the inside of the wheel cylinder. If it is scored in any way, the cylinder must be honed with a wheel cylinder hone or fine emery paper, and finished with crocus cloth if emery paper is used. If the inside of the cylinder is excessively worn, the cylinder will have to be replaced, as only 0.003″ (0.0762mm) of material can be removed from the cylinder walls. When honing or cleaning the wheel cylinders, keep a small amount of brake fluid in the cylinder to serve as a lubricant.

7. Clean any foreign matter from the pistons. The sides of the pistons must be smooth for the wheel cylinders to operate properly.

8. Clean the cylinder bore with alcohol and a lint-free rag. Pull the rag through the bore several times to remove all foreign matter and dry the cylinder.

9. Install the bleeder screw and the return spring in the cylinder.

10. Coat new cylinder cups with new brake fluid and install them in the cylinder. Make

sure that they are square in the bore or they will leak.

11. Install the pistons in the cylinder after coating them with new brake fluid.

12. Coat the insides of the boots with new brake fluid and install them on the cylinder. Install the brakes.

FRONT DISC BRAKES

Inspection

1. Raise the vehicle until the wheel and tire clear the floor. Place safety stands under the vehicle.

2. Remove the wheel cover. Remove the wheel and tire from the hub and disc.

CAUTION: *Brake shoes contain asbestos, which has been determined to be a cancer causing agent. Never clean the brake surfaces with compressed air! Avoid inhaling any dust from any brake surface! When cleaning brake surfaces, use a commercially available brake cleaning fluid.*

3. Visually inspect the shoe and lining assemblies. If the lining material has worn to a thickness of 0.030″ (0.762mm) or less, or if the lining is contaminated with brake fluid, replace all pad assemblies on both front wheels. Make all thickness measurements across the thinnest section of the pad assembly. A slight taper on a used lining should be considered normal.

4. To check disc runout, tighten the wheel bearing adjusting nut to eliminate end-play. Check to make sure the disc can still be rotated.

5. Hand spin the disc and visually check for runout. If the disc appears to be out of round or if it wobbles, it needs to be machined or replaced. When the runout check is finished, loosen the wheel bearing adjusting nut and retighten to specifications, in order to prevent bearing damage.

6. Visually check the disc for scoring. Minor scores can be removed with fine emery cloth. If it is excessively scored, it must be machined or replaced.

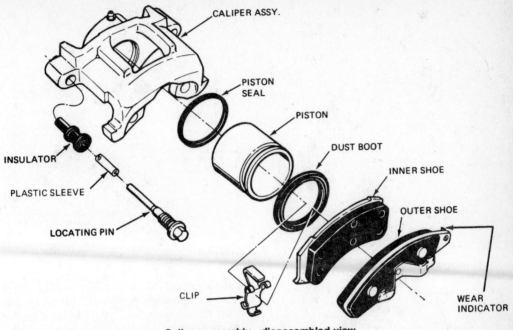

CALIPER ASSY.

PISTON SEAL

PISTON

DUST BOOT

INNER SHOE

OUTER SHOE

INSULATOR

PLASTIC SLEEVE

LOCATING PIN

CLIP

WEAR INDICATOR

Caliper assembly—disassembled view

7. The caliper should be visually checked. If excess leakage is evident, the caliper should be replaced.

8. Install the wheel and hub assembly.

Brake Pads

REPLACEMENT

1. Remove the master cylinder cap, and check the fluid level in the primary (large) reservoir. Remove brake fluid until the reservoir is half full. Discard this fluid.

2. Raise and safely support the vehicle. Remove the wheel and tire assembly from the hub. Be careful to avoid damage to or interference with the caliper splash shield or bleeder screw fitting.

CAUTION: *Brake shoes contain asbestos, which has been determined to be a cancer causing agent. Never clean the brake surfaces with compressed air! Avoid inhaling any dust from any brake surface! When cleaning brake surfaces, use a commercially available brake cleaning fluid.*

3. Remove the caliper locating pins.

4. Lift the caliper assembly from the integral spindle/anchor plate and rotor. Remove the outer shoe from the caliper assembly.

5. Remove the inner shoe and lining assembly. Inspect both rotor braking surfaces. Minor scoring or building of lining material does not require machining or replacement of the rotor.

6. Suspend the caliper inside the fender housing with a wire hooked through the outer

leg hole of the caliper. Be careful not to damage the caliper or stretch the brake hose.

7. Remove and discard the plastic sleeves that are located inside the caliper locating pin insulators. These parts must not be reused.

8. Remove and discard the caliper locating insulator. These parts must not be reused.

9. Use a 4" (101mm) C-clamp and a block of wood 2¾" x 1" and approximately ¾" thick (70mm x 25mm x 19mm) to seat the caliper hydraulic piston in its bore. This must be done to provide clearance for the caliper assembly to fit over the rotor when installed. Remove the C-clamp from the caliper (the caliper piston will remain seated in its bore).

10. Install new locating pin insulators and plastic sleeves in the caliper housing. Do not use a sharp edge tool to insert the insulators in the caliper housing. Check to see if both insulator flanges straddle the housing holes and if the plastic sleeves are bottomed in the insulators as well as slipped under the upper lip.

11. Install the correct inner shoe and lining assembly in the caliper piston. All vehicles have a separate anti-rattle clip and insulator that must be installed to the inner shoe and lining prior to their assembly to the caliper. The inner shoes are marked LH or RH and must be installed in the proper caliper. Also, care should be taken not to bend the anti-rattle clips too far in the piston or distortion and rattles can result.

12. Install the correct outer brake shoe and lining assembly (RH/LH), making sure that the

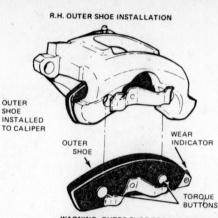

R.H. OUTER SHOE INSTALLATION

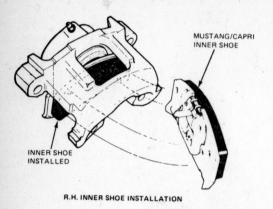

MUSTANG/CAPRI INNER SHOE

INNER SHOE INSTALLED

R.H. INNER SHOE INSTALLATION

OUTER SHOE INSTALLED TO CALIPER

OUTER SHOE

WEAR INDICATOR

TORQUE BUTTONS

WARNING: OUTER SHOE TORQUE BUTTONS MUST BE SOLIDLY SEATED IN CALIPER HOLES OR TEMPORARY LOSS OF BRAKES MAY OCCUR.

Disc brake shoe installation

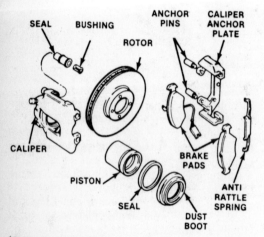

SEAL BUSHING ANCHOR PINS CALIPER ANCHOR PLATE

ROTOR

CALIPER

PISTON

SEAL

DUST BOOT

BRAKE PADS

ANTI RATTLE SPRING

Merkur front disc brakes

causing agent. *Never clean the brake surfaces with compressed air! Avoid inhaling any dust from any brake surface! When cleaning brake surfaces, use a commercially available brake cleaning fluid.*

1. Remove the caliper assembly from the vehicle as outlined in Pad Replacement. Disconnect the brake hose. Place a cloth over the piston before applying air pressure to prevent damage to the piston.

2. Apply air pressure to the fluid port in the caliper with a rubber tipped nozzle to remove the piston. On Continental and Mark VII models, use layers of shop towels to cushion possible impact of the phenolic piston against the caliper iron when piston comes out of the piston bore.

clip and/or buttons located on the shoe are properly seated. The outer shoe can be identified as right hand or left hand by the war indicator which must always be installed toward the front of the vehicle or by a LH or RH mark. Refill the master cylinder.

WARNING: *Make certain that the two round torque buttons are seated solidly in the two holes of the outer caliper leg and that the shoe is held tightly against the housing by the spring clip. If the buttons are not seated, a temporary loss of brakes may occur!*

13. Install the wheel and tire assembly, and tighten the wheel attaching nuts to 80-105 ft. lbs.

14. Pump the brake pedal prior to moving the vehicle to position the brake linings.

15. Road test the vehicle.

CALIPER SERVICE

CAUTION: *Brake shoes contain asbestos, which has been determined to be a cancer*

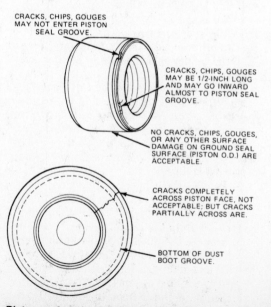

CRACKS, CHIPS, GOUGES MAY NOT ENTER PISTON SEAL GROOVE.

CRACKS, CHIPS, GOUGES MAY BE 1/2-INCH LONG AND MAY GO INWARD ALMOST TO PISTON SEAL GROOVE.

NO CRACKS, CHIPS, GOUGES, OR ANY OTHER SURFACE DAMAGE ON GROUND SEAL SURFACE (PISTON O.D.) ARE ACCEPTABLE.

CRACKS COMPLETELY ACROSS PISTON FACE, NOT ACCEPTABLE; BUT CRACKS PARTIALLY ACROSS ARE.

BOTTOM OF DUST BOOT GROOVE.

Piston surface irregularities, disc brake

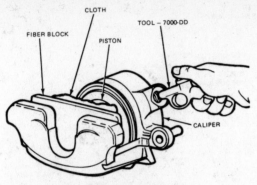

Removing the piston from the caliper

Do not use a screwdriver or similar tool to pry piston out of the bore, damage to the phenolic piston may result. If the piston is seized and cannot be forced from the caliper, tap lightly around the piston while applying air pressure. Use care because the piston can develop considerable force from pressure buildup.

3. Remove the dust boot from the caliper assembly.

4. Remove the rubber piston seal from the cylinder, and discard it.

5. Clean all metal parts and phenolic piston with isopropyl alcohol. Then, clean out and dry the grooves and passageways with compressed air. Make suer the caliper bore and component parts are thoroughly clean.

6. Check the cylinder bore and piston for damage or excessive wear. Replace the piston if it is pitted, scored, corroded, or the plating is worn off. Do not replace phenolic piston cosmetic surface irregularities or small chips between the piston boot groove and shoe face.

7. Apply a film of clean brake fluid to the new caliper piston seal, and install it in the cylinder bore. Be sure the seal does not become twisted but is firmly seated in the groove.

8. Install a new dust boot by seating the flange squarely in the outer groove of the caliper bore.

9. Coat the piston with brake fluid, and install the piston in the cylinder bore. Be sure to use a wood block or other flat stock when installing the piston back into the piston bore. Never apply C-clamp directly to a phenolic piston, and be sure pistons are not cocked. Spread the dust boot over the piston as it is installed. Seat the dust boot in the piston groove.

10. Install the caliper over the rotor as outlined.

Hub and Disc

REMOVAL

1. Raise and safely support the vehicle. Remove the wheel.

CAUTION: *Brake shoes contain asbestos, which has been determined to be a cancer causing agent. Never clean the brake surfaces with compressed air! Avoid inhaling any dust from any brake surface! When cleaning brake surfaces, use a commercially available brake cleaning fluid.*

2. Remove the caliper. Slide the caliper assembly away from the disc and suspend it with

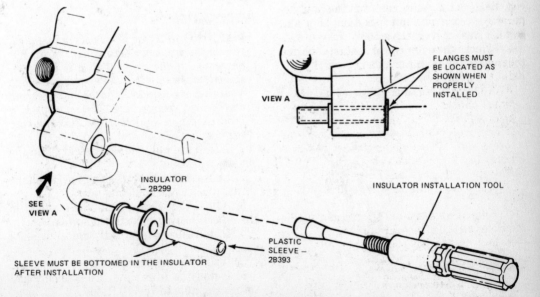

Insulator and sleeve installation

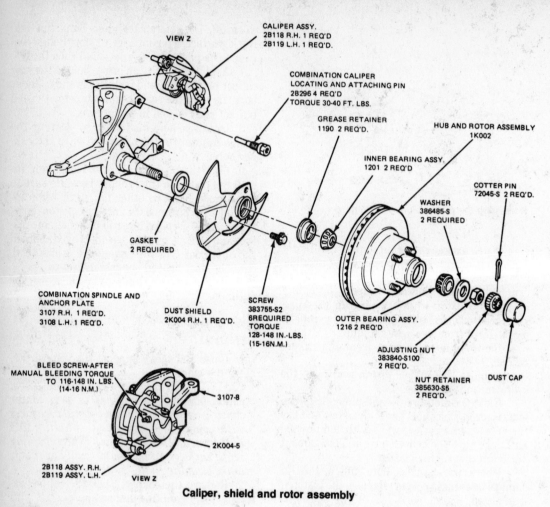

Caliper, shield and rotor assembly

a wire loop. It is not necessary to disconnect the brake line.

3. Remove the grease cap from the hub. Remove the cotter pin, nut lock, adjusting nut, and flat washer from the spindle.

4. Remove the outer wheel bearing cone and roller assembly from the hub.

5. Remove the hut and disc assembly from the spindle.

INSTALLATION

WARNING: *If a new disc is being installed, remove the protective coating with carburetor degreaser. If the original disc is being installed, make sure that the grease in the hub is clean and adequate, that the inner bearing and grease retainer are lubricated and in good condition, and that the disc breaking surfaces are clean.*

1. Install the hub and disc assembly on the spindle.

2. Lubricate the outer bearing and install the thrust washer and adjusting nut.

3. Adjust the wheel bearing as outlined in the Wheel Bearing Adjustment section.

4. Install the nut lock, cotter pin, and grease cap.

5. Install the caliper assembly.

6. Install the wheel and tire assembly and torque the nuts to 75-110 ft. lbs.

7. Lower the vehicle and road test it.

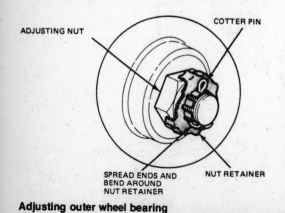

Adjusting outer wheel bearing

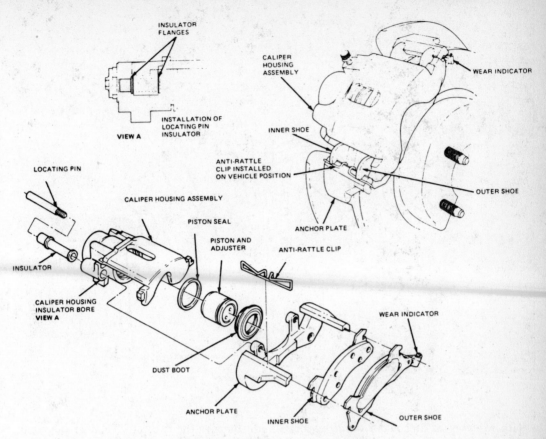

INSULATOR FLANGES

VIEW A

INSTALLATION OF LOCATING PIN INSULATOR

CALIPER HOUSING ASSEMBLY

WEAR INDICATOR

INNER SHOE

ANTI-RATTLE CLIP INSTALLED ON VEHICLE POSITION

OUTER SHOE

ANCHOR PLATE

LOCATING PIN

CALIPER HOUSING ASSEMBLY

PISTON SEAL

PISTON AND ADJUSTER

ANTI-RATTLE CLIP

INSULATOR

CALIPER HOUSING INSULATOR BORE VIEW A

WEAR INDICATOR

DUST BOOT

ANCHOR PLATE

INNER SHOE

OUTER SHOE

Rear disc brake caliper and anchor plate

REAR DISC BRAKES

Disc Brake Pads

REMOVAL AND INSTALLATION

1. Remove the caliper as outlined below. It is not necessary to disconnect the brake line. Simply wire the caliper to the frame to prevent the brake line from breaking.

CAUTION: *Brake shoes contain asbestos, which has been determined to be a cancer causing agent. Never clean the brake surfaces with compressed air! Avoid inhaling any dust from any brake surface! When cleaning brake surfaces, use a commercially available brake cleaning fluid.*

2. Remove the pads and inspect them. If they are worn to within ⅛" (3mm) of the shoe surface, they must be replace. Do not replace pads on just one side of the car. Uneven braking will result.

3. To install new pads, remove the disc and install the caliper without the pads. Use only the key to retain the caliper.

4. Seat the special tool firmly against the piston by holding the shaft and rotating the tool handle.

5. Loosen the handle ¼ turn. Hold the handle and rotate the tool shaft clockwise until the caliper piston bottoms in the bore. It will continue to turn after it bottoms.

6. Rotate the handle until the piston is firmly seated.

7. Remove the caliper and install the disc.

8. Place the new inner brake pad on the anchor plate. Place the new outer pad in the caliper.

9. Reinstall the caliper according to the directions given earlier.

Caliper

REMOVAL AND INSTALLATION

1. Raise the vehicle, and install safety stands. Block both front wheels if a jack is used.

2. Remove the wheel and tire assembly from the axle. Use care to avoid damage or interference with the splash shield.

3. Disconnect the parking brake cable from the lever. Use care to avoid kinking or cutting the cable or return spring.

CAUTION: *Brake shoes contain asbestos, which has been determined to be a cancer causing agent. Never clean the brake surfaces*

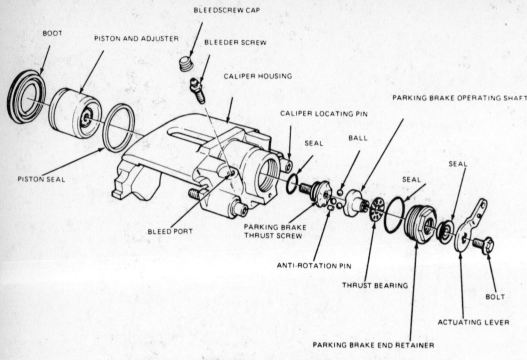

BLEEDSCREW CAP

BOOT   PISTON AND ADJUSTER   BLEEDER SCREW

CALIPER HOUSING

PARKING BRAKE OPERATING SHAFT

CALIPER LOCATING PIN

SEAL   BALL

SEAL

SEAL

PISTON SEAL

BLEED PORT   PARKING BRAKE
THRUST SCREW

ANTI-ROTATION PIN

THRUST BEARING

BOLT

ACTUATING LEVER

PARKING BRAKE END RETAINER

Rear caliper exploded view

with compressed air! Avoid inhaling any dust from any brake surface! When cleaning brake surfaces, use a commercially available brake cleaning fluid.

4. Remove the caliper locating pins.

5. Lift the caliper assembly away from the anchor plate by pushing the caliper upward toward the anchor plate, and then rotate the lower end of the anchor plate.

6. If insufficient clearance between the caliper and shoe and lining assemblies prevents removal of the caliper, it is necessary to loosen the caliper end retainer ½ turn, maximum, to allow the piston to be forced back into its bore. To loosen the end retainer, remove the parking brake lever, then mark or scribe the end retainer and caliper housing to be sure that the end retainer is not loosened more than ½ turn. Force the piston back in its bore, then remove the caliper.

CAUTION: *If the retainer must be loosened more than ½ turn, the seal between the thrust screw and the housing may be broken, and brake fluid may leak into the parking brake mechanism chamber. In this case, the end retainer must be removed, and the internal parts cleaned and lubricated; refer to Caliper Overhaul.*

7. Remove the outer shoe and lining assembly from the anchor plate. mark shoe for identification if it is to be reinstalled.

8. Remove the two rotor retainer nuts and the rotor from the axle shaft.

9. Remove the inner brake shoe and lining assembly from the anchor plate. Mark shoe for identification if it is to be reinstalled.

10. Remove anti-rattle clip from anchor plate.

11. Remove the flexible hose from the caliper by removing the hollow retaining bolt that connects the hose fitting to the caliper.

12. Clean the caliper, anchor plate, and rotor assemblies and inspect for signs of brake fluid leakage, excessive wear, or damage. The caliper must be inspected for leakage both in the piston boot area and at the operating shaft seal area. Lightly sand or wire brush any rust or corrosion from the caliper and anchor plate sliding surfaces as well as the outer and inner brake shoe abutment surfaces. Inspect the brake shoes for wear. If either lining is worn to within ⅛" (3mm) of the shoe surface, both shoe and lining assemblies must be replaced using the shoe and lining removal procedures.

13. If the end retainer has been loosened only ½ turn, reinstall the caliper in the anchor plate without shoe and lining assemblies. Tighten the end retainer to 75-96 ft. lbs. Install the parking brake lever on its keyed spline. The lever arm must point down and rearward. The parking brake cable will then pass freely under the axle. Tighten the retainer screw to 16-22 ft. lbs. The parking brake lever must rotate freely

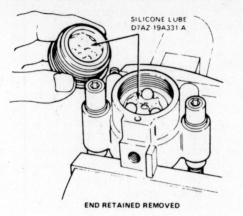

SILICONE LUBE
D7AZ-19A331-A

END RETAINED REMOVED

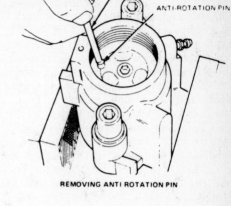

MAGNET OR TWEEZERS

ANTI-ROTATION PIN

REMOVING ANTI ROTATION PIN

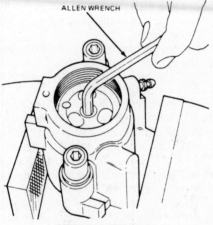

ALLEN WRENCH

REMOVING THRUST SCREW

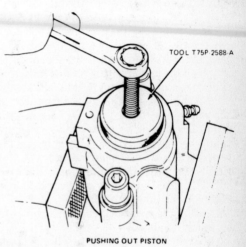

TOOL T75P-2588-A

PUSHING OUT PISTON

Rear caliper service

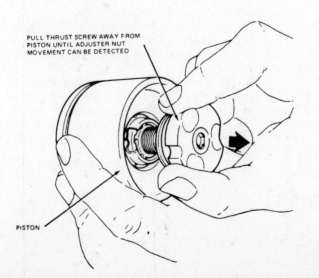

PULL THRUST SCREW AWAY FROM
PISTON UNTIL ADJUSTER NUT
MOVEMENT CAN BE DETECTED

PISTON

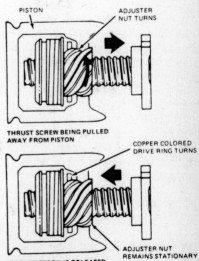

PISTON

ADJUSTER
NUT TURNS

**THRUST SCREW BEING PULLED
AWAY FROM PISTON**

COPPER COLORED
DRIVE RING TURNS

ADJUSTER NUT
REMAINS STATIONARY

THRUST SCREW IS RELEASED

Rear caliper adjuster operation

after tightening the retainer screw. Remove the caliper from the anchor plate.

14. If new shoe and lining assemblies are to be installed, the piston must be screwed back into the caliper bore, using Tool T75P-2588-B or equivalent to provide installation clearance. This tool requires a slight modification for use on Continental rear disc brakes. This modification will not prevent using the tool on prior year applications. New tools purchased from the Special Service Tool catalog under the T75P-2588-B number will already be modified. Remove the rotor, and install the caliper, less shoe and lining assemblies, in the anchor plate. While holding the shaft, rotate the tool handle counterclockwise until the tool is seated firmly against the piston. Now, loosen the handle about ¼ turn. While holding the handle, rotate the tool shaft clockwise until the piston is fully bottomed in its bore; the piston will continue to turn even after it becomes bottomed. When there is not further inward movement of the piston and the tool handle is rotated until there is a firm seating force, the piston is bottomed. Remove the tool and the caliper from the anchor plate.

15. Lubricate anchor plate sliding ways with lithium or silicone grease. Use only specified grease because a lower temperature type of lubricant may melt and contaminate the brake pads. Use care to prevent any lubricant from getting on the braking surface.

16. Install the anti-rattle clip on the lower rail of the anchor plate.

17. Install inner brake shoe and lining assembly on the anchor plate with the lining toward the rotor.

18. Be sure shoes are installed in their original positions as marked for identification before removal.

19. Install rotor and two retainer nuts.

20. Install the correct hand outer brake shoe and lining assembly on the anchor plate with the lining toward the rotor and wear indicator toward the upper portion of the brake.

21. Install the flexible hose by placing a new washer on each side of the fitting outlet and inserting the attaching bolt through the washers and fitting. Tighten to 20-30 ft. lbs.

22. Position the upper tab of the caliper housing on the anchor plate upper abutment surface.

23. Rotate the caliper housing until it is completely over the rotor. Use care so that the piston dust boot is not damaged.

24. Piston Position Adjustment: Pull the caliper outboard until the inner shoe and lining is firmly seated against the rotor, and measure the clearance between the outer shoe and caliper. The clearance must be $\frac{1}{32}$-$\frac{3}{32}$" (0.8-

2.4mm). If it is not, remove the caliper, then readjust the piston to obtain required gap. Follow the procedure given in Step 13, and rotate the shaft counterclockwise to narrow gap and clockwise to widen gap (¼ turn of the piston move it approximately $\frac{1}{16}$" [1.6mm]).

WARNING: *A clearance greater than $\frac{3}{32}$" (2.4mm) may allow the adjuster to be pulled out of the piston when the service brake is applied. This will cause the parking brake mechanism to fail to adjust. It is then necessary to replace the piston/adjuster assembly following the procedures under Overhaul.*

25. Lubricate locating pins and inside of insulator with silicone grease.

26. Add one drop of Loctite® E0AC-19554-A or equivalent to locating pin threads.

27. Install the locating pins through caliper insulators and into the anchor plate; the pins must be hand inserted and hand started. Tighten to 29-37 ft. lbs.

28. Connect the parking brake cable to the lever on the caliper.

29. Bleed the brake system. Replace rubber bleed screw cap after bleeding.

30. Fill the master cylinder as required to within ⅛" (3mm) of the top of the reservoir.

31. Caliper Adjustment: With the engine running, pump the service brake lightly (approximately 14 lbs. pedal effort) about 40 times. Allow at least one second between pedal applications. As an alternative, with the engine Off, pump the service brake lightly (approximately 87 lbs. pedal effort) about 30 times. Now check the parking brake for excessive travel or very light effort. In either case, repeat pumping the service brake, or if necessary, check the parking brake cable for proper tension. The caliper levers must return to the Off position when the parking brake is released.

32. Install the wheel and tire assembly. Tighten the wheel lug nuts. Install the wheel cover. Remove the safety stands, and lower the vehicle.

33. Be sure a firm brake pedal application is obtained, and then road test for proper brake operation, including parking brakes.

CALIPER OVERHAUL

1. Remove the caliper assembly from the vehicle as outlined.

CAUTION: *Brake shoes contain asbestos, which has been determined to be a cancer causing agent. Never clean the brake surfaces with compressed air! Avoid inhaling any dust from any brake surface! When cleaning brake surfaces, use a commercially available brake cleaning fluid.*

2. Remove the caliper and retainer.

3. Lift out the operating shaft, thrust bearing, and balls.

4. Remove the thrust screw anti-rotation pin with a magnet or tweezers.

NOTE: *Some anti-rotation pins may be difficult to remove with a magnet or tweezers. In that case, use the following procedure.*

    a. Adjust the piston out from the caliper bore using the modified piston adjusting tool. The piston should protrude from the housing at least 1″ (25mm).

    b. Push the piston back into the caliper housing with the adjusting tool. With the tool in position on the caliper, hold the tool shaft in place, and rotate the handle counterclockwise until the thrust screw clears the anti-rotation pin. Remove the thrust screw and the anti-rotation pin.

5. Remove the thrust screw by rotating it counterclockwise with a ¼″ allen wrench.

6. Remove the piston adjuster assembly by installing Tool T75P-2588-A or equivalent through the back of the caliper housing and pushing the piston out.

WARNING: *Use care not to damage the polished surface in the thrust screw bore, and do not press or attempt to move the adjuster can. It is a press fit in the piston!*

7. Remove and discard the piston seal, boot, thrust screw C-ring seal, end retainer O-ring seal, end retainer lip seal, and pin insulators.

8. Clean all metal parts with isopropyl alcohol. use clean, dry, compressed air to clean out and dry the grooves and passages. Be sure the caliper bore and component parts are completely free of any foreign material.

9. Inspect the caliper bores for damage or excessive wear. The thrust screw bore must be smooth and free of pits. If the piston is pitted, scored, or the chrome plating is worn off, replace the piston/adjuster assembly.

10. The adjuster can must be bottomed in the piston to be properly seated and provide consistent brake function. If the adjuster can is loose in the piston, appears high in the piston, or is damaged, or if brake adjustment is regularly too tight, too loose, or non-functioning, replace the piston/adjuster assembly.

WARNING: *Do not attempt to service the adjuster at any time. When service is necessary replace the piston/adjuster assembly.*

11. Check adjuster operation by first assembling the thrust screw into the piston/adjuster assembly, pulling the two pieces apart by hand approximately ¼″ (6mm), and then releasing them. When pulling on the two pieces, the brass drive ring must remain stationary, causing the nut to rotate. When releasing the two parts, the nut must remain stationary, and the drive ring must rotate. If the action of the components does not follow this pattern, replace the piston/adjuster assembly.

12. Inspect ball pockets, threads, grooves, and bearing surfaces of the thrust screw and operating shaft for wear, pitting, or brinelling. Inspect balls and anti-rotation pin for wear, brinelling, or pitting. Replace operating shaft, balls, thrust screw, and anti-rotation pin if any of these parts are worn or damaged. A polished appearance on the ball paths is acceptable if there is no sign of wear into the surface.

13. Inspect the thrust bearing for corrosion, pitting, or wear. Replace if necessary.

14. Inspect the bearing surface of the end plug for wear or brinnelling. Replace if necessary. A polished appearance on the bearing surface is acceptable if there is no sign of wear into the surface.

15. Inspect the lever for damage. Replace if necessary.

16. Lightly sand or wire brush any rust or corrosion from the caliper housing insulator bores.

17. Apply a coat of clean brake fluid to the new caliper piston seal, and install it in the cylinder bore. Be sure that the seal is not twisted and that it is seated fully in the groove.

18. Install a new dust boot by seating the flange squarely in the outer groove of the caliper bore.

19. Coat the piston/adjuster assembly with clean brake fluid, and install it in the cylinder bore. Spread the dust boot over the piston, like it is installed. Seat the dust boot in the piston groove.

20. Install the caliper in a vise and fill the piston/adjuster assembly with clean brake fluid to the bottom edge of the thrust screw bore.

21. Coat a new thrust screw O-ring seal with clean brake fluid, and install it in the groove in the thrust screw.

22. Install the thrust screw by turning it into the piston/adjuster assembly with a ¼″ allen wrench until the top surface of the thrust screw is flush with the bottom of the threaded bore. Use care to avoid cutting the O-ring seal. Index the thrust screw, so that the notches on the thrust screw and caliper housing are aligned. Then install the anti-rotation pin.

WARNING: *The thrust screw and operating shaft are not interchangeable from side to side because of the ramp direction in the ball pockets. The pocket surface of the operating shaft and the thrust screw are stamped with the proper letter (R or L), indicating part usage.*

23. Place a ball in each of the three pockets of the thrust screw, and apply a liberal amount of silicone grease on all components in the parking brake mechanism.

24. Install the operating shaft on the balls.

25. Coat the thrust bearing with silicone grease and install it on the operating shaft.

26. Install a new lip seal and O-ring on the end retainer.

27. Coat the O-ring seal and lip seal with a light film of silicone grease, and install the end retainer in the caliper. Hold the operating shaft firmly seated against the internal mechanism while installing the end retainer to prevent mislocation of the balls. If the lip seal is pushed out of position, reset the seal. Tighten the end retainer to 75-95 ft. lbs.

28. Install the parking brake lever on its keyed spline. The lever arm must point down and rearward. The parking brake cable will then pass freely under the axle. Tighten the lever retaining screw to 16-22 ft. lbs. The parking brake lever must rotate freely after tightening.

29. Arrange the caliper in a vise and bottom the piston with modified Tool T75P-2588-B.

30. Install new pin insulators in the caliper housing. Check to see if both insulator flanges straddle the housing holes.

31. Install the caliper on the vehicle.

Brake Discs

REMOVAL AND INSTALLATION

1. Raise the car and support it. Remove the wheels.

CAUTION: *Brake shoes contain asbestos, which has been determined to be a cancer causing agent. Never clean the brake surfaces with compressed air! Avoid inhaling any dust from any brake surface! When cleaning brake surfaces, use a commercially available brake cleaning fluid.*

2. Remove the caliper, as outlined earlier.

3. Remove the retaining bolts and remove the disc from the axle.

4. Inspect the disc for excessive rust, scoring or pitting. A certain amount of rust on the edge of the disc is normal. Refer to the specifications chart and measure the thickness of the disc, using a micrometer. If the disc is below specifications, replace it.

5. Reinstall the discs, keeping in mind that the two sides are not interchangeable. The words **left** and **right** are cast into the inner surface of the raised section of the disc. Proper reinstallation of the discs is important, since the cooling vanes cast into the disc must face opposite forward rotation.

6. Reinstall the caliper.

7. Install the wheels and lower the car.

PARKING BRAKE

Brake Cables

CAUTION: *Brake shoes contain asbestos, which has been determined to be a cancer causing agent. Never clean the brake surfaces with compressed air! Avoid inhaling any dust from any brake surface! When cleaning brake surfaces, use a commercially available brake cleaning fluid.*

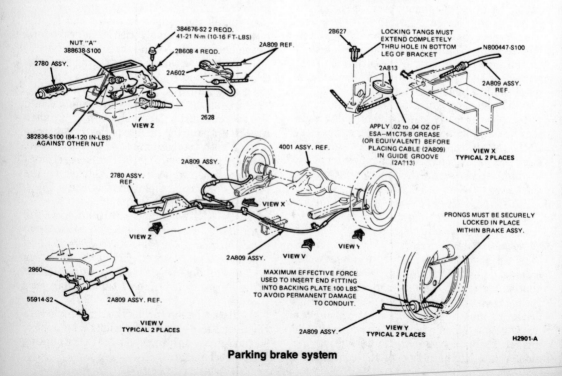

Parking brake system

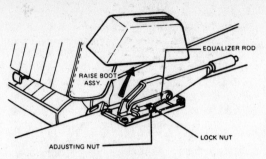

Parking brake control assembly

REMOVAL AND INSTALLATION

Mustang and Capri

1. Release the parking brake.
2. Remove the cable adjusting nut.
3. Raise and support the rear end on jackstands.
4. Disconnect the cable ends from the equalizer.
5. Remove the cotter pin that attaches the conduit to the bracket and remove the retaining clip that attaches the cable to the underbody.
6. On cars with rear drum brakes:
   a. Remove the brake drums.

b. Remove the brake shoes and disconnect the cable end from the self-adjusting lever.

c. Compress the pronged retainers and remove the cable assembly from the backing plate.
7. On cars with rear disc brakes, remove the clevis pin securing the cable to the caliper actuating arm.
8. Installation is the reverse of removal. Adjust the parking brake.

Merkur

1. Raise and support the rear end on jackstands.
2. Loosen the adjuster locknut.
3. Remove the drums and brake shoes.
4. Disconnect the cables from the brake lever on the secondary shoe.
5. Spread the retaining clip on the cable casing and pull the cable from the backing plate.
6. Remove the clip and clevis pin attaching the cable equalizer to the parking brake lever rod.
7. Open the routing clamps and disengage the cable from the control arms. Thread the cables through the body brackets and remove it.
8. Installation is the reverse of removal.

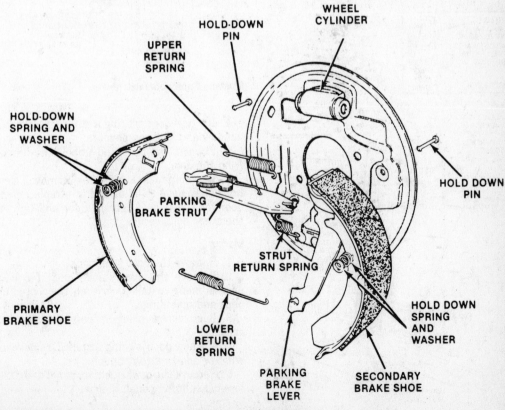

Merkur rear drum brakes

Body

10

EXTERIOR

Doors

REMOVAL AND INSTALLATION

Mustang and Capri

1. Remove the door trim panel.
2. Remove the watershield, and, if a new door is being installed, save all the moulding clips and mouldings.
3. Remove the wiring harness, actuator and speakers.

SEALER
E4G213-A
OR ADHESIVE
M2G150-A APPLY
OVER ENTIRE
SURFACE

UPPER HINGE ASSY 22800

SECTION A

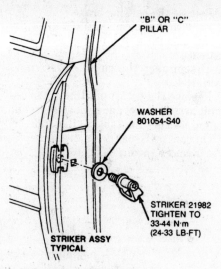

"B" OR "C" PILLAR

WASHER 801054-S40

STRIKER 21982 TIGHTEN TO 33-44 N·m (24-33 LB-FT)

STRIKER ASSY TYPICAL

Mustang Capri door latch striker

4. If a new door is being installed, remove all window and lock components.
5. Support the door and unbolt the hinges from the door.
6. Installation is the reverse of removal. New holes may have to be drilled in a replacement door for the trim. Align the door and tighten the hinge bolts securely.

Merkur

1. Remove the door trim panel.
2. Remove the watershield, and, if a new door is being installed, save all the moulding clips and mouldings.
3. Remove the wiring harness, actuator and speakers.
4. If a new door is being installed, remove all window and lock components.
5. Remove the cowl side trim panel and dash lower insulating panel. Remove the lower safety covering.
6. Support the door and unbolt the hinges.

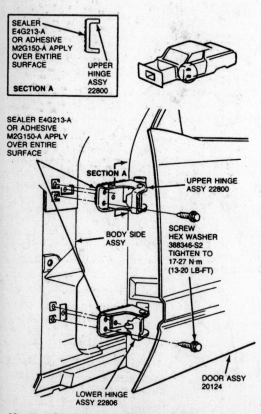

SEALER E4G213-A
OR ADHESIVE
M2G150-A APPLY
OVER ENTIRE
SURFACE

SECTION A

UPPER HINGE ASSY 22800

BODY SIDE ASSY

SCREW HEX WASHER 388346-S2 TIGHTEN TO 17-27 N·m (13-20 LB-FT)

DOOR ASSY 20124

LOWER HINGE ASSY 22806

Mustang/Capri side door hinge assembly

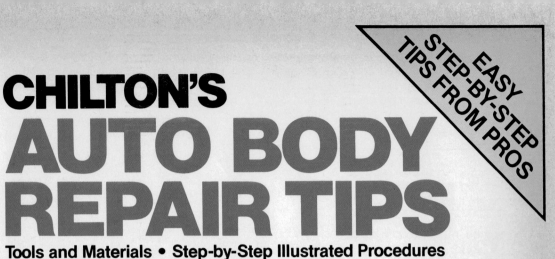

CHILTON'S
AUTO BODY
REPAIR TIPS

EASY
STEP-BY-STEP
TIPS FROM PROS

Tools and Materials • Step-by-Step Illustrated Procedures
How To Repair Dents, Scratches and Rust Holes
Spray Painting and Refinishing Tips

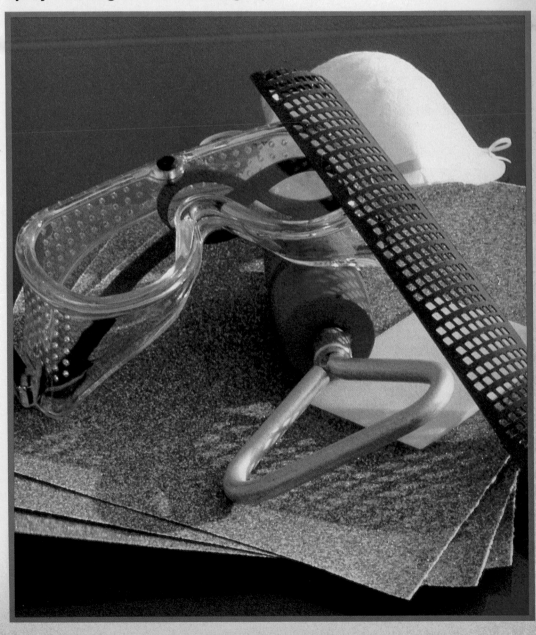

With a little practice, basic body repair procedures can be mastered by any do-it-yourself mechanic. The step-by-step repairs shown here can be applied to almost any type of auto body repair.

TOOLS & MATERIALS

You may already have basic tools, such as hammers and electric drills. Other tools unique to body repair — body hammers, grinding attachments, sanding blocks, dent puller, half-round plastic file and plastic spreaders — are relatively inexpensive and can be obtained wherever auto parts or auto body repair parts are sold. Portable air compressors and paint spray guns can be purchased or rented.

Auto Body Repair Kits

The best and most often used products are available to the do-it-yourselfer in kit form, from major manufacturers of auto body repair products. The same manufacturers also merchandise the individual products for use by pros.

Kits are available to make a wide variety of repairs, including holes, dents and scratches and fiberglass, and offer the advantage of buying the materials you'll need for the job. There is little waste or chance of materials going bad from not being used. Many kits may also contain basic body-working tools such as body files, sanding blocks and spreaders. Check the contents of the kit before buying your tools.

BODY REPAIR TIPS

Safety

Many of the products associated with auto body repair and refinishing contain toxic chemicals. Read all labels before opening containers and store them in a safe place and manner.

• Wear eye protection (safety goggles) when using power tools or when performing any operation that involves the removal of any type of material.

• Wear lung protection (disposable mask or respirator) when grinding, sanding or painting.

Sanding

1 Sand off paint before using a dent puller. When using a non-adhesive sanding disc, cover the back of the disc with an overlapping layer or two of masking tape and trim the edges. The disc will last considerably longer.

2 Use the circular motion of the sanding disc to grind *into* the edge of the repair. Grinding or sanding away from the jagged edge will only tear the sandpaper.

3 Use the palm of your hand flat on the panel to detect high and low spots. Do not use your fingertips. Slide your hand slowly back and forth.

WORKING WITH BODY FILLER

Mixing The Filler

Cleanliness and proper mixing and application are extremely important. Use a clean piece of plastic or glass or a disposable artist's palette to mix body filler.

1 Allow plenty of time and follow directions. No useful purpose will be served by adding more hardener to make it cure (set-up) faster. Less hardener means more curing time, but the mixture dries harder; more hardener means less curing time but a softer mixture.

2 Both the hardener and the filler should be thoroughly kneaded or stirred before mixing. Hardener should be a solid paste and dispense like thin toothpaste. Body filler should be smooth, and free of lumps or thick spots.

Getting the proper amount of hardener in the filler is the trickiest part of preparing the filler. Use the same amount of hardener in cold or warm weather. For contour filler (thick coats), a bead of hardener twice the diameter of the filler is about right. There's about a 15% margin on either side, but, if in doubt use less hardener.

3 Mix the body filler and hardener by wiping across the mixing surface, picking the mixture up and wiping it again. Colder weather requires longer mixing times. Do not mix in a circular motion; this will trap air bubbles which will become holes in the cured filler.

Applying The Filler

1 For best results, filler should not be applied over 1/4" thick.

Apply the filler in several coats. Build it up to above the level of the repair surface so that it can be sanded or grated down.

The first coat of filler must be pressed on with a firm wiping motion.

Apply the filler in one direction only. Working the filler back and forth will either pull it off the metal or trap air bubbles.

REPAIRING DENTS

Before you start, take a few minutes to study the damaged area. Try to visualize the shape of the panel before it was damaged. If the damage is on the left fender, look at the right fender and use it as a guide. If there is access to the panel from behind, you can reshape it with a body hammer. If not, you'll have to use a dent puller. Go slowly and work the metal a little at a time. Get the panel as straight as possible before applying filler.

1 This dent is typical of one that can be pulled out or hammered out from behind. Remove the headlight cover, headlight assembly and turn signal housing.

2 Drill a series of holes ½ the size of the end of the dent puller along the stress line. Make some trial pulls and assess the results. If necessary, drill more holes and try again. Do not hurry.

3 If possible, use a body hammer and block to shape the metal back to its original contours. Get the metal back as close to its original shape as possible. Don't depend on body filler to fill dents.

4 Using an 80-grit grinding disc on an electric drill, grind the paint from the surrounding area down to bare metal. Use a new grinding pad to prevent heat buildup that will warp metal.

5 The area should look like this when you're finished grinding. Knock the drill holes in and tape over small openings to keep plastic filler out.

6 Mix the body filler (see Body Repair Tips). Spread the body filler evenly over the entire area (see Body Repair Tips). Be sure to cover the area completely.

7 Let the body filler dry until the surface can just be scratched with your fingernail. Knock the high spots from the body filler with a body file ("Cheesegrater"). Check frequently with the palm of your hand for high and low spots.

8 Check to be sure that trim pieces that will be installed later will fit exactly. Sand the area with 40-grit paper.

9 If you wind up with low spots, you may have to apply another layer of filler.

10 Knock the high spots off with 40-grit paper. When you are satisfied with the contours of the repair, apply a thin coat of filler to cover pin holes and scratches.

11 Block sand the area with 40-grit paper to a smooth finish. Pay particular attention to body lines and ridges that must be well-defined.

12 Sand the area with 400 paper and then finish with a scuff pad. The finished repair is ready for priming and painting (see Painting Tips).

Materials and photos courtesy of Ritt Jones Auto Body, Prospect Park, PA.

REPAIRING RUST HOLES

There are many ways to repair rust holes. The fiberglass cloth kit shown here is one of the most cost efficient for the owner because it provides a strong repair that resists cracking and moisture and is relatively easy to use. It can be used on large and small holes (with or without backing) and can be applied over contoured areas. Remember, however, that short of replacing an entire panel, no repair is a guarantee that the rust will not return.

1 Remove any trim that will be in the way. Clean away all loose debris. Cut away all the rusted metal. But be sure to leave enough metal to retain the contour or body shape.

2 Grind away all traces of rust with a 24-grit grinding disc. Be sure to grind back 3-4 inches from the edge of the hole down to bare metal and be sure all traces of paint, primer and rust are removed.

3 Block sand the area with 80 or 100 grit sandpaper to get a clear, shiny surface and feathered paint edge. Tap the edges of the hole inward with a ball peen hammer.

4 If you are going to use release film, cut a piece about 2-3″ larger than the area you have sanded. Place the film over the repair and mark the sanded area on the film. Avoid any unnecessary wrinkling of the film.

5 Cut 2 pieces of fiberglass matte to match the shape of the repair. One piece should be about 1″ smaller than the sanded area and the second piece should be 1″ smaller than the first. Mix enough filler and hardener to saturate the fiberglass material (see Body Repair Tips).

6 Lay the release sheet on a flat surface and spread an even layer of filler, large enough to cover the repair. Lay the smaller piece of fiberglass cloth in the center of the sheet and spread another layer of filler over the fiberglass cloth. Repeat the operation for the larger piece of cloth.

7 Place the repair material over the repair area, with the release film facing outward. Use a spreader and work from the center outward to smooth the material, following the body contours. Be sure to remove all air bubbles.

8 Wait until the repair has dried tack-free and peel off the release sheet. The ideal working temperature is 60°-90° F. Cooler or warmer temperatures or high humidity may require additional curing time. Wait longer, if in doubt.

9 Sand and feather-edge the entire area. The initial sanding can be done with a sanding disc on an electric drill if care is used. Finish the sanding with a block sander. Low spots can be filled with body filler; this may require several applications.

10 When the filler can just be scratched with a fingernail, knock the high spots down with a body file and smooth the entire area with 80-grit. Feather the filled areas into the surrounding areas.

11 When the area is sanded smooth, mix some topcoat and hardener and apply it directly with a spreader. This will give a smooth finish and prevent the glass matte from showing through the paint.

12 Block sand the topcoat smooth with finishing sandpaper (200 grit), and 400 grit. The repair is ready for masking, priming and painting (see Painting Tips).

Materials and photos courtesy Marson Corporation, Chelsea, Massachusetts

PAINTING TIPS

Preparation

1 SANDING — Use a 400 or 600 grit wet or dry sandpaper. Wet-sand the area with a 1/4 sheet of sandpaper soaked in clean water. Keep the paper wet while sanding. Sand the area until the repaired area tapers into the original finish.

2 CLEANING — Wash the area to be painted thoroughly with water and a clean rag. Rinse it thoroughly and wipe the surface dry until you're sure it's completely free of dirt, dust, fingerprints, wax, detergent or other foreign matter.

3 MASKING — Protect any areas you don't want to overspray by covering them with masking tape and newspaper. Be careful not get fingerprints on the area to be painted.

4 PRIMING — All exposed metal should be primed before painting. Primer protects the metal and provides an excellent surface for paint adhesion. When the primer is dry, wet-sand the area again with 600 grit wet-sandpaper. Clean the area again after sanding.

Painting Techniques

P aint applied from either a spray gun or a spray can (for small areas) will provide good results. Experiment on an old piece of metal to get the right combination before you begin painting.

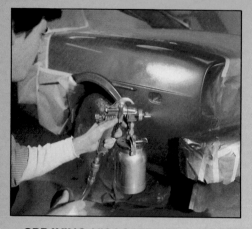

SPRAYING VISCOSITY (SPRAY GUN ONLY) — Paint should be thinned to spraying viscosity according to the directions on the can. Use only the recommended thinner or reducer and the same amount of reduction regardless of temperature.

AIR PRESSURE (SPRAY GUN ONLY) — This is extremely important. Be sure you are using the proper recommended pressure.

TEMPERATURE — The surface to be painted should be approximately the same temperature as the surrounding air. Applying warm paint to a cold surface, or vice versa, will completely upset the paint characteristics.

THICKNESS — Spray with smooth strokes. In general, the thicker the coat of paint, the longer the drying time. Apply several thin coats about 30 seconds apart. The paint should remain wet long enough to flow out and no longer; heavier coats will only produce sags or wrinkles. Spray a light (fog) coat, followed by heavier color coats.

DISTANCE — The ideal spraying distance is 8"-12" from the gun or can to the surface. Shorter distances will produce ripples, while greater distances will result in orange peel, dry film and poor color match and loss of material due to overspray.

OVERLAPPING — The gun or can should be kept at right angles to the surface at all times. Work to a wet edge at an even speed, using a 50% overlap and direct the center of the spray at the lower or nearest edge of the previous stroke.

RUBBING OUT (BLENDING) FRESH PAINT — Let the paint dry thoroughly. Runs or imperfections can be sanded out, primed and repainted.

Don't be in too big a hurry to remove the masking. This only produces paint ridges. When the finish has dried for at least a week, apply a small amount of fine grade rubbing compound with a clean, wet cloth. Use lots of water and blend the new paint with the surrounding area.

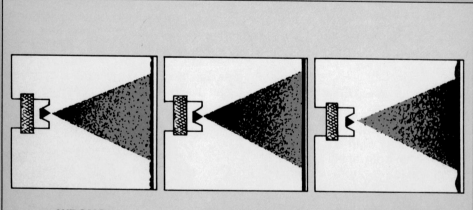

WRONG

Thin coat. Stroke too fast, not enough overlap, gun too far away.

CORRECT

Medium coat. Proper distance, good stroke, proper overlap.

WRONG

Heavy coat. Stroke too slow, too much overlap, gun too close.

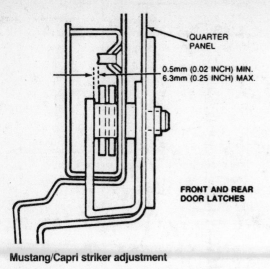

Mustang/Capri striker adjustment

QUARTER
PANEL

0.5mm (0.02 INCH) MIN.
6.3mm (0.25 INCH) MAX.

FRONT AND REAR
DOOR LATCHES

7. Installation is the reverse of removal. New holes may have to be drilled in a replacement door for the trim. Align the door and tighten the hinge bolts securely.

ADJUSTMENT

Door alignment is obtained by loosening the hinge-to-door bolts and moving the door as required to obtain a proper fit. Similarly, the latch striker must be loosed and repositioned for proper engagement with the latch.

Door Lock Cylinder

REMOVAL AND INSTALLATION

NOTE: *The key code is stamped on the driver's door lock cylinder to aid in replacing lost keys. Remember, if you replace a door lock cylinder you'll have to replace your ignition lock cylinder as well.*

1. Remove the trim panel and watershield.
2. Disconnect the lock control-to-door lock cylinder rod from the lock cylinder arm.
3. Remove the door lock cylinder retainer and slide the cylinder from the door. If a new lock cylinder is being installed transfer the arm to the new cylinder.
4. Installation is the reverse of removal.

Hood

REMOVAL AND INSTALLATION

1. Open and support the hood.
2. Matchmark the hood-to-hinge positions.
3. Have an assistant support the hood while you remove the hinge-to-hood bolts.
4. You and your assistant can remove the hood.
5. Installation is the reverse of removal.

ALIGNMENT

1. Side-to-side and fore-aft adjustments can be made by loosening the hood-to-hinge attachment bolts and positioning the hood as necessary.
2. Hood vertical fit can be adjusted by raising or lowering the hinge-to-fender reinforcement bolts.
3. To ensure a snug fit of the hood against the rear hood bumpers, it may be necessary to rotate the hinge around the 3 attaching bolts.

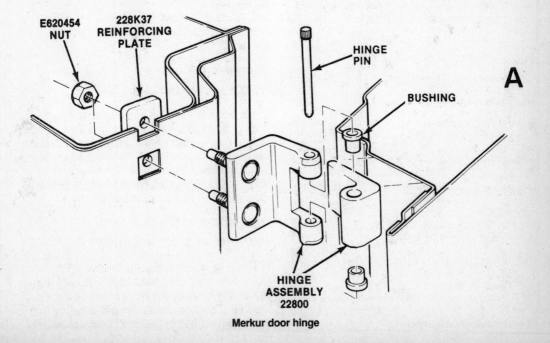

E620454
NUT

228K37
REINFORCING
PLATE

HINGE
PIN

BUSHING

A

HINGE
ASSEMBLY
22800

Merkur door hinge

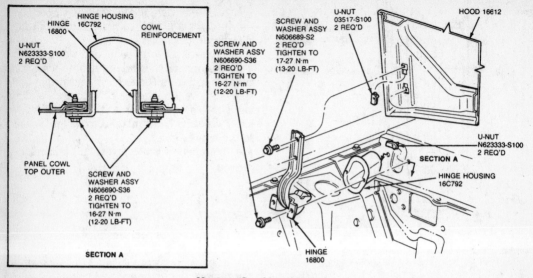

Mustang/Capri hood hinge

Trunk Lid/Hatch Door

REMOVAL AND INSTALLATION

Mustang and Capri

The trunk lid can be removed by removing the hinge-to-trunk lid bolts and sliding the trunk lid off of the hinges. The gas struts used to support the trunk lid must be removed with the lid in the fully open position.

Merkur

1. Open the liftgate and disconnect the electrical connections.
2. Release the loom grommets. Connect drawstrings to the looms, pipes and pull the drawstrings through the liftgate.

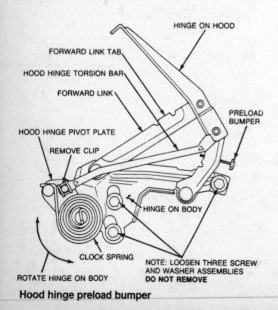

Hood hinge preload bumper

3. Support the liftgate with props and remove both lift cylinders. To remove the lift cylinders, insert a small prybar into the groove in the lift cylinder head and pry the spring clip open. Pull the cylinder out of the pivot.
4. Remove the molded upper covering to expose the hinge nuts.
5. Remove the hinge nuts and remove the liftgate.
6. Installation is the reverse of removal.

ALIGNMENT

1. Fore-aft fit may be adjusted by loosening the hinge-to-lid bolts and positioning the lid as necessary.
2. Vertical fit can be adjusted by adding or deleting shims located between the the hinges and trunk lid.

Windshield

REMOVAL AND INSTALLATION

The windshield is retained by a urethane adhesive. Several special tools and a special urethane compound are required for windshield replacement. Replacement bonding must meet Federal Motor Vehicle Safety standards. For these reasons, bonded windshield replacement should be left to a professional shop.

Rear Window Glass

REMOVAL AND INSTALLATION

The rear window glass is retained by a urethane adhesive. Several special tools and a special urethane compound are required for windshield replacement. Replacement bonding must meet Federal Motor Vehicle Safety standards.

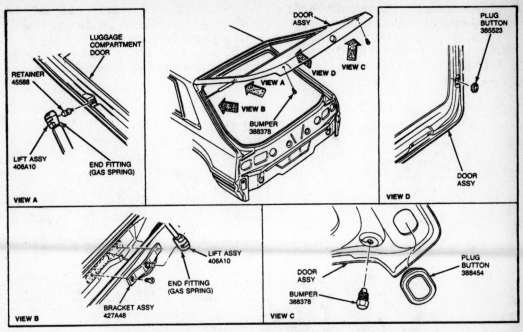

Mustang/Capri luggage compartment door, hinge and lift assembly

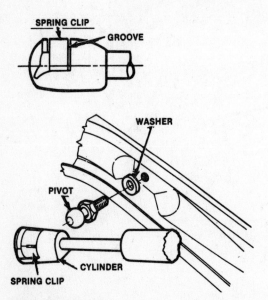

Merkur liftgate prop

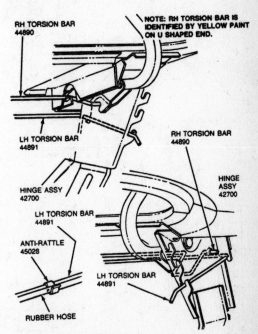

Mustang sedan trunk lid torsion bar

For these reasons, bonded windshield replacement should be left to a professional shop.

Front Bumpers

REMOVAL AND INSTALLATION

Mustang and Capri

1. The bumper is removed by removing the 8 attaching bolts.

2. Squeeze the bumper pad retaining tabs with pliers and push them through their holes until the pads are removed.

3. Installation is the reverse of removal. Torque the bracket-to-bumper bolts to 20 ft. lbs.; the isolator-to-reinforcement bolts to 35 ft. lbs.

Merkur

1. Disconnect the wiring at the fog lamps and turn signals.

2. Remove the 4 nuts at each wheel well that secure the bumper to the bumper bar brackets.

3. Remove the plastic support straps which support the lower side of the bumper trim.

4. Remove the trim beam from the bumper by removing the license plate bracket and the 3 retaining screws. Remove the plastic pushpin at the center of the bumper.

5. Remove the 4 bolts and 1 nut from the bumper arm mounting plate and the 3 screws

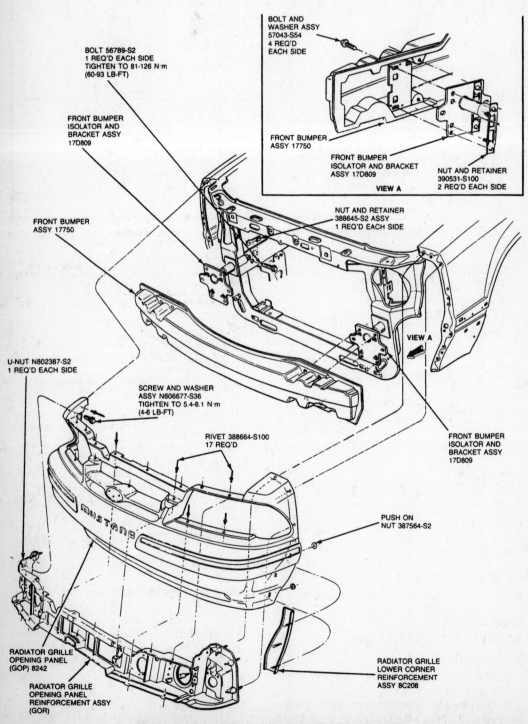

Mustang radiator grille opening panel. The Capri is similar

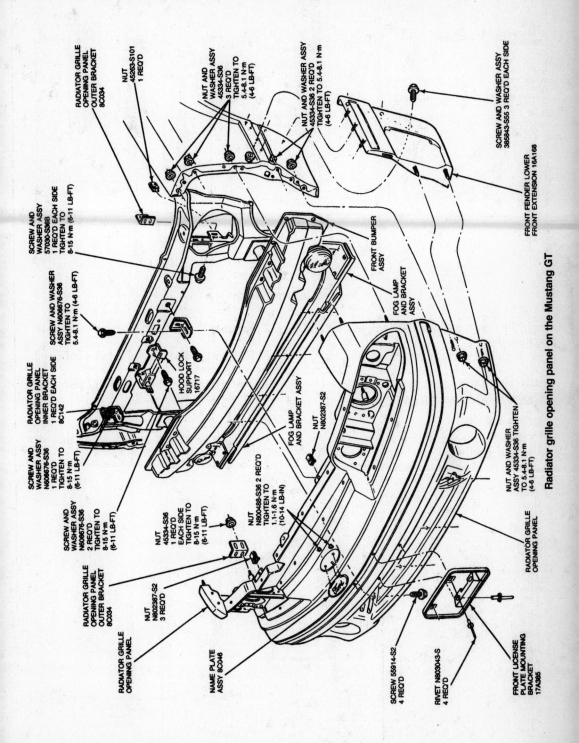

RADIATOR GRILLE OPENING PANEL OUTER BRACKET 8C034

NUT 45263-S101 1 REQ'D

NUT AND WASHER ASSY 45334-S36 3 REQ'D TIGHTEN TO 5.4-8.1 N·m (4-6 LB-FT)

NUT AND WASHER ASSY 45334-S36 2 REQ'D TIGHTEN TO 5.4-8.1 N·m (4-6 LB-FT)

SCREW AND WASHER ASSY 57030-S268 1 REQ'D EACH SIDE TIGHTEN TO 8-15 N·m (6-11 LB-FT)

SCREW AND WASHER ASSY 385843-S55 3 REQ'D EACH SIDE

FRONT FENDER LOWER FRONT EXTENSION 16A168

SCREW AND WASHER ASSY N606676-S36 1 REQ'D TIGHTEN TO 8-15 N·m (6-11 LB-FT)

RADIATOR GRILLE OPENING PANEL INNER BRACKET 1 REQ'D EACH SIDE 8C142

SCREW AND WASHER ASSY N606676-S36 TIGHTEN TO 5.4-8.1 N·m (4-6 LB-FT)

FRONT BUMPER ASSY

FOG LAMP AND BRACKET ASSY

RADIATOR GRILLE OPENING PANEL

SCREW AND WASHER ASSY N606676-S36 2 REQ'D TIGHTEN TO 8-15 N·m (6-11 LB-FT)

HOOD LOCK SUPPORT 16717

FOG LAMP AND BRACKET ASSY

NUT N802387-S2

NUT AND WASHER ASSY 45334-S36 TIGHTEN TO 5.4-8.1 N·m (4-6 LB-FT)

RADIATOR GRILLE OPENING PANEL

NUT 45334-S36 1 REQ'D EACH SIDE TIGHTEN TO 8-15 N·m (6-11 LB-FT)

NUT N800488-S36 2 REQ'D TIGHTEN TO 1.1-1.6 N·m (10-14 LB-IN)

RADIATOR GRILLE OPENING PANEL OUTER BRACKET 8C034

NUT N802387-S2 3 REQ'D

NAME PLATE ASSY 8C046

SCREW 55914-S2 4 REQ'D

RIVET N803043-S 4 REQ'D

FRONT LICENSE PLATE MOUNTING BRACKET 17A385

Radiator grille opening panel on the Mustang GT

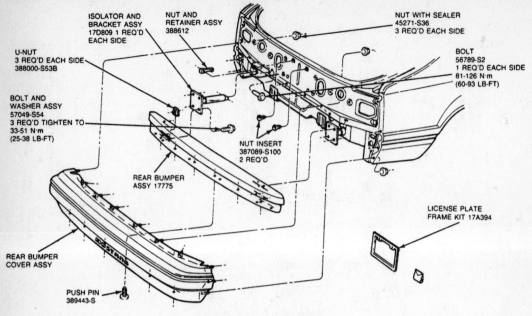

Mustang/Capri rear bumper

from the fog lamp housing. Remove the front bumper beam.

6. Installation is the reverse of removal.

Rear Bumpers

REMOVAL AND INSTALLATION

Mustang and Capri

1. Remove the 6 pushpins retaining the cover to the bottom of the reinforcement. The pushpins must be destroyed to remove them.

2. Remove the nuts attaching the cover to the body.

3. Remove the 6 isolator-to-bracket bolts and remove the bumper.

4. Installation is the reverse of removal. Torque the bolts to 20 ft. lbs.

Merkur

1. Remove the 4 nuts at each wheel well attaching the bumper to the brackets.

2. Open the liftgate and remove the nuts and

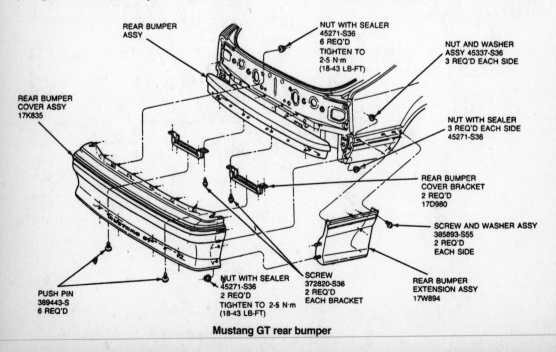

Mustang GT rear bumper

washers retaining the rear trim. Detach the trim from the body along the upper edge by pulling it rearward.

3. Pull the bumper assembly horizontally away from the body.

4. Remove the 4 screws from the bumper arm mounting plate and remove the bumper.

5. Installation is the reverse of removal.

Grille

REMOVAL AND INSTALLATION

Mustang and Capri, except GT

1. Remove the license plate bolts or rivets.
2. Remove the lower grille-to-radiator support screws.
3. Remove the upper grille-to-support brackets.
4. Remove the grille-to-fender nuts and detach the reinforcement assembly.
5. Remove the headlamp side marker, park and turn lamps from the reinforcement.
6. Remove the 2 pushnuts per side attaching the lower corner reinforcement assembly.
7. Drill out the grille-to-reinforcement rivets and remove the grille.
8. Installation is the reverse of removal.

Merkur

1. Open the hood.
2. Remove the 4 grille retaining screws.
3. Lift the grille to disengage the 4 locating lugs and remove the grille.
4. Installation is the reverse of removal. The grille panel should be carefully positioned so that the rubber gap moulding around the headlamp and fender is properly positioned.

INTERIOR

Door Trim Panels

REMOVAL AND INSTALLATION

Mustang and Capri

1. Remove the window handle retaining screw and remove the handle.
2. Remove the door latch handle retaining screw and remove the handle.
3. Remove the screws from the armrest door pull cup area.
4. Remove the retaining screws from the armrest.
5. On cars with power door locks and/or pow-

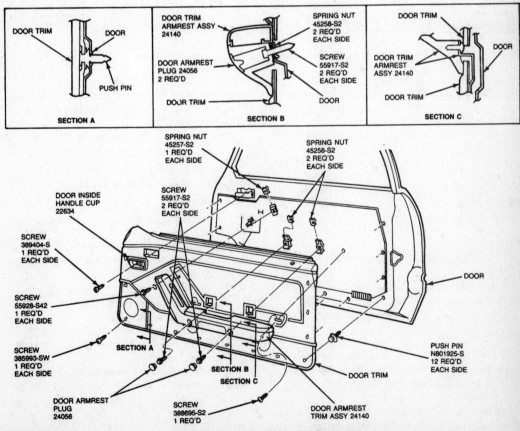

Base model Mustang/Capri door trim panel

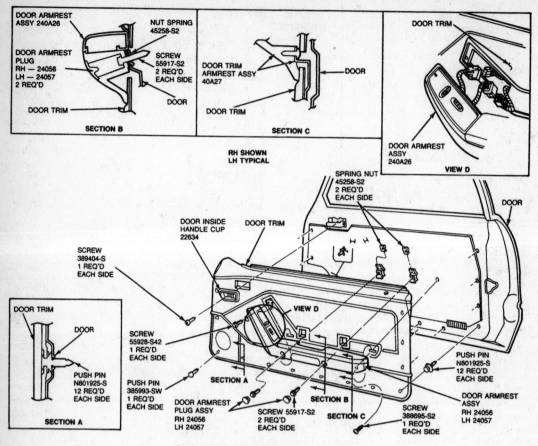

Optional Mustang/Capri door trim panel

er windows, remove the retaining screws and power switch cover assembly. Remove the screws holding the switch housing.

6. Remove the mirror remote control bezel nut.

7. Remove the door trim panel retaining screws.

8. With a flat, wood spatula, pry the trim retaining clips from the door panel. These clips can be easily torn from the trim panel, so be very careful to pry as closely as possible to the clips.

9. Pull the panel out slightly and disconnect all wiring.

10. If a new panel is being installed, transfer all necessary parts.

11. Installation is the reverse of removal.

Merkur

1. Depress the spring retainer and remove the power door switch. Disconnect the wiring.

2. Remove the door handle bezel.

3. Remove the map pocket.

4. Using a wood spatula, pry out the 4 trim panel clips along the bottom edge of the door. Pry right along side each clip to avoid tearing

the panel. Hold the panel outward with light pressure and pry out the remaining clips all around the door.

5. Installation is the reverse of removal.

Door Glass

REMOVAL AND INSTALLATION

Mustang and Capri

1. Remove the door trim panel and watershield.

2. Remove the screw attaching each glass rear stabilizer to the inner panel, and remove the stabilizer.

3. Loosen the 2 screws that attach the door glass front run retainer to the inner door panel.

4. Lower the glass to gain access to the glass bracket rivets.

5. Drill out the glass bracket attaching rivets and push out the rivets.

WARNING: *Before removing the rivets you should insert a suitable block support between the door outer panel and the glass bracket, to stabilize the glass during rivet removal.*

6. Remove the glass.

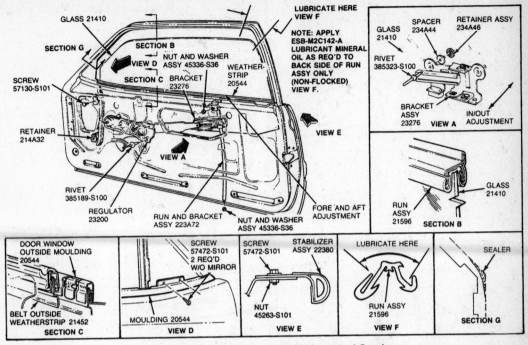

Door window mechanism on the Mustang and Capri

7. Installation is the reverse of removal. Replace the rivets with ¼-20 × 1" nuts and bolts. When the glass is operating properly, tighten the bolts to 20 in. lbs.

Merkur

1. Remove the door trim panel.
2. Remove the power mirror.
3. Remove the attaching screw and unclip the door glass run extension.
4. Lower the window until the ball and socket joints connecting the window bracket to the regulator are visible through the lower door opening.
5. Separate the ball and socket joints and lower the window to the bottom of the door.
6. Detach the window weatherstripping from the rear half of the window opening.
7. Remove the glass from the door.
8. Installation is the reverse of removal.

Door Glass Regulator

REMOVAL AND INSTALLATION

Mustang and Capri

1979-83

1. Remove the door trim panel and watershield.
2. Support the glass in the full up position.
3. Drill out the motor bracket-to-inner panel attaching rivet and remove the rivet. Disconnect the motor wires at the connector.

On the models with power windows, drill out the regulator attaching rivets and remove the rivets.

4. Disengage the regulator arm from the glass bracket and remove the regulator from the door.
5. If equipped with power windows, secure the regulator in a vise and drill a $5/16$" hole through the regulator sector gear and the plate. Install a ¼" bolt and nut in the hole to prevent the sector gear from moving when the motor and drive assembly is removed.
6. Remove the motor assembly from the regulator and install it on a new regulator.
7. Installation is the reverse of removal. Replace the rivets with ¼-20 × ½" machine screws. Remove the regulator restraining bolt and nut if the old regulator was re-used.

1984-88

1. Remove the trim panel and watershield.
2. Prop the window glass in the full up position.
3. Disconnect the window motor wiring if so equipped.
4. Drill out the 3 rivets (manual windows) or 4 rivets (electric windows), attaching the regulator to the inner door panel.
5. Remove the upper screw and washer and the lower nut and washer, attaching the run and bracket to the inner door panel. Slide the run tube up between the door belt and glass. It's a good idea to cover the glass with a protective cloth.

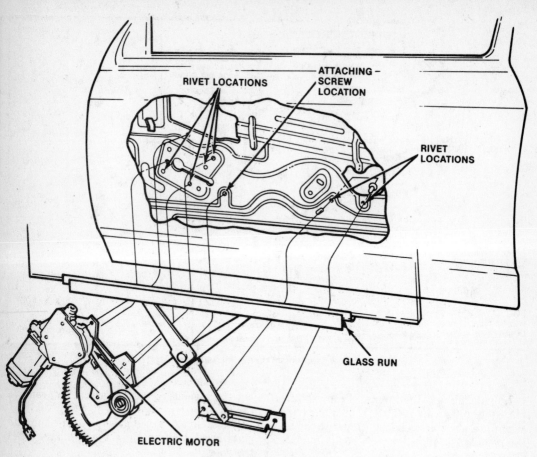

RIVET LOCATIONS

ATTACHING –
SCREW
LOCATION

RIVET
LOCATIONS

GLASS RUN

ELECTRIC MOTOR

Merkur window mechanism

6. Remove the regulator slide from the glass bracket and remove the regulator through the door access hole.

7. Installation is the reverse of removal. Replace the rivets with ¼-20 × 1″ bolts and nuts.

Merkur

MANUAL REGULATOR

1. Remove the door trim panel.
2. Lower the glass to the down position.
3. Separate the regulator from the glass by pulling the retaining balls on the regulators from the sockets in the channel rollers.
4. Drill out the 4 rivets holding the regulator panel assembly and 2 rivets holding the regulator guide slide.
5. Remove the regulator attaching screw.
6. Remove the regulator through the lower door opening.
7. Installation is the reverse of removal. Replace the rivets with bolts, lockwashers and nuts.

POWER REGULATOR

1. Remove the door trim panel.
2. Raise the glass to the full up position and prop it up.

3. Disconnect the power window motor wiring.
4. Drill out the 4 rivets holding the regulator panel assembly and 2 rivets holding the regulator guide slide.
5. Remove the regulator attaching screw.
6. Remove the regulator through the lower door opening.
7. Installation is the reverse of removal

Electric Window Motor

REMOVAL AND INSTALLATION

Mustang and Capri

1979-83

1. Remove the trim panel and watershield.
2. Remove the speakers.
3. Disconnect the motor wires and the connector.

NOTE: *On 1980 models, sheet metal interference may obscure the upper motor mount screw. This interference may be removed by grinding.*

CAUTION: *If equipped with power windows, secure the regulator in a vise and drill a* ⁵⁄₁₆″ *hole through the regulator sector gear*

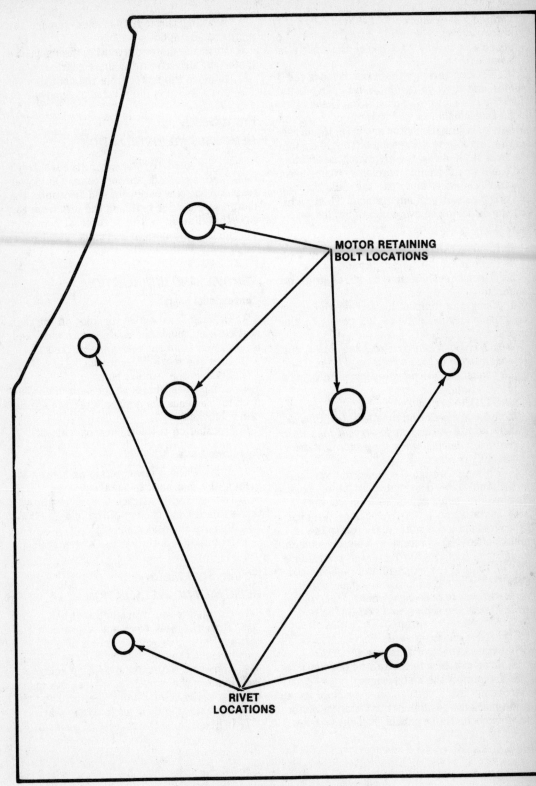

**MOTOR RETAINING
BOLT LOCATIONS**

**RIVET
LOCATIONS**

Template for the Merkur window mechanism

and the plate. Install a ¼" bolt and nut in the hole to prevent the sector gear from moving when the motor and drive assembly is removed.!

4. Working through the holes, remove the 3 motor and drive-to-regulator attaching bolts. Remove the motor and drive from the door.

5. Installation is the reverse of removal. When installing the motor and drive to the regulator, install the 3 screws just snugly enough to hold it. Remove the regulator restraining bolt and nut if the old regulator was re-used. Connect the wires and cycle the glass through its run to ensure gear engagement. Then, tighten the attaching screws to 50-85 in. lbs.

1984-88

1. Remove the trim panel and watershield.
2. Disconnect the battery ground.
3. Disconnect the motor wires and the connector.
4. Using the dimples located on the inner door panel, drill ¾" holes for access to the motor.

WARNING: *When drilling the holes, the glass must be in the up position. The hole saw pilot must not extend more than ¼" beyond the hole saw.*

CAUTION: *Drill a ⁵⁄₁₆" hole through the regulator sector gear and the plate. Install a ¼" bolt and nut in the hole to prevent the sector gear from moving when the motor and drive assembly is removed!*

5. Working through the holes, remove the 3 motor and drive-to-regulator attaching bolts. Remove the motor and drive from the door.

6. Installation is the reverse of removal. When installing the motor and drive to the regulator, install the 3 screws just snugly enough to hold it. Remove the regulator restraining bolt and nut if the old regulator was re-used. Connect the wires and cycle the glass through its run to ensure gear engagement. Then, tighten the attaching screws to 50-85 in. lbs.

Merkur

1. Remove the door trim panel.
2. Raise the glass to the full up position.
3. Disconnect the motor wiring.
4. Using the accompanying template as a guide, mark the position of the 3 window motor retaining bolts with a punch. Drill out ¾" holes.

5. Working through the holes, remove the motor retaining bolts.
6. Push the motor outward to disengage the motor and drive from the drive gear.
7. Remove the motor from the door.
8. Installation is the reverse of removal.

Front Seats

REMOVAL AND INSTALLATION

Seats are removed by removing the seat track bolts and seat belt anchor bolts. On power seats, tilt the seat backward and disconnect the motor wiring prior to lifting the seat from the car. Installation is the reverse of removal. Torque the fasteners to 30 ft. lbs.

Rear Seats

REMOVAL AND INSTALLATION

Conventional Seats

1. Bearing down with your knee on the rear seat cushion, push the cushion rearward and disengage it from the retaining brackets.
2. Rear the rear seat armrests.
3. Remove the seatbelt bolts.
4. Grasp the seatback at the bottom and lift it up to disengage the hanger wire from the retainer brackets.
5. Installation is the reverse of removal.

Fold-Down Seats

1. Remove the 2 lower retaining screws attaching the seat back to the floor.
2. Lift up and disengage the upper clips of the seatback from the top of the folding floor.
3. Remove the seat assembly.
4. Installation is the reverse of removal.

Power Seat Motor

REMOVAL AND INSTALLATION

1. Unbolt the seat track and seat belts.
2. Turn the seat over and disconnect the wiring.
3. Remove the seat from the car.
4. Remove the 3 motor mounting bolts.
5. Remove the cable-to-seat track clamps.
6. Open the wire retaining straps and remove the motor and cables from the seat.
7. Installation is the reverse of removal.

How to Remove Stains from Fabric Interior

For rest results, spots and stains should be removed as soon as possible. Never use gasoline, lacquer thinner, acetone, nail polish remover or bleach. Use a 3′ x 3″ piece of cheesecloth. Squeeze most of the liquid from the fabric and wipe the stained fabric from the outside of the stain toward the center with a lifting motion. Turn the cheesecloth as soon as one side becomes soiled. When using water to remove a stain, be sure to wash the entire section after the spot has been removed to avoid water stains. Encrusted spots can be broken up with a dull knife and vacuumed before removing the stain.

Type of Stain	How to Remove It
Surface spots	Brush the spots out with a small hand brush or use a commercial preparation such as K2R to lift the stain.
Mildew	Clean around the mildew with warm suds. Rinse in cold water and soak the mildew area in a solution of 1 part table salt and 2 parts water. Wash with upholstery cleaner.
Water stains	Water stains in fabric materials can be removed with a solution made from 1 cup of table salt dissolved in 1 quart of water. Vigorously scrub the solution into the stain and rinse with clear water. Water stains in nylon or other synthetic fabrics should be removed with a commercial type spot remover.
Chewing gum, tar, crayons, shoe polish (greasy stains)	Do not use a cleaner that will soften gum or tar. Harden the deposit with an ice cube and scrape away as much as possible with a dull knife. Moisten the remainder with cleaning fluid and scrub clean.
Ice cream, candy	Most candy has a sugar base and can be removed with a cloth wrung out in warm water. Oily candy, after cleaning with warm water, should be cleaned with upholstery cleaner. Rinse with warm water and clean the remainder with cleaning fluid.
Wine, alcohol, egg, milk, soft drink (non-greasy stains)	Do not use soap. Scrub the stain with a cloth wrung out in warm water. Remove the remainder with cleaning fluid.
Grease, oil, lipstick, butter and related stains	Use a spot remover to avoid leaving a ring. Work from the outisde of the stain to the center and dry with a clean cloth when the spot is gone.
Headliners (cloth)	Mix a solution of warm water and foam upholstery cleaner to give thick suds. Use only foam—liquid may streak or spot. Clean the entire headliner in one operation using a circular motion with a natural sponge.
Headliner (vinyl)	Use a vinyl cleaner with a sponge and wipe clean with a dry cloth.
Seats and door panels	Mix 1 pint upholstery cleaner in 1 gallon of water. Do not soak the fabric around the buttons.
Leather or vinyl fabric	Use a multi-purpose cleaner full strength and a stiff brush. Let stand 2 minutes and scrub thoroughly. Wipe with a clean, soft rag.
Nylon or synthetic fabrics	For normal stains, use the same procedures you would for washing cloth upholstery. If the fabric is extremely dirty, use a multi-purpose cleaner full strength with a stiff scrub brush. Scrub thoroughly in all directions and wipe with a cotton towel or soft rag.

Mechanic's Data

11

General Conversion Table

Multiply By	To Convert	To	
	LENGTH		
2.54	Inches	Centimeters	.3937
25.4	Inches	Millimeters	.03937
30.48	Feet	Centimeters	.0328
.304	Feet	Meters	3.28
.914	Yards	Meters	1.094
1.609	Miles	Kilometers	.621
	VOLUME		
.473	Pints	Liters	2.11
.946	Quarts	Liters	1.06
3.785	Gallons	Liters	.264
.016	Cubic inches	Liters	61.02
16.39	Cubic inches	Cubic cms.	.061
28.3	Cubic feet	Liters	.0353
	MASS (Weight)		
28.35	Ounces	Grams	.035
.4536	Pounds	Kilograms	2.20
—	To obtain	From	Multiply by

Multiply By	To Convert	To	
	AREA		
.645	Square inches	Square cms.	.155
.836	Square yds.	Square meters	1.196
	FORCE		
4.448	Pounds	Newtons	.225
.138	Ft./lbs.	Kilogram/meters	7.23
1.36	Ft./lbs.	Newton-meters	.737
.112	In./lbs.	Newton-meters	8.844
	PRESSURE		
.068	Psi	Atmospheres	14.7
6.89	Psi	Kilopascals	.145
	OTHER		
1.104	Horsepower (DIN)	Horsepower (SAE)	.9861
.746	Horsepower (SAE)	Kilowatts (KW)	1.34
1.60	Mph	Km/h	.625
.425	Mpg	Km/1	2.35
—	To obtain	From	Multiply by

Tap Drill Sizes

National Coarse or U.S.S.

Screw & Tap Size	Threads Per Inch	Use Drill Number
No. 5	40	39
No. 6	32	36
No. 8	32	29
No. 10	24	25
No. 12	24	17
$\frac{1}{4}$	20	8
$\frac{5}{16}$	18	F
$\frac{3}{8}$	16	$\frac{5}{16}$
$\frac{7}{16}$	14	U
$\frac{1}{2}$	13	$\frac{27}{64}$
$\frac{9}{16}$	12	$\frac{31}{64}$
$\frac{5}{8}$	11	$\frac{17}{32}$
$\frac{3}{4}$	10	$\frac{21}{32}$
$\frac{7}{8}$	9	$\frac{49}{64}$

National Coarse or U.S.S.

Screw & Tap Size	Threads Per Inch	Use Drill Number
1	8	$\frac{7}{8}$
$1\frac{1}{8}$	7	$\frac{63}{64}$
$1\frac{1}{4}$	7	$1\frac{7}{64}$
$1\frac{1}{2}$	6	$1\frac{11}{32}$

National Fine or S.A.E.

Screw & Tap Size	Threads Per Inch	Use Drill Number
No. 5	44	37
No. 6	40	33
No. 8	36	29
No. 10	32	21

National Fine or S.A.E.

Screw & Tap Size	Threads Per Inch	Use Drill Number
No. 12	28	15
$\frac{1}{4}$	28	3
$\frac{6}{16}$	24	1
$\frac{3}{8}$	24	Q
$\frac{7}{16}$	20	W
$\frac{1}{2}$	20	$\frac{29}{64}$
$\frac{9}{16}$	18	$\frac{33}{64}$
$\frac{5}{8}$	18	$\frac{37}{64}$
$\frac{3}{4}$	16	$\frac{11}{16}$
$\frac{7}{8}$	14	$\frac{13}{16}$
$1\frac{1}{8}$	12	$1\frac{3}{64}$
$1\frac{1}{4}$	12	$1\frac{11}{64}$
$1\frac{1}{2}$	12	$1\frac{27}{64}$

Drill Sizes In Decimal Equivalents

Inch	Decimal	Wire	mm
1/64	.0156		.39
	.0157		.4
	.0160	78	
	.0165		.42
	.0173		.44
	.0177		.45
	.0180	77	
	.0181		.46
	.0189		.48
	.0197		.5
	.0200	76	
	.0210	75	
	.0217		.55
	.0225	74	
	.0236		.6
	.0240	73	
	.0250	72	
	.0256		.65
	.0260	71	
	.0276		.7
	.0280	70	
	.0292	69	
	.0295		.75
	.0310	68	
1/32	.0312		.79
	.0315		.8
	.0320	67	
	.0330	66	
	.0335		.85
	.0350	65	
	.0354		.9
	.0360	64	
	.0370	63	
	.0374		.95
	.0380	62	
	.0390	61	
	.0394		1.0
	.0400	60	
	.0410	59	
	.0413		1.05
	.0420	58	
	.0430	57	
	.0433		1.1
	.0453		1.15
	.0465	56	
3/64	.0469		1.19
	.0472		1.2
	.0492		1.25
	.0512		1.3
	.0520	55	
	.0531		1.35
	.0550	54	
	.0551		1.4
	.0571		1.45
	.0591		1.5
	.0595	53	
	.0610		1.55
1/16	.0625		1.59
	.0630		1.6
	.0635	52	
	.0650		1.65
	.0669		1.7
	.0670	51	
	.0689		1.75
	.0700	50	
	.0709		1.8
	.0728		1.85

Inch	Decimal	Wire	mm
	.0730	49	
	.0748		1.9
	.0760	48	
	.0768		1.95
5/64	.0781		1.98
	.0785	47	
	.0787		2.0
	.0807		2.05
	.0810	46	
	.0820	45	
	.0827		2.1
	.0846		2.15
	.0860	44	
	.0866		2.2
	.0886		2.25
	.0890	43	
	.0906		2.3
	.0925		2.35
	.0935	42	
3/32	.0938		2.38
	.0945		2.4
	.0960	41	
	.0965		2.45
	.0980	40	
	.0981		2.5
	.0995	39	
	.1015	38	
	.1024		2.6
	.1040	37	
	.1063		2.7
	.1065	36	
	.1083		2.75
7/64	.1094		2.77
	.1100	35	
	.1102		2.8
	.1110	34	
	.1130	33	
	.1142		2.9
	.1160	32	
	.1181		3.0
	.1200	31	
	.1220		3.1
1/8	.1250		3.17
	.1260		3.2
	.1280		3.25
	.1285	30	
	.1299		3.3
	.1339		3.4
	.1360	29	
	.1378		3.5
	.1405	28	
9/64	.1406		3.57
	.1417		3.6
	.1440	27	
	.1457		3.7
	.1470	26	
	.1476		3.75
	.1495	25	
	.1496		3.8
	.1520	24	
	.1535		3.9
	.1540	23	
5/32	.1562		3.96
	.1570	22	
	.1575		4.0
	.1590	21	
	.1610	20	

Inch	Decimal	Wire & Letter	mm
	.1614		4.1
	.1654		4.2
	.1660	19	
	.1673		4.25
	.1693		4.3
	.1695	18	
11/64	.1719		4.36
	.1730	17	
	.1732		4.4
	.1770	16	
	.1772		4.5
	.1800	15	
	.1811		4.6
	.1820	14	
	.1850	13	
	.1850		4.7
	.1870		4.75
3/16	.1875		4.76
	.1890		4.8
	.1890	12	
	.1910	11	
	.1929		4.9
	.1935	10	
	.1960	9	
	.1969		5.0
	.1990	8	
	.2008		5.1
	.2010	7	
13/64	.2031		5.16
	.2040	6	
	.2047		5.2
	.2055	5	
	.2067		5.25
	.2087		5.3
	.2090	4	
	.2126		5.4
	.2130	3	
	.2165		5.5
7/32	2188		5.55
	.2205		5.6
	.2210	2	
	.2244		5.7
	.2264		5.75
	.2280	1	
	.2283		5.8
	.2323		5.9
	.2340	A	
15/64	.2344		5.95
	.2362		6.0
	.2380	B	
	.2402		6.1
	.2420	C	
	.2441		6.2
	.2460	D	
	.2461		6.25
	.2480		6.3
1/4	.2500	E	6.35
	.2520		6.
	.2559		6.5
	.2570	F	
	.2598		6.6
	.2610	G	
	.2638		6.7
17/64	.2656		6.74
	.2657		6.75
	.2660	H	
	.2677		6.8

Inch	Decimal	Letter	mm
	.2717		6.9
	.2720	I	
	.2756		7.0
	.2770	J	
	.2795		7.1
	.2810	K	
9/32	.2812		7.14
	.2835		7.2
	.2854		7.25
	.2874		7.3
	.2900	L	
	.2913		7.4
	.2950	M	
19/64	.2953		7.5
	.2969		7.54
	.2992		7.6
	.3020	N	
	.3031		7.7
	.3051		7.75
	.3071		7.8
	.3110		7.9
5/16	.3125		7.93
	.3150		8.0
	.3160	O	
	.3189		8.1
	.3228		8.2
	.3230	P	
	.3248		8.25
	.3268		8.3
21/64	.3281		8.33
	.3307		8.4
	.3320	Q	
	.3346		8.5
	.3386		8.6
	.3390	R	
	.3425		8.7
11/32	.3438		8.73
	.3445		8.75
	.3465		8.8
	.3480	S	
	.3504		8.9
	.3543		9.0
	.3580	T	
	.3583		9.1
23/64	.3594		9.12
	.3622		9.2
	.3642		9.25
	.3661		9.3
	.3680	U	
	.3701		9.4
	.3740		9.5
3/8	.3750		9.52
	.3770	V	
	.3780		9.6
	.3819		9.7
	.3839		9.75
	.3858		9.8
	.3860	W	
	.3898		9.9
25/64	.3906		9.92
	.3937		10.0
	.3970	X	
	.4040	Y	
13/32	.4062		10.31
	.4130	Z	
	.4134		10.5
27/64	.4219		10.71

Inch	Decimal	mm
	.4331	11.0
7/16	.4375	11.11
	.4528	11.5
29/64	.4531	11.51
15/32	.4688	11.90
	.4724	12.0
31/64	.4844	12.30
	.4921	12.5
1/2	.5000	12.70
	.5118	13.0
33/64	.5156	13.09
17/32	.5312	13.49
	.5315	13.5
35/64	.5469	13.89
	.5512	14.0
9/16	.5625	14.28
	.5709	14.5
37/64	.5781	14.68
	.5906	15.0
19/32	.5938	15.08
39/64	.6094	15.47
	.6102	15.5
5/8	.6250	15.87
	.6299	16.0
41/64	.6406	16.27
	.6496	16.5
21/32	.6562	16.66
	.6693	17.0
43/64	.6719	17.06
11/16	.6875	17.46
	.6890	17.5
45/64	.7031	17.85
	.7087	18.0
23/32	.7188	18.25
	.7283	18.5
47/64	.7344	18.65
	.7480	19.0
3/4	.7500	19.05
49/64	.7656	19.44
	.7677	19.5
25/32	.7812	19.84
	.7874	20.0
51/64	.7969	20.24
	.8071	20.5
13/16	.8125	20.63
	.8268	21.0
53/64	.8281	21.03
27/32	.8438	21.43
	.8465	21.5
55/64	.8594	21.82
	.8661	22.0
7/8	.8750	22.22
	.8858	22.5
57/64	.8906	22.62
	.9055	23.0
29/32	.9062	23.01
59/64	.9219	23.41
	.9252	23.5
15/16	.9375	23.81
	.9449	24.0
61/64	.9531	24.2
	.9646	24.5
31/32	.9688	24.6
	.9843	25.0
63/64	.9844	25.0
1	1.0000	25.4

AIR/FUEL RATIO: The ratio of air to gasoline by weight in the fuel mixture drawn into the engine.

AIR INJECTION: One method of reducing harmful exhaust emissions by injecting air into each of the exhaust ports of an engine. The fresh air entering the hot exhaust manifold causes any remaining fuel to be burned before it can exit the tailpipe.

ALTERNATOR: A device used for converting mechanical energy into electrical energy.

AMMETER: An instrument, calibrated in amperes, used to measure the flow of an electrical current in a circuit. Ammeters are always connected in series with the circuit being tested.

AMPERE: The rate of flow of electrical current present when one volt of electrical pressure is applied against one ohm of electrical resistance.

ANALOG COMPUTER: Any microprocessor that uses similar (analogous) electrical signals to make its calculations.

ARMATURE: A laminated, soft iron core wrapped by a wire that converts electrical energy to mechanical energy as in a motor or relay. When rotated in a magnetic field, it changes mechanical energy into electrical energy as in a generator.

ATMOSPHERIC PRESSURE: The pressure on the Earth's surface caused by the weight of the air in the atmosphere. At sea level, this pressure is 14.7 psi at 32°F (101 kPa at 0°C).

ATOMIZATION: The breaking down of a liquid into a fine mist that can be suspended in air.

AXIAL PLAY: Movement parallel to a shaft or bearing bore.

BACKFIRE: The sudden combustion of gases in the intake or exhaust system that results in a loud explosion.

BACKLASH: The clearance or play between two parts, such as meshed gears.

BACKPRESSURE: Restrictions in the exhaust system that slow the exit of exhaust gases from the combustion chamber.

BAKELITE: A heat resistant, plastic insulator material commonly used in printed circuit boards and transistorized components.

BALL BEARING: A bearing made up of hardened inner and outer races between which hardened steel ball roll.

BALLAST RESISTOR: A resistor in the primary ignition circuit that lowers voltage after the engine is started to reduce wear on ignition components.

BEARING: A friction reducing, supportive device usually located between a stationary part and a moving part.

BIMETAL TEMPERATURE SENSOR: Any sensor or switch made of two dissimilar types of metal that bend when heated or cooled due to the different expansion rates of the alloys. These types of sensors usually function as an on/off switch.

BLOWBY: Combustion gases, composed of water vapor and unburned fuel, that leak past the piston rings into the crankcase during normal engine operation. These gases are removed by the PCV system to prevent the build-up of harmful acids in the crankcase.

BRAKE PAD: A brake shoe and lining assembly used with disc brakes.

BRAKE SHOE: The backing for the brake lining. The term is, however, usually applied to the assembly of the brake backing and lining.

BUSHING: A liner, usually removable, for a bearing; an anti-friction liner used in place of a bearing.

BYPASS: System used to bypass ballast resistor during engine cranking to increase voltage supplied to the coil.

CALIPER: A hydraulically activated device in a disc brake system, which is mounted straddling the brake rotor (disc). The caliper contains at least one piston and two brake pads. Hydraulic pressure on the piston(s) forces the pads against the rotor.

CAMSHAFT: A shaft in the engine on which are the lobes (cams) which operate the valves. The camshaft is driven by the crankshaft, via a belt, chain or gears, at one half the crankshaft speed.

CAPACITOR: A device which stores an electrical charge.

CARBON MONOXIDE (CO): a colorless, odorless gas given off as a normal byproduct of combustion. It is poisonous and extremely dangerous in confined areas, building up slowly to toxic levels without warning if adequate ventilation is not available.

CARBURETOR: A device, usually mounted on the intake manifold of an engine, which mixes the air and fuel in the proper proportion to allow even combustion.

CATALYTIC CONVERTER: A device installed in the exhaust system, like a muffler, that converts harmful byproducts of combustion into carbon dioxide and water vapor by means of a heat-producing chemical reaction.

CENTRIFUGAL ADVANCE: A mechanical method of advancing the spark timing by using flyweights in the distributor that react to centrifugal force generated by the distributor shaft rotation.

CHECK VALVE: Any one-way valve installed to permit the flow of air, fuel or vacuum in one direction only.

CHOKE: A device, usually a moveable valve, placed in the intake path of a carburetor to restrict the flow of air.

CIRCUIT: Any unbroken path through which an electrical current can flow. Also used to describe fuel flow in some instances.

CIRCUIT BREAKER: A switch which protects an electrical circuit from overload by opening the circuit when the current flow exceeds a predetermined level. Some circuit breakers must be reset manually, while other reset automatically

COIL (IGNITION): A transformer in the ignition circuit which steps of the voltage provided to the spark plugs.

COMBINATION MANIFOLD: An assembly which includes both the intake and exhaust manifolds in one casting.

COMBINATION VALVE: A device used in some fuel systems that routes fuel vapors to a charcoal storage canister instead of venting them into the atmosphere. The valve relieves fuel tank pressure and allows fresh air into the tank as fuel level drops to prevent a vapor lock situation.

COMPRESSION RATIO: The comparison of the total volume of the cylinder and combustion chamber with the piston at BDC and the piston at TDC.

CONDENSER: 1. An electrical device which acts to store an electrical charge, preventing voltage surges.
2. A radiator-like device in the air conditioning system in which refrigerant gas condenses into a liquid, giving off heat.

CONDUCTOR: Any material through which an electrical current can be transmitted easily.

CONTINUITY: Continuous or complete circuit. Can be checked with an ohmmeter.

COUNTERSHAFT: An intermediate shaft which is rotated by a mainshaft and transmits, in turn, that rotation to a working part.

CRANKCASE: The lower part of an engine in which the crankshaft and related parts operate.

CRANKSHAFT: The main driving shaft of an engine which receives reciprocating motion from the pistons and converts it to rotary motion.

CYLINDER: In an engine, the round hole in the engine block in which the piston(s) ride.

CYLINDER BLOCK: The main structural member of an engine in which is found the cylinders, crankshaft and other principal parts.

CYLINDER HEAD: The detachable portion of the engine, fastened, usually, to the top of the cylinder block, containing all or most of the combustion chambers. On overhead valve engines, it contains the valves and their operating parts. On overhead cam engines, it contains the camshaft as well.

DEAD CENTER: The extreme top or bottom of the piston stroke.

DETONATION: An unwanted explosion of the air fuel mixture in the combustion chamber caused by excess heat and compression, advanced timing, or an overly lean mixture. Also referred to as "ping".

DIAPHRAGM: A thin, flexible wall separating two cavities, such as in a vacuum advance unit.

DIESELING: A condition in which hot spots in the combustion chamber cause the engine to run on after the key is turned off.

DIFFERENTIAL: A geared assembly which allows the transmission of motion between drive axles, giving one axle the ability to turn faster than the other.

DIODE: An electrical device that will allow current to flow in one direction only.

DISC BRAKE: A hydraulic braking assembly consisting of a brake disc, or rotor, mounted on an axle, and a caliper assembly containing, usually two brake pads which are activated by hydraulic pressure. The pads are forced against the sides of the disc, creating friction which slows the vehicle.

DISTRIBUTOR: A mechanically driven device on an engine which is responsible for electrically firing the spark plug at a predetermined point of the piston stroke.

DOWEL PIN: A pin, inserted in mating holes in two different parts allowing those parts to maintain a fixed relationship.

DRUM BRAKE: A braking system which consists of two brake shoes and one or two wheel cylinders, mounted on a fixed backing plate, and a brake drum, mounted on an axle, which revolves around the assembly. Hydraulic action applied to the wheel cylinders forces the shoes outward against the drum, creating friction and slowing the vehicle.

DWELL: The rate, measured in degrees of shaft rotation, at which an electrical circuit cycles on and off.

ELECTRONIC CONTROL UNIT (ECU): Ignition module, module, amplifier or igniter. See Module for definition.

ELECTRONIC IGNITION: A system in which the timing and firing of the spark plugs is controlled by an electronic control unit, usually called a module. These systems have not points or condenser.

ENDPLAY: The measured amount of axial movement in a shaft.

ENGINE: A device that converts heat into mechanical energy.

EXHAUST MANIFOLD: A set of cast passages or pipes which conduct exhaust gases from the engine.

FEELER GAUGE: A blade, usually metal, of precisely predetermined thickness, used to measure the clearance between two parts. These blades usually are available in sets of assorted thicknesses.

F-Head: An engine configuration in which the intake valves are in the cylinder head, while the camshaft and exhaust valves are located in the cylinder block. The camshaft operates the intake valves via lifters and pushrods, while it operates the exhaust valves directly.

FIRING ORDER: The order in which combustion occurs in the cylinders of an engine. Also the order in which spark is distributed to the plugs by the distributor.

FLATHEAD: An engine configuration in which the camshaft and all the valves are located in the cylinder block.

FLOODING: The presence of too much fuel in the intake manifold and combustion chamber which prevents the air/fuel mixture from firing, thereby causing a no-start situation.

FLYWHEEL: A disc shaped part bolted to the rear end of the crankshaft. Around the outer perimeter is affixed the ring gear. The starter drive engages the ring gear, turning the flywheel, which rotates the crankshaft, imparting the initial starting motion to the engine.

FOOT POUND (ft.lb. or sometimes, ft. lbs.): The amount of energy or work needed to raise an item weighing one pound, a distance of one foot.

FUSE: A protective device in a circuit which prevents circuit overload by breaking the circuit when a specific amperage is present. The device is constructed around a strip or wire of a lower amperage rating than the circuit it is designed to protect. When an amperage higher than that stamped on the fuse is present in the circuit, the strip or wire melts, opening the circuit.

GEAR RATIO: The ratio between the number of teeth on meshing gears.

GENERATOR: A device which converts mechanical energy into electrical energy.

HEAT RANGE: The measure of a spark plug's ability to dissipate heat from its firing end. The higher the heat range, the hotter the plug fires.

HUB: The center part of a wheel or gear.

HYDROCARBON (HC): Any chemical compound made up of hydrogen and carbon. A major pollutant formed by the engine as a byproduct of combustion.

HYDROMETER: An instrument used to measure the specific gravity of a solution.

INCH POUND (in.lb. or sometimes, in. lbs.): One twelfth of a foot pound.

INDUCTION: A means of transferring electrical energy in the form of a magnetic field. Principle used in the ignition coil to increase voltage.

INJECTION PUMP: A device, usually mechanically operated, which meters and delivers fuel under pressure to the fuel injector.

INJECTOR: A device which receives metered fuel under relatively low pressure and is activated to inject the fuel into the engine under relatively high pressure at a predetermined time.

INPUT SHAFT: The shaft to which torque is applied, usually carrying the driving gear or gears.

INTAKE MANIFOLD: A casting of passages or pipes used to conduct air or a fuel/air mixture to the cylinders.

JOURNAL: The bearing surface within which a shaft operates.

KEY: A small block usually fitted in a notch between a shaft and a hub to prevent slippage of the two parts.

MANIFOLD: A casting of passages or set of pipes which connect the cylinders to an inlet or outlet source.

MANIFOLD VACUUM: Low pressure in an engine intake manifold formed just below the throttle plates. Manifold vacuum is highest at idle and drops under acceleration.

MASTER CYLINDER: The primary fluid pressurizing device in a hydraulic system. In automotive use, it is found in brake and hydraulic clutch systems and is pedal activated, either directly or, in a power brake system, through the power booster.

MODULE: Electronic control unit, amplifier or igniter of solid state or integrated design which controls the current flow in the ignition primary circuit based on input from the pickup coil. When the module opens the primary circuit, the high secondary voltage is induced in the coil.

NEEDLE BEARING: A bearing which consists of a number (usually a large number) of long, thin rollers.

OHM: (Ω) The unit used to measure the resistance of conductor to electrical flow. One ohm is the amount of resistance that limits current flow to one ampere in a circuit with one volt of pressure.

OHMMETER: An instrument used for measuring the resistance, in ohms, in an electrical circuit.

OUTPUT SHAFT: The shaft which transmits torque from a device, such as a transmission.

OVERDRIVE: A gear assembly which produces more shaft revolutions than that transmitted to it.

OVERHEAD CAMSHAFT (OHC): An engine configuration in which the camshaft is mounted on top of the cylinder head and operates the valve either directly or by means of rocker arms.

OVERHEAD VALVE (OHV): An engine configuration in which all of the valves are located in the cylinder head and the camshaft is located in the cylinder block. The camshaft operates the valves via lifters and pushrods.

OXIDES OF NITROGEN (NOx): Chemical compounds of nitrogen produced as a byproduct of combustion. They combine with hydrocarbons to produce smog.

OXYGEN SENSOR: Used with the feedback system to sense the presence of oxygen in the exhaust gas and signal the computer which can reference the voltage signal to an air/fuel ratio.

PINION: The smaller of two meshing gears.

PISTON RING: An open ended ring which fits into a groove on the outer diameter of the piston. Its chief function is to form a seal between the piston and cylinder wall. Most automotive pistons have three rings: two for compression sealing; one for oil sealing.

PRELOAD: A predetermined load placed on a bearing during assembly or by adjustment.

PRIMARY CIRCUIT: Is the low voltage side of the ignition system which consists of the ignition switch, ballast resistor or resistance wire, bypass, coil, electronic control unit and pick-up coil as well as the connecting wires and harnesses.

PRESS FIT: The mating of two parts under pressure, due to the inner diameter of one being smaller than the outer diameter of the other, or vice versa; an interference fit.

RACE: The surface on the inner or outer ring of a bearing on which the balls, needles or rollers move.

REGULATOR: A device which maintains the amperage and/or voltage levels of a circuit at predetermined values.

RELAY: A switch which automatically opens and/or closes a circuit.

RESISTANCE: The opposition to the flow of current through a circuit or electrical device, and is measured in ohms. Resistance is equal to the voltage divided by the amperage.

RESISTOR: A device, usually made of wire, which offers a preset amount of resistance in an electrical circuit.

RING GEAR: The name given to a ring-shaped gear attached to a differential case, or affixed to a flywheel or as part a planetary gear set.

ROLLER BEARING: A bearing made up of hardened inner and outer races between which hardened steel rollers move.

ROTOR: 1. The disc-shaped part of a disc brake assembly, upon which the brake pads bear; also called, brake disc.
2. The device mounted atop the distributor shaft, which passes current to the distributor cap tower contacts.

SECONDARY CIRCUIT: The high voltage side of the ignition system, usually above 20,000 volts. The secondary includes the ignition coil, coil wire, distributor cap and rotor, spark plug wires and spark plugs.

SENDING UNIT: A mechanical, electrical, hydraulic or electromagnetic device which transmits information to a gauge.

SENSOR: Any device designed to measure engine operating conditions or ambient pressures and temperatures. Usually electronic in nature and designed to send a voltage signal to an on-board computer, some sensors may operate as a simple on/off switch or they may provide a variable voltage signal (like a potentiometer) as conditions or measured parameters change.

SHIM: Spacers of precise, predetermined thickness used between parts to establish a proper working relationship.

SLAVE CYLINDER: In automotive use, a device in the hydraulic clutch system which is activated by hydraulic force, disengaging the clutch.

SOLENOID: A coil used to produce a magnetic field, the effect of which is produce work.

SPARK PLUG: A device screwed into the combustion chamber of a spark ignition engine. The basic construction is a conductive core inside of a ceramic insulator, mounted in an outer conductive base. An electrical charge from the spark plug wire travels along the conductive core and jumps a preset air gap to a grounding point or points at the end of the conductive base. The resultant spark ignites the fuel/air mixture in the combustion chamber.

SPLINES: Ridges machined or cast onto the outer diameter of a shaft or inner diameter of a bore to enable parts to mate without rotation.

TACHOMETER: A device used to measure the rotary speed of an engine, shaft, gear, etc., usually in rotations per minute.

THERMOSTAT: A valve, located in the cooling system of an engine, which is closed when cold and opens gradually in response to engine heating, controlling the temperature of the coolant and rate of coolant flow.

TOP DEAD CENTER (TDC): The point at which the piston reaches the top of its travel on the compression stroke.

TORQUE: The twisting force applied to an object.

TORQUE CONVERTER: A turbine used to transmit power from a driving member to a driven member via hydraulic action, providing changes in drive ratio and torque. In automotive use, it links the driveplate at the rear of the engine to the automatic transmission.

TRANSDUCER: A device used to change a force into an electrical signal.

TRANSISTOR: A semi-conductor component which can be actuated by a small voltage to perform an electrical switching function.

TUNE-UP: A regular maintenance function, usually associated with the replacement and adjustment of parts and components in the electrical and fuel systems of a vehicle for the purpose of attaining optimum performance.

TURBOCHARGER: An exhaust driven pump which compresses intake air and forces it into the combustion chambers at higher than atmospheric pressures. The increased air pressure allows more fuel to be burned and results in increased horsepower being produced.

VACUUM ADVANCE: A device which advances the ignition timing in response to increased engine vacuum.

VACUUM GAUGE: An instrument used to measure the presence of vacuum in a chamber.

VALVE: A device which control the pressure, direction of flow or rate of flow of a liquid or gas.

VALVE CLEARANCE: The measured gap between the end of the valve stem and the rocker arm, cam lobe or follower that activates the valve.

VISCOSITY: The rating of a liquid's internal resistance to flow.

VOLTMETER: An instrument used for measuring electrical force in units called volts. Voltmeters are always connected parallel with the circuit being tested.

WHEEL CYLINDER: Found in the automotive drum brake assembly, it is a device, actuated by hydraulic pressure, which, through internal pistons, pushes the brake shoes outward against the drums.

ABBREVIATIONS AND SYMBOLS

A: Ampere

AC: Alternating current

A/C: Air conditioning

A-h: Ampere hour

AT: Automatic transmission

ATDC: After top dead center

μA: Microampere

bbl: Barrel

BDC: Bottom dead center

bhp: Brake horsepower

BTDC: Before top dead center

BTU: British thermal unit

C: Celsius (Centigrade)

CCA: Cold cranking amps

cd: Candela

cm^2: Square centimeter

cm^3, cc: Cubic centimeter

CO: Carbon monoxide

CO_2: Carbon dioxide

cu.in., in^3: Cubic inch

CV: Constant velocity

Cyl.: Cylinder

DC: Direct current

ECM: Electronic control module

EFE: Early fuel evaporation

EFI: Electronic fuel injection

EGR: Exhaust gas recirculation

Exh.: Exhaust

F: Fahrenheit

F: Farad

pF: Picofarad

μF: Microfarad

FI: Fuel injection

ft.lb., ft. lb., ft. lbs.: foot pound(s)

gal: Gallon

g: Gram

HC: Hydrocarbon

HEI: High energy ignition

HO: High output

hp: Horsepower

Hyd.: Hydraulic

Hz: Hertz

ID: Inside diameter

in.lb.; in. lb.; in. lbs: inch pound(s)

Int.: Intake

K: Kelvin

kg: Kilogram

kHz: Kilohertz

km: Kilometer

km/h: Kilometers per hour

kΩ: Kilohm

kPa: Kilopascal

kV: Kilovolt

kW: Kilowatt

l: Liter

l/s: Liters per second

m: Meter

mA: Milliampere

mg: Milligram

mHz: Megahertz

mm: Millimeter

mm^2: Square millimeter

m^3: Cubic meter

MΩ: Megohm

m/s: Meters per second

MT: Manual transmission

mV: Millivolt

μm: Micrometer

N: Newton

N-m: Newton meter

NOx: Nitrous oxide

OD: Outside diameter

OHC: Over head camshaft

OHV: Over head valve

Ω: Ohm

PCV: Positive crankcase ventilation

psi: Pounds per square inch

pts: Pints

qts: Quarts

rpm: Rotations per minute

rps: Rotations per second

R-12: A refrigerant gas (Freon)

SAE: Society of Automotive Engineers

SO$_2$: Sulfur dioxide

T: Ton

t: Megagram

TBI: Throttle Body Injection

TPS: Throttle Position Sensor

V: 1. Volt; 2. Venturi

μV: Microvolt

W: Watt

∞: Infinity

<: Less than

>: Greater than

Index